Families in Canada

Families in Canada
Social Contexts, Continuities, and Changes

Third Edition

James M. White
University of British Columbia

Lyle E. Larson
Professor Emeritus
University of Alberta

J. Walter Goltz
Emeritus Professor of Sociology
North American Baptist College

Brenda E. Munro
University of Alberta

PEARSON
Prentice
Hall

Toronto

National Library of Canada Cataloguing in Publication

Families in Canada : social contexts, continuities, and
changes / James M. White ... [et al.].—3rd ed.

Second ed. written by Lyle E. Larson, J. Walter Goltz and Brenda E. Munro.
ISBN 0-13-177628-2

1.Family—Canada.   I.White, James Martin II. Larson, Lyle E., 1937– . Families in Canada.

HQ560.F33 2005   306.85'0971   C2004-902424-8

ISBN 0-13-177628-2

Vice President, Editorial Director: Michael J. Young
Executive Acquisitions Editor: Jessica Mosher
Executive Marketing Manager: Judith Allen
Associate Editor: Patti Altridge
Production Editor: Martin Tooke
Copy Editor: Alex Moore
Proofreader: Heather Bean
Production Coordinator: Patricia Ciardullo
Page Layout: Laserwords
Art Direction: Mary Opper
Cover Design: Michelle Bellemare
Cover Image: Getty Images
Interior Design: Gail Ferreira Ng-A-Kien

Statistics Canada information is used with the permission of the Minister of Industry, as Minister responsible for Statistics
Canada. Information on the availability of the wide range of data from Statistics Canada can be obtained from Statistics
Canada's Regional Offices, its World Wide Web site at http://www.statcan.ca, and its toll-free access number 1-800-263-1136.

4 5 6 7 DPC 09 08 07

Printed and bound in Canada.

This book is dedicated to our spouses and companions, who have supported, encouraged, and enriched this project in ways too numerous to count and with a debt too rich to be repaid.

James M. White

Lyle E. Larson

J. Walter Goltz

Brenda E. Munro

2004

Brief Table of Contents

Table of Contents

Chapter 4: History of the Family   67

PART IV: DEFINING AND MAINTAINING MARRIAGE RELATIONSHIPS   169

Chapter 8: The Institutional Framework of Marriage   169

Chapter 9: Marital Quality and Communication 190

Chapter 10: Work, Marriage, and Family 218

Preface

Families in Canada, Third Edition, is a comprehensive introduction to the study of marriage and family life historically, cross-culturally, and with particular emphasis on Canadian society. Wherever possible, we use research data collected in Canada. Canadian research is sometimes quite difficult to locate, but we have conducted a careful search based on the location of the author, the title of the published work, and the source of data. The location—where the actual research project was conducted—is often buried in the methods section of published articles. Canadian sources are identified with asterisks (*) in the Suggested Readings section of each chapter and in the Bibliography at the back of the book. We also use data collected in other countries, primarily the United States, to ensure a comprehensive overview of family life in North America.

Our goal is to provide a solid background for those who may wish to pursue the study of sexuality, intimate relationships, marriages, families, and the interface between families and society, in more specific detail in advanced courses. This book represents not only a valuable text but also a reference source for students and scholars as they continue their study of the family and marriage.

Important Themes

There are several ways in which *Families in Canada*, Third Edition, provides a somewhat different focus from other textbooks. We emphasize five themes: eclecticism, comprehensiveness, diversity, continuities and changes, and objectivity.

Eclecticism

We have deliberately chosen to identify and use a variety of conceptual and methodological approaches that are common in family study. The research that has been conducted to test or illustrate these perspectives is presented throughout the book. The study of families is a scientific area of study that transcends traditional faculties and departments. Although each of us, as authors of this textbook, has a sociological orientation, we have also included materials from other disciplines, including anthropology, history, economics, social psychology, psychology, psychiatry, family science, and human ecology. Research in these varied settings reflects a variety of methodologies, including both quantitative and qualitative styles of obtaining information. Therefore, our introduction to the study of families reflects this variety of perspectives, methods, and issues.

Comprehensiveness

By the term *comprehensive* we mean that we specifically intended to provide an overview of what is known about families in North America as we begin this new millennium, with particular reference to family life in Canada. When there were salient gaps in Canadian data, we chose to supplement the Canadian material with complementary research in the United States to ensure a well-rounded view of the issues. Even so, we have not included everything. Some issues and topics have not been addressed; many issues could have been examined in greater detail. Many of these are the focus of books designed for senior courses on the family, some of which will be driven by particular theoretical perspectives, such as Marxist or feminist approaches.

Diversity

The traditional single-earner family, in which the father is the paid employee and the mother is primarily responsible for rearing the children, is no longer the most prominent family form in Canadian society. *Families in Canada*,

Third Edition examines a diversity of families—single-earner families, two-earner families, single-parent families (never married, divorced, separated, and widowed), and remarried families. Diversities in sexuality and mating are also reviewed. Understanding the *social context* of families is important since there are many variations due to cultural, subcultural, and historical multiformity. Indeed, this rich diversity of Canadian family life is part of our roots and our heritage. One of our specific goals is to represent controversies, scholarly debates, and competing perspectives in theory, research, and the interpretations of patterns and trends. Wherever possible we have tried to present objectively and fairly at least two sides of each issue.

Continuities and Changes

We have tried to emphasize two other salient themes in understanding patterns and trends among families in Canadian society. There are many aspects of family life in Canada that are very stable. Marriage is still popular for the majority of us, although we are more likely to put marriage off much longer. Having one or more children is still one of the most important things that most of us do during our lifetime. While there are real changes occurring in the nature and meaning of sexuality, marriage, and parenting, some of these changes may be temporary, while others may change the social landscape in a significant way. These twin themes reflect the long-standing struggle between generations and the ongoing search for intimacy. We have tried to capture both continuities and changes in a meaningful way throughout the textbook. We hope that you will sense that not all change is "real" change.

Objectivity

Chapter 2 emphasizes that objectivity is the result of unbiased collection and reporting of information. This means the following: (1) being fair to relevant points of view; (2) being committed to the principle of avoiding bias; and (3) maintaining an open mind to the evidence even if the data is inconsistent with our own personal values.

Organization of the Book

We introduce some of the basic issues in studying families in Part I. Chapter 1 examines the complexities of defining marriages and families, stability, and change in family life, and provides a brief overview of the demographic characteristics of families in the 1996 Canadian census. The major theories and methods used in family study are examined in Chapter 2.

Part II, Families in Differing Times and Places, examines the macro-sociological issues in family life in traditional cultures and ongoing continuities and changes (Chapter 3), in history (Chapter 4), and specifically in Canadian society (Chapter 5).

Part III, Intimacy and Premarital Relationships, examines changing standards of sexual interaction and dating in Chapter 6, and the development of intimate relationships, mate selection, and cohabitation in Chapter 7.

Defining and Maintaining Marriage Relationships is the focus in Part IV. Chapter 8 deals with marriage laws, the transition to marriage, marital commitment, and the impact of marital status on adult well-being. Marital adjustment, satisfaction, conflict, sexuality, extramarital sexuality, and marital enrichment are the focus of Chapter 9. The employment experience of women, its effects on marriage and family life, and the issues that men and women face as marital partners in dual-work and single-work households are emphasized in Chapter 10.

The fifth section of the book focuses on the issues in bearing and rearing children in families over the life span. Chapter 11 emphasizes census and vital statistics about families, pregnancy, birth, parenthood during infancy, and raising young children. The second section of Chapter 11 focuses on parent and adolescent relationships, and the impact of children and adolescents on their parents. Chapter 12 deals with the processes of aging in families and families in later life including kinship relationships and caregiving.

Part VI emphasizes families in transition and crisis. Chapter 13 focuses on divorce, single-parent families, remarriage patterns, and the characteristics of remarried families. The impact of divorce and remarriage on child development and individual well-being of the children of divorce over the life span is also explored. Chapter 14 deals with families dealing with various types of crises including illness, death, and violence.

Part VII only contains one chapter. The purpose of Chapter 15 is to briefly review the policy issues facing Canadian families at the beginning of the 21st century. This includes identifying the variety of scholarly perspectives on the meaning of current patterns and trends, and summarizing the diversity of policy recommendations designed to improve individual and family well-being.

Features for Students

A number of pedagogical features are included to help the student understand and recall the material in each chapter.

Chapter Objectives

Each chapter opens with a set of brief statements about the most important concepts and issues that are examined. These objectives are intended to help students to read the material more effectively.

Summary

The end of each chapter contains a brief summary of some of the key points and concepts.

Key Terms

Important terms and concepts are boldfaced and defined in the text in each chapter, listed alphabetically at the end of each chapter, and identified and defined in the glossary at the end of the book. These terms are the most basic and commonly used in the discipline. A good understanding of these concepts will lead to a more accurate sense of the nature and meaning of family issues in Canada.

Questions for Review

A set of review questions is also provided to enable the student to rethink the material in the chapter.

Questions for Discussion

Each chapter contains a few discussion questions for students to use either in self-reflection or in conversations with other students who have also read the chapter. We hope that these aids will help the student understand the material and facilitate preparation for examinations.

Boxes, Charts, Figures, and Tables

Highlight boxes are used in many different ways in this book, including summarizing important concepts, expanding on certain subjects to provide clarification, noting recent research studies, presenting interesting quotations of relevance to the discussion, or relating stories of individuals dealing with particular issues.

Tables typically contain important statistical data from Canadian Vital Statistics or the Census. Figures and charts are used to graphically illustrate important patterns and trends. Each of these features is designed to convey important information and to help students understand more about the issues and topics under discussion.

Further Readings

At the end of each chapter, the student will find a set of recommended supplementary readings for further study. A brief explanation of each of the recommended books is provided.

Acknowledgments

The third edition of *Families in Canada: Social Contexts, Continuities, and Changes* certainly owes a debt to all those who contributed to the previous editions of this book. This edition has profited from the critical comments and corrections offered by the numerous undergraduate classes studying the family. Furthermore, the Family Studies Research Volunteer Program, under the direction of Dr. Sheila Marshall and the volunteer coordinator Lyanne Westie, supplied many undergraduate research volunteers who contributed critical readings of many of these chapters. Finally, this third edition must acknowledge the contribution of our family members who have assisted with various tasks such as bibliographic searches and initial proofing of manuscript pages. Special thanks to Amy, Kelly, and Rebecca White for their assistance.

James M. White
University of British Columbia

Lyle E. Larson
Professor Emeritus
University of Alberta

J. Walter Goltz
Emeritus Professor of Sociology
North American Baptist College

Brenda E. Munro
University of Alberta

CHAPTER 1

Understanding Marriages and Families

After studying this chapter, you should be able to do the following:

- Discuss three assumptions that help to explain why the family is such an important social unit in our society.
- Discuss the differences between definitions of the family used in applied and policy settings versus definitions of the family used in social science research and theory.
- Explain the normative definitions of marriage and family.
- Distinguish between social change and social stability.
- Identify some of the basic issues facing families in contemporary society.
- Describe the basic demographic characteristics of marital status, family status, and family structure in Canada.

Introduction

In almost all societies, families are the basic unit of human organization. Most of us are born into and raised in families. Married couples with children, families whose children have left home, or married couples without children occupy most domestic dwellings in Canada. Many of us will invest substantial amounts of time, effort, and emotion in our families—more so than in any other social institution or domain (work, education, religion, or politics). Few people, whatever their marital status, are willing or able to escape the pervasive influence of their families, past or present, on their everyday lives. And Canada is not unique in being a couple- and family-oriented society. This social structure, with minor and interesting variations, has prevailed in societies throughout time.

The purpose of this chapter is to introduce you to some of the basic concepts and issues in the study of marriages and families. The first section identifies several reasons why families are so important to most of us. The second section raises some of the current issues in

formulating definitions of *marriage* and *family*. The third section outlines several of the basic concepts such as family change and stability. And the last section provides a brief description of families in Canada today.

The Importance of the Family

Whatever its form, and wherever it is found, the family is the primary source of meaningful relationships from birth to death. Husband/wife, parent/child (and stepparent/stepchild), father/daughter, mother/daughter, brother/sister, brother/brother, sister/sister, grandmother/grandchild, uncle/nephew, cousin/cousin—these are some of the relationships that symbolize what it means to be a family. In its many diverse and subcultural forms, the family is a universal social institution that has withstood the forces of time.

Why has the family been such a resilient social institution? With existing social science knowledge, it isn't possible to answer this question completely, let alone definitively. But we can suggest three principal assumptions about how the family serves individuals and society. We would argue that families have maintained a unique role throughout history by performing the functions described below. These assumptions are generally consistent with structural–functional and social institutional, as well as several psychological, theories. In the chapters that follow, we will consider societal and technological changes that may alter the meaning and importance of families in decades to come.

Assumption I

Families are primarily responsible for the reproduction and nurturant care of children.

Robert Winch (1971), among many scholars, has identified both the reproductive and nurturant functions as essential to the continued existence of society. Clearly, society would disappear if its dying members were not replaced. Similarly, without the transmission of beliefs and values unique to a particular society, that society would cease to exist.

One of the major functions of marriage has been for the partners to conceive and give birth to children. Until recently, reproduction resulted exclusively from sexual intercourse between a man and a woman. Newer developments in artificial insemination and *in vitro* fertilization (including human embryo transplants) have separated conception from sexual intercourse. In addition, these innovations have made it possible for women without male partners to give birth to children. Although these technological advances will both reduce the problem of infertility and alter the meaning of parenthood for some, the family's basic role in reproduction will likely prevail.

In most societies of the world, the family has been primarily responsible for the socialization of children. A child's beliefs, values, and knowledge are traditionally acquired within the family context, a pattern that remains prevalent in many countries. In Canada and many similar societies, however, much of a child's socialization now takes place in public or private schools. Daycare centres and family day homes increasingly support single-parent and two-income families. Even so, families remain predominantly responsible for the nurturant care of their children. **Nurturant care** is defined as the provision of the essential emotional and social needs of human beings. In the early development of small children, these needs are critical because children are

dependent on others for years after birth. They must learn how to walk and talk, to take care of themselves, and to relate with love and appreciation to others. Many of the child's religious, political, and moral values are learned in the home. Indeed, parents are the child's main interpreters and mediators of culture, and what the child learns at school is often processed through the parents' reactions and values.

Despite its flaws (such as neglect and abuse), which are largely due to the imperfections of adult members, the family remains the primary love- and care-giving social institution for child rearing.

Assumption II

Families are primarily responsible for the establishment of an individual's social identity, social role, and social status.

The concept of **social identity** refers to the names and status that we are assigned at birth. In most societies, one main source of identity is the name we are assigned by our family or kinship group. Surnames, first names, maiden names, and married names are all important sources of self-definition. The significance of this simple form of identification is illustrated by the trauma of an individual who suffers amnesia and has no way of identifying a place in the world to others or even to him or herself. There may come a time when a number, such as our social insurance number, becomes nearly as important as our family name. However, family identity will probably always mean more to individuals throughout their lives.

The concept of **social roles** refers to the expectations that society and families have for the social categories we are assigned. These categories include roles such as child, son, daughter, grandson, granddaughter, and so forth. Many of our social roles are learned in the family in which we are raised. The family into which we are born is defined as our **family of orientation** (or family of origin). If our parents' marriage dissolves and one or both of them remarry, we will also acquire roles such as stepson or stepdaughter, perhaps half-brother or half-sister as well. Some of these labels may have negative connotations, for both individuals and the families, in the larger society of which these families are a part. If we marry and have children of our own, we form what is defined as a **family of procreation**. In this family, we may also acquire the roles of husband or wife, father or mother, daughter-in-law or son-in-law, and eventually grandfather or grandmother, father-in-law, or mother-in-law. These roles, and the expectations that accompany them, will influence much of what we think and do throughout our lives, despite the many other roles (such as that of employee) that we will also play. McGoldrick and Carter (1982) note that families, unlike all other organizations, take on new members only by birth, adoption, or marriage. Furthermore, family members cannot entirely escape a family role through separation or divorce; they can only do so through death.

The concept of **social status** refers to the value or esteem assigned to the position that an individual occupies in the social system. Few societies are without *ascribed* or assigned roles. Many societies also permit selected roles to be *achieved* or earned. The family into which a child is born—over which the child has no control—determines most of that child's social statuses. These include social class (such as working or middle class), ethnicity (such as Ukrainian, Japanese, or Aboriginal), and religion (such as Catholic, Muslim—or atheist). Some of these labels will have negative connotations in the larger society in which the family of orientation resides; other labels may command special favours or unique esteem.

Assumption III

Families are the primary source of intimacy and need fulfillment for the individual throughout the life span.

The need for physical, sexual, intellectual, and emotional closeness with others seems to be a basic human need (Fromm, 1956; Maslow, 1968; Murstein, 1974). Although work and play groups may satisfy some of these needs, the **family** is most often the primary source of reference and closeness. The family household is the place to return after a day's work and, for most people, the family represents a special place of refuge and support. Family events typically give life its meaning, including being raised and loved, dating, getting married, giving birth, caring for children, and becoming a grandparent.

Contemporary society, in contrast, is characterized by more impersonal, mechanistic relationships (Durkheim, 1960; Tönnies, 1963; Wirth, 1938). Urban life, in particular, is a prototype of formal exchange between individuals in organizations. Social roles dictate interaction patterns throughout the day. Social roles pattern with whom one talks, what one says, how one says it, how long one talks; whom to touch, where to touch, when to touch; with whom to sit, where one sits, when to sit, and so on. People seldom share their feelings on the job, on the elevator, or on the bus. Conversation tends to be casual and impersonal (the weather or other acceptable topics). Toffler (1970) describes men and women in modern society as *modular* (prefabricated and artificial) and *mobicentric* (linked to transience and movement)—characteristics that lead to temporary friendships, temporary relationships, and temporary families. In the urban "lonely crowd," the need for intimate relationships has become even more important than in traditional societies (Veroff, Douban, and Kulka, 1981, for example). Marriage and family life, while seemingly more problematic and unfulfilling than in more traditional societies, continues to be the major source of meaning and intimacy for most people.

According to Brehm (1992), intimacy is the close relationship between two people that involves three characteristics: interdependence, need fulfillment, and emotional attachment. Brehm defines *interdependence* as the mutual impact that partners have on each other. Interdependence in families occurs frequently, tends to have a strong and enduring impact, and is pervasive because it affects relationships in many different areas of life. *Need fulfillment* refers specifically to basic human needs that are essential to individual well-being. Weiss (1969), as cited in Brehm (1992), argues that every individual has the following five important needs that must be fulfilled in relationships with others:

- **The need for intimacy** We need someone with whom we can share our feelings freely.

- **The need for social integration** We need someone with whom we can share our concerns.

- **The need for being nurturant** We need someone whom we can take care of.

- **The need for assistance** We need someone who will help us out when we need it.

- **The need for reassurance of our own worth** We need someone who will tell us that we matter.

Almost all definitions of intimacy also include the need to experience warmth or affection (emotional attachment). Feelings of love are a powerful force in human relationships. They smooth over mistakes and encourage intimacy in marital and parent–child relationships.

Intimacy needs, however, are not always fulfilled in families. They may be ignored, abused, or exploited. Even as families are the primary source of need fulfillment and well-being, they are also the place where conflict and violence are most likely to occur. Homicide, physical violence, and child abuse or child neglect are part of family life for far too many husbands and wives and children. At least one in 10 married women is physically abused in Canada each year. Child neglect or abuse occurs in perhaps 20 percent of Canadian families. Chapters 6, 7, 11, and 14 will investigate the potential hazards of extreme intimacy.

Even so, most Canadian studies indicate high levels of preference for and satisfaction with family life. A study by Bibby (1995) illustrates these values. Of the top 10 wants, the first four were the following: being loved (82 percent), family life (86 percent), freedom (87 percent), and happiness (89 percent). Most Canadian respondents (94 percent) reported being happy with their marriages. Bibby also found that 93 percent of the respondents said that family life and friends provided "quite a bit" or a "great deal" of enjoyment.

The search for intimacy leads to marriage and the family; and when it is not found, the same route is tried again. Each of the above three assumptions illustrates why the family continues to be the basic social institution in all known societies.

Defining Marriage and Family

To many Canadians, defining marriage and family is not an issue. Many of us use common-sense definitions. For example, a marriage is a man and a woman living together with the legal right to do so. Or, a family is a married couple with children. While these definitions make sense to most of us, they exclude many people whose marriage and family situations differ. These standard definitions are even less viable when applied to other societies, historically or cross-culturally.

How we define marriages and families is critically important when those definitions are linked to entitlements, benefits, or sanctions. For example, there may be a "family rate" for admission to ice skating rinks or swimming pools. More importantly, provincial or federal transfers may be tied to the number of families below a certain income level or of a certain type. Workplace family policies such as flex time or employee pension fund access may be tied to these definitions. Finally, we should not underestimate the "legitimizing" function of definitions. Definitions of marriage and family say which relationships are normative and accepted and, hence, these become part of an ideology about "family." To be other than normative and accepted is to be defined as an outsider.

On the other hand, social scientists seldom think of the definitions they use in research and theory as being so powerful. In previous generations, academic definitions were thought to get at the essence of the thing being defined. Once the essential attributes of "marriage" or "family" were known, it was believed, we would have a form of knowledge. In the study of the family, this was illustrated by the search for definitions with universal application. A universal definition of family, for example, would require the relationship defined by the concept of family to be the primary social institution in all societies of the world. The diversity of forms of marriages and families have made this attempt at universalism less than successful. However, academics have learned that the purpose of our definitions is quite unlike the purposes of policy makers who have control over resources such as entitlements and benefits. Academic definitions are useful for doing research and for proposing explanations of phenomena. Thus definitions fall into two groups: those that inform researchers and social scientists, and those that policy makers use to disburse legitimacy and entitlements.

We divide the discussion of definitions into those definitions *used in policy or ideology formulations* and those used in *social science research*. This is not to say that these do not share commonalities. Although on some rare occasions the terms *marriage* and *family* may be interchanged in daily conversation, for most of us a *marriage* denotes a couple or dyadic relationship proscribed by a legal contract. A *family*, on the other hand, most often refers to what social scientists call the "nuclear" family that consists of at least one adult and his or her biological or adopted offspring.

Although these two terms seem to identify the common ground for most academic research and policy definitions, they also prove difficult to define. For example, an increasing number of couples never have children.

Are childless couples "families"? Are couples with adult children who no longer live at home still families? Does a married couple that continues to live with the husband's family of orientation become a separate family only when the husband and wife leave and establish a second residence? Is a "common-law" relationship the same as a marriage? Questions such as these have given rise to emotional debates among specialists in the family about how to define the terms *marriage* and *family*. Professional organizations, therapists, social workers, and many others have taken strong positions as to what are acceptable or unacceptable definitions. Our purpose in this section is to briefly summarize this diversity of views and to provide specific working definitions that most accurately represent the basic characteristics of marriage and family for social scientists.

Policy and Ideological Definitions

Legal Definitions Most industrialized or modern societies of the world have established laws or normative regulations that define the rights and duties of spouses, parents, and children. In Canadian law, marriage is defined as "the voluntary union for life of one man and one woman to the exclusion of all others. Marriage is a status that is conferred on individuals by the State" (Payne and Payne, 1994:15). Currently, the federal definition of marriage as being a union between a man and a woman has been declared in violation of the Charter of Rights and Freedoms by courts in Quebec, Ontario, and British Columbia. These courts both ruled that to only define marriage as between heterosexuals was discriminatory against gays and lesbians. As a result, the Minister of Justice for Canada is seeking opinions and input into the process of developing a different definition. In the ministry discussion paper, one of the options is for the federal government to abandon the area and not bother with a marriage act. Indeed, today's complex issues, such as gay marriage and the legal status of cohabitation as a "common-law" marriage, make the legal definition contentious.

As Payne and Payne point out, the concept of the family does not have a precise legal definition (1994:1). Even so, it is clear from their careful review of the legal issues and precedents relating to families that the presence—past or current—of children in the household signifies that a family relationship exists. It is emphasized that family law in Canada "deals with the pathology of family breakdown and its legal consequences

for spouses and their children" (Payne and Payne, 1994:1). The Paynes indicate that the terms *marriage* and *family* are not interchangeable in Canadian law. Laws related to marriage are discussed in more detail in Chapter 8.

Inclusive Definitions We are using the term *inclusive* to refer to the conceptual dimension of formulating or rejecting definitions of "marriages" and "families" that are assumed to be out of date or inconsistent with current social reality. The **inclusive definitions** perspective regards marriages and families not as social institutions but as private, voluntary social groups or relationships. This approach often emphasizes the importance of *familial feelings or a family-like situation* when including certain persons or groups in the definition of the family.

There is now considerable pressure from lesbian and gay couples to receive the same recognition and benefits as do heterosexual married couples. Quite a few family scholars, lawyers, provincial legislators, and members of parliament have been advocating rights for gay couples similar in purpose to those of married couples. Many feminist scholars have lobbied for these rights in their own professional organizations, with universities, corporations, and governments. The main impetus for rights similar to those of married couples, however, has come from lesbian or gay couples themselves. Almost every day, media outlets such as daily newspapers publish newsworthy stories about yet another discrimination case before the courts, or the decision by some employer to grant health and pension benefits to an employee's same-sex partner. Indeed, the province of British Columbia amended its *Family Relations Act* on July 22, 1997, to redefine "spouse" to include any two people who have lived in a marriage-like relationship for at least two years, including two persons of the same gender. It was the first jurisdiction in North America to have taken such a step.

The federal government of Canada has chosen to restrict employment benefits to "a 'same-sex partner' relationship... when, for a continuous period of at least one year, an employee has lived with a person of the same sex in a homosexual relationship, publicly represented that person to be his/her partner and continues to live with that person as his/her partner" (*Moore and Akerstrom, Complainants vs. Treasury Board, Department of Foreign Affairs and International Trade, Canada Employment and Immigration Commission, Public Service Alliance of Canada and Professional Association of Foreign*

Service Officers, Respondents, April, 1997:3). The term *spouse* was explicitly withheld in this ruling. It appeared at that time that the Government of Canada was committed to preserving the legal concept of marriage for heterosexual couples. Since then, two provincial supreme courts have ruled that marriage is not exclusively the domain of heterosexuals and the federal minister of justice is drafting new legislation to change the marriage act in accordance with these rulings. In 1996, the United States government voted to define marriage as the union of one man and one woman. This bill was signed into law by then-president Bill Clinton. These matters are discussed further in Chapter 8.

The inclusive approach to defining families is a recent development in the scholarly community. In this approach, definitions are powerful ideological tools used by conflicting groups to legitimate their claims. For example, the benefits of marriage could be seen to be currently controlled by those with a "heterosexist" ideology. Definitions in this perspective are often seen as "reality making" rather than as "tools" for research. In every society, some individuals see marriage or the family very differently from the way the majority does. And in postmodern societies such as Canada, where divorce, remarriage, and shifting values are common, there is likely to be a greater variety of individual meanings or definitions for marriage or family.

Phenomenological Definitions In an article, Holstein and Gubrium (1995) analyzed the ways in which individuals experience reality from what is called a phenomenological and ethnomethodological theoretical perspective. A "family" is each individual's interpretation of who their "kin" really are. The researchers argue that meanings and interpretations have no connection to rules, norms, or culture. The individual's "local subculture" is his or her reality. A good example of an inclusive definition is the following: "the constellation of family is limited only by the limits of participants' creativity" (Rothberg and Weinstein, 1966:57). Rothberg and Weinstein provide seven definitions for "sexual minority" families in emphasizing the stress of being a gay family in a "heterosexist" context.

Ideology of Diversity and "Families" These definitions are reasoned attempts to deal with the increasing diversity of primary or close relationships in postmodern societies. According to Cheal (1993),

a Canadian sociologist, the 1980s and 1990s witnessed a shift from the modern family to the postmodern family. The family is no longer a fixed form. The term *families* has replaced the term *family.* Bernardes (1993) discounts the "normal nuclear family" as being less than 2 percent of families in the United Kingdom. He argues that "the nuclear family is such an unrealistic myth that even presenting it as a viable goal has done harm in generating unrealistic expectations" (p. 36). The major thrust of this position is that the traditional family unit is dead, and that it is time scholars find out what families are like in the "real" world. The focus in research, theory, and university-level teaching, it is argued, should be devoted to the increasing diversity of marital and family forms.

Part of the problem with this assumption is that the definition of the "traditional" or "normal" nuclear family is typically a distortion of reality. Instead of 2 percent (Bernardes, 1993) or 10 percent (Coontz, 1992), about 40 percent of all families in Canada at this time can be described as two original spouses with children either at home or no longer living at home.

Ideology of Professions and Situational Definitions **Situational definitions** is the applied dimension of developing a "working terminology" to facilitate the training of professional caregivers. Social workers, for example, will be directly involved in helping individuals with broken relationships establish "family-like" bonds. We are using the word "situational" because it aptly illustrates a common approach among social agencies when dealing with special situations in which children or adults find themselves, due to poverty, multiple divorces, or remarriages, or due to the choice to enter an alternative lifestyle. Crosbie-Burnett and Lewis developed a good example of a situational definition of a family in their work with Alcoholics Anonymous families struggling with alcohol abuse (1993), the "pedi-focal" definition. They define a **pedi-focal family** system as "all those involved in the nurturance and support of an identified child, regardless of household membership [where the child lives]" (p. 244). This definition means putting the needs of children above those of adults, focusing on the needs of dependent children regardless of changes in the relationships among the adults connected to the child. In such situations, adults who are not biologically related to the child become "fictive kin." In such situations, children belong to the community and are the responsibility of any adults who are able to contribute to the child's well-being.

In working with various family issues, the definitions used typically reflect the particular issues with which the agencies involved must deal. Hanson and Lynch (1992:285), for example, define the family as follows: "For the purposes of this article, a family is considered to be any unit that defines itself as a family including individuals who are related by blood or marriage as well as those who have made a commitment to share their lives." This is a good example of a convenient and relevant definition for agencies that work with a diversity of "family lifestyles." Hanson and Lynch's particular audience was teachers who work with pupils with special education needs. McNeece (1995), writing from a social work practice perspective, emphasizes the value of definitions such as "a family is a group of people who love and care for each other" (Seligmann, 1990, as quoted in McNeece, 1995:5), and "two or more individuals who consider themselves family and who assume typical family obligations" (Hartman, 1990, as quoted in McNeece, 1995:5). Perhaps the most explicit example of a situational definition of a family is "the informal unit where those who cannot take care of themselves can find care in the time of need" (Bould, 1993:138). An example of such a situational "family" unit is aptly illustrated by Tina's story in Box 1.1.

Stories such as Tina's are consistent with situations in which an individual's perceptions of reality are the only "family-like" reality they know. Tina saw her friends as "family," even though most of these individuals lived in other households. Tina's friends seemed to behave like family toward Tina, as well, even though she had no legal or biological ties with any of them.

All scholars in the field would agree with the importance of in-depth research on the increasing variety of close relationships or variant experiences related to marriage-like and family-like lifestyles. Considerable research has been published relating to common-law unions, divorces, remarriages, single parents, stepparenting, custody, the connections (rights, duties, relationships) with a diversity of kin, and the patterns and effects of these for children and adults over the life span. Indeed, multiple cohabitation, divorce, and remarriage occur for a significant number of individuals. There is still much more to learn about these issues. Scholarly research is still in its infancy regarding alternative lifestyles or living arrangements, such as gay and lesbian couples, gay parenting, children in gay households (through adoption, the merger of two households where one of the partners already has a child, etc.), surrogate parenthood, single women bearing children through artificial insemination, and other variations. Many experts in the family field have concluded that "there is no single correct definition of what a family is" (e.g., Fine, 1993:235).

Box 1.1	Current Issues: A "Situational Family" Unit

Tina, a homosexual male who dressed as a female, lived with her lover Phil for 11 years until Phil died of AIDS. Tina also had AIDS. Tina's friends realized that she could not take care of herself, so Bill, an ex-lover, offered a room in his house. He furnished the room with Tina's favorite things, and bought a new bed and furniture for her care and comfort. Bill's work schedule often forced him to be away day and night. Caregiving tasks were divided among six friends with regular duties. Tom, who is HIV positive, drove Tina to her doctors' appointments. Ann's weekly job was cooking mild foods that could be stored for future meals. Every Saturday she sat with Tina until Alex arrived after he finished his work at 5 p.m. He and Tina watched videos that were provided by another friend. Lucy came by twice a week and changed the bed, did laundry, and tidied up Tina's room. Bill kept in touch with Tina's parents and her older brother. When Tina died, Bill notified Tina's family. Tina had not had any contact with her family for 10 years, except for one visit to inform her family that she had AIDS. Bill invited the family to come to the memorial service and to stay with him. The same people who served as caregivers for Tina were now providing tours, meals, and company for the visiting parents and brother. The biological family had not realized that their child had such a caring "family" who loved him so dearly. Tina's mother still keeps in touch with Ann, a member of Tina's "family," and sends her holiday cookies and letters.

Source: Bould, 1993:140.

Even so, Fine also points out that the "multiple definitions in the literature... [are] related to the *values* [emphasis ours] of those who supply the definition" (p. 235). This is probably a fairly accurate explanation for the mini-explosion of definitions intended to include any configuration of persons who want to think of themselves as a family.

Social Scientific Definitions

Disciplinary Definitions The most obvious source of diversity among social scientific definitions of the family is the different assumptions and concepts that academic disciplines bring to the study of the family. An economist might define family as an economic unit based on the work and cooperation of individuals in the unit. A psychologist, however, might be more interested in the multiple personalities interacting in the group. Historians may conceptualize family as being extended over generations and periods of history. Anthropologists and ethnographers are more likely to focus on kinship systems whereas linguists are more likely to examine family terms of reference and address. These different definitions do not compete with each other for the "truth" because there is no true definition. In the social scientific disciplines, definitions serve to focus our research and studies of a phenomenon. Because of the different perspectives, the phenomenon is constituted and conceptualized differently. As we shall see in later chapters, these different disciplinary perspectives serve to enrich our knowledge.

Theoretical Definitions Several disciplines may share theories. Each theory provides its own definition of the family, which is formulated according to the theory's major concepts and assumptions (Doherty et al., 1993). For example, Smith (1995) recorded different definitions of the family for each of eight conceptual or theoretical approaches. The definition of family for symbolic interactionist theory is "a unit of interacting personalities." This theory, discussed in Chapter 2, focuses on interaction between two-person dyads within a family unit. If there is one female child, for example, there are three interacting dyads: husband–wife, father–daughter, and mother–daughter. This theory assumes that the thoughts and perceptions of, say, the husband/father, influence interactions *with*, and actions *of*, the daughter.

As will be pointed out in Chapter 2, the purpose of a conceptual approach in the social sciences is to develop law-like explanations of the central phenomena addressed by the theory. Sometimes theories about families examine family stability and coherence over time. Other theories might focus on the conflict between family members to explain outcomes such as divorce or child abuse. Like the diversity of disciplines, the plethora of theories adds incredible richness to our perspective. There is a notable difference between theoretical claims and disciplinary perspectives.

Disciplinary perspectives simply reflect different foci and conceptual tools. Many times this is also true of different theoretical perspectives such as the examples above. There is, however, a problem when two theories claim that they can explain the same phenomenon. For example, if a psychodynamic theory claimed that spousal abuse is caused by the personality of the abuser and a more sociological theory claimed that the lower resources of the victim cause spousal abuse, we would be forced to test which of these theories is empirically most adequate. We might find that only one is true or that both may be predictive of spousal abuse. When both theories are correct, we must forge a new and more adequate theory combining elements of both. As we shall see in Chapter 2, this is an important way in which theories assist the social sciences in accumulating knowledge.

Definitions Using "Norms"

Many of the social scientific disciplines and theories share the concept of the *norm*. "Cultures are held together by distinctive systems of norms and values. Norms are agreed-upon societal rules and expectations specifying appropriate and inappropriate ways to behave in a particular society. Normative expectations tell what to do, how to do it, where to do it, and why it is to be done. Expectations... vary by age, gender, and position in society" (Abu-Laban and Abu-Laban, 1994:53). These norms typically include folkways, mores, laws, and values relating to nearly everything one does, and they are associated with specific groups or organizations that are considered by the majority of a particular society to facilitate individual and societal well-being. These groups or organizations are referred to as **social institutions**, and include government, economic, health, family, and related systems. The concept of "normatively defined" relates to the discipline of sociology, not necessarily to a particular theory. Even so, several theories, including both macro-sociological and micro-sociological theories, use various aspects of the normative dimension of social influence.

Powerful forces influence definitions of *marriage* and *family* in all societies and influence what individuals "do" in marriages and families. These forces include official laws, expectations emanating from many sources (friends, kinship groups, religious connections, education, employment requirements, community standards, etc.), and socialization within one's family of orientation. Even though variations from these expectations are not uncommon (e.g., cohabitation, divorce, remarriage and, more recently, alternative lifestyles), the majority—51 percent or more—of marriage and family participants in most societies want to establish and maintain meaningful and lasting marriage and family bonds, regardless of how each society tends to define the particular form and function of these bonds.

Much of our historical evidence indicates that the **nuclear family** is the basic building block of most family systems in most societies. Although this extensive discussion of definitions has been necessary, it is self-evident that the majority of people in most modern and postmodern societies know what the process of becoming and being a family is all about. Common-law unions, divorce, remarriage, single-parent families, etc., are part of the story for many families. The core of this family unit, and almost all family units in most societies, is at least one parent and one child. The definition that follows is based on the folkways, mores, laws, and values of most societies.

A family is an intergenerational social group organized and governed by social norms regarding descent and affinity, reproduction, and the nurturant socialization of the young. White (1991:7)

This version of the family is the predominant form in all known societies. The term *intergenerational* supports the notion that families are based on the presence of a biological or adopted bond that spans from an adult of one generation to a child or adult child of another generation. This definition therefore includes single-parent families of whatever form (unmarried, divorced, or remarried). The family may include the parents' biological offspring, adopted children, and children conceived through artificial insemination or surrogate parenthood. In the phrase *organized and governed by social*

norms, the salient role of society is emphasized (laws such as inheritance and custody, expectations, a learned sense of responsibility for the care of children) in determining what the family is expected to mean to those who bear and rear children. As long as society approves, the type and number of parents should not be specified, because these structural factors vary from society to society. Some societies require a biological father and mother; others require only a mother or a grandmother, or both.

Reiss (1965) documented that most societies are directly involved in the *nurturant socialization* of their dependent children. Nurturant care entails loving, protecting, feeding, supporting, and meeting the emotional and physical needs of one's children. Of course, this does not always occur. Indeed, in Chapter 12, we discuss the significant number of children in Canada who are neglected or abused. Most families in most societies are also involved in teaching and training their children in the unique values of their culture and subculture (e.g., race, ethnic and religious values). As discussed in the second assumption about families earlier in this chapter, adults remain members of their family of orientation throughout their lifetime. When a child is born to or adopted by a member of this family of orientation, this parent–child unit becomes a family of procreation.

The family as normatively defined is based on the most fundamental structure and the primary purpose of caring for offspring. Such a definition makes no official or legal comment on many possible characteristics, including age, sex, or physical features, of a parent or child. There is, however, the question regarding the rapidity of change in the norms governing and defining the family.

There have been few explicit research studies of how the average person defines marriage and the family. A 1992 study in Sweden (Levin and Trost, 1992) provided 16 one-sentence statements of different "collections of individuals" to 948 respondents. The results were as follows: married couple with children (99 percent said this was a family); divorced couple with a child (83 percent); non-married, cohabiting couple with a child (97 percent). In contrast, only 30 percent considered a homosexual couple with a child to be a family, and only 23 percent considered a once-cohabiting couple with a child that are no longer living together to be a family.

An Ipsos/Reid national poll (2004) of adults documented an almost even split on same-sex marriages. Forty-seven percent said that the government should change the legislation to allow homosexual couples to legally marry, while 48 percent of the sample were opposed (http://www.ipsos-na.com/news/pressrelease.cfm?id=2038)

The normative definition of the family is clearly not the same as marriage. Certainly one way to ascertain the normative definition of marriage would be to turn to contemporary laws defining marriage, since these laws are formal reflections of social norms. The problem with such an approach would be that it would restrict us to one society in one historical period. We would prefer a broader approach. Indeed, in Chapter 3 we will find that in many societies and over historical time most marriages would have broken our contemporary laws, especially laws against bigamy restricting multiple mates. From a cross-cultural perspective, marriage is a social institution with specific functions in most societies of the world.

Marriage is a normatively defined and publicly acknowledged intimate and sexual relationship between at least one man and at least one woman established with the intention of permanence.

This definition assumes that most societies play a significant role in defining what marriage is and what it is not. The majority of men and women within most societies enter a relationship that is publicly accepted. A marriage may be a legal relationship requiring a license, a public ceremony with witnesses and verbal pronouncements, and perhaps a blood test. Typically, however, marriage as a normatively defined relationship is a matter of norms that are carried in the hearts and heads of the members of the community, tribe, or kinship groups, and enforced by positive and negative sanctions. A number of societies still permit more than one spouse (primarily more than one wife; a small number, two or more husbands; a few, two or more of each), but most societies expect the majority of marriages to have at least one male and one female. This relationship provides the normative basis or eligibility for sexual intercourse, affectionate interaction, emotional intimacy, and reproduction. Although these marriage functions are normative, couples in many societies may in reality simply live in the same residence without affection or intimacy. The intention of permanence is still considered an important dimension of marriage in most societies, but, as is well known, **divorce rates** are high in postmodern societies. Despite this evidence seemingly to the contrary,

however, the desire for a marriage that will last is still prevalent in Canadian society.

Many societies approve of several types of marriage; however, homosexual relationships between two men or two women are excluded from our definition because they are not institutionalized as marriages (that is, accepted as normative and approved by the majority of any society). However, 47 percent of the respondents in the Ipsos-Reid poll seem to approve of the concept of same-sex marriage. Indeed, 58 percent of the respondents in Quebec supported same-sex marriages.

Although currently Canada does not recognize same sex marriages, there are a host of court cases arguing that this denial of legitimation violates the Charter of Rights. It is apparent that many postmodern societies have implemented or permitted the use of alternative terms for various alternative lifestyles. Denmark and other Scandinavian countries, for example, use the term **domestic partnership** for lesbian and gay couples. Indeed, the same term is now widely used in both Canada and the United States. Although officially undefined, it is often used to identify a "conceptual alternative living arrangement" to marriage, in an effort to obtain similar rights and benefits to those that marriage bestows as a social institution. Live-in partners of homosexual employees of the province of Manitoba, for example, are eligible for such benefits as Canada Pension and health care. As indicated earlier in this chapter, British Columbia and the federal government have taken a similar step. Many other jurisdictions have acknowledged this concept, including corporations, universities, city governments, and provincial and state governments in both Canada and the United States (Wisensale and Heckart, 1993).

The **normative definitions** presented above cover most marriages and families in Canada. Our predominant marital form fits the definition—that is, most marriages are based on the legal definition of marriage and are entered into with the intentions of, or desire for, intimacy and permanence. Similarly, most families involve two parents and their biological offspring, thus exceeding the minimum definition of the family that we will be using. Even so, the traditional marriage and family pattern seems to be changing. More than half of Canadian mothers have two jobs, one in their own household and the other in the workplace. More than 30 percent of our marriages are remarriages. Single-parent families now constitute almost 25 percent of all Canadian families with children at home. It is likely that this family form will continue to increase. People practise many other "alternative lifestyles" or mating forms, although not necessarily with normative approval. Indeed, even if the legal definition of marriage changes to include same sex couples, it may be some time before Canadian tolerance of same sex marriages evolves into normative approval of these unions. Marriage and family experiences also vary by ethnicity, social class, recentness of immigration, religion, and region, as well as by many other factors. For these reasons and others, this book uses the plural "families" in its title.

We use these definitions of *marriage* and *family* to guide our discussions in the remainder of this chapter and the book. We urge our readers to not accept these definitions as "true" but as a reflection of current and historical norms constructing family and marriage. The risk in uncritically accepting normative definitions is that social change may quickly overtake us. Our cross-cultural and historical normative perspective suggests some degree of stability in regard to these definitions. On the other hand, our world appears to change at an ever-increasing rate. The processes of urbanization and modernization have been eclipsed by the postmodern phenomena of information societies and globalization. The very notion of stability may be an anachronism.

Family Change and Stability

The Dialectic Between Stability and Change

Change, process, and stability are important concepts in family analysis; this book is as much about change and process as it is stability. There is often a struggle between forces that pressure society to retain or reestablish the "tested and true" values, and those that foster or demand the establishment of different values and behaviours. Much is happening in family life: marriage rates are down—sharply, in the province of Quebec—but may go up again; cohabitation rates are up—also sharply in Quebec—but may go down; divorce rates have levelled off and seem to be decreasing, but may begin to increase again. Despite these apparent changes, many of these rates have been as high or low in the past. Marriage rates were low in the early 1900s and divorce rates were extremely high during World War II.

The most important question we can ask regarding stability and change is: "Are apparent changes simply random variations or do these patterns represent real social change?" **Change**, by formal definition, means that an observation of something at Time 1 is different than the observation of the same object at Time 2. Substantively, this refers to movements in both form and function that tend to make preceding forms and functions outdated.

The problem for almost all students of social change is to discriminate between random variations in stable patterns and changes in the patterns. This is worthy of some further clarification and we use the diagrams in Figure 1.1 to illustrate these concepts.

As Graph 1 illustrates, if the average of the up-and-down pattern reveals a consistent increase (or decrease, as in Graph 2) in some family attribute, it is generally postulated that real change is occurring. The stable upward trend (solid line) in Graph 1 is computed from the observations (dotted line). Be careful to note that the observations randomly vary about the trend line. In general, observations are never all on a trend line or average but rather fall on one side or the other side. When all of these positive and negative variations are added together they will sum to zero, meaning that there are the same quantity of observations on each side of the line. This is random variation.

In Graph 4 the average is not trending up or down but the observations are varying randomly about the stable, unchanging average. Indeed, there are as many observations (dotted) above as below the average line (solid). If one were to take only two observations, it would be quite possible to end up with data supporting a downward or upward trend when in fact we have a flat trend. We can learn a few basic principles from this example. First, it is important to have not just two but multiple observations when one is studying change and stability. Second, random variation is not the same as actual change.

Graphs 1, 2, and 3 show actual changes. We have lots of examples of social change in Canada. For instance, the increase in cohabiting relationships seems to be a good example of real change in Canada. Another good example seems to be the sharp increase in the percentage of mothers employed in the labour force. We will discuss this change and its implications in Chapters 11 and 12; the incidence of cohabitation will be investigated in detail in Chapters 7 and 8.

In addition, Graph 3 in Figure 1.1 illustrates a change in the trend pattern. This could be the beginning of a social process that is cyclical or patterned. **Social process** refers to recurring attitudinal or behavioural patterns that seem to reflect change in the short term, but that in the long term tend to reflect cycles or recurring patterns. For example, economists often talk of the business cycle and in Chapter 3 we will discuss a cyclical view of the family. Graph 3 might also show how apparent change may actually be a short-term trend that reverses itself in the long run. Age at marriage is a good example of this type of pattern. From the year 1941 to the year 1971, the average age of Canadian males at first marriage steadily dropped from about 28 years to about 24 years. But from 1971 to the present, the trend reversed itself, with the average age rising to about 29 years. Graph 4, which is really simply an extension of Graph 3, shows what may happen in the very long term,

over many generations. The average of all the multiple shifts turns out to be a horizontal straight line, indicating no net change (Graph 4). This graph illustrates the most typical model of social process—apparent changes come and go with what seem to be "real changes," while the basic patterns of family life actually remain quite stable over time. As we will see throughout this book, real change seems to be occurring in certain areas of family life, but hindsight is usually a more reliable teacher than prediction. For example, John Watson, the famous behaviourist, predicted in 1934 that in 50 years the family would no longer exist.

We are writing this book at a time when many people believe that significant change is occurring in courtship, marriage, and the family in Canadian society. Perhaps this is correct. However, it is important to remember that marriages and families have existed as long as have human beings. The structures and

Figure 1.1   Change vs. Process

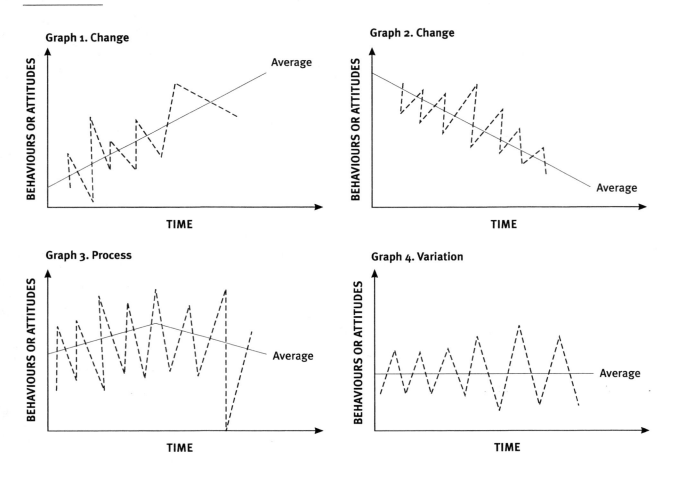

relationship patterns have varied from society to society, but the basic family patterns within a society have resisted change. Current family patterns have evolved from less efficient ways of meeting the basic needs of people, but traditions alter slowly. When changes occur in family life, they typically lag far behind changes in other social institutions. Modern changes in technology, for example, have seemed to unsettle family tradition by removing many of its functions (Ogburn and Nimkoff, 1955). At the same time, however, new family functions are established, and latent (dormant or unmet) functions become more important. In fact, some scholars argue that there have been significant cycles in family life throughout history (for example, Zimmerman, 1947), and that family life is a good example of social process. While the family is subject to changes in the larger society and is significantly influenced by them over time, the basic needs of the individual eventually seem to lead to the reconstruction of traditions that facilitate strong and vital family life. We will investigate social change and processes in the history of marriages and family in Chapter 4. In addition, Chapter 15 will review family change in more detail.

Is the family in a demise phase, as some scholars argue? Or is the family still strong, either maintaining its current form and function, or changing, slowly or rapidly? These are topics of major interest to us all. The degree of controversy among family scientists is illustrated in Box 1.2. Although these quotations reflect perspectives covering more than three decades of speculation, they remain characteristic of viewpoints today.

Linton's words, written years ago, suggest that a person's family is the most important entity in his life. A certain amount of change is inevitable as the family adjusts to the changing demands of society, but, for the most part, the similarities from generation to generation far exceed the differences. Thompson and Walker, feminist scholars in the United States, emphasize the reality and importance of diversity in family lifestyles. They argue that scholars must stop looking for "bad things" in family lifestyles, and instead focus on positive outcomes. Bernardes, a British family scholar, believes that the continued search for or study of "the family" is an "immoral" action by any scholar. He emphasizes that the diversity of all family lifestyles must be the focus of both theory and research if the study of family is to remain a legitimate scholarly discipline.

Social Issues Affecting Family Well-Being

Marriage and family patterns are directly related to the sociocultural context in which they occur. These patterns, whether in the Ukraine, for example, or in Canada, have their own history and their own current trends and patterns. An analysis of family stability and change, therefore, should include an investigation of

---

Box 1.2	Cultural Insights: Families and Marriages—Views of Stability and Change

The ancient trinity of father, mother, and child has survived more vicissitudes than any other human relationship. It is the bedrock underlying all other family structures. Although more elaborate family patterns can be broken from without or may even collapse of their own weight, the rock remains. In the Götterdämmerung, which overwise science and over-foolish statesmanship are preparing for us, the last man will spend his last hours searching for his wife and child (Linton, 1959:52).

It is time to ask new questions about families in all their diversity . . . . Scholars must stop asking about the price of deviance that faces individuals, families and society when women work outside the home, when women strive for autonomy and equality in family life, when children are in child care, when couples divorce, when parents remarry, and when women, especially mothers, live without men (Thompson and Walker, 1995:858).

We must entirely reject the concept of "the family" as theoretically adequate and, as a consequence, recognize the enormous difficulty, in principle, of studying what actors refer to as "family life". . . . family ideology is so deeply integrated into our consciousness that most people cannot support the idea that *the family* [emphasis ours] does not exist for any length of time (Bernardes, 1993:40).

the historical processes and family pattern trends of a given sociocultural context. In this way, we can clarify the dynamic relationships between families and their societies in the late 1990s and into the 21st century.

We will examine many issues in the chapters that follow. Over a decade ago, the National Council on Family Relations released a Task Force Report on 19 critical areas of concern in assisting families to prepare for the future (Olson and Hanson, 1990). The report identified patterns, changes and trends that required adjustment and action in many areas of marriage and family life: by the individuals and families who experience them, by the public and private agencies that provide social services and support, and by government organizations that establish policies to reduce or prevent their negative consequences. As will become evident in several chapters in this book—particularly in Chapter 15—the definition of the "well-being" of marriages and families varies among family scholars.

Poverty and other sources of economic distress are major causes of many of the issues that threaten individual and family well-being (cf. Taylor et al., 1991; Ross et al., 1991; Menaghan and Parcel, 1991; McLanahan and Booth, 1991; Voydanoff, 1991). We examine the impact of poverty on families in detail in Chapter 5.

The multiple issues in the linkages between men, women and family life are emphasized throughout this book, primarily in Chapters 11 through 15. Many of the issues identified above are complex, indeed more complicated than can be examined thoroughly in this book. Issues such as poverty and gender differences involve entrenched political, religious, and ideological biases. Moreover, scientists often have divergent views on the definition and meaning of the issues, as well as on whether solutions are needed or whether appropriate solutions can be formulated.

As we discussed in the Preface, we have adopted an eclectic approach to the study of marriage and family life in this book. This approach should help to shed light on the complexity of the issues and the diversity of viewpoints prevalent today.

Characteristics of Marriage and Family Patterns in Canada

In subsequent chapters, we will examine in detail the variety and diversity of demographic marriage and family patterns in Canada, as well as the changes that have occurred since the beginning of the 20th century. In this section, several basic characteristics of marriage and family for Canada as a whole are summarized, using three basic sources of information: 1) the Census conducted every five years, 2) the annual reports of the Vital Statistics Department, and 3) selected publications that will help clarify these official data sources. On May 15, 2001, the federal government conducted its Census of the Canadian population. The decade Census enumerates the population of Canada. About 80 percent of the population was asked to answer seven questions and the remaining 20 percent was asked the seven basic questions plus an additional 52 questions. The mid-decade Census in 1996 asked five or six basic questions of the entire population, and more detailed questions of a 20- to 30-percent probability sample of the total population. Selected data will also be used from the 2001 Census. Each year, vital statistics are collected to provide annual records of ongoing significant events in the lives of all Canadian residents. "Vital statistics provides for the continuous registration of all births, deaths, marriages, and divorces as they occur" (McVey and Kalbach, 1995:17).

Throughout this book, we will examine Canadian statistics in regard to many areas, including work, education, and divorce. The immediate goal of this chapter is to get a "snapshot" of Canadian families in 2001. The selected Census data reviewed are in the areas of cohabitation, marital status, and family structure.

Cohabitation and Common-Law Unions

Without any doubt, the increases in cohabitation over the last three decades of the 20th century constitute a revolution in the coupling patterns of young adults. Although later chapters will have much more to say about this, it is important at this juncture to clarify the terms *cohabitation* and *common-law union*. **Cohabitation** usually refers to a couple sharing a common domicile and adopting the adult roles of husband and wife without having been married. Various researchers define these parameters differently and thus there are some definitional disputes. **Common-law unions** should be used as a more technical term referring to heterosexual cohabiting couples that have met or surpassed the time limits set by each province to qualify as a common-law marriage. In many provinces, a couple living together for more than one year is recognized as a common-law marriage. Since no province recognizes same sex marriages at this time, it would be impossible to have homosexual cohabiting unions counted as common-law marriages. In the Census, however, this is not the case. In the 2001 Census, common-law partners are defined as two persons of opposite sex or of the same sex who are not legally married to each other, but live together as a couple in the same dwelling. In the following discussion, it is important to realize that the term "common-law" now refers to cohabitation and no longer refers to a type of marriage.

The data presented in Table 1.1 indicate that less than 10 percent of the population of Canada is currently cohabiting. This result, however, conceals the actual popularity of cohabitation by comparing it to the population of Canada. There are many persons who are not available for cohabitation in the population of Canada, such as currently married and infant children. A much clearer picture emerges if we examine some of the age-specific rates of cohabitation in Table 1.2.

When we examine cohabitation or common-law by the age groups that are most likely to be participating in the common-law relationship, we find that some of the percentages are double what they were in Table 1.1. This is not surprising. Rather, what is surprising is that these percentages are so low. When we move into our discussion of cohabitation in Chapters 6, 7, and 8, we will find that many young adults use cohabitation as a "step" or "stage" before marriage. In addition, cohabitation is often a relatively brief and transitory period of time. As a result of the transitory nature of cohabitation, the best indicator we might have for any

TABLE 1.1   Common-Law Relationships in Canada (2001 Census, Statistics Canada)

	POPULATION	MALE	FEMALE
In common-law relationship	2 284 830 (7.6 %)	1 146 055 (7.8%)	1 138 755 (7.4 %)
Not in common-law	27 722 265 (92.4 %)	13 560 795 (92.2%)	14 161 470 (92.6 %)
Total	30 007 090 (100 %)	14 706 850 (100%)	15 300 240 (100%)

Source: Adapted from 2001 Census, http://www12.statcan.ca. (Table 95F0405XCB01004).

TABLE 1.2   Selected Age-Specific Common-Law Relationships in Canada (2001 Census, Statistics Canada)

AGE GROUP	POPULATION	MALE	FEMALE
	Total	In common-law	In common-law
20–24 years	1 955 810	95 115 (9.7 %)*	150 115 (15.4%)
25–29 years	1 898 195	178 775 (17.4%)	192 665 (16.3%)
30–34 years	2 096 740	179 225 (17.4%)	173 710 (16.3%)
35–39 years	2 522 855	183 665 (14.7%)	175 110 (13.7%)

* Percentages are computed by dividing the number of common-law relationships for each age group and gender by the total population in the age group and gender category.

Source: Adapted from 2001 Census, http://www12.statcan.ca. (Table 95F0405XCB01004).

age group would be if they "ever cohabited" before marriage. Such data is not available from the Census but is available from other sources. This data and the details of this discussion will have to wait until these later chapters.

Marital Status

Table 1.3 allows us to examine marital status over the last five years. The categories used in this table are currently single, married, widowed, or divorced. The married category includes all those who are currently legally

TABLE 1.3   Population by Marital Status and Sex, 1998–2002

	1998	1999	2000	2001	2002
TOTAL					
Both sexes	30 248 412	30 509 323	30 790 834	31 110 565	31 413 990
Male	49.5%	49.5%	49.5%	49.5%	49.5%
Female	50.5%	50.5%	50.5%	50.5%	50.5%
SINGLE					
Both sexes	42.3%	42.3%	42.3%	42.3%	42.4%
Male	53.5%	53.5%	53.6%	53.6%	53.6%
Female	46.5%	46.5%	46.4%	46.4%	46.4%
MARRIED*					
Both sexes	48.4%	48.2%	48.1%	47.9%	47.8%
Male	49.9%	49.9%	49.9%	49.8%	49.8%
Female	50.1%	50.1%	50.1%	50.2%	50.2%
WIDOWED					
Both sexes	4.9%	4.9%	4.9%	4.9%	4.9%
Male	17.7%	17.9%	17.9%	18.3%	18.5%
Female	82.3%	82.1%	81.9%	81.7%	81.5%
DIVORCED					
Both sexes	4.4%	4.5%	4.7%	4.8%	4.9%
Male	42.6%	42.6%	42.6%	42.6%	42.6%
Female	57.4%	57.4%	57.4%	57.4%	57.4%

*Includes persons legally married, legally married and separated, and persons living in common-law unions.

Source: Adapted from Statistics Canada, CANSIM II, Table 051-0010.

married (even though they may be separated) and those that are currently cohabiting. The category "married" as used in this table emphasizes the relationship dimension of the term rather than strict legal definition.

According to Table 1.3, approximately 47.8 percent of Canadians were married in 2002. About 42.3 percent were single, 4.9 percent divorced, and 4.9 percent widowed in 2002. It is perhaps more interesting to examine the percentage increases over the five-year period. In this calculation, using the 1998 numbers as the base, the population for the country increased by 3.8 percent. If the underlying social process in the year 2002 is the same as in 1998, then the proportional differences between, for example, divorce in 1998 and divorce in 2002 should simply match the population increase of 3.8 percent. Indeed some of the processes appear to approximate the population increase. People in the single status increased by 3.96 percent. On the other hand, those in the married category decreased to 2.65 percent, representing slower growth in this category than the growth in the total population. Widowhood increased more rapidly than the population at 4.1 percent growth. And astoundingly, divorce increased by 15.8 percent over this period of five years. Although this would seem to be a major and dramatic jump in divorce, in Chapter 13 we will discover that there are many ways to compute divorce statistics. More importantly, we should be aware that an increase in "divorce status" does not necessarily mean an increase in divorce. Over the five years covered in Table 1.3, we could have a constant rate of divorce but a decline in remarriage. This would produce an increase in the number of people in the divorce status category without having any increase in divorce. Indeed, Chapter 13 will help clarify the complex processes that produce the data in Table 1.3.

You should also note that in Table 1.3 certain categories of marital status are unevenly distributed by gender. Specifically, widowhood is a more prevalent status among females and, though less dramatically, divorce status is also more prevalent. The explanation of these gender imbalances is somewhat different. Males have higher mortality at earlier ages than females and hence are more likely to leave widows. In regard to divorce status, the explanation is that as with all statuses there is a considerable degree of transience. During a lifetime, one person may sequentially experience statuses such as single, married, divorced, married, widowed, and married once again. The number of divorced females is in part dependent on the remarriage rates. As we will see in

Chapter 13, males have a higher probability for remarriage than females. The fact that whenever there is a divorce a male and a female both enter the divorced status would suggest we would find the same numbers for both genders. However, the higher transition rates for males out of the status of divorce explain the gender difference. Obviously, there is more to this gender difference than discussed here and we can look forward to exploring this in depth in several future chapters.

Family Status and Family Structure

In assembling its Census data, Statistics Canada distinguishes between household and the Census family. The term **household**, as used by Statistics Canada,

> . . . refers to a person or group of persons who occupy the same dwelling and do not have a usual place of residence elsewhere in Canada. It may consist of a family group (Census family) with or without other non-family persons, of two or more families sharing a dwelling, of a group of unrelated persons, or of one person living alone.

The term **Census family**, in contrast,

> . . . refers to a now-married couple (with or without never-married sons and/or daughters of either or both spouses), a couple living common-law (again, with or without never-married sons and/or daughters of either or both partners), or a lone parent of any marital status, with at least one never-married son or daughter living in the same dwelling.

Table 1.4 shows that in 2001 most of the population of Canada (30 007 094) resided in private households (29 522 305) with an average of 3 people (this varied by province). The percentage of households relative to the population for Canada was 39 percent whereas for Ontario it was 37 percent and for Manitoba 39.6 percent. Only about 30 percent of all households contained children. Lone person households composed about 26 percent of total households in Canada. As we found with marital status, such statistics may be somewhat misleading since any individual's life may be composed of multiple transitions between types of households. For example it is not unusual for young single persons to live on their own before marriage, then form a couple, then a family, eventually returning to a lone person household in old age. Several chapters in this book, including Chapters 2 and 4, will focus on the study of such transitions.

TABLE 1.4 Household Type, in Private Households, 2001 Counts, for Canada, and Selected Provinces — 20 Percent Sample Data

POLITICAL REGION	HOUSEHOLD TYPE					
	Population in private households (number)	Total private households	Couple family households with children[1]	Couple family households without children[2]	One-person households	Other family house hold-types[3]
Canada	29 522 305	11 562 980	3 530 180	3 237 620	2 976 875	1 818 300
Newfoundland and Labrador	507 245	189 040	68 065	58 405	34 060	28 515
Prince Edward Island	133 070	50 795	16 830	14 530	11 580	7860
Nova Scotia	895 305	360 020	104 465	109 065	89 005	57 485
New Brunswick	717 535	283 820	88 125	87 375	63 585	44 730
Quebec	7 097 855	2 978 115	842 180	809 855	880 770	445 315
Ontario	11 254 730	4 219 415	1 376 975	1 179 330	990 165	672 950
Manitoba	1 090 625	432 550	127 910	118 405	121 760	64 475
Saskatchewan	956 635	379 675	110 970	108 210	105 150	55 35
Alberta	2 918 920	1 104 100	359 945	308 490	255 375	180 285
British Columbia	3 858 730	1 534 335	423 460	437 915	418 135	254 825
Yukon Territory	28 160	11 365	3295	2785	3265	2010
Northwest Territories	36 955	12 565	4680	2510	2785	2590
Nunavut	26 525	7175	3280	740	1250	1905

1. Refers to couple family households with at least one child under 25 years of age.
2. Includes couple family households with all children 25 years of age and over.
3. Includes multiple family households, lone-parent family households, and non-family households other than one-person households.

Source: Adapted from http://www12.statcan.ca/english/census01/products/highlight/PrivateHouseholds/Page.cfm?Lang=E&Geo=PR&View=1a&Table=1&StartRec=1&Sort=2&B1=Counts.

According to the 2001 Census (Table 1.5), about 75.3 percent of all families with children at home reside with a married or common-law couple. A relatively large percentage of children (65.3 percent) live with married parents. A surprising 24.7 percent of all families with children are lone parent families and the great majority of these lone parent families are female headed (80 percent). Although lone parent families are only about a quarter of all families with children at home, they have the greatest number of children at home (1.5) compared to couple families with only 1.1 children at home. If we multiply the number of lone families by the average number of children in these families we find that approximately 1 966 777 children would be in lone

TABLE 1.5   Number of Children at Home and Family Structure for Census Families in Private Households, for Canada, Provinces, Territories, Census Metropolitan Areas, and Census Agglomerations, 2001 Census—20 Percent Sample Data

	FAMILY STRUCTURE						
	Total family structure	Total couple families	Married couples	Common-law couples	Total lone-parent families	Female parent	Male parent
Total families with children at home	5 311 795 (100%)	4 000 605 (75.3%)	3 469 700 (65.3%)	530 905 (10%)	1 311 185 (24.7%)	1 065 365 (20%)	245 825 (4.7%)
One child at home	2 285 110	1 483 435	1 229 055	254 375	801 675	638 430	163 240
Two children at home	2 087 355	1 716 265	1 518 475	197 790	371 085	307 640	63 450
Three or more children at home	939 325	800 905	722 170	78 730	138 425	119 295	19 130
Average number of children at home per family	1.1	1.1	1.1	0.8	1.5	1.5	1.4

Source: Adapted from Statistics Canada, 95F0312XCB01004.

parent families. If we do the same computation for total couple families and take the ratio, we find that a much greater percentage of children (29.8 percent) are potentially exposed to scarcer parental resources than are children in couple families. Though this is simply an estimate, it nonetheless serves to awaken us to the potential for disadvantages that might be tied to lone parent families. This topic will be further discussed in much greater detail in Chapters 10, 11, and 13.

It should be mentioned that Census data provides us with a "snapshot" of Canadian families in the Census year 2001. This type of data also provides the basis for possible errors in causal attributions and policy directions. The major problem is one to which we have previously alluded: families and individuals might occupy a status or category for a relatively short period of time. For example,

"cohabitation" or "lone parent families" represent statuses or categories in which it is important to know how many people are currently, but it is perhaps even more important to know the "flow" or "transition" rate into and out of these categories. Indeed, if most people move from cohabitation to marriage in a relatively short duration of time it would be unwise to make policy decisions about these categories, given the frequent change in constituents and hence attributes. This cautionary remark also prefaces an even broader perspective on Census data.

Data does not speak for itself, but must be interpreted. There is no such thing as a *prima facie* fact since all facts are composed of background assumptions and methodological assumptions. We will find that the next chapter introduces many of the theoretical and methodological assumptions used in the study of the family.

SUMMARY

- Marriages and families have proven to be resilient institutions, having weathered the test of time and change. Their strength seems to derive from their primary role in three areas: reproduction and the nurturant care of children; the establishment of an individual's social identity, social role and social status; and as a source of intimacy and need fulfillment for the individual throughout the life span.

- Although most of us have clear ideas about what marriage and family mean to us, these important social institutions have multiple meanings, both within our own society and among most societies throughout the world.

- There are two basic types of marriage and family definition: *ideological and policy definitions* and *social scientific definitions*. One example of policy type definitions is *legal definitions* that specify the requirements that distinguish married from non-married persons, their legal rights as married persons, and the legal rights of their children and other relatives. Social scientists formulate theoretical definitions that are consistent with the particular conceptual approach they are using to understand and explain selected dimensions of marriages or families.

- Normative definitions used in the social sciences focus on the folkways, mores, laws (formal norms), and values of a society relating what to do, how to do it, where to do it, and why to do it that way. Therefore, normative definitions of marriage and families reflect the powerful forces of the law, the expectations of society and culture, and socialization experiences in subcultures and families of orientation.

- Marriages and families are challenging phenomena to study. Some scholars point to social processes to emphasize the *stability and unchanging patterns* of marriage and family life. Other scholars point to social changes to emphasize the *changing nature* of marriage and family life. What may seem to be social change in the early 2000s may, in the long term, turn out to be social process.

- The dominant patterns of marriage and family life in Canada seem clear. Most non-single Canadians are married, and most married people have children. Although only about 8 percent of Canadians are currently cohabiting, Canadians in the age range of 20–35 years have almost double that percentage. In regard to marital status, the relative numbers in this status declined from 1998 to 2002. This is in sharp contrast to the 15 percent increase for those of divorce status. We did caution that this could easily mean that divorce rates were stable but that there could be a decline in the remarriage rate. Indeed, Census data can easily be misinterpreted because it only provides a "snapshot" of a category rather than the flow or transitions in and out of the categories. Finally, although most Canadian children live at home live with two parents, about 25 percent of the families with children at home are lone parent families containing almost 30 percent of the children.

KEY TERMS

Census family (17)

Change (11)

Cohabitation (14)

Common-law unions (14)

Divorce rate (10)

Domestic partnership (10)

Family (3)

Family of orientation (2)

Family of procreation (2)

Household (17)

Ideological and policy definitions (5)

Inclusive definitions (5)

Intimacy (3)

Legal definitions (5)

Normative definitions (10)

Nuclear family (9)

Nurturant care (2)

Pedi-focal family (6)

Situational definitions (6)

Social identity (2)

Social institution (8)

Social process (12)

Social roles (2)

Social scientific definitions (8)

Social status (3)

QUESTIONS FOR REVIEW

1. Identify and discuss the three key assumptions that help to explain why marriage and family life are important in society.

2. Identify the types of definitions of *marriage* and *families*. Briefly describe the differing foci and purposes of each of the approaches to defining *marriage* and *families*.

3. What is the current legal definition of *marriage* in Canada? (Hint: at the time of writing of this chapter the Minister of Justice was undecided about the direction a new definition should take.)

4. Distinguish the situational and inclusive definitions of the family. Why are these definitions both similar and different? Identify a good example of an inclusive definition.

5. What is meant by the term *normatively defined* and how does this concept relate to the definitions of *marriage* and *family* that the authors have used in this textbook? Discuss the advantages and disadvantages of these definitions over other ways of defining families.

6. Distinguish between change and social process. Cite an example of each pertaining to marriage or family patterns in Canada.

7. Use Census data to describe the basic characteristics of marital status, family status and family structure.

QUESTIONS FOR DISCUSSION

1. What does marriage really mean to you? Is your "meaning" different from that of your relatives and friends? Why do you think there are differences?

2. What does your family mean to you? Do other members of your family feel differently? Why? How should social institutions (such as the church, government, courts, or the media) deal with family issues?

3. Should same-sex relationships be included in the definition of *marriage*? If so, under what conditions? If not, what are your reasons?

4. What is your view of same-sex couples being allowed to adopt children? To conceive, by whatever means? To rear children?

5. What is your reaction to what marriages and families seem to be like in Canadian society? Should these ways of life change? How? Should they remain unchanged? In what ways?

SUGGESTED READINGS

Che-Alford, Catherine Allan, and George Butlin. 1994. *Families in Canada.* Catalogue No. 96-307E, Statistics Canada and Prentice Hall Canada. This short booklet contains a succinct overview of various definitions of the family, demographic trends and family diversity, living arrangements of children, and work–family issues.

Conway, John F. 1990. *The Canadian Family in Crisis.* Toronto: James Lorimer. A critical review of changes in family life and the effects of these changes on children, women, men, and the family in Canada. Conway contends that structural inequities in Canadian society are one of the major sources of the crises in family life.

Department of Justice, *Marriage and Legal Recognition of Same-sex Unions: A Discussion Paper,* November 2002, http://canada.justice.gc.ca/en/dept/pub/mar/6.html.

Mandell, Nancy and Ann Duffy (eds.). 1995. *Canadian Families: Diversity, Conflict and Change.* Toronto: Harcourt Brace & Company. This is an anthology of nine chapters authored by Canadian scholars. The issues addressed include an overview of family histories, contemporary diversities, lesbian and gay men in families, Native people and immigrants, public policies, divorce, poverty, and violence.

National Council on Family Relations (2000). *Journal of Marriage and the Family 62,* 4. This special issue provides a decade review of research in most areas of family studies.

Vanier Institute of the Family. 1996. *Canada's Families: They Count.* Ottawa: Vanier Institute of the Family. This unique publication is a "desktop flip chart" with plastic laminated pages. It provides a detailed demographic record of almost anything statistical related to family life that one might want to know. This publication is produced in colour and is easy to read.

CHAPTER 2

Family Theories and Methods

After studying this chapter, you should be able to do the following:

- Describe the differences between personal experience and the scientific method.
- Define the differences between theoretical frameworks and theories.
- Define the different levels of family analysis.
- Define the key concepts and assumptions of each of the conceptual approaches typically used in understanding and explaining families.
- Delineate the different types of research design used in family research.
- Explain the basic measuring and sampling procedures in family research.
- Describe how family scholars analyze data collected from or about families.

Introduction

Young children between the ages of two and four are full of questions: Where did I come from? Why is he my brother? What is that for? Children are excited about knowledge, and their frequent questions are often penetrating. For social scientists, the learning quest begins with analytical questions of three basic types: What is? (or sometimes Who is?); How is it this way? (dealing with the conditions under which it is this way, such as when and where); and, Why is it this way? Through these questions, scientists clarify what they want to know. The examples below illustrate these questions:

- What are alternative lifestyles? What is cohabitation? What is marriage? What is the family? Who marries or is married?
- How does a person become married? Do people get married in different ways? When do people marry? Where do they marry? How do people become a family?

- Why do people get married? Why don't some people get married? Why do people have children? Why do some people choose not to have children?

The first set of questions is the most primitive and deals with description: a rose is a plant, a deer is an animal, a marriage is a social institution. Like the questions asked by children, each answer often raises another question. The second set of questions seeks clarification of those factors that will facilitate more precision: Are all relationships marriages? Are all marriages social institutions? Do all marriages have the same functions? The third set of questions is most concerned with explanation. **Explanation** refers to the "why" of what people think and do. If we know why some individuals act in obsessive and compulsive ways, we may also be able to predict what these people will do in intimate relationships. Can we predict who will cohabit and who won't? Can we predict who will marry and who will not? Can we predict who will stay married and who will not? Are educated persons more likely to have fewer children? The goal of social science is to be able to answer the why question—the most interesting and the most difficult scientific task.

Family social scientists are interested in understanding why individuals enter, maintain, and sometimes leave intimate bonds; why some marriages fail and others last for a lifetime; why the social institution of the family exists and continues to persist in all societies of the world. In this chapter, we take a close look at the ways in which family social scientists examine these and many other interrelated questions. In the first section, we discuss two ways of understanding families. The second section summarizes the various levels at which family research is conducted. In the third section, we consider the issues in theorizing, and the various theories. The final section looks at the methods that family scientists use.

Ways of Understanding Families

Personal Experience

There are several ways to study why family members and families behave in different ways. Perhaps the most prominent way of knowing is through personal experience. In interacting with our own parents, brothers and sisters, and spouses and children, we develop a personal point of view about what it means to be a family. What we come to believe about men and women as dates, lovers, sexual partners, husbands/wives, fathers/mothers, or grandfathers/grandmothers also influences the ways we relate to others. Personal experience is based on the evidence we have collected, whether positive or negative, in our interactions with members of our family. Based on our experiences and the knowledge we derive from them, we expect others to behave in certain ways. We often assume that we know the reasons for their behaviour. These predictions are a primitive form of theorizing, because our experiences guide and influence our response to others. In fact, it is difficult to separate our perceptions of other families and our particular preferences toward family lifestyles from our own experiences (e.g. Swenson, 1999:14–15).

Our experiences also include frequent exposure to the ideas of others. These ideas are often couched as "common sense." Sex, marriage, and family life are frequent topics of discussion with friends. We observe the families of close friends and often get to know a lot about their families. Many of us learn about what families are like or should be like in schools or churches. The media (books, magazines, television, movies, and even music) also offer us many images of family life, ranging from news accounts of what the "experts" are saying, to the supposed wisdom of the columnist, to the tragedy and comedy of the soap opera.

This book emphasizes other methods of understanding the family, such as analytical description, explanation, and research. Personal experiences have several limitations. First, our own experiences tend to distort our view of marriage and the family. Those who have had negative experiences are more likely either to see negative attributes or to exaggerate positive attributes in other families. The person who leaves a spouse for a more attractive person, for example, may be more likely to see the good side of divorce, despite its negative impact on children. Our own experiences tend to bias what we see. Second, personal experiences provide a limited view of family reality, not the whole picture. Knowing something of the patterns and practices of families in other communities, other parts of Canada, as well as in other cultures, leads to new understandings and insights. Third, family members tend to explain their own problems by blaming others in their families. As someone once wisely said, "Nothing can ever be sliced so thinly that it still doesn't have two sides." Finally, our "common sense" as developed through exposure to external sources fails to provide objective methods for studying the family. Not long ago, "common sense" had people believing in the inherent inferiority of women and the correctness of slavery. Certainly, the track record for common sense should provoke a good deal of mistrust and cynicism about its claims to knowledge about families. Understanding and explaining human development requires a broader, more objective point of view than personal experience can provide.

Scientific Method

The hallmarks of a scientific approach to knowledge and explanation are objectivity and replicability. Objectivity, like truth, is an ideal. In the hands of the practicing scientist it is an attempt to be a value-free collector and reporter of information. **Objectivity** typically involves three dimensions: a) being fair to relevant points of view, b) being committed to avoiding bias, and c) maintaining an open mind to the evidence even if the data is inconsistent with one's own personal values. On of the critical tenets of objectivity in science is that results can be replicated by other independent observers using the same measures. Thus it is important that researchers employ a standard set of procedures that other researchers can follow to see if they obtain the same results. These procedures involve at least the four steps below, the first three of which illustrate the practice of objectivity in the work of acquiring knowledge:

1. Clarifying When we clarify, we identify exactly what it is we need to know more about. This involves defining the concepts that directly relate to the ideas, questions, or problems we want to know about family life. The more precise the definition of the issue, the more it is likely that accurate measures can be developed. For example, different concepts of marriage may need to be defined before we can understand and explain marriages.

2. Formulating We need to formulate a reliable way of locating and measuring those things we want to know. The measures must be precise enough to distinguish the concepts. Love, for example, may have different meanings to males and females, unmarried and married persons, or persons who have been married five years versus 50 years. Each concept of love must be measured with precision.

3. Collecting The information must be collected in such a way that other researchers can scrutinize it. The methods used (for example, a survey questionnaire, or direct observation) must be administered so that any other researcher can duplicate the technique in a follow-up study. This dimension of scholarship is referred to as **replicability.** If the finding cannot be replicated using the same procedures, the results may not be reliable.

4. Analyzing and Interpreting What does the information mean? This step is the natural conclusion to the use of scientific methodology in obtaining information about families. The theoretical approach, methods, and results are typically reported in professional journals or books, and contribute to the scholarly explanation of attitudes and behaviours in families.

Although objectivity is the scholarly password among social scientists, scholarship can still be influenced by the values of the scholar. It is sometimes difficult to ignore one's own marriage or family experiences when conducting research on the structure and process of marriage and family life. Scholars also struggle with biases and prejudices. Accordingly, the scientific method is only as dependable as the degree to which objectivity is maintained at each step of the process. For example, if a researcher assumes that parenthood is dissatisfying to most working parents, then the questions, concepts, definitions, and measures may be slanted toward the negative. Obviously, there is a "down side" to parenthood, but if the positive aspects of parenting are ignored in the research project, the social realities of parenthood are distorted.

Typically, scholarly work fulfills the first three steps (clarification, formulation and collection) with rigor. The personal values of scientists, however, seem more evident in the final step, when they analyze the information they collect. They may downplay findings that are inconsistent with the theory tested, or overemphasize weak findings in support of their assumptions. Each of these considerations suggests that objectivity may be difficult to achieve in social science research. Ideological bias and the personal values of the researcher may influence all aspects of research activity. Therefore, just as scholars must critically review the research of others, so should students be skeptical of research findings. While the scientific method is a reliable source of knowledge about families, its explanatory value depends on systematic review and assessment. Scholarship should involve a strong commitment to the principles of objectivity. This is especially true in the area of interpretation of data since, as we shall see shortly, different theoretical assumptions can lead us to see and interpret the same behaviour very differently.

Levels of Analysis in the Study of Families

Families can be studied at several different levels: for example, individual family member, family group, or even the institution of the family. The distinctions provided by levels of analysis are important for both theory and method. Almost any conceptual approach in the social sciences, including many in the physical sciences (genetics and neurology, for example), has multiple levels of analysis. Let's take an example from biology. If we wanted to explain why a person became sick with a particular disease, we could examine the person's overall psychological and physical health. We might ask questions about an individual's happiness as well as about health behaviours such as smoking and alcohol consumption. On a cellular level we might examine the proportion of T-cells in the blood stream and other cellular aspects of the immune system. And, at a much broader epidemiological level, we might examine the probability of this person getting ill when they reside in a particular city or country. In other words, we may analyze the cellular level, the individual level, or the population level. The data findings and theory we develop may be somewhat different at varying levels of analysis. For example, the definition of death for an organism such as a human or mammal might be the cessation of brain waves or heart beat. However, such measures of death are clearly at the level of the organism. At the cellular level these measures are less meaningful. Indeed, after the organism dies many cells such as hair cells continue to grow for some time.

The family can also be analyzed on multiple levels. For example, if we research a topic like marital satisfaction we might examine an *individual's* satisfaction with her marriage. However, such an analysis would miss the interactional component that would be captured in the *dyad* or *relationship*. The relationship processes are different from those that can be examined at the individual level. For instance, we can measure agreement or consensus in a relationship between two people (dyad), but this would not be a meaningful measure with only one individual. Further, if we were to measure a concept like family solidarity or cohesion we would need to examine the family at a *group level*. If we were to examine the norms that compose the Canadian family we would move to an *institutional level* of analysis. So some measures are appropriate for one level of analysis but not for other levels (White, 1991).

In general we divide levels of analysis into two broad categories, the macroscopic (group and institutional) and the microscopic levels (individual and dyad). Understanding these levels will assist us in understanding research such as in the example of "marital satisfaction," and it will also assist in understanding theory. For example, Bronfenbrenner (1979) defines

four levels of scope in the analysis of families: the macrosystem, exosystem, mesosystem, and microsystem. These basic concepts are a central dimension of *ecological theory*, to be discussed later in this chapter. Bulcroft and White (1997) detail several levels of analysis in studying families but, for simplicity, we will only emphasize the macrosystem and the microsystem.

Macrosystem

The macrosystem level of family analysis deals with cultural and societal issues analyzed as institutions and populations. Macro-sociologists and anthropologists do most of their research at this level. What are families like in Canadian society compared with families in the United States, Japan, or Russia? What is the role of culture (values, norms, customs) in defining and influencing the family as a social institution? How do other social institutions (government, religion, economics, health) influence the family, and vice versa? Are there important trends and patterns in family life over time? These questions illustrate the importance of intrasocietal analysis (one society), cross-cultural analysis (from two to several hundred societies) and historical analysis (in one or more societies). Societal structures, patterns and processes (such as type of government, poverty, urbanization, technological change, revolution, war, social policies and social change) are examined in the study of family patterns and processes. The sources of information include demographic data (data about populations, such as an official census), ethnographic accounts of tribes and unique cultures, and cross-cultural surveys. To illustrate the contrast between the most general and the most specific levels of analysis, we turn next to the microsystem.

Microsystem

This level of family analysis is the most specific. Psychologists, social psychologists, and micro-sociologists do most of their work at this level, studying interpersonal relationships in everyday life. At this level of analysis, the main question is the following: Why do we feel, think, and do the things we do to and with each other? In the context of the family, intrapersonal, interactional, and developmental issues are examined in relationships between husbands and wives, parents and children, individuals and in-laws, and the many other relationships connected with the establishment and breakdown of marriages and families. Psychological analysis focuses on the connection between a person's inner thoughts and feelings and how that person acts. Social psychologists are interested in the connection between a person's attributes (feelings, thoughts, behaviours) and that person's interaction with others. At the microsystem level, scholars also deal with the influence of parents, as well as others, on the development of children.

Here are some of the questions that microsystem researchers ask: What are the similarities and differences between marriage relationships and unmarried heterosexual relationships? Do homosexual and heterosexual relationships differ? Do married couples act differently after they have children? Do family relationships in large families differ from those in small families? Are there differences in child-rearing patterns between two-parent and single-parent families?

Theory and Belief

One question students seldom ask is "Why do we need or want theories?" Certainly, many students have an intuition or feeling that theories are important, but they often have not paused to ask why this is so. In this section we want to briefly define "theory" and distinguish it from a similar term, "belief." After this we will discuss the usefulness of theory.

A belief is an idea about the world that we hold to be true. For example, if you believe in a supreme being, you would hold that this is true rather than false or imaginary. Of course there are degrees of belief, but all of these would have some assertion of truth.

On the other hand, a theory is a set of propositions that may be used to explain an occurrence or event. For example, if I drop this book and it falls to the floor, I could invoke the theory of gravity, with its many propositions about mass, to explain this particular incident. Indeed, a theory is a generalization that can cover or explain a great many particular events. Scientific theories are not only general, but they must be capable of empirical disconfirmation. That is, we have to be able to know under what conditions the theory could be refuted. The great bulk of scientific theories from Copernicus to the present time have been disproved or modified. For instance, Newtonian mechanics was replaced by the special and general theory of relativity.

The major difference between belief and scientific theory is that theories must be refutable and indeed given sufficient time, usually are refuted. Thus, scientific theories are better and better explanations of our world—but none would warrant being identified with absolute truth and true belief. Theories are more like grand hypotheses that we tentatively use until they are modified or displaced by a better theory.

This leaves us with the question, "If theories are not absolutely true, then what good are they?" White and Klein (2002) list seven uses for scientific theory: accumulation, precision, guidance, connectedness, interpretation, prediction, and explanation. We will briefly discuss a few of these. Scientific theories assist us in *accumulating* information. Some would say that we live in an information society, yet many of us may be swimming in information with little hope of making sense of it all. Theories allow us to use their concepts and relations to organize masses of information. To the extent that the theory provides a general and broad *explanation*, we find that the theory transforms information into knowledge. Theories *guide researchers* to test assumptions that are critical to the theory and would lead to the theory's rejection or modification. And finally theories allow us to look to the past and *interpret* the past by the theory.

Note that many of these functions could be shared by "beliefs." Beliefs can organize data and explain events. However, beliefs cannot be refuted since they would then become theories and hence, tentative.

Theoretical Frameworks in the Study of Families

The study of the family has traversed many distinctions about its theory and theorizing. Between 1950 and 1970, scholars referred to loose clusters of ideas as conceptual approaches (White, 2005). Conceptual approaches organize ideas, questions, and concepts to help clarify some aspect of family life. Hill and Hansen (1960) argue that what distinguishes one conceptual approach from another are the underlying assumptions. The assumptions typically represent beliefs about human nature, family, and society. Assumptions are not necessarily true or false; instead, they are conceptual tools used to see what one can learn by simply assuming that something is true. Sigmund Freud, the founder of psychoanalytic theory, for example, assumed (believed) that each person is born with antisocial drives (Bayer, 1981). He used this assumption to develop concepts such as the id, ego, and superego, and to formulate propositions about why individuals feel, think, and behave as they do. Later, family scholars had to develop a number of low level and middle range theories that could be united through assumptions and concepts shared with other such theories. These sets of common assumptions and concepts are now called **theoretical frameworks** (White and Klein, 2002; Boss et al. 1993).

The notions of conceptual approach and theoretical framework, according to Klein and White (1996:8–9), are more or less synonymous. Klein and White, however, define the term *ideology* as very different from an approach. Ideologies are seen as moralistic sets of beliefs in that they evaluate the rightness or wrongness of the evidence discovered in the empirical test of any particular conceptual approach. The researchers point out that ideologies sometimes facilitate the development of a scientific theoretical perspective. For example, Marxist ideology eventually led to the development of the *conflict approach* to be discussed later in this chapter. Yet, these could not be called theories or theoretical frameworks unless they can be overturned by empirical data.

Assumptions are not always articulated in a theoretical framework, but they are implicit in the definitions of concepts. Concepts are the building blocks of the approach; explanatory statements called propositions use them. A **proposition** is a statement that specifies the general relations between two concepts, such as "X causes Y." When these concepts are reduced to specific concrete measures for a particular situation we

have a hypothesis. The hypothesis is what the social scientist expects to find in the actual study of some aspect of human phenomena. The term *hypothesis* is not used interchangeably with *proposition*. A **hypothesis** uses the measures (or indicators) that are actually available in the data being analyzed by the researcher. Consider the following examples of a conceptual proposition and the hypothesis used to measure it:

> *Proposition:* "Positive affect" is significantly related to "marital satisfaction."

> *Hypothesis:* "Frequent touching" will be significantly correlated with "each spouse's score on the Dyadic Adjustment Scale of marital satisfaction."

In this example, the concepts of "positive affect" and "marital satisfaction" represent the researcher's conceptual perspective. However, the actual measures available—"frequent touching" and "the Dyadic Adjustment Scale score"—represent a much narrower meaning of these concepts. These more limited hypotheses are merely two of several possible ways of measuring (operationalizing) the concepts in the proposition. Box 2.1 illustrates several propositions from selected conceptual approaches. We will discuss seven theoretical frameworks, including some of those noted in Box 2.1, in the next section.

A theoretical framework or conceptual approach is important for two reasons. First, it narrows the scope of the analysis to more manageable limits. By focusing (as with a microscope) on a small unit of analysis, we can learn a great deal about the phenomenon that we would miss by using a more comprehensive perspective.

Box 2.1   Examples of Propositions

"Feelings of tension and frustration from uncompleted sexual experiences are more frequent for women than men." (Exchange approach; Nye, 1979:19)

"The more important a role expectation is to a person, the greater the effect that the quality of role enactment has on that person's satisfaction." (Symbolic interaction approach; Burr et al., 1979:71)

"Greater amounts of stressors and strains are associated with decreased adult functioning after separation

and divorce, when personal resources are taken into account." (Stress approach, Double ABCX model; Tschann et al., 1989:1036)

"Parent assault will be positively related to the extent to which the adolescent associates with intimate others who engage in violence and assault, including friends and parents." (Combines various approaches in the study of family violence and juvenile delinquency; Agnew and Huguley, 1989:704)

Theoretical frameworks (or approaches) are steps toward building general theories. These frameworks often contain several theories at a lower level of abstraction, but only the assumptions and concepts unite them at this point. Over time, we expect to see theoretical frameworks evolve into broad and general theories with uniting propositions. Second, theoretical frameworks are tools to provide helpful and efficient building blocks in the development of theory. By developing propositions and testing hypotheses about specific aspects of the family, and eventually linking verified findings (or those found to be mostly true), researchers enhance the likelihood of more comprehensive explanations of family phenomena.

Theoretical frameworks use the processes of *theorizing*, and they may contain smaller theories, but they are still in the process of becoming major theories. According to Zetterberg (1965), the unique characteristic that distinguishes any theory is that the propositions are "law-like." The concept of **theory** is defined as propositions (or theorems) that have been systematically and empirically tested (they are found to be valid, reliable and statistically significant) in multiple studies, conducted under different conditions, in different places, at different times, by independent researchers. However, this definition does not mean that established theories are the final word. Theories are always in process, subject to challenge and refinement. Scholarly work contributes to the improvement of theoretical explanations. While the social sciences have very few law-like theories, there are many conceptual approaches and theoretical frameworks that have proved useful in understanding and explaining marital and family phenomena.

In the following section, we will briefly examine several theoretical frameworks following White and Klein (2002). Box 2.2 identifies the basic explanatory argument of each of these theoretical frameworks.

Box 2.2   Seven Theoretical Frameworks in Family Study

Primarily macrosystem theories

Conflict
Because individuals and groups are self-oriented, family bonds are inherently conflictual and competitive.

Feminist
The links between gender, economics, politics, and patriarchy are the source of inequalities between women and men in the household. Patriarchy distorts theorizing and research.

Ecological
Adaptation by individuals in families and in their ever-changing social and economic environment is a natural and inevitable process. A variety of forces and resources interact in establishing acceptable ways of forming personal and interpersonal family meanings. Biological factors, in interaction with socialization factors, influence human development and the nature of mating and bonding between human beings.

Primarily microsystem theories

Symbolic interaction
Individual meanings and interpretations determine how a family member acts and reacts in interaction with others.

Social exchange
Individuals enter, stay, or leave relationships based on the personal benefits (profit margin) they receive compared with past or alternative relationships.

Family development
Most individual behaviours in families are in response to learned expectations from society, one's family of orientation, and private agreements established in the family of procreation. These expectations change over the life span.

Systems
When individuals share time and space in families, they establish family-level characteristics. These holistic bonds are unique and distinct from the sum of the individual characteristics of each family member.

Various perspectives are defined in the family literature. A more elaborated set of theories is identified in the *Sourcebook on Family Theories and Methods* (Boss et al., 1993); however the depth and detail of those discussions are inappropriate for our purposes. The most recent textbook on family theories (White and Klein, 2002) includes seven major theoretical frameworks. Several other approaches are defined as subsets of these major theories.

Macrolevel Theoretical Frameworks

Most macrolevel theoretical frameworks are in some way descended from a currently moribund theoretical framework known as the structural-functional perspective. This framework was especially influential in the decades leading up to and immediately after the Second World War. In order to understand macrolevel theory, a brief discussion of structural-functionalism is necessary.

The structural-functionalist approach focuses primarily on the macrosystem level of analysis, although the original theorists tried to explain all system levels in the tradition of a grand theory. This approach emphasizes the interdependency of the many parts of a society (Parsons and Bales, 1955; Bell and Vogel, 1960; Coser, 1964; McIntyre, 1981; Kingsbury and Scanzoni, 1993). Each part is assumed to perform an important function for each other part, directly or indirectly. The term *function* refers to the purpose or contribution that a social unit or social institution fulfills to maintain society. Various functions serve societal needs, family needs, and individual needs. Perhaps the most basic assumption is that certain minimum purposes or needs, or functional prerequisites, must be fulfilled in order for society to survive.

Structural-functionalism also emphasizes that the family itself has functional prerequisites or needs that must be satisfied if the family unit is to survive. In this sense, each family unit is like a miniature society. The survival of each family unit, therefore, is also dependent on the fulfillment of four basic functions: a) economic cooperation—a mutually acceptable division of labour; b) role differentiation—the distribution of power and responsibility; c) solidarity—the importance of building meaningful relationships among family members; and d) integration—inculcating shared values and attitudes about the meanings

of family, purpose and goals in living (Parsons and Bales, 1955; Scanzoni, 1970).

A structural-functional approach emphasizes *functions* (contributions of various parts to the whole), *dysfunctions* (actions with negative consequences), and *eufunctions* (the presence of some behaviour that has no known function) in systems and subsystems. Functions may also be manifest (known) or latent (apparent with the passage of time).

The major problem with this approach is that certain functions, such as divorce by mutual consent, may be functional for the well-being of certain individuals and types of marital relationships, but also dysfunctional for the majority of individuals, married couples, and society at large. In addition, determining whether a function is a functional prerequisite to societal well-being, or simply a time-based function that can be replaced by new functional alternatives, may involve more speculation than fact (Kingsbury and Scanzoni, 1993). Indeed, Klein and White (1996) have chosen to drop the structural-functional approach in their book on family theories. They take the position that functionalist concepts are now a subset of the systems approach and ecological approach.

Although structural-functionalism has largely been abandoned as a distinct school of thought, its influence permeates contemporary social science thinking. We used the structural-functional approach in parts of the section on defining *marriage* and *the family* in Chapter 1. We will also revisit aspects of this approach in Chapter 3, and more generally in Chapters 4 and 15. As you read subsequent chapters in this textbook, the most relevant conceptual approach will be identified wherever it is important to the issues or research under review.

Conflict Framework The conflict approach has its origins in the work of Karl Marx and Friedrich Engels (Moore, 1967). Marxist ideology responded to the economic inequities between the rich—the dominant *bourgeoisie* (the upper class)—and the oppressed *proletariat* (the working people). Women, wives, and mothers were exploited because they received lower pay when employed, and no payment or benefits as housewives or mothers. Capitalism promoted the patriarchal system, Marxism argued, and the patriarchal family promoted the capitalist system.

Most conflict theorists emphasize power. At the macrolevel, these scholars emphasize that the family is strategically involved in the reproduction and maintenance of capitalist society. The mechanisms of power are twofold: first, children are socialized to adopt patriarchal and capitalistic values; and second, the traditional division of household labour reinforces existing power structures in society (Farrington and Chertok, 1993). The political economy approach, still largely ignored by American family theorists,[1] is closely connected to basic conflict theories. Canadian family scholars have emphasized the role of economic structures and processes in the development and structure of family relationships. They have considered, for example, the impact of industrialization on family life (Gaffield, 1990), social class variations in family life, the impact of the economy on household labour and women's roles, and government influences on personal choices among men and women (Baker, 1990b). Other scholars using a political economy approach argue that economic arrangements between men and women in the workplace and in the household, whatever their form, are determined by systems of power and ideologies designed to maintain the status quo (Maroney and Luxton, 1987). In the section on the feminist approach, we will discuss links between the political economy and feminist perspectives.

At the microlevel, the conflict approach basically assumes that individuals are more self-oriented than other-oriented, and are inclined to pursue their own interests at the expense of others (Sprey, 1979). Therefore, conflict in the family is inevitable and natural, since the family is both a social institution and a small group. At the microlevel, the unequal distribution of power in the family creates "power exertion processes" and "power resistance strategies" to keep family power structures in place and suppress change (Szinovacz, 1987; Farrington and Chertok, 1993). Each member of a family, therefore, faces the never-ending necessity of dealing with other members' conflicting interests. Three interconnected concepts are fundamental to this approach: competition, conflict, and consensus. The essence of competition is that whenever one spouse wins, the other loses. Conflict involves direct confrontation (attack) whenever the need arises; the marriage relationship is in a condition of continual conflict for an extended period of time until agreement is reached or the relationship ends. Consensus, in the conflict perspective, refers to those areas in which a couple has achieved agreement.

Conflict and competition are certainly aspects of family existence and, as Chapters 7, 13, and 14 will document, conflict and violence are significant factors in dating, marriage, and family life. However, the conflict approach de-emphasizes the role of consensus in everyday life and denies that peace-making is also a significant thrust in both families and societies. White and Klein (2002) also point out the fact that conflict is a dynamic process, i.e., there is an inherent interpersonal and societal struggle to remove inequities, which eventually may lead to the reduction of conflict.

Feminist Framework The feminist framework is a macro-sociological framework that basically views the family as incorporating the gender inequality found in the larger society. Until the mid-20th century, the feminist perspective was largely limited to the pursuit of justice and equality. Remarkable women, beginning in the 17th century, persisted in the drive for full citizenship (including the right to vote), legal rights, an end to sex discrimination in education and employment, and the elimination of sex stereotyping (Osmond and Thorne, 1993). In the 1960s and 1970s, major changes occurred in the approach to gender issues. Two perspectives seem to have emerged. The most prominent feminist perspective is a macro-sociological approach that seeks to understand family behaviours as reflecting and recreating the "patriarchal" systems of oppression found in the larger society.

Even though the feminist framework is largely macroscopic, it does include several psychological and social-psychological themes that are used to understand and explain gender differences. For example, it emphasizes conflicts between the subjective experiences of women and men (Bernard, 1972). Bernard has documented that there are "his" and "hers" definitions of the same marriage. Several feminist authors have argued that women have a unique way of knowing and thinking about the meaning of society, morality, family, and children (Gilligan, 1982; Ruddick, 1982). Other feminists use psychoanalytic assumptions (Chodorow, 1978; Gilligan, 1982) and emphasize the importance of emotions, intimacy, body functions, ways of knowing and reasoning, or the symbolism in language to describe conscious and unconscious psychosexual development. Osmond and Thorne (1993) suggest that this approach values young girls and adult women and encourages the thinking that gender differences can be transformed.

The predominant frame of reference—Marxist feminist theory (similar to radical feminism and socialist feminism)—is a subset of macro-resource conflict theory (Klein and White, 1996). Firestone (1970) argued that women are victims of their biology in four ways: 1) without birth control, women are controlled by pregnancy, lactation, and the care of infants; 2) infants are largely dependent on female adults for survival; 3) mother–child interdependency shapes what it means to be a mother and child; and 4) the fact of reproduction defines the meaning of gender for women. Patriarchy is blamed for pornography, prostitution, sexual harassment, rape, and for societal pressures in favour of heterosexuality and against abortion, contraception, and sterilization. Marxist dogma appeals to feminist theorists because it supports the rights of the oppressed and the need for radical changes in the structure of society (Osmond and Thorne, 1993).

As mentioned in the summary of the conflict perspective, feminist scholars in Canada have been exploring the connections between the political economy perspectives and feminist theories. They believe that the economic system stimulates the oppression of women based on biological sex differences that underlie all other forms of inequality. Politically defined economic systems subordinate women as housewives, child-bearers, and child-rearers (Maroney and Luxton, 1987). Maroney and Luxton identify four unique hypotheses:

- gender differentiation is as pervasive as social class;

- gender inequality is inherent within and between social classes;

- gender and economic issues cannot be separated;

- reproduction is based on economic factors, not maternal instinct.

Thompson and Walker summarize "the place of feminism in family studies" (Thompson and Walker, 1995) and identify five basic premises of feminist scholarship:

1. The central concept of feminist theory is the social construction of gender. "Feminists examine the structural, cultural, historical and interpersonal conditions that create distinctions and perpetuate power relations between women and men" (Thompson and Walker, 1995:848). Socialization is not as important as stratification. Men only do housework if the demand is high and women aren't available. Research focuses on why women and men collude to accept men's justifications for ignoring housework, and examines types of caring, fairness and conflict, and different types of household labour. Indeed, feminists argue that much of nonfeminist scientific theory and research is conceptualized in a patriarchal system. Feminist scholars see gender as the fundamental basis of inequality between men and women.

2. Feminist theorists are committed to gender equality and social change. One simple definition of feminist theory is "analysis of women's subordination for the purpose of figuring out how to change it" (Gordon, 1979:7). This is an advocacy perspective, not unlike Marxist ideology. Feminist scholars "are outspoken in their commitment to gender equality" (Thompson and Walker, 1995:852). According to Cheal (1991), feminist theory is a broadly based movement for publicizing the private problems of women, such as domestic violence, child care needs and financial dependence.

3. Feminist theories question "the family." Scholars argue that patriarchy idealizes the "traditional family" (father as provider, mother as homemaker) and promotes the myth that there is a universal definition of the family (Thorne, 1982a; Eichler, 1988). Thompson and Walker (1995:858) suggest that the "prevailing notions" of "the family" do not match the experiences of women. It is emphasized that who or what constitutes family cannot be taken for granted, and that it is time to ask questions about families in all their diversity, "rather than search for the bad things that are assumed to befall any family that does not match this standard" (p. 858). Heterosexuality is seen as a political institution (Rich, 1980). The meanings of marriage and family are no longer societal "givens" (Alpert, 1988; Weston, 1991; Preston, 1992). They argue that "the family is now an openly contested issue, and the debate in the journals is lively." Feminists reject structural-functionalist and universal definitions of the family, as described in Chapter 1, in preference to inclusive definitions.

4. Feminist theorists and researchers put their beliefs into action. The college and university classroom is the primary location in which the feminist perspective is operationalized, i.e., put into action. Advice on how to effectively practise this theory in the classroom is now regularly published in professional family journals (Walker, 1993; Thompson and Walker, 1995). Allen (1988; and Allen, 1995) was one of the first feminist teachers to initiate a literature on feminist teaching strategies in family courses and share her own experiences as a feminist scholar. The annual conference of the National Council on Family Relations provides a forum for feminist pedagogy. Classroom instruction emphasizes the strengths and achievements of diverse groups, such as different social classes, races, ethnicities, genders, and sexual orientations (Walker, 1993). Teaching emphasizes the positive aspects of diverse groups and lifestyles and minimizes comparisons between underrepresented groups and the mainstream standard (Walker, 1993; Crawford and Marecek, 1989). Male scholars with a feminist orientation are also putting their beliefs into action in the classroom (Marks, 1995).

5. The feminist approach emphasizes the centrality of women's lives and experiences. This includes the study of women's experiences as mothers and women's ties with kin. They do not study fathering unless the fathering issues use the "construction of gender as the central concept" (Thompson and Walker, 1995). The reason for this is that the feminist perspective makes a distinction between the culture and the conduct of fatherhood. As indicated earlier in this chapter, a conceptual approach is a "device to see what one can see with a different set of glasses." In other words, feminist theorists are using a particular approach to see what they can learn that might otherwise be missed using a different perspective.

Feminist theorizing is the most explicit example of the value of choosing an *a priori* set of assumptions and seeking to define and explain issues that arise from a particular point of view.[2] Feminist scholars are asking important questions. Two textbooks provide differing ideas on what it means to be a family in Canada (Eichler, 1988; Mandell and Duffy, 1988). Eichler emphasizes the significant departures from monolithic, conservative, sexist, and microsystem biases in current family literature, citing changes in household management, reproduction, child care, and family policies. Mandell and Duffy have edited a book of readings that illustrates the diversity of feminist views on reconstructing the Canadian family. The concepts and methods in the feminist approach may contribute important new insights to our understanding of family phenomena. We include feminist theorizing and research throughout this textbook.

Culture influences feminist thinking and research activity as it does masculinist theorizing and research activity. Socialization, culture, and professional training in the social sciences affect both male and female ways of knowing. Osmond and Thorne (1993), two prominent feminist scholars, argue that feminist theory must now focus on families as both a locus of conflict and subordination, and as the major source of cooperation and solidarity. White and Klein (2002) and Chafetz (1997, 1999) distinguish between feminism that is mainly ideological and feminist theory that is more focused on scientific explanation. In the chapters to follow we will focus more on the second form of feminist theory and explanation.

Ecological Framework According to White and Klein (2002), the ecological perspective has evolved from several diverse influences, including plant ecology; the ways in which human populations adapt to particular environments; concerns about excess population growth combined with limited food supply or insufficient living spaces; and the interaction between biological and social factors in population growth. The most basic premise is the principle of adaptation. Human ecology deals with the interactions and interdependence of humans (individuals, groups, and societies) with the environment, both organic and inorganic (Bubolz and Sontag, 1993). The "key process is adaptation by humans of and to their environments" (p. 421). Families live in an ever-changing social and economic environment.

Ellen Richards, who died in 1911, was the first female student at MIT (Massachusetts Institute of Technology) and one of the pioneers of water purity analysis. Richards later founded and was the first president of the American Home Economics Association (Clark, 1973, as summarized in Klein and White, 1996:212). Family ecology developed out of the discipline of home economics. The "family is conceived as a life-support system dependent on the natural environment for physical sustenance and on the social environment for human contact and meaning" (Hook and Paolucci, 1970).

Each family unit, whatever its form, is said to have a family ecosystem that includes the *human-built environment*, the *sociocultural environment*, and the *natural physical-biological environment* (Bubolz and Sontag, 1993:432). This conceptual approach assumes that all types of families take in energy and information, process these "data," and seek ways to adapt to the environment. These adaptations occur through communication, decision-making, and managing physical, material, and technological resources to carry out daily activities. This approach accepts diverse family structures including "sets of interdependent but independent persons who share some common goals, resources, and a commitment to each other over time" (Bubolz and Sontag, 1993:435). Bubolz and Sontag (1993: 426) also emphasize the importance of core and universal values in family ecological systems: survival (economic adequacy), justice, freedom, and peacefulness. Questions such as the following are asked: "What changes are necessary to bring about human betterment? How can families and family professionals contribute to the process of change?" (Bubolz and Sontag, 1993:429).

There are several other ecological approaches. We will mention only one. Bronfenbrenner (1979, 1986), a psychologist who specializes in human development, emphasizes the importance of the individual's family context—the microsystem, and three other systemic levels with which the microsystem interacts and which influence human development—the mesosystem, exosystem, and macrosystem. In his 1986 publication, Bronfenbrenner develops a new concept: the *chronosystem*. The individual traits and abilities of each child born into a family interact with the interpersonal and social environment throughout the life span. Bronfenbrenner's contributions to both family ecology and human development theory are significant. Research on day care and its effects on infants and young children by Belsky and his colleagues (e.g., 1984), and studies of child mistreatment in high-risk neighbourhoods by Garbarino and his colleagues (e.g., 1980) are excellent examples of research related to Bronfenbrenner's version of the ecological approach. (See also Chapter 11.) Klein and White (1996:240) indicate that the ecological perspective is still in its youth. The connections and interactions between families and their diverse environments are still much like a catalogue of concepts, issues, and diagrams.

Each of these conceptual approaches stimulates differing methodological and conceptual strategies in the search for scientific knowledge about intimacy, marriages, and families. Box 2.3 briefly illustrates how each of these approaches would theorize about or study divorce. As we emphasized in Chapter 1, our approach in this book is eclectic and not restricted to only one or two of these conceptual schemes. Although we will attempt to use the theories and research relevant to the topics examined, our real purpose in this book is to introduce the material applicable to each chapter. Accordingly, this chapter identifies theoretical approaches, but many others will specifically focus on the research rather than the theory. In the last section of this chapter, we briefly deal with research methods in family study: design, measurement, sampling, and data analysis.

Microlevel Theoretical Frameworks

Similar to the way that macrolevel theories were influenced by one particular predecessor (structural-functionalism), microlevel theories can be seen as reacting to the mechanistic determinism (stimulus-response) of psychological reinforcement theory that was associated with Skinner (1953). As a result, most of the microlevel theories tend to be social-psychological approaches. These approaches often see the individual as the unit of analysis but recognize the environment as socially, culturally, and psychologically important in explaining individual behaviour in the family.

Symbolic Interaction Framework The symbolic interaction approach emphasizes the role of individual interpretations of reality and role definitions in marital and family interactions (Charon, 1979; Burr et al., 1979; LaRossa and Reitzes, 1993; White and Klein, 2002). The concepts highlight symbols (language, gestures, and other cues), variant perceptions, the person's capacity to receive and evaluate stimuli and response, the importance of self-esteem, and interpersonal family processes such as role-playing, communication problems, decision making,

Box 2.3   Studying Divorce from Seven Theoretical Frameworks

Conflict

Divorce is probably inevitable. How do economic structures keep marriages together despite self-interest and continuing conflict?

Feminist

How does patriarchy influence divorce rates and divorce outcomes for women and their children? What are the sources of gender inequity in divorce for men and women?

Symbolic interaction

What are the perceptions and interpretations of the actions and interactions of marital partners who have obtained divorces? In what ways did these interpersonal perceptions influence their behaviours?

Social exchange

What are the relative costs and rewards of staying together versus leaving the marital relationship? What are the relative costs and rewards of remaining divorced?

Family development

What were the expectations of the marital partners before divorce? What were the expectations of society and of their families of orientation? At what stage did the divorce occur?

Systems

What were the holistic characteristics of the family (or marital) system prior to divorce, compared with other family systems in which divorce has not occurred?

Ecological

In what ways did the environment undermine the stability of the family? In what ways did the family's ecological adaptations such as "communication or managing material resources" contribute to the breakdown of the family? What type of family ecology was formed in response to divorce?

---

and socialization. Perhaps the main postulate of symbolic interaction theory is that people are not robots in relationships, simply acting in routine ways and performing exclusively in the ways they have been taught. They think about their actions and the actions of significant others.

The symbolic interaction approach, in contrast to stimulus-response approaches, emphasizes stimulus-interpretation-response (SIR), which means that the stimulus is interpreted before the individual responds or reacts. This interpretation involves learned symbols. Actions have different meanings for both the actor and the spouse (or child) who experiences the action. Indeed, human beings act toward others on the basis of the cognitive or perceptual meanings that the actions of others have for them. When intimate partners, spouses, or family members interact, their perception of the situation itself, and of the intentions of the other actors in that situation, influence their interpretations. Importantly, symbolic interactionists assume that perceptions and the meanings derived from them however accurate or inaccurate, are real; and that

these meanings are, therefore, real in their consequences for human relationships.

Symbolic interactionists emphasize the importance of reaction, rather than action alone. They assume the human mind is like a computer that has stored every thought, feeling, and action ever experienced in interaction with others. This information may be employed in unexpected ways when the person reacts to stimuli such as the actions of spouses, parents, and others.

Because this approach relies on the thoughts and feelings of the individual in action and interaction, its postulates are more difficult to test. Although the assumptions and predictions are designed to explain interaction, survey data is most often collected from individuals, rather than from the two or more members of a family unit who are interacting. Perhaps the major limitation of this theoretical approach is that the data is largely based on self-reports. Attitudes, emotions, interpretations, and related phenomena that are "inside the head" can only be known to the degree that they are accurately reported in surveys or psychological inventories. Furthermore, individual respondents may have widely varying levels of self-awareness and self-understanding. But despite its limitations, this approach is perhaps the most popular microsystem approach in family study. In addition, it deals more directly with the everyday realities of interacting with spouses and children than does any other frame of reference. LaRossa and Reitzes (1993) argue that the study of the family at the microlevel depends on the symbolic interaction approach.

Social Exchange Framework Costs and rewards are central tenets of the social exchange approach (Blau, 1964; Chadwick-Jones, 1976; Nye, 1979; Sabatelli and Shehan, 1993; White and Klein, 2002). Although exchange theory has occasionally been used to examine macrosystem issues, most theoretical work occurs at the microsystem level. Exchange theorists argue that individuals evaluate the relative costs and rewards of entering, staying in, or leaving any relationship, including a marital or family relationship. If the relationship is perceived to provide a higher degree of profit (the rewards exceed the costs) than other relationships, the person is likely to stay. This process of evaluation involves two comparisons. The *comparison level* (CL) refers to a person's evaluation based on what she feels she deserves. Each person has her own standard of aspiration and expectation. The *comparison level for alternatives* (CLalt) refers to the minimum profit or outcome that an individual will accept relative to the alternative opportunities that the person perceives are available. This evaluation process leads, in the short term or long term, to entering, staying, or leaving behaviours. Family exchange theorists often emphasize the principle of reciprocity: the significance of duties, rights, and equities in marital and family bonds (Scanzoni, 1970; Scanzoni, 1978). People are obliged to help those who help them, and should not be unfair to or undermine those who have helped them. Exchange theory is one of the more precise theories in the family field, in that it defines specific conditions that regulate interpersonal, sexual, premarital, marital, and family phenomena.

The exchange argument—that nobody does anything in the long term without getting what they perceive as a fair exchange for their effort—seems like a powerful explanation of marriage and family relationships. We should consider, however, the exceptions to the reciprocity rule. Parents often sacrifice for their children without any apparent gain. Some individuals care for a paralyzed spouse in spite of daily sacrifices. Husbands and wives continue to live together even when they might gain more from alternative relationships. Not all intimate bonds, therefore, can be reduced to the profit principle. However, exchange theorists have an answer: no one does anything for another person without believing in a reward either in this life or the life hereafter. Here is an excellent example of the power of an assumption. Assumptions may not be testable; they are merely beliefs that underlie the theoretical approach. "Despite the criticisms... exchange theory is one of the most popular social science theories applied to the family" (Klein and White, 1996: 85).

Family Development Framework Klein and White (1996:89) point out that family development is the only theory that is uniquely focused on the family. Each of the other approaches can be used in the study of other social groups and institutions. The developmental approach is primarily microsystem-oriented and may be classified as a middle-range theory. It focuses on the impact of expectations (norms) on what family members do to and with each other (Hill and Rodgers, 1964; Rodgers, 1973). Accordingly, what husbands and wives do is strongly influenced by what various players *expect* them to do: society (Canada, ethnic group, religious group, and so on), the family in which they were socialized, and their spouses. Family members occupy socially defined positions (mother, son, wife) that are made up of roles (sets of norms). A key feature of this approach is the life-span dimension. Developmental scholars assume that norms change in each of the family stages in the family life span, often referred to as the *family career*. Accordingly, the expectations are different for couples without children from those for parents with infants or teenagers. Mattessich and Hill (1987) specified seven basic family life stages based on three criteria: changes in family size, age composition, and the occupational status of the breadwinner(s). These stages are adapted below as follows:

■ childless couples

■ childbearing families, with infants and preschool children

- childbearing families with grade-school children
- families with teenagers
- families with young adults still at home (one or more children 18 years of age or older)
- families in the middle years (children launched from parental household)
- aging families

These stages, with some variation, continue to be used in research on the family career. White (1991), Rodgers and White (1993), Klein and White (1996), White and Klein (2002) have updated the theory to emphasize the significance of these changes in connection with other transitions, such as cohabitation, births in later stages, separation, divorce, remarriage, or death. Early developmentalists also defined a special set of crucial norms called *developmental tasks* for each stage of the life span. If an individual, couple, or family fails to fulfill these expectations, progress to the next stage is hindered. If this occurs, normal relationship development is also hindered, and the likelihood of relationship failure increases. Although this concept remains an important dimension of the approach, the focus has shifted to a more general notion: "If a family or individual is 'out of sequence' with the normative ordering of family events, the probability of later life disruptions is increased" (Klein and White, 1996:132). The normative ordering or sequencing of family stages must also interface with other social institutions, such as education, work, or the economy. These are important innovations in the developmental approach and may offer greater explanatory power as these aspects of the theory are tested in ongoing research. Nonetheless, many development theorists continue to explain family behaviours, family stability, and family satisfaction largely on the basis of which expectations between and among members of the family are fulfilled over time.

As emphasized above, the developmental approach emphasizes the normative dimension of interpersonal behaviour. Accordingly, it ignores the innovative and creative dimensions of relationships—those actions and interactions that cannot be anticipated by knowing what the members of families are expected to do. Critics of developmentalism have long argued that events such as cohabitations, separations, divorces, remarriages, and alternative careers, such as never-married parenthood

and childlessness, have been neglected. White (1991) and Klein and White (1996) have accepted the challenge. Individual and family developmental issues, and the divergent pathways of family careers, are difficult to measure, let alone accurately assess over time. In the interim, the traditional conceptual tools will continue to be useful in understanding family patterns over the life span.

Systems Framework The systems approach was first developed by von Bertalanffy (1950), a biologist who asserted the importance of studying the molecule as a unit, rather than studying the various forms of biological life (germs, amoeba) that live inside the molecule. The application of this approach to human units of organization followed (Broderick and Smith, 1979; Kantor and Lehr, 1975; Montgomery, 1981; Whitechurch and Constantine, 1993; Broderick, 1993).

The systems approach emphasizes the characteristics of system and subsystem behaviours over time. The family, as a holistic unit, is a system, and the husband–wife relationship is a subsystem. The parts do not equal the whole; or, to put it another way, the whole is more than the sum of the parts. This means that if we know the exact characteristics of a husband and a wife, we still cannot accurately describe or predict what these two persons will be like as a couple, nor how they will act as a couple with other couples. The couple has an identity as a couple that is separate and distinct from the identities of the two individuals. The same principle applies to the family as a unit.

The systems perspective focuses not on how fathers influence their sons or on how sons influence their fathers, but on the characteristics of the father–son relationship as a unit (subsystem). How does the father–son relationship differ from the mother–son relationship? How does the Johnson family differ from the Jones family? Is one family unit more disorganized, the other more egalitarian? Why? Do family behaviours differ from one time to another? How are behaviours sequenced and interconnected over time? Are there recurring cycles or phases?

Typologies of marital and family systems are increasingly common in the systems literature. Fitzpatrick (1988), for example, uses empirical data to define three types of married couples: traditionals, independents and separates. Olson et al. (1979), using detailed measures of family cohesion and family adaptability, defined 16 types of family systems. Many systems analysts examine how families receive and process information (Kantor and Lehr, 1975). *Closed family systems* resist accepting new information. *Random family systems* receive information without regulation or evaluation. *Open family systems* weigh information in the interest of growth and change.

Systems theory emphasizes an important aspect of marital and family relationships: the unique characteristics of the unit. Broderick (1993) presents a process view of the family system that includes the family relationships and the evolution of shared meanings and realities within the family. Although the approach has generated many good ideas, useful comparisons between units, and many interesting hypotheses, it remains largely descriptive rather than explanatory. White and Klein (2002) point out that systems theory has proven very useful in family therapy and in the study of marital and family communications and interaction.

Research Methods in Family Study

An immense amount of research on premarital, marital, and family relations is conducted each year. The *Inventory of Marriage and Family Literature*, published each year by the National Council on Family Relations, lists thousands of new articles by author, subject, and key words (e.g., Toullatos and Czaplewski, 1992). The publication, which also includes books, provides a listing of 3703 articles and 488 books published between September 1990 and December 1991. This publication has now been "assimilated" by the Family Studies Data Base (FSDB). The FSDB is issued quarterly on a CD-ROM to both library and private subscribers. It is the single most useful resource for students, researchers, and teachers on any topic or issue related to sexuality, marriages, families, parenting, and hundreds of other key words. About half of all family research is designed to test one or more dimensions of a conceptual approach.

The study of the family is similar to other social scientific and scientific fields in that all have witnessed an astounding increase in the amount of data amassed. It is critical that students be armed with theories to explain and interpret this array of data and, just as importantly, students should have basic research and

methodological skills so that they can assess which research is valid, reliable, and trustworthy. Indeed, the critical capacity that students gain from this understanding of research will transfer to almost every endeavor they will undertake as consumers, professionals, educators, and parents.

Research Question: The Beginning

Every research project, whether it be a term paper or a national survey of Canadians, should begin with a research question. At the simplest level, a research question might be formulated in a "why" or "how" question such as "Why do people get divorced?" or "How do married couples decide to have a first child?" Certainly these naïve questions give way to more sophisticated questions as one reads and gains more background in an area. In the end we can see three major sources from which research questions emerge.

1. Theory In this case, the research question emerges from a careful reading of theory and the identification of particular propositions that have not been tested. Of course, the most fruitful tests would be those that would refute or disprove the theory and lead us to a better formulation.

2. Empirical Studies As we review empirical studies in an area, we might find that there are gaps in our empirical knowledge. For example, we might find that on the one hand working women do much more housework than men, and on the other hand, these women are satisfied with the division of labour in their marriage. The "gap" in this literature would be captured in the question "How can women doing so much work be satisfied with the division of labour?"

3. Naïve Curiosity Although this may not be the most sophisticated way of approaching research, it nonetheless might produce important findings. Some simple questions are extremely difficult to address, such as "Why do people have babies?" This naïve question becomes more interesting when we add information such as that children are an economic liability rather than asset and that filial piety and responsibility for the elderly is declining. Simple curiosity will always be a source of hypotheses.

Research Design

Once the types of questions in a research project are formulated, the next step is developing the strategy for conducting the study. The first step in developing a research design is to change the research question into a hypothesis. The reason for this is simple. In logic we cannot ascertain the truth or falsity of a question but only the truth or falsity of a statement. Since every statement has its opposite, we really have two hypotheses. For example, if we say "people want to have babies because they think the child will take care of them in their old age" then the obverse of this is that this is not the reason they want babies. Once the research question is turned into a statement, we have a *"substantive" hypothesis,* and its obverse, which is called the *"null" hypothesis.* If one is true then the other must be false, and vice versa.

A research design is simply the logic that would allow us to determine the truth or falsity of a hypothesis in an unambiguous manner. For example, we might claim that billiard ball A imparts "force" to an inert billiard ball B thus creating B's movement across the billiard table. This claim would have to undergo successive trials where other possible causes of motion were eliminated as explanations. The mental setting up of these possible situations is the research design. There are numerous types of research designs, only a few of which we will discuss below.

Most research designs are drawn from what is called the *classical experimental design.* In the classical design, there are two groups: an experimental group that will receive the "treatment" and the control group that will not receive any "treatment." Figure 2.1 shows a classical experimental design with four cells. The "R" on the left hand side of the table indicates that people are randomly assigned to either the experimental test group or the control. This random assignment guarantees that the only differences between these two groups are the random variations you would expect between people. Within the four cells of the table are the "effects." At time 1 there should be no differences (except random differences) between the control and test groups. At time 2, after the test group received the treatment, there should be a significant change in the score of the treatment group (3→8) and no change for the control since nothing happened to them except the change of time.

Figure 2.1   Classical Experimental Design

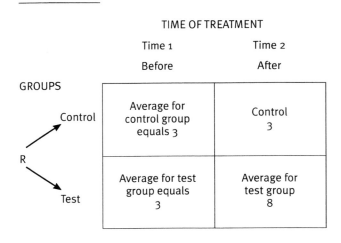

Most students are well aware of the limitations of the classical experimental design, and it has been replaced by host of other designs such as the Solomon design (see Kidder and Judd, 1986). For example, we said that nothing would change for the control except the passage of time—but what if we were interested in an outcome that was developmental, such as a child talking? We might put our test group children into an early language class and just leave the control with their parents. However, we might find that both groups change as a function of the length of time between tests. Indeed, we might find that if before and after times were a year apart, there would be no difference in language ability, but if the duration were two months we might find that the test children acquired language more quickly. Another problem with this design is the placebo effect: just knowing that you are in a study may make you change attitudes or behaviours independent of any test or treatment. Regardless of the flaws, the classical experimental design remains the foundation on which most other designs build.

Many times we cannot control random assignment to groups or the timing of treatments because we want to find out what people in actual families are doing and thinking. In this case we sacrifice the internal validity of experimental designs for the higher generalizability and reality of the field situation. For most of the social sciences this means some form of *correlational design.* A correlational design addresses the hypothesis in a slightly different way. Returning to our example of the billiard balls, correlational design would posit that over many observations there is a high positive correlation between A hitting B and B moving, and a low or "zero" correlation between B moving when A does not hit it. Correlational designs are used when we want to observe families and individuals in natural settings and have data that is readily generalizable to the real world rather than the laboratory.

There are many drawbacks to correlational designs, but the single biggest one is captured in the commonly uttered phrase "correlation is not causation!" (MacIver, 1964) For example, if we were to observe house and building fires in a city over a year and then tabulate the correlation between the "amount of fire damage" and the "number of fire engines" at the fire, the resulting correlation might lead us to conclude that fire engines cause fire damage. After all, the more fire engines attending the fire, the worse the fire damage. This is an example of "spurious" correlation or causation. In such cases we usually find that the correlation between two variables is actually due to an unknown or unmeasured third variable. In the case of the fire damage and fire engines, the third variable would be the number of "alarms" the fire marshal turns in for the fire. The fire marshal assesses the potential degree of the fire and decides how many alarms should be sent. The number of alarms determines how many fire engines are sent, but it also is a crude indicator of the amount of fire damage that is occurring. Figure 2.2 demonstrates this case of spurious causation (MacIver, 1964).

The design we adopt for our research must attempt to give us the best chance of assessing the validity of the research hypothesis. As we have seen, some designs, such

as the experimental design, will be very strong in assessing causation (internal validity) but weak in terms of generalizing to the real world where a host of other complicating variables are operating. Other designs, such as the correlational design, might be adaptable to the real, complex social environment (external validity), but have significant drawbacks in terms of causation (spuriousness). The researcher must choose whether the research question hypothesizes causation or would be better tested in an ecologically valid setting.

Measurement

Hypotheses contain concepts and relations. For example, the hypothesis "the higher the socioeconomic status of the husband, the greater the amount of housework he will perform" contains two concepts: "socioeconomic status of husband" and "amount of housework performed." There is one relation between these two concepts that says as one concept increases, so does the other. A researcher must first determine what indicators will be used to measure the concepts and propositions. The term *operationalize* refers to the process by which indicators are developed to measure each concept and relation. Concepts may be carefully defined, but they may be very difficult to measure. In the example of husbands doing housework, socioeconomic status is relatively easy to operationalize since there are many good indexes available that have been well tested for reliability and validity. On the other hand, the measurement of "amount of housework" is much more difficult. Certainly, we could use hours of work performed in the home, but that would value vacuuming the rugs the same as repairing a broken water pipe. Clearly, if one examined the

Figure 2.2   Example of Spurious Correlation

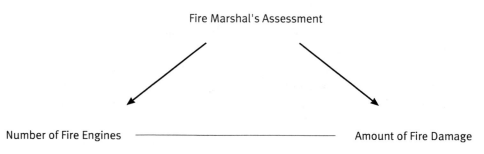

market value of this labour, a house cleaner is less expensive than a plumber. Indeed, there are many possible ways to measure amount of housework and in the last analysis, the operationalization would have to be guided by theory in addition to the research question.

There are two basic types of measurement: quantitative and qualitative measures. **Qualitative measures** require decoding by the researcher and are thus based on the researcher's sensitivity to and immersion in the subject area. Qualitative measures often emphasize open-ended interviews or observations. Hypotheses are often not used (Glaser, 1978, for example), or the goal of the research may be an in depth description. Such designs typically involve case studies of family members who openly share their realities and experiences with the researcher. Several follow-up sessions may be required to obtain a complete understanding of the family's experiences. This type of research typically de-emphasizes the use of numbers or frequencies to analyze what people say about their experiences. Instead, qualitative studies permit people to define and redefine meanings continually in their own experience, a process that enables them to find themselves and clarify their own understandings (Hutchinson, 1986). Qualitative studies often use *volunteer, nominated* or *snowball* samples. Snowball samples involve personal referrals by key respondents to obtain additional participants in the study. A Canadian study of childless couples (Veevers, 1980) is an excellent example of volunteer and snowball techniques. Martin (1993) studied nine couples and three mothers whose healthy babies died of Sudden Infant Death Syndrome. The results of this important work clarify the dynamics of the grief process.

Family members may be observed (in homes, shopping malls, laboratories) or interviewed. Written materials such as magazines, government reports, historical documents, and published or unpublished policies by organizations may be examined in what is often called *content analysis*. Clinical studies are also good examples of qualitative designs. They involve in-depth examinations of couples or families undergoing some degree of relationship distress. Researchers usually interview each individual and give various psychological tests. They may accumulate and analyze clinical records for multiple clients in search of apparent patterns or typologies (such as differing types of families). Participant observation and related forms of field observation are other examples of qualitative design.

Jules Henry, working with research associates, lived with eight different families from early morning until late evening for one week. His book, *Pathways to Madness* (Henry, 1971), is a popular description of the everyday lives of eight troubled family systems which appeared "normal" in public. Anthropologists may live with a colony or tribe of people observing mores and lifestyles, taking field notes, and recording impressions on a daily basis. Qualitative studies are typically exploratory in purpose because they have insufficient information or subjects to formulate reasonable hypotheses. A qualitative design also helps the researcher to set aside any preconceived ideas in the interest of learning how the individuals in families define their own reality. For this reason, this type of research plan may be preferred to quantitative techniques.

Quantitative measures, in contrast, typically involve a clear idea of what the researcher wants to know and the development of specific questions to measure phenomena. Quantitative measures by definition involve ways of counting or obtaining frequencies of behaviours or attitudes. Observations and the responses to questions are systematically counted. Quantitative methods are by far the most common type of research design, and the *survey* is the most popular quantitative tool. Nearly 65 percent of all marriage and family research studies rely on surveys to gather data (Galligan, 1982).

Questionnaires may be mailed out, delivered to households, or administered in specific locations. The response categories usually provide limited choices varying from two (such as *Yes* or *No*), to a number on a scale of 1 to 10, where 1, for example, is "very strongly agree" and 10 is "very strongly disagree." Interviews are conducted in person or by telephone. Interviewers may ask structured questions, such as those found in the typical questionnaire, but they often use more open-ended questions and follow-up probes to the responses received.

Another form of quantitative measurement is direct observation of families in field studies, in the laboratory with two-way mirrors and video cameras, and in natural settings such as the family home. What family members say, and to whom they say it, can be systematically recorded by hand or with audiotape. Their nonverbal behaviour as they talk—such as facial expressions, gestures, or even posture—can also be recorded by hand, by video recorder, or by a small computer programmed with codes for various behaviours. Verbal and physical interactions can be counted.

Experimental design, another research technique, usually includes several features. Families are randomly divided into a target group and a control group. The target group families will be given different information (called the *treatment effect*) from the control group families. All families will be pre-tested before the treatment effect, and post-tested to see if the treatment effect makes a difference. The major advantage of this design is that it allows researchers to control factors that often influence research findings. Very little pure experimental research has been done with marriages or families, but wherever possible, various aspects of experimental design are used. Behaviour modification research, for example, uses treatment effects and pre-test/post-test designs, typically without control groups (Patterson, 1988). Surveys may include longitudinal designs (sampling the same subjects in two or more time periods), and may occasionally create control groups by excluding certain questions in the "second wave."

Quantitative measurement involves three major components. The first is determining the types of variables to be measured. There are three basic types of variables: nominal, ordinal, and interval. A **nominal variable** contains two or more categories that are qualitatively different, where the difference or distance between each category cannot be determined mathematically. The variable "sex," for example, contains two categories: female and male. Usually, a person is not part male and part female. An **ordinal variable** means that the differences among the values or categories of a variable can be rank ordered. The responses to a question about divorce, for example, can be organized into low, medium and high agreement. The mathematical differences between these categories of agreement are not equal, but they are rank ordered. An **interval variable** may be defined when the differences among categories or values of a variable can be measured mathematically, because the distance between each value of the variable is equal. Income is a good example of an interval variable.

The second component deals with the issue of **validity**. Does the indicator used actually measure the concept as defined? Can the researcher show that the indicator and the concept mean the same thing? For example, is "love" (the concept) accurately measured by the "number of years a couple have lived together" (the indicator)? The third component concerns **reliability**. Does the indicator used measure the same thing each time it is used in different studies, in different locations, and at different times? Indicators may be reliable but invalid measures of the concept. Likewise, an indicator may be a valid measure of the concept, but prove to be an unreliable indicator in multiple tests.

Sampling

After resolving design and measurement issues, the next step in research is to decide which subjects are to be studied. In the Canadian Census, conducted every 10 years, information is collected from every household in Canada. One member in every household (over the age of 18) is interviewed or is responsible for filling out the questionnaire. Most research projects, however, cannot afford to collect data from every household. Indeed, the Canadian Census draws a random sample of households, one member of which is asked to complete the long form of the Census questionnaire. Therefore, researchers frequently draw a sample from a defined population.

There are two basic types of samples: probability and non-probability. **Probability samples** are based on a known population; each member of that population has an equal chance of being included in the sample. If the households of the city of Calgary, Alberta, were the population, each household within the city limits would need to be identified. After determining how many subjects are required for data analysis, the researcher might randomly choose every tenth household. When probability samples are drawn, the results can be generalized to that larger population. **Non-probability samples**, on the other hand, are simply groups of persons that happen to be readily available, such as a classroom of students or some of the subscribers to a magazine. The characteristics of the population are unknown or inadequately identified. Non-probability samples are not the same as random samples.

Probability samples are often impossible to draw because the complete population of a particular type of family (single-parent families, for example) cannot be accurately identified. Researchers sometimes draw *stratified random samples* from areas of a city where a higher proportion of certain types of families is known to exist. This sampling procedure permits probability samples of the divorced, the never-married, seniors, or related groups that are specifically identified.

Non-probability samples are often the only option, and are sometimes more useful for the purposes of a study. If we wanted to study family specialists, for example, we might draw a purposive sample by obtaining membership lists from the National Council on Family Relations or the Canadian Association of Sociologists and Anthropologists. Similarly, if a graduate student wanted to study families in which one or more children died under the age of 20, she might have to contact hospitals, doctors and churches to obtain a list of members or referrals. The results, however, cannot be generalized to a population of grieving parents unless the entire population of such parents has been identified. These and related sampling techniques provide the necessary subjects for the research project. Such studies provide important insights, but the findings can only be generalized to the population of parents actually studied.

Data Analysis

Once the data have been collected, they must be prepared for analysis. This preparation involves coding each of the variables and preparing frequency distributions. Several variables may need to be merged into a scale to create an index of marital quality, or family satisfaction, or religiosity, and so forth. Most data are entered into computers and analyzed with data analysis software.

Data analysis typically makes use of three types of variables: dependent variables, predictor (often called independent) variables, and control variables. **Dependent variables** represent the aspect of family life that the researcher wants to explain. The **predictor variables** are those that the researcher has chosen, based on theory or a literature review, as the most likely variables to help explain the dependent variable(s). Note the titles of selected articles that appear in Box 2.4 in two issues of the *Journal of Marriage and the Family* (February 1997; August 1997), and three recent issues of the *Journal of Family Issues* (March 1996; May 1997; and September 1997).

Control variables are typically background variables that are expected to modify or clarify the relationship between the independent (or *predictor*) and dependent variables. They include variables such as age, gender, education, occupation, and related factors. In other studies, however, they may be used as major predictor variables. Indeed, what one family scholar frequently uses as a dependent variable, another might use as a predictor variable. Once the connections between or among the variables are specified, the researcher must determine how the data will be analyzed. Many researchers emphasize the connections or relationships among the variables.

Two of the Canadian studies identified in Box 2.4 will be used to briefly illustrate these three types of variables. In the Roxburgh (1997) study, the "effect of children" is the predictor variable. The "mental health of women in the paid labor force" is the dependent variable. The age and marital status of the mother are the control variables. The "effect of children" is

---

Box 2.4   Examples of Dependent and Predictor Variables

Note: The dependent variable is <u>underlined</u> and the predictor variable is in *italics*.

"<u>Interpersonal Congruency</u>: *The Role of the Family* in Political Attitudes of Youth" (Dalhouse and Frideres, 1996*).

"*The Influence of Spouses' Behavior and Marital Dissolution* on <u>Marijuana Use</u>: Causation or Selection" (Yamaguchi and Kandel, 1997).

"*The Effect of Children* on the <u>Mental Health of Women in the Paid Labor Force</u>" (Roxburgh, 1997*).

"*Gender, Status,* and <u>Domestic Violence</u>: An Integration of Feminist and Family Violence Approaches" (Anderson, 1997).

"<u>Marital Instability after Midlife</u>" (Wu and Penning, 1997*).

* Based on data collected in Canada.

measured by the degree and types of stressors that working mothers might experience because they have children. The study by Wu and Penning (1997) only identifies the dependent variable in the title of the article. Although the title of a research article typically contains apparent "hints" as to the major variables of a study, titles are seldom a definitive way of identifying these variables. The independent variable in this study is based on Becker's theoretical model (1981) of "marital-specific capital," which includes the presence of children, a larger number of children, age differences between the spouses, and related measures.

Statistics are frequently used to assess the strength of these linkages among variables (or the relative influence of the predictor variables) and the significance of the findings. The strength of the relationship between variable X and variable Y may be determined by the size of the percentage difference. For example, if 80 percent of adult daughters care for their aging in-laws, and only 25 percent of adult sons provide similar services, this difference alone documents the role of daughters in elder care.

The strength of the relationship, however, is most often assessed with statistical correlations. A **correlation** is a mathematical procedure used to measure the statistical strength of the relationship between two or more variables. A perfect correlation between two variables, depending on the type of statistic used, typically equals +1.00 or −1.00. If we use the elder-care example above, a perfect correlation would mean that all daughters took care of elders and that no sons at all took care of their aging in-laws. When there are several predictor variables (for example, gender, age, employment, religion, and geographical distance of caregiver), multiple regression correlational techniques might be used. Multiple regression involves correlational analysis while controlling for each of the other variables, one variable at a time. This technique is used to assess which variables are the most powerful predictors of the dependent variable.

Researchers use a test of significance to assess the reliability of the correlations between the variables. Is the relationship (correlation) random, or is it too strong to be simply a random relationship? A **significance test** assesses the probability that the results were obtained by chance. If the same study were replicated with another sample of similar subjects, the test of significance determines that five in 100 studies

(=.05) would have different results. The smaller the ratio, the more significant the correlations (for example, =.001 means one chance in 1000 studies). Significance tests are affected by the size of the sample. The larger the sample, the more likely it is that a small correlation (such as +.20 or −.20) will be significant.

After researchers have completed their statistical analysis, they must interpret the results. What do the findings mean? Do they confirm the hypotheses? How do the findings differ from previous research? What are the limitations of the study? What suggestions can be made for further research to clarify what is still unknown or unclear? Data analysis should be cautious and self-critical, even while clearly interpreting what the results seem to mean. Research on pre-marriage, marriage, and family relationships is not unlike other research in the social sciences. The scholarly questions must be conceptualized carefully and operationally defined with precision, and the data must be collected and analyzed with rigor.

Ethics in Family Research

Most of us consider our intimate relationships—our friendships, marriages, and families—to be very private. Family researchers, indeed all researchers in the social sciences, are committed to the principle of confidentiality in data collection. Scholars protect individual responses and observations of individual behaviours by assigning identification numbers to each individual being studied. Names and addresses of participants are typically destroyed unless subjects grant written permission for a follow-up as part of a longitudinal research design. By law, therapists must report cases of incest, child abuse, and related criminal actions; but researchers, in contrast, at least at this time, are not required to report such problems to public authorities. The integrity of the research process requires that the data obtained from subjects remain confidential.

Observational research designs and the types of questions posed in surveys must carefully weigh the dangers of causing psychological distress against the scientific value of the study. When researchers ask people to participate in a research project, they must accurately inform subjects of the study's general purpose so that each person's consent to participate is informed. Deception has no place in scientific research. Where possible, and if appropriate, subjects should receive a summary and be debriefed about the results of the study.

ENDNOTES

1. The *Sourcebook of Family Theories and Methods: A Conceptual Approach* (Boss et al., 1993) only briefly mentions the political dimensions of economic inequities in families (Goldner, 1993: 623–624).

2. Many theorists have not defined their underlying assumptions in the development of a particular theory. The underlying assumptions have often been identified by second-generation students of theory (cf. Nye and Berardo, 1981).

SUMMARY

■ Personal experience in developing knowledge about others is useful, but has significant limitations as a method in social science research. Objectivity and replicability are the basic principles in the use of the scientific method. The knowledge acquired and methods used in research must be open to scrutiny and confirmation by other scientists.

■ These analytical questions are organized into a conceptual approach, which can be defined as a set of assumptions, concepts, and propositions about specific aspects of human phenomena. A conceptual approach narrows the scope of family analysis and is an important building block in the formulation of a theory. A conceptual approach becomes a theory when the propositions have been empirically verified in multiple research studies under differing conditions, places, and times, by independent researchers.

■ We defined seven different conceptual approaches in family study. Three approaches primarily concern macrosystem family issues: conflict, feminist, and ecological theories. Four other approaches primarily emphasize microsystem family issues: symbolic interaction, exchange, developmental, and systems theories. We will use each of these approaches throughout the text, when appropriate, to illustrate and document what is known and not known about families.

■ Family research involves four issues. The design of a study decides the way the data will be collected. The alternatives include case studies, clinical records, participant and direct observations, Census data, surveys and experiments. Measurement concerns the accuracy and precision of the indicators used to quantify the concepts. These measures need to be valid and reliable. The sampling techniques determine the choice of subjects. The ideal technique is a probability or random sample from a known population, but, due to financial considerations or the specific purposes of the study, non-probability samples are frequently used. Once the data are collected, they must be prepared for analysis. This task includes defining variables, choosing appropriate statistical procedures, and interpreting the results.

KEY TERMS

Control variable (42)
Correlation (43)
Dependent variable (42)
Explanation (22)
Hypothesis (27)
Interval variable (41)
Nominal variable (41)
Non-probability sample (41)
Objectivity (23)
Ordinal variable (41)
Predictor variables (42)
Probability sample (41)
Proposition (27)
Qualitative measures (40)
Quantitative measures (40)
Reliability (41)
Replicability (24)
Significance test (43)
Theoretical framework (27)
Theory (28)
Validity (41)

QUESTIONS FOR REVIEW

1. Identify the similarities and differences between personal experience and the scientific method as ways of understanding families.

2. Define *objectivity* and *replication*.

3. Describe the differences between a theoretical framework and a theory. Why are theoretical approaches important in science?

4. Identify the levels of analysis used in the study of the family.

5. Accurately describe the key explanatory argument of each of the seven theoretical frameworks described in this chapter.

6. Distinguish between qualitative and quantitative measures. Identify the strategies involved in using each measurement approach.

7. Define interval, ordinal, and nominal variables.

8. Distinguish between probability and non-probability samples.

9. Explain the use of dependent, predictor, and control variables.

QUESTIONS FOR DISCUSSION

1. How has your own personal experience shaped your values? In what ways have your experiences enabled you to predict what individuals and people in families do?

2. Think about the differences between any two approaches included in this chapter. Use these theories to try to explain something that has occurred in your life or is occurring to someone you know. Do both theories provide useful insights?

3. Discuss similarities and differences between the conflict and the feminist approaches.

4. Think about some aspect of family life that is of concern to you. What type of research design do you think would help you to gather the kind of information that you need to understand the situation better?

SUGGESTED READINGS

Boss, Pauline G., William J. Doherty, Ralph LaRossa, Walter R. Schumm, and Suzanne K. Steinmetz. 1993. *Sourcebook of Family Theories and Methods: A Contextual Approach.* New York: Plenum Press. This book is the most comprehensive resource available on family theories and methods. In 27 chapters, the book reviews the history of family theories and methods, 16 relevant theoretical traditions, and seven methodological traditions applicable to the study of the family.

Bulcroft, R. and J.M. White. 1997. "Family research methods and levels of analysis," *Family Science Review 10*, pp. 136–153. This is a detailed discussion of the issues regarding levels of analysis written for the advanced undergraduate or graduate student. It also discusses the individualistic and ecological fallacies.

Kidder, L.H. and Judd, C.M. 1986. *Research Methods in Social Relations (5th Edition).* New York: Holt, Rinehart and Winston.

White, J.M. and D.M. Klein. 2002. *Family Theories (2nd edition).* Thousand Oaks, CA: Sage Publications. This book reviews the explanation, philosophy, and history of theory in family studies. The conceptual approaches summarized in this chapter are reviewed in this book.

White, J.M. 2004. *Advancing Family Theories.* Thousand Oaks, CA: Sage Publications. This is a more advanced treatment of many of the topics raised in the White and Klein (2002) book. This advanced work concentrates on many issues in the area of philosophy of the social sciences and would prove interesting reading for any student of the social sciences.

CHAPTER 3

Kinship Organization of Marriage and Family

After studying this chapter, you should be able to do the following:

- Identify the major categories of kinship, and accurately classify kinship connections and variations.
- Identify the major types of lineage, residence, and authority in kinship systems.
- Describe the major connections between lineage and residence.
- Distinguish types of extended family such as traditional extended family, stem family, joint family, and matrifocal family.
- Define the major types of marriage, and describe the ways in which these marital systems differ from each other.
- Identify the main arguments associated with the "convergence" theory of modernization.
- Describe some of the major forces that facilitate and resist change in industrializing societies.

Introduction

There is a variety of marital, family, and kinship systems throughout the world. These systems have varied throughout history and continue to vary cross-culturally today. As indicated in Chapter 1, there is considerable debate about the meanings of marriage, family, and even kinship. Our purpose in this chapter is to summarize the many ways that the basic forms of marriage, family, and kin are expanded or reshaped and lived out throughout the known world. Some of the reasons why these various systems have emerged and continue to persist will be discussed. We will also discuss some of the factors that change kinship organization in many societies. The first two sections of this chapter examine kinship and marital systems in traditional societies. In the third section, several major societies are briefly reviewed to better understand cultural shifts and significant changes in process.

Anthropologists and ethnographers have collected most of the information presented here. Ethnographers are researchers who have lived in these societies, talked with people about how society members are related to each other, constructed diagrams of kinship relationships, and published their findings. The precise and detailed study of kinship systems, in which scholars attempt to specify how all variations work, is a highly technical and specialized area in anthropology. The study of kinship, however, is just as important to understanding modern cultures as it is to understanding traditional cultures.

There are many reasons for studying kinship. We will highlight just a few of the most important of these reasons. First, the study of kinship emphasizes for the student the exact ways that his or her culture connects his or her family to the past and the future. We are all aware that our great-uncle or aunt is related to us, but we are less aware that some day we might well be occupying that position for our sister's children's children. A second reason for studying kinship is that it provides tools to understand other cultures. For example, if we wish to understand arranged marriages, betrothal customs, or even concubinage in other cultures, we must study kinship. Indeed, kinship norms and rules organize much of family life in most cultures. A third reason for studying kinship is that it organizes family relationships in ways that have great theoretical importance. The two dominant theoretical perspectives on kinship stress quite different elements of social organization: descent and alliance. As we shall see, both of these theoretical perspectives assist us in gaining a broad theoretical understanding. Finally, the last reason for studying kinship is practical: kinship provides us all with a "road map" of what we regard as "right and wrong" and "natural and unnatural." For example, is it proper for a young man to marry his dead brother's wife? Many of you would see no problem with such a union based on genetics; however, until recently many provinces in Canada prohibited such unions. On the other hand, many of you might view a marriage to a first cousin as incestuous, but the Marriage Act (1990) does not specifically prohibit it. Indeed, cousin marriages are preferred in some cultures. The practical significance of all this is that each culture's kinship system supplies a "cognitive map," not just for understanding kin relations but for evaluating the "morality" of these. In a tolerant multicultural society, the study of kinship helps to prepare us for understanding our own diverse culture as well as the global village in which we live.

Kinship Systems

As Stanton (1995:97) points out: "[O]f all types of human affiliation, kinship is, with few rare exceptions, the most permanent and has the greatest long-term impact on the life, behavior, and social identity of an individual." It may also be emphasized that variation in kinship systems, both historically and cross-culturally, has been the major source of subcultural and cross-cultural diversity throughout the known world. Urban migration within and between countries, contemporary air travel, hard surface highways, international tourism, global communications systems, and many other sources of contact among peoples of differing cultures, lifestyles, and ideologies are a reality of life as we begin the 21st century. Indeed, Canada, for most of its history, has been regarded as an example of multiculturalism that works. Therefore, although our laws regulate the degree and scope of diversity in our 10 provinces and three

territories, we value and often celebrate ethnic and racial traditions. In the following pages, we describe some of the influences that have shaped the characteristics of marriage and kinship systems. As a result of conflicting influences, the systems in most societies are much more complex than can be described here. If you are interested in reading more about how complex many of these kinship systems are, you will find useful, but somewhat technical, discussions in Lévi-Strauss (1969), Schusky (1983), and Murdock (1949).

The structural-functional approach to kinship studies dominated the first half of the 20th century in the work of anthropologists such as Malinowski (1922) and Radcliffe-Brown (1931). These scholars tended to emphasize the importance of descent and lineage in understanding kinship. Because of this emphasis, this approach is commonly referred to as **descent theory**. In the middle of the 20th century the noted French anthropologist Claude Lévi-Strauss and others developed a second major approach. It argued that kinship rule organized social exchanges in most societies. These exchanges are viewed as creating social and political alliances between groups. Thus this second broad perspective is often called **alliance theory**. These two approaches might not seem contradictory, however they clash profoundly when they offer competing explanations of cousin marriages. We will not visit this debate in great detail but it is important for the student to recognize that each of these theories focuses on a different aspect and process of kinship organization. We will have cause to discuss these processes later in this chapter.

Types of Kin Relationships

There are two types of kinship relationships: those in which one is related by blood—often referred to as **consanguineal kin**—and those in which one is related through marriage, called **affinal kin**. Figure 3.1 illustrates these relationships within families of origin and procreation. The referent person is designated as Ego.

Even though we often depict kinship as a "tree" of relationships, kinship is not simply a genealogical family tree. In a sense, all of us are related through our distant ancestors—indeed, some believe that our common ancestors were the biblical Adam and Eve. Kinship is, first and foremost, a social definition. The limits of these social definitions vary widely among various ethnic groups and cultures. As suggested by

Figure 3.1   Basic Kinship—Family of Orientation and Procreation

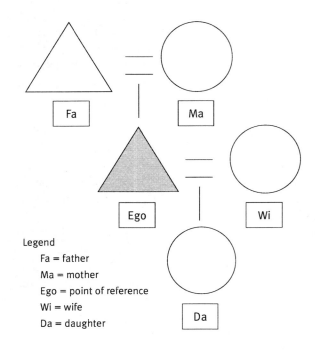

Legend
Fa = father
Ma = mother
Ego = point of reference
Wi = wife
Da = daughter

Source: Schusky, 1965.

Stanton (1995), all cultures have rules for defining who one's important relatives are. The important relatives—those who are in the appropriate lineage system—are those who have rights and duties related to inheritance, authority, economic privilege, participation in ceremonies and rituals, choice of marriage partner, taking of sides in a conflict, and many other aspects of life.

What Does Kinship Organize?

The title of this chapter suggests that kinship systems organize marriage and family life. Indeed, kinship is an institutional system in most societies. Kinship systems define with whom one may mate and marry and the complex rights and duties of various kin positions. This organization is achieved by means of social rules or "norms." Some of these norms may be so commonly accepted that they become formalized as laws. For example, in North America we have bigamy laws prohibiting marriage to more than one person at a time. The result of such laws is to make polygamy—multiple

mates—illegal. Yet in many societies, polygamy is seen as desirable and normative. Another example of the strength of the social norms regulating kinship is the way that different societies define incest. All societies forbid incest among nuclear family members. The minor exception to this taboo occurs when a royal or priestly bloodline is in jeopardy of not being passed on to a succeeding generation (e.g., the Incas of Peru). In many cultures, however, first cousin marriage is preferred or encouraged while in some other cultures it is viewed as incest. It is the very strongly felt taboo of incest that justifies both of these perspectives because the incest taboo is the basis for defining who we can and can't marry. For example, if matrilineal first cousins are in a different clan than Ego but patrilineal cousins are in Ego's clan, then it would be considered incest to marry someone of the same clan but permitted or encouraged to marry a person of another clan. In the case of two clan systems (moieties), the matrilineal cousin would be the preferred mate.

Scholars usually divide the kinship norms that organize family and marriage into sets of social rules governing mate selection and finance, marriage types, descent, inheritance, residence, and authority. We cover each of these below.

The Purpose of Kinship Organization

Many students can easily understand *how* kinship organizes areas of family life; however, it is often more obscure *why* kinship systems do this. In today's world, most contemporary societies are attempting to allow a diversity of perspectives and ways of living within the broad parameters of social order. Diversity is often accommodated and the traditions and cultures of minorities are protected, or at least considered. However, today's world is not the one in which kinship systems developed.

Kinship developed in all societies before written history, before the codification of laws, and most likely before all other forms of social order—it is the most basic social order. Kinship uses the most basic relationships among humans—those relationships defined by marriage and birth—to structure the norms and rules that govern the intergenerational transmission of wealth and status as well as the governance of family members (authority). The evolutionary reasons for this can be easily imagined.

Imagine a society in which there are just a man and a woman, say Adam and Eve. Adam and Eve inhabit a finite and bounded territory. Within this territory Adam is responsible for tending and harvesting a garden and fishing the river. Eve hunts deer and small mammals for meat. Adam and Eve have two children, Eric and Amy. Adam teaches Eric to garden and fish while Eve teaches Amy to hunt. Eventually, Eric and Amy reach reproductive age and want to find mates. If Eric brings a female home, she will want to assume the gender-typed work of hunting, and if Amy marries a male he will expect to garden and fish. If we skip down a few generations, we can easily see how the finite territory will shrink, as will the fishing and hunting resources. One way around this would be to develop a rule of residence that states that the male offspring should live with their bride's family or on new territory. However, even if we have such a rule of residence we will still need a rule about inheritance of the territory once Adam and Eve die. Very simply, kinship systems evolve and develop to solve these obvious problems (Schusky, 1965)[1].

Obviously, many contemporary societies are highly codified and have laws that govern many if not all of the areas once regulated by kinship norms. The reason we study kinship today is that even in these advanced societies, much of formal law is nonetheless based on older kinship systems. For example, why do we in North America feel that monogamy is the natural and correct way to conduct marital relationships when cultures such as those in China, India, and Africa have long practised polygamy? Understanding kinship systems is critical to understanding our own culture and the cultures of others as we increasingly come into daily contact with the various members of our global village.

Basic Kinship Terms

We discussed Figure 3.1 as helping to provide a road map of kinship. In actual fact, kinship systems are much more elaborate and complex than Figure 3.1 suggests. This section introduces the nomenclature of basic kinship terms used in the international study of kinship. It then introduces a few of the major types of kinship structures so that we can gain an impression of the richness and complexity of kinship.

If you ask your father if you can borrow the car tonight, you would most likely address him in a familiar term such as "Dad." This is called a "term of address." On the other hand, if we ask you "From whom did you borrow the car?" you would probably say your "father." That would be a "term of reference." A term of reference tells us how that person is related to you. It is these terms that most interest us in sketching out the kinship of a society. These terms also provide us with some difficulty. Imagine a society that speaks a different language. We ask a respondent in that culture "From whom did they borrow the car?" and get the answer "shadrw." We still do not know if "shadrw" is a generic "term of reference" or a "term of address." Most ethnographers are interested in the kin terms of reference, so we could state that we are interested in only these terms. Let's say that our translator tells us that "shadrw" is indeed like our English term "father." However, we become concerned when we find that our respondents also use this name for their maternal and paternal uncles. Can they all be fathers? As we shall see shortly, the answer is yes, but for the moment we have another problem.

Since kinship is socially defined, we do not want to confuse kin terms with biology nor do want to impose our culture's kin terms on cultures we wish to study. We must be open to a "father" being other than the biological father, as is the case in our culture with adoption. It quickly becomes evident that we need a shorthand that can assist us with identifying the kinship positions but that carries as little cultural baggage as possible. Below are the basic terms for constructing kinship systems.

International	North American
ABBREVIATION	**TERM**
Fa	father
Ma	mother
Da	daughter
So	son
Br	brother
Si	sister
Wi	wife
Hu	husband

The kinship terms above can be used to identify other kin positions without carrying any one culture's content and connotations. For instance, a first cousin of your father's side could be FaBrSo, FaBrDa, FaSiSo, or FaSiDa. Although this system may seem abstract, you will see its usefulness in the next section.

Kinship Classification Systems

Ethnographers and anthropologists have studied kinship since the beginning of the 1800s. As a result, they have developed a classification system. Lewis Henry Moran developed the first classification system in 1870 (Schusky, 1965), and since that time several have been proposed. Today most systems are classified as being similar to one of the following classification types: Eskimo, Hawaiian, Iroquois, Sudanese, Crow, and Omaha. Although any one society may have some idiosyncratic differences from the classification that best fits that society, the classification systems provide a clear and useful way to get a broad perspective on kinship. Below, we examine just a few of the major kinship classifications in order to get an idea about how these work.

First, let's examine Hawaiian (also known as Polynesian) kinship. Polynesian kinship is especially interesting to us because the example regarding "shadrw" was drawn from this classification scheme. Figure 3.2 shows the Hawaiian classification system.

In systems such as in Figure 3.2, sex and generation are the basis of kin terms. In Hawaiian kinship systems, Ego often resides with his cousins in a common household. Ego's aunts and uncles of the same generation as his mother and father also are called father and mother. In such kinship systems, Ego would have a great deal of social security in having siblings to look after one another and play together as well as having ample parents for supervision. Given what you know about the incest taboo being universal for nuclear family members, would you guess that Ego might be expected to marry his female cousins?

The second system we examine is Eskimo. Classification systems are often named for the social or cultural group that was first studied with that system, even though we have since found other groups that are even better examples. Eskimo kinship is shown in Figure 3.3. Eskimo forms of kinship are somewhat similar to Hawaiian since they distinguish kin by generation and sex but not by lineage. However, in Eskimo kinship systems Ego's nuclear family is set off from all other relatives. Here we find the need to distinguish all those who are Ego's Fa and Mo's collateral (same generation) as having the names of Au or Un. Likewise Ego's collaterals are only distinguished by Co (they are Ego's collaterals) but they are not distinguished by sex. Do you think Ego could marry either his FaBrDa or MoSiDa?

Most North American families use the system in Figure 3.3. It emphasizes the nuclear family to the exclusion of other relatives. It names all Ego's collateral cousins (Co) in the same way. This system appears not to emphasize lineage on either the mother's or father's side.

The last kinship classification system we examine, the Crow system, is more complex (see Figure 3.4). Hawaiian and Eskimo are the two simple systems while the other four (Crow, Sudanese, Iroquois, and Omaha)

Figure 3.2   Hawaiian Classification System

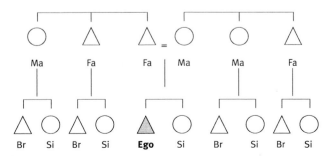

Source: Adapted from Schusky, 1965:20.

Figure 3.3   Eskimo Classification System

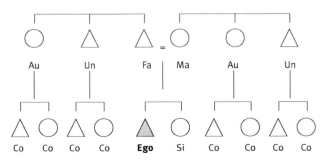

Source: Adapted from Schusky, 1965:20.

Figure 3.4   Crow Classification System

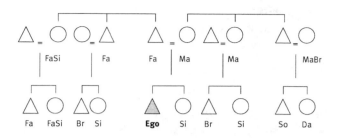

Source: Adapted from Schusky, 1965:33.

are much more complex. Hawaiian and Eskimo are bilateral systems that view both the mother and father's kin as equally important. The Crow and the other systems are unilineal systems. The Crow system is matrilineal, which means that the mother's side of the family is most important in reckoning descent and lineage.

In the Crow system, Ego has a special relationship with mother's brother. Indeed, in many matrilineal societies it is mother's brother who acts much like a social father to Ego. In such systems, Ego would receive his name, status, training, and wealth from his mother's brother rather than his biological father. The Crow system also introduces one of the most basic and important distinctions in kinship (except for Hawaiian and Eskimo). Most classification systems clearly define cross and parallel cousins. A parallel cousin is the offspring of Ego's parent's same-gender sibling. So, for example, FaBrSo and MaSiSo are parallel cousins. Note that included in Crow-type kinship among Ego's "brothers and sisters" are his parallel cousins on both sides (FaBrSo, FaBrDa, and MoSiSo, MoSiDa). The maternal set of cross-cousin are "taboo" since you cannot marry your son or daughter. These distinctions for MaBrSo and MaBrDa maintain the matrilineage as non-incestuous. The male cross-cousins on the father's side are termed "father" and will be so for subsequent generations. This line represents a type of clan organization or "sib" on the father's side. In Crow kinship, property and lineage are reckoned through the mother's side but the sib membership is from the father's side of the family.

You may be wondering what this all has to do with you. It is pertinent to understanding the importance that your assumptions about kinship, incest, marriage, and lineage play in how you see the world. The naturalness of your system to you is often matched by your

inability to see the perspective of others, especially in this important area. The following incident reported by Schusky (1965) serves as an example of this difficulty:

A French explorer among the Illinois Indians decided the savages were so stupid they could not remember kinship terms and were likely to call anyone "mother," even small babies who "could not possibly be their mothers." Of course, once the principles of unilineal systems are understood, the terminology becomes perfectly logical. (Schusky, 1965:29)

The social norms and rules that construct kinship allow every culture to avoid "incest" with a son or daughter regardless of whether the person is a biological relative or is FaBrDa or FaBrSo. We now turn to a discussion of the social rules or normative systems that construct kinship and its particular map of social reality.

Rules of Marriage and Marriage Finance

Marriage in many societies (especially unilineal societies) involves one kin group losing a son or daughter and the other kin group gaining a son or daughter. Most societies have developed a form of marriage finance that relates directly to losing and gaining members. **Dowry** is a system where the parents of the bride pass some form of wealth to the parents of the groom. It is perhaps an oversimplification of dowry to say that it is to increase the marital prospects of the young woman and, hence, serves to transfer her from the long-term economic support of her parents to that of the groom and his kin group. Certainly, in many societies this might have been the case; however, families can use dowry and other forms of marriage finance to increase their daughter's and their own social status through marriage. As Levi-Strauss has pointed out, marriage alliances are not just between individuals but also between social groups. Arranged marriages are testimony to the long-held and cross-cultural conviction that marriages are too important to the family to be left to the romanticized ideals of the young.

The second major form of marriage finance is **bride price**. Bride price is some form of wealth paid to the parents of the bride. Similar to dowry, these payments, we might speculate, are to pay for the loss of the young woman's services to her parents and family. However, as with dowry, this interpretation needs to be seen in the wider context of forming alliances between kin social groups and family estates. Interestingly, today's custom of an engagement ring may have evolved from bride price. Most systems of bride price (and dowry) have evolved to more directly transferred money or wealth. The wedding ring represents a direct form of bride price that is far more portable than cattle, pigs, or sheep. As well, in many dowry systems such as those in Ireland and India, dowry payments might be considered the property of the wife and add to her resources and power in the marriage. In some cases, if the wife divorces and returns to her family of origin she may take her dowry with her.

Marital systems are a subset of kinship systems. Kinship systems in small traditional societies control who one marries (or with whom one cohabits[2]) as well as where married persons live and how long they will live there. Kinship systems also control the conditions under which marriage units are ended, if such endings are permitted (e.g., divorce, temporary or permanent separations, etc.). The rules vary among patrilineal, matrilineal, bilineal, and bilateral kinship systems. Although these matters are important in understanding these societies, we have chosen to focus on the major types of marriage and selected characteristics of these marital systems. We will also briefly examine selected examples of marital and family systems.

There are two basic types of marriage, monogamy and polygamy, and three more uncommon forms of marriage, polyandry, polygynandry, and cenogamy. **Monogamy** is the marriage of one man and one woman, and is the most common marital form actually practised in most societies, regardless of the cultural preference or normative ideal. Even in many cultures where the ideal might be multiple wives or husbands, monogamy is most common. The typical explanation for this is the sex ratio—number of males versus females as a function of birth—throughout the world. As a consequence, the maximum opportunity for each individual to obtain a marriage partner is enhanced when the sex ratio is 100 males for every 100 females. Another argument is that most men and women are too poor to have more than one wife or husband. Only 14.5 percent of the 1157 societies listed in the *Ethnographic Atlas* preferred monogamy (Murdock, 1967). But usually where monogamy is preferred no alternative form of marriage is permitted. Among industrial and postindustrial societies,

monogamy is the only legal form of marriage. Many persons, however, end up practising *serial monogamy* through divorce and remarriage, sometimes several times during their lifetime.

Polygyny is a specific example of plural marriage, and refers to a marriage between one man and two or more wives. There are certainly examples in Canada of polygyny, such as in the community of Bountiful, British Columbia, but such cases are the exception in this country. Murdock's (1967) analysis of societies, however, notes that the majority preferred the polygynous marital form (981 societies out of 1157, or 85 percent). In 42 percent of these so-called polygynous societies, polygyny is only practised occasionally. In such societies polygyny is a status symbol—if possible, the citizens of such cultures strive to achieve the benefits of a polygynous marriage. Queen et al. (1985) indicate that kings often had hundreds of wives, chiefs had dozens, and commoners had two or three. Wives were valued for two things: economic productivity and producing children. The economic factor, as a primary motive in collecting wives, is illustrated in the following quote:

> It is by no mere accident that polygynous households average more pigs than monogamous ones. Informants stated explicitly that some men married second and third wives in order to enlarge their herds. They laughed at the writer's suggestion that a man might become polygynous in order to increase his sexual enjoyment. (Oliver, 1955:352)

Polygyny, along with other forms of plural marriage, continues to be a distinctive feature of African marriage (Garenne and van de Walle, 1989). It is estimated that the prevalence of *polygamy*—this concept refers to *all* forms of multi-spouse marriage—in African societies ranges from 20 to 50 percent of all marriages, making polygyny in Africa "10 times as high as . . . in Asia's polygamous societies" (Caldwell and Caldwell, 1990:120). A recent study of polygyny and marital satisfaction in Cameroon (Gwanfogbe et al., 1997) found that strong husband support was the primary predictor of marital satisfaction among wives, even if their nutritional needs were inadequate. Older husbands are preferred, due to greater financial stability and emotional maturity.

Another study of Ghanaian women in polygynous marriages provides several up-to-date insights (Klomegah et al.,1997). The author argues the following in defense of polygynous marriage in a subsistence economy: enhanced food production; increased birthrates enabling a larger labour force and emotional support for mothers; old-age security for parents; and facilitated alliances among the extended family, the clan, and the ethnic community. In Ghana, 68 percent of marriages are monogamous and 32 percent are polygynous. The typical polygynous household has three wives (55 percent); 34 percent include two wives, and 11 percent have four to six wives. Eighty-four percent of wives who have obtained a high school education are in a monogamous marriage. In other words, only 16 percent of polygynous wives have obtained a high school degree. Women in monogamous marriages are concentrated in urban locations (75 percent) and tend to be employed in professional, technical, managerial, and social service positions, while wives in polygynous marriages tend to be agricultural, clerical, or sales workers.

Although there is disagreement among scholars, jealousy among wives seems to be a common problem in polygynous households. One of the major solutions is **sororal polygyny**, in which the co-wives are either sisters or other female kin. Indeed, this type of polygyny is the most common. In such circumstances, the co-wives tend to live together in a common household. The other solution is **non-sororal polygyny**, in which unrelated wives each live in separate households (Lee, 1982). There is some evidence that multiple wives, in both Ghana and Kenya, want to have fewer children and to cease having children sooner than do their husbands (Dodoo, 1998). This may be an indication that attitudes are beginning to change among women in polygynous households.

Polyandry is the reverse of polygyny—one woman and two or more husbands. Only seven societies preferred this marital system (0.6 percent of all societies identified in the *Ethnographic Atlas*), although others have been identified (Ingoldsby, 1995:124). Cassidy and Lee (1989) suggest that polyandry is a response to societal poverty, resulting in a low birthrate and limited economic roles for women. The implication of this system is that **female infanticide** is practised to control the number of females able to birth children. Several males are therefore able to have sexual intercourse with only one wife, and therefore reduce the number of children born. Some societies practise **fraternal polyandry**. The Toda are a small tribe living in villages in southern India. The predominant occupation is caring for herds of sacred buffalo. Todas exhibit an apparent example of polyandry. When a woman marries a man, she also automatically marries his brothers. This practice reduces jealousy among the brothers. **Non-fraternal polyandry**—in which the husbands and fathers are not brothers—is less common (Queen et al., 1985).

Cenogamy is a form of group marriage—a situation in which a group of men are all married to the same group of women, and vice versa. They all know each other and typically share the same residence (Ingoldsby, 1995). Polyandry is often directly associated with cenogamy, particularly when female infanticide is discontinued. When the ratio of females to males increases, a polyandrous marriage unit may take in sisters of the female spouse and non-kin females that have no place to live. The Todas are a commonly used example of this form of group marriage (Queen et al., 1985).

Perhaps the most explicit example of cenogamy that occurred in the United States was a religiously based form of group marriage practised by a group called the Oneidan Perfectionists, founded by John Humphrey Noyes in the early 1830s (as summarized by Ingoldsby, 1995; Foster, 1981). Noyes considered monogamy to be a kind of selfish love, and replaced monogamy with the idea of "complex marriage." Noyes believed that it was natural for all men to love all women, and vice versa, and therefore each adult in that community was married to all the adults of the opposite sex. Having sex with a person of the opposite sex, however, required the submission of a request to a Central Committee, and women could turn down such requests. Although this group of men and women was permitted to have sexual intercourse with approval, they could not conceive children until nearly 20 years had passed. Noyes implemented *coitus reservatus* as a birth control procedure; the group limited sexual relations for men unable to control ejaculation to women past menopause.

Polygynandry, occurring in polyandrous cultures, differs from cenogamy in that both men and women may have plural spouses, but the spouses are not the same persons. The woman visits her various husbands, and the man visits his various wives, but each may not know the spouses of their partner. Box 3.1 describes a unique example of polygynandry in northern Nigeria. As pointed out by Sangree and Levine (1980), Nigerian polygynandrous tribes have their own system of

Typically, a young woman marries three men on the same day, but lives with each of them in specific order. The young woman begins with the "first marriage," which her parents arrange. After betrothal, the girl is free to select her second husband as her "love marriage." The third groom is, like the first husband, selected by her parents, and is referred to as the "home marriage." Most men also enter into each of these three types of marriages, so marriage is polygynous for them, even though it is polyandrous for the women. A woman usually stays with her "first husband" for a year; she then must move in with her "love husband." After a year in the love marriage, the third husband may claim his wife. After the initial two years, the wife may move back and forth among husbands as she desires. As Chalifoux (1980) points out, more than half of Abisi women refuse to go to their home husband. These men, including the rejected suitors, have paid a "bride price" in the form of free labour to the girl's parents. There is also a fourth marriage, typically referred to as the "grass marriage." This husband is typically an older man, who, being more successful financially, entices the thrice-married woman with financial security. When the girl's parents learn of this marriage, the union is confirmed by payment of a goat and two hoes.

Source: Ingoldsby and Smith, 1995.

marriage. Each husband, typically unrelated to the other husbands, has his own separate residence, and the wife serves each husband on a rotating basis. In this context, Chalifoux (1980) describes a particular tribe called the Abisi—a population of about 3300 people divided into six clans. The major reason the Abisi marital system is referred to as polygynandrous in that the plural marriages of each sex are separate. The focus is on polyandry for the women, with polygyny as a natural by-product for the men.

Rules of Descent and Inheritance

Descent and inheritance are different. Descent refers to how Ego sees kin relationships. Inheritance, on the other hand, refers to how a kinship system passes wealth from generation to generation. Usually, the descent system is a good predictor of the inheritance system. However, inheritance systems might favour a certain gender and birth order such as the first born (primogeniture) son or last born (ultimogeniture) son. We will say more about specific cases of inheritance when we survey family history in the next chapter.

The lines of descent in a kinship system of a given society may be based on the idea that one is related to people on both the mother and father's sides of the family, or descent may acknowledge kinship with people in only one parental line. **Unilineal** or single-line kinship systems trace descent through only one side. If the society takes the position that individuals are only related to their father's side, then one's father is only related to his father's side, and the same is true of his father's father. As a result, the only people seen as related to each other are those who can trace their descent through the same line of male ancestors: through the father, the father's father, the father's father's father, and so on. This kinship system is called **patrilineal** because the members are all descended from the same line of fathers. In contrast, people who share only a common female relative, such as a grandmother or great-grandmother, are not seen as kin. Unilineal systems, and, more specifically, patrilineal systems, have been the most common kind of system among all nonindustrial human societies. Murdock (1949), in his study of nonliterate societies, found that patrilineal kinship systems were the most common (43 percent). The other unilineal system is the **matrilineal** system, which traces descent only through the line of mothers. In the matrilineal system, an individual is only related to those who share a common female ancestor, in the line that includes one's mother, one's mother's mother, one's mother's mother's mother, and so on. People who share only a common male ancestor are not seen as an individual's kin. In the following pages, we shall see that the kind of kinship system within which people live has a powerful influence on their lives.

A **double-descent** or bilineal system is a kinship system in which a person is kin to both the mother's line of mothers and the father's line of fathers. Note that here a person is not kin to her father's mother's kin, nor to her mother's father's kin, although she is kin to her father's father's kin and her mother's mother's kin. This system is unique in that the person in this family unit has distinctive rights and privileges through the father's line, and a different set of rights and privileges through the mother's line. An example of this would be political rights from one line, and social rights from the other line. The major point is that in a double-descent system whatever is inherited from the mother is not also inherited from the father, and vice versa.

There is a fourth system of lineage called a **bilateral**, or two-sided, system. Both the father's and the mother's lines in each generation regulate and offer benefits to Ego. Both Canada and the United States use a bilateral form of lineage, as do many large industrialized societies. However, the patterns of influence are not as clear-cut. Assumptions and expectations are not always fulfilled. For example, holiday get-togethers sometimes cause major eruptions among in-laws over who goes or comes where and with whom. Inheritance "rights" are sometimes a source of emotional, if not legal, conflict.

Rules of Residence

In traditional societies, survival considerations determined where newly married couples lived because where they lived determined whom they were able to help, economically and militarily. Eleven possibilities existed in these societies; six are commonly found and discussed below, while five mixed types are infrequently observed and not explored here (Nimkoff, 1965).

By far the most common living arrangement, found in 313 out of 560 societies studied, is patrilocal residence, where the married couple lives with the groom's father's band. The second most common arrangement, with 85 cases, was matrilocal residence, where the couple lives in the bride's mother's band or village. In **bilocal** residence—30 cases—the married couple might live with either the groom's father's family, or the bride's mother's family. There were 27 cases of **neolocal** residence, where the married couple typically

establishes a residence separate from either parental group, as is the case in our society. **Avunculocal** residence requires the couple to move to the groom's mother's brother's household. Although this arrangement is rather rare, found in only 13 of the 560 societies, it makes sense in some societies, as will be seen. Finally, there was one quite common mixed type, **matripatrilocal** residence (59 cases), in which the couple lives first with the bride's mother's household, and thereafter with the groom's father's household. In many matripatrilocal societies the couple lives at the bride's mother's residence until a baby is born, since often the couple is not seen as really married until parenthood. The groom might work for his father-in-law during this period, earning the right to marry.

Notice that these residence arrangements have quite different consequences. Neolocal residence results in some degree of isolation for the married couple, since they are physically separated from the parents and siblings. Canada and the United States are typically classified as having a neolocal form of residence. **Matrilocal** residence means that the wife lives in the same band as her parents, all her sisters, and her unmarried brothers, while her husband lives apart from his parents and siblings. Patrilocal residence keeps the husband in his parents' band with all his brothers and unmarried sisters, while it separates the wife from her band—as does matripatrilocal residence, once the couple moves to the husband's father's band. Avunculocal residence serves to keep together the men who trace their descent through the same line of mothers, instead of through the same line of fathers, as with patrilocal residence. Bilocal residence, which allows the couple to live with either set of parents, is often found where resources are scarce, thus letting the husband and wife choose to live where survival is best assured.

Neolocal residence is rare in small traditional societies, because the couple needs to live with a band to improve its chances of survival. Couples living alone were vulnerable to starvation or attack by hostile bands; therefore, neolocal residence was found primarily in peaceful societies such as that of the Inuit, in which warfare was virtually unknown. You might ask: Why pay so much attention to residence patterns when we are talking about kinship systems? The answer is that residence rules have determined which people have stayed and lived together. In time, these people came to see each other as relatives, whereas people who did not stay together came to be seen as non-relatives, even if they were related to each other genetically. We tend to think of kinship as something "natural": naturally, we are related (genetically) to our mother and our father and our siblings. Through them, we are related to their mothers and fathers (our grandparents) and to their siblings (our uncles and aunts), and to their siblings' offspring (our cousins). And we are related "by marriage" to our spouse's relatives, and to our siblings' spouses—our brothers-in-law, sisters-in-law and parents-in-law. (But note that we do not feel that we are related to the parents or siblings of these in-laws.)

As suggested earlier, it is clear that society determines who we identify as our relatives. The typically Canadian idea of relatives includes both **genetic relatives**, who are related to us because we share common ancestors, and affinal relatives, who are related to us through marriage. Although the kinship rules in most small traditional societies may seem very strange to outsiders, this is natural as all kinship systems seem odd to members of a different system.

As Table 3.1 shows, a close relationship has been found between residence rules and how descent is traced in small traditional societies. **Patrilocal** bands tend to have patrilineal kinship systems tracing descent through the line of fathers. Avunculocal systems have matrilineal descent, and matripatrilocal systems often have bilateral descent. However, the data in the table show that the relationship between residence rules and rules of descent is not as close as the preceding discussion suggests. There are many inconsistencies, particularly in the bilateral and matrilineal descent columns. These inconsistencies are probably the result of changes in some aspects of the kinship system, without parallel changes in other parts of the system. Various circumstances might have dictated these changes, but we will not discuss them here.

Rules of Authority

Authority is one sub-form or subset of power. Authority is commonly defined as "legitimate power." In relation to kinship, this implies that the kinship system recognizes or bestows power in the hands of specific kin positions. For example, most patrilineal societies bestow power on Ego's father or the eldest male in the clan or group. Such systems of authority are

TABLE 3.1   The Relationship Between Residence and Descent in Non-literate Societies

RESIDENCE	DESCENT				
	PATRILINEAL	MATRILINEAL	BILATERAL	DOUBLE	TOTAL SMALL-TRADITIONAL SOCIETIES
Patrilocal	202	14	74	23	313
Matrilocal	3	38	43	1	85
Bilocal	1	0	29	0	30
Neolocal	1	2	24	0	27
Avunculocal	0	12	1	0	13
Matripatrilocal	28	2	28	1	59
Other	4	12	15	0	31
Total small-traditional societies	239	80	214	27	560

Source: Adapted from Nimkoff, 1965:25.

termed *patriarchal* and are the most common pattern of authority among societies. Although it would be tempting to assume that the power arrangements in matrilineal societies would be *matriarchal* or power seen as legitimately held by a female head, this is not the case. In many matrilineal societies authority is invested in the mother's brother. Even though power is legitimated by how a male is related to the female lineage, the authority is still in the hands of the male. One exception to this is the matrifocal family discussed later in this chapter. Females head these families but, as we will see, there are often no adult males present in these three-generation families. Thus it is debatable whether or not this would constitute a matriarchy. Indeed, there are no existing well-documented historical records to support the prolonged existence of a normatively defined matriarchy in any society.

On the other hand, family forms of legitimate power keep evolving. No one can doubt that developed post-industrial societies have evolved toward egalitarian systems of authority. An *egalitarian* system is one in which both sides (husband and wife, father and mother) share power equally. We will discuss the issues of power and authority in today's families in greater detail in Chapter 10.

Extended Families

Earlier in this chapter, reference was made to the **nuclear family** (composed of father, mother, and children) as the basic building block of all kinship systems. During your lifetime, most of you will inhabit both the nuclear families of orientation and procreation (see Figure 3.1). If both of these nuclear families were to live in a common residence or within close proximity to each other, we would say they are an extended family. Although the term "extended family" was originally intended to convey the meaning of a common residence, it has been somewhat relaxed to fit adjacent residences in urban areas (e.g., Young and Wilmott, 1957). Extended families are simply family units that contain more members than the core nuclear family, in the interest of mutual assistance, the inheritance of property, and the perpetuation of certain kinship values that seem necessary for the preservation of the family system. We discuss the principal form of extended family below.

Patrilineal Extended Family: The Traditional Chinese

The nuclear family (defined in Chapter 1) becomes an **extended family** when it is vertically "extended" to include a third, grandparental generation, in addition to the parent and offspring generations, or even a fourth generation. Three-generation households are sometimes found in North American society, when an elderly parent comes to live with and be cared for by a married daughter, or less often by a married son.

Such multigenerational extended families were common in China before the communist revolution. The Chinese extended family was patrilineal, although often more complex than the patrilineal families found in nonliterate societies. A very large family might consist of the patriarchal family head, his wife and concubines, his married sons and their wives and unmarried children, his unmarried sons and daughters, and his married grandsons (sons' sons, not daughters' sons) and their wives and children (if any). For an extended family to be so large, the birth rate had to be high, which was customary, and the infant and childhood death rates had to be quite low, which was characteristic of wealthy families. When these conditions existed, extended families could grow very large. A whole village might consist of a single extended patrilineal family or clan, all related to a single male ancestor (Baker, 1979). Poor peasants in China also preferred the extended family form, but their families were much smaller in size because of high infant and child mortality rates. Furthermore, the parents often did not live long enough to see their offspring married.

Why did the Chinese family take this form? The answer is found in the many functions of this family system, and the many things that it accomplished, both for its members and for the society as a whole. These included lending money to members, helping families pay for elaborate weddings and funerals, keeping law and order in the village, serving as the government agent in collecting taxes, establishing schools, maintaining the graves of ancestors, and looking after clan property (Chao, 1977). Although only large clan organizations could accomplish all of these tasks, even poor families benefited from this type of family organization. It kept the parents and their male offspring together as a single work unit, whose joint efforts might make it possible to buy more land for the growing family.

Unsuccessful families, however, were driven into tenant farming and poverty, risking starvation and early death, and were sometimes forced to sell their children as slaves. Such extended families remained small.

Another advantage of this family form was that it kept the sons at home where they could provide for their elderly parents, a practice strongly encouraged by the Chinese Confucian ethic. It was reinforced by the Chinese Imperial Government, which, through its practice of collective responsibility, held the patriarchal family head responsible for the conduct of all its members (Queen et al., 1985).

The Stem Family

There are more modest ways of extending the basic nuclear family that have been practised for various economic reasons. One common example is the **stem family**, which extends the patrilineal parental family (which may include the paternal grandparents in the household) by the addition of a married son and his family. Typically, either the eldest or the youngest son stays with his parents on the family farm or estate. He inherits the whole property and is responsible for providing and caring for his parents until they die.

Among British nobility, the eldest son usually inherits the property as well as the family title (Lord, Earl, Count, for example). As you will recall, this inheritance rule is called *primogeniture*, and its advantage is that the first son to reach maturity is obliged to assist his father on the farm or estate. Alternatively, the advantage of *ultimogeniture*, which specifies inheritance by the youngest son, is that this son is more likely to be reaching his prime when his father is aging and most needs assistance. Under both these rules, other brothers had to make their own way. Among British nobility, the church, the army, and the navy were the preferred placement opportunities, and family influence was important in obtaining attractive appointments. The surplus sons of commoners (non-nobles) had to make out as best they could, which after the 17th century typically meant moving to the rapidly growing cities or to overseas colonies, including Canada.

The stem extended family has been the dominant family form in Ireland, allowing rural land holdings to be held intact for generations (Arnsberg and Kimball,

1940). It has also been argued that the stem family was common in rural Quebec, as we will discuss in Chapter 6.

The Joint Family

The other common smaller extended family is the joint family, which is still often found in India today. The **joint family** typically consists, in one household, of a parental couple, their married sons and their sons' offspring, and their own unmarried sons and daughters. Authority is vested in the eldest male, who has the right and responsibility to make all decisions, including those determining the education, the occupation, and the spouse of others in the household (Ishwaran, 1982). The Indian joint family never grows as large as some Chinese extended families, however. Following the death of the father, the eldest son assumes patriarchal authority over others in the household. The family divides when the brothers have married sons of their own who establish new joint families.

The joint family has obvious advantages: the economies of a single household, and the strong bonds among the brothers and their wives. Brothers may or may not work together, but they help each other in times of need. Wives share housework and child rearing, and assist each other when a sister-in-law is ill or absent. They also provide each other with comfort and support—a significant advantage in a patriarchal society such as India, where wives would otherwise lack support if abused, and are not emotionally close to their husbands (Goode, 1970). While the joint family system only maintains family lands undivided if there is just one surviving son in the family, it does provide assistance and support to the elderly. It has obvious assistance and economic advantages that are not found in our own nuclear family system.

The Matrifocal Family

We have been describing variations of the patrilineal family system, where the central figure of the family is the father. However, there are other family systems that appear somewhat matriarchal, although a society in which women dominate families has never been found. The most obvious examples are the matrifocal or mother-centred families, in which the husband or father-figure is absent, found in Jamaica, in some Latin

American countries, and increasingly in Canadian lone-mother families. The matrifocal family is a type of *constricted family unit,* typically without a resident father. Although the matrifocal family is the most common type of constricted family, it may be noted that there are a variety of lone-parent-led families that will not be discussed in this chapter, including father-led families and single-parent families headed by professional, well-educated, or financially secure parents, whatever the parent's gender.

Matrifocal families are often found in impoverished areas where young men are unable to earn incomes that would enable them to get married and support a family. Their inability to marry does not deter them from sexual relationships, however, so many women become pregnant before marriage. After the baby is born, these women remain in their parental homes, and eventually seek work while their mothers care for the children. These women often do marry, frequently after having borne two or more children. The husband, who may have fathered one or more of the children, is usually well past adolescence and able to help support a family, but his economic insecurity often destabilizes the marriage. This pattern is common in Jamaica, where husbands often disappear when they are unemployed. The stable, dependable, sustaining family members typically include the mother and her daughter(s) and her daughter(s)' children; together, they make up the matrifocal household (Roberts and Sinclair, 1978).

Blumberg and Garcia (1979) have identified five necessary conditions for a viable matrifocal family:

1. The social unit that is paid for work and accumulates property must be either the man or the woman. If the income-earning unit is the family, the household will not be matrifocal.

2. Women must have independent access to income opportunities. Either economic opportunities must be open to women through their own work or the work of their children, or there must be state-provided social assistance.

3. The customs and laws of the society must permit women to control property and to assume the responsibilities of head of the household.

4. Women must be able to adapt their subsistence opportunities to their child-care responsibilities. They may find work that can be done at home, ask mothers or other female relatives to baby-sit, have older children look after younger ones, or receive welfare payments.

5. The subsistence resources available to a lone mother must not be much less than those commonly earned by the men of her social class. If women's earnings are much less, it would be more advantageous for women to be wives in patriarchal families than to head up matrifocal families.

Blumberg and Garcia note that "all these conditions most frequently exist among the economically marginal in wage labour societies, accounting for the concentration of female-centred and female-headed families" in such societies. They are most prevalent among the lowest income levels, the "surplus labour classes" of a society (1977:109).

These conditions apply to industrialized societies, as well as to Jamaica and other developing nations. There are many lone-mother, matrifocal families in Canada today, as we will discuss in Chapter 5. In both Canada and the United States, for example, earning opportunities are often unavailable to poor single mothers, because they do not have access to child-care arrangements; instead, they subsist on minimally adequate social welfare payments. In both developing and modern industrial societies, matrifocal families are found in lower social class groupings, where often the men earn less income than do the women. When this is the case, it does not "pay" a woman to marry within her own class and try to make the marriage work (Blumberg and Garcia, 1977). This situation approaches that seen in a matrilineal society, in which women control the economic resource (land). Although women heading matrifocal families do not have more resources than the men in their class, they do not have many less, so marriage provides few advantages over lone motherhood. Students interested in further study of family systems will find the sources listed at the conclusion of this chapter very helpful.

Kinship, Modernization, and Cross-Cultural Changes

Technological innovations are occurring rapidly in both traditional and industrializing societies. Are marital and family systems in small traditional societies changing? Chapter 1 drew an important distinction between change and process. Four graphs were used to illustrate different types of change over time. There are ups and downs in marriage and family systems throughout history. The purpose of this section of the chapter is to review relevant theory relating to change in marriage and family systems, and current research in several countries that examines trends in family life.

Modernization and Kinship

Perhaps the most widely read theoretical treatise relating to social change and family life is *World Revolution and Family Patterns* (Goode, 1963). Goode was interested in the transition from advanced agricultural economic systems to industrial economies. Therefore, this theory largely ignored small traditional societies such as those discussed earlier in this chapter. Goode's approach is often referred to as *convergence theory*. Goode predicted the inevitable convergence of family systems into a conjugal (or monogamous) marital form and a nuclear family form. He argued that the processes of industrialization, urbanization, and general modernization (increasing societal complexity) are directly related to a decrease in the prevalence of the extended family system and the increase in the conjugal family system. Goode further suggested that the nuclear family would emerge as the dominant family form throughout the industrialized world, even though many societies came from various different starting points. The power of the kinship system, it was argued, is either a barrier or a victim to the processes of modernization (Inkeles and Smith, 1974). Parsons and Bales (1955) also proposed that differentiation in modernizing societies is the primary explanation for the rise of the isolated nuclear family. They further argued that the nuclear family is characterized by its structural isolation, the emotional intensity of family life, rigid role segregation of the husband and wife, individual achievement, and social and geographical mobility.

The typical critique of Goode's assumptions, as well as those of Parsons and Bales, is that there is considerable contact in many societies between the nuclear family and many extended kin, as well as gift sharing, financial aid, the return of older children to the nest, care for elderly parents, and frequent contact by letters and telephone (e.g., McDonald, 1992). In other words, the nuclear family in our modern postindustrial society is not, in fact, "isolated." The kinship systems of large agricultural and industrializing societies are typically the major sources of resistance to change. Nonetheless, increasing technological innovations, occupational and professional options, higher levels of educational achievement, intracultural and cross-cultural mobility, and many other attributes of modernization are powerful forces opposing traditional ways. Accordingly, in the next section, we evaluate the modernization hypothesis in light of several research studies in various industrializing societies. As the evidence will show, modernization has impacted not only our own society, but also family systems in many industrializing societies. In some cases, the shifts appear modest or even uncertain, while in others they seem significant. Even so, it will be apparent that kinship systems—as well as nuclear and extended family ties—are a resistant and resilient source of control and meaning in everyday life. The battle for, and against, change continues even in Canada and the United States despite continuing educational and technological innovations.

Family Ties

China is a particularly interesting example of change because of the communist revolution (summary based on Riley, 1994). Prior to the revolution, older men held the authority, while the young, and women, had little power or influence and were dependent on family elders. Elders completely controlled marriage, including the timing of weddings and the choice of partners. The post-revolutionary government outlawed many of the old rules concerning marriage, such as child marriage without meeting the prospective spouse until the wedding and arranged marriages. The state took control of all production, job assignments, and decisions about schooling. Family elders lost power. Even so, ties among parents and their children remained strong throughout the revolution. Indeed, family ties—the loss of control notwithstanding—were *strengthened* by the communist revolution. As Riley points out, the most important change in marriage has been the dramatic rise in the age at marriage. In this post-revolution period, housing shortages and the absence of a dating culture has led to a continuing influence of parents in the lives of their daughters. The principle of *guanxi*—a system used to exchange favours to fulfill a private goal or need—is a continuing influence. Riley believes family ties will "mix" with the new economic policies. Despite the optimism in this research project, the "mix" is likely to be an ongoing factor in continued change.

Al-Haj (1995) examined the modernization thesis among a society of Arabs within the nation of Israel. The traditional kinship system was group-centred and required the subjection of the individual to the group. Al-Haj points out that the Arab minority (16 percent of the total population in Israel) is experiencing innovations in several ways: increased education and standard of living, and exposure to mass media, politicization, and bilingualism. Al-Haj found that while the kinship system continues to have a significant influence politically and socially, its economic role has become marginal. Pragmatic values have replaced traditional ideological commitments to kinship structures and regulations. The role of kin has sharply changed in the interest of social and political mobilization and economic mobility. Al-Haj seems to indicate that these sharp changes are necessary, but—it is hoped—temporary. This may well be an excellent example of social process, i.e., the old kinship system may be reestablished when the current political situation is changed.

Sibling Relationships

Cicirelli (1994), using data available from many societies, compared sibling relationships in nonindustrialized and industrialized societies. His conclusions are interesting and aptly illustrate the evolution of family patterns. The differences are compared in Table 3.2. Cicirelli concludes from his analysis that sibling relationships are obligatory in nonindustrialized societies and discretionary in industrialized societies. In reviewing the impact of modernization on cultural differences such as sibling relationships, Cicirelli, with minor reservations, concludes that most cultures will move toward an industrialized society model.

Consanguineous Marriage

One of the more traditional major societies is the nation of Iran. Iran, like many Middle Eastern cultures, has experienced considerable internal religious turmoil in connection with rapid industrialization related to the discovery and production of oil resources. *Consanguineous marriage* is a common type of marriage in many societies, and typically refers to a marriage with a third cousin or closer relative. As suggested earlier in

TABLE 3.2   Sibling Relationships in Nonindustrialized and Industrialized Societies

NONINDUSTRIALIZED SOCIETIES	INDUSTRIALIZED SOCIETIES
Sibling relationships are crucial to family function and adaptation to larger society.	Sibling relationships are secondary to spousal and parent–child relations. No major effect on family function or adaptation to larger society.
Child caretaking role is shared with other siblings. Sibling caretaking is merged with educational responsibility. Siblings are socialization agents of younger siblings.	Parents have control over child caretaking. Older siblings are only incidentally involved.
Sister–brother and brother–brother are the closest relationships.	Sister–sister relationships are the closest.
Older siblings have authority over younger siblings.	Sibling relationships are variable, ranging from extreme closeness to rivalry to indifference.

Source: Cicirelli, 1994.

this chapter, marriage to a close relative minimizes the risk of incompatibility between marital partners and their families. Givens and Hirschman (1994) studied nearly 5000 Iranian women in a fertility survey conducted in 1976–1977. They found that women who married at a later age, who achieved higher levels of education, and who worked before getting married were much less likely to marry cousins. Interestingly, however, there has been a sharp resistance to modernization among traditional Iranian kinship systems. Indeed, it was found that between the 1950s and 1970s, the incidence of marriage to cousins increased—a kind of religious counterculture movement. It is evident that traditional families have a strong stake in marriage selection. The authors of this study indicate that Saudi Arabia, Lebanon, and Jordan have similar trends and conflicts. They also indicate that the forces of modernization are likely to eventually erode cultural preference for the marriage of cousins.

Marriage Timing

The age at marriage, particularly among women, is perhaps one of the most powerful factors influencing the processes of modernization. Using data from an Asian marriage survey, King et al. (1986), as reported in Domingo and King (1992), found a sharp trend toward later marriages. In 1930, for example, 60 percent of marriages occurred at age 15 in Pakistan, 43 percent in Indonesia, and 10 percent in the Philippines. Among women born between 1951 and 1960, in contrast, fewer than 10 percent in Indonesia and 5 percent in the Philippines were married at age 15. Domingo and King reexamined the Asian marriage survey database, and found that economic development is the primary reason for change in the age at marriage, i.e., more work opportunities and higher wages for women, predominantly in Pakistan and Indonesia. Daughters are increasingly valued for their productive contributions, and not just for their reproductive capacity and the formation of alliances; they are more often contributing to the "good of the family" through nontraditional means, by providing income and prestige. There is a loosening of traditional parental control. Consequently, the age at marriage has increased; the role of parents in mate selection has decreased, particularly in urban areas; and the idea of meeting one's husband-to-be before marriage is increasingly common in urban areas.

In both Thailand and the Philippines, women have made greater progress toward what are typical patterns in North American societies. The impact of delayed marriage is also apparent in Egypt and Jordan (Heaton, 1996). Both countries exhibit increasing female educational achievement and involvement in the workforce. Educated and employed women are more likely to use contraceptives and to have smaller families. The delayed age of marriage in Sri Lanka, however, seems to lead to quite different outcomes (Malhotra and Tsui, 1996). Family and cultural factors remain central in the determination of marriage timing. Women attending school, including those who achieve higher academic levels, are not considered ready for marriage. Partly due to the lack of white-collar jobs, many educated women are unable to obtain satisfactory employment. Arranged marriage is more common among educated women, because education acts as a dowry substitute and increases a woman's value in the marriage marketplace. This society is an excellent example of the complexities in testing the modernization hypothesis. Ethnic, cultural, and family factors play a significant role in the marriage patterns and outcomes for women in Sri Lanka. The economic system lags behind the educational expertise available. Education and delayed marriage are not automatic indicators of either social change or social process in all societies.

The Gender Factor in Family Change

Perhaps the single most powerful argument in support of the modernization thesis is that industrializing economies have created a demand for the participation of women in the formal labour force. Chafetz and Hagan (1996) analyzed data for 21 industrial countries, all listed in the *World Development Report* as "industrial market economies." The data analyzed for the last 30 years reveal the following:

1. women's labour force participation rates expanded dramatically in response to increased demand for their labour;
2. post-secondary enrollment rates increased for women;
3. first-marriage rates decreased, most notably among young women;

4. divorce rates increased;

5. total fertility fell to below replacement level;

6. first births were increasingly deferred to the late 20s and beyond (Chafetz and Hagan, 1996:197).

Chafetz and Hagan also note several other family-related factors that have significantly changed, which were not examined in their analysis: increasing rates of out-of-wedlock births; increasing numbers of children raised in single-parent families and with stepparents and step siblings; increasing feminization of poverty, especially for mothers and their dependent children. They rightly point out that decision-making among women is an attempt to satisfy two sets of goals: "achievement within the labor force and commitment to romantic partners and children" (212). Overall, their data clearly document the obvious: industrialization has changed the way in which many, if not most, men, women, and children live in families in industrialized societies.

Higher Education versus Local Tradition

We conclude this chapter with two research studies in two quite different industrializing societies—Libya and India. Each society illustrates the sharp antithesis between forces of modernization, such as higher education, and local traditions and customs.

Libya Al-Nouri (1995) argues that higher education in Libya has been the single most powerful force in encouraging social change. Traditional family patterns included parallel-cousin marriage, polygyny, female chastity, subordination of women, encouragement of femininity in young girls—and adulthood meant getting married and having children. Young boys were expected to be courageous and generous. As adults, men were expected to be the breadwinners, and women, the housekeepers. In contrast, modernization in Libya has led to an acceptance, as a given, of college training for both sexes. According to Al-Nouri, the positive outcomes of university education in Libya have included the liberation of women, reduction of differences between men and women, secularism, social mobility, and professional ambition for both men and women. The continued development of scientific and educational institutions is one of the top priorities of the state's agenda. There are now two major universities and several smaller ones. Oil-rich Libya is able to provide the latest and best in facilities and labs, as well as high salaries. Investment in hard sciences, however, far exceeds investment in the social sciences. Strangely enough, Libya may be a classic example of a traditional society that has been transformed rapidly by education and technology. Resistance among rural families and tribal groups remains, but seemingly in a subdued and uncertain "state of reluctant acceptance." Significant conflicts between traditional and modern lifestyles may be on the horizon.

India In contrast to the Libyan study—largely an examination of the characteristics of a changing society—the Indian study examines gender equality in two types of working couples. As of 1981, only 14 percent of females were employed full time, compared to 52 percent of men (Bharat, 1995:373). Of the 326 couples involved in the study, 58 percent were defined as wives with a professional career, and 42 percent as non-career wives. In traditional Indian culture the husband is considered the wife's lord and master, provider and protector—but not her companion. Professional men and women in this study, as well as non-career women, considered companionship and family roles more important than sexual, domestic, or provider roles. The roles of companion, friend, children's guide, and worker for the family's best interest were the most important. In contrast, the provider and domestic roles were gender-biased, i.e., husbands saw themselves as the primary breadwinners, and their wives as primarily responsible for domestic duties, such as meals, household management, and child care. Career wives shared these views, but were more liberal than their husbands. It should be emphasized that these findings are actually very similar to much of the research in Canada and the United States. The importance of this study is that it illustrates an often-misunderstood fact about cross-cultural research in traditional societies. Even if social change is not widespread, most societies have professionally trained people (doctors, engineers, accountants, etc.) who are married and, typically, educated in excellent institutions that are located in industrializing, industrial, and postindustrial societies. Their lifestyles may be quite different from the rank-and-file of a given society.

As indicated above, the overwhelming majority of us now live in a global village. Mass communication and transcultural mobility can potentially take each of us to nearly any corner of the earth. The staples of change—education, communication, goods and services, contrasting and contradicting values, and human connections—however well-intentioned—may enhance or hinder individual, marital, family, kinship group, and societal well-being. There are rights and wrongs, as well as betters and bests, in human exchange. Some ways of life turn out to be much wiser in the long term. Others turn out to be premature and perhaps destructive. We can all learn from each other.

ENDNOTES

1. This example is drawn from Schusky (1965).
2. Cohabitation, as we understand this term in North America, is not the equivalent of marriage, although there are legal signs that this assumption may be in the process of changing. Cohabitation, however, as used in the study of small nontraditional societies, is almost identical to marriage. Marriage is not a legal concept in the small traditional societies examined in this section. It is a normative union, defined by kinship regulation and control. Kinship "rules" are much like laws as we know them.

SUMMARY

- Kinship is a social definition of who is related to whom.
- Kinship is defined by affinal and consanguineal relationships.
- Kinship terms are either *terms of reference* or *terms of address*. For the most part ethnographers study terms of reference because these show social organization, whereas terms of address show the closeness and meanings of the relationship to Ego. For example, one refers to their father (term of reference) so that others will understand the relationship, but Ego may address his father as "Dad," a term of address. We usually express kinship terms of reference by the positional shorthand such as FaSiSo and reserve the specific cultural term "cousin" as denoting the content of the role.
- Descent is of two types: Unilineal systems are either patrilineal (through the line of the father) or matrilineal (through the line of the mother). Bilineal kinship

systems establish certain rules through the patrilineal line, and other regulations through the matrilineal line. Bilateral kinship systems enable both the husband and wife lines to influence the marital unit and the nuclear family unit.

- Monogamy and polygamy are the two major types of marriage. Bride price and dowry are the two major forms of marriage finance.
- Patriarchal, matriarchal, and egalitarian forms of authority are all types of "legitimate power."
- There are six major types of kinship residence systems: patrilocal, matrilocal, bilocal, neolocal, avunculocal, and matripatrilocal. Residence rules specify where an individual is required to live when marriage occurs.
- Stem families, composed of a parental couple and the family of the son who will inherit the family property, have been common in Ireland.
- Joint families, composed of a parental couple, their immature offspring, and often their sons' families, or of the families of brothers, their children, and their immature siblings, are still common in India.
- The matrifocal family is headed by the mother, consists of her immature children, and may be extended to include grown daughters and perhaps daughters' children. Economics is behind the large numbers of matrifocal (lone-mother) families in the Western world. Where families are not economically productive units, and where unmarried mothers are able to support themselves as well as or better than husbands could support them, matrifocal families are numerous.

KEY TERMS

Affinal kin (47)

Alliance theory (47)

Avunculocal (55)

Bilateral (55)

Bilocal (55)

Bride price (51)

Cenogamy (53)

Consanguineal kin (47)

Descent theory (47)

Double-descent (55)

Dowry (51)

Extended family (57)
Female infanticide (53)
Fraternal polyandry (53)
Genetic relatives (56)
Joint family (58)
Matrilineal (54)
Matrilocal (55)
Matripatrilocal (55)
Monogamy (52)
Neolocal (55)
Non-fraternal polyandry (53)
Non-sororal polygyny (53)
Nuclear family (57)
Patrilineal (54)
Patrilocal (56)
Polyandry (53)
Polygynandry (53)
Polygyny (52)
Sororal polygyny (53)
Stem family (58)
Unilineal (54)

QUESTIONS FOR REVIEW

1. How would you distinguish between consanguineal and affinal kin? What are the differences among the three types of kin categories?

2. Compare and contrast the definitions of *patrilineal*, *matrilineal*, and *bilateral* systems.

3. Avunculocal residence is associated with what kind of lineage system? Why?

4. How does the stem family differ from the Indian form of extended family?

5. Why is polygyny the most popular form of marriage in most societies of the world while monogamy is the most commonly practised?

6. How would you distinguish a group marriage, or cenogamy, from polygyny?

7. Carefully review the convergence theory, and briefly explain why it has had such an impact on understanding changes in family systems.

8. What is a matrifocal family, and what are the conditions under which it becomes common?

QUESTIONS FOR DISCUSSION

1. What are the major reasons kinship systems influence the everyday life of children?

2. Discuss with classmates your reactions to the lifestyle of the Abisi tribe in Nigeria. How do your reactions differ?

3. Explain why you agree or disagree with the following statement: In almost all societies, men's expectations of the family responsibilities of women have been more important than women's expectations of the family responsibilities of men. Give examples to illustrate your argument.

4. Critically evaluate the convergence hypothesis. In what ways is Professor Goode right? In what ways do you consider his argument inadequate?

5. Explain why you agree or disagree with the following statement: Beliefs about sexual and family morality are functions of the kinship systems of the society in which they are found. Support your argument with appropriate examples.

SUGGESTED READINGS

Ben-Rafael, Eliezer. 1997. *Crisis and Transformation: The Kibbutz at Century's End*. New York: State University of New York Press. This small book is an excellent review of the history and development of the Kibbutz system. The book reveals the struggles and radical changes that have occurred within the system.

Goode, William J. 1963. *World Revolution and Family Patterns*. Glencoe, IL: Free Press. At the time of its publication, this book was considered one of the most important books published to date. Although the book has had many critics, it continues to challenge many of the alternative explanations of family change.

Holy, L. 1996. *Anthropological Perspectives of Kinship*. Chicago: Pluto Press. This book provides an excellent and well-written introduction to the study of kinship appropriate for undergraduate students.

Journal of Comparative Family Studies, edited by Dr. George Kurian, Department of Sociology, University of Calgary. This journal focuses on publishing research conducted in other cultures. It is a valuable resource for further study on marital, family, and kinship systems around the world.

Murdock, George P. 1965. *Social Structure*. New York: The Free Press. This work presents a comprehensive description and analysis of the variety of kinship systems found in small traditional societies. You may also wish to consult Dr. Murdock's 1967 "Ethnographic Atlas: A summary," *Ethnology* 6 (April):109–236.

Schusky, E. 1965. *Manual for Kinship Analysis*. New York: Holt, Rinehart and Winston. This concise book remains as one of the clearest and most detailed "manuals" on deciphering the complexities of kinship. It is most appropriate for advanced undergraduate and graduate students.

CHAPTER 4

History of the Family

After studying this chapter, you should be able to do the following:

- ■ Outline Zimmerman's theory of the cycle of family change and discuss its possible relevance to Canadian families today.
- ■ Discuss the similarities and the differences between Zimmerman's and Ogburn's theories of family change.
- ■ Indicate how the Hebrew family has influenced contemporary Western families.
- ■ Discuss how Christianity has influenced contemporary Western families.
- ■ Describe the major influences that contributed to the formation of the modern family, as identified by Goode.
- ■ Identify some of the major demographic changes that have taken place in the Canadian family since the Second World War.

Introduction

What are the origins of the contemporary North American family? To what early family systems can it be traced? In what ways has it changed, and what caused these changes? In this chapter, we look for answers to these questions by briefly outlining the historical origins of the North American family system. We begin by examining key theories of family change. We then assess the roots of the Euro-Canadian family in the Hebrew, Roman, Early Christian, and medieval English and French family systems. In the concluding section we discuss family patterns in Canada during the 19th and 20th centuries, including major demographic characteristics. We will take an historical approach that identifies the key features of the family systems from which most Canadian families today seem to have evolved.

Few of the theories we discussed in Chapter 2 attempt to explain the transformations in the family during the past 3500 years. Accordingly, we will begin by describing a few of the theories that have tried to explain these transformations. We examine these theories not because they are necessarily true, but because

they lead us to consider other factors. First, discussing the earliest theories permits us to critique their seemingly common-sense ideas. Second, the two most recent theories, which emphasize important aspects of contemporary families, help us to consider the origin of these aspects and their possible consequences for Canadians today.

Theories of Family Change

Two students of the family, Bachofen (1861) and Morgan (1877), assumed that the earliest form of marriage was not polygyny or polyandry, but group marriage. However, we now know that some animal species mate with only a single partner, sometimes for life, and early humans may have had similar relationships. Early theorists believed that within a group marriage, the identity of a child's mother was obvious, but the identity of the child's father was not, and therefore descent would be traced through the known parent—the mother—resulting in a matrilineal kinship system, with patrilineality a later development. This theory, however, lacks supporting archaeological or ethnographic evidence. These theorists also believed that all family systems followed a single evolutionary sequence, an idea that now seems unlikely. Finally, early family-change theorists believed that people in simple societies associated lineage with genealogical ties. But more recent study indicates that in most nonliterate societies, conceptions of kinship and descent primarily reflect group affiliation (i.e., who lives with whom) rather than genealogy. Accordingly, over thousands of years a human society might have alternated between patrilocality and matrilocality a number of times, as survival advantage dictated.

While the early writers stimulated interesting discussion with their theories, it is now clear that many of their ideas were probably mistaken. The two theorists we describe next may not be entirely right either, but their arguments are more relevant to contemporary society—and more provocative as well. Both theorists viewed family through the lens of macrosocial conflict (White and Klein, 2002). Zimmerman (1947) believed the family was in a continual dialectic between power over the individual being invested in the family versus power invested in the external social institutions of the state and church. Ogburn (1955), however, perceived family change as taking place through society's continual adjustment to technological change and the removal of the functions that families serve.

Carl Zimmerman developed a cyclical theory of family change in his book *Family and Civilization* (1947). He argued that there are essentially three kinds of family systems. The **trustee family** is a patriarchal, extended family in which the rights and privileges of the individual are subordinate to the family group; the welfare of the family is supreme. The patriarchal head of the trustee family is virtually all-powerful and has control of life and death over his wife and children. The **atomistic family** represents the opposite extreme, with the family exercising very few constraints on the rights and privileges of its ultra-individualistic members. Zimmerman saw the **domestic family** as an ideal balance between the excessive family domination and the rampant individualism of the other two family systems.

Zimmerman believed that family change was cyclical because of the interdependency between the family and the state. Where the trustee family is dominant, the state is organized to work through the extended family, exercising its authority through the family head, as was earlier true in China. Zimmerman believed that "under the authority of the trustee family, civilization moves toward greatness . . . . Order is created out of chaos and wealth accumulates" (Schultz, 1972:102). However, this success leads to disintegration, because unchecked authority results in abuse of authority, and families begin to feud.

Because of the need to restore order in society, power slowly shifts from the extended family to other institutions. The trustee family evolves into the domestic family as power over family members is increasingly assumed by church and state. During this phase, civilization flourishes, Zimmerman maintained, because people are not stifled by their families and are free to be creative. Individuals now have rights, and divorce becomes acceptable, although rare; marital separation is more common. In the domestic family, members feel more free to flout the family's authority, and therefore the power of the state steadily increases to compensate for declining familial control.

With the increasing power of the state and the declining authority of the family, the atomistic family gradually replaces the domestic family. Individual autonomy is now supreme; personal rights are paramount. Obligations to both the parental family and to one's spouse and children are seen as secondary to the individual's right to self-development. No longer a divinely instituted relationship, marriage is now a civil contract, to be ended when it is no longer convenient.

Evidence for the current preeminence of the atomistic family is far stronger now than when Zimmerman wrote *Family and Civilization* some 50 years ago. It is seen in the high rates of divorce, illegitimacy, childless marriages, youth problems, and, Zimmerman believed, in feminist movements. He asserted that this phase of individualism inevitably leads to societal disintegration, because atomistic and broken families cannot rear children capable of maintaining an orderly society. But in a disintegrating society, the government is unable to provide protection and support, and people will once again become heavily dependent on strong family organization. The trustee family will reemerge, and the cycle of family change will begin again.

Zimmerman's study of history led him to believe that in the 2500 years since early Roman society began, this family cycle has repeated twice. The first cycle came to an end after the Roman Empire disintegrated, about 500 A.D., and the second cycle has lasted until now. The social problems now found in many

Western societies, including the high and often growing rates of family breakdown, drug abuse, crime, and homelessness, could be seen as indications of increasing societal disintegration. Zimmerman might predict that some of you will live to see the reappearance of the trustee family among your grandchildren.

Zimmerman's book was not well received by family sociologists when it appeared in 1947. In the period following the Second World War, when it became possible once again for young North Americans to get married and have children, there was little interest in the kind of sweeping theory that he proposed. Family scholars generally ignored his work, preferring to conduct survey studies of courtship behaviour and marital adjustment. They did not appreciate his questioning the viability of the nuclear, atomistic family, which seemed so strong and stable at that time.

Since the 1960s, the relevance of Zimmerman's approach has become better appreciated, Wilke argues (1976). The atomistic family seems well adapted to society today, and there are strong legal and institutional supports for individualism, which Zimmerman recognized, but he questioned whether the children raised in increasingly atomistic families would learn the values and disciplines necessary to perpetuate their society. Whether or not we accept Zimmerman's predictions, it is clear that only in a society such as ours could the extreme individualism we find today have evolved. It is an extreme that is perhaps both our blessing and our curse. Individualism seems to be a source of many problems that we have not yet been able to solve, but which we may need to solve if our society is not to disintegrate, as Zimmerman would predict.

Zimmerman's theory assumes that there is an inverse relationship between the family and the state, which means that when the authority of the state is stronger, the solidarity of the family is weaker. William F. Ogburn's theory of family change is based on a more modest version of this assumption (Ogburn and Nimkoff, 1955). His analysis began with the observation that technological inventions, such as the wheel, the steam engine, and jet aircraft, are quickly adopted because their advantages are so obvious. But inventions such as these often have unanticipated effects on society, including the family system. In simple societies, the family provides for the health, security, socialization, education, worship, and recreation of its members. But with improvements in technology, societies become more complex, and the state inevitably becomes more powerful. Ogburn agreed with Zimmerman that as the state gathers strength, families weaken and functions erode. Worship moves from the home into churches and temples; security becomes the responsibility of the state; and hospitals, schools, workshops, factories, and commercial recreation all appear, relieving the family of more traditional functions.

Ogburn argued that the more "advanced" society becomes and the more it develops specialized institutions, the more the family loses functions and the more insignificant the family becomes. We could argue that this theory is truer today than ever before: no longer is there any clear need to get married, as there is in nonliterate societies where husbands and wives are dependent on each other.

Both Zimmerman and Ogburn saw the family as highly responsive to changes in society, and these insights are certainly valid. Zimmerman focused on a pattern of changes that results in a pathological form of the family and leads to societal disintegration. Ogburn analyzed how the significance of the family declines when its former functions are taken over by specialized institutions, and he pointed to increasing indications of family disorganization: divorce, premarital sex, desertion, and juvenile delinquency. But he was generally optimistic about the family; he saw it becoming ever more specialized to meet the interpersonal needs of its members, and meeting these needs increasingly well.

In the remainder of this chapter, we trace the sources of the modern Euro-Canadian family form, considering the influences of the patriarchal families of ancient Israel, ancient Rome, and early Christianity. The theories of Zimmerman and Ogburn will help us to understand the changes that have taken place. We then examine family patterns in Canada during the 19th and 20th centuries, including some demographic characteristics of Canadian families today.

Roots of the Euro-Canadian Family

The origins of Western civilization and of Canadian society are found in the Judaic, Greco/Roman, and early Christian civilizations. Israel was the source of our basic concepts of morality and religious concepts of the family; Rome was the source of our philosophy and science, and the civil concepts that have shaped family ideals and (to a lesser extent) family practices in Canada today. But with the fall of the Roman Empire, families in the Middle Ages began to reflect the influences of the church, and the conditions of feudal society.

Three legal systems have made significant contributions to Western marriage law, and thus to Canadian law. Roman matrimonial law contributed the requirement of monogamous marriages with spousal consent, and the expectation that marriages would be concluded at once, rather than in different phases. Canon law added the prohibition of marriage between close relatives, introduced ecclesiastical marriage, and, since 1184, has defined marriage as a sacrament that could not be dissolved by the spouses. Secular law introduced the concept of marriage as a civil contract between two parties. This concept was adopted by Protestant law, which later allowed divorce and civil marriage (Payne and Payne, 1994).

The Ancient Hebrew Family

Our knowledge of the Hebrew family is based on the Old Testament and other Jewish sources. The earliest description of marriage and the family for the Hebrews appears in Genesis 2:21–28. Male and female were both created in the image of God, placed in a monogamous marital relationship, commanded to bear children (the "goodness" of sex is assumed in this account), and commanded, as a couple, to exercise stewardship over creation.

There are two factors that complicate our understanding of the nature of the ancient Hebrew family. One is the considerable time involved (more than 1200 years); significant changes in cultural and social patterns took place within that time span. The other is the range of kinship terminology that is often missed in translations of Hebrew. The word *family* is used to translate a number of Hebrew words, including *tribe*, *clan*, and *father's house*, none of which accurately reflects what "family" means to us today. Tribe (*sebet*) was the primary unit of social and territorial organization in Israel, and reflected the names of the 12 sons of Jacob (Israel), with Joseph's two sons divided into Manasseh and Ephraim. Clan (*mispaha*) is often translated as *family*, which is misleading, since the clan could comprise quite a large number of families,

"though its most specific meaning is 'a residential group of several families,' or, more commonly 'a clan'" (Perdue, 1997:177). "Clan" signifies an intermediate role, since it denotes a kinship organization that is smaller than a tribe, but larger than a family. Father's house or household (*betab*) was the third level of Israel's kinship structure, which invoked the "strongest sense of inclusion, identity, protection, and responsibility" (Wright, 1992:762). "Households in ancient Israel were multi-generational and consisted of two or three families, related by kinship and marriage, who lived in a residential complex of two or three houses connected together. Families were patrilineal . . . patrilocal . . . and at least became largely patriarchal" (Perdue, 1997:166).

Sociologically, the *betab* (household) was the most important small unit in the nation, and fulfilled four major functions for the Israelite man, woman and child. The *betab* was the basic unit of Israel's system of land tenure, with each *betab* having its own inheritance of land. It was also the centre of judicial law and administration of justice. This included internal, domestic jurisdiction under which the head of the household could act judicially with respect to marriage and divorce, matters relating to slaves (except murder or physical injury), and parental discipline. "The *betab*, therefore, was the primary framework of legal authority within which the Israelite found himself from childhood, and to which he remained subject for a considerable period of his life—even into adulthood and parenthood, while his father was alive" (Wright, 1992:764). It should be noted that this legal authority applied not only to females, but to all males within the household. Judicial administration also entailed the external, public administration of justice. The heads of houses acted judicially in the local civic assembly—"the gate"—which was most likely a group of elders comprising senior males from each household. The didactic function was the third major function, with the father being charged with the primary responsibility of communicating the faith, history, law, and traditions of the nation to his household. The mother, however, also had considerable input in the didactic function, as indicated in Proverbs 1:8; 31:10–31. Finally, the family fulfilled the important function of maintaining Israel's relationship with God (Wright, 1992).

Marriage arrangements in Israel were under the jurisdiction of family law, rather than civil or criminal law. Marriages were normally arranged between families. They needed to be outside the degrees of kinship of the *betab*, but usually within the kinship of the *mispaha* (clan). Marriage within the *mispaha* was obligatory in the case of daughters who, in the absence of sibling brothers, had inherited the land of their father. While romantic relationships did take place in the Hebrew world (Gen. 24:67; 29:16–20; Judges 14:3; I Sam. 1:5; 18:20; 25:44; 2 Sam. 3:15; 11:27), sexual relationships were not only romantic, but political and economic. Marriage was a covenant with political and economic responsibilities that brought together two households willing to exchange substantial goods and services with each other over a period of time. It is for this reason that men and women themselves rarely chose their own marital partner (Matthews and Benjamin, 1993). It is clear from Genesis 2:24, as well as from the prophetic writings, that monogamy was the ideal marital relationship. It is equally clear that polygyny, but not polyandry, was practised. "It seems very likely that an additional wife or concubine was taken primarily for the purpose of acquiring or adding to one's children, that monogamy was probably the general rule among ordinary people (for economic reasons), and that the taking of many wives was purely a symbol of prestige and power (or political alliances) indulged in by royalty, though condemned by Deuteronomy 17:14–17" (Wright, 1992:766).

In Israel, the arrangement of a marriage was frequently accompanied by the exchange of gifts, cementing the relationship between bride and groom, as well as between families. It is in this context that the Israelite *mohar* (the money or equivalent given by the bridegroom to the bride's family) is to be understood. While this may have the outward appearance of a purchase, de Vaux (1965:27) argues that this custom of the *mohar* seems to be not so much the "price paid for a woman, as a compensation given to a family, and, in spite of the apparent resemblance, in law this is a different consideration." Similarly, Wright argues that the common translation of "bride-price" is very misleading in its depiction of marriage in Israel as being solely a matter of purchase. "This view, and its oft-repeated correlates, that wives in Israel were chattel property and that adultery was simply a property offence, cannot be supported by a careful study of the laws and narratives about wives in the OT" (1992:766). Safrai and Stern

(1976) point out that while a wife's status was inferior to that of her husband in some legal aspects, socially, the woman's position in the house was highly esteemed and was protected by various laws and beliefs. Both early and late sources emphasize that sexual relations required the wife's consent, and that the husband had no right to force himself on her. Similarly, Perdue (1997) points out that women wielded significant influence over males in their household, as depicted in biblical and early Jewish literature (Sarah, Genesis 12–23; Rebekah, Genesis 24–27; Samson's wife, Judges 14:17; Bathsheba, I Kings 1:15–21; and the "capable wife" of Proverbs 31:10–31).

The sexual code of the ancient Hebrews was firmly grounded in patriarchal values. Matthews and Benjamin (1993) point out, however, that patriarchy is not sexism, which leads to prejudice and oppression based on the faulty assumption that women are biologically inferior to men, and which uses power to deprive women of autonomy.

> The Bible itself grants women much more access to the administrative, judicial, and economic systems than many of today's generalizations about women and the Bible acknowledge. The status of women in early Israel may be no model for the reconstruction of contemporary society on more inclusive principles, but neither is it a unilateral endorsement for the subordination of women. And the world of the Bible may not be feminist, but neither is it completely male oriented. It may not be liberated, but it is liberating . . . . Patriarchy in ancient Israel was based not on the subordination and exploitation of women, but rather on the efforts of all the men and women in its household to survive. (Matthews and Benjamin, 1993:22–23)

In general, only men could divorce their spouse, although under certain conditions, such as a husband unable to fulfill his marital obligations, a wife could divorce her husband (Safrai and Stern, 1976). "By the Roman period, the wife could divorce her husband for: impotence, change of religion, refusal to support her, commission of a serious crime, extreme dissoluteness, and affliction with a loathsome disease (leprosy)" (Leslie and Korman, 1985:147–148). Divorced women were not stigmatized; like widows, they were often awarded property, and could remarry.

The ancient Hebrews regarded children as a blessing from God, and considered a childless couple a tragedy. When Rachel was unable to bear children, for example, she said to Jacob, "Give me children, or else I die" (Genesis 30:1). Children were subject to the authority of both father and mother, and were educated according to Hebrew laws. Hebrew scriptures strongly emphasized the proper training and instruction of children (Deuteronomy 6:4–9). The duty of honour and obedience on the part of children is stressed throughout the Old Testament and Hebrew Bible; rebelliousness and disobedience were perceived as serious breaches of responsibility to the community, and were disciplined strictly (Deuteronomy 21:18–21).

While a man's children were legally regarded as the personal property of the father with a calculable economic value, the frequent conclusion that this gave the father absolute power over them (*patria potestas*) may be mistaken. In fact, Deuteronomy 21:18–21 clearly places the execution of a stubborn, rebellious son in the hands of a court of elders, and the investigation includes the testimony of both father and mother; the consent of both parents necessary for the charge to be legally actionable provided an added element of protection for the son (Wright, 1992). Matthews and Benjamin (1993) also indicate that the father was not a despot within the family. While he was "to be fruitful and multiply, and fill the earth and subdue it" (Genesis 1:28), and while *subdue* can imply the use of force, fathers were not expected to be ruthless.

The Roman Patriarchal Family

The early Roman family resembled the Hebrew family in that it was patrilineal and patriarchal, but it differed in being strictly monogamous. Yet significant changes in the traditional family system occurred following the Roman victories in the Punic Wars during the 3rd century BC. Some condemned these changes, including the early Christians who praised the values of the earlier Roman family (Gies and Gies, 1987).

The Roman patriarchal, trustee-family household included all of the sons, their families, unmarried daughters, and patrilineal grandchildren of the *pater familias*, or patriarch. Upon the patriarch's death, each son became the *pater familias* of his own household. The powers of the *pater familias* exceeded even those of the Hebrew father. His power over his children was called *potestas*, and continued through his lifetime. By law, he could sell his children or grandchildren, and even decide at their birth whether they were to live or die. If

he decided that they were to die, they were exposed in the countryside, or some other family could take them as slaves. He arranged for the marriages of his children and patrilineal grandchildren, seeking unions that were politically or economically advantageous without concern for the wishes of the couple. He could also require them to divorce against their wishes (Goodsell, 1934). In time, the negotiation of marriage passed from the *pater familias* to professional matchmakers.

The marriage contract gave no remuneration to the bride's family. Rather, the bride was required to bring a **dowry** to the husband's family. The husband controlled the dowry as long as the marriage survived, but often returned it to the woman upon divorce. This dowry payment discouraged ill-treatment of the wife, because the husband's family had to repay it to the wife if the marriage failed.

Divorces were rare until after the Punic Wars. As among the Hebrews, only men could initiate divorce proceedings. However, the Roman practice imposed restrictions, sometimes requiring the approval of a council composed of male members from both families. Adultery made this step unnecessary, and gave the husband the right to punish or even kill his wife. Nevertheless, Roman women clearly had higher status than did Hebrew women because of the dowry practice, and because marriages were monogamous. Men could not undercut the position of their wives by taking a concubine, or second or third wife, and these features of Roman marriage probably limited any tendency for men to think of wives as easily disposable.

The status of women improved significantly during the Punic Wars. Women became less subject to patriarchal authority because the men were away fighting. Moreover, having to manage the family farm or other enterprise by themselves, women became used to more autonomy. These developments led to an unprecedented relative emancipation of women, but there were other influences, as well. A new form of marriage (*sine manu*), under which a married woman remained a member of her father's family (instead of her husband's family) and thus retained the right to inherit property, became increasingly common. Wealthy fathers began a practice of giving property to their daughters. If a woman was later divorced, this property reverted to her ownership. Similarly, the dowry paid when a woman married reverted to her ownership after divorce. It also became common, at this time, for the groom to make a gift of property to his bride when they married. This property remained under his control, unless he was at fault in a later divorce, in which case it became the property of the wife (Goodsell, 1934).

In the family, as in most other relations, wealth meant power. With increased wealth, women were less dependent on fathers or husbands, so the bases of the traditional patriarchal family were gradually and irreversibly transformed. In time, the Roman marriage came to be based on the free consent of the bride and groom, with women often achieving a surprising degree of equality. As the power of husbands was reduced and wives became more independent, the divorce rate increased rapidly—some famous Romans of the time are reported to have married three, four, or even five times—but at the same time women gained a degree of independence never before dreamed of in the ancient world.

The standards governing family life began to erode as well, undercut by the dissolute lifestyle of the wealthy. Marriage became more optional, as Zimmerman indicated in his description of the atomistic family. Abortion became more common, and the exposure to the elements or abandonment of infants was widely practised. The numbers of unmarried adults grew so rapidly that around 9 AD penalizing laws were passed preventing those unmarried and aged 20 to 55 from inheriting property, except from close relatives. Some couples married temporarily simply for convenience (Queen et al., 1985).

There were further inevitable changes as the atomistic family took root. By the end of the 1st century, when the Empire was at its most powerful and just before it went into decline, Roman sexual, marriage, and family patterns had evolved in ways that may seem familiar today. Rates of divorce, adultery, abortion, prostitution, and homosexuality were all high. Marriage rates were so low that bachelors were subject to special taxes. As we shall see later in this chapter, there are reasons to argue that the Canadian family may be no less atomistic today than the Roman family was before the Empire fell (Goodsell, 1934).

The Diverse Impact of Christianity

Our knowledge of early Christianity's influence on the family is based on the New Testament, writings of the early church fathers, and other historical sources. In the first section, we consider the teachings of Jesus and Paul on marriage and family life. In the second, we examine the institutionalization of the church in later centuries and the writings of early church fathers.

The Establishment of the Early Christian Community Early Christians generally accepted the practices of the Judeo-Roman world, but the teachings of Jesus and the many letters written by the apostle Paul had a powerful influence on marriage and family customs. Jesus emphasized mutual respect and consideration in all relationships (Matthew 7:12), and affirmed the importance of affection, faithfulness and the permanence of marriage (Matthew 19:4–9), although he permitted divorce on the grounds of infidelity. Later, Paul described the qualities of loving relationships in I Corinthians 13, and emphasized that wives and husbands should submit to each other (Ephesians 5:21–33). He also stressed equality and reciprocity in a married couple's sexual relationship (I Corinthians 7:3–6), and emphasized that the man and woman mutually have each other's bodies, which is in strong opposition to the widespread patriarchal assumption that the man owns the woman (Osiek and Balch, 1997:115).

The statement that many early Christians "saw sexual activity as utterly evil and degrading and the sexual impulse as something to be repressed and excised (destroyed) if happiness or salvation was to be achieved" (Deane, 1963:54) must be balanced by Paul's statement in I Cor. 7:3–5: "The husband should not deprive his wife of sexual intimacy, which is her right as a married woman, nor should the wife deprive her husband. The wife gives authority over her body to her husband, and the husband also gives authority over his body to his wife. So do not deprive each other of sexual relations." Far from teaching the sinfulness of sexual relations, Paul clearly teaches the normative nature of sex within the marriage bond. Both partners are put on the same level with respect to marital obligations. Conjugal rights are equal and reciprocal. Both husband and wife are to be sensitive to the sexual needs of the other. The relationship is lifted from one of self-gratification to one of mutual moral sensitivity.

The early New Testament church also brought about important changes in the treatment of children. Although the ruling Roman society strongly emphasized the patriarchal approach of the absolute authority of the father, Christianity taught the mutual responsibility of parents and children, and insisted that children were as worthy as adults in the eyes of God. Jesus himself introduced this change in approach, saying "Let the children come to me. Don't stop them! For the Kingdom of Heaven belongs to such as these" (Matthew 19:14). Hare (1993) suggests that the disciples represent, in this anecdote, a traditional viewpoint, in which children are accorded a low status in society and are prohibited from participating in organized religion. In contrast, Jesus insists that children are just as valuable to God as are adults. He suggests that from a sociological point of view, the child's increased status under Christianity may be one reason why the religion spread so rapidly in the Roman world. "Christianity offered a family religion in which both sexes and all ages could participate together" (Hare, 1993:224).

Just as Paul emphasized the mutual obligations of husbands and wives, he also clearly emphasized the mutual obligations of parents and children. On the one hand, children are clearly instructed to obey their parents, but on the other hand, fathers (who were the primary disciplinarians) are instructed not to exercise the kind of discipline that would exasperate or embitter their children (Ephesians 6:4, Colossians 3:20–21). The New Testament also stressed the importance of providing for orphans and widows (Acts 6., I Timothy 5., James 1:27).

The Institutionalization of the Church Near the beginning of the 3rd century AD, views on sexuality, marriage and family life apparently began to shift. The early church fathers interpreted Paul's epistles to mean that sexual passion was contrary to spirituality, and that celibacy expressed religious devotion and purity. Using selected passages from I Corinthians 7, early church authorities taught that Paul urged celibacy over marriage, endorsed widowhood over remarriage, and confirmed men's domination of women (Andry, 1981; Whiteley, 1974). What is often overlooked is that Paul's teaching regarding celibacy is firmly anchored in an eschatological perspective that suggested in view of the imminent end of the world, it would be better not to marry. Celibacy is not regarded by Paul as being obligatory for all Christians, but is seen as a special gift, for some, that results in freedom to be totally dedicated

to working for the Kingdom of God. Beginning in the 2nd or 3rd century, the basis for the celibate life starts to change. Rather than being determined by a call to the total service of God, or by a life lived in the expectation of the end of the world, it comes to be considered a superior degree of perfection which is attained only by special people. This led to a double standard that divided Christians into two classes, with monks being first-class citizens, and the married being second-class citizens.

The conviction of the superiority of virginity over married life became a mark of the church fathers (Rordorf, 1969). Indeed, many early church fathers asserted that all sexual activity was sinful. Perhaps the most influential writer, Saint Augustine (354–430 AD), taught that "sexual intercourse between husband and wife, even if it is not strictly limited to the purpose of procreation, is permissible, although such sexual activity is not good, and indeed is a sin" (Deane, 1963:54–55). Sexuality and sexual interest were considered temptations embodied by women, a perception that persisted well into the Middle Ages. Saint John Chrysostom, one early church father, described women as "a necessary evil, a natural temptation, a desirable calamity, a domestic peril, a deadly fascination and a painted ill" (quoted in Ralph de Pomerai, 1930:137). Women were considered to represent the evils of sex and to partake of the sin of Eve:

> You are the devil's gateway: You are the unsealer of that forbidden tree: You are the first deserter of the divine law: You are she who persuaded him whom the devil was not valiant enough to attack. You destroyed so easily God's image, man. On account of your desert—that is, death—even the Son of God had to die. (Tertullian, *On the Apparel of Women*, Book I Chapter I, Vol. 4, p. 14, quoted in Queen and Habenstein, 1974:203)

As Tuchman (1978) observed, the medieval church ordered women to bind their breasts and cover their bodies in order to avoid leading men into temptation; women were seen as "the church's rival, the temptress, the distraction, the obstacle to holiness, the Devil's decoy" (p. 211). Institutionalized Christianity also perpetuated the Hebrew belief in the subordination of women, weakening the egalitarian advances in the teachings of Jesus and Paul. Selected passages in Ephesians (5:22–24) and I Corinthians (14:33–35) were used to instruct women to obey their husbands in all matters.

The glorification of virginity and celibacy affected ideas about the family. Husbands and wives were seen as having abandoned more spiritual celibate lives, although marriage itself was considered an honourable state, especially within the context of permissible Roman practice. Sexual intercourse was to be performed only for procreation, not for pleasure or intimacy, so contraception was strictly forbidden. Extended family ties were de-emphasized, probably because many families had both Christian and non-Christian members. The church forbade marriage between various categories of relatives, including relatives of godparents, and between Christians and non-Christians. In the first three centuries AD, divorce followed Hebrew and Roman customs and remained a private family matter, but in 407 AD, the Council of Carthage declared the indissolubility of marriage. Marriage was perceived as a permanent sacrament, with adultery the only grounds for divorce. Despite this ruling, however, divorce was permitted in some parts of Europe for the next 600 or 700 years (Goodsell, 1934; Queen et al., 1985).

The Medieval English Family

The medieval English family pattern both filtered and perpetuated Hebrew, Roman, and early Christian influences. A central feature of this family system was the legally specified dependence of women on men: in English common law the wife was virtually the ward of her husband. Her dowry, her personal property, and even her clothing became the property of her husband, to do with as he saw fit. A court decision from that time declared the following: "It is adjudged that the wife has nothing of her own while her husband lives, and can make no purchase with money of her own" (quoted in Pollock and Maitland, 1911:432).

In actual practice, however, women often had more power than this ruling might suggest. The military responsibilities of manorial lords required them to be away for long periods. At these times the lady had to direct the affairs, and perhaps even organize the defence, of the manor. The wives of serfs found themselves in the same situation when their husbands went to war, having to carry on as best they could—or risk starvation. In peacetime as well, the wives of tenant farmers and of craftsmen worked side by side with their husbands. Women were capable of taking over their husbands' tenant farms, and often went into business for themselves. They sometimes contracted debts that were not the responsibility of their husbands, though this was forbidden by common law (Gies and Gies, 1987; Queen et al., 1985).

One basis for the freedoms enjoyed by medieval wives was the legal rights they held before marrying, which were the same as those of a man. A woman could hold land, own property in her own name, inherit an estate, enter into a contract, make a will, and sue or be sued in court (Queen et al., 1985). But since it was expected that women would marry, were many able to remain single and so enjoy these rights? At least during "the calamitous fourteenth century" (Tuchman, 1978), which brought the Black Death and the Hundred Years War, there may have been many women for whom husbands could not be found. The independence that women gained during this century, like the independence that Roman women gained during the Punic Wars, probably established precedents that continued in force thereafter.

Though church directives respecting marriage were by now quite explicit, in practice they were often not followed. When significant property or political advantage were not involved, marriages were informal. As a result, there was much casual polygamy, concubinage, and easy separation and divorce. Among the propertied classes, parents, liege-lords, or patrons arranged marriages for reasons of economic or political advantage. Often marriages were contracted for children: records show some were married when only eight years old. Such marriages could be annulled, however, if they refused the arrangement, before the girl was 12 and the boy was 14 years of age—though there must have been strong pressure against their doing so (Queen et al., 1985).

The church insisted on the permanence of marriage, with divorce possible only when granted by the Pope. However, the church could annul a marriage if the spouses were too closely related to each other through genetic, affinal, or even godparent ties. Other grounds included adultery, leprosy, and impotency. As well, a married couple who fought frequently and bitterly could be granted a judicial separation by a court, but they were unable to remarry.

Protestantism was important in reshaping the later English family, in part because ministers lacked the spiritual powers of Catholic priests and so the power of the church was reduced. This happened at a time of other important societal changes. Moving to one of the growing cities or to an overseas colony enabled many people to escape from traditional authorities, start a new life, and marry a person of their own choice.

As during both earlier and later periods, the actual sexual standard during the 17th century was a double one. Indeed, during the preceding century, it was not uncommon to find wealthy men openly maintaining a mistress without risk to either their marriages or their personal reputations. Chastity was still required of women, because they and their children were legally the property of the father and husband. An adulterous affair by the wife was thus a crime against the husband's property (Queen et al., 1985). As well, a husband could gain legal separation from an adulterous wife, and if he could prove adultery to Parliament, he could obtain a divorce with permission to remarry. But this also enabled a wife who wanted to marry her lover to shame her husband into getting a divorce, which alone made it possible for her to remarry.

Treatment of children throughout the Middle Ages, and indeed until the 19th century, was very different from what we know. Most shocking to us is the fact that many babies were simply abandoned, discarded by their parents. Boswell (1988) concludes that in many areas this was true of between one-quarter and one-third of all babies born. The apparent reasons were the absence of effective birth control measures, and the need to restrict the number of heirs to inherit property. People wanting "cheap help" rescued and raised some of these "foundlings," and in time "foundling hospitals" were established to care for those who survived. There are parallels here to contemporary abandonment or murder of babies by unwed mothers who don't know what else to do, and to elevated rates of abuse of stepchildren. These matters are discussed further in Chapter 14.

Strangely, "In medieval society the idea of childhood did not exist" (Ariès, 1962:129); indeed children did not count, because they often died early. They were not seen as having a distinctive nature, and once past babyhood they had no special status, but were seen as "small adults" and soon began learning adult work. This helps explain the frequent practice of child-marriage. But Ariès notes that many women cared for babies and small children solicitously. By the 16th century, attitudes of enjoying and "coddling"

children were common among the lower classes, where "upbringing" did not matter. Reacting against this, "people of quality" disdained coddling, and viewed small children as unworthy of attention. "Childhood" was finally recognized during the 17th century, and churchmen and moralists came to see children as "fragile creatures of God who needed to be both safeguarded and reformed" (Ariès, 1962:133).

The French Family in the 17th Century

The 17th-century family in France shared some features with the late Middle Ages family and with the 18th-century English family described in the following section. This was the family form imported by the habitants to New France (Quebec). It is indicative of this family system that there was no term meaning "nuclear family" (husband, wife and children) until early in the 19th century. The closest approximation was *maison*, meaning household, which often included additional relatives (Wheaton, 1980). Both "blood" and "in-law" relatives were very important in this family system, as in the Hebrew family system discussed earlier, but there was no clear specification of the rights and duties of people in various kinship relationships (Hunt, 1970).

In 17th-century France, the church insisted on the consent of a couple to be married, but descriptions from that time emphasize the importance to families of negotiating an advantageous match. The groom's family wanted to maximize the size of the dowry; the bride's father wanted a helpful son-in-law. However, the financial requirements for marriage (dowry for the bride, independent quarters for the groom) were so difficult to acquire that marriage was frequently delayed. Though marriage for love was disparaged, it was, in fact, easily achieved, since a marriage was valid if a couple made a statement of mutual consent and then lived together. After 1556, the frequency with which young people frustrated the marriage arrangements made by their parents led to progressively more stringent laws requiring parental permission for a marriage. For a time, the penalty for violating this law was death, but custom was so strong that marriages without permission were common for another century or more (Hunt, 1970).

The expectation arose that the groom in prearranged marriages should appear to "court" and should profess love for his fiancée (Hunt, 1970). But any tendency for love and physical attraction to become the basis for mate selection was inhibited by Catholic insistence on sex as sinful except for purposes of procreation. Women were often viewed as sexual temptations to sin and thus to damnation, and as potentially unfaithful wives (Wheaton, 1980). Accordingly, there was no Great Transformation to increased sensuality-based attraction, love, courtship, marriage, and marital companionship, such as occurred in England (see the next section).

This real fear of women, Hunt argues, caused men to disparage them. Certainly women continued to have the low status in 17th-century France that they had held in Europe ever since the fall of Rome. Indeed, a woman's only real value was as a mother (Hunt, 1970). But wives were, in fact, productive workers and household administrators, managing servants and keeping accounts in prosperous families. Moreover, a woman enjoyed certain privileges, including full rights of inheritance in her parents' estate and ownership of property in her own name. (Her husband managed it, but he could be discharged for mismanagement.) She could make a will disposing of her property to whomever she chose. These were rights that English women did not gain for more than a century (Hunt, 1970). So, compared with others at this time, the situation of French women was rather fortunate, but patriarchalism and female subservience were unchallenged.

Childhood mortality was high, with between one-third and one-half of children dying by the age of five. Nevertheless, children were seen as an economic liability because more children were born than could be used productively or provided for through inheritances. Crude abortion efforts, abandonment of babies, and even infanticide were common. Babies kept by their parents were often malnourished, even semi-starved, because nursing mothers' food resources and work schedules left them unable to lactate sufficiently. The semi-starvation that babies often experienced caused many to be greedy and seen as gluttonous, thus reinforcing church teachings that children were tainted by original sin (Hunt, 1970).

Despite the apparent harshness of life, particularly for children, in preindustrial Western societies, it was "human" to an extent unimaginable today, as Laslett emphasizes in his book *The World We Have Lost* (1979). The work group was a family group; the members played family roles and they had family feelings for each other, patriarchal though the family was. Laslett argues that when the whole society was organized like this, "in spite of all the subordination, the exploitation and obliteration of those who were young, or feminine, or in service, everyone belonged to a group, a family group. Everyone had his circle of affection . . . ." (Laslett, 1979:5).

Feelings of family solidarity were strong, perhaps in part because kinship obligations were ill-defined. In its less affluent version, this was the family system brought to New France. Here the availability of land made having large families more advantageous, but the habitant father's right to choose the son to inherit the family farm made for obedient formality in father–son relationships. During the 17th century, more than 14 000 French immigrants came to New France. Most of these immigrants were single men, who were either soldiers or indentured workers. Females made up less than 15 percent of immigration, and so Louis XIV recruited almost 800 young French women of marriageable age, who came to the colony between 1663 and 1673. Of the French immigrants who arrived before 1700, only 5000 remained, while the rest returned to France. A serious imbalance between males and females persisted, with two males for every female. An important effect of this imbalance was that females tended to get married much earlier than men. The average age at first marriage for females born between 1640 and 1679 was 20, while the average age for males was 28 (Dumas and Péron, 1992).

The English Family Since the 18th Century

With increasing trends toward industrialization during the 18th century, the family became more focused on the interpersonal needs of its members. The result was a Great Transformation in family relationships, which laid the foundations of the modern family (Shorter, 1975). In partner selection, there was a shift from emphasis on family position and dowry size to choice based on romantic love. In mother–infant relationships, mother-love came to limit the productive-worker involvement of many women. Privacy and intimacy in family relationships progressively displaced intense involvement with the village or neighbourhood. In brief, when survival declined as the determinative issue, sentiment became the preeminent influence.

The 18th-century wife was still under the patriarchal authority of her husband, and, indeed, legally was his property, as was all she owned before marriage. But many women were eager to retain control over their property, and two ways to accomplish this were found. Before marriage a woman could give her property in trust to someone, thus placing it beyond reach of her husband. She could also place a clause in the marriage contract preventing the husband from interfering in her management of her property. Relatives bequeathing property to a married woman could place it with a trustee responsive to her wishes. In time, the husband came to be viewed as the wife's trustee for property she had inherited. These possibilities for financial independence reduced the subordination of middle- and upper-class wives to their husbands. At the same time, lower-class women often enjoyed greater equality because of the importance of the contributions they made to the family economy (Goodsell, 1934).

Protestantism contributed to the decline of the earlier interest in the wealth and social standing of a prospective mate. Puritans placed increased emphasis on the personal qualities of the future husband and wife; partners were to be chosen for their inner virtues. Some even believed people should have the right to choose whom they would marry. Parental control thus began to weaken, as children were allowed to reject a mate chosen for them.

These changes led to a "sexual revolution" (Shorter, 1975)—a dramatic increase in premarital sexual intercourse between about 1725 and 1850. This gave further encouragement to sentimental relationships between young people. Courtship manners and patterns began to develop, and love for a "suitable" partner became the basis for betrothal. First appearing among the working classes where wealth and social standing were not at stake, this pattern soon spread to the upper classes. With marital partners chosen on the basis of love, it became possible for husband and wife to be friends. Conservative voices were still heard proclaiming the folly of marriage for love, but there were opposing voices, as well. In 1700, one woman wrote, "And if a Woman can neither Love nor Honour she does ill in promising to Obey" her husband (Mary Astell, 1700:52, quoted in Queen et al., 1985:179).

By the end of the 18th century, an estimated 75 percent of upper-class marriages were love matches. The aristocracy was still expected to marry within its class, but even here occasional exceptions were found. The idea that an important goal in marriage was companionship was beginning to take root. Marriages were often of short duration, however, because mothers died during childbirth. Death rates among men were high, as well, and remarriages were common. Widowers tended to remarry promptly, but widows were less marriageable—unless they had inherited property (Shorter, 1975; Goodsell, 1934).

Before the Great Transformation, there was little interest in children, particularly among the privileged. Working-class people wanted children for the work they would perform, but pregnancy, childbearing, and care of small children were burdens to women throughout most of their fertile years. Contraceptive efforts were practised but were generally ineffective, and abortion was common, though condemned by the church. Many babies were abandoned. Puritanism taught that children were tainted by "original sin," predisposing them to willful wickedness. Parents were duty-bound to break their children's wills and their spirits (Trumbach, 1978).

No significant changes took place in earlier regulations governing annulment, legal separations, and divorces. Church regulations specifying obstacles to marriage based on "blood," in-law, or godparent relationships made it possible to obtain an annulment, if such relationships could be proved. Divorce, and thus remarriage, was permitted only in cases of adultery. During the Cromwellian period when there was a Protestant Parliament, divorce for other grounds became a legal possibility. Few were granted, however, and the validity of a subsequent remarriage was uncertain (Shorter, 1975).

Family Patterns in Canada

Indigenous Canadian Families

The appearance of humans on the North American continent is commonly agreed upon as roughly 50 000 to 10 000 years ago during the ice age (Dickason, 2002). There remains some disagreement as to the exact nature of this "appearance." While many scholars argue that the most likely source of the original inhabitants was migration via a land bridge from Asia to Alaska, the stories and myths of many aboriginal peoples would suggest a genesis in North America. Regardless of the exact origins, by about 10 000 years ago there were many distinct groups settled across the Americas (Dickason, 2002).

Most of our knowledge about the first peoples of Canada comes from either archaeological evidence or from historical records of when Europeans first came to Canada. At the time of first contact by the Norse Vikings, about 1000 AD, most of Canada's indigenous peoples were hunter-gatherers but already comprised diverse cultures. There were at least 12 different linguistic families with over 80 distinct tribal organizations. It was clear to the Europeans that the Aboriginal inhabitants of the Americas lacked the political and military organization to successfully defend their land from invasion. The waves of European contact include not only the French and English but also the Russians, Spanish, Dutch, and Swedish. The first contact for most indigenous peoples in Canada was with the French or English (Dickason, 2002).

There is not one family form that characterizes all of the indigenous peoples of Canada. As we have previously discussed in Chapter 3, many of the major kinship classification systems are named after Amerindian groups such as Crow, Omaha, and Eskimo. Even though these names represent the Europeanized versions of the true tribal names, they nonetheless show that kinship among North America Aboriginal groups included matrilineal and patrilineal, matrilocal, and patrilocal. Beyond that, clan systems involved both political clans and totemic clans. For example, many of the Aboriginal groups along the Pacific coast were matrilineal and practised both clan and village exogamy. The complexity of many Aboriginal kinship systems is also tied to the practices of child socialization and care. For example, in matrilineal societies it would be quite ordinary to find a child being socialized by his mother's brother and other lineage members. Indeed, Aboriginal socialization practices may have anticipated Hilary Clinton's insights on child socialization (*It Takes a Village*, 1996) by many centuries.

First contact with Europeans was not a uniform process, since different tribal groups came into contact with different Europeans at very different times. Although in some cases warfare marked the first contact, in many instances there was trade. More importantly for the family and kinship networks of Aboriginals, some of this contact involved the conscientious attempts by Europeans to acculturate and assimilate Aboriginal groups through intermarriage. Dickason (2002:145) provides one such example where the French sent French families among the Huron in order to intermix and eventually intermarry. However, this policy at times could backfire, as is the case where one Iroquois stated " 'we have learned to change Frenchman into Hiroquois' but added diplomatically, 'let us rather say that they will become French and Hiriquois at the same time'" [sic] (Dickason, 2002:146).

The complexity of family forms and kinship among the Aboriginal groups of Canada makes generalizations about families exceedingly difficult. Suffice it to say that family was one of the most well organized areas of social life in most Aboriginal groups. As contact increased during the 1800s, imposed social structures such as the residential schools systematically destroyed the social organization of the family as well as language and culture. The consequences of such policies are discussed in the next chapter.

French Canadian Families

The **habitant family** of 17th and 18th century was spread throughout parts of Canada but was most concentrated in rural Quebec. The habitant family pattern was shaped by four main influences: the Catholic Church, the ready availability of land, the need for farm labour, and suspicion of English Canadians. The result was a close-knit kinship system composed of patriarchal families that were very large (Queen et al., 1985). There is an ongoing debate amongst historians as to whether or not the French Canadian family represented a "stem family" as described in Chapter 3. While some scholars contend that the French Canadian family followed a similar pattern to that described by LePlay (1871) for France (Queen et al, 1985), other scholars argue that the French Canadian family was not a stem form (Gerin, 1932; Verdon, 1987; Bouchard, 1987). Current evidence would seem to favour the rejection of the stem family hypothesis (see Bouchard, 1992; Dagenais, 2000; LaPierre-Adamcyk, LeBourdais and Marcil-Gratton, 2003). The characteristics of the habitant family that most scholars do agree upon are the patriarchal authority pattern and the large family sizes; even in the 1950s many families had 9 or 10 children—and as many as 18 or 20 (see Box 4.1).

Box 4.1 The Kinship Network of the French Canadian Family

A remarkable feature of the French Canadian family system was that people retained contact with multitudes of relatives. The closest contacts, often daily or weekly, were with parents, siblings, and grown offspring, and often involved an exchange of services. Even when relatives had moved away to Montreal or to New England, as happened frequently, contact was maintained through letters, telephone calls, and visits. The solidarity of this kinship system meant that French Canadians were aware of great numbers of relatives, a network weakened only partially by geographical scattering (Garigue, 1960). This vast kinship knowledge was not restricted to rural areas where relationships were functionally important. In interviews with Montreal residents in 1956, Garigue (1960) found that the number of relatives his respondents could identify ranged from 75 to 484, and averaged 215 covering up to six generations (Garigue, 1980).

Piddington illustrates the inbred nature of many kinship networks with an example from his research in a French Canadian community in Manitoba. An informant might respond to a question about his relatives by saying, "He is my brother-in-law because his second wife is my wife's sister; he is also my uncle because his first wife was my mother's sister; and he is also my cousin, like everybody else" (1971:457). Because authority is associated with respect and social distance from underlings (Homans, 1950), Quebec fathers have had rather emotionally distant relationships with their children. They preferred to spend their free time discussing politics and other matters of interest with male friends (Garigue, 1980). Moreover, competition among brothers for the father's approval (and the farm) often prevented them from having close relationships with each other. As a result, relationships between women and men became more important, and women gained influence. Husbands commonly consulted with their wives, and often with sisters and mothers as well, before making an important decision. As the focus of men's emotional relationships, women thus became the "effective leaders of the kin group" (Garigue, 1980:129).

The French Canadian family system created its own tensions, especially between the father and his older sons, over the question of inheritance. Conflict was often exacerbated by a growing resistance to the traditional expectation that sons and daughters would give their wage income to the father to spend for the family's benefit. Moreaux's research shows that the women in the family, including the mother, often tended to unite against the men, leading Moreaux to describe the power distribution in these families as a "fragile equilibrium" (Moreaux 1971:140).

A man married when he could support himself on his own farm or from wage employment. Mate selection reflected familial interests, and was made, after a long acquaintanceship, from among families sharing bonds of kinship, obligation, or political interest. Despite the opposition of the church, cousin marriage was quite common, including marriage of first cousins for which the priest often granted religious permission. A marriage contract was negotiated specifying the size of the bride's dowry, the money or property she was to bring to the marriage, and in time a church wedding was held. Celebrations of the wedding sometimes went on for days, moving from house to house. The first baby often arrived within the first year, and others followed at frequent intervals thereafter. Since parents had many children, who had many in turn, people had many cousins, and grandparents had many grandchildren. Men as well as women were strongly committed to familial relationships. They saw their relatives often if they were in the same community, visiting them and exchanging services with them.

This family system persisted for centuries, apparently with little change, because of the church's influence and the farm-family tradition. Families were committed to **impartible inheritance**—passing the family farm intact to the son who was likely to be the most successful farmer. This son and his wife stayed on the farm, helping his father until he took over the property, and then providing for his parents until they died. Because land was cheap, it was not difficult to help other sons start farms of their own, most often near the same village. Those who did not farm found work in the nearby logging camps; others became priests. Daughters who did not marry either lived with a brother and made a welcome contribution to the household, or joined a convent. Sons were obedient to their father's authority, since the father decided which one would inherit the farm (Queen et al., 1985). The father would also assist to resettle other sons nearby (LaPierre-Adamcyk, LeBourdais, and Marcil-Gratton, 2003).

Changes during the Quiet Revolution of the 1960s transformed French Canadian family life, as some of the statistics cited earlier in the chapter indicate. When farms increased in size and decreased in number, the farming population declined sharply between 1951 and 1976, from 18.9 percent to 3.1 percent of the total Quebec population (Queen et al., 1985). Children are no longer productive investments, Quebec cities have become cosmopolitan, and traditional church teachings are increasingly ignored. Individualism is now the dominant value. The following has resulted:

- The significance of kinship ties has weakened.
- Motherhood has become less "sainted," and women may choose between motherhood and other options.
- The patterning of family roles and interaction has changed.
- The authority of fathers has weakened.
- Children are less dutiful toward their parents.
- The solidarity of the family, economically and emotionally, has weakened (Queen et al., 1985).

The very low marriage and birthrates in Quebec today reveal that traditional family values have been abandoned more rapidly here than anywhere else in Canada. But the process began almost 50 years ago: 1931 was the last year in which the Quebec total fertility rate, at 4.0 children per woman, was the highest in Canada. Change quickly followed. By 1968, a baby-boom year for the country as a whole, the Quebec total fertility rate of 3.8 was the lowest among the Canadian provinces, and the rate continued to drop, reaching a low point of 1.4 children in 1987, substantially below the **replacement level**—the level at which new births compensate for deaths in a society. The next year, the Quebec government began efforts to increase the birthrate by offering substantial baby bonuses, which have been raised several times. In 1991, these bonuses paid mothers $500 for the first baby, $1000 for the second, and no less than $6000 (paid in installments) for each child thereafter. The Quebec birthrate per 1000

women of childbearing age has now increased somewhat, from 46.1 in 1987 to 53.1 in 1990; all-Canada figures increased during the same period by a lesser amount, from 53.6 to 56.9 (*Health Reports*, 1992).

Rejection of Catholic teaching is also seen in French Canadian attitudes toward premarital sex. In 1968, the incidence of premarital intercourse among young Francophones was lower than among Anglophones (47 and 50 percent, respectively). By 1988, the pattern was reversed, with 85 percent of young Francophones in comparison with 74 percent of young Anglophones reporting they were sexually experienced. Many more Francophone than Anglophone men and women advocated the liberal "sex for fun" standard—52 and 37 percent, respectively, for Francophone men and women, and 37 and 20 percent for Anglophones—in preference to the more conservative "sex if in love" and "sex only if married" standards. Most telling of all is the tendency for young French Canadians to reject marriage, at least verbally. Some 50 percent of Francophones, and only 14 percent of Anglophones, agreed with the statement "I would prefer to live with someone [of the opposite sex] rather than bother to get married," and 26 percent of Francophones compared with 5 percent of Anglophones agreed that "Since living together is becoming so common, I doubt that I will ever get married" (Hobart and Grigel, 1992).

These recent changes in French Canadian sexual and family relationships illustrate the speed with which even a tightly integrated and traditional family system, strongly supported by religion, may change in response to conditions in a modern, secular society.

However, French communities that remained physically and socially isolated have resisted acculturation and assimilation, suggesting that the drastic changes in French Canadian family patterns are mainly a product of urbanization and extensive contact with Anglo-Saxons and other Canadians. Such has been the case of French Acadians (descendants of the French settlers from the colony of Acadia) in the Maritime provinces. As a study of an Acadian village—Ste. Marie—in New Brunswick shows, family patterns and relationships in an enclosed French community have not undergone a significant change over time. Large numbers of children per family are still common in the village studied, and the majority of women get pregnant during their first year of marriage. Wives are expected to be fertile, and not wanting children is something villagers attribute only to *Les Anglais*. Although the basis for forming multi-family households has changed, such arrangements are still common in the village, where 40 percent of the village households included at least one grandparent at the time of the study. In the past, cooperation among family members in carrying out fishery and farming activities necessitated parents living with their married son, or two brothers and their nuclear families living together. Currently, however, no married son was found to be working with his father, and poor health or aging of a parent has become the main reason for living permanently with parents (Davis, 1985).

As in the traditional French Canadian family, however, the extended family in this Acadian village has retained most of its traditional functions. Adult siblings continue to be very close and often establish households on adjoining pieces of land, maintaining daily visits. Also, it is not uncommon in Ste. Marie to find the sibling of a woman married to the sibling of that woman's husband. When a parent dies or becomes incapacitated, his or her sibling is still expected to take care of the children, sometimes for years. Parents consider it a duty of their married children to remain in frequent contact, to the extent that if the child does not visit them for several days, they would assume he has been away on a trip. The study also shows that relationships with kinsmen, or *parents*, such as uncles, aunts and cousins, continue to be based on traditional expectations. These kin have an obligation to be present at and participant in important ceremonial occasions, such as weddings, and to provide assistance in times of crisis.

Endogamy is found to be quite high among these Acadians, as all marriages at the time of the study were between Acadians. Villagers do not marry the Anglo-Canadians who live in the parish, and believe that marrying a Catholic is important to keep their language, religion, and culture pure. Traditional division of labour persists between spouses, despite the fact that many wives are wage-earners and are, for historical reasons, generally more educated than their husbands. Women assume the main responsibility for housework, child care, and the garden, and make decisions in a few areas only, such as selecting purchases for the home and children. Acadian children are expected to perform various household chores and care for their siblings. At as young as 10 years of age, children are entrusted with the feeding, entertaining and reprimanding of their younger siblings (Davis, 1985).

There is evidence from a study of six French settlements in Saskatchewan that living in multiethnic communities has a weakening effect on ethnic retention among rural French Canadians. While they continued to be opposed to marrying a non-Catholic in their majority (81.2 percent), more than half (54 percent) of the 202 French Canadians interviewed were not opposed to marrying a non-French. Moreover, while favouring ethnic retention, almost half (46 percent) of the respondents were resigned to ethnic identity loss, feeling that it was becoming increasingly impossible or pointless to stress ethnic distinctions. This belief was particularly prevalent among the young, and the third-generations who have been settled in western Canada for a longer time. The study further provides evidence that the larger the French population in each community, and therefore the less the contact with other ethnic groups, the higher the adherence to ethnic identity retention. Favouring ethnic retention decreased from 89.4 percent in almost completely French communities, to 58 percent in communities with a French proportion of 50 to 74 percent (Anderson, 1985).

Preindustrial Canadian Families

Preindustrial European settlement varied significantly according to the place of settlement. Settlement patterns depended on primary occupation (fishing versus farming) and location (towns and villages versus cities). Residence patterns also depended on the land to be settled: long, narrow strips of land along the St. Lawrence River, or along a road, isolated homesteads in the Ontario bush country, or dispersed farmsteads around the general store on the prairies. Despite such variations, in many respects pre-Confederation families shared similarities in that they were all colonials, having a relationship to the land that was like that of peasants in their country of origin. "And while some lived in villages, fur trading posts, and cities, the vast majority of the population lived on farms and engaged in some combination of agriculture, fishing, lumbering, and the fur trade, according to the seasons of the year and the region in which they lived" (Nett, 1993:48).

The preindustrial economy of this period was based on family economies, both in rural and urban locations. Most production of goods and services took place in individual residences, with each member of the family contributing to such production. Economic survival depended on the full participation of all family members. Families operated as collective units, and age was a more important determinant of contributions to the family economy than was sex (Nett, 1993).

Joy Parr's (1982) overview of Canadian families during the last century describes several contrasting patterns. She points out that since Quebec settlers came from various areas, French patterns of community life were not reproduced in Quebec. But in time, neighbours increasingly were kin members, and social contacts were with other family members who provided an important source of support and assistance. Authority and dependence were centred in the family, with neighbourhood and community often being identified with the family. When they grew up, however, most children migrated to the cities to find work (Parr, 1982).

Similar situations were characteristic of families in rural Ontario. With some exceptions, most settlers began as nuclear families, but their households gradually grew larger and more complex. Children made important contributions to family production, and, since food and clothing were a part of the productive efforts, families were generally large. Schooling was concerned with mastering practical skills, and was controlled by the community rather than by the state. "Some successful families were able to repay their children's contributions of farm labour with gifts of land nearby; other parents [moved to back townships] so the kin group might remain together. But more often . . . young people left their native communities as single individuals or couples to set up their own farms at a distance or to pursue a trade" (Parr, 1982:13).

In both Quebec and Ontario, family members worked together to make farm life economically viable, and their communal labour created strong solidarity. Working with their same-sex parents, children learned their designated roles. Caring for small children and domestic animals, as well as growing and preserving food, baking, and washing and mending clothes were all women's work (Wilson, 1991). Women were also responsible for the medical, spiritual, and educational welfare of their families. Mothers passed on to their daughters their skills in making and using medicines and other household products (Errington, 1988). Increasingly during the 19th century, however, families moved to the city. By the end of the century, over one-third of families were city-dwellers, almost 10 percent living in Quebec City, Montreal, Ottawa and Toronto (Wilson, 1991).

Most women in the city who had paid employment were young and single, because there were strong sentiments against employing wives. Low wages and few opportunities for advancement made marriage and motherhood attractive. However, in towns where industries such as garment-making were expanding, employment of working-class mothers and children became common. The continued importance of the family as an economic unit, in which members turned over their earnings and shaped their career choices in the service of their families, was a carryover from rural life (Wilson, 1991).

Because of the importance of child labour in Canada at this time, England sent over thousands of orphans, who were put to work in factories and on farms. In towns, children were more available to attend classes, so schools were established and children left school at a later age. As Gaffield's (1982) description of developments in Prescott County, Ontario, shows, mill owners often established schools to encourage community stability and to train children in work disciplines. According to sawmill owners, children's experiences of sitting in rows, responding to bells and obeying the teacher taught punctuality, sobriety, and deference. Schooling thus offered two promises: to maintain social order by keeping children busy, and to train employees for the mill, both physically and psychologically. In fact, in the history of childhood in Ontario during the 19th century, schooling was a dominant experience (Gaffield, 1982).

Life in North America permitted more freedom in intimate relationships than had been possible in England, but practical considerations were important. As women could not earn much money, most wanted a husband who was a "good provider," so the patriarchal authority of the provider-husband persisted. Cultural disparagement of women continued into the early decades of this century, with women seen as emotional, illogical, and incapable of careful thought. In Victorian times, women were supposed to have no sexual feelings; sex was "a man's privilege and a woman's duty."

Typically, Canadian marriages were neither physically nor emotionally close, so there was little intimacy in married life. Instead, women drew emotional support from strong, often lifelong, friendships with other women (Kersten and Kersten, 1991). As we discuss in the following section, the lot of most women was early marriage and long years of childbearing and child care, terminated by relatively early death.

Emergence of the Modern Family

The most ambitious effort to describe the modern family and to analyze the reasons for its emergence was made by William Goode (1970). He argued that the changing needs of an industrial society, together with the popular ideology of personal freedom, explains the appearance of the conjugal family around the world. A **conjugal family** is one in which the most important bond is the marriage bond. Goode emphasized that these families have few obligations toward and little influence on related conjugal families. Newly married couples are typically neolocal, establishing a new residence separate from the bride's or groom's parents, whose role in their lives is relatively unimportant. This distance, in turn, decreases interaction with relatives and further reduces the family influence.

Relatives, even siblings, now have almost no vested interest in the mate selection of their kin, because they are little affected by each other's well-being. Marriages are no longer arranged by family, but are based on mutual attraction—although parents may still exercise control over where young people meet. Age at marriage tends to increase because people must be sufficiently mature to make wise marital choices and to support the independent, neolocal households they establish. Fertility patterns change as well; children are born not to serve the needs of the extended family, but to satisfy the parenting interests of the married couple (Goode, 1970).

The close, functional relationships found between members of patrilineal or matrilineal kinship groups are not relevant to the conjugal family unit. As a result, unilineal kinship reckoning becomes multilineal, because "his" family and "her" family are equally insignificant. The kinship group, distanced and less functional, no longer provides emotional support, but couples now feel they should be able to count on their mates. No doubt, many couples do provide each other

with this support, but many others do not. As marriage is primarily based on affection (at least at the outset), and spouses rely exclusively on each other for emotional satisfaction, marriage is an unstable relationship, vulnerable to breakup and divorce. Thus, high divorce rates are another characteristic of the conjugal family (Goode, 1970).

Goode acknowledged that the ties between conjugal family members and their secondary kin are typically closer than his theoretical analysis suggests. Indeed, he admitted that the most common type of visiting is with relatives (Goode, 1970). However, he explained this activity as an extension of the family network, whereby the emotional ties within the parental nuclear family lead people to visit parents, siblings and other favourite relatives, even after individuals marry and have their own families. Goode also noted, however, that this extended kin group, known as **kindred**, is somewhat different for the husband, wife and children in a multilineal system. Different subgroups may make competing claims on these people, and may help to sharpen conflicts between husband and wife when their relationship begins to fall apart.

Goode argued that industrial society was the dominant influence on the evolution of the conjugal family. As an industrial society values achievement and performance, rather than birth characteristics, it must therefore be an open-class society, where people can move to the job that they can perform most effectively. Both geographic and social family mobility are necessary. Because the conjugal family is neolocal and thus separated from kin, it has fewer family members and kin obligations to leave behind if a promotion in another centre is offered.

Upper-class families are less vulnerable to the influence of industrialization, however, because they have the resources to resist these pressures. Middle-class families can take advantage of new opportunities, while changing more slowly. Lower-class families, in contrast, must adjust quickly, because they have no control over their access to employment. Because upper-class and some middle-class families can provide job opportunities, their children have good reason to respond to parental influence. Lower-class parents, however, do not have such leverage, so their offspring more often ignore them after coming of age.

In response to arguments against his analysis, Goode acknowledged that industrialization does little to change lower-class families in most societies, because these families have always been small due to poverty. He also emphasized that his analysis denies neither the importance of family ideology nor the influence of the family on the industrialization process. The ideology that glorifies the conjugal family, proclaiming the right of the individual to choose a spouse, a place to live, and which kin obligations to accept, appeals strongly to young people and to women, and is "destructive of the older traditions in almost every society" (1970:18–19). While this ideology has an independent impact on traditional societies, its spread is greatly facilitated by the industrialization process, which reduces the functional significance of the kinship group.

Canadian Families During the 19th and 20th Centuries

As you will recall from Chapter 1, **demography** refers to the study of the age and gender composition of a population, and the processes that may sustain or change that composition. There are only four basic processes affecting the age and gender mix of a population: births, deaths, immigration of people to a country, and emmigration from a country. These processes, in turn, have other causes. For example, births are affected by marriage rates (how many people stay single) and the age at which people marry. Migration rates are affected by economic conditions in both the country of origin and the country of destination.

In this section, we study historical demographic indications of the changes that have affected the Canadian family since the mid-19th century. Much of this data is available from *Historical Statistics of Canada* (11-516-XIE, Statistics Canada). It is important to remember that these statistics need to be interpreted. Recall that Goode and others have argued that we are moving toward a "conjugal" family form. In part this argument is founded on population changes that could be indirectly measured by the extent to which we have moved away from being rural, getting married and having large families.

Urban-Rural Table 4.1 shows that in 1871, shortly after Confederation, the population of Canada was about eighty percent rural. By 1921, the population was almost evenly split between rural and urban living arrangements. From 1921 to 1976, the population has become increasingly urbanized. This process of urbanization has naturally been accompanied by industrialization and Canada becoming one of the major "developed" nations of the world.

Marriage The marriage rate is a measure frequently used to indicate the status of marriage in Canada, and indicates the number of marriages per 1000 total population in a given year. Figure 4.1 provides the marriage rate for Canada and the United States for selected years and Table 4.2 shows the marriage rate from 1921 to 1974 along with the average age for brides and groom, divorces and net family formation.

Figure 4.1 indicates that the marriage rate has fluctuated in both countries over time. The Depression of the 1930s, with its cutbacks in economic activity and major increases in unemployment, led to the abandonment or postponement of many marriages. The Second World War resulted in an increase in the marriage rate until 1946, followed by a slight decline in the last two years of the war as a result of conscription. Following the war years, the marriage rate continued to decline, with the exception of the 1970s; this decade may be regarded as an offshoot of the baby boom. In recent years, more and more Canadians are choosing to postpone marriage, as revealed by the figures for age at first marriage.

Table 4.2 shows that the marriage rate in Canada has shifted significantly over time. From 1921 to 1936, the marriage rate was low. Interestingly, this period encompassed both the boom time of the 1920s and the bust time of the 1930s economic depression. Marriage rates increased sharply during the Second World War and immediately after. During the decade of the 70's the marriage rate rose once again.

The changes in marriage rates can be contextualized by the "net family formation" shown in Table 4.2. Net family formation is measured as the sum of marriages plus married female immigrants minus divorces, female emigrants, and deaths of married persons. The assumption here is that "net family formation" shows the actual potential for families during any given year. As we can see from Table 4.2, net family formation in Canada has increased from 37 000 to 111 000. During this period the Canadian population increased by a factor of 2.6 while family formation grew by a factor of 3.0—clearly net family formation has grown in Canada.

TABLE 4.1 Population, Rural and Urban, Census Dates, 1871 to 1976

YEAR	TOTAL	1941 DEFINITION[1]	
	POPULATION	URBAN	RURAL
1976	22 992 605	17 366 970[2]	5 625 635[2]
1971	21 568 310	14 114 970	7 453 340
1966	20 014 880	12 625 784	7 389 096
1961	18 238 247	11 068 848	7 169 399
1956	16 080 791	9 286 126	6 794 665
1951[3]	14 009 429	7 941 222	6 068 207
1941	11 506 655	6 252 416	5 254 239
1931	10 376 786	5 572 058	4 804 728
1921	8 787 949	4 352 122	4 435 827
1911	7 206 643	3 272 947	3 933 696
1901	5 371 315	2 014 222	3 357 093
1891	4 833 239	1 537 098	3 296 141
1881	4 324 810	1 109 507	3 215 303
1871	3 689 257	722 343	2 966 914

1. For urban, rural figures for census of 1901 to 1956, based on 1956 definition, see note to series A15-19 in original volume.
2. Based on the definition of the 1976 Census.
3. Includes Newfoundland beginning in 1951. The total population of Newfoundland in 1951 is distributed as follows: basis 1941 definition, urban, 104 377; rural, 257 039; total, 361 416.

Source: *Historical Statistics of Canada* (2nd Edition) 11-516-XIE, Statistics Canada.

Table 4.2 reveals great stability in the average ages of brides and grooms in Canada. It must be remembered that the average age includes all those married in a given year and hence would include second and third marriages. We would expect more of these second and third marriages to be associated with high divorce rates, yet in Table 4.2 we find that the age of brides and grooms is fairly stable from 1961 to 1974. In general then we can conclude that historically the age at marriage has been falling in Canada. We will get a very different picture once we turn our analysis to trends in the last 25 years in Chapters 9 and 13.

Reproduction The most comprehensive measure of the reproductive performance of a population at any one time is the total fertility rate. The **total fertility rate** is the "total number of births a woman would have during the course of her childbearing years if the age-specific rates remained in effect during this time" (McVey and Kalbach, 1995:266). The total fertility rate thus reflects the combined tendencies toward having more or having fewer babies that may be characteristic of women at different ages, in a given year.

Balakrishnan et al. (1993) suggest that the family has slowly evolved from a rigid institution to an individual relationship based solely on affective solidarity, and more independence and autonomy for each spouse. In the past, children were seen as a justification for marriage, whereas the young couple of today must decide whether they want a child or not, and when to

TABLE 4.2 Number of Marriages and Rates, Average Age at Marriage for Brides and Bridegrooms, Number of Divorces and Rate, Net Family Formations, Canada, 1921–1974

| Year | Marriages | | Average Age at Marriage (Years)[1] | | Divorces[2] | | Net Family Formation[2] |
	Number	Rate (per 1000 Population)	Brides	Bridegrooms	Number	(Rate per 100 00 population)	(000s of Families)
1974	198 824	8.9	24.7	27.4	45 019	200.6	111
1973	199 064	9.0	24.8	27.3	36 704	166.1	111
1972	200 470	9.2	24.7	27.1	32 389	148.4	105
1971	191 324	8.9	24.8	27.3	29 685	137.6	100
1970	188 428	8.8	24.9	27.3	29 775	139.8	103
1969	182 183	8.7	24.9	27.3	26 093	124.2	103
1968	171 766	8.3	24.4	26.8	11 343	54.8	111
1967	165 879	8.1	24.4	26.8	11 165	54.8	117
1966	155 596	7.8	24.4	27.0	10 239	51.2	101
1965	145 519	7.4	24.5	27.2	8974	45.7	81
1964	138 135	7.2	24.5	27.3	8625	44.7	69
1963	131 111	6.9	24.6	27.5	7686	40.6	60
1962	129 381	7.0	24.6	27.5	6768	36.4	58
1961	128 475	7.0	24.7	27.7	6563	36.0	67
1960	130 338	7.3	24.7	27.7	6980	39.1	67
1959	132 474	7.6	24.8	27.7	6543	37.4	67
1958	131 525	7.7	24.8	27.8	6279	36.8	7
1957	133 186	8.0	24.9	27.8	6688	40.3	103
1956	132 713	8.3	25.0	27.9	6002	37.4	84
1955	128 029	8.2	25.1	28.0	6053	38.6	74
1954	128 629	8.4	25.2	28.1	5923	38.8	86
1953	131 034	8.8	25.3	28.2	6160	41.6	91
1952	128 474	8.9	25.3	28.3	5650	39.1	90
1951	128 408	9.2	25.3	28.3	5270	37.7	93
1950	125 083	9.1	25.3	28.5	5386	39.3	71

(Continued)

TABLE 4.2 Continued

Year	Marriages		Average Age at Marriage (Years)[1]		Divorces[2]		Net Family Formation[2] (000s of Families)
	Number	Rate (per 1000 Population)	Brides	Bridegrooms	Number	(Rate per 100 00 population)	
1949	124 087	9.2	25.41	28.71	6052	45.1	74
1948	126 118	9.6	25.4[1]	28.6[1]	6978	54.5	79[2]
1947	130 400	10.1	25.3	28.6	8213	65.6	72
1946	137 398	10.9	25.3	28.6	7757	63.2	104
1945	111 376	9.0	25.5	29.0	5101	42.3	50
1944	104 656	8.5	25.6	29.2	3827	32.1	48
1943	113 827	9.4	25.4	29.0	3398	28.9	55
1942	130 786	10.9	25.2	29.0	3091	26.6	72
1941	124 644	10.6	25.1	28.9	2462	21.4	68
1931	68 239	6.4	24.9	29.2	700	6.8	29
1921	71 2563	7.93	25.5	29.9	558	6.4	37

1. Excluding the province of Quebec for 1921 to 1925: Newfoundland for 1921 to 1948; and the Yukon Territory and the Northwest Territories for 1921 to 1949.
2. Excluding Newfoundland for 1921 to 1948. For the definition of net family formation see the text.
3. Excluding the Yukon Territory and the Northwest Territories.

Source: *Historical Statistics of Canada* (2nd Edition), 11-516-XIE, Statistics Canada.

Figure 4.1 Marriage Rates, Canada and U.S.A., 1921–1995

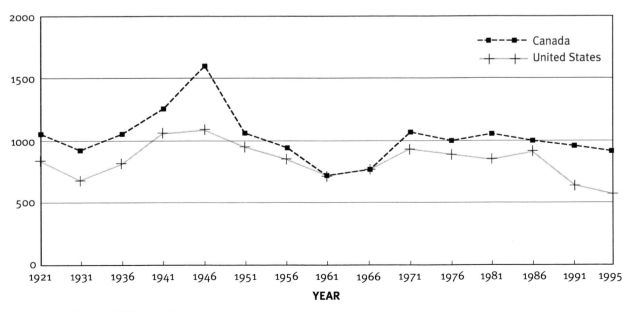

Source: McVey, 1998.

have it. "The decision to have a child is now tied to the need of reaching a better emotional balance. The presence of children is seen as a means to complete the fulfillment of what is expected from the couple's relationship" (1993:13).

Table 4.3 shows the total fertility rates for all of Canada from 1926 to 1974. In 1926, the rate was about 3.5 children per woman. The net reproduction rate was about 1630 births per 1000 women, meaning that Canada was above replacement level (1.0). Table 4.3 shows that by 1974, total fertility had dropped to 1.87 births per woman and net reproduction was significantly below replacement level at 886 births per 1000 women. Canada's long downward trend in births was interrupted by increased fertility during the decades of the 40s to the 60s. The downward trend in fertility really resumed in the middle of the 1960s. Indeed, in 1965 Canada still was above replacement level (1.48) with total fertility at about 3.1 children per woman. In less than a decade this rate fell precipitously to below replacement level (.88) with a total fertility of 1.9 children per woman. Thereafter, the rate declined, largely because employment opportunities for women were increasing and the availability of birth control pills ensured that pregnancy did not have to interfere. Growing numbers of women postpone childbearing in order to pursue higher education and enter the labour market. At roughly the same time (1960 to 1974) the percentage of illegitimate births more than doubled (4.3 percent to 9 percent). This may in part be due to increasing numbers of common-law relationships in which there are growing numbers of children being born to couples who are not legally married. In 1994, unmarried women accounted for one in four births, compared with only 1 in 17 in 1974 (Ford and Nault, 1996).

When women bear 1.9 children on the average, some women have more children, of course, and some women have none. The percentage of married women who are childless has tended to vary according to the influence of economic conditions, and has been quite high in the past. For example, the incidence of childlessness throughout their childbearing years among women born between 1861 and 1976 was 12.8 percent. The economic deterrent of the Depression and the absence of husbands during the Second World War increased this rate to 15.4 percent for women born between 1902 and 1911. The percentage then fell to

7.2 among women born between 1932 and 1936, reflecting both the prosperity of the 1960s and 1970s, and the increased ability of doctors to deal with infertility problems (Gee, 1987; Ram, 1990). Balakrishnan et al. (1993) found that of all the ever-married, currently married, and never-married women aged 18 to 49 in their survey, 9.6 percent expected to remain childless.

Size of Families and Households

Since the average woman during the mid-1800s was having more than six children (and some were having as many as 10 or 12), we might assume that households were correspondingly large. They were not, however, because of high infant and childhood death rates—in some families, half of those born died during childhood. Moreover, since women tended to bear children throughout their 25 or more fertile years, some of the older children would have left home by the time the youngest ones were born (Nett, 1981). Table 4.4 shows the available statistics on the average size of the family since 1921. In 1921 the number was just 4.3. It decreased because of the Depression to 3.7 by 1951, and then increased to 3.9 in 1961, during the baby boom post-war years. During the last 100 years, the process of urbanization has changed the nature of the Canadian family (see Tables 4.1 and 4.4): as more families became urban, they also became smaller.

In the past, families often had additional people living with them—a parent or an unmarried aunt, a sister of the husband, or a hired hand. These additions were few, however, so the average number of persons per household in Canada has never been very large. In 1861, the average number peaked, with 6.3 people living in the average Canadian household. Since then, the number has declined steadily, to 5.0 by 1901, to 4.4 in 1931 (a Depression year), and to 3.9 in 1961, when most of the baby boom children had been born. By 1991, the average Canadian household included only 2.7 persons.

If we compare the average family size and average household size data, we can conclude that until 1961, the household size was larger than the family size, clearly reflecting the presence of non-nuclear family members. Remarkably, since 1965 the average household family size has been smaller than the average family size. The reason is that some of these households have only a single member, and the number of people

TABLE 4.3 Live Births, Crude Birth Rate, Age-Specific Fertility Rates, Gross Reproduction Rate, and Percentage of Births in Hospital, Canada, 1921–1971 (all fertility rates based on live births per thousand women for the specified group)

| YEAR | LIVE BIRTHS | | | | FERTILITY RATES BY AGE OF MOTHER[1] | | | | | | | | | |
	Total number	Number illigitimate[2]	Percentage illegitimate[2]	Crude birth rate[3]	15–19 years	20–24 years	25–29 years	30–34 years	35–39 years	40–44 years	45–49 years	Total fertility rate[1]	Net reproduction rate (per thousand woman)[1]	Percentage of births occurring in hospital[4]
1971	362 187	32 698	9.0	16.8	40.1	134.4	142.0	77.3	33.6	9.4	0.6	2187	1029	99.6
1961	475 700	21 490	4.5	26.1	58.2	233.6	219.2	144.9	81.1	28.5	2.4	3840	1795	96.9
1951	381 092	14 537	3.8	27.2	48.1	188.7	198.8	144.5	86.5	30.9	3.1	3503	1701	79.1
1941	263 993	10 430	4.0	22.4	30.7	138.4	159.8	122.3	80.0	31.6	3.7	2832	1377	48.9
1931	247 205	8 543	3.5	23.2	29.9	137.1	175.1	145.3	103.1	44.0	5.5	3200	1555	26.8
1921	264 879[6]	3 334[5]	2.0[5]	29.3[3]	–	–	–	–	–	–	–	–	–	–

[1] Data for the Yukon Territory and the Northwest Territories not available prior to 1950; Newfoundland excluded throughout.

[2] Excludes the Yukon Territory and the Northwest Territories prior to 1950.

[3] Number of live births per thousand population; excludes the Yukon Territory and the Northwest Territories, 1921 to 1923.

[4] Excluding the province of Newfoundland; excludes the Yukon Territory and the Northwest Territories, 1926 to 1949.

[5] Excluding the province of Quebec, 1921 to 1925; excluding Newfoundland, 1921.

[6] Excludes the Yukon Territory and the Northwest Territories.

Source: Adapted from the Statistics Canada publication "Historical Statistics of Canada," Second Edition, Catalogue 11-516, 1983.

TABLE 4.4   Number of Families and Average Number of Persons Per Family, 1881–1976

YEAR	TOTAL		URBAN		RURAL	
	NUMBER	AVERAGE	NUMBER	AVERAGE	NUMBER	AVERAGE
1976	5 727 895	3.5	4 372 090	3.4	1 355 805	3.7
1971	5 070 682	3.7	3 923 380	3.6	1 147 305	4.1
1966	4 525 266	3.9	3 413 178	3.8	1 113 088	4.3
1961	4 147 444	3.9	2 985 055	3.7	1 162 389	4.3
1956	3 711 500	3.8	2 583 568	3.6	1 127 912	4.3
1951	3 287 384	3.7	2 123 540	3.5	1 163 844	4.1
1941[1]	2 525 299	3.9	1 437 415	3.7	1 087 884	4.3
1931[1]	2 419 360	3.9	1 333 579	3.7	1 085 781	4.1
1921[1]	2 001 512	4.3	1 023 736	4.0	977 776	4.6
1911[2]	1 488 353	–	–	–	–	–
1901	1 070 747	–	–	–	–	–
1891	921 643	–	–	–	–	–
1881	812 136	–	–	–	–	–

1. Excludes Newfoundland the Yukon Territory and the Northwest Territories.
2. Excludes Newfoundland only in 1911 and earlier years.

Source: Adapted from the Statistics Canada publication "Historical Statistics of Canada," Second Edition, Catalogue 11-516, 1983, Series A254-259.

living alone has been increasing rapidly. In Canada in 1961, 9.3 percent of all households had only one person, and during the next 39 years the figure more than doubled, to 23 percent by 1991. This rapid rise occurred in part because the increase in the age at marriage meant that there were more single young adults. In addition, the life expectancy of women increased more rapidly than that of men; there were more widows, during the prosperous 1970s and early 1980s, who were able to have their own households (Ram, 1990; Statistics Canada, 1992b: Table 6). However, the depressed economy during the late 1980s and early 1990s drove many single young people out of their apartments. Among those aged 15 to 19, the proportion living alone fell from 4 percent to 3 percent between 1986 and 1991 (*The Daily*, July 7, 1992).

Divorce All marriages are eventually broken, of course, by death if not by divorce or separation, but the causes have changed over time. In 1861, 5.3 percent of the population aged 15 years of age and older was widowed, and the proportion divorced was less than 0.01 percent (Census of Canada, 1608–1876). The proportion of widows rose to 6.4 percent in 1901, dropped to 5.6 percent in 1911, began to increase slowly to a peak of 6.6 percent in 1951, and then increased more rapidly in the 1980s (Census of Canada, 1901, 1911 and 1951).

An often-quoted statistic, particularly in the mass media, is that the Canadian divorce rate is about 30 or 40 percent. While this statistic may be true in that about half as many divorces are granted as marriages are performed each year, the difficulty is that two different populations are being compared. The couples who divorce in a particular year do not normally come from the group who married that year, but are, rather, drawn from the entire group of married people in the country. A more accurate figure is provided by the number of divorces in a particular year in relation to the number of marriages in existence (regardless of when they were entered into) in a given year. Another figure frequently used is the crude divorce rate (the number of divorces per 1000 population). Table 4.2 provides the crude divorce rates as well as the marriage rates from 1921 to 1974.

The crude divorce rate has undergone some dramatic changes. First, the divorce rate increased during World War II and immediately after to a high of 65.6 in 1947. The war years and war marriages clearly are implicated in these rates. The next major jump was from the 54.8 divorces per 1000 in 1968 to the 124.2 divorces per 1000 in 1969. This major increase is tied to the liberalization of the Divorce Act that took place in 1968. Changes in the grounds for divorce made it possible for more divorces to occur than under the previous law. Divorces continued to rise under the new Act and reached record highs in the 1970s.

Increased divorce and delayed marriage have changed the marital status profile of Canadian adults. In 1861, for example, among Canadians aged 15 and older, 38 percent were single, 57 percent were married, 5.3 percent were widowed, and none were recorded as separated or divorced (Census of Canada, 1608–1876, 1878). By 1891, the number of single people had increased to 42 percent and the number of those married had decreased to 51 percent, probably because of the many male immigrants arriving during the 1880s. Widows and widowers made up 6.2 percent of the population, and less than 0.01 percent were separated or divorced (Census of Canada, 1890–1891, 1893).

Thereafter, the proportion of single people began to decline and the proportion of married people increased, so that, in 1921, they accounted for 36 and 58 percent of the population, respectively. The proportion of widowed people stayed at 6.2 percent, and the percentage of divorced reached 0.1 percent of the population 15 years of age and older. Because the Depression caused many people to postpone marriage, in 1931 the proportion of single people increased to 38 percent, married people declined to 56 percent,

and widowed and divorced people remained unchanged at 6.2 and 0.1 percent, respectively (Census of Canada, 1921, 1931). During the marriage boom after the Second World War, two-thirds of adults were married, and the percentage of single people declined sharply to 26.5 in 1961. Widowhood peaked at 6.6 percent in 1951, a figure that probably reflected Second World War casualties, and despite the surge in divorces at the end of the war, only 6 percent of all Canadian adults were divorced in 1961 (Census of Canada, 1951, 1961).

Remarriage Remarriage rates were high during the 19th and early 20th centuries. Husbands and wives often died prematurely, and the surviving spouse needed to marry a new partner. As the life expectancies of men and women increased, and while divorce rates were low, the remarriage rate fell. But with the increase in divorce, the proportion of all marriages that were remarriages grew as well. In 1951, remarriage was more common for men than for women, and more common for those divorced than for those widowed. Accordingly, the remarriage rate was 346 per 1000 divorced men, 183 per 1000 divorced women, 31 per 1000 widowed men, and 9.9 per 1000 widowed women. By 1989 the remarriage rates for divorced women and men had equalized, but had fallen substantially to 87 and 89 per 1000, respectively. One reason for this drop is that many divorced people chose to cohabit with someone instead of marrying, at least for a time, and these relationships do not count as remarriages. Chapters 13 and 14 offer a full discussion of remarriage.

Historical Trends The historical trends that we have described in this section show that the Canadian family has undergone significant changes during the last 100 years. Family size has become smaller, fertility is below replacement level, and divorce has steadily increased while the marriage rate has remained relatively stable. Certainly, the indicators we have presented do not contradict Goode's hypothesis relating the decline of the extended family to industrialization. However, as we shall see in chapters to follow, none of these indicators is as unambiguous and clearly defined as we might expect. To understand divorce, fertility, marriage, and family size we must understand the complex processes that are linked to changes in these indicators. Subsequent chapters examine these indicators as they are linked to the changing diversity of the Canadian population, including changing dating patterns, changing work patterns, and changing marital expectations.

SUMMARY

- Zimmerman developed a theory of family change, describing a transition from a strong, traditional "trustee family" to a very fragile atomistic family, which somewhat resembles the North American family today. Ogburn suggested a theory that was similar, but emphasized the continued importance of the family.

- The ancient Hebrew family was strongly patriarchal, a pattern that has persisted well into the 20th century in most Western societies. The Hebrew family (household) fulfilled four major functions: it was the basic unit of Israel's land tenure; it was the centre of judicial law and administration of justice; it was the centre of didactic instruction; and it maintained Israel's relation to God.

- Women were able to achieve greater equality with men at the height of the Roman Empire due to increased wealth, but the family was still basically patriarchal.

- The teachings of Jesus and the apostle Paul emphasized mutual respect in the family, and also affirmed the importance of affection, faithfulness and the permanence of marriage. Beginning with the 3rd century, the Christian church taught that virginity and celibacy were more spiritual states than marriage. Marriage, however, was considered a permanent sacrament, so divorce was limited to cases of infidelity. Early church fathers taught that children are born innately sinful, and that child-rearing must therefore be very strict. This belief continues to influence some Christian families today.

- The Great Transformation, which began during the 17th century, in time changed the preoccupation of people from survival to sentiment. It transformed partner selection from choice based on family position to choice based on romantic love, made love central to the mother–infant relationship, and increased the intimacy of family relationships.

- In Canada during this century, wives have changed from homemaking mothers to mothers employed outside the home. The education of children has become an urgent preoccupation. As the influence of kinship relationships has dwindled, couples expect to satisfy their emotional needs within the marriage.

- Canadian demographic data show that family patterns have changed during the past century, and particularly in the past 30 years. Since 1960, Canadian marriage and birthrates have fallen and divorce rates have increased.

- Goode's analysis of the impact of the industrialization of modern societies indicates that this led to decline of the extended family and emergence of the nuclear family as the pre-eminent family form.

KEY TERMS

Atomistic family (68)

Conjugal family (84)

Demography (85)

Domestic family (68)

Dowry (72)

Habitant family (79)

Impartible inheritance (80)

Kindred (84)

Replacement level (81)

Total fertility rate (86)

Trustee family (68)

QUESTIONS FOR REVIEW

1. List some of the distinguishing features of Zimmerman's trustee family, domestic family, and atomistic family.

2. What source of change does Ogburn identify in his theory of family change, and how does he avoid being pessimistic about the future of the family?

3. What features does Goode identify as distinctively characteristic of the modern family today?

4. What influences on the evolution of today's modern family does Goode identify?

QUESTIONS FOR DISCUSSION

1. What has been the effect of Christianity on the status of the family?

2. In your judgment, what is the likelihood that the contemporary North American family will evolve once again into Zimmerman's trustee family? Why do you think so?

3. If the patriarchal family form were to dominate North American society once again, do you think that wives and children would be seen as men's property? Why, or why not?

4. It can be argued that the full effects of the transition to the modern form of the family, which Goode describes, are only now becoming apparent. How will these full effects probably influence the future of the family?

5. Which demographic statistics make you hopeful about the future of the Canadian family, and which make you more pessimistic?

SUGGESTED READINGS

Balakrishnan, T.R., Evelyne Lapierre-Adamczyk, and Karol K. Krotki. 1993. *Family and Childbearing in Canada*. Toronto: University of Toronto Press. This book provides an analysis of databases on the 1984 National Fertility Study. It examines trends in fertility, sociocultural and economic factors, as well as attitudes toward marriage, family, abortion, and contraception.

Dickason, O.P. 2002. *Canada's First Nations: A History of Founding Peoples from earliest Times* (3rd Edition). Oxford: Oxford University Press.

Gee, Ellen M. 1987. "Historical Change in the Family Life Course of Canadian Men and Women," in Victor Marshall (ed.). *Aging in Canada* (second edition). Toronto: Fitzhenry and Whiteside. An excellent documentation of the demographic changes in the Canadian family during the past 100 years.

Gies, Frances and Joseph Gies. 1987. *Marriage and the Family in the Middle Ages*. New York: Harper and Row. A fascinating description of marriage and family patterns during the 1000 years from the beginning to the end of the Middle Ages.

LaPierre-Adamcyk, E., C. LeBourdais, and N. Marcil-Gratton. (2003). "French Canadian Families." In J. Ponzetti et al. (Eds.) *International Encyclopedia of Marriage and Family* (Vol. 2, pp.697–702). New York: MacMillan Reference.

McDaniel, Susan A. 1994. *Family and Friends*. Ottawa: Statistics Canada. Based on the 1990 General Social Survey, this volume concentrates on family and friends. It examines various social trends in families, including union formation and dissolution, children and fertility intentions, living arrangements, household division of labour, contacts with family and friends, and older Canadians.

McVey Jr., Wayne W. and Warren E. Kalbach. 1995. *Canadian Population*. Toronto: Nelson Canada. As indicated in the preface, the objective of this book was to provide the basic information about Canada's population, including its origins, the factors related to its growth and geographical distribution, and the demographic, social, and economic characteristics of Canadian individuals and families.

Queen, Stuart A., Robert W. Habenstein, and Jill S. Quadagno. 1985. *The Family in Various Cultures*. New York: Harper and Row. Good, concise analyses of the ancient, classical, and European influences on the Western family, together with descriptions of family forms that have appeared in the United States and Canada.

Shorter, Edward. 1975. *The Making of the Modern Family*. New York: Basic Books. This is an interesting and very readable analysis of the "pre-modern" European family, and of the influences under which it evolved into the modern family form.

Zimmerman, Carl. 1947. *Family and Civilization*. New York: Harper and Row. This is the book in which Zimmerman developed his theory of the trustee, domestic and atomistic families, and the conditions that gave rise to each form.

5

Variations in Canadian Families

After studying this chapter, you should be able to do the following:

- Explain some of the consequences of urban life for the marriage and family patterns of Native Canadian people.
- Understand some of the implications of historical immigration policy.
- Describe the features of the first-generation Canadian family, changes in roles and relationships among its members, and its kinship and ethnic networks.
- Explain the probabilities that Canadian men, women, and children may experience poverty.
- Describe the situations of women who are least at risk and most at risk of experiencing poverty in Canada, and list the reasons for your distinction between these two groups.

Introduction

At the end of the last chapter, we examined Canadian statistics. These statistics average across all families and, hence, conceal the variation between families that composes the rich tapestry that is Canada. It is the particular history and composition of each ethnic, social, and cultural community in Canada that creates this tapestry. Some of these groups, such as the English and French, have already received some attention while other groups have not. It is not the intention of this chapter to provide an exhaustive list of these various groups, but rather to use a few examples to demonstrate how this diversity not only shapes the lives of family members but also provides an important component of the Canadian mosaic. As will be shown in the discussion below, policies of immigration have dictated when immigrants can construct or reconstruct their families and kinship networks in Canada, and, consequently, determined the timing by which

each community has been able to produce generations beyond the first generation of immigrant families. This variable has had tremendous influence on the degree of integration or assimilation into the fabric of society that each ethnic community has been able to achieve from the time it was first established in Canada.

Traditionally, sociologists identify five *sources of variability*—ethnicity, religious beliefs, social class, rural–urban differences, and regional differences. These affect marriage and family behaviours in many ways; however, the ways in which they affect families are much more complex than is apparent. For example, we most often find that several of these operate conjointly so that new immigrants may settle together in ethnic enclaves so as to maintain their beliefs and religion; an example can be seen with the Icelandic immigrants that settled in and around Gimli, Manitoba. Another way that these five variables are complex is in the many sub-dimensions each one incorporates. For example, ethnicity incorporates sub-variables such as time of immigration, cultural identity, visible minority status, and many others. In the sections to follow, we emphasize certain variables rather than others and focus on the complexity of the interactions of these five variables in regard to Native groups, immigration, and poverty.

Aboriginal Canadian Families

Native Canadians include Treaty Native Canadians, Inuit, and Métis, and each of these includes numerous bands and tribal groups. While some of this discussion deals with Native Canadians generally, our focus is

primarily on those of Native Canadian origin because they are the most numerous (see Table 5.1). We prefer to use one of two descriptive phrases in this textbook, Aboriginal or Native Canadian.

Changing Family Relationships

The opportunities and diversions available in towns and cities have long attracted many Native Canadians from their home settlements and reserves. Between 1961 and 1981, the proportion of the Native Canadian population living off-reserve doubled to about 30 percent, probably in response to perceived employment

TABLE 5.1   Population by Aboriginal Group, Provinces and Territories, 2001

	TOTAL POPULATION	TOTAL ABORIGINAL POPULATION	TREATY NATIVE CANADIAN	MÉTIS	INUIT	NON-ABORIGINAL POPULATION
CANADA	29 639 030	983 090	638 445	298 480	46 165	28 662 725
Newfoundland and Labrador	508 075	18 965	8560	5665	4740	489 300
Prince Edward Island	133 385	1395	1105	230	20	132 040
Nova Scotia	897 570	17 065	13 515	3180	370	880 555
New Brunswick	719 715	17 155	12 500	4440	215	702 725
Quebec	7 125 580	80 025	54 005	16 420	9600	7 046 175
Ontario	11 285 550	190 070	138 505	49 900	1665	11 097 239
Manitoba	1 103 695	150 545	92 890	57 290	365	953 655
Saskatchewan	963 150	131 085	86 250	44 555	280	832 960
Alberta	2 941 150	157 325	89 000	67 065	1260	2 784 930
British Columbia	3 868 875	171 210	124 910	45 385	915	3 698 850
Yukon	28 525	6640	5860	610	170	21 980
Northwest Territories	37 105	18 910	11 225	3680	4005	18 375
Nunavut	26 665	22 725	105	55	22 565	3945

Source: Adapted from the Statistics Canada website <http://www12.statcan.ca/english/census01/products/highlight/Aboriginal/Page.cfm?Lang=E&Geo=PR&View=1a&Table=1&Sort=2&B1=Counts01&B2=Total>

opportunities (Siggner, 1986). By 2001, over 50 percent of registered Native Canadians lived off reserves, many in industrial areas of Ontario and British Columbia (Table 5.2). Although cities may be perceived as having employment opportunities, Frideres (1983) has noted that "the vast majority" of Natives entering cities lack the necessary qualifications to get work or even to succeed in school.

Many of the Aboriginals' problems are related to their lower socioeconomic status. Their unemployment rate in 1991 reached 24.6 percent in total, and 30 percent among the registered Native Canadians living on reserves. Just over half (57 percent) participated in the labour force that year, mainly working in construction, service, and clerical jobs. Aboriginals have lower educational attainment than do those in the general population, where twice as many achieved less than grade nine education in 1991 (23.9 percent vs. 13.8 percent), and only 2.6 percent obtained a university degree compared to 11.6 percent of non-Aboriginals (Royal Commission on Aboriginal People, 1996). There is some indication, however, that the Native Canadians' lot is slowly improving. The life expectancy among those living on the reserve has increased by 3.3 years for males, and 4.1 years for females, from 1981 to 1986. Infant mortality has decreased by approximately half, and the proportion of dwellings with more than one person per room has fallen from 33.4 percent to 28.9 percent for the same period. Enrollment of children in school was also more than

TABLE 5.2   Persons Registered Under the *Indian Act*, Provinces and Territories, 2001

	TOTAL[1]	TOTAL LIVING ON RESERVE[1]	TOTAL LIVING OFF RESERVE
CANADA	558 180	274 215	283 955
Newfoundland and Labrador	3605	750	2855
Prince Edward Island	850	375	475
Nova Scotia	10 870	7270	3605
New Brunswick	10 530	5940	4585
Quebec	49 110	32 510	16 600
Ontario	107 395	39 910	67 490
Manitoba	90 650	51 250	39 395
Saskatchewan	84 075	43 710	40 365
Alberta	80 775	36 365	44 410
British Columbia	103 550	44 690	58 860
Yukon	5075	1835	3240
Northwest Territories	11 585	9600	1985
Nunavut	100	0	100

1. Estimates based on 20 percent sample data.

Source: Adapted from the Statistics Canada publication "Aboriginal Identity Population (3), Registered Indian Status (3), Age Groups (11B), Sex (3), and Area of Residence (7) for Population, for Canada, provinces and territories, 2001 Census - 20% Sample data," Catalogue 97F0011, January 21, 2003.

90 percent in 1991, and the number of band-operated schools has doubled over the last decade, an indication that Native Canadian people are taking more control over the education of their children (Native Canadian and Northern Affairs Canada, 1993).

A 1991 Statistics Canada (1993b) survey of all Native Canadians gives information on some of their current concerns. This study suggested that about two-thirds (64 percent) live away from reserves. The 2001 Census recorded a different proportion and is probably more accurate at this time. Table 5.2 shows that just over half of Native Canadians are currently living off reserves. The earlier survey did document that Natives experience extreme poverty (identified as not having enough food during the preceding year), reported by about 9 percent of those on and off the reserve. Native Canadians living off reserves report consuming alcohol (88 percent) more often than those on reserves (79 percent). These two groupings have somewhat different perceptions of the problems they experience. Those on reserves more often cite as problems unemployment (78 percent versus 60 percent among those off-reserve), alcohol abuse (73 percent versus 56 percent), drug abuse (59 percent versus 43 percent), family violence (44 percent versus 36 percent), and suicide (34 percent versus 21 percent) (Statistics Canada, 1993b: Table 4.3). These figures suggest that off-reserve Native Canadians feel they have fewer problems than those living on reserves. When asked about appropriate solutions, about 11 percent of both groups said there was a need for more police and more family counseling services, but only 1 percent advocated banning alcohol from the community (Statistics Canada, 1993b).

Native Canadian Women and Children

Native Canadian women suffered a form of discrimination for 117 years that was not experienced by Native Canadian men or Canadian women: A status Native Canadian woman who married a non-Native Canadian man lost her registered status and with it her right to live on her home reserve, to receive subsidized education, and to benefit from free medical care. These losses were sharpened by the fact that when a Native Canadian man married a non-Native Canadian woman, not only did the man retain his status, but his non-Native Canadian wife became a registered Native Canadian as well and retained these rights even after divorcing her Native Canadian husband. As recently as 1973, the Supreme Court of Canada upheld these provisions of the *Native Canadian Act*, which were strongly supported by Native Canadian men, most of whom continue to be strongly patriarchal. These provisions are a source of considerable bitterness for Native Canadian women, about half of whom have married non-Native Canadians since 1970 (Jamieson, 1978, 1986).

A law passed in 1985, which eliminated the policy and reinstated as registered Native Canadians women who had earlier lost their status (Jamieson, 1986), finally ended this century-long discrimination. But the new legislation cannot immediately heal scarred gender relations among Native Canadians. Many women remain resentful toward the men, who succeeded in blocking their reinstatement for so long, while the men resent Native Canadian women who married non-Native Canadians and who may now bring these men into reserve communities. On the other hand, family reunification is now possible because women who were expelled from their home reserves are now able to rejoin their extended families (Ponting, 1986).

Increasingly, Aboriginal people are turning to traditional beliefs and teachings for strength and guidance in seeking solutions to their family problems (Canadian Council on Social Development and Native Women's Association of Canada, 1991). Recently, the Canadian Royal Commission on Aboriginal Peoples has examined Native health policy issues. It concluded that there is a need for a holistic approach to Natives' health that emphasizes the interconnectedness of health and environment in their traditional culture. Aboriginals are historically and culturally at one with nature, and the commission expressed the view that an Aboriginal health model should be treated like a welfare program that addresses poverty and housing conditions among a wide range of emotional, mental, physical, spiritual, sexual, and cultural issues. The Commission considered community healing particularly essential to improving indigenous people's health; the whole community needs to break the long cycle of oppression and deprivation, and the resulting years of suffering and moral decay (O'Neil, 1997).

Current Family Patterns and Conditions

The divorce rate among Native people is similar to that for non-Natives. Frideres (1993) notes, however, that many Native women never formally marry—although they live with a man and bear children—in part because an unmarried Native mother may receive more baby-bonus payments than a mother who is married and separated. Native Canadian women are also eligible for various educational and vocational training programs only if they are unmarried. Native Canadians often avoid the legal and child-support costs associated with formal divorce by simply separating; alternatively, the husband may desert his family (Hagey et al., 1989c; Frideres, 1993).

Continuing poverty is an important cause of these family conditions. In 1985, 46 percent of status Native Canadians obtained most of their income from government transfer payments of various kinds, up from 34 percent in 1980 and more than twice the 20 percent figure for all Canadians. Between 1980 and 1985, when the economy was in recession or just recovering, all Canadians experienced a drop in employment income, but while the national average was a 4 percent drop, Native Canadians suffered a 13 percent decrease. This discrepancy demonstrates the vulnerability to economic recession of the many Native Canadians with low levels of education and skilled-employment training. In consequence, while the average family income of all Canadians in 1985 (with a 3.1-person average family) was about $38 000, for status Native Canadians (with an average family size of 3.9), average family income was only about $22 000. Native Canadians off-reserve were slightly better off ($23 000) than those on-reserve ($21 000), and they had smaller families on average (3.8 and 4.2 persons, respectively) (Hagey et al., 1989b, 1989c).

Because of illnesses resulting from poverty and poor housing, and because of their higher-risk lifestyles, the death rates of Native Canadians are almost one third higher than for all Canadians (about 945 per 100 000 population, in contrast to 648). Notably, more than one-third of all Native Canadian deaths during the past decade has been due to accidents and violence, more than four times the 8 percent rate for all Canadians. "Native people have five times the rate of child welfare, four times the death rate, three times the violent death, juvenile delinquency and suicide rates, and twice the rate of hospital admissions of the average Canadian population" (Frideres, 1993:207). The Native Canadian homicide rate is twice that of the Canadian population, as well. All of these high misfortune rates have damaging and often tragic consequences for Native Canadian family life. We do not have the space to discuss the sources of these conditions, but they result, Frideres (1993) believes, from "the cultural imperialism of the Canadian government" and the "racist philosophy" seen in a society that perceives Native people as inferior (208).

A recent publication by the Quebec Native Women's Association (1996) used a variety of sources, such as vital statistics, academic and scientific articles, news items, personal stories, and qualitative interviews, to provide a profile of Quebec Aboriginal families (**AmerNative Canadians**). A third of these families are found to be residing off-reserve. Aboriginal Canadians of AmerNative and Inuit origin living in Montreal have increased by 100 percent since 1986. Often, however, the attraction of urban life is short-lived, and many women who live in Montreal feel isolated, excluded and abandoned. The study compares the Aboriginal and Quebec populations on many demographic and family features. Twice as many Aboriginals have less than grade nine education, and their unemployment rate is two to three times higher than that of Quebec populations in general. Even among the highest income groups, such as the Cree and the Hmo-Wendula nations, the average income is still 25 percent less than the average Quebec family income ($35 000).

Multi-family households are on the decline, but their proportion (6.8 percent) is still eleven times higher than that of other families in Quebec. Among certain nations, such as the Alikamek, the proportion of extended-family households reaches 20 percent. Some variations are found between Aboriginals who live on the reserve and those who live in the city. Families on the reserve tend to be larger (4.5 members) than families living elsewhere, where the average is closer to the general Quebec average (3.3 members compared to 3.1). Women in urban areas also tend to have a higher level of education than do women on the reserve (Quebec Native Women's Association, 1996).

Canadian Immigration Policies and the Family

Immigration laws and policies, and the changing needs of the economy, have largely determined the structure of the family in Canada over the years. Since families had to be large enough to provide the labour power needed to acquire full title of the land, large peasant families from the Ukraine were recruited at the turn of the century to establish farms in western Canada. Early Ukrainians immigrated as families with the intention of reestablishing a permanent peasant subsistence agricultural community (Satzewich, 1993). In contrast, Chinese men were recruited to work on the construction of the British Columbia section of the Pacific Railroad, and came as labourers with the intention of earning enough money to return to China and enhance their family economy. Once the railroad was completed, the Chinese immigrants were subject to racialization policies that stemmed from public perceptions that they were too competitive and presented a threat to the white labour force. Federal legislation imposed a head tax on the Chinese labourers and their family members who were left in China, which restricted the reunification and formation of Chinese nuclear families. Chinese males also did not want to bring their spouses and children to an environment in which people exhibited racist hostility against them (Satzewich, 1993).

Racial policies continued until 1962, favouring northern and western European immigrants and facilitating their movement as a unit through financial resettlement assistance (Corbett, 1997). These discriminatory laws have had many implications for Canadian families. Like their Australian counterparts, it took immigrants from non–English-speaking countries decades to reconstruct their families (Collins, 1993). Separated from their families, Asian immigrants to the U.S. redefined and extended the concept of family.

For the women left behind in the home country, it was a different story. They had to maintain what became known as the *split household,* which lasted, in certain cases, for several generations. While the husband produced income abroad, the wife and other relatives carried out the functions of socialization and household reproduction tasks (Glenn, 1983). A common theme in popular U.S. literature of the time involved wives forgotten in the homeland. Wives in the home country became virtual widows, expected to serve their husband's family and remain sexually faithful, while their husbands abroad were free to visit prostitutes or take on other wives (Hutter, 1993; Espiritu, 1997).

The point system established in 1967 opened the door for families from nontraditional countries to come to Canada. Today, Canadians from other than Aboriginal, British and French origins account for 27 percent of the total population, and three out of five immigrants are from non-European countries (*Transition,* 1994). The point system, however, continued to favour immigrants with skills, because of the demand for skilled and professional labour. Since they are more likely to acquire the appropriate required skills, those from middle- and upper-middle-class backgrounds are overrepresented among the new waves of immigrants (Man, 1995). While it facilitated the reunion of immigrants with their relatives, the 1978 *Immigration Act* has further discriminated against low-income immigrants, who would not be able to sign the required undertaking to sponsor their immediate relatives for up to 10 years (Satzewich, 1993).

This sponsorship policy has also resulted in marginalization of family-sponsored immigrants. Because they are considered dependents, and therefore not destined for the labour market, family-class immigrants are denied access to federal job and language training programs (Boyd, 1990). The sponsorship policy poses an additional problem for women because it does not qualify them for many provincial and municipal social programs. Those who find themselves in abusive marriages are unable to access resources to seek help, and are left vulnerable to the goodwill of their male sponsor (Canada Employment and Immigration Advisory Council, 1991). Often, the male sponsor uses the threat of deportation and loss of her children to keep a battered wife subservient, and to prevent her from reporting the abuse and seeking help (Chotalia, 1994; Jang and Morello-Frosch, 1990).

One long-term implication of these immigration policies is the gap they have created in the degree of successful integration of different ethnic groups into the fabric of Canadian society. Groups that were obstructed from forming their nuclear and extended families took a longer time to produce third and further generations in Canada. Because of their high proportion, first-generation families and their second-generation offspring have been the main focus in studies of most ethnic communities. Often, in the literature, the term *immigrant* is used interchangeably with *ethnic*. From an ethnocultural perspective, there is very little research on third-generation families, and almost none on fourth-generation and beyond. The assumption seems to be that ethnicity plays a minimal role in the life of families beyond the second generation, and therefore does not deserve exclusive attention. While it is true that the desire for cultural retention is stronger among first-generation immigrants (Dhruvarajan, 1993), there is not enough research to examine the dynamics of its influence on family life in subsequent generations. For instance, despite the fact that French Canadians are one of the largest ethnic communities, studies on the French family tend to adopt mainly a demographic or a political perspective, with little attention to the role ethnic beliefs or practices play in influencing family patterns and the dynamics of family relationships.

The literature on Canadian ethnic families is also relatively limited compared to its counterpart in the U.S. Whenever relevant, the discussion below on contemporary Canadian families will draw on data from the U.S., as well as Australia, because of common immigration laws, and adjustment and living circumstances, among immigrants in the three countries. We will briefly describe the family and kinship systems among Native Canadians, French Canadians, and more recent Canadians, emphasizing the recent and ongoing changes they are experiencing. Finally, we illustrate the importance of social class influences by discussing how poverty affects Canadian families.

First-Generation Families in Canada

The Changing Structure and Functions of Kinship and Ethnic Networks

While the extended family as a residential unit is not the norm in most contemporary societies, it continues to maintain important functions in many countries from which immigrants originate. When an immigrant leaves these kinship systems, he loses his major support structure. According to Krupinski (1977), the extended family normally defines the parameters of socially accepted behaviour and imposes varying degrees of sanctions if those parameters are overstepped.

The immigrant families he studied in Australia complained of social isolation and lack of emotional support because of the absence of extended families. For example, Hong Kong families lived in close proximity to their relatives and developed a close-knit support network, and received assistance in housework and child care while they went to work. Husbands took it for granted that they would share the breadwinner role while remaining solely responsible for the management of the household. In Canada, these women found it difficult to balance work and family responsibilities in the absence of grandparents, and were reluctant to seek their husbands' help for fear of being perceived as incapable of performing the "good wife" role (Man, 1995).

Feelings of an emotional void and loneliness, and lack of support in raising children and mediating marital problems, were all reported by immigrants and refugees as consequences of separation from the extended family (Muir, 1988; Dasgupta, 1992; Seifeddine, 1997). Because the spouses are too dependent on each other for happiness and companionship, isolation from kin can also cause stress in the marital relationship. In Man's (1995) study, migration heightened the incompatibility and lack of communication between some spouses, leading to marriage breakdown. In order to cope with the absence of immediate family members, immigrants maintain close contacts with their relatives abroad through letters, phone calls, and gift exchanges (Witterbrood and Robertson, 1991; Seifeddine, 1997; Langford, unpublished). Family sponsorship programs in Canada have allowed immigrants to reconstruct part or all of their families, depending on their financial capabilities (see Johnson, 1988, 1989, 1990). Over time, East Indian communities in British Columbia recreated their kin universe in Canada (Srivastava, 1975).

Kinship and ethnic networks facilitate adaptation of first-generation families by providing them with various forms of needed support. For Vietnamese refugees in Canada, ethnic enclaves are found to be important sources of jobs and training, and a buffer against isolation. Moreover, through patchworking, or bringing and sharing diverse resources, these families secure protection against economic instability and fluctuation in the supply of resources (Kibria, 1994). A study of Korean immigrants in Toronto actually shows that ethnic social support is directly related to lower levels of depression, while general social support from the broader community has a minimal influence (Noh and Avison, 1996). The author explains these findings in terms of sociocultural similarity hypothesis, where support from a provider of a similar background is more likely to result in empathic understanding. Members of the larger community may be viewed as less aware of or sensitive to the particular difficulties faced by an immigrant family.

The Double Bind of Kinship and Ethnic Ties

Ethnic networks can be a mixed blessing for the family. While providing its members with emotional and practical support, these networks also have the potential to segregate or ghettoize them, impeding their integration into the larger society. The more self-sufficient the ethnic community is in terms of having its own sociocultural and economic structures and institutions, the less the contact needed with the larger society, and the more enclosed the community (Thomas, 1990). In fact, case studies of Lebanese extended families in Nova Scotia show that members who rely only on their ethnic networks tend to have low levels of acculturation in terms of friendship with other Canadians and membership in mainstream organizations (Jabbra, 1983).

As Table 5.3 demonstrates, many members of ethnic groups may self-identify with more than one group. For example, a person from the country of Vietnam may identify with that nationality while also identifying him or herself as ethnic Chinese. Indeed, Chinese ethnic groups are resident in most countries of the world. Table 5.3 shows that many people (over 11 million) in Canada identify with more than one ethnic group. For more statistical information, consult the 2001 Census.

Religiosity can also affect the enclosure of ethnic families. Groups that are unified by strong religious beliefs are found to have the greatest capacity to be segregated (Thomas, 1990). Dhruvanajan (1993) found Indian Canadian men and women who rank high on religiosity to be significantly more likely to have friends from their own ethnic groups, encourage children to value their own religion and culture, and speak their ethnic language. Groups with strong religious affiliations also tend to have higher rates of endogamy, or marrying within one's own group. The highest rates

of endogamy in Canada are for Asians, Jews, Italians, and French (Thomas, 1991). By minimizing the loss of group members to "outside" groups, ensuring the homogeneity of the community, and reproducing ethnicity, in-group marriages may also result in enclosure and minimal contact with the larger society.

As we have noted, immigrants may identify with multiple groups based on cultural practices and religion, but they may also identify with a geographic or political region. Table 5.4 shows the contributions various world regions have made to Canada's ethnic mixture. Note that before 1961 most of Canada's immigrants arrive from the United Kingdom and Europe. In the last decade (1991–2001), the great bulk of immigrants have originated from parts of the Asian continent. Unlike many of the immigrants from Europe, the newer waves of immigration are more likely to be visible minorities (Table 5.4). Being included in a visible minority could be a matter of self-identification but it could also be a matter of stereotyping and prejudgment by others. It is fairly obvious that ethnic identity is a complex and multidimensional issue for immigrants and provides both opportunities for support and belonging as well as opportunities for prejudice and discrimination.

Another case of double bind is the ethnic family enterprise. While providing the family with financial security and the opportunity for employment, businesses such as restaurants and clothing subcontractors are labour-intensive and survive only at the expense of unpaid or minimally paid labour of wives, children, relatives and other co-ethnics (Espiritu, 1997). Large, well-established ethnic communities can also have adverse effects on individuals and families (Johnson, 1988).

Economic Integration and Family Well-Being

There is strong evidence that economic integration among first-generation Canadians is the major vehicle to their overall integration into the larger society. Immigrants who are successful in their occupations report feeling themselves part of Canada (Thomas, 1990). A recent graduate of an employment training program, a Cuban refugee in Canada, underscores his belief that one gains access to society through employment: "I began to feel

TABLE 5.3   Population by Selected Ethnic Origins, Canada, 2001

	TOTAL RESPONSES	SINGLE RESPONSES	MULTIPLE RESPONSES
TOTAL POPULATION	29 639 035	18 307 545	11 331 490
ETHNIC ORIGIN			
Canadian	11 682 680	6 748 135	4 934 545
English	5 978 875	1 479 525	4 499 355
French	4 668 410	1 060 760	3 607 655
Scottish	4 157 210	607 235	3 549 975
Irish	3 822 660	496 865	3 325 795
German	2 742 765	705 600	2 037 170
Italian	1 270 370	726 275	544 090
Chinese	1 094 700	936 210	158 490
Ukrainian	1 071 060	326 195	744 860
Native Canadian	1 000 890	455 805	545 085
Dutch (Netherlands)	923 310	316 220	607 090
Polish	817 085	260 415	556 665
Indian	713 330	581 665	131 665
Norwegian	363 760	47 230	316 530
Portuguese	357 690	252 835	104 855
Welsh	350 365	28 445	321 920
Jewish	348 605	186 475	162 130
Russian	337 960	70 895	267 070
Filipino	327 550	266 140	61 405
Métis	307 845	72 210	235 635
Swedish	282 760	30 440	252 325
Hungarian (Magyar)	267 255	91 800	175 455
American (USA)	250 005	25 205	224 805
Greek	215 105	143 785	71 325
Spanish	213 105	66 545	146 555
Jamaican	211 720	138 180	73 545
Danish	170 780	33 795	136 985
Vietnamese	151 410	119 120	32 290

Source: adapted from the Statistics Canada website <http://www12.statcan.ca/english/census01/products/highlight/ETO/Table1.cfm?Lang=E&T=501&GV=1&GID=0>

TABLE 5.4   Visible Minority Population by Age, 2001

	TOTAL	0–14	15–24	25–44	45–64	65–74	75 AND OVER
Total population	100% (29 639 030)	19.4%	13.5%	30.5%	24.4%	7.1%	5.1%
Total visible minority population	13.4% (3 983 845)	23.6%	15.9%	33.9%	19.9%	4.3%	2.3%

Source: Adapted from the Statistics Canada publication "Visible Minority Groups (15), Sex (3) and Age Groups (8) for Population, for Canada, Provinces, Territories, Census Metropolitan Areas and Census Agglomerations, 2001 Census - 20% Sample data," catalogue 95F0036, April 23, 2003.

integrated when I obtained work . . . . We will always return to the same point. Everything comes from this. If you have work, you become connected" (Hartzman, 1991:15). When unemployed, immigrants report they feel a sense of alienation and isolation from other Canadians, with whom they would often have no opportunity for socializing other than the workplace (Seifeddine, 1997).

The case of the Rodriguez family, a Mexican family who immigrated to the United States, is typical of many immigrant couples. Like many other women in similar manual-skill jobs, Mrs. Rodriguez found herself making more money than her husband in the new country. Though he never spoke about it to anyone in his family, Mr. Rodriguez felt like a failure as a husband and a father. His wife was finding it easier to communicate with the larger community, and with the children, who became closer to her. They started to ignore their father, who they saw as rigid and old-fashioned because he could not speak English. Mr. Rodriguez was finding himself more and more marginalized and excluded from the family's daily affairs, and turned to alcohol to forget about his problems (Partida, 1996).

A comparison of American states on the incidence of wife assault shows that social disorganization, which includes migration and other forms of geographical mobility, is significantly linked to wife abuse. Even more closely related to the rate of wife assault is gender inequality, as measured by the extent to which women in each state have parity with men in economic, political, and legal spheres. The higher the status of women in each state, the lower the rate of wife assault found (Strauss, 1994). What these findings suggest is that immigrant women are at a hightered risk of domestic violence. Many immigrant women come from patriarchal cultures where gender inequalities are large and wife abuse is widespread. A cross-national study found that the proportion of women who report being physically or sexually assaulted by their partner ranges from 42 percent to 74 percent in many Latin American, South Asian and African countries, compared to 20 percent in the United States (Fischbach and Herbert, 1997). The struggle to create a home, obtain good employment, and develop language skills often leaves the immigrant couple with little time to deal with issues within the marriage, and adds to the risk of immigrant women being abused by their partner. Mutual dependency and financial worries could also force unhappy couples to stay together and lead to further frustration and violence (O'Hara, 1994).

Employment problems have particular implications for professional first-generation couples. There is a lack of recognition for foreign educational and professional credentials, both by accreditation bodies and Canadian employers, that results in unemployment or underemployment of immigrant professional men and women (Thomas, 1991, Canada Employment and Immigration Advisory Council, 1991). Data from the 1991 Census indicate that, among adults aged 25 to 44 who have worked in the 18 months before the Census, visible minorities (25 percent) were more likely to have a university degree than were other adults (17 percent). Nonetheless, they were less likely to be employed in higher professional (39 percent) and managerial (13 percent) occupations, compared to other adults of similar education (52 percent in professional and 18 percent in managerial positions). Similarly, among those aged 25 to 44 with other types of postsecondary education,

26 percent of visible minorities were in professional, semiprofessional, or managerial occupations, compared with 32 percent of other adults. According to data on the same age group, manual labour jobs were more common among highly educated visible minorities, with 12 percent of those with a postsecondary education and 4 percent with a university degree doing such jobs, compared to 8 percent, and 2 percent, respectively, of other adults (*The Daily*, 1995). Since two-thirds of adults in visible minorities are immigrants who came to Canada since 1972 (*The Daily*, 1995), job discrimination reflected in the above occupational differential is mainly directed toward first-generation Canadians.

One response to unemployment and underemployment among these well-educated couples has been self-employment (Muir, 1988). Using the data from the 1986 Census of Canada, Beaujot et al. (1994) found support among the foreign-born population to the *blocked mobility hypothesis*, which proposes that there are certain labour market disadvantages for groups that create barriers to their social mobility. The authors found immigrants with a non-Canadian bachelor's degree to be twice as likely as those with a similar Canadian education to be self-employed in nonprofessional occupations. The 1991 Census of Canada also shows that the foreign-born population tends to be self-employed at a substantially higher rate than the Canadian-born, and that some, such as the Korean, Greek, and Israeli communities, are extremely entrepreneurial (Razin and Langlois, 1995).

While they provide opportunities to produce income and to have autonomy at work, small businesses are risky, and they survive at the expense of long hours and work shifts that the couple may not have been used to before. Needless to say, these circumstances may lead to frustration and leave them little time to spend together. Among first-generation men, underemployment has been reported to result in feelings of loss, devastation, inadequacy, and despair, putting stress on their relationships with their wives and children (Drachman et al., 1996; Lee and Westwood, 1996). Similarly, highly educated women who become unemployed in Canada report that they find themselves dependent on their husbands for the first time in their lives, and experience a new, relatively powerless relationship with them (Man, 1995).

Family Roles and Relationships

Change in Women's Roles and Marital Relationships When immigrant families move into a new country, new ideologies and structural conditions may challenge the traditional roles of their members and lead to a change in these roles. Perhaps the most crucial catalyst for change in these families has been the labour force participation of women. Women in first-generation families mainly go to work out of economic need and the inability of the husband to support the family and achieve upward mobility on his own (Pedraza, 1991; Anderson and Lynam, 1987; Dossa, 1988; Haddad and Lam, 1988). In fact, married migrant women all over the world often display higher labour force participation rates than all migrant women taken together (Zlotnik, 1995). In Canada, immigrant women are mainly concentrated in low-status non-unionized jobs, such as the garment and needle trades (Thompson, 1990). This is partly due to their lack of language and job training skills (Canada Employment and Immigration Advisory Council, 1991), and partly due to institutionalized racism and the tendency among employers to view workers' ethnic cultural differences as problems (Witterbrood and Robertson, 1991). Espiritu (1997) reports that U.S. employers in the garment, microelectronics, and cannery industries prefer to hire Asian immigrant women because of stereotypical assumptions that immigrant women can afford to work for less, and the patriarchal assumption that women are more suited physiologically to certain kinds of detached and routine jobs.

Ironically, this same exploitation by employers enhances working women's status in first-generation families, and helps them challenge the patriarchal authority of the husband and his traditional role as the breadwinner of the family. Immigrant women in the lower echelons of the Canadian labour force see the demeaning nature of their work as secondary to the benefits of having money they can call their own, developing a sense of competence, breaking isolation, and sharing financial decision-making with their husbands (Anderson and Lynam, 1987). Similarly, wives' sharing of the breadwinning role has led to an increase in the sharing of important family decisions among working-class Italian immigrant couples in Toronto (Haddad and Lam, 1994). Punjabi female cannery workers report that their husbands listen more to them now than before they worked, and that they do not seek his permission anymore when they go somewhere or buy something (Williams, 1989).

This change in women's roles among first-generation families does not come without a cost, however. When men experience unemployment or underemployment, while their wives are able to find employment and acquire new independence, they feel the threat to their breadwinner identity and suffer from damaged self-esteem. The result is often resentment, depression, confused identity, and marital stress and conflict that escalates sometimes into divorce (Gill and Mathews, 1995; Drachman et al., 1996; Espiritu, 1997; Miederna and Nason-Clark, 1989). The following example explains this change in a Korean couple who immigrated to the U.S. in the early 1980s. Mr. Kim was an editor-in-chief for a major local newspaper in Korea, while his wife was a homemaker. In the U.S., however, they opened a dry-cleaning business with the savings they brought with them, and managed the business together. He ironed shirts and pants while she worked as a seamstress and cashier. Soon Mrs. Kim started demanding more participation in housework from her husband. She also felt more competent in managing the store, and often criticized his slow work. The more assertive Mrs. Kim got, the angrier and more noncompliant Mr. Kim became. The years of conflict finally culminated in marital separation (Drachman et al., 1996).

Sharing domestic labour appears to be the largest area of conflict among first-generation couples with a working wife. Husbands are more agreeable about sharing decision-making than domestic labour. In their study of working-class Italian couples in Toronto, Haddad and Lam (1994) found only four couples in which men did a large portion of the domestic labour. Korean wives in the U.S. are highly active in their economic roles, mainly working in the family firm. Yet, their long working hours, which often reach 60 or more per week, are not balanced by their husbands taking on a larger share of housework, nor is there such an expectation from either the husband or the wife. Wives with children may reduce their share by relying on children and cohabiting kin. Otherwise, they are expected to assume responsibility for most of the household tasks (Min, 1992; Kim and Hurh, 1988).

Overburdened working women in first-generation families also often have to perform their domestic tasks in isolation from immediate family, adding to their stress (Haddad and Lam, 1994; Man, 1995). This can seriously jeopardize their health, as strongly evidenced in a cross-national study of the association between international migration and suicide. Role conflict resulting from female participation in the labour force affects suicide even more than does stress related to migration itself (Stack, 1981).

Attitudes toward domestic labour and gender roles are deeply ingrained in the collective mind of the cultural group, and men who try to change them on an individual basis may be faced with criticism or subtle ostracism. This is reflected in the comments of a Somalian refugee husband in Edmonton, who admits that he does all the cleaning and cooking on the weekend, while giving his wife some time off so that she can go out with her friends. He never lets his friends see him doing that, however, neither does he tell them about it because they might call him "a woman" (Langford, unpublished). Fear of ridicule from their community is also what drives Hmong American men to make and sell handicrafts secretly, because these activities have traditionally been done by women (Ceilanshah, 1994).

Generally, a husband's participation in the domestic sphere depends on his gender-role attitudes and his willingness to relinquish patriarchal privileges and make necessary adjustments to the new reality. Among 117 immigrant fathers/husbands in Toronto, Haddad and Lam (1988) found three gender-role categories. The *adapters*, who felt their performance of domestic chores was a necessary strategy to maximize the family well-being, significantly increased their share in domestic labour. The *situationalists*, who believed they simply had no choice in the matter, participated minimally in family work, while the *traditionalists* exhibited no change in gender-role attitude and resisted doing any domestic work. There is also evidence that these gender-role attitudes change with time spent in Canada. Husbands of Indian and Pakistani women who had resided in Canada for a longer period of time helped in housework, unlike the newly arrived who had been in Canada for no more than five years, and who tended to feel ashamed of doing "feminine" work (Siddique, 1977). Often, first-generation working women themselves may not attempt to openly challenge the husband's gender-role attitudes, or seek radical restructuring of the traditional family system. Gender intersects with ethnicity, race, and social class to produce a sense of powerlessness that these women experience as low self-esteem (Kuppersmith, 1994).

Intergenerational Conflict As Trussman (1991) argues, young people *enculturate*, whereas adults, who come to a new society with clearly defined identities, can only *acculturate*. **Enculturation** refers to the process by which one learns one's own culture whereas **acculturation** refers to the process of incorporating aspects of other cultures into one's own culture. While the first generation may be secure in its identity, the second generation is trapped between two worlds with sometimes conflicting sets of values (Swanson, 1996). They have been described as the generation that plays a transitional role between the old and the new culture, often falling victim to both (Elkholy, 1990). The cultural gap that migration creates between first-generation parents and their adolescent children, and the resulting intergenerational conflict, is well-documented in the literature (Noivo, 1993; Rosenthal, 1984; Ambert, 1992). Among Indian Canadian families of British Columbia, Srivastava (1975) found that second-generation adolescents consider their parents too authoritarian and demanding of more influence in choice of their marriage partners. They are questioning the relevance of traditional Indian ways, and favouring Canadian patterns because they are important to the teen culture.

One major area of conflict between first-generation parents and their adolescent children has been dating. While chaperoned or group dating may be acceptable in some cultures from which parents originate, the North American style of dating is often not a socially accepted behaviour. Consequently, it causes parents much concern and anxiety. An Edmonton study of second-generation youth actually identifies "dating" as the issue around which most conflict with parents revolves (Seifeddine, 1994). Parents are particularly concerned about the daughters' dating because the family honour may be affected by her sexual conduct, and, therefore, they tend to use a double standard in allowing their son more freedom than his sister (Vasta, 1980; Haddad and Smith, 1996; Swanson, 1996, Basran, 1993; Dhruvaragan, 1993).

When it comes to marriage, first-generation parents continue to prefer and encourage in-group marriage among their children to preserve their ethnicity. This is particularly so for daughters. Ahmed et al. (1996) explain this phenomenon among South Asian Muslims in America. Since children normally follow the father's faith, a daughter's children are considered more likely to lose their Islamic affiliation, and parents try to forbid their daughter from marrying a non-Muslim. First-generation parents resort to many measures to ensure endogamy for their children. When a Lao male is ready for marriage, he is introduced to appropriate Lao women by family and relatives, and if he chooses a mate, he may proceed with a traditional courtship which involves visiting the girl in her home (Muir, 1988). Arab Muslim parents organize annual conventions of ethnic and religious clubs, and use large wedding ceremonies as opportunities to bring young people together (Swanson, 1996). Others have picked up the custom prevalent among South Asians to advertise for a partner in Islamic magazines under Matrimonials, listing the qualities desired in the mate (Haddad and Smith, 1996).

The practice of arranging for children's marriage to young men and women from their home country is still common among many South Asian parents. It has caused problems for many Canadian-born young Asians, because of the difficulty for the foreign-born husband, in particular, to adjust to the way of life of his Western-raised wife (Ahmad et al., 1993). Today, while still preferring their offspring to marry within a field of eligibles defined by class, religion, and caste, many Indo-Canadian parents accept the fact that their children will not be subjected to arranged marriages (Basran, 1993; Dhruvanaja, 1993). The double standard in dating and marital choice has left many young Muslim women in Canada with fewer eligible mates and little choice but to marry outside their faith, at an estimated rate of 30 percent (Haddad and Smith, 1996).

Later Generations and Family Change

As mentioned earlier, there are few studies on families of second and later generations that examine the influence of ethnicity on family life. The existing evidence suggests, however, that ethnic identity does not necessarily disappear, although it may change in later generations. Ethnicity continues to play an important role in the life of second and even third generations (Kourvetaris, 1997). Three types of second-generation families have been identified: 1) families who have completely abandoned the ethnic way of life; 2) families who have only identified with working-class families who live in ethnic colonies; and 3) (the most prevalent) families who have adjusted to living between two worlds, taking what they consider to be the best of each. While ethnicity as a way of life may disappear with the third generation, it continues to exist as a symbol of heritage and ethnic pride.

Findings of one study that examined ethnic change in a random sample of 477 French Canadians provide further evidence that acculturation is a complex, multidimensional process, and does not culminate in rejection of ethnicity among later generations. Various modes of ethnic change were found. Most respondents scored high on French ethnic affiliation, while scoring moderately to moderately high on acculturative tendency. In other words, while they were more likely to use French in social interaction, have close French friends, and be married to French partners, they were also equally attached to both French and English Canadian cultures and likely to support cultural exchange (Laroche et al., 1996).

Families in Poverty

Regardless of ethnic identity or culture, poverty has profound effects for families, especially the children. The context of poverty is important in two ways. First, the context of poverty is always in relation to some larger system of social class and stratification. Second, the context of poverty involves judgments of absolute deprivation and relative deprivation. For example, if one lived in a well-to-do neighborhood, relative deprivation might be judged by the type of car one owns; in a poor neighborhood it might be judged by owning or not owning any type of car.

Poverty needs to be examined in the broader context of social inequality and stratification. Since the earliest times, historians have documented inequalities within social systems. In many cases these inequalities may be passed on from one generation to another, such as being born to a particular caste in a caste system or other type of ascriptive closed system. However, even

more open, achievement-oriented systems may maintain class distinctions intergenerationally by the distribution of wealth such that sources of social mobility for children are dependent on the parent's wealth. There are academic arguments that social class background and values predominate in the distribution of resources. There is also the view that every society holds certain positions and occupations as more important than others due to prolonged training or skills, and rewards are therefore stratified accordingly (Davis and Moore, 1945). Most students are familiar with the measurement of *socio-economic status* (SES) as an attempt to calibrate where any person falls in the stratification system based on the person's education level, occupational prestige, and yearly income. Every society is stratified, but the degree of intergenerational mobility is often used to characterize whether the system is a caste-like system with little or no social mobility, or is a highly mobile system that is truly based on a person's abilities and motivation. Canada, like the United States, has an ideology that supports social mobility and equality of opportunity for all. In such systems, we would expect to find that intergenerational social mobility is high. However, absolute levels of poverty may so affect a child's chances of success in completing school, acquiring skills, and attending university, that even though opportunities may be based on merit and performance, the child is nonetheless excluded due to the level of poverty.

The second context of poverty is its dual meaning as both relative poverty and absolute poverty. A person may be poor *relative* to other people but not be poor in absolute terms. In absolute terms, a poor person is simply not able to afford necessities of life such as adequate food or shelter. Both aspects of poverty are reflected in the criterion used by Statistics Canada to measure poverty. The average Canadian household spends 38.5 percent of its total income on food, clothing, and shelter. This figure provides the basis for deciding where the **low income cut-off (LICO)** should be set. In general, the figure is set about 50 percent higher, at the point where a household must spend 58.5 percent of the total income on necessities. The amount of the LICO, of course, varies with the number of people in the household (see Table 5.5). Families living on the poverty line must often do without what they want or need, and those living below this LICO are often termed "poor." It must be understood that

Statistics Canada does not see the LICO as a measure of poverty but only as a relational characterization of the families that are less well off. On the other hand, the Federal/Provincial/Territorial Working Group on Social Development Research and Information has been mandated to design an absolute measure of poverty based on a "basket of goods and services" required for basic living. The work was completed in May 2003 and initial data using the Market Based Measure (MBM) suggests that it will provide a more conservative indicator of poverty in families. In addition, Statistics Canada is developing a measure termed the Low Income Measure (LIM) that is computed as 50 percent of median family income adjusted for the size of the family. No analyses of the 2001 Census data are available using this newer measure (see Statistics Canada, Cat. No. 13F0019X1B).

Many societal influences determine the number and the characteristics of people who are poor: wage levels, income distribution to different class levels, economic cycles of prosperity and recession. Individual factors such as educational attainment, employability, and physical or mental handicaps are relevant as well.

Effects of the first three societal influences are seen in recent fluctuations in poverty rates. In 1969, 23.1 percent of all Canadians had incomes below the LICO. By 1980, this figure had dropped to 15.3 percent. It jumped to 18.2 in 1984, fell to 13.6 percent in 1989, and rose to 16.0 in 1991, slightly fell again to 15 percent in 1993, only to rise to 17.1 percent in 1994 and 17.8 percent in 1995. The number of persons with income below the low income cut-offs in 1995 was estimated at 5 205 000. Many of these families had children; 21 percent of children under 18 lived in low-income families in 1995, up from 19.5 percent in 1994 (Ross et al., 1996).

These changes were primarily due to fluctuations in the economy. The 1996 Statistics Canada Income Survey indicated that almost half of Canada's poor under the age of 65 are *working poor*. This is mainly due to the fact that the minimum wage is no longer a living wage. In 1992, in almost all provinces, a 40-hour work week at minimum wage was below the poverty line. The federal minimum wage provided only 55 percent of the poverty line in 1992, which means that almost half of the minimum-wage workers were poor. Economic

TABLE 5.5 **National Council of Welfare Estimates of Statistics Canada's Before-Tax Low Income Cut-Offs (1992 Base) for 2002***

FAMILY SIZE	COMMUNITY SIZE				
	CITIES OF 500 000+	100 000– 499 999	30 000– 99 999	LESS THAN 30 000	RURAL AREAS
1	$19 256	$16 516	$16 401	$15 261	$13 307
2	$24 069	$20 644	$20 501	$19 077	$16 633
3	$29 934	$25 676	$25 497	$23 725	$20 687
4	$36 235	$31 080	$30 864	$28 719	$25 041
5	$40 505	$34 743	$34 501	$32 103	$27 993
6	$44 775	$38 406	$38 138	$35 486	$30 944
7+	$49 043	$42 069	$41 774	$38 870	$33 896

* Based on inflation of 2.2 percent from 2001 to 2002.

Source: Adapted from National Council of Welfare, Fact Sheet, http://www.ncwcnbes.net/htmdocument/principales/povertyline.htm.

conditions also had an impact on the welfare poor. Social assistance benefits were about 15 to 50 percent of the average income in most provinces in 1994, and they continue to decline (Cohen, 1997).

The marital relationships of poor couples often suffer, when despair, fear, and hostility become their dominant feelings. Unemployment is associated with low levels of marital and family satisfaction. Family harmony, husband–wife consensus, and communication and solidarity are weakened when stress and conflict become more frequent (Voydanoff, 1991). These tendencies worsen when families live in neighbourhoods where there is widespread poverty, inadequate housing, poor health, hunger, and neighbourhood disorganization (Zimmerman and Chilman, 1988). This weakening of the family structure is particularly tragic because people living in poverty badly *need* family solidarity. Inevitably, the results are higher rates of family violence (Gelles and Straus, 1988) and of separation and divorce (Voydanoff, 1991).

We do not need the LICO or the LIM to tell us that many children and their families have low income. Table 5.6 clearly shows that lone parent families with children under 18 only have on average about 37 percent of the income of married couples with children under 18. The highest minimum wage in Canada is for British Columbia at $8 per hour (2001) and the lowest is PEI at $5.80 per hour. Assuming an eight-hour day

and seven-day week, a minimum wage worker would earn between $16 640 and $12 064 per year.

Research on divorced mothers has generally found that the greater their economic distress, the greater their social adjustment problems (Voydanoff, 1991). Most have to move into poorer neighbourhoods and are forced to change residences more often than two-parent families do, a circumstance that limits their ability to develop a neighbourhood support group. Like other poor parents, lone mothers are more often worried, dissatisfied with their lives, and psychologically distressed; in comparison with other mothers, they make more use of community mental-health services (McLanahan and Booth, 1991).

There is also a high poverty rate among new Canadians who arrived in Canada after 1979 (33 percent), but the incidence of poverty decreases with the amount of time spent in Canada. Adding to the financial difficulties they experience in the early settlement period, immigrants and refugees now have to pay a head tax of $975 (Cohen, 1997).

Poverty among the Old and the Young

Most seniors do not work, and their poverty rate has tended to be high, despite any savings they may have, because of inflation—the 1950 dollar is worth about one-tenth of a 1990 dollar. In 1969, 41 percent of

TABLE 5.6   Median Family Income (1995 and 2000) by Selected Family Type

FAMILY TYPE	INCOME (NO. OF INDIVIDUALS)	
	1995	2000
Census family	$ 51 150 (7 837 865)	$ 55 016 (8 371 025)
Married couple families	$ 56 851 (5 779 720)	$ 61 607 (5 901 425)
Married couple no children	$ 44 837 (2 244 085)	$ 48 544 (2 431 720)
Married couple with children under 18 years old	$ 61 719 (2 663 545)	$ 67 505 (2 545 755)
Common law	$ 48 598 (920 640)	$ 61 748 (1 158 405)
Lone parent families	$ 26 057 (1 137 505)	$ 30 791 (1 311 190)
Lone parent with children under 18 years old	$ 20 520 (734 010)	$ 24 818 (819 715)

Source: Adapted from Statistics Canada, Cat. No. 97F0020XCBO1003.

elderly families (headed by persons aged 65 and older) were poor, but this proportion dropped to 22 percent by 1980 as the payments provided by Old Age Security pensions, which began in 1951, and Guaranteed Income Supplements, initiated in 1966, became increasingly adequate for meeting the needs of the aged. During the 1980s, the incomes of elderly couples improved greatly, thanks to increases in government social security and pension plan provisions. The poverty rate of couples over age 64, which was about 15 percent higher than the rate for childless younger couples in 1980, fell until the rates for both were about 9 percent in 1991. Elderly unattached women (over age 64) were much more often poor than were elderly unattached men (47.4 versus 33.4 percent) in 1991, and their rate even increased to 50.6 percent in 1995. The poverty rate of elderly women is much higher than that of elderly men because women less often have private pension coverage, and tend to live longer. (National Council of Welfare, 1988, 1992, 1993; Cohen, 1997).

Such a discrepancy was also true for younger unattached women and men, whose poverty rates were 37.6 and 30.5 percent, respectively. While the elderly often experience poverty because they can no longer work, young adults (under 25 years) are often poor because they cannot find work or cannot qualify for well-paid jobs. In 1986, 30 percent of young families (under age 25) were poor, as compared with 11 percent of families headed by 35- to 44-year-olds. The incidence of poverty was twice as high for unattached individuals under age 25 as it was for those in the 35 to 44 age group (48 versus 22 percent). In 1995, the 18 to 24 age group was identified as a high-risk group, with an astounding poverty rate of 65.9 percent. What is more alarming is the poverty rate among women in this age group compared to the men's rate (71.4 percent versus 57.6 percent). Among single mothers under 25, the overwhelming majority (90 percent) were poor in 1995 (Cohen, 1997).

Among the elderly and the young, more women than men live in poverty (National Council of Welfare, 1988), in part because of changes in marriage and family life during the 1970s and 1980s. Although they made up 51 percent of the population, women represented 59 percent of the poor in both 1975 and 1987. Anti-poverty programs during this 12-year period clearly failed to reduce the gender difference. The continuing

high poverty rates are caused by motherhood and child-care responsibilities, the inequalities women experience in the labour market, and the financial consequences of separation, divorce, and widowhood (National Council of Welfare, 1990).

As the story in Box 5.1 suggests, many women at the deepest level of poverty are young single mothers who often have little schooling (National Council of Welfare, 1990; 1992). Divorce is much more impoverishing for women than for men. Typically, mothers are awarded child custody, and while only 9 percent of divorced men not having child custody are poor, 58 percent of divorced women with custody of their children have incomes less than the LICO. The proportion of those who are poor increases with the number of children, from 43 percent for mothers of one child to 89 percent for mothers of four or more. Clearly, the court-ordered spousal and child support payments in Canada are too low. In 1986, they averaged just 18 percent of the before-tax income of the husbands, leaving these men living well above the poverty line. But even low support payments make a difference; 75 percent of divorced mothers not receiving them lived in poverty, compared to 58 percent of those who did (National Council of Welfare, 1990).

Poverty among Children

Because so many children have poor mothers, the rate of poverty among children is very high. In 1994, 19.5 percent of Canadian children lived in poverty (Ross et al., 1996). Child poverty is the most damaging of all types of poverty to the individual and the society. It is costly in terms of wasted lives, wasted talent and motivation, the resulting high costs of physical and mental health care, and expense to the police, judicial, and penal systems. Table 5.7 shows that child poverty is extremely high (57 percent) among lone parent female families. Figure 5.1 shows that while 25.4 percent of all children are below the poverty line, particular groups such as aboriginal children and visible minority children are at much greater risk.

For society, the most serious consequences of poverty result from its physical, psychological, and social damage to children. The effects of poverty on physical health begin before birth: people born into poverty face a greater risk of death, mental retardation, cerebral palsy, epilepsy, visual defects, and low IQ, and,

Research Insights: When Young Girls Have Babies

Nancy Doherty lives in a dreary strip of high-rise apartments known for cheap rents and cockroaches. Eighteen years of age and on welfare, she is the mother of eight-month-old Jessica. In November, squeezed between the pressures of single parenthood and the demands of attending high school full time, Doherty dropped out of Grade 11. "It was real easy at first getting up at 5 a.m., out of the door at 7 to take Jessica to day care and then off to school," she says. "But it caught up with me. I was just so tired and I was always late . . . I just couldn't help it." The future frightens her: "I'm always thinking, what would happen if I die?" she says. "I have no daddy around for Jessica. I mean, I have nothing."

For teenage mothers, the resolve to build a better life for their children often alternates with despair that they are too young—and powerless—to do so. According to the latest statistics, more than 60 percent of the 39 000 Canadian teens who became pregnant in 1989 kept their babies. But up to 80 percent of teenage mothers are the sole providers for their children; at least one in five has used services for abused women, while one in six has been treated for drug or alcohol addiction. Adrift in a working world that demands expertise and experience that they do not have, and unable even to legally sign a lease until age 18, many young single mothers live in poverty.

Often the odds are against them. Belinda Stuart's parents divorced when she was eight. Her relationship with her mother "fell apart" when she was 14, and she left home to live more than two years either with friends or on the street. During that time, she was raped and had an abortion. Then relatives in Ottawa took her in. "That's the way I see life. When I got pregnant, I said, 'Well, figures.' I fall into little statistics all the time. The homeless one, the one that's beaten, the one who's raped."

Only 12 public high schools in all of Canada operate subsidized day-care facilities on school grounds and offer programs designed for young mothers. One 20-year-old mother who has a 10-month-old daughter with Down's syndrome says, "Doctors look down on teenage moms. You have to convince them your child is sick." Most teen mothers agree that while a 25-year-old can freely discipline a child in public, a 17-year-old cannot. "One smack and they take your child away," says one.

Source: Adapted from Fulton, 1993:32–33.

Figure 5.1   **Aboriginal Children, Visible Minority Children, and Children with Disabilities (0–14 Years) Living in Poverty**

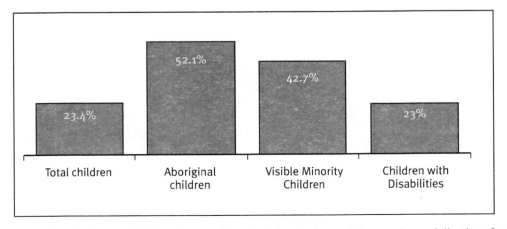

Source: Aboriginal Children in Poverty in Urban Communities: Social exclusion and the growing racialization of poverty in Canada: Notes for Presentation to Subcommittee on Children and Youth at Risk of the Standing Committee on Human Resources Development and the Status of Persons with Disabilities on Wednesday, March 19th 2003, John Anderson, Canadian Council on Social Development, (http://www.ccsd.ca/pr/2003/aboriginal.htm).

TABLE 5.7   Child Poverty Rates among Children in Female Lone-Parent Families, by Province, Canada, 1980–1989

	1980	1981	1982	1983	1984	1985	1986	1987	1988	1989
					INCIDENCE (%)					
Atlantic Provinces	58.0	74.0	71.2	69.0	74.2	70.1	68.4	70.6	66.2	65.7
Newfoundland	60.8	71.5	77.1	80.8	63.9	72.2	67.9	77.2	68.9	66.5
PEI	44.4	58.7	58.3	68.1	56.7	57.5	48.5	60.0	49.5	52.5
Nova Scotia	57.9	72.8	67.9	62.8	74.5	67.7	66.8	62.3	62.1	62.6
New Brunswick	59.1	78.1	73.6	70.1	80.5	72.8	73.7	76.6	70.6	70.2
Quebec	64.8	57.0	71.7	68.0	70.7	68.3	63.4	70.2	60.2	57.4
Ontario	57.4	57.8	62.0	64.0	63.4	65.5	55.8	51.3	52.6	49.7
Prairie Provinces	54.1	52.8	56.2	67.7	64.9	62.5	60.0	62.2	63.3	65.8
Manitoba	60.4	65.8	62.4	68.8	53.3	66.4	70.0	58.3	66.2	69.5
Saskatchewan	60.7	66.4	52.4	53.6	67.3	59.5	64.8	67.5	66.9	62.8
Alberta	50.1	40.0	54.3	65.0	67.6	61.8	53.8	62.0	60.5	65.0
British Columbia	56.1	60.7	62.1	51.2	63.2	64.5	67.0	71.8	66.0	62.1
CANADA	58.9	58.2	64.2	64.8	66.6	65.9	61.1	63.3	59.4	57.5

Source: Prepared by the Canadian Council on Social Development, using data from Statistics Canada, Cat. 13-569-XPB.

accordingly, have more learning disabilities and behavioural problems (Greene, 1991; Ross et al. 2000).

A 1990 Ontario Health Survey found that teens in low-income families were twice as likely to smoke and almost three times as likely to use alcohol as were wealthy teens. Moreover, 54 percent of the poor teens reported always using birth control compared to 68 percent of the wealthy, and these latter were twice as likely to use a condom. Perhaps most alarming is the survey finding that the number of teenage women who had been pregnant in the last five years in low-income families was almost five times higher than that of other teens, at a rate of 18 percent. Another factor, and a probable cause of some of these problems, is that as many as 15 percent of poor children chronically experience hunger and malnourishment. It is estimated that almost a quarter of a million children (225 000) per month were using food banks during the early months of 1991, while others were obtaining food from soup kitchens, drop-in centres, and breakfast programs (Ross, et al. 1996).

SUMMARY

■ The major *analytic* sources of variability in marriage and family practices in Canadian society are ethnicity, religion, social class, rural–urban lifestyle, and regional differences.

■ The effect of social class influences on the family is clearly seen in studies of poverty. Divorce makes lone-mother families poor, and poor families often divorce.

■ Poverty is related to age, with higher incidences among adults who are young and who are elderly. While poverty among the elderly has declined thanks to government support payments first introduced in the 1960s, the depressed economic conditions of recent years have increased poverty among young people.

- The deepening impoverishment of single mothers has increased the number of poor children in Canadian society. The effects of poverty on children raise serious concerns about their future adjustment as adults, and about how their growing numbers will affect the future of Canada.

KEY TERMS

Acculturation (107)
AmerNative Canadians (99)
Enculturation (107)
Low income cut-off (LICO) (108)

QUESTIONS FOR REVIEW

1. What are the most important sources of variation in Canadian family life today, and what aspects of family life do they affect?

2. What parallels do you see between the changes now taking place in Aboriginal Canadian families and in white Canadian families?

3. There has been a prolonged debate in Canada about how we can conceptualize and measure poverty in Canada. What role do the LICO and LIM play in measuring poverty?

4. To what extent do you think "poverty" is relative to the standard of living in a country and to what extent does it represent an absolute set of basic requirements for sustenance?

QUESTIONS FOR DISCUSSION

1. If we assume that a particular family form is "well adapted," to *whom* or *what* is it adapted? Discuss how the ways that Canadian marriage and family practices have changed since 1960 are adaptive, and the ways that these changes are maladaptive to quality of family life.

2. In what ways might the traditional Native Canadian or the Hindu family system be better adapted than the typical Canadian family to the conditions of urban life today? In what ways would these traditional families be less well adapted?

3. Since Canadian society is not yet willing, or able, to ensure that each person in this country has a decent standard of living, which groups' needs should be provided for first, and which groups' needs should be considered last?

SUGGESTED READINGS

Goode, William J. 1970. *World Revolution and Family Patterns*. New York: Macmillan. This classic work on the sociology of the family argues that worldwide urbanization is causing a massive decline in the variability of family and kinship systems around the world. It contains excellent discussions of family change in the West, China, India, Africa, and other parts of the world.

Greene, Barbara. 1991. *Canada's Children: Investing in Our Future*. Ottawa: Supply and Services Canada. This report by the Parliamentary Subcommittee on Poverty provides excellent recent and detailed information on the situation of children in LICO families today, and on the effects of poverty on children.

Ishwaran, K. 1980. *Canadian Families: Ethnic Variations*. Toronto: McGraw-Hill Ryerson. Brief sketches are provided on the family systems of 13 different ethnic or religious groups in Canada, written by scholars who have made special studies of each. Chapters are included on Mennonite, Doukhobor, Polish, Japanese, and French Canadian families, among others.

National Council of Welfare. This government-funded organization produces a dozen or more reports every year that detail the most recent LICOs for different categories of people who live in poverty. You will find them in the Government Publications section of your library or at http://www.ncwcnbes.net/.

CHAPTER 6

The Formation of Intimate Relationships: Dating and Sex

After studying this chapter, you should be able to do the following:

- Describe the main changes in dating conventions in Canada over the course of the present century.
- Identify four important functions of dating.
- Discuss four main areas in which problems associated with dating arise.
- Summarize the findings of research into violence in dating relationships.
- Identify the factors that contribute to, and the stages of, relationship formation, stability, and dissolution.
- Describe how stage models of close relationships explain the development of interpersonal relationships.
- Outline the major trends in attitudes and behaviour with respect to changing sex standards in our society.
- Describe the broad social and cultural context within which these changing sex standards are taking place.
- Identify Reiss's four premarital sex standards, and describe recent changes in young people's adherence to them.
- List three significant gender differences in attitudes toward love.

Introduction

As we discussed in Chapter 1, **intimacy** is the close relationship between two people, characterized by interdependence, need fulfillment, and emotional attachment. Traditionally in our society, many people seek close relationships that result in marriage. But not all intimate relationships between individuals lead to marriage, and today an increasing number of couples are forming intimate relationships in which the goal of marriage is not paramount. The majority of young people, however, still end up in marital relationships.

Based on a search of scholarly publications and books, Moss and Schwebel (1993) found 61 unique definitions of *intimacy*. Using this research, they arrived at the following definition:

> Intimacy in enduring romantic relationships is determined by the level of commitment and positive affective, cognitive and physical closeness one experiences with a partner in a reciprocal (although not necessarily symmetrical) relationship (1993: 33).

Five components of intimacy are specified by this definition: commitment, affective intimacy, cognitive intimacy, physical intimacy, and mutuality. These components will be examined in this and succeeding chapters. **Dating** consists of "going-together" activities and interaction that enable couples to explore varying levels

115

of interpersonal intimacy and commitment. **Courtship** consists of "going-together" activities and interaction that enable couples to explore deeper levels of interpersonal intimacy and commitment in order to determine if marriage is feasible and desirable for them. Young people at earlier ages and at lower levels of intimacy typically regard their activities as dating, and as fulfilling the purpose of recreation or "having fun." Those older and at deeper levels of intimacy are more likely to regard their activities as courtship, and as fulfilling the purpose of mate selection. One person in a relationship may interpret these going-together activities as "dating," while the other person interprets them as "courtship." *Love* occupies a prominent position in attitudes towards dating, courtship, and marriage.

The Dating Continuum

Adolescence is a period of growing interest in and interaction with persons of the other sex. The onset of puberty is associated with clearly marked differences between the sexes, and an increasing concern with intimacy. According to Brehm et al. (2002), the search for intimacy became an important characteristic of the early 1980s. Willard Waller (1937) presented one of the first sociological descriptions of dating. He differentiated between *dating,* seen as a "dalliance" relationship or recreational activity, and *courtship,* defined as a serious relationship stressing qualities related to personality and character. Today, the distinction between dating and courtship is being replaced with the concept of a dating continuum. The **dating continuum** consists of various identifiable stages from least serious to most serious (casual dating, frequent dating, steady dating, engagement).

Conventions of Dating

Over the past century, the conventions of dating have changed considerably in both Canada and the United States. We can distinguish three broad periods. First, prior to the 1920s, the dating system was quite restrictive and closely regulated. Dating activities were often supervised by parents or chaperones, and most often took place in the female's home. Dating was normally interpreted as a serious commitment to marriage.

The second period encompasses the years 1920 to 1960. Shortly after the First World War, dating practices began to change significantly. Dating became less strictly supervised. Dating activities were still governed by a fairly extensive system of rules, expectations, and values derived from parents and peer groups, but standards of acceptable behaviour varied widely, and depended on the individual's level of personal involvement in the relationship. According to Murstein (1980), changes in dating conventions were generally associated with an increase in urban living, the availability of the automobile as a means of transportation without parental supervision, the availability of the telephone as a means of communication without parental supervision, the increasing popularity of co-educational colleges, the changing status of women, and greater opportunities to participate in leisure-time activities.

The third broad period of dating practices stretches from 1960 to the present. Beginning in the 1960s, new standards governing dating behaviour developed. As Bowman and Spanier (1978) point out, these standards are marked by three characteristics. First, dating now allows *more freedom for females.* The dating system has changed from being largely male-dominated to one in which females possess greater freedom to initiate dating contacts. In the previous period, men were expected to call and make arrangements for dating activities, provide the means of transportation, and take responsibility for expenses. Although females experience greater freedom in this area today, total equality has not been achieved. Laner and Ventrone (1998) found that changing social norms have had little effect on male and female roles, especially in early relationship development.

Second, dating today is characterized by *less formality.* Advance planning is no longer as important as it once was. Couples tend to participate in more spur-of-the-moment activities that require little planning or expense, but place more emphasis on opportunities for interaction. Casual dress is more common.

The third characteristic of dating practices today is the *increase in group activities.* Group activities that take place on short notice often provide the context in which young people meet, form friendships, and develop intimate relationships.

Francis (1992) describes the terminology that high school students now use in referring to dating experiences. *Hanging out* means that they are friends. *Seeing each other* implies that they have a romantic interest, but not an exclusive relationship. *Going together* suggests that the relationship is exclusive. Francis supports the findings of Bowman and Spanier that many dating activities take place in groups, and tend to be informal in nature. Girls call boys as frequently as boys call girls. Who pays for activities depends on who has the money. In senior high school, however, adolescents begin to experiment with developing close relationships that are more serious and intense. Nett (1993) suggests that the term that covers the various patterns known as courting, dating or getting together is courtship.

Dating experiences today range from traditional dating conventions to the more informal "getting together" approach. The movement toward more informal dating practices with fewer rules and regulations places a greater responsibility on the young person to make personal decisions. Ramu suggests that "[m]odern courtship practices continue to involve anticipatory socialization, attempts to cultivate self-esteem, sexual experimentation, participation in recreational activities and the opportunity to develop criteria for the selection of potential mates" (1993:45).

Functions of Dating

Although the trend in dating practices may be toward less formal and more group activities, dating continues to serve young people as a channel through which to develop personal interests in one another and to engage in activities that inevitably move toward increasing levels of emotional closeness and commitment. Skipper and Nass (1966) identified four important functions of dating or "going-together" activities. First, dating can be a form of *recreation*. Particularly for younger people, the purpose of dating is often simply to have a good time. The focus is on activities that provide entertainment and immediate enjoyment. Dating is expressive (an end in itself) rather than instrumental (a means to an end, such as marriage).

Second, dating can be a form of *socialization*. It provides an opportunity for males and females to become better acquainted, to learn how to respond to members of the other sex, and to learn how to adjust to one another. The dating relationship differs from a brother–sister relationship in terms of style and level of interaction, and it may be particularly important for those who have no other-sex siblings of similar age. Dating also

provides information about one's own personality in a variety of situations and relationships, and may highlight areas in need of change or improvement.

Third, dating can be a form of *status grading* or *status achievement*. Dating a highly desirable partner may raise a person's status and prestige in his peer group. In societies in which kin members arrange marriage, the family performs the status function, since the family determines the category of person an individual will marry. In Canada, where autonomous selection prevails, the dating system helps to determine the desirability of persons, and hence their status.

Fourth, dating can be a means of *mate selection*. It provides an opportunity for unmarried young people to associate with each other and, over a period of time, develop intimate relationships leading to cohabitation, engagement, and marriage. The function of mate selection may not be a conscious goal at younger ages or at the earlier stages of dating, but it becomes increasingly important at older ages and at later stages of dating that involve deeper levels of commitment.

Based on a sample of high school students in three different cities in southwestern Ontario, Peters (1980) found that for most students, dating served the function of recreation (41 percent) or socialization (29 percent). No students said that they dated for the purpose of popularity or prestige, but some students may have been unconscious of this motivation, and those who were conscious of it may have been reluctant to admit it. Few viewed dating from the perspective of other-sex comparison or mate selection (11 percent), although more females (15 percent) than males (5 percent) dated in order to discover if their partner would be suitable as a spouse.

In a study of older adolescents, Miller et al. (1993) found three general dating goals: 1) avoiding conflict in a relationship; 2) maintaining emotional intimacy with one's partner; and 3) achieving narcissistic goals, such as making a positive impression or engaging in sexual intimacy. It appears that older adolescents are more willing than those who are younger to recognize narcissistic goals in dating.

The Process of Relationships

The development of interpersonal intimacy has shifted from formal, structured relationships to more casual, informal associations that may or may not lead to engagement and marriage. Accordingly, the study of close, interpersonal relationships has shifted from an emphasis on *structure* to a concern with *process*.

The Development and Dissolution of Close Relationships

What are the factors that contribute to the accurate prediction of the stability of premarital relationships, or the prediction of eventual marriage? Lloyd et al. (1984) found that the length of the relationship at the time the study was initiated accounted for a significant proportion of the explained variance. When the length of the relationship was statistically controlled, four variables remained as significant predictors of relationship stability at three- and seven-month follow-up periods: level of involvement, reward level for self, reward level for partner, and perceived chance of marriage. The researchers concluded that these four variables might represent "both an investment in the relationship and an assessment of its future potential which, irrespective of its length, predicts who will remain in the relationship and who will break apart" (Lloyd et al., 1984:75).

In a sample from a western Canadian university, Kingsbury and Minda (1988) grouped relationships into three distinct periods: a growth period (initiation and building); a maintenance period (continued interaction); and a relationship termination period (deterioration and termination). They then classified their subjects into one of these three groupings and compared them on seven relationship characteristics. Subjects in the growth and maintenance groups scored significantly higher than those in the termination group on perceived emotional, sexual, intellectual, and recreational intimacy, as well as on measures of self-disclosure (trust), equity, and relationship satisfaction. Few differences were found between males and females. These findings suggest that intimacy, self-disclosure, and relationship satisfaction are essential if relationships are to continue.

Lloyd and Cate (1985) investigated the role that conflict plays in the development and dissolution of intimate relationships. Their study outlined the developmental trend of conflict from casual dating to the dissolution of the relationship. The researchers applied

a model of five relationship stages for both males and females. The stages were as follows:

Casual The partners see each other but do not identify themselves as a couple.

Couple The partners identify themselves as a couple, but have not reached total commitment to the relationship.

Commitment The partners demonstrate total commitment to the relationship.

Uncertain The partners are not sure about the future of the relationship.

Certain The partners are sure the relationship will end.

Lloyd and Cate found that the developmental trend of conflict was significant through these five stages over time. On a scale ranging from 5 to 45, the level of conflict increased significantly from the casual stage (mean=10.34) to the couple stage (mean=14.67) to the committed stage (mean=17.72) to the uncertain stage (mean=25.61). It then leveled off at the certain stage (mean=25.56). The largest mean increase in conflict occurred between the committed stage and the uncertain stage. The same pattern was found for both males and females.

Lloyd and Cate surmised that increasing conflict beyond the couple stage may indicate the following: 1) problems in negotiating conflict; 2) the discovery of incompatible criteria for a relationship; or 3) the desire for a long-term commitment. These findings suggest that conflict is an important variable in the differentiation of relationships that reach a high level of interdependence and eventually result in marriage, and those that reach a high level of interdependence yet subsequently dissolve.

The breakup of close relationships has received growing research attention, but there are few studies based on data collected from both ex-partners. Sprecher (1994) collected data from both partners of 47 heterosexual couples who broke up while they were participating in a larger study. First, partners were compared with respect to their perspectives on the breakup and on their emotional reactions. She found a lack of similarities in the emotional responses to the breakup, with the exception of guilt, resentment, and loneliness. "The more a respondent experienced each of these emotions, the less his or her partner experienced the same emotion"

(Sprecher, 1994:208). This may be because the partner who left might experience guilt, but not resentment and loneliness, whereas the partner who was abandoned might experience resentment and loneliness, but not guilt. There was agreement, however, on which partner had made the decision to break up, as well as the reasons for the breakup.

Sprecher also compared men as a group with women as a group to determine if there were gender differences in the understanding of the breakup. An earlier study that measured gender differences (Hill et al., 1976) found that men demonstrated more distress than did women following a breakup, women were more likely to be perceived as the initiator of the breakup, and women found more reasons for the breakup than did men. These gender differences were not replicated in the present study. Men did not get more distressed than did women after the breakup, and no differences were found in the reasons provided for the breakup. Women were more likely to be perceived as the initiator of the breakup, but only by themselves and not by their male partners.

A study of relationship conflict in 75 gay, 51 lesbian, and 108 heterosexual couples found that conflict issues clustered into six groups, including power, social issues, personal flaws, distrust, intimacy, and personal distance. Heterosexual couples argued more frequently regarding social issues, whereas gay and lesbian couples argued more frequently over distrust. The area of distrust may be more problematic for gay men and lesbians because previous partners are more likely to remain in their social support networks. Frequent conflict regarding these six areas was negatively related to each partner's current relationship satisfaction. Frequent arguing about power was also related to a decrease in relationship satisfaction over time. Power may be the most important factor in the chain of events leading to relationship dissolution (Kurdek, 1994).

Stage Models of Close Relationships

To address the question of mate selection more extensively, some theorists have formulated comprehensive models that combine the most useful single factors. These models are based on a sequence of stages (or levels) of interpersonal relationship development by which couples move from acquaintanceship to dating, and ultimately to marriage.

Reiss (1960, 1980) developed a model that focuses on social and cultural factors, but which also attempts to take account of the psychological level of emotions in the development of heterosexual love relationships. Reiss conceptualized the development of love in terms of four processes: *rapport,* or ease in being with someone; *self-revelation,* or disclosure of personal information; *mutual dependency,* or doing things that require the other person to be present; and *intimacy need-fulfillment,* or the desire to share experiences with someone who loves and appreciates us. These four processes are interdependent. They flow into one another positively to strengthen a love relationship, or move negatively to weaken a love relationship.

Larson's model of the development of love is similar to the Reiss model, but more elaborate. It is likewise based on social psychological theory and existing empirical evidence (Larson, 1976a: 133–146). Love is conceptualized as a continuum from low positive affect to high positive affect. The higher the level of positive affect, the more intimate and fulfilling the meaning and dimensionality of positive affect becomes. Larson's model is intended to explain the lifetime of a relationship, including dating, engagement, and marriage. The model contains seven steps (using a staircase analogy): limited rapport, rapport, limited transparency, creative interdependency, crucial transparency, self-discovery, and vital transparency. Each of these steps are defined below:

Step 1 Limited rapport ("This is a person with characteristics that I like.")

Step 2 Rapport ("I feel at ease when with my partner.")

Step 3 Limited transparency ("I feel free to tell my partner things that I would not generally tell anyone else.")

Step 4 Creative interdependency ("My first priority in my life is to build and strengthen my relationship with my partner.")

Step 5 Crucial transparency ("I feel free to tell my partner my most important and most private feelings and thoughts.")

Step 6 Self-discovery ("My relationship with my partner is the primary and most frequent way in which I learn new and important things about myself.")

Step 7 Vital transparency ("Nothing I might do or say can weaken my relationship with my partner.")

Larson describes *surface relationships* as an important stage of positive affect that would typically include steps 1, 2, and 3. Such relationships typically involve frequent interaction, considerable comfort, enjoyment, pleasure, and companionship. These relationships involve a degree of exclusivity and a decision to assign priority to each other. Many marriages are based on this level of positive affect. *Intimate relationships*, in contrast, are characterized by a commitment to build deeper and more resilient levels of positive affect as represented in steps 4 through 7. Love is an individual emotion. Therefore, each partner may be "standing" on different steps, and she or he may move up and down the steps. Marriage may occur at any step, as may a sexual relationship. The higher the step, and the greater the mutuality, the more intimate and meaningful the relationship is.

While Larson defined love simply as a positive affect, other social scientists have attempted to grapple more directly with the nature of love by formulating more complex definitions and models.

The Nature of Love

The criteria for mate selection in societies that emphasize nuclear family systems are based primarily on interpersonal attraction or the romantic ideal of love. In our society, love is the primary prerequisite for getting married, and the key ingredient of successful marriages. Its loss is frequently regarded as the fundamental reason for marital breakups.

Murstein (1986) distinguishes between love as feeling and love as behaviour. He points out that love as feeling is problematic because of its variability, in that "today's passionate love may be regarded tomorrow as yesterday's infatuation" (Murstein, 1986:101). But he also points out that love as behaviour is problematic because it is possible to beat one's spouse and yet claim to love him or her deeply, or to behave lovingly and yet claim mere friendship. Murstein concludes that love should be defined as a judgment or "a decision on the part of an individual to regard another person as a love object, the conditions for defining love varying from one individual to another" (Murstein, 1986:103).

Conducting research about love is difficult because of the elusive nature of the concept itself. Love has been defined in many different ways (see Box 6.1). In an attempt to clarify the concept, social scientists have distinguished among different types of love. Let us begin by considering the romantic ideal of love.

The Romantic Ideal of Love

Romantic love involves a strong physical and emotional attraction to another person, frequently leading to their idealization. Idealization is the irrational overlooking of faults and magnifying of virtues in a person to the point where one creates an unreal picture of the beloved. Consequently, one comes to the unwarranted belief that love can "conquer all"—regardless of the loved one's shortcomings, compatibility problems, opposition of parents, and any social differences. Romantic love is frequently associated with *premarital* relationships, and is *not* what the average husband and wife normally mean when they say that they love each other.

The Western concept of romantic love derives many of its major tenets from the concept of courtly love developed during the Medieval period of history. The major characteristics of courtly love harken back to the Greek and Roman concepts as developed by Plato and Ovid, and rediscovered in Europe during the 10th to 12th centuries. The gradual wider acceptance of the concept of romantic love among people other than those in the ruling classes created problems over the acceptability of extramarital sexuality. Shifting romantic love to the premarital period and viewing it as the basic requirement for marriage gradually resolved this dilemma. This development was associated with the movement away from arranged marriages and toward autonomous marriages (Reiss, 1980).

Upon coming to the New World, many European settlers adopted freer courtship practices than prevailed in Europe. In Canada, the role of romantic love in mate selection has changed over the past 300 years. During the 18th century, marriage contracts demonstrated the importance of negotiating property and monetary considerations in marriage agreements, rather than the importance of love. Although participants chose their own mates, romantic love was not nearly as important as it became later. It was not until the end of the 19th century that romance became well-established as the basis for the choice of marital partners (Nett, 1981). Today, romantic love is viewed by many as an essential

Box 6.1　　　　Current Issues: What Is Love?

Let me not to the marriage of true minds
Admit impediments. Love is not love
Which alters when it alteration finds,

. . . .

Love alters not with his brief hours and weeks,
But bears it out even to the edge of doom.
If this be error and upon me proved,
I never writ, nor no man ever loved.

— *William Shakespeare*

When love is at its best, one loves so much that he
cannot forget.

— *Helen Hunt*

Love is patient, love is kind. It does not envy, it does
not boast, it is not proud. It is not rude, it is not self-
seeking, it is not easily angered, it keeps no record
of wrongs. Love does not delight in evil but rejoices
with the truth. It always protects, always trusts, always hopes, always perseveres.

— *I Corinthians 13:4–7*

'Tis better to have loved and lost, than never to
have loved at all.

— *Tennyson*

Love arrives on tiptoes and bangs the door when it
leaves.

— *Robert Lembke*

Love doesn't make the world go' round. Love is
what makes the ride worthwhile.

— *Franklin P. Jones*

How do I love thee? Let me count the ways,
I love thee to the depth and breadth and height
My soul can reach, when feeling out of sight
For the ends of Being and ideal Grace.

— *Elizabeth Barrett Browning*

component in the development of a happy marriage (Grunebaum, 1997).

Dion and Dion (1991) investigated the relationship between individualism (with its emphasis on personal autonomy and self-fulfillment) and romantic love. Individualism has been documented as a salient cultural value in Canada and the United States. Psychological individualism, reflecting a preference for personal autonomy and self-sufficiency, was associated with a lower likelihood of ever having been in love. Among those who had experienced romantic love, individualism was associated with less affective involvement with their partner. Finally, individualists were less likely to characterize their romantic love experiences as demonstrating tender, deep, and rewarding qualities. "The individualist in love appears therefore to be a relatively emotionally detached lover, without a strong attachment and commitment to the relationship or to his or her partner" (1991:31). Personal enjoyment with different partners tends to be preferred over an exclusive, intense involvement with one partner.

Companionate or Mature Love

The concept of romantic love, important as it is in Western society, does not adequately capture the elements of love that go beyond emotional attachment, physical attraction, and idealization. A number of researchers differentiate romantic love from companionate or mature love. **Companionate (mature) love** includes physical attraction and emotional attachment, but it also involves a realistic assessment of the partner and of the relationship, resulting in both intimacy and commitment.

Walster and Walster, for example, distinguish between passionate love and companionate love. *Passionate love* is defined as "a wildly emotional state, a confusion of feelings: tenderness and sexuality, elation and pain, anxiety and relief, altruism and jealousy." By contrast, *companionate love* is "a lower key emotion. It's friendly affection and deep attachment to someone" (Walster and Walster, 1978:2).

Brehm et al (2002) adopts the differentiation between passionate and companionate love, but argues that they should be viewed as two ends of a continuum. Based on a sample of residents in Calgary, Munro and Adams (1978) found evidence for a differentiation between romantic and conjugal love and for a functional linkage between role structure and attitudes toward love. Unmarried and newly married couples (whose role formation is not clearly developed) displayed high levels of romantic love. When children were born to a couple, their belief in the power of the romantic ideal of love decreased and more rational attitudes associated with conjugal love increased. The researchers postulated that the introduction of children affected the type of role structure influencing the couple. Once the children left home, the couple's interpersonal salience increased, and the partners showed an increase in both romantic attitudes and more rational attitudes toward love.

Sprecher and Regan (1998) surveyed university students to better understand differences between passionate and companionate love. Couples were at various stages of relationships, ranging from exclusive dating to marriage. Unlike previous research, this study found that couples experienced considerable degrees of both kinds of love, and that the two types of love were highly correlated.

What attributes are associated with a more mature conception of love? A sample of undergraduate students at the University of British Columbia was requested to list attributes of love. The five most frequently listed attributes were caring, happiness, friendship, the freedom to talk about anything, and warm feelings. When subjects were provided with a list of attributes and asked to rate how central each feature was to the concept of love, the five attributes receiving the highest ratings were trust, caring, honesty, friendship, and respect (Fehr, 1988).

Fehr (1994) points out that most of the empirical research on love has focused on romantic/passionate love, but that romantic love may not be as salient to the research participants as it is to the researchers. She therefore set out to determine how laypeople respond to prototypes of different types of love, such as friendship love, sexual love, familial love, passionate love, puppy love, and others. This research was conducted with Canadian university students. Subjects were asked to indicate which types of love were most similar to their own views of love. Companionate varieties of love, such as friendship love or familial love, were identified by subjects as being closest to their own definitions of love. In contrast, passionate-like prototypes, such as passionate, infatuation, puppy, and sexual love, were least like subjects' own views of love. Fehr suggests that social psychologists may need to pay more research attention to companionate styles of love.

Multidimensional Models of Love

As we have seen, researchers have recognized various sorts of love. Very often, love is conceptualized as a continuum, with passionate love (infatuation) or romantic love at one end, and mature love (companionate love) at the other. John Lee has formulated a more comprehensive, multidimensional model of love.

Lee (1974) argues that various styles of love are equally valid. He asserts that the fast-changing, pluralistic society in which we live makes a fulfilling *mutual* love more difficult to attain than ever before. Rather than viewing differences in the experience of love as differences in quantity (more, less), he suggests that we would do better to view such differences as differences in styles of loving. Lee builds his multidimensional model on three basic styles of love: *eros*, *ludus*, and *storge*. Each corresponds to the three primary colours (red, blue, and yellow). Lee then derives three secondary styles of love: *mania*, *pragma*, and *agape* (Lee, 1974, 1975, 1977, 1988). Just as red and blue are blended to form purple, so *eros* and *ludus* are blended to form *mania*. Similarly, *eros* and *storge* are blended to form *agape*, and *ludus* and *storge* are blended to form *pragma*.

■ **Eros** Romantic, passionate love, or love of beauty, is marked by an irrational and powerful attraction to the physical appearance of the other. The intensity of attraction often leads to early sexual relations, but it is the fascination with beauty that is the basis for personal, psychological, and sexual intimacy. Erotic lovers frequently enjoy exclusive relationships, but erotic love is quick to develop and quick to decay, and usually does not become a lasting relationship.

■ **Ludus** Playful love treats love as a game in which one does not become too involved. The obsessive passion is not for the partner, but for the game of love itself. Ludic love is permissive and pluralistic. The ludic lover often avoids deep involvement by cultivating several partners at the same time or by not seeing particular partners too often. Cynical lovers may seek to get partners as emotionally involved as possible, while themselves avoiding entangling commitments or emotional dependence. Love is seen as fun and games, rather than as intimate or committed.

■ **Storge** Friendship or companionate love is a "slow-burning" relationship that is rarely hectic or urgent. It comes gradually with the passage of time and the enjoyment of shared activities. It is based on long-term friendship and companionship, and only gradually takes on romantic overtones. It is stable and trusting but lacks dramatic passion. "In storge, there are fewer campaigns to fight and fewer wounds to heal. There is a lack of ecstasy, but also a lack of despair" (Lee, 1974:48).

■ **Mania** Possessive or obsessive love was called by the Greeks "the madness from the gods." Sleep, hunger, and the normal experiences of life are replaced by obsessive thoughts of the beloved. *Mania* involves intense mental preoccupation with the relationship, but it provides little satisfaction. The manic lover experiences peaks of ecstasy and depths of despair. Intense jealousy is a frequent response to a lack of attention. Although completely wrapped up in the love object, the manic lover is likely to be possessive rather than giving, clinging rather than trusting.

■ **Pragma** Realistic love is "love with a shopping list," or love based on a careful evaluation of one's own "marketability" compared with the good and bad points of the partner. It is rational and practical, quite unlike *eros*. Computer dating services are based on a pragmatic philosophy of love. More intense feelings, however, may develop once a solid match is made.

■ **Agape** Selfless or altruistic love is a generous, unselfish giving of oneself. The agapic lover is kind, caring, and sensitive to the other's needs, without making demands for the self. Agapic love is an expression of the will as well as the emotions. Lee says that he has not found an unqualified example of *agape*, but a few respondents had brief episodes of such love in otherwise selfish relationships.

Lee argues that the advantages of his typology of love are that it recognizes different types of love, and enables us to investigate which types of love are most compatible. Each of us may be predisposed toward a particular style of loving. Partners with different love styles will find it hard to sustain a successful relationship with each other unless each is willing to compromise. It is possible for one person to experience a variety of love types. And people may adopt different love types in different relationships.

A cross-sectional study examined differences in the endorsement of the above six styles of love among four family-life-stage groups (college-age single youth, young childless married adults, married adults with children living at home, and married adults with "launched" children). The notion of a developmental progression of love attitudes across the life span was not evident. The study did find a number of differences between young singles and all married adults regardless of family life stage. Young singles held manic and ludic love attitudes more strongly than did any of the married groups, and also demonstrated the lowest levels of agapic love attitudes. No significant gender differences were found in love attitudes (Montgomery and Sorell, 1997).

Gender Differences in Love

In our society, many people assume that females are more emotional than males and therefore that females are more likely than males to fall in love or to experience romantic feelings. The empirical evidence, however, suggests that males experience greater idealization or romanticism in the courtship process.

Hobart (1958) found that as a relationship changed from the non-dating stage to the preferred-date stage to the going-steady stage, romanticism increased with more intimate stages of courtship for males, but not for females. He also found that being away from one's partner was more likely to heighten romanticism for males than for females. Knox and Sporakowsi (1968) found that females were more realistic than males in their attitude toward love. Fengler (1974) found few differences between males and females in levels of romanticism during stages of noninvolvement, but found divergent paths in states of high romantic involvement (frequent dating or going steady), with males being more romantic than females.

In their study of dating couples, Rubin et al. (1981) discovered that men scored significantly higher than their female partners on a romanticism scale measuring such idealistic notions as "love strikes at first sight" and "love can overcome differences of race, religion and economics." According to their study, men were more likely than women to fall in love quickly, whereas women tended to be more deliberate and discriminating about entering into a romantic relationship. On the other hand, women fell out of love more readily than men. Men were more negatively affected by the breakup of a relationship than were women, tending to report higher levels of depression, loneliness, and unhappiness, and less freedom than their former girlfriends (Rubin et al., 1981). Similarly, Kanin et al. (1970) found that females were more deliberate in identifying the experience of love in a relationship, but once the current relationship was accepted as a love relationship, the female became more romantic than the male. Harris (in Walster and Walster, 1978) described the different approaches of men and women by suggesting that women could be described as LIFO (last in, first out) of romance, while men were FILO (first in, last out).

A recent study (Lawrance et al., 1996) investigated whether young men's and women's behaviour in heterosexual situations follows traditional, culturally defined gender role prescriptions that suggest men are more instrumental or assertive, while women are more expressive. They also sought to determine if expectations have shifted, leading to a convergence of young men's and women's gender-relevant personality attributes. While they found some evidence of convergence in men's and women's perceptions of ideal attributes, they concluded that men's and women's gender-relevant attributes continue to reflect traditional gender-typed perceptions. Men's attributes were more *instrumental* than women's, while women were more *expressive* than men.

Changing Premarital Sex Standards

Changing Sexual Attitudes

General trends in attitudes and behaviour regarding sex standards documented in the past couple of decades include the following:

- Attitudes toward premarital sex have become consistently more permissive, and more permissive attitudes are associated with more permissive sexual behaviour, including the experience of premarital intercourse.

- Increases in permissive attitudes and behaviour have been significantly greater for females than for males, resulting in greater convergence of sexual behaviour between the sexes. Despite the convergence, however, men still continue to demonstrate more permissive attitudes than do women.

- There has been a decrease in adherence to the abstinence standard, and a corresponding increase in adherence to the "love" and "fun" standards; significantly more males than females accept recreational sex, or permissiveness without affection.

- There has been an increase in the number of sexual partners among those who are sexually experienced, and a decrease in the average age of first intercourse. Increases in premarital sexual permissiveness are associated with increasingly serious stages of the relationship.

- During the past decade, the movement toward greater sexual permissiveness is more notable among Francophone than Anglophone young people.

- Increasing consistency has been found between sexual attitudes and actual sexual behaviour (Bibby and Posterski, 1992; Herold, 1984; Hobart, 1990a; Hobart and Grigel, 1990; King et al., 1988).

Reiss (1967) identified four premarital sex standards:

- **Abstinence** Premarital intercourse is unacceptable behaviour for both men and women in all circumstances.

- **Double standard** Premarital intercourse is more acceptable for males than for females. In Canada, the double standard had virtually disappeared by 1988. Reiss found evidence for a **transitional double standard**, which accepts the right of males to engage in premarital intercourse, but suggests that females may do so only if they are in love or are engaged.

- **Permissiveness with affection** Premarital intercourse is acceptable provided a stable relationship with love or strong affection is present. Reiss suggests that intercourse among couples who are engaged or in love has always been the least condemned type of premarital intercourse.

Permissiveness without affection Approval of premarital intercourse for both men and women regardless of affection in the relationship. Recreational sex was a standard held by only a small minority in the 1960s.

Hobart obtained data from university and trade school students in three different decades—1968, 1977 and 1988 (Hobart, 1972, 1974, 1976, 1984, 1990a). These findings remain the best source of Canada-wide trends with respect to male and female Anglophone and Francophone students primarily in regard to professed sex standards (attitudes) and sex behaviour. The initial study (Hobart, 1972) found both male and female Francophone students to be *less* permissive than male and female Anglophone students (see Figures 6.1 and 6.2). In the 1968 data, Hobart had already isolated, in two ways, tendencies toward the emergence of a "new morality":

■ A majority of both Anglophone and Francophone subjects approved of premarital sex for women when couple members were engaged or in love.

■ A massive increase in the premarital intercourse experience of women was reported, suggesting the erosion

of the expectation of female virginity required under the old morality.

Significant changes in adherence to the various premarital sexual standards took place between 1968 and 1977:

■ a decline in the profession of the double standard

■ an increase in the profession of the fun standard

■ an increase in consistency between professed and practised norms, and

■ the emergence of more egalitarian sexual standards between males and females (Hobart, 1984).

The 1988 data showed further changes in adherence to the various premarital sexual standards for both male and female and Anglophone and Francophone respondents (Hobart, 1990a):

■ The abstinence standard declined for all four groups (Anglophone men and women; Francophone men and women), with the sharpest decreases taking place

Figure 6.1   Anglophone Premarital Sex Standards

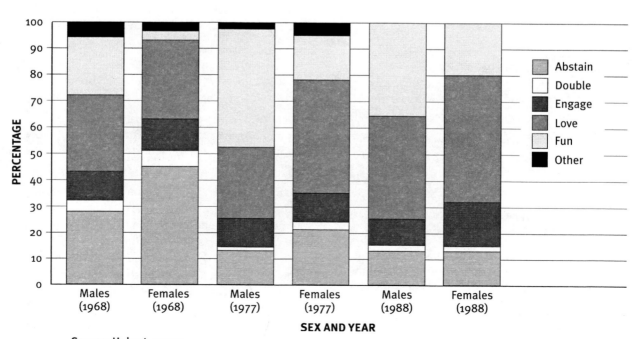

Source: Hobart, 1990a.

Figure 6.2   Francophone Premarital Sex Standards

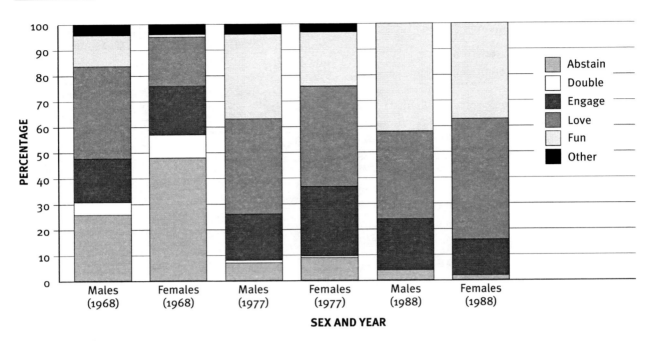

Source: Hobart, 1990a.

between 1968 and 1977, and with smaller changes taking place during the 1980s.

■ The greatest decline in support for the abstinence standard over the 20-year period was found among Francophone women (from 48 percent to 2 percent), and the smallest decline was found among Anglophone men (from 28 percent to 13 percent).

■ Francophones and females experienced substantially more decline in support of the abstinence standard than did Anglophones and males (Hobart, 1990a).

A ranking of the three most frequently chosen premarital sexual standards reveals some significant changes over the 20-year period (see Table 6.1).

■ For *Anglophone males*, the two most frequently chosen standards in 1968 were the love standard and the abstinence standard, whereas in 1988 they were the love standard and the fun standard.

■ In contrast, the two most frequently chosen standards for *Anglophone females* in 1968 were the abstinence

standard and the love standard. In 1988 these had changed to the love standard and the fun standard.

■ For *Francophone males*, the two most frequently chosen premarital standards in 1968 were the love standard and the abstinence standard, whereas in 1988 they were the fun standard and the love standard.

■ In contrast, the two most frequently chosen standards for *Francophone females* in 1968 were the abstinence standard and the engagement standard. In 1988 they were the love standard and the fun standard.

The large-scale abandonment of the abstinence standard documented above, particularly among Francophones, has been accompanied by an increase in adherence to the love and fun standards. In 1988, these two standards were the top-ranked standards among all four groups surveyed. Together they accounted for 86 percent of Francophone males, 84 percent of Francophone females, 75 percent of Anglophone males, and 69 percent of Anglophone females. Thus, the great majority of respondents accepted the premarital

TABLE 6.1   Rank Ordering of Premarital Sex Standards, 1968–1988

YEAR	STANDARD	PERCENTAGE	YEAR	STANDARD	PERCENTAGE
	Anglophone Males			**Francophone Males**	
1968	Love	30	1968	Love	36
	Abstinence	28		Abstinence	26
	Fun	22		Engagement	17
1977	Fun	45	1977	Love	38
	Love	28		Fun	33
	Abstinence	13		Engagement	18
1988	Love	39	1988	Fun	52
	Fun	36		Love	34
	Abstinence	13		Engagement	7
	Anglophone Females			**Francophone Females**	
1968	Abstinence	45	1968	Abstinence	48
	Love	30		Engagement	19
	Engagement	12		Love	18
1977	Love	44	1977	Love	39
	Abstinence	21		Engagement	28
	Fun	18		Fun	22
1988	Love	49	1988	Love	47
	Fun	20		Fun	37
	Engagement	17		Engagement	14

Source: Adapted from Hobart, 1990a.

sex standards of permissiveness either with or without affection. Permissiveness without affection was adopted by one out of every two Francophone males, by one out of every three Anglophone males and Francophone females, and by one out of every five Anglophone females.

An important update on these findings (Bettor, Hendrick, and Hendrick, 1995) makes a strong distinction between casual and serious relationships. Respondents in this study were asked to evaluate sex vignettes of very different heterosexual dating couples.

Persons in *serious relationships* were viewed as passionate, friendship-oriented, practical, possessive, and altruistic in their love styles—desirable as dating and marriage partners. In contrast, couples in *casual relationships* were seen as "game-playing," instrumental and sexually permissive. Hensley (1996) also found that *Ludus love* [game-playing love] remains largely a male style of sexual interaction and continues to be associated with having multiple sex partners. It seems evident that "permissiveness with affection" continues to be the primary sex script.

We now turn to a different set of normative categories recently used in the U.S. to describe attitudes toward premarital intercourse, as well as several other moral values (Michael et al., 1994:234). Table 6.2 summarizes selected data for three major competing value systems in American society: traditional, relational, and recreational. As will be seen below, there are actually seven more specific types of value systems regarding sexual activity.

As Table 6.2 shows, less than 20 percent of the American public believe that premarital sex is always wrong. However, 60 percent believe that premarital

TABLE 6.2   Normative Orientations toward Sexuality

	PREMARITAL SEX IS ALWAYS WRONG	PREMARITAL SEX AMONG TEENAGERS IS ALWAYS WRONG	WOULD NOT HAVE SEX UNLESS IN LOVE	SAME GENDER SEX IS ALWAYS WRONG
Traditional Orientations				
Traditional	100.0	99.5	87.5	96.4
Pro-choice traditional	23.6	90.3	66.0	94.4
Relational Orientations				
Religious	0.0	78.6	98.0	81.9
Conventional	0.4	29.1	83.8	65.4
Contemporary religious	0.8	33.6	65.3	6.4
Recreational Orientations				
Pro-Life	6.5	65.7	10.1	85.9
Libertarian	0.0	19.7	19.5	9.0
Total Sample	19.7	60.8	65.7	64.8

1. *Traditional people:* Religious beliefs always guide their behaviour. This group constitutes one-third of sample. Most are opposed to homosexuality, premarital sex, teenage sex, extramarital sex, and want restrictions on legal abortion. The difference between the two groups is that *"pro-choice traditionals"* believe that women should be able to have an abortion.

2. *Relational people* believe that sex should be limited to a loving relationship, but not necessarily limited to marriage. This group constitutes about one-half of sample. The *"religious"* think that their religious faith should shape their behaviour but oppose homosexuality and abortion. *Conventionals* are more tolerant toward teenage sex and abortion but oppose extramarital sex and same-gender sex. The *contemporary religious* tend to be accepting of homosexuality.

3. *Recreational people* believe that sex does not need to have anything to do with love. About 25 percent of the sample holds this view. *"Pro-life"* persons oppose homosexuality and abortion but are accepting of teenage and extramarital sex. *"Libertarians"* in contrast are the most accepting of almost any sexual behaviours. Religion is not a factor in their value systems.

sex among teenagers, and that extramarital sex and same-gender sex is always wrong. It is apparent, however, that there are significantly different sexual world views. The researchers in this study argue that these competing views explain why it is so difficult to formulate social policies. Sexual issues are complex, contentious, and divisive. Only 16 percent of this sample were under the age of 24—the group most applicable to this chapter. Among the men in this age group, 17 percent were classified as traditional, 47 percent as relational, and 36 percent as recreational. Women under the age of 24 were distinctly more conservative in their perspectives: 23 percent traditional, 25 percent recreational, but higher than the men at 52 percent relational. As may be expected, both men and women became more traditional, less relational, and less recreational, the older the age group.

In another study among college men and women in the U.S. who were attracted to each other, men expected sexual intercourse after fewer dates (an average of eight) than women (an average of 12 dates) (Cohen and Shotland, 1996). In situations of emotional involvement without attraction, about 53 percent of the women and 59 percent of the men assumed that sexual intercourse might be expected if the emotional involvement continued. Both men and women who were both emotionally involved and physically attracted to each other assumed that sexual intercourse was a high probability (80 percent of women and 90 percent of men). Comparative studies in other societies illustrate both different and changing values. For example, more than half of college students in the U.S. disapprove of 15-year-old girls and 15-year-old boys engaging in sexual intercourse with a steady dating partner—about 50 percent of college men disapprove, compared to about 68 percent of college women. In contrast, only 15 percent of Swedish men and 13 percent of Swedish women disapprove (Weinberg, Lottes and Shaver, 1995). Swedish men and women in college are less likely to disapprove of sexual intercourse among 15-year-olds not significantly involved (an average of 48 percent of men and 56 percent of women). In contrast, about 75 percent of American men disapprove, compared to 92 percent of women. Sweden offers a classic example of permissive attitudes toward sexuality and cohabitation.

Changing Sexual Behaviours

Significant changes among adolescents in Canada are also evident with respect to sexual *behaviour*. Table 6.3 provides a summary of most of the studies of premarital sexual behaviour conducted in Canada between 1974 and 1996. We would encourage the reader to review the patterns illustrated in Table 6.3. By the mid-70s over half of males in high school had had sexual intercourse. The percentage of females involved in sexual intercourse was 10 to 20 percent lower than males. These patterns were quite similar for university students. By the late 1980s, the percentage of young people engaging in premarital sexual intercourse had climbed over the 70-percent threshold and had reached the 85-percent threshold among Francophone Canadian males and females. There were similar increases in sexual behaviour among high school students.

A Canadian study (Meston, Trapnell, and Gorsalka, 1996)—note that the percentages in Table 6.3 are averages for Asian and non-Asian respondents—indicates that university students continue to be sexually active. Among non-Asian males and females (82 percent of whom were Canadian-born), 71 percent of the males had engaged in sexual intercourse one or more times, compared to 76 percent of females. In contrast, among Asian males and females, 63 percent of males and 52 percent of females had had sexual intercourse. Ninety-four percent of the students were between the ages of 18 and 25. Twenty-one percent of non-Asian males had had six or more sexual partners, compared to 28 percent of non-Asian females. Among Asian males and females, only 3 percent of females had had more than six sexual partners, compared to 7 percent of Asian males.

It would appear that premarital sexual behaviour is quite similar among high school students in the United States. An average of 53 percent of high school students have had intercourse at least once between 1990 and 1995 (Warren et al., 1998). White male sexual behaviour decreased about 7 percent during this period. There was a small increase in sexual behaviour among white females from 47 percent to 49 percent. Black students initiated sexual intercourse earlier than did white students and were more likely to have engaged in sexual intercourse in the past three months. The differences are large. For example, in 1995, 59 percent of

TABLE 6.3 Premarital Sex among Canadian Students

| RESEARCHER | LOCATION | DATE | PERCENT ENGAGING IN PREMARITAL SEX | |
			M	F
HIGH SCHOOL STUDENTS				
Hundleby	Ontario Grade 9	1974	22	15
	Ontario Grade 10	1974	33	25
Stennet et al.	Ontario Grade 13	1974	53	39
Herold	Toronto Grades 12, 13	1975	57	33
King et al.	National Grade 9	1988	31	21
	National Grade 11	1988	49	46
	National dropouts	1988	89	81
Bibby and Posterski	National	1992	62	49
UNIVERSITY STUDENTS				
Mann	Ontario, Western	1965	35	15
Barrett	Ontario, Toronto	1968	40	32
Hobart	Alberta, Ontario, Quebec	1968	56	44
Mann	Ontario, York	1969	51	31
Perlman	Manitoba	1970	55	37
Perlman	Manitoba	1975	62	45
Pool and Pool	Ontario, Carleton	1975	N/A	66
Pool and Pool	Ontario, Ottawa	1975	N/A	53
Herold and Thomas	Ontario	1975	64	55
Hobart	Anglophone	1977	73	63
	Francophone	1977	59	65
Barrett	Ontario, Toronto	1978	62	58
Herold, Way and Kitchen	Ontario, Guelph	1982	60	52
Hobart	Anglophone	1988	72	76
	Francophone	1988	86	84
King et al.	National sample	1988	77	73
Meston et al.	British Columbia, Vancouver	1996	71	76

Source: Adapted from Herold, 1984:13; and other sources cited.

Black males had had sexual intercourse, compared with 32 percent of white males. Black males and females were also about four times as likely as white males and females to have had four or more sexual partners.

Santelli et al. (1998), using a 1992 Youth Risk Data Base aged 14 to 21 years of age, found that 15 percent of females and 35 percent of males who had engaged in sexual intercourse in the past three months had had sex with two or more partners. Females who had had six or more sexual partners rose from 8 percent for 14-year-olds to 31 percent for 21-year-olds, and males from 14 to 45 percent.

The most prodigious study of sexual behaviour in the U.S. (Laumann et al., 1994) found that in the past 12 months, among youth under 25 years of age, only 11 percent had had no sex partners, 57 percent had had one partner, 24 percent had had two to four partners, and 8 percent had had five or more partners. The data for the previous five years indicates that 12 percent had had no sex partners, 22 percent had had one, 38 percent had had two to four, 18 percent had had five to 10, and 7.5 percent had had 11 or more. Females were more likely to have one sexual partner, while only 7.8 percent had had more than five sexual partners. Valois et al. (1997), in a study of more than 1000 high school students, document that the higher the number of sexual partners, the greater the prevalence of aggressive and reckless behaviours.

Might a change be under way? An important study using a different population of 17- to 19-year-old never-married males has found a bi-modal curve in sexual behaviour (Ku et al., 1998). The percentage of males who had ever had sexual intercourse increased from 66 percent in 1979 to 76 percent in 1988, and decreased to 68 percent in 1995. While this shift did not occur for Black males, young white males in this study apparently are being influenced by more conservative sexual attitudes, AIDS education programs, and the fear of AIDS. It is unknown whether this trend will continue.

The Context of Changing Sex Standards

Research in both Canada and the United States continues to indicate a high level of approval for premarital sexual intercourse. Sexual intercourse is no longer exclusive to the bond of marriage. Most couples enter marriage not only sexually *experienced* but also having been sexually *active*. These changes have not taken place in a vacuum, but are clearly related to current social and cultural conditions. As Laumann et al. (1994) demonstrate, the contemporary social context permits a diversity of value systems that not only permit, but even encourage, sexual experimentation among both adolescents and married and unmarried adults over the life span. As peer groups have become increasingly autonomous, they have developed a "youth culture" in which premarital sexual involvement is both accepted and expected. Table 6.4 indicates that sex norms may be in flux due to competing ideologies.

TABLE 6.4   Attitudes toward Premarital Cohabitation (percentages)

	ANGLOPHONE			FRANCOPHONE		
	1968	1977	1988	1968	1977	1988
Definitely good	6.5	17.0	19.8	25.3	35.8	71.2
Good sometimes	18.6	42.9	26.2	20.4	32.8	20.0
Good and bad	30.9	24.8	37.3	40.6	21.0	6.9
Bad sometimes	1.6	5.5	7.1	0.5	4.7	0.8
Definitely bad	42.4	9.8	9.8	13.3	0.7	1.7
Total Number	682	622	1727	392	4.5	420

Source: Hobart and Grigel, 1992:321.

Hobart (1993b) maintains that factors contributing to changes in premarital sex standards include the increased availability and acceptability of contraception and abortion; the increased acceptability of unwed pregnancy and motherhood; increased levels of employment among women; and the liberalization or loss of credibility of religious definitions of sexual morality. The most profound social influences, however, include the following: a shift from familistic to individualistic values; an increased emphasis on egalitarian heterosexual relationships; and an increased valuation of hedonistic gratification seen in the "fun" standard. Counterinfluences, however, include the significant threat to health of sexually transmitted diseases, and in particular the continuing threat of AIDS.

A study of "college virgins" (Sprecher and Regan, 1996) identified the top five reasons among men and women for being a virgin. Their findings appear in rank order in Table 6.5. Virgin men are significantly more concerned about AIDS than are virgin women. Women are significantly more concerned about getting pregnant than are men, and are significantly more concerned about the length of the relationship. In this study, among female virgins, the belief that premarital sex was wrong ranked number 7 (number 11 for men) and religious beliefs ranked number 8 (number 10 among men). Perhaps the most interesting distinction between men and women relates to their feelings about being a virgin. Virgin women were significantly more likely to feel proud and happy and less embarrassed and guilty. Given the obvious concerns about AIDS and pregnancy, Hawkins and Gray (1995) asked college students what they are doing to achieve safer sex behaviours. Their choices illustrate the contemporary student's mind-set. In rank order from the *most* often chosen "safety step" to the *least* often chosen, the findings were as follows:

1. discuss contraception prior to sexual behaviour
2. be more selective as to whom one has sex with
3. reduce number of sexual partners
4. discuss partner's sexual health prior to engaging in sex
5. use condoms
6. abstain from sex

There seems to be only modest evidence that the current major sexual concerns are salient factors in the continuing sexual revolution.

Although virgins are still considered a unique group of young people, there appears to be a trend toward virginity before marriage, as well as a return of non-virgins to the premarital abstinence standard (Goodstein and Connelly, 1998). Another factor is that the U.S. Congress has set aside $50-million in grants each year for states to teach sexual abstinence. Combined with the addition of non-federal matching funds, nearly half a billion dollars have been earmarked for teaching abstinence (Dobson, 1998). Dobson also reports that 2.4 million youth have pledged to stay abstinent as a result of the True Love Can Wait movement.

TABLE 6.5   Reasons for Remaining Virgins

MEN	WOMEN
(1) Not been in relationship long enough or in love long enough [M = 2.78*]	(1) Not been in relationship long enough or in love long enough [M = 3.16*]
(2) Fear of pregnancy [M = 2.66*]	(2) Fear of pregnancy [M = 3.16*]
(3) Worry about getting AIDS [M = 2.84*]	(3) Worry about getting AIDS [M = 2.96]
(4) Worry about getting another STD [2.53]	(4) Not met a person I want to have sex with [2.91*]
(5) Too shy or embarrassed to initiate sex with partner [2.39*]	(5) Don't feel ready to have sex yet [2.84*]

Note: M stands for the mean or average score. The asterisk indicates that the differences between men and women are significant at the .004 level.

Source: Sprecher and Regan, 1996.

Correlates of Premarital Sexual Behaviour

We have documented the rapid decrease in commitment to the abstinence standard of premarital sexual relations, accompanied by the rapid increase in the endorsement of the love and fun standards. What are the primary factors related to these major changes in premarital sexual behaviours?

Use of Alcohol and Drugs

King et al. (1988) found that young people who used cigarettes, alcohol, and drugs were much more likely to engage in sexual intercourse. Sexually experienced young people were more likely to drink alcohol once a week, and to consume larger amounts of it at one sitting, than were sexually inexperienced respondents. They concluded that because half of the young people who often had sexual intercourse also used both alcohol and marijuana, they were at a higher risk of Human Immunodeficiency Virus (HIV) infection. Their frequent sexual experiences, combined with the use of substances that inhibited their intentions and competence to practise "safer sex," increased their risk of infection. More recent research has shown that the greater the number of sexual partners, among high school students, the more likely it is that these students are engaged in other "risk" behaviours, including the frequent use of alcohol, illicit drugs and cigarettes, and TV/video game viewing (Valois, Kammermann and Drane, 1997). These activities, as pointed out earlier in this chapter, are significantly correlated with the results of other aggressive and reckless behaviours: HIV infections, sexually transmitted diseases, and unintended pregnancy. Santelli et al. (1998) also found that alcohol use, illicit drug use, and young age at first coitus were significantly associated with multiple sexual partners, increasing from 8 percent to 48 percent among females, and from 23 percent to 61 percent among males.

Family Structure

An important change in the past few decades is the increasing proportion of married couples with children who have experienced a divorce or separation. Kinnaird and Gerrard (1986) found that daughters from divorced and reconstituted families reported higher rates of intercourse than did those from intact families. Fifty-three percent of respondents from intact families reported engaging in premarital intercourse, compared with 70 percent from divorced families, and 80 percent from reconstituted families. In contrast, among daughters who came from divorced homes, 57 percent of the sexually experienced had their first experience of intercourse at age 16 or younger, compared to 33 percent from reconstituted families and 19 percent from intact families. More recent research also indicates that children raised in single-parent homes, or who have left home before the age of 16, are more likely to experience nonvoluntary first intercourse (Abma, Driscoll, and Moore, 1998; also see Moore, Nord, and Peterson, 1989). The finding that young adolescents from intact homes are less likely to report engaging in sexual intercourse is also documented by a number of other studies (Newcomer and Udry, 1987; Miller and Bingham, 1989; Flewelling and Bauman, 1990).

Newcomer and Udry (1987), for example, indicate that adolescents experience less control in single-mother households because two parents are able to provide more supervision than one. Fathers may carry more authority than mothers and create more fear of a confrontation. Single mothers are also more likely to work full time, and thus have fewer opportunities to monitor adolescent activities. Single mothers may also be dating and sexually active, thus modeling unmarried sexual involvement. Thornton and Camburn (1987) found that divorced mothers were less religious and demonstrated more sexually permissive attitudes than did mothers who had not been divorced. Thornton (1991) reported that children whose mothers married at a younger age, or who were pregnant at the time of their marriage, were more likely than others to enter their own marital or cohabiting unions at a significantly earlier age.

Sexual Socialization

The earliest and most powerful socializing agency the young person encounters is the family. Gibbs (1993) found that 30 percent of young people aged 13 to 15 indicated that they had learned more about sex from their parents than from their friends (26 percent), from school (26 percent), or from entertainment (15 percent). In contrast, young people aged 16 to 17 indicated that

that they had learned more about sex from their friends (37 percent) than from their parents (22 percent), entertainment (18 percent), or from school (15 percent). A Time/CNN poll revealed that 60 percent of parents encouraged their daughters not to engage in premarital sex, while less than half told their sons the same thing. The result reflects the double standard: more than two-thirds of respondents agreed that sex enhances a boy's reputation, while a girl who has sex sees her reputation suffer (Gibbs, 1993).

Family members were cited as an important source of information about sex for a sizeable proportion of persons in every age group (between 32 percent and 49 percent), and the primary source of information for respondents in grades 7 and 9. Friends became the primary source of information among high school and university respondents. More females than males preferred mothers as a source of information, while more males than females preferred fathers (King, 1988).

Sexual socialization by parents, while important, affects only a minority of Canadian young people. Sex education programs in the schools have also received mixed evaluations. School was cited as the second most important source of information by about one-third of grades 7 and 9 respondents, and by about one-quarter of high school and university respondents (King et al., 1988).

Research documents widespread increases in adolescent pregnancies, abortions, and sexually transmitted diseases. This situation has led some parents, educators, and legislators to call for the inclusion of abstinence education in all sex education programs. Some young people are responding to the dangers that they perceive to be associated with premarital sexual experience by returning to the abstinence standard. These young people recognize that they are in the minority, and consequently experience negative reactions from their peer group.

Family Relationships and Interaction The parent factor, by intention or default, has always been salient in the lives of adolescents. Sexual behaviour is not an exception to this rule. Low parental monitoring, permissive parental values, sexual abuse by parents, low neighbourhood monitoring, lack of discussion between mothers and daughters about birth control, among a field of other factors, are all strongly associated with sexual intercourse (Small and Luster, 1994; Luster and Small, 1994). Only 1 percent of female teenagers with no risk factors were sexually active, compared to 42 percent with three risk factors, and 80 percent with eight or more risk factors. In a related study among adolescent girls, the combination of strong mother–daughter bonds, opposition to premarital sex by mothers, and minimal discussion about birth control by mothers resulted in girls being 12.5 times less likely to engage in premarital sex (Jaccard, Dittus, and Gordon, 1996). Apparently, however, frequent discussion of birth control with mothers was correlated with increased sexual activity. In general, a strong positive relationship with moms among Black adolescent girls also sharply reduced the frequency of sexual intercourse and made more consistent the use of contraceptives.

Mothers are the central figure in discussions about all matters related to premarital sexual activities—HIV, AIDS, STDs, birth control, etc. (Miller et al., 1998). Older siblings have also been found to have a powerful influence on younger sibling sexual behaviour, both pro and con (Widmer, 1997). When the cross-cultural factor is added to the "power of positive family ties," the resistance to sexual activities outside marriage is even more powerful. For example, in Taiwan less than 2 percent of teens have had sexual intercourse (Chang, 1996).

In Hobart's studies (1990a), among both male and female Anglophone college students, permissive premarital sexual attitudes were correlated with permissiveness of mothers and fathers. Father permissiveness was the only major predictor of permissive attitudes among male and female Francophones. Relative to sexual *behaviour*, the major predictors among Anglophones were the following: father's level of education, mother's occupational status, family breakup, and the number of communities lived in. "Communities lived in" was also a strong predictor of permissive sexual behaviour in a recent U.S. study (Stack, 1994). No parental factor played a role in Francophone sexual behaviour.

Dating Relationship Development

Sexual behaviours have an impact on dating relationships. Cate et al. (1993) found that guilt, obligation, pressure, and permissive sexual attitudes were negative predictors of a positive relationship for both females and males. In contrast, love for partner, degree of commitment at time of first intercourse, and positive attitudes toward premarital sexual intercourse were significant factors in sexual satisfaction. These findings were more significant for females than for males. The degree of control young women have over their first sexual intercourse experience is important (Abma, Driscoll, and Moore, 1998). About 25 percent report that their first experience was nonvoluntary and unwanted. Among women whose first sexual partner was seven or more years older than themselves, although considering the event to be voluntary, nearly 40 percent rated it low on the "wanted" scale. Consent does not necessarily mean desire. It was also found that children from single-parent homes, or who had left home before the age of 16, were more likely to have experienced nonvoluntary first intercourse.

In a longitudinal study of unmarried women engaged in exclusive sexual relationships in 1983 and who were studied again in 1991, only 10 percent, on average, of the women had a secondary sexual partner: 18 percent of those still dating, 20 percent of those now cohabiting, and 4 percent of those now married (Forste and Tanfer, 1996). Although most of this study dealt with the degree of similarity between partners, the most important conclusion is that dating and cohabiting women are more similar to one another than they are to married women. Daters and cohabitors were significantly less committed to their relationships. With time, sexual exclusivity in both dating and cohabiting relationships decreases.

Peer-Group Relationships

In a comparison of adamant virgins, potential non-virgins, and non-virgins in Ontario, Herold and Goodwin (1981b) found that the most significant predictor of the transition to non-virginity was peer experience with premarital intercourse. Shah and Zelnick (1981) found that women with sexual views resembling those of their friends were most likely to have had premarital sexual experience, and to have had more sexual partners. Having friends who were sexually experienced was the strongest predictor of permissive sexual attitudes and behaviour for both Anglophone males and

females, and for Francophone females—but not for Francophone males (Hobart, 1990a; Hobart and Grigel, 1990).

The peer-pressure factor in sexual behaviour continues to be a source of "sexual aggressiveness" among men, much more so than among women (Boeringer, Shehan, and Akers, 1991). A 1998 study confirms the notion that coercive peers reinforce each others' actions (Christopher, Madura, and Weaver, 1998). Sexual aggression is related to the desire for control. The typical "assumption" among sexually aggressive males is that women really control whether sex occurs, and therefore they must have wanted the sex that the male aggressor obtained. Success reinforces that myth.

Religion and Moral Reasoning

Does religious participation have a negative impact on sexual permissiveness? In a Canadian sample, Herold (1984) found that among females who attended religious services at least once a week, 41 percent accepted premarital intercourse with affection. In contrast, almost all (86 percent) of those who rarely or never attended church approved of premarital intercourse with affection. Comparative figures for males were 63 percent and 87 percent, respectively. A national study of Canadian youth found that 35 percent of university students who had not experienced sexual intercourse attended church weekly, whereas only 13 percent of sexually experienced youth attended church on a weekly basis (King et al., 1988). However, a more recent study of the sexual attitudes and behaviour of Canadian young people discovered that religion had a weak relationship with premarital sexual attitudes and behaviour (Hobart, 1990a; Hobart and Grigel, 1990).

It would seem that religion no longer has a significant impact on premarital sexual attitudes and behaviour among Canadian young people. Thornton and Camburn (1989:643) hypothesized that "church attendance and religious importance are likely to produce less permissive attitudes and less engagement in premarital sex, while the acceptance of premarital sex is likely to reduce religious participation." The data confirmed the hypothesis: youth who attended church frequently and who placed a high value on religion's role in their lives had less permissive sexual attitudes and lower levels of sexual experience. Permissive attitudes and premarital sexual behaviour reduced religious participation.

In another study, high school and college females reported feeling guilty after their *first* experience of sexual intercourse, but few reported guilt feelings regarding their *current* sexual experience—as sexual experience increases, sex guilt diminishes (Herold and Thomas, 1978).

Competing perspectives and *social changes* regarding premarital sexuality are now the norm. Petersen and Donnenwerth (1997) collected data from four groups: Conservative Protestants, Mainline Protestants, Catholics, and Nones (people without any religious connection), every third year from 1972 to 1993. The opposition to premarital sex among Conservative Protestants, who attended church frequently, "simply did not change over the 21 years." Similarly, the Nones held highly permissive views of premarital sex and did not change their views in the same period of time. In contrast, infrequent Conservative church attenders as well as Mainline Protestants and Catholics, adopted increasingly more permissive views toward premarital sex over the 21-year period. Even so, the less religious public appears to respect their peers who remain virgins. For example, secular university students considered hypothetical females the most moral and trustworthy if they were described as delaying sex in a relationship and were regular church-goers (Isaac, Bailey and Isaac, 1995). A follow-up study (Bailey and Vietor, 1996) found that higher standards of sexual purity are expected of religiously active females. However, if it was learned that these moral attributes had been violated or weren't true, their valuation was lowered. This is referred to as the "halo" or "religious boomerang" effect. It is apparent that while religious persons are admired and respected for being "righteous" about sexual matters, false testimony knocks them from the religious pedestal.

Are young religious women more likely to remain virgins? Virgin women, aged 11 to 19 in 1984, were studied for a four-year period, reaching the ages of 15 and 23 at the conclusion of the study (Brewster et al., 1988). At the end of the four-year period, among white women, 61 percent of those classified as Christian Fundamentalists were still virgins, compared to 42 percent of Catholics and 39 percent of "all others" (including "no religion" and "Nonfundamentalist" Protestants). Among Black women, the percentage of virgins was significantly lower: Fundamentalist, 45 percent; Roman Catholic, 30 percent; others, 29 percent. These findings illustrate the strength of the religious factor among young women involved in the conservative Christian community. Over the four-year period, Catholic and "other" women were much more likely to lose their virginity. In contrast, there was a sizeable increase in the proportion of those maintaining their virginity among white Protestant Fundamentalist women. This pattern, however, did not apply among *Black* Fundamentalist women. Another important factor in this study is the use of contraceptives. Among the 39 percent that *did not remain virgins* and who were associated with white Fundamentalist churches, 41 percent did not use contraceptives, compared to 75 percent of the Black teenage women. Thirty-seven percent of white women used condoms and 18 percent used the pill. In contrast, significantly fewer Black women used these methods: 16 percent used condoms and 7 percent used the pill. Roman Catholic young white women were *less likely* to use the pill, while Black Catholic women were *more likely* to use the pill.

The authors point out that while Black churches discourage sexual activity and childbearing outside marriage, they are also more communalistic and forgiving. This research evidence is consistent with the research reported earlier in this chapter (Laumann et al., 1994; Michael et al., 1994). National programs such as those sponsored by Focus on the Family (and other religious organizations), with the financial help of donors, such as the advertisements in newspapers throughout the country, e.g., "Abstinence: It Works Every Time," and programs such as True Love Can Wait, may have a significant impact on parents and teens who are involved with conservative religious organizations, as well as among the "dating public."

Problems Associated with Dating

In our discussion of the conventions and functions of the dating system in Canada, we emphasized that dating has been and continues to be a changing institution that places importance on the decisions and choices of the participants. Since nearly 90 percent of our population eventually gets married, it is rather easy to assume that the dating system has an impressive success record that encompasses most persons in our society. What is often overlooked is that dating is a problematic relationship for many persons at some time or other in their lives. For example, the growing number of divorces and separations may reflect weaknesses in the current dating and courtship system. Individuals may experience adverse effects when serious dating relationships break down, which carry over into later marriage relationships. The breakdown or dissolution of dating relationships has, until recently, received little research attention. The problematic aspects of dating merit further examination.

Securing Dates

Significant numbers of young people who are interested in dating have problems securing a date. They find the experience frustrating and traumatic. Herold (1984) reported that in the 1980s, one-third of Canadian high school students were not currently dating, and that 15 percent of university females and one-third of university males were not currently dating. Herold found that common problems experienced by both males and females in securing dates were feelings of shyness, self-consciousness, and unease. These problems contributed to an increase in anxiety and unhappiness, and to a lowering of self-esteem.

How do young people overcome some of the problems experienced in securing dates? According to a study of how dating partners meet (Knox and Wilson, 1981), most university students reported that they came to know their current dating partner through a friend. Others reported that they met dating partners at a party, at work, in class, or as a result of growing up together. It appears that young people experiencing difficulties in securing dates should turn to their friends for assistance, or should more actively participate in various networks that provide opportunities for interaction with prospective dates.

In a study of how French couples met over the past half-century, Bozon and Héron (1989) found that during the 1920s, two out of every three marriages were the outcome of meeting in the neighbourhood, at work, at a dance, or during a private visit. During the 1970s, in contrast, these four forms of encounter only accounted for one-third of all marriages. In the 1920s, neighbourhood meetings accounted for more than one out of five marriages (over 20 percent), whereas in the 1980s they accounted for less than 5 percent. During the 1980s, meetings at work accounted for the largest proportion of marriages (almost 15 percent).

Network Interference

Although the dating system in Canada emphasizes the free choice of participants, considerable research evidence indicates that family and friends influence dating choices. **Network interference** refers to the attempts of family members or friends to influence the dating choices of individuals. In one university sample, 60 percent of the women and 40 percent of the men indicated that their parents tried to influence whom they dated (Knox and Wilson, 1981).

Another study measured the degree of interference of network members (parents, siblings and friends) by the respondents' perception of whether the network members felt that less time should be spent with the partner. The perceived degree of interference was lowest in the early and late stages, and greatest in the middle stages of relationships. A one-year follow-up study classified respondents as those whose relationship had declined during the intervening period, those who had experienced no change, and those whose relationship had advanced. Those whose relationship had declined had experienced the highest level of network interference (Johnson and Milardo, 1984), indicating that such interference can undermine dating relationships. Network interference may arise from the fact that as couples become more romantically involved, their friendship networks shrink, and they become less involved even with those friends who are still in their network, thus leading network members to oppose the relationship (Johnson and Leslie, 1982).

Sprecher and Felmlee (1992) found that social network approval of the relationship from family and friends had a positive effect on the quality of the relationship (love, satisfaction and commitment). Perceived support for the relationship from one's own family and friends more strongly influenced satisfaction, love, and commitment than did perceived support from one's partner's family and friends. Network support also affected the stability of relationships. Decreased social network support was associated with a higher level of relationship breakup, particularly for females. These findings provide strong support for the argument that parents have an important role in influencing romantic relationships—and that peers have an even greater effect.

Leslie et al. (1986) show that not only do parents seek to influence the dating choices of their children, but young people also actively seek to influence their parents' reactions to their dating choices. The study found that 85 percent of the respondents reported at least one attempt to influence their mother's thinking, and 77 percent reported at least one attempt to influence their father's thinking. The strongest predictor of the number of influence tactics was the relationship stage, with individuals at the more serious stages being most likely to seek to influence their parents. Daughters reported less support by parents for their relationship, but they were more likely than sons to attempt to influence their parents. How can we account for this difference between daughters and sons? Perhaps it is simply a matter of perception. Or it may reflect the assumption that daughters need more protection. Perhaps daughters are more active in maintaining relationships with the extended family, and thus parents have a greater stake in the selection of a suitable partner.

Sprecher and Felmlee (2000) studied the effects of network approval longitudinally on the evolution of close relationships. The five waves of this longitudinal study of romantic couples showed findings that were different for males and females. Females who expressed liking for the male partner's family at the outset of the study and who perceived their relationship as approved by their friendship network were significantly less likely to break up. Males' friends seem to increase their approval as a function of the duration of the relationship. Marriage was predicted by the approval of the male's friendship network.

The findings of these studies provide evidence of limitations to the autonomous system of mate selection that is presumed to operate in our society. Not only do parents seek to influence the prospective mate selection of their offspring, but children desire and actively solicit the approval of parents for their choices, particularly when the relationship has progressed to more serious stages. In addition, it seems clear that the approval of peers and friendship networks plays a role in the continuance or breakup of romances.

Gender Differences in Perceptions and Expectations

Research has found significant differences between genders in the dating experience. Males and females have a different understanding of dating interaction, and they frequently pursue different goals in establishing intimate relationships. In their 1992 study of almost 4000 high school students across Canada, Bibby and Posterski found that almost nine out of 10 teenagers (87 percent) approved of premarital sex when the people involved *love* each other. But when the people involved just *like* each other, the number of females approving dropped from 86 percent to only 51 percent, while the male figure declined only slightly from 88 percent to 77 percent. Only two in 10 females approved of sexual relations after only a few dates, compared with seven out of 10 males. Thus, females were less likely than males to approve of casual sexual relations in dating. The researchers suggest that these differences may be the outcome of the higher values females place on relationships, and their tendency to link sexual involvement to significant social ties.

Hobart (1981) studied recent changes toward egalitarianism in male and female gender roles in Canada. He found a greater surge toward egalitarianism among Francophones than among Anglophones over an 11-year period (1968–1977). He also found that the more serious the relationship, the greater egalitarianism there tended to be. In other words, "advanced courtship status" was positively related to egalitarianism scores. This may be because higher levels of emotional involvement lead to idealized expectations of mutual sharing of marital role responsibilities. This correlation between advanced courtship and egalitarianism was found among both Anglophone and Francophone men, but not among either of the female groups. He also found that men were more vulnerable than women to romantic distortion of marital role expectations during advanced courtship.

How does the movement toward greater egalitarianism among males and females affect dating practices? In a comparison of the participation of feminists and nonfeminists in date initiation and date expense sharing, Korman (1983) found that feminists were more likely to initiate dates than were nonfeminists, and that they were also more likely to share expenses on such dates. Of the nonfeminists who initiated dates, 44 percent reported that the male paid all expenses. By contrast, only 8 percent of the feminists who initiated dates reported that the male paid all expenses. Although feminists participated more in date expense sharing than did nonfeminists, Korman found that feminists (62 percent) were just as likely as nonfeminists (58 percent) to believe that when the men paid for the dates, they expected women to engage in more sexual activity than the women really desired.

In a longitudinal study, Peplau et al. (1977, 1995) investigated the personal and relationship correlates of sex role attitudes of 231 college-age dating couples during college, and again 15 years later. Contrary to expectations, sex role attitudes assessed during college were not related to general patterns of marriage, childbearing, and employment. Thus, for example, traditional sex role attitudes were not related to the likelihood of marriage, timing of first marriage, or age at first marriage. Traditional women (43 percent) were more likely than other women (26 percent) to marry their college sweetheart, and were much less likely to have the marriage end in divorce in the 15-year period. (None of the traditional marriages versus half of the egalitarian marriages ended in divorce.) The sex role attitudes of men and women were not related to the number of children, the timing of children, or plans for future children. Contrary to predictions and their own expectations, traditional women were just as likely to be employed full time as those with egalitarian sex roles. One significant difference was that traditional women were less likely than other women to obtain graduate degrees.

Violence and Coercion

Growing concern has been expressed about violent behaviour in the family, focusing on wife abuse and child battering. However, relatively little attention has been devoted to violence in the dating relationship, which is an important setting for the study of violence generally. The dating relationship involves a high degree of intimacy and privacy, but because there are few legal or social obstacles to its dissolution, we might expect the incidence of violence to be very low (Deal and Wampler, 1986). However, studies have revealed a surprising amount of violence in this setting. The incidence of dating violence is hard to determine precisely. Reports have indicated that from 20 percent to 47 percent (Deal and Wampler, 1986; Hanley and O'Neill, 1997)) of dates turn violent. The forms of violence reported have included threatening, pushing, slapping, punching, striking with an object, choking, assault with a weapon, and rape. The more serious forms of dating violence do not occur as frequently as the other forms, but still represent an important social problem.

A study of dating violence in a Canadian sample of college males stated that 43 percent of respondents reported perpetrating physical abuse, and 25 percent reported engaging in physical abuse on more than one occasion (Barnes et al., 1991). A more extensive study, which involved a national representative survey (DeKeseredy and Kelly, 1993) of 1307 men and 1835 women who were students at 44 Canadian colleges and universities defined woman abuse as "any intentional physical, sexual or psychological assault on a female by a male dating partner" (1993:146). The incidence of sexual abuse (referring to experiences in the last 12 months) measures experiences such as unwanted sexual contact, sexual coercion, attempted rape, and rape. The global incidence rate for female victims of sexual abuse was 28 percent, whereas only 11 percent of the males reported having victimized a female dating partner. Prevalence figures (measuring experiences since leaving high school) were considerably higher, with 45 percent of the women reporting that they had been sexually abused since leaving high school, and 20 percent of the men reporting at least one abusive incident in the same time period. On the global scale, the incidence of physical abuse is reported by 14 percent of men, while 22 percent of females report experiencing physical abuse. Again, the prevalence of physical abuse is higher, with almost 35 percent of women reporting having been physically assaulted and 18 percent of the men reporting having used physical abuse since leaving high school. Psychological abuse is even more prevalent, with 74 percent of men reporting having been psychologically abusive, and 79 percent of women reporting being victims of psychological abuse. The prevalence figures were somewhat higher, with 86 percent of women and 80 percent of men reporting this behaviour since high school.

The exact causes of date violence are not yet clear. Stets's (1992) data suggests that males that are involved in date violence are unable to "take the role of the other." She uses this interpretation from Symbolic Interaction theory to argue that some males lack empathic abilities and that this lack of empathy with the partner is a good predictor of date violence. Hendy et al. (2003) found that violence received as a child from mothers was associated with males in romantic relationships instigating violence and with females receiving violence. Although these two positions may be complementary, it is unclear at this time if mothers' violence to boys is related to a lack of empathic ability and later violence in romantic relationships.

The differences between males and females in reporting experiences of abuse "raise important questions of a social and legal nature regarding the interpretations that men and women have of consent within dating relationships. These bear directly on current discussions about whether consent has been given or one partner has simply complied because they felt pressure to do so or were unable to refuse—the no means no debate" (DeKeseredy and Kelly, 1993:156). A further breakdown of these figures is found in Box 6.2. An earlier study using a convenience sample of 333 undergraduate male students at four Ontario universities found that 69 percent of the respondents reported having psychologically abused their female partners, 12 percent had engaged in physical abuse, and 3 percent had sexually abused a dating partner or girlfriend (DeKeseredy, 1988b).

In an investigation of three dating violence profiles, Gray and Foshee (1997) found that 66 percent of students who reported violence in their relationship reported that such violence was mutual, whereas 14 percent of participants were victims only, and 20 percent were perpetrators only. Individuals who engaged in mutual violence received and perpetrated significantly more violence than those who were victims only or perpetrators only. Individuals in mutually violent relationships were more accepting of dating violence than were those in one-sided relationships, and had also been victims of partner violence in other dating relationships. The majority of individuals experiencing violence reported that their relationship was "good" or "very good," and from 55 to 63 percent of those experiencing violence were still dating their partner. Twenty-six percent of males compared to only 8 percent of females reported being victims only of dating violence, whereas 29 percent of females compared with only 4 percent of males reported being perpetrators only of dating violence.

Riggs and Caulfield (1997) examined how the expected consequences of using physical violence in a dating relationship affected the actual use of violence by male college students in their current dating relationship. They found that physical aggression is related to the expected consequences of that aggression. Men who used physical aggression were more likely to expect that it would result in winning the argument. Men who did not use physical aggression in their current dating relationship were more likely to expect that the use of violence would result in an interruption, or the dissolution, of the relationship.

Studies have shown there are a number of gender differences with respect to perpetrating violence and being victimized by violence in close relationships. Females reported engaging in a wider variety of violent actions, but males were more likely to engage in more extreme forms of violence resulting in injury (Lane and Gwartney-Gibbs, 1985; Stets and Henderson, 1991). Males exhibited a more regular pattern of dating violence, involving multiple incidents with multiple partners (62 percent males as opposed to 24 percent females), whereas females were more likely to perpetrate violence on a single occasion with a single partner (51 percent of females versus 20 percent of males). Cohabiting students were more likely to be victimized by violence than were either singles or marrieds (Makepeace, 1986). Female victims reported suffering more negative effects, including anger and emotional trauma, from violence in relationships (Follingstad et al., 1991).

Hanley and O'Neill (1997) tested dating couples on violence and commitment. They found that in one-third of the couples, at least one respondent reported the occurrence of violence. When violence was defined as occurring only when reported by both members, the prevalence rate dropped from 33 percent to 19 percent. Violent couples were more likely to use verbal aggression as well as physical violence. Violent couples had been dating longer and demonstrated higher levels of commitment to one another than did nonviolent couples. The authors suggest that reports of mutual violence may be incongruent because of the different ways

Box 6.2   Research Insights: Abuse on Canadian University Campuses

A national survey of 1835 female college and university undergraduates found the following:

Psychological abuse

- 989 (62 percent) said her partner did or said something to spite her
- 857 (53 percent) said they were insulted or sworn at
- 614 (37 percent) said they had been accused of having affairs or flirting with other men
- 491 (30 percent) said they were put down in front of friends or family
- 433 (27 percent) said men they dated had thrown, smashed or kicked something
- 174 (11 percent) said men threatened to hit or throw something at them

Physical abuse

- 319 (20 percent) said they had been pushed, grabbed, or shoved
- 85 (5 percent) said they had been slapped
- 85 (5 percent) said they had something thrown at them
- 61 (4 percent) said they had been kicked, bitten or hit with a fist
- 54 (3 percent) said they had been hit with an object
- 32 (2 percent) said they had been choked
- 21 (1 percent) said they had been beaten
- 9 (1 percent) said they had been threatened with a knife or a gun

- 2 (0.1 percent) said a knife or gun was used on them

Sexual abuse and assault

- 318 (18 percent) said they engaged in sex play unwillingly because they were overwhelmed by a man's continual arguing and pressure
- 198 (12 percent) said they had sexual intercourse unwillingly because they were overwhelmed by a man's continual arguing and pressure
- 129 (8 percent) said they had sexual intercourse unwillingly because they were drunk or high
- 121 (7 percent) said that a man had attempted sexual intercourse when they were drunk or high, but intercourse did not occur
- 67 (4 percent) said that a man had attempted sexual intercourse by threatening or using some degree of physical force, but intercourse did not occur
- 54 (3 percent) said they engaged in sex play unwillingly because physical force was threatened or used
- 34 (2 percent) said they had sexual intercourse unwillingly because physical force was threatened or used

Source: Dekeseredy and Kelly, 1993:152–153.

---

in which men and women view aggression. A second explanation of underreporting violence is that individuals in violent relationships are justifying their decision to remain in the relationship by reporting less violence than actually occurs.

A weakness of many of the studies on dating violence is that they do not examine the context of such violence. How much violence perpetrated by females, for example, is a reaction to unwanted sexual advances by the male partner, and hence a matter of self-defence or self-protection? How frequently do women hit men

in response to violence initiated by the men? These issues need to be carefully examined in future research.

What precipitates violence in close relationships? Makepeace (1981) reported that the most frequent precipitating cause of violence was jealousy regarding the real or perceived involvement of the partner with another person. Next in order of importance was disagreement regarding drinking and sexual denial. Barnes et al. (1991) reported that the two strongest predictors of abuse of a dating partner were violence in the family of origin and frequent use of alcohol. Deal and Wampler (1986) concluded that only two variables—previous violent experiences and self-esteem—were associated with premarital violence. Previous violent experiences accounted for almost all of the premarital violence reported.

Christopher et al. (1993) found that sexual promiscuity, violent attitudes, and hostility were important predictors of male sexual aggression against women. Positive relationships have also been found between abuse of dating partners and higher levels of stress among men, as well as higher levels of support and social ties with abusive peers (DeKeseredy, 1990; DeKeseredy and Kelley, 1995).

In a multivariate investigation of dating aggression, Foo and Margolin (1995) measure the unique and combined contributions of the following variables to dating aggression: exposure to aggression in the family of origin, attitudes justifying dating aggression, child-to-parent aggression; child sexual abuse; violent sexual victimization; alcohol use; and socioeconomic status. They found that the determinants of dating violence appear to be different for males and females, in that the variables examined account for 41 percent of variance in males' dating aggression but only 16 percent of the variance in females' dating aggression. The primary overlap between males and females is found in the attitude that humiliation by one's dating partner justifies dating aggression. While self-defence is a highly endorsed condition for justifying dating aggression, it does not predict actual aggressive behaviour.

Using regression analysis, Small and Kerns (1993) found five factors that predicted the experience of unwanted sexual activity: parental monitoring, history of sexual abuse, peer conformity, alcohol use, and authoritative parenting. Parental monitoring was the strongest predictor, followed closely by a history of sexual abuse and peer conformity. Excessive alcohol use and authoritative parenting made independent, but weaker, contributions to unwanted sexual activity. Parental monitoring involves keeping tabs on children's whereabouts, but also involves making an effort to know their friends. Adolescents with parents who appropriately monitor them are less likely to get into situations where sexual coercion is likely to occur. A prior history of sexual abuse may have traumatized adolescents, so they may have difficulty setting sexual boundaries, they may feel powerless in the face of sexual aggression, and they

may be confused about normal dating and sexual behaviour. Adolescents who experienced higher peer conformity were more vulnerable to unwanted sexual activities. The tendency to yield to the wishes and desires of others to the exclusion of one's own needs may be related to the cultural stereotype that being feminine is related to pleasing others. The use of alcohol may result in the victim being less able to defend herself, the lowering of both persons' inhibitions, and an increase in aggression of the assailant. Adolescents from homes with authoritative parents have usually been previously involved in making decisions affecting their personal lives, and are thus better prepared to make assertive and responsible decisions on their own.

One of the most disturbing aspects of violence in dating relationships is the proportion of persons who remain in such relationships despite the lack of barriers keeping them in the relationship. Apparently, many victims perceive abuse as legitimate behaviour in intimate relationships. Perhaps they perceive no other preferable alternatives, particularly when reinforced by the cultural norm that "any partner is better than no partner." Lloyd (1991) suggests that physical violence and sexual exploitation ("the dark side of courtship") do not lead to relationship breakups because of two particular features of the dating and courtship system. The first is the traditional aspect of courtship for men and women, which emphasizes male control and female dependence and relationship maintenance. In the minds of the partners, this perception may justify the use of force by the male and compliance by the female. The second feature is the role of romanticism in courtship. Romanticism leads to the downplaying of violence, or to the attribution of violence to external factors such as spontaneous or impulsive behaviour, or to situational factors such as undue stress. Some victims of abuse have indicated that their relationship actually improved after an act of violence. Romanticism may also lead to the belief that violence will disappear over time or be conquered by love. Henton et al. (1983) found that more than one-third of their respondents who had experienced aggression interpreted it as a sign of love.

Using a national representative sample of young never-married persons who date, Stets (1992) applied insights provided by symbolic interaction theory to explain dating aggression. The non-consensual process of conflict, the cognitive process of role-taking, and the expressive process of interpersonal control were examined with respect to their effect on dating aggression. The research showed that these factors were important, particularly in explaining more persistent, recurring acts of aggression. Cognitive processes (particularly the ability to take the role of the other), and expressive processes (or actions that express the self and control the other) were related to frequent patterns of minor and severe aggression, but were not associated with the one-time occurrence of aggression. Stets concludes that interaction variables are better able to predict the forms and frequencies of dating aggression than are such demographic variables as age, gender, race, and socioeconomic status. "This suggests that dating aggression has less to do with individuals' background characteristics and more to do with the kinds of interaction patterns that occur in relationships" (Stets, 1992: 175).

The relationship between adolescent-courtship violence and subsequent domestic violence has been largely neglected despite the fact that courtship may be a transitional phase or training ground in the later use of violence. Ryan (1995) discovered that many of the characteristics that have been found to be associated with wife-battering men in previous studies were also found in college men who admitted to engaging in low-level courtship violence.

Date Rape

One aspect of dating violence that has been receiving increasing public attention is the problem of acquaintance rape, or date rape (see Box 6.3). **Date rape** occurs when a nonconsenting woman is forced by her partner to engage in unwanted sexual activities while on a date. The definition of what constitutes date rape is rather ambiguous, and creates problems for those studying the issue. One study presented male and female subjects with a detailed description of a date that culminated in sexual intercourse. Three factors varied in the description: the amount of force by the male (low or moderate); the onset of protest by the female (early, moderate, or late during foreplay); and the type of protest (pleading, or pleading plus physical struggle). In evaluating the incident, more egalitarian subjects were less likely to perceive the victim as blameworthy. The more force was used, the more the female protested,

and the earlier the protest took place, the more likely the incident was to be viewed as rape. When little force was used, and the woman's protests were late in onset, both male and female subjects were likely to blame the woman and to perceive her as desiring sex (Shotland and Goodstein, 1983). Sawyer et al. (1998) found that students perceived rape as being sexual intercourse that occurred after the word "no" had been verbalized, regardless of the presence or absence of coercion. When "no" was not verbalized, but coercion was clearly present, both men and women reported only moderate levels of rape attribution.

In their survey of recent research related to date rape, Ward et al. (1991) identify four major themes: the increasing incidence of sexual assault among college students (estimates range from a low of 15 percent to a high of 78 percent); the underreporting of assaults; the reluctance to use the "rape" label to describe incidents in intimate relationships; and the frequent link between sexual assault and the use of alcohol. A weakness of much of the research is that it dichotomizes rape as either "stranger" or "acquaintance/date" rape. Though many women fear the stranger in the parking lot or the back alley, there is increasing evidence that this stereotype does not adequately characterize sexual assault. Ward et al. suggest a four-fold typology that takes account of the context that brings the victim and perpetrator together: *stranger rape*, the stereotypical view of rape; *party rape*, in which the victim and perpetrator are strangers but are part of the same social situation; *acquaintance rape*, in which the victim and perpetrator know each other; and *date rape*, in which a dating relationship exists between the victim and perpetrator.

In their study, Ward and her colleagues asked respondents about unwanted sexual contact (attempted or actual kissing, fondling, or touching in a sexual manner); unwanted attempted sexual intercourse (any form of attempted sexual penetration); and unwanted completed sexual intercourse (any form of sexual penetration, including vaginal intercourse, oral sex, and anal intercourse). Thirty-four percent of their sample of women said they had experienced unwanted sexual contact; 20 percent experienced unwanted attempted sexual intercourse; and 10 percent experienced unwanted sexual intercourse. The majority of unwanted sexual advances took place in a casual relationship. All of the reports of attempted and completed intercourse with a

Box 6.3   Research Insights: Date Rape

A major survey of U.S. colleges showed approximately one in seven female students had experienced date rape, a psychologist told the Commons subcommittee . . . . And Rhonda Steinberg, president of the Canadian Psychological Association, said the problem could be as bad in Canada, although she has yet to complete a similar survey of Canadian universities. "I have no reason to believe it's any different here," said Steinberg, a professor at Simon Fraser University in British Columbia. "I don't think we're any less violent. We're just quiet about it."

In date rape, the offenders are friends, classmates, even former lovers. "One would expect that because of (the male students') knowledge ... that they would know better," Steinberg told MPs. "They don't."

The subcommittee is completing a study of violence against women, ranging from wife abuse to sexual assaults on children.

Steinberg said she used the university date rape statistics to show violence against women isn't limited to the poor, uneducated, lower-class groups she said were normally associated with such behaviour. "The major reason that this occurs is that women in this society are seen as fair game," she said.

Women are often portrayed in the media as vulnerable, and men are often socialized to believe they can take advantage of that because they have power, said Steinberg.

Source: Cox, 1991:A4.

"stranger" took place during or immediately following a party, and commonly involved the use of alcohol. Though women fear walking alone at night, unwanted sexual experiences are more likely to occur in the context of a "normal" social situation, usually after parties.

DeKeseredy (1988a) draws attention to the fact that many studies of dating violence attribute partial responsibility to the female victims for precipitating the violence. This mitigates the assailant's guilt, and places the blame on the victim. It also diverts attention from the trauma and suffering of victims of violence, and obscures the true nature of male violence against women. Schuler (1990) asserts that the guilt, confusion, and fear experienced by date rape victims can last for years, and is often worse than what victims of a stranger-rape experience. Date rape leads to a lack of trust, since it was a friend who betrayed the victims and violated their bodies. Shapiro and Schwartz (1997) found that women who had experienced date rape reported more trauma symptoms and lower sexual self-esteem than did women who had never been raped.

A shattering example of the attitudes of some men toward rape was seen in the response to the Queen's University student council's anti-rape campaign slogan, "No means no!" Some men responded with such slogans as "No means more beer," "No means harder," "No means kick her in the teeth," and "No means she's a dyke." When women on campus protested, some received harassing telephone calls, and the controversy continued for more than a month. Thorne-Finch (1992) questions why men would ever have treated rape as a laughing matter, and argues that this scandal shows that there has been little change in our society in attitudes toward women.

Benokraitis (1993) points out that since rape is learned behaviour, it can also be unlearned. Solutions must be sought on three different levels. On the *individual level*, women must learn to take greater control of their lives, and to be more informed about the risks of dating relationships. They need to be aware of the contributing factors of alcohol and conducive environments for sex. On the *organizational level*, campus authorities need to be pressured to take serious action against students who engage in sexual aggression on campus. On the *societal level*, a significant proportion of our attitudes and behaviour relating to sex, dating, and rape needs to be revamped. The male conception of women as sex objects needs to be altered, through legislation if necessary.

SUMMARY

- The dating continuum distinguishes various stages of dating relationships. Changing conventions governing dating behaviour are continuing to emerge, including more freedom for females, less formality, and fewer group activities. Dating fulfills a number of different functions including recreation, socialization, status grading or achievement, and mate selection.

- The study of close, interpersonal relationships has changed from an emphasis on structure in relationships to a concern with the process of relationships. This includes the study of the development, the maintenance or stability, and the dissolution of close relationships. A number of stage models have been created, based on a sequence of stages of interpersonal relationships.

- In our society, love is seen as the primary ingredient in mate selection, and our definition of love is strongly influenced by the romantic ideal. Many definitions distinguish between romantic and companionate, or conjugal, love. Others define love from a multidimensional perspective.

- Selected trends in attitudes and behaviour with respect to premarital sex include an increase in the approval and incidence of premarital sexual behaviour; a more rapid increase in sexual permissiveness and behaviour for females than for males; an increase in the number of males and females who approve of intercourse both with and without affection; a decrease in the average age at which first intercourse is experienced; and an increase in the number of sexual partners among the sexually experienced.

- Changing sex standards within our society are related to greater autonomy in relationships with the other sex; the development of a "youth culture" supporting premarital sex; the increased availability and acceptability of contraception and abortion, and acceptance of unwed pregnancy and motherhood; the increased number of women in the labour force; and the decreased influence of religion over individuals. Changes in values such as increased individualism, increased egalitarianism in relationships, and an increased emphasis on hedonism have also influenced changing sex standards.

- Premarital sexual attitudes and behaviour have been described by four premarital sex standards: abstinence; the double standard; permissiveness with affection; and permissiveness without affection. The most significant change is the decline of the abstinence standard, and the corresponding increase in the permissiveness with or without affection standards.

- A number of correlates of premarital sexual attitudes and behaviour have been found. Children from divorced or separated homes have higher rates of premarital intercourse, and experience first intercourse at an earlier age. There is little parental participation in intentional sex instruction, but what does take place is primarily due to the efforts of mothers. As well, studies show that the relationship between partners themselves is a more powerful influence on the experience of premarital sex than is formal sex education in the school or the home; young people who have experienced premarital sex tend to have friends with more permissive attitudes toward, and more frequent experience of, premarital sex; and both religious affiliation and participation are negatively related to premarital sexual permissiveness.

- Dating is problematic for many persons at some time in their lives. Problems include difficulties in securing dates, network interference, gender differences in perceptions and expectations, and the incidence of violence and coercion.

- A common assumption is that females are more romantic than males, but considerable research evidence indicates the opposite. Males and females differ not only in levels of romanticism, but also in the ways in which they experience love. Females are more likely to emphasize companionate, dependent, and pragmatic relationships, whereas males are more likely to emphasize romantic and game-playing approaches to love.

- Studies of date rape have revealed the increasing incidence of sexual assaults among college and university students, the underreporting of such assaults, the reluctance to apply the "rape" label, and the frequent presence of alcohol. Rape is more likely to occur among acquaintances, friends, and dating partners than among strangers, and consequently has more traumatic effects.

KEY TERMS

Agape (123)

Companionate (mature) love (121)

Courtship (116)

Date rape (143)

Dating (115)

Dating continuum (116)

Eros (122)

Intimacy (115)

Ludus (122)

Mania (123)
Network interference (137)
Pragma (123)
Romantic love (120)
Storge (123)

QUESTIONS FOR REVIEW

1. How would you define intimacy? How is intimacy related to dating and courtship?
2. What is the relative importance of romantic love in individualistic and collectivistic societies? How are values with respect to romantic love changing in these societies?
3. Review the major features of dating prior to the 1920s; from the 1920s to the 1960s; and since the 1960s.
4. Discuss the major functions of dating, and how these are related to different stages of dating and courtship.
5. Discuss the role of conflict in different stages of a dating or courtship relationship.
6. Define love as you understand it. Differentiate between romantic love and companionate love, and indicate what is meant by love in a multidimensional perspective. How do males and females differ in their experience and expression of love?
7. Review the key problems that young people encounter in the areas of securing dates, network interference, gender differences in perceptions and expectations, and violence and coercion.

QUESTIONS FOR DISCUSSION

1. What changes in dating and courtship practices would you project for the 21st century, based on current trends?
2. How would you define love? How important is love in the development of a stable, growing relationship or marriage?
3. Why do people remain in a violent dating relationship despite the absence of barriers keeping them there?
4. What are the causes of violence in a dating or courtship relationship?

SUGGESTED READINGS

Brehm, S., R. Miller, D. Perlman, and S. Campbell. 2002. *Intimate Relationships*. Boston, MA: McGraw-Hill Inc. The discussion is a unique combination of scholarly and practical approaches to developing and maintaining relationships.

Hendrick, Susan S. and Clyde Hendrick. 1992. *Romantic Love*. Newbury Park: Sage. An examination of romantic love from a social psychological perspective, which also uses insights from sociobiology, philosophy, history, family studies, and sociology. Gender differences in close relationships are examined.

CHAPTER 7

Mate Selection, Courtship, and Cohabitation

After studying this chapter, you should be able to do the following:

- Differentiate between autonomous and arranged selection of mates.
- Discuss the influence of the sex ratio on marriage for each sex, and the contributing factors to the "real" marriage squeeze among middle-aged women.
- Define exogamy and endogamy, and provide examples of how each limits autonomous mate selection; review the impact of age, religion, and ethnicity on marital homogamy.
- Discuss the changing incidence and meaning of premarital cohabitation for young people.
- Describe the effects of premarital cohabitation on marital quality and stability.
- Discuss gay and lesbian relationships, and explain the problems inherent in comparing gay and lesbian mate selection to heterosexual mate selection.

Introduction

As has been seen in Chapter 6, the ways in which individuals form intimate relationships may vary considerably based on the trajectory of the relationship as well as peer and parental support. Heterosexual contact and interaction before marriage is strongly related to the type of society in which one lives. Canadian society primarily fosters an autonomous system of mate selection. In this chapter, we examine the shift from dating to courtship and mate selection.

There is no clear marker or event that separates dating from mate selection. Indeed, the two can be intertwined. However, for many young people there is a subtle change in thinking from "that would be fun" to "am I seriously interested in this person as a mate?" A dating partner might evolve into a serious relationship, but the very definition of dating is tied to recreation and fun. Mate selection, by contrast, on the other hand is tied to the conscious and "unconscious"

screening of potential mates. Although mate selection is an extension of the formation of intimate relationships discussed in Chapter 6, it is also much more. Mate selection is for the purpose of reproduction and, hence, partners are selected by criteria that relate to longer term relationships than dating.

Choosing a Marriage Partner

"Your choice of a marriage partner is one of the most important choices you will make in your life." Generations of parents across the country have often repeated some form of this statement. Many of us have heard it in our own home. The use of the word *choice* indicates our particular cultural bias, which defines marriage as an individual decision with relatively little influence from institutions or other persons. Most young people in our society accept as a given the freedom to choose their own mate, and they regard other approaches as strange or even inconceivable. Nevertheless, a cross-cultural consideration of mate selection reveals that the process varies considerably from society to society, as described in Chapters 3 and 4.

According to Reiss (1980), *courtship institutions* are a universal aspect of every human society. All courtship institutions share one common function: the selection of future mates. However, societies vary in the degree to which either young people or their parents are socially sanctioned to arrange marriages. We might view the different structures used for courtship institutions as lying on a continuum. **Arranged marriages,** at one end of the continuum, are those in which the parents of the participants exercise complete control of the selection of the marriage partner. Parents, kin, or intermediaries choose marriage partners on the basis of social class, caste, religion, education, or other similar criteria. **Autonomous marriages,** at the other end of the continuum, are those in which the participants themselves have free choice in their selection of a marriage partner.

A general trend toward autonomous marriages is found among some second-generation immigrants to Canada from countries in which arranged marriages are common. As many as 90 percent of South Asians born and raised in Canada still choose a marriage arranged by their parents or a mediator. A significant change, however, is that more authority is being given to young people to make up their own minds about whom they will marry. Previously, the participants often had not even met before their marriage; today, an increasing number have the "final say" in response to their parents' choice, and some even go out together following the initial meeting and agreement to marry. Today, parents more often screen potential partners rather than determine the final selection. One Pakistani woman comments as follows: "The best recipe I can come up with is if a man likes someone, and she likes him too, then get the family involved for a marriage" (Jimenez, 1992a).

Dion and Dion (1993) link individualism and collectivism to culture-related and gender-related differences in close relationships. They find support for three propositions: Romantic love is an important basis for marriage in societies where individualism is a dominant cultural value. Psychological intimacy in a marital relationship is more important for marital satisfaction and personal well-being in individualistic societies. While individualism contributes to the value of romantic love as a basis for marriage, it makes the development of intimacy more problematic because of individualism's emphasis on autonomy and self-fulfillment, which leads to an ambivalence about emotional dependence in an intimate relationship. An emphasis on individualism was negatively related to reported caring, need and trust of one's partner (Dion and Dion, 1991). In contrast, in collectivistic societies, romantic love is less likely to be valued as a basis for marriage. Intimacy is likely to be diffused across a network of family relationships. In such societies, interpersonal dependency is regarded as much more positive and constructive (Dion and Dion, 1993).

A more recent study (Dion and Dion, 1996) emphasizes that there have been changes in values with respect to romantic love and its impact on marital choice in traditionally collectivistic societies, and particularly among persons from such societies who have immigrated to Canada and other Western countries. An increased emphasis on individualism leads to an increased emphasis on personal growth and fulfillment in marriage, and the assumption that marriage should promote self-development. When fulfillment does not take place, the basis for marriage may be questioned. Dion and Dion maintain that in recent decades heightened individualism has contributed to higher rates of marriage failure and divorce. "If so, it remains to be seen whether young adults in these societies (e.g., Japan, Taiwan) and young adults whose parents emigrated from traditionally collectivistic societies to Canada, Australia, or the United States show increasingly high rates of divorce and remarriage" (Dion and Dion, 1996: 15,16).

Based on a biosocial theoretical approach, Pérusse (1994) tested an evolutionary model of mate choice, which hypothesized that such choice is based on resources that each sex contributes to reproduction. Support for his model was indicated by the following findings:

1. The acquisition of mating partners by men (but not by women) was strongly correlated with their social status. He concludes that male social status is an important criterion of female mate choice.

2. The number of partners acquired by women in the preceding year was inversely correlated with age, and thus positively associated with reproductive potential. The number of partners acquired by men

in the preceding year was not associated with age. This leads to the conclusion that males, at least partly, base their mate choice on their prospective partners' capacity to procreate.

3. A significant relationship was found between marital dissolution and extramarital relations for women but not for men, suggesting that men place greater importance than do women on sexual exclusivity in mating.

Having considered the cultural variation in choosing marriage partners, we might react with a sense of relief that we live in a society that practises autonomous mate selection. The label of autonomous mate choice for our society, however, is somewhat misleading. Indeed, there is probably no society in which a person is completely free from outside influences when choosing a marriage partner. Important factors that come into play include the socialization process, which results in our attraction to selected persons, family pressures to marry certain kinds of persons, and cultural expectations that marital choices fall within certain parameters.

Arranged Marriages

Arranged marriages are contracted by parents, relatives, or a matchmaker who does not assume that the young individual's choice is of paramount importance. Indeed, in arranged marriages it is often said that "marital decisions are too important to be left to the young." Arranged marriages often emphasize the importance of the marriage to social institutions such as the family and kinship, religion, and social status structures.

Most theories about the nature of arranged marriage focus on kinship. The French anthropologist Claude Lévi-Strauss (1949) developed a complex theory about the role of kinship in marriage. He proposed that arranged marriages represent social exchanges between kinship groups. In many societies these social exchanges were an exchange of mates between clans or totemic groups but not necessarily within one generation. As a result, kinship allied these groups over successive generations. As Lévi-Strauss points out, such systems of exchanges would serve to dampen any hostilities between social groups while encouraging other forms of social exchange and trade. This perspective has become known as "alliance theory" since it focuses on the role of arranged marriages in forming the social alliances.

Another function of arranged marriages is to ensure stability and membership in certain social institutions. The two most important of these are the pattern of institutionalized stratification (social class or caste) and institutional religion. Parents and matchmakers are often most concerned that the marriage replicates the existing social structure. For example, in traditional Indian marriages, caste boundaries and caste endogamy is strictly observed. Religious endogamy is another principal concern in the formation of unions. Both of these social structures depend on ascriptive and relatively closed systems for their permanence, and arranged mate selection has been one of the major tools for the preservation of the status quo. Among immigrant groups, arranged marriages that are endogamous to the ethnic group can be used to preserve language and culture and to hold off trends of assimilation.

Today, arranged marriages in most societies are changing character as those societies move from highly traditional, ascriptive forms of status to forms that emphasize individual achievements rather than artifacts of birth. Seldom do parents arrange a marriage partner for their child when the child is first born, and increasingly intermediaries such as matchmakers replace the functions that parents and kin once played. For example, in India, it is common that the first stage is for a third party to match horoscopes of prospective boys and girls. The matching is usually circumscribed by religious and social status considerations. After this point, the family will allow for their child to meet the prospective mates, and the desires of the young person are considered. There are other considerations, such as the size of the dowry, that might overshadow the young person's preferences and fit with the economic plans of the family.

Arranged marriages in China follow a much more formally acknowledged protocol known as the "three letters and six etiquettes." The three letters explicitly lay out gifts (dowry and bride price) to be exchanged by each family. The etiquettes refer to the proper sequence of events, including the matchmaker establishing that the birth date and hour of birth for the boy and girl are compatible. However, before these take place the parents identify a list of prospects; this list is usually guided by the parents' concern with religion and social status.

There is little doubt that those arranging marriages are becoming increasingly concerned with the desires and preferences of the young. It is interesting that as we move to autonomous choice of mates, we often find that divorce rates increase. This may be because divorce rates are always low in traditional societies, but it could also be that a broader range of evaluations of potential mates are made when the parents and kin and matchmakers are all involved in the process. However, we might be over emphasizing the "freedom" young people have in the "autonomous" choice of mates, since the actual process of selecting a mate appears to be constrained by many factors.

The Limits of Autonomy in Mate Selection

As we have seen, Canadian young people frequently assume that their choice of a mate is completely autonomous—in other words, that they are free to marry anyone they please. However, a number of factors do place limits on autonomy, whether we consciously recognize their influence or not.

Kerckhoff and Davis (1962) introduced a "filter" model of mate selection. This model has undergone multiple restatements and modifications over time (e.g. Murstein 1970). It is best viewed as a heuristic model to help us understand the usual decisions and processes that mate selection and courtship follow within autonomous systems. Interestingly, this model also points out that what we call an "autonomous system" involves the values we have learned from significant people in our lives such as parents and is subject to continuing pressures from peers, parents, and kin as well as social institutions. We will use this model to help us organize the many theories about mate selection into a coherent perspective.

Pool of Eligibles and Gender Preference

Imagine that you could, at least in principle, choose anyone in the world as a marriage partner. You would have a confusing array of possibilities. This would imply that the pool of eligibles for mating would be composed of everyone in the world. Fortunately, for most of us, such an assumption would be unrealistic. The first criteria we might bring to narrowing down the pool of eligibles is that we might prefer one sex over another. This would immediately shrink the pool of possible mates by half. The basic notion of filtering models such as in Figure 7.1 (e.g., Kerckoff and Davis, 1962; Murstein, 1970) is that this huge pool of eligibles is "screened out" or "filtered" through successive filters until only one or a few individuals remain for the final choice. In reality, this process may be more metaphorical or heuristic than descriptive of how individuals actually proceed in their mate selection.

Propinquity and Sex Ratio

It used to be said in earlier decades that partners were most likely to be selected from within close proximity (**propinquity**) to one's home and neighborhood. Today, with the Internet and other sorts of long distance communications in addition to easy and accessible travel, distance is no longer such a barrier to forming close relationships. Indeed, Statistics Canada (2003) reports that 12 percent of married relationships do not co-reside with one another.

Even though propinquity is no longer as predictive as it once was, we usually need to communicate and become acquainted over a period of time before we are ready to marry. Of course, to every rule there are exceptions; one such is "speed dating," where successive prospects are interviewed in the course of one evening. Even more "arm's length" is Internet dating, where two people might correspond and become close but not meet in person for some time, as in the movie "You've

Figure 7.1   Filtering Process in Autonomous Mate Selection

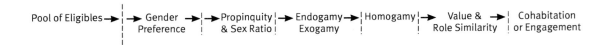

Pool of Eligibles → | → Gender → | → Propinquity | → Endogamy → | Homogamy | → Value & → | Cohabitation
Preference & Sex Ratio Exogamy Role Similarity or Engagement

Got Mail" (Warner Bros., 1998). Research has not been able to keep up with all of the technological changes in regard to dating and mate selection (e.g. White, 2003) let alone the changes in family and spousal communication, so we are only speculating that most young people will still prefer face-to-face interaction in regard to mate selection.

Another factor that limits autonomy in mate selection is the impact of the sex ratio on marriage patterns. The **sex ratio** is the number of males for every 100 females in a particular population. A low sex ratio (fewer men than women) results in an oversupply of women. A high sex ratio (fewer women than men) results in an oversupply of men. In a study of marriage among Canadian women, Trovato (1988) found support for the hypothesis that a higher sex ratio is associated with relatively high marriage rates and relatively low age at first marriage for women. As the sex ratio increases, there is an undersupply of eligible women, resulting in an increase in the importance of marriage and the family in people's lives. South and Lloyd (1992) supported the finding that a lower sex ratio reduced the marriage rates for women. They also found evidence that it increased the ratio of nonmarital ("out of wedlock") to marital births, and that it lowered the average divorce rates. A number of factors influence the sex ratio for marriageable adults, including sex ratio at birth, migration, hypergamy (the tendency of women to marry men older than themselves), the greater tendency of men to marry following divorce, the termination of common-law unions, and mortality rates and life expectancy (Riordan, 1994).

Glick and his colleagues introduced the term **"marriage squeeze"** in 1959 to refer to a low sex ratio created by the baby boom (Glick, 1988). Girls born during the baby boom (between 1945 and 1965) faced a shortage of men in the usual age range when they were ready to marry because of their propensity to marry men who were older than themselves—men born during the pre-boom years. Glick (1988) speculated that the marriage squeeze indirectly contributed to the growth of the women's liberation movement during the 1970s, as many of these unmarried women entered the workforce and turned to careers instead of getting married. Their experience of discrimination in the labour force may have prompted many of them to turn to the women's movement for support. Using data

from the 1979–1986 waves of the *National Longitudinal Survey of Youth*, Lichter et al. (1995) tested the hypothesis that shortages of suitable marriage partners lower the probability of marriage for women and increase the likelihood that never-married women will enter heterogamous marriages. While they found that a high sex ratio (more men than women) increases the likelihood of a woman marrying a high-status rather than a low-status man (in terms of occupation and education), they found little evidence that actual mate surpluses or deficits resulted in an increase of heterogamous marriage (status or age).

Also according to Glick, demographic data indicate that during the 1990s and through the turn of the next century, the marriage squeeze will be reversed, with fewer women than men in the marriage market. This prediction is borne out in Canada, where in 1991 there were 120 unattached men aged 15 to 29 for every 100 unattached women the same age. The Northwest Territories, the Yukon, and Quebec had the highest ratios of unattached men aged 15 to 29 (128, 127 and 124, respectively) for every 100 comparable women. Nova Scotia and Ontario had the lowest ratio, with 118 unattached young men for every 100 women. The highest sex ratios are found among those who are younger, and the sex ratio progressively declines with age. According to the 1991 Census the sex ratio declined from the 120 reported among those aged 15 to 29, to 98 for those aged 30 to 49, to 62 for those aged 50 to 64, and reached its lowest level among those aged 65 and older (a sex ratio of 30). This low sex ratio among seniors is largely due to the shorter life expectancy of men and the greater tendency of unmarried women to survive to old age (Riordan, 1994). When figures from the general population rather than from the single population are used, the 1996 Census indicates the following sex ratios: for those aged 15 to 29, the sex ratio is 101.1; for those aged 30 to 49, it is 98.1; for those aged 50 to 64, it is 97.8; and for those aged 65 and older, it is 72.9 (McVey, 1998).

Another factor influencing the availability of potential spouses is **hypergamy**, where a woman marries "up" in terms of age or other factors such as social class, socioeconomic status, education, and intelligence. It is considered appropriate for men to marry persons their own age or younger, and for women to marry persons their own age or older. Hypergamy norms are not problematic during adolescence or early adulthood since approximately equal numbers of eligible men and women exist. With advancing age, however, there are proportionately fewer and fewer unmarried men, who are able to choose from a larger pool of younger women. In contrast, there are proportionately more women, who have an increasingly smaller pool of eligible men from which to choose. At age 40, more than one-third of women have no available potential male partners to marry, and at age 50, half of women are without available partners. Veevers (1988, 2003) referred to this situation as the "real" marriage squeeze. This squeeze may contribute to a reaffirmation of the double standard in middle age. By midlife, the wife's pool of eligibles has shrunk, while the husband's has expanded. The application of the **principle of least interest**—the person least interested in continuing the relationship has the most power in the relationship (Waller, 1937)—results in the onus for maintaining the relationship falling on the wife, tipping the balance of power in the husband's favour.

Though we live in a society that emphasizes autonomous mate selection, we have seen that a number of structural factors such as age, religion, ethnicity and race, the sex ratio, and other factors such as social class place limits on autonomy. Now that we have considered the prior effects of these factors, we can turn to the role of personal and psychological factors related to individual choice. The next section considers the processes by which people seek intimate relationships.

Endogamy and Exogamy

The filters of exogamy and endogamy can be variously organized by rules that prescribe marrying inside a social group such as a clan or outside a geographical site such as a village or town. The principle of **exogamy** requires a person to select a marriage partner from outside certain prohibited groups. The widespread taboo against incest, which prohibits sexual relationships with close kin, falls into this category.

The principle of **endogamy** requires a person to select a marriage partner from inside certain acceptable social or cultural groups, despite the absence of formal regulations. **Homogamy** (assortative mating) is the tendency of persons to select mates with similar social or personal characteristics, despite the absence of formal

requirements. **Heterogamy** is the tendency of persons to select mates with different social or personal characteristics. Research shows that there is assortative matching on a wide range of variables, especially age, education, social class, race or ethnicity, and religion. We examine three variables for which recent Canadian data are available—age, religion, and ethnicity.

Age Homogamy

Based on the 1991 Census and the 1990 General Social Survey, Gentleman and Park (1994) report on age differences between spouses. Figure 7.2 reveals that husbands were older than wives in about 73 percent of the sample, wives were older than husbands in about 17 percent of the sample, and about 11 percent of the couples were the same age. Whereas 26 percent of husbands were one to two years older than their wives, only 10 percent of wives were one to two years older than their husbands. While 41 percent of husbands were three to nine years older than their wives, only six percent of wives were three to 9 years older than their husband (see Figure 7.2).

Do age differences have any impact on marital stability? Gentleman and Park found that divorce rates were lowest when the husband is two to 10 years older than his wife, or when their age differences were extremely large. They also found that divorce was more likely to take place when the wife was older than the husband than when the husband was older than the wife.

United States census data indicate that since 1900 marriages have shifted from being primarily heterogamous with respect to age, to being predominantly homogamous (see Table 7.1). In 1900, almost two-thirds (63 percent) were heterogamous, with 47 percent of the women being married to older men and 16 percent being married to men who were younger than themselves. By 1960 only 37 percent of marriages were heterogamous, and by 1980 only 30 percent were heterogamous. Age-heterogamous marriages are associated with a number of factors: foreign birth, lower educational levels, lower family income, lower occupational status, and non-employment of wife (Atkinson and Glass, 1985).

Despite the tendency toward assortative mating on the basis of age and other criteria, this tendency may be modified as women grow older without being married.

Figure 7.2   Age Differences of Married Couples

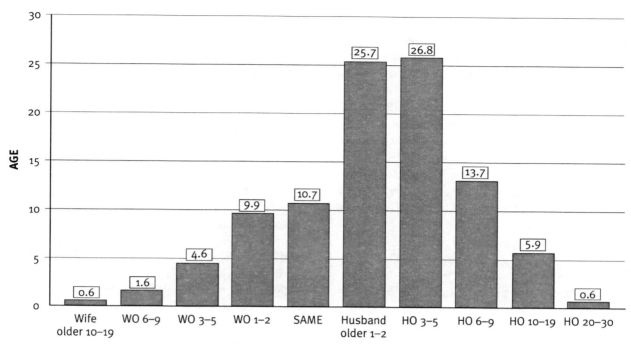

Source: Adapted from Gentleman and Park (1994:230).

TABLE 7.1   Age Homogamy/Heterogamy, by Year

	1900	1960	1980
	%	%	%
Husband older	47.1	33.0	26.9
By 5–9 years	20.1	23.0	19.5
By 10+ years	27.0	10.0	7.4
Spouses same age (± 4 years)	37.1	63.3	69.9
Wife older	15.8	3.7	3.1
By 5–9 years	5.3	2.8	2.5
By 10+ years	10.5	.9	.6

Source: Atkinson and Glass (1985:687).

In a study of women who delay marriage until after age 30, Lichter (1990) found that 30 percent of such women married a man who was at least five years older, and that 12 percent of delayed marriages included a husband who was at least 10 or more years older (compared with 20 percent and 5 percent respectively of marriages before age 30). Older women were also more likely to marry previously married men (about 33 percent of marriages after age 30 compared with 10 percent of marriages before age 30). Delayed marriage was also associated with the willingness to marry a lower-status man, as measured by level of education completed.

Despite the trend toward age-homogamous marriages, it is still true that for most societies, the woman is younger than the man in the majority of couples (Bozon, 1991). Bozon suggests that this is related to the social significance of age for men and women at the time when they decide to form a couple. He points out that younger women prefer men who are older than themselves, whereas older women prefer men who are closer to their age. The reverse is observed for men. Younger men prefer women who are closer to their own age, whereas older men choose women who are appreciably younger than themselves. This preference of younger women for older men is interpreted as a traditional attitude that corresponds to a traditional sexual division of labour, as seen in Box 7.1. This preference becomes less clear-cut in situations where women's status is not determined by the status of their spouse, as in cases of rapid acquisition of higher education and entry into the workforce. This view is supported by the current shift to more age-homogamous marriages, which corresponds with the increasing education and resulting equality of women.

There has been a convergence in the age differential of brides and grooms, decreasing from 3.3 years in 1941 to 2.2 years in 1971 and to 1.9 years in 1995 (see Figure 7.3). Age at first marriage has been increasing for both males and females since 1971, but has increased more for females than for males, resulting in a smaller age differential at first marriage. Couples who choose to marry are doing so at older ages. In 1993, fewer than 4 percent of marriages in Canada involved brides under 20, compared with nearly 30 percent in 1973. Similarly, in 1993 only 1 percent of all marriages involved bridegrooms under 20, compared with 8 percent in 1973. By 1993, one-third of men and one-fifth of women who married for the first time were over 30, compared with 10 percent of men and 5 percent of women in 1973 (Data Releases, 1995). Bumpass et al. (1991) point out that the increase in age at first marriage should not be interpreted as an increase in singlehood. The growing rates of cohabitation suggest that young people are forming unions at almost as early an age as they did previously. When first cohabitation is included with first marriage, a slight decline in age at first union is found.

Religious Homogamy

Religious homogamy can be defined in a number of different ways. It most frequently refers to those marriages in which both spouses identify a common religious affiliation at the time of marriage. But religious homogamy may also be defined in terms of the religion in which each spouse was raised, or the religion of the parents of the spouses, or the religion of each spouse at the time of measurement of the variable. The studies reported here use the first definition.

An early report (Heer, 1971) found that *interfaith* marriages (*religious heterogamy*) in Canada and in each Canadian province had increased among Catholics, Protestants, and Jews from 1922 through 1957. A follow-up study (Heer and Hubay, 1976) found a steady increase in interfaith marriages in Canada as a whole, from 6 percent in 1927 to 22 percent in 1972. In a further update of religious intermarriage in Canada, Larson and Munro (1985) found that from 1974 to 1982, religious intermarriage continued to increase among Catholics and Jews, but remained stable among Protestants. However, when subcategories of the Protestant denomination were considered separately, the researchers found significant variation from one group to another (Larson and Munro, 1990). Table 7.2 provides data that indicate religious heterogamy significantly increased in Canada between 1981 and 1990. In fact, the number of interfaith marriages more than doubled during this time from 21.8 percent to 48.6 percent. Religious homogamy is highest among the Jewish and non-Christian faiths, and lowest among mainline Protestant religions.

| Box 7.1 | Current Insights: Traditional Attitudes and Age Heterogamy |

Interview with a secretary born in 1959. Five years younger than her husband. She was 17 when they met.

"I think what made up my mind was Philip's maturity. For a start, he was older than me. He had finished his course, I was only just starting mine... I think it was his protection that I needed... I had the impression I was learning things with him and he made me feel secure, I felt protected... a bit like a father figure, I'd say, yes, a father" (Bozon, 1991: 124).

Figure 7.3   Median Age at First Marriage

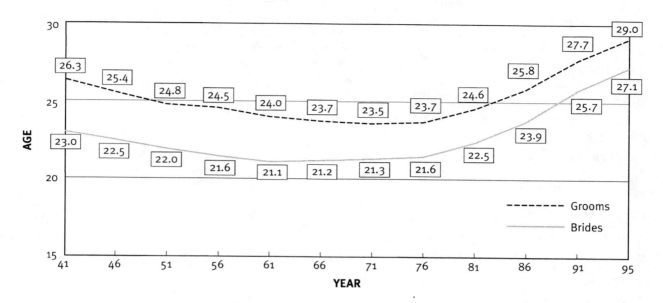

Source: Statistics Canada, 1992. Selected Marriage Statistics, 1921–1990, Catalogue No. 82–552; Data Releases, 1992, 1997. Health Reports.

What are the reasons for the increase in religious intermarriage? A frequent explanation is religious distribution; that is, the proportion of the total population that identifies itself with each religious group (Heer and Hubay, 1976). The smaller the religious group relative to the total population, the larger the proportion of heterogamous marriages we might expect. However, we know from our discussion of assortative matching that the selection of marriage partners is not random. Therefore, we need to focus on the characteristics of religion itself. Larson and Munro (1985) suggest that the increase in religious intermarriage signals a decrease in the significance of religion as a major source of values in an individual's life, or an indication of increasing secularization.

Kalmijn (1991) reports the interesting finding that while intermarriage between Catholics and Protestants (religious heterogamy) increased dramatically between the 1920s and 1980s, educational heterogamy decreased over this period. He suggests that there has been a shift from religious background to education as a basis of marital choice. Marital couples are increasingly heterogeneous with respect to religion, but homogeneous with respect to education.

What is the potential impact of this increase in religious heterogamy on marital stability? Based on data from the 1987–1988 National Survey on Family and Households, Lehrer and Chiswick (1993) found that marital stability does not vary across the various types of homogamous unions. Interfaith unions, however, have generally higher rates of breakup than intrafaith unions. This finding is consistent with the view that less efficiency and higher levels of conflict characterize heterogamous unions. Similarly, Maneker and Rankin (1993) cite evidence that religious homogamy is associated with longer marriage duration, and the couples with no religious affiliation are at greatest risk of filing for early divorce.

What is the impact of religious heterogamy or homogamy on children's religion? According to Bibby, (1997), 85 percent of married couples in 1995 belonged to the same religious group, and between 94 percent and 99 percent of same-faith couples reported that their children had the same religious identity. Similarly, parents who are not identified with any religion generally have children who have no religion. Children raised in interfaith marriages are most likely to be raised in their mother's faith tradition, even if

TABLE 7.2   Heterogamous Marriage by Denomination, Canada, 1981 and 1990*

	1981		1990	
	HUSBAND	**WIFE**	**HUSBAND**	**WIFE**
MAINLINE PROTESTANT				
Anglican	34.7	37.8	65.9	66.8
Lutheran	35.0	35.7	75.2	76.7
Presbyterian	38.2	36.7	64.7	64.6
United Church	24.7	28.1	55.8	64.9
Other Protestant	21.5	25.0	48.9	65.9
CONSERVATIVE PROTESTANT				
Baptist	3.6	33.9	57.2	58.7
Mennonite	15.4	14.2	36.2	35.6
Pentecostal	16.3	25.4	38.6	43.9
Salvation Army	30.4	31.3	65.1	68.3
CATHOLIC				
Greek Orthodox	26.0	19.5	63.8	51.2
Roman Catholic	10.9	12.8	40.7	42.4
Ukrainian Catholic	34.7	29.8	21.3	27.5
OTHER RELIGIONS				
Jewish	10.2	7.6	29.3	26.2
Non-Christian	13.9	8.1	29.3	26.2
No Religion	47.7	23.4	44.1	48.6
TOTAL	21.8	21.8	48.6	48.6

*The figures given in the table represent percentages of husbands and wives engaging in heterogamous (interfaith) marriages.

Sources: Heaton (1991:367); Statistics Canada (1991:10,11).

that is "no religion." When one marriage partner reports having no religion, the majority of children (56 percent) of these marriages have some religious affiliation. This is accounted for by the fact that it is usually men who report having no religion, and that in interfaith marriages it is usually the mothers who pass on their religion.

Ethnic Homogamy

Richard (1991) compared the prevalence and patterns of ethnic intermarriage in Canada in 1871 and 1971. Canadian Census data reveal that in 1871, a substantial 83 percent of all husbands married spouses of the same ethnic origin, while only 17 percent had ethnically heterogamous marriages. Ethnic homogamy was highest for the French (97 percent) and the Irish (83 percent). In 1971, the proportion of husbands with ethnically homogamous marriages had declined to 63 percent, while the proportion of interethnic marriages had doubled to 37 percent. Ethnic homogamy was highest for the French (86 percent) and the Italians (77 percent).

What is the impact of ethnic intermarriage on the maintenance of ethnic identity? Goldstein and Segall (1991) found that mixed marriages were associated with a lower level of ethnic identity among the children of such marriages. Based on this data, we can predict that the increasing rate of interethnic marriages will result in declining ethnic identity among Canadians in the future—despite our official emphasis on multiculturalism—unless immigration rates continue to be very high. While ethnic intermarriage may be a sign of social integration in Canada, the same is not true in other countries, as Box 7.2 demonstrates.

What is the impact of interethnic marriages on marital stability? Ho and Johnson (1990) found that interethnic marriages in Hawaii had a higher proportion of divorces than did intraethnic marriages. The relative income level of ethnic groups was also associated with marital stability, with greater instability in marriages in which the income of the bride's ethnic group is higher than that of the groom's ethnic group.

There is little doubt that such measures of social homogamy as age, religion, and ethnicity continue to influence our choice of marital partner. The assumption that assortative mating also operates with respect to personal characteristics is not clearly documented in the literature. Surra and Longstreth (1990) found that common leisure activities were positively related to the interdependence of dating couples. Likewise, Houts et al. (1996) report that in a sample of working-class and middle-class couples, individuals with more similar role preferences and leisure interests experience a higher level of compatibility.

Value and Role Similarity

Murstein (1970, 1987) introduced the notion that after the initial filtering of possible mates, subsequent screening developed according to the criteria of similarities of values and compatible understanding of roles in a relationship. Murstein (1987) argues that mate selection is a process marked by three relatively distinct stages or phases: stimulus, value similarity, and finally role compatibility (S-V-R). He proposes that partners are first drawn to one another on the basis of physical attraction and physical cues such as attire and looks. After the initial attraction phase, partners then assess their value similarity through increasingly deeper disclosure. Finally, partners assess their role compatibility in terms of gender roles and marital roles. As these assessments proceed through the three phases, the relationship deepens and involvement becomes more permanent. Partners successfully assessing and negotiating their relationship through these three stages will eventually reach marriage.

Individual and Interactional Theories

In the final analysis, no matter how much one person desires or wants to marry another, mate selection remains an interactional phenomenon rather than solely an individual choice. Social exchange theory has provided the basis for much of the interpretation of dyadic processes in mate selection. For example, Nye (1979) discussed the costs and rewards that each individual weighs when seeking a mate. This perspective has led to the common phrase in the academic literature that treats these interactional processes as a "marriage market" (e.g. Bulcroft and Bulcroft, 1999). The marriage market is marked by each person attempting to make their most marketable and valuable assets public while seeking to conceal their liabilities and costs. These assets and liabilities may be somewhat different based on gender; however, some qualities are generally regarded similarly by both sexes. For example, characteristics such as "being easy to get along with" are highly regarded by both genders (see Green and Kenrick, 1994; Jensen-Campbell, Graziano, and West, 1995). There can be little doubt that as more young people cohabit before marriage, the concealment of negative attributes or overstatement of positive attributes will becomes increasingly difficult. Indeed, according to Gwartney-Gibbs (1985), premarital cohabitation is occupying a new stage in the mate selection process.

Cohabitation and Mate Selection

The rapid increase in premarital intimacy has been associated with the postponement of marriage or an increase in the age at first marriage, and with an increase in **cohabitation**. Cohabitation without marriage is no longer seen as a deviant phenomenon in Denmark or Sweden, and may have become a social institution. Sweden and Denmark have the highest unmarried cohabitation rates in the world, where it is estimated that as many as 99 percent of those marrying have previously cohabited

(Trost, 1981). Cohabitation in Sweden is not seen as preparation for, or an alternative to, marriage, but rather as a *form* of marriage. One of the distinguishing marks of cohabitation in Sweden is the presence of children, with about the same proportion of cohabiting (42 percent) as newly married couples (49 percent) having one or more children (Lewin, 1982).

Cohabitation in Canada and the United States has increased dramatically over the past three decades. During this time cohabitation has changed from a deviant form of coupling to a socially accepted form of relationship. It is rapidly becoming a common route to marriage and a common relationship type in Canada. Turcotte and Bélanger (1997) report that the majority (57 percent) of first conjugal unions formed in Canada between 1990 and 1995 were common-law unions. An even higher proportion is found in Quebec, where 80 percent of all first unions formed in this period were common-law unions.

Attitudes toward Cohabitation

In their national sample of high school students, Bibby and Posterski (1992) found that 88 percent believed it was acceptable for a couple who were not married to live together. There was little variation by region, gender, or "race." In another 1992 study, a marked decline was found in the proportions of Anglophones who said that cohabitation relationships were "definitely bad," from 42 percent in 1968 to 10 percent in 1988. A substantial but smaller increase was found in the proportion of Anglophone students expressing unqualified approval of cohabitation (from 7 percent to 20 percent). The most dramatic change was found in the attitudes of Francophones: the proportion indicating that cohabitation was "definitely bad" fell from 13 percent to 2 percent between 1968 and 1988, while those saying it was "definitely good" increased from 25 to 71 percent during this 20-year period (Hobart and Grigel, 1992).

Incidence of Cohabitation

In 1981, cohabiting unions represented 5.6 percent of all husband–wife families in Canada (McKie, 1986). In 1986, 7.2 percent of all husband–wife families were living in common-law unions, representing an increase of

37 percent over 1981 (Turcotte, 1988). By 1990, common-law couples made up 10 percent of all husband–wife families, and by 1996 this had increased to 12 percent (Statistics Canada, 1997). The Family History Survey of 1984 indicated that 16.5 percent of adult Canadians between the ages of 18 and 65 had cohabited at one time or another. Of these, 92 percent had only cohabited once, 7 percent had cohabited twice, and the remainder had cohabited up to six times (McKie, 1986). By 1990, 28 percent of men and 29 percent of women had lived in at least one cohabiting relationship, with the most rapid increase found among people aged 40 to 49 (Stout, 1991). Cohabitation is much more common among younger people than among older people. In fact, of those people *living as couples* in 1990, 82 percent of those aged 15 to 19 and 50 percent of those aged 20 to 24 were living in common-law unions (Stout, 1991). By 2002, the Statistics Canada report *Changing Conjugal Life in Canada* reports that 53.3 percent of females age 20 to 29 are likely to have cohabitation as their first conjugal type of experience (see Figure 7.4).

There is a relationship between religion and pre-marital cohabitation. An earlier study (Watson, 1983) found that more than half of cohabitors claimed no religious affiliation, but of those who did, Catholics were the most likely to have cohabited (79 percent); Fundamentalist Protestant groups were least likely to have cohabited (25 percent); and those who were affiliated with Mainline Protestant groups were in an intermediate position (59 percent). In a more recent study, Balakrishnan and Chen (1990) found no difference between the overall premarital cohabitation rates of Catholics and Protestants (22.4 percent and 22.3 percent, respectively). The rate for "other religions" was somewhat lower (14.1 percent), but was considerably higher for those who report no religion (42.3 percent), almost double the overall rate of 23.3 percent. Premarital cohabitation is also strongly related to religiosity. Turcotte and Bélanger (1997) report that women who attend religious services every week are only half as likely to experience a first common-law union as those who attend only occasionally.

Cohabitation, Courtship, and Marriage

Cohabitation has different meanings for different participants. For some, cohabitation may be merely a matter of convenience with "no strings attached," rather than a relationship implying commitment and permanence. For others, it may be seen as a prelude to marriage or as the last stage of courtship, which permits couples to determine their mutual compatibility under conditions of a "trial marriage." Some may see it as a temporary substitute for marriage while awaiting the resolution of an application for divorce or other practical problems. Others may see cohabitation as a permanent alternative to marriage

Figure 7.4 **Probability of Women Experiencing a Marriage or Common-Law Union as a First Union, Canada, 2001**

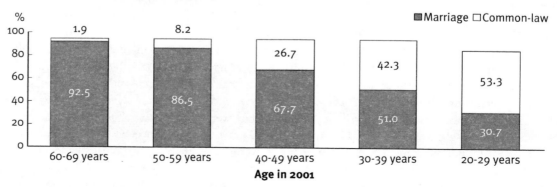

Source: Statistics Canada, Cat. No. 89-576-XIE, Chart 1.

or as a rejection of legal marriage. Common-law unions may also be entered into for economic reasons, such as to share living expenses. One study (Morrison and Oderkirk, 1991) points out that current transfer programs and income tax programs provide proportionally greater income tax benefits to cohabiting and lone parents than to married-couple families in Canada. Cohabitation, however, is not yet a permanent alternative to marriage, since the vast majority of cohabiting couples ultimately marry (McKie, 1986; Turcotte, 1988; Bumpass and Sweet, 1989, Statistics Canada, 2002, 89-576-XIE).

Another frequently studied question is whether cohabitors differ in any important characteristics from those who follow a more traditional courtship-and-marriage route. Significant differences have been found in a number of important variables. Age was related to cohabitation, with the largest proportion of Canadians currently cohabiting tending to fall between the ages of 25 and 45. Cohabitors were likely to be less educated, contrary to the popular conception that cohabitation is concentrated among college students (Spanier, 1983; Tanfer, 1987; Bumpass et al., 1991). Cohabiting men and women also tended to be grouped at the lower end of the income scale (Spanier, 1983; Watson, 1983). Spanier (1983) reported that unmarried cohabiting men were less likely to be employed than were married men, but unmarried cohabiting women were more likely to be employed than were married women. Higher rates of cohabitation also tended to be found in larger cities (Spanier, 1983). According to the 1991 Census, common-law couples were more likely to have both partners in the labour force (77 percent) than were married couples (58 percent).

Is cohabitation a part of the courtship process, or is it a distinct institutional form (a "looser bond"), with different goals, norms and behaviours? Schoen and Weinick (1993) argue that if cohabitations are "informal marriages," then partner choice in cohabitation would resemble partner choice in marriage. They found that in their choice of a partner, cohabiting couples gave greater weight to achieved characteristics (such as education), and less weight to ascribed characteristics (such as age, race and religion) which reflect longer-term considerations. They concluded that cohabitation is *not* a part of the courtship process, but

rather that it is a "looser bond," representing a relationship distinct from marriage.

Cohabitors also tend to be less traditional than do non-cohabitors. They demonstrate unconventional behaviour, such as the use of illicit drugs, and report poorer relationships with parents and other family members (Newcomb, 1986). Yllo and Straus (1981) found that cohabiting couples were more violent than were married couples, although the opposite might be expected because cohabiting couples are legally free to leave an unsatisfactory relationship. Not only were cohabiting women more likely than married women to be the victims of violence, but they were also more likely to be violent toward their partners. Stets (1991) reported higher levels of aggression among cohabitors (14 percent) than among those who were married (5 percent). Cohabitors possessed a demographic profile associated with higher rates of violence; they tended to be younger, they did not participate in social organizations or demonstrate strong ties to their relationships; and they were more likely to have psychological and behavioural problems such as depression and alcohol abuse.

A number of personal and relationship factors have also been found to differentiate cohabitors from non-cohabitors. With respect to personality traits, male cohabitors were *less* congenial, law-abiding, orderly, and religious, and were *more* androgynous and rated themselves as more attractive than did non-cohabitors. Female cohabitors were *less* deliberate, diligent, law-abiding, self-accepting, clothes-conscious, and religious, and were *more* liberal, extroverted, and androgynous (less feminine) than were non-cohabitors. They also had more leadership qualities (Newcomb, 1986, Newcomb and Bentler, 1980).

With regard to sex roles, male cohabitors were less traditional, but they were not more likely to describe their relationship as more egalitarian than were non-cohabiting males. Cohabiting females were more likely to see their relationship as male-dominated with respect to power, or to see themselves at a power disadvantage, than were non-cohabiting females (Risman et al., 1981). Despite this evidence, cohabiting males and females were more likely to report higher levels of satisfaction with the relationship, and cohabiting males were more likely to report greater sexual satisfaction than were non-cohabiting couples (Risman et al., 1981).

Cohabitation and the Stability of Marriage

The single most important question that has emerged over the last three decades of research on cohabitation is in regard to the relationship between premarital cohabitation and the quality and permanence of latter marriage. The overall finding appears quite simple: premarital cohabitation increases the risk of later divorce or separation. Certainly this finding is robust and consistent in the research literature from the beginning studies by Watson (1983) to the most recent by Teachman (2003). It would be an oversimplification, however, to conclude that all types and forms of cohabitation have the same effect on later marriage. In order to understand the complexities in this area of research and why the simple conclusion is somewhat suspect, it is necessary to take an historical perspective on this area of research.

One of the earliest researchers in Canada studying the effect of cohabitation is Watson (1983). He tested the assumption that cohabiting couples demonstrate higher levels of adjustment during their first year of marriage, since the difficulties that are normally faced during the first year of marriage should already have been resolved. In contrast to this expectation, this Canadian study found that non-cohabitors had significantly higher marital adjustment scores than did cohabitors. In a later longitudinal follow-up of this study, no significant differences in marital adjustment were found between cohabitors and non-cohabitors (Watson and DeMeo, 1987). A follow-up study of both samples was conducted after four years of marriage. At the end of the first year of marriage, the marital adjustment scores were significantly higher for non-cohabitors. By the fourth year of marriage, marital adjustment had declined for both, but had declined more rapidly for non-cohabitors, so that the difference was no longer significant. The negative effect of cohabitation on marital quality disappeared once cohabiters and marrieds had the same duration of time in the relationship. Indeed, because cohabitors had been living together longer at the date of marriage than had noncohabitors, it is reasonable that they would experience lower initial scores that would increasingly converge with noncohabitors as they spent longer periods living together. This was the first recognition that duration of relationship needed to be controlled if any comparison was to be made between these two groups, cohabitors and noncohabitors.

Using data from the 1984 Canadian Fertility Study, Balakrishnan et al. (1987) found a 50-percent higher risk of marital dissolution among women who had cohabited prior to marriage as compared with those who had not. Sixty-five percent of the women whose marriage was preceded by cohabitation were still married to the same partner, compared with 81 percent whose marriage had not been preceded by cohabitation. This is contrary to the expectation that less successful relations would be weeded out previous to marriage, and that the later age at marriage associated with cohabitation would contribute to greater marital stability for cohabitants. Also using data from the 1984 Canadian Fertility Study, Krishnan (1998) found that women whose marriages were preceded by cohabitation were more likely to experience broken marriages. He also found that those who attended church more frequently were less likely to experience the disruption of their marriage, even after other sociodemographic variables were controlled. White (1987) contradicted both of these studies; however, subsequent critiques, debate, and reanalysis showed premarital cohabitation to be negatively related to marital stability (Trussell and Rao, 1989; White, 1989, Halli and Zimmer, 1991). These debates highlighted some of the complexities that would continue to surface in the literature such as linking the cohabitation to the future spouse or to some other person, the changing social norms making cohabitation more acceptable, and the duration of the cohabitation.

Booth and Johnson (1988) examined four models of how premarital cohabitation might affect marital quality:

■ **Cohabitation is a training period for marriage** Relationships that do not work are terminated, and successful relationships lead to marriage.

■ **Cohabitation is an alternative to marriage** Couples who cohabit do so because they are less committed to marriage and hold liberal views regarding the permanence of marriage; they also demonstrate greater willingness to take risks, and to participate in other unconventional behaviours.

■ **Cohabitation is a form of early marriage** High satisfaction effects are found during cohabitation; subsequent marriage would lead to lower levels of marital satisfaction.

■ **Cohabitation has a negative effect on marriage** Cohabitants who marry may experience doubts or guilt feelings, or they may de-emphasize the permanent nature of marriage.

No support was found for the models that cohabitation provided superior training for early marriage or that it accelerated the effects of early marriage. Some support was found for the model that cohabitors represent poor marriage risks because of unconventional lifestyles, as well as for the model that cohabitation itself may have a negative influence on marriage.

The next study (Teachman and Polonko, 1990) to address the effects of premarital cohabitation on marital stability reached the same overall conclusions as did its predecessor. Teachman and Polonko (1990), however, examined sub-types within the pool of all premarital cohabitors. Most surprisingly, they found that when you divide premarital cohabitations into those who cohabited six months or less and those who cohabited more than six months before marriage, the direction of effects changes. Those who cohabited six months or less had more stable marriages than non-cohabitors, but those who cohabited more than six months had less stable marriages. This has led to speculation that there may be at least two types of cohabitations: those who use cohabitation as a stage before marriage and those that are more haphazard in their goals for the cohabitation. Those using cohabitation as a conscious prelude to marriage show salutary effects and those who are more haphazard show negative effects.

Shoen (1992) analyzed marriage cohorts for the U.S. and found that while overall premarital cohabitation has a negative effect on later marital stability, it has a positive effect for the most recent marital cohorts. This finding sparked a debate about the effects of the social context and definition of cohabitation and the effect that being defined as a deviant relationship might have on the participants. The argument is that when cohabitation is defined as "deviant" by the social norms of the society—as for earlier marriage cohorts—then only those that were "liberal" in their views of divorce and marriage would be attracted to such a lifestyle choice. However, as time passes and cohabitation becomes more socially acceptable, cohabitation will attract an increasingly "normal" group of participants whose divorce rates will mirror the rates for the population in general.

A U.S. study, for example, used data from the National Survey of Families and Households to examine whether the greater instability of marriages begun by cohabitation could be accounted for by the greater unconventionality of cohabitors. The findings supported the suggestion that cohabitation was more attractive to never-married individuals who were more unconventional in their attitudes toward sexual behaviour, single parenting, and marital permanence. Unconventional attitudes, however, were not strong predictors of differences in stability between cohabitors and non-cohabitors (DeMaris and MacDonald, 1993). In a related study, DeMaris and Rao (1992) found that cohabitors have a hazard of dissolution that is about 46-percent higher than the hazard for non-cohabitors, and that these differences remain significant even when adjusting for the time spent in cohabitation. Likewise, Nock (1995) compared marriages and cohabiting relationships. Among cohabitants, Nock found lower levels of commitment and happiness with the relationship. Cohabitors also had poorer relationships with parents than did comparable married individuals.

By 1995, the literature in regard to the effect of premarital cohabitation had evolved into two specific theories. The first theory is that because the social acceptability of premarital cohabitation has been negatively defined, premarital cohabitation has attracted specific types of people. The people attracted to cohabitation have had traits such as liberal views about divorce, being non-religious, and liberal sexuality. This first theory argues that these people are divorce-prone regardless of whether they cohabit or not. It just so happens that the values they carry predispose them to cohabit as well as divorce. Therefore, the negative relationship between premarital cohabitation and later marital stability is spurious. In other words, there is nothing about cohabitation that "causes" later marital disruption. This theory is known as the "**selection hypothesis**." One corollary to the selection hypothesis is that as cohabitation becomes more accepted and "normal" we would expect it to attract a less select group of people whose divorce rates would approach that of the population at large. The second theory is contrary to the selection hypothesis in that it argues that the experience of premarital cohabitation affects the participants' attitudes and beliefs about marriage and relationships in a profound way. The experience of premarital cohabitation has a negative effect on people regardless of the background the participants bring to the cohabitation. This theory is commonly known as the "**experience hypothesis.**"

Hall and Zhao (1995) tested the hypothesis that there is a "selection effect" reflecting the fact that co-habitors are a select group differing in salient ways from those who do not cohabit, and that these differences make cohabitors more vulnerable to divorce. After controlling the effects of four sociodemographic factors that differentiate cohabitors, they found that premarital cohabitation was still associated with a greater risk of divorce. These four factors were the presence of stepchildren, marital status homogamy, parental divorce, and age heterogamy.

Lillard, Brien, and Waite (1995) used a complex statistical model to examine the selection hypothesis. However, unlike Hall and Zhao (1995), Lillard et al. used most of the previously identified attitudes and characteristics that are commonly associated with divorce proneness to account for the marital stability of their sample. After divorce was accounted for by these characteristics, Lillard et al. then determined whether premarital cohabitors were still more likely to get divorced. Lillard et al. (1995) argue that there is no negative effect for premarital cohabitation on marital stability once these divorce-prone characteristics are taken into consideration. In other words, Lillard et al. provide strong evidence that the selection hypothesis is correct and that the relationship between premarital cohabitation and marital stability is spurious and not causal.

Although the "experience hypothesis" has not been as well researched as the "selection hypothesis," it nonetheless has received some empirical support (Axinn and Thornton 1992; Axinn and Barber, 1997). These researchers argue that the experience of premarital cohabitation weakens the participants' commitment to marriage and that the experience of cohabitation demonstrates to the participants that intimate and fulfilling relationships are available outside of marriage. Besides correlations of attitudes and beliefs about marriage, it is difficult to demonstrate that cohabitation is other than selection.

To the uninitiated, the research into premarital cohabitation may appear to be confusing and haphazard. However, there is a consistent, programmatic focus to this research over its development. This research may be summarized as follows:

1. **Research question:** What is the relationship between premarital cohabitation and marital quality? The answer to this question seems to be that premarital cohabitors that marry have greater time in the living relationship before their wedding day, and so they show less marital satisfaction (quality) until the comparison group of non-cohabitors has had sufficient time to suffer the same initial declines (Watson, 1983; Watson and DeMeo, 1987). It should be noted that other researchers have identified characteristics that make married life more difficult for cohabitors who marry (DeMaris and McDonald 1983; Nock, 1995) but these characteristics may be due to "selection" into cohabitation.

2. **Research question:** What is the relationship between premarital cohabitation and later marital instability (e.g. divorce)? The answer to this question is that premarital cohabitors who marry have a higher rate (30 to 50 percent higher) than those who marry without prior cohabitation. (Balakrishnan et al., 1987; Booth and Johnson 1988; Teachman and Polonko, 1990; Schoen 1992; Demaris and Rao, 1992; Lillard et al., 1995; Axinn and Barber 1997; Teachman, 2000, 2003). Figure 7.5 shows the most recent statistics for Canada supporting this relationship.

3. **Research question:** Are there subtypes of cohabitation that show different effects for cohabitation on marriage? The answer to this is that there are clearly different subclasses or types of cohabitation with different effects on later marriage. Teachman and Polonko (1990) showed clearly that shorter-duration cohabitations have positive effects on marriage, and Schoen (1992) demonstrated that marital cohorts seem to have differential effects with the most recently married having positive effects for cohabitation on marital stability.

4. **Research question:** Is the negative effect of premarital cohabitation on marital stability due to the "experience" of cohabitation or the divorce-prone characteristics of those who choose to cohabit? Lillard et al. (1995) provide strong evidence that it is a selection effect. However, we must be cautious since both could be operating simultaneously and research has not totally excluded the "experience hypothesis."

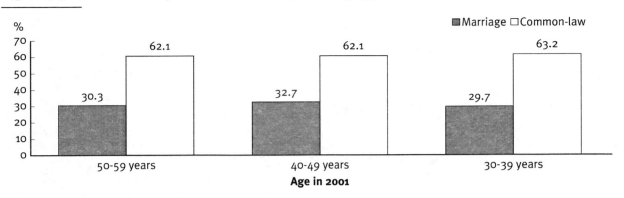

Figure 7.5   Probability for Women to Separate by Type of First Union, Canada, 2001

Source: Statistics Canada, Cat. No. 89-576-XIE, Chart 5.

Refocusing Research on Dating, Mate Selection, and Cohabitation

Gwartney-Gibbs (1986) and others have stated that premarital cohabitation represents a new stage in the mate selection process. She argues that the older models of mate selection only identified dating, going steady, and engagement, whereas we have now added cohabitation to that sequence. As we have seen, much of the research in the area of premarital cohabitation focuses on its effects on later marital stability. Recently, two scholars have redirected the focus for research on premarital cohabitation. Sandra McGinnis (2003) has argued that we cannot study premarital cohabitation without knowing more about the patterns of mate selection for those who are not cohabiting. McGinnis argues that the marriage formation process has changed not just because we have added cohabitation but also because our expectations about sex, marriage, and commitment have also changed. In a similar vein, Jay Teachman (2003) has argued that we have isolated our studies of premarital cohabitation from other changes in dating and mate selection, most notably changes in regard to premarital sexual activity. Both of these scholars have taken steps to move researchers away from what could be termed an isolated perspective on premarital cohabitation, and to refocus studies on premarital cohabitation within the overall context of mate selection.

McGinnis (2003) suggests a model of marriage entry that is founded on the individual weighing the costs and rewards associated with different paths. She uses a sample that includes other forms of mate selection stages besides cohabitation so that she can compare the effects of various paths on the outcome of getting married. For example, she finds that cohabitation compared to going steady reduces the perception of costs to getting married and also reduces the perception of benefits. The comparison with "going steady" shows that cohabitation increases both the expectation and intention to marry over that experienced by those "going steady." Contrary to the perspective that the "experience" of cohabitation has a negative effect on attitudes about marriage, McGinnis states that "...the findings in regard to costs imply that cohabitation does not have uniformly negative effects upon views of marriage" (2003:114).

Teachman (2003) notes that researchers have focused on premarital cohabitation as a central change in mate selection practices over the past three decades. He points out that at the same time, premarital intercourse has also changed dramatically. He argues that both of these phenomena need to be considered together as affecting later marital stability. He notes that both DeMaris and McDonald (1993) and Teachman and Polonko (1990) found that where cohabitation was limited to one partner and that partner becomes the marriage spouse, premarital cohabitation has no negative effect on later marital stability. It is only when there are multiple cohabiting partners that effects become negative. He speculates that this may support two different types of cohabitation: those planning to marry and those who see cohabitation as an alternative to marriage. Like cohabitation, premarital intercourse with multiple partners might have different effects on later marriage. Teachman tested the interaction of multiple cohabitors and multiple sexual partners on later marital disruption of a U.S. sample of women. He found that "women whose intimate premarital relationships are limited to their husbands—either premarital sex alone or premarital cohabitation—do not experience an increased risk of divorce" (2003:453). However, the strongest negative effects on marital stability were found for those women with multiple cohabitations and those with multiple sexual partners.

The refocusing of premarital cohabitation studies to include variables in the broader context of mate selection is a needed development to assist scholars in making these findings more relevant and coherent. This is not meant to say that we do not know a great deal about premarital cohabitation as a stage in mate selection. We know that planned and time-limited cohabitations are more likely to lead to marital success. We know that haphazard cohabitation, multiple cohabiting partners, and multiple sexual partners are all associated with poor marital outcomes. As our research stands today, there are still many questions that need to be addressed, especially concerning comparisons between other stages and forms of mate selection and premarital cohabitation.

Gay and Lesbian Relationships

The research on gay and lesbian cohabitation is very difficult to compare to the literature on heterosexual mate selection for several reasons. First, in many research contexts, being homosexual or practising homosexual acts may be illegal or subject to negative informal sanctions such as "gay bashing." As a result, it is difficult to recruit subjects. A second reason that comparisons are difficult is that until recently (June 2003 in Canada), there was no comparable institution to marriage for homosexual couples. Thus, comparing mate selection processes is impossible since

the outcomes are so different. Although gay cohabiting relationships exist, they could not lead to marriage and such relationships have been difficult to sample in any rigorous manner. Given the difficulties with research in this area, it is surprising to find the quality of data that we do have.

The major source on homosexual and lesbian behaviours was published in 1994 (Laumann et al., 1994). This study is highly critical of the so-called Kinsey Report, in that probability sampling was not used in preference to "purposely recruiting" volunteers (1994:289). Two other prominent studies are also questioned because probability samples were not used, i.e., Blumstein and Schwartz (1983) and Bell and Weinberg (1978) (see Laumann et al., 1994:36). Using a national sampling research procedure in the U.S., Laumann and his colleagues (1994:303–304) used data from nearly 4000 men and 5000 women to examine relationships among same-sex partners. In contrast to estimates by Kinsey, only 2.7 percent of men and 1.3 percent of women had had sex with one or more same-sex partners in the previous 12 months. These numbers were higher in the past five years (men, 4.1 percent; women, 2.2 percent). College graduates were more likely to be involved with homosexual partners, with 3.5 percent of men and 2.5 percent of women reporting a homosexual act in the past 12 months, and 6.9 percent of men and 5.8 percent of women reporting a homosexual act since the age of 18. More than 10 percent of homosexual men living in the 12 largest cities in the U.S. had had a same-sex partner in the previous year. Among homosexual men, the mean number of partners in the past year was 1.8; in the past five years, 4.9; and since the age of 18, 16.5. Including homosexual and bisexual partners, the mean number of partners since the age of 18 was 42.8. In contrast, the number of partners among homosexual women was about half that of homosexual men.[1] Homosexual men and women were more likely to identify themselves as either Jewish or "no religion." The majority did not attend church. Black men and women had more sexual partners than did white men and women, both in the previous year and in the past five years.

Schreurs and Bunk (1995) investigated relationships among 50 lesbian and 50 heterosexual couples. They found that lesbian couples demonstrated higher degrees of emotional and recreational intimacy, and that they reported a more positive attitude toward emotional intimacy than did heterosexual couples. Women in lesbian relationships reported higher levels of emotional intimacy than either men or women in heterosexual relationships. Women in both lesbian and heterosexual relationships placed higher value on emotional intimacy than did men.

Kurdek (1996) used longitudinal data to study the deterioration of relationship quality for gay and lesbian cohabiting couples. Couples who separated over a five-year period reported a decrease in feelings of positivity to the other, an increase of conflict within the relationship, and an increase in personal autonomy in the period preceding the separation. Decreases in positivity were linked to separation, especially when personal autonomy increased.

In an exploration of the reasons (love, lust, fear) given by gay men for engaging or not engaging in specific sexual practices, the authors found that subjects made choices based on individual needs, values, and life circumstances. They found that most men considered themselves to be taking adequate precautions against infection, even though an outside observer might disagree on "objective" grounds (Ames et al., 1995).

Data collected from 165 homosexual men who reported engaging in unprotected anal sex found that the perception of risk varied according to whether behaviours took place with steady or non-steady partners. The majority of men who engaged in sexual risk behaviours within their primary relationship did not subjectively appraise their behaviour as risky. Those who had unprotected anal sex with casual partners were more likely to be aware of the risk involved (Bosga et al., 1995).

Sexual jealousy in the relationships of homosexual and heterosexual men was compared between 1980 and 1992 (Bringle, 1995). Homosexual and heterosexual relationships were found to be similar on the level of relationship involvement. Homosexual respondents, however, reported *lower* levels of experiencing and expressing sexual jealousy, *less* exclusive relationships, *more* extra-dyadic sexual relations by their partners, a *larger number* of relationships, and relationships of *shorter* duration. Both homosexual and heterosexual men in 1992 (as compared with 1980) reported *higher* levels of experiencing and expressing sexual jealousy in relation to their partner's extra-dyadic sexual behaviour, *more* exclusive relationships, *fewer* relationships, and relationships of *longer* duration. Bringle suggests that these changes may be related to the increase in sexually transmitted diseases in general, and to the fear of AIDS in particular.

Mate Selection in the New Millennium

Vast changes have taken place in standards of interpersonal intimacy in the past three decades. There has been an important decline in acceptance of the abstinence standard from 1968 to 1988, accompanied by increased endorsement of the fun standard, or of permissiveness without affection. Many hail these changes as liberation from restrictive sexual norms and requirements. Contrary to the finding by Teachman (2003), Rubin (1985) argues that it is important that both men and women have premarital sex, on the basis that it may enhance relationships and contribute to successful marriage. He asserts that the vast majority of people who have experienced premarital sex have not sustained any injuries as a result. Money (1986) argues for the principle of sexual inviolacy, which guarantees equal sexual rights for all, while tolerating the maximal amount of social diversity and individual eccentricity. This principle holds that no one has the right to impose on anyone else his version of what is or is not erotic or sexual.

Others, however, suggest that the sexual freedom established during the past few decades has not resulted in the increase in happiness that was assumed would follow the liberation from binding sexual mores: "We have been liberated from the taboos of the past only to find ourselves imprisoned in a 'freedom' that brings us no closer to our real nature or needs" (Marin, 1983:52). On the basis of his experience as a therapist, Marin argues that the loneliness and dissatisfaction expressed by many persons is more an expression of the need for friendship and community rather than the expression of genuine sexual passion. The sexual revolution has resulted in the rejection of many old illusions, but it has not taught us how to create more intimate relations or how to demonstrate "generosity" or genuine concern for the welfare of the others (Marin, 1983).

Canada as a country has pursued a policy of multiculturalism and tolerance that accommodates many different religious and secular approaches to mate selection. Undoubtedly much of the sexual freedom gained in the last century will continue to flourish in the 21st century. But this freedom will be increasingly modified and rearranged to accommodate ethnic practices such as arranged marriages and matchmaking, as well as cohabitation as a prelude to marriage. In the chapters to follow, we will address the patterns and functions of marriage in Canadian society. It will be in those chapters and the final chapter of this book that we must address the question "Will cohabitation become a truly popular alternative to marriage?" If the answer is affirmative, then mate selection processes will have replaced the institution they serve.

ENDNOTE

1 The data presented by Laumann et al., 1994:313–317 on the number of sexual partners among both homosexual men and homosexual women is uniquely obtuse and difficult to interpret accurately. However, we are confident that our interpretation of this data is correct.

SUMMARY

■ Autonomous mate selection is constrained by factors such as propinquity and the values of favouring similarity of partners such as homogamy and value similarity.

■ The filter model of mate selection provides a convenient metaphor for the ways that mates are filtered out of the pool of eligibles. This model allows us to incorporate both macro-societal influences, such as the way universities assure similarity of values and motivation in their student bodies, and individual psychological principles, such as value similarity.

■ Murstein's Stimulus-Value-Role theory of mate selection is a sequential theory that accounts for initial attraction, increasing disclosure of values, and finally to the assessment of role compatibility. It is nonetheless not a dyadic theory of mate selection.

■ Significant increases in cohabitation have recently been reported. Attitudes toward cohabitation have become more favourable in the general population and among adolescents. The experience of cohabitation has also increased among Canadian young people. Cohabitors are less traditional and more individualistic than are non-cohabitors. Most studies of cohabitation

found it to be associated with lower quality and stability of subsequent marriages. This relationship is weaker among recent cohorts, since cohabitation has become more common.

■ Teachman (2003) and McGinnis (2003) are refocusing studies on cohabitation on the broader context of these processes in mate selection by emphasizing comparisons with other forms of mate selection. They examine cohabitation as just one of the components in contemporary mate selection.

KEY TERMS

Arranged marriage (148)
Autonomous marriage (148)
Cohabitation (158)
Endogamy (152)
Exogamy (152)
Experience hypothesis of cohabitation (163)
Heterogamy (152)
Homogamy (152)
Hypergamy (151)
Marriage squeeze (151)
Principle of least interest (152)
Propinquity (150)
Selection hypothesis of cohabitation (162)
Sex ratio (151)

QUESTIONS FOR REVIEW

1. What are the major differences between autonomous and arranged mate selection?

2. How is autonomous mate selection constrained? What factors are involved as constraints?

3. Why are dyadic approaches to mate selection termed "interactional"?

4. Explain the difference between the selection and experience hypotheses regarding the effect of cohabitation on later marriage.

5. How is the marriage squeeze related to the sex ratio?

6. How have cohabitors differed from more traditional couples?

7. In what ways is the study of cohabitation becoming refocused?

QUESTIONS FOR DISCUSSION

1. What are the primary changes in adherence to varying premarital sexual standards? How will the incidence of AIDS change these patterns in the next decade?

2. What is the impact of cohabitation on marital quality and stability? Is this impact likely to change in the next few decades? How?

3. To what extent do our theories about mate selection (e.g., filtering process, Murstein's S-V-R, etc.) pertain to more traditional societies that practise arranged marriage?

4. To what extent do you think "romanticism" is part of your concept of love? What about concepts of love in more traditional cultures? If divorce rates are any indication, would we expect more traditional cultures to believe that autonomous mate selection and dating is a positive development for the future of marriage and family?

SUGGESTED READINGS

Bibby, Reginald W. and Donald C. Posterski, 1992.* *Teen Trends: A Nation in Motion.* Toronto: Stoddart. An extensive examination of the attitudes, values, beliefs, outlook, expectations, and behaviour of Canadian teenagers between the ages of 15 and 19.

Michael, Robert T., John H. Gagnon, Edward O. Laumann, and Gina Kolata. 1994. *Sex in America: A Definitive Survey.* Toronto: Little, Brown and Company. This book, and its more sophisticated companion— *The Social Organization of Sexuality: Sexual Practices in the United States*—is the most comprehensive summary of what is known about sexual behaviour in the 1990s.

Teachman, Jay. 2003. "Premarital Sex, Premarital Cohabitation, and the Risk of Subsequent Marital Dissolution Among Women," *Journal of Marriage and Family* 65, 444–455.

Statistics Canada. 2002.* *Changing Conjugal Life in Canada.* Catalogue No. 89-576-XIE.

CHAPTER 8

The Institutional Framework of Marriage

After studying this chapter, you should be able to do the following:

- Describe how marriage law regulates the marital agreements that two people make with each other, and explain the benefits of marriage laws.
- Discuss the four elements of capacity that are required to contract a valid marriage.
- Summarize the current status of Canadian law as it affects common-law marriages.
- Summarize the current status of Canadian law as it affects homosexual partnerships.
- Describe the nature and limitations of domestic contracts.
- Describe the background and meaning of the various rituals and customs associated with contemporary marriage ceremonies.
- List the major areas in which the transition from independence to interdependence takes place, and describe the eight general developmental tasks discussed by Duvall and Miller.
- Describe the differences among personal, structural, and moral commitment, and summarize the impact of religion on marital commitment.
- Assess the relationships that have been found between marital status and personal well-being, as well as between gender and personal well-being.

Introduction

When we are young we like to romanticize marriage with statements implying that "love will conquer all difficulties." The highly romanticized perspective on marriage tends to avoid or downplay the institutional nature of marriage. Although most of us get married because we are "in love," some of us are more conscious of the institutional nature of marriage. Those among us who insist on prenuptial agreements or want to examine the genetic profile of the potential spouse indicate this.

A social institution is an area of social life (polity, religion, family, etc.) that is organized and governed by informal and formal norms. Some people are clearly aware that marriage is a socially organized and regulated institution. Every society establishes the formal norms about the *legal* relationships of husbands and wives through laws relating to marriage and marriage-like relationships. The social norms and expectations of family, friends, and spouse determine marriage as a *social* relationship. Certainly some of these expectations may be consciously negotiated, or may simply evolve through the process of interaction, but many of these social expectations are considered to be basic to the marital relationship (e.g., sexual consummation).

In this chapter we will examine the impact that the changing legal requirements as incorporated in Canadian marriage laws are having on the way that

Canadians experience and think about marriage. We will also consider how social expectations determine celebrations such as the wedding ceremony. We examine the basic developmental tasks that all couples confront in the transition to marriage, and the role-making aspects of establishing joint roles as husband and wife. Finally, we will investigate the role of commitment in marital relations, and the impact of marriage on the personal well-being of adults.

Canadian Marriage Laws

Our society widely applies religious sanctions in launching a marriage and in promoting its stability, but it is atypical in this emphasis. The concept of marriage in Western societies has had an interesting evolution. In early England, marriage was a compact between two kin groups, as is true today in most preliterate societies and in societies that practise arranged marriages. As we saw in Chapter 4, an increase in the power and control of the church resulted in the regulation of marriage by canon law. The growth of the power of the state led to conflict between the state and the church, and ultimately marriage came under state control. Most countries, including Canada, sanction either a civil or religious wedding, though in some countries the civil ceremony is required, while the religious one is optional. Still, the great majority of Canadian young people anticipate having a religious wedding. Despite the fact that only 18 percent of Canadian high school students attend religious services on a weekly basis, 85 percent expect to have a "church wedding" (Bibby and Posterski, 1992). While most young people turn to the church for the solemnization of their wedding, the clergyman in actual fact is acting as an agent of the state, and the state sets the conditions under which a particular marriage is legitimized. Thus, marriage in the eyes of the state is first and foremost a legal contract regardless of how much "in love" the partners may be.

Marriage and the Law

In contrast to divorce law, which is under federal jurisdiction, marriage laws are primarily under the jurisdiction of the individual provinces. In Quebec, the *Civil Code* governs marriage, whereas the nine other provinces and the territories have enacted marriage acts. Although these laws vary somewhat from province to province, they do agree in important ways. The federal Marriage (Prohibited Degrees) Act of 1990 is mainly concerned with defining the consanguineal and affinal relationships that are prohibited from marriage (e.g., father–daughter, son–mother, etc.). Provincial marriage acts are fairly uniform in making provision for both religious and civil marriage ceremonies, setting out additional prohibited degrees of consanguinity (blood ties) or affinity (ties through marriage) between bride and groom, making provision for at least two witnesses, providing for the issuance of marriage licences, specifying who is authorized to solemnize a marriage, and determining the minimum age at marriage with and without parental consent. Some provinces require a medical examination prior to marriage. Marriages between people of the same sex and people already married to someone else are prohibited (*Canadian Family Law Guide*, 1991).

Many couples entering marriage fail to realize that marriage is not simply a contract between two people living together, but is a status conferred on individuals by the state. Contrary to other contracts, marriage is not merely a private arrangement between two persons, but has a public character, and is subject to laws dictating and controlling the rights, obligations, and incidents of marriage, independent of the wishes of those who marry. While marriage is based on a contract between two individuals, the state establishes conditions as to its creation, duration, and consequences (Payne and Payne, 1994).

In general, parties to a marriage have a legal obligation to support each other financially, both during the marriage and after a separation or divorce. Husbands and wives have obligations to each other in terms of property they have accumulated during their marriage. They also have obligations to any children born of the marriage (Cohen, 1984).

Why is the state interested in regulating marriage? Eichler (1988) speculates that it is not because it wants to regulate sexual activities, since neither premarital nor extramarital sexual intercourse are prohibited or illegal. Marriage laws benefit the state in two ways: married spouses have an obligation to care for each other and provide each other with the necessities of life; and marriage provides a social identity for the children and makes the parents responsible for their children's economic, social, emotional and physical well-being. To the extent that these obligations are met, the state is relieved of responsibility in these areas.

What is noteworthy about this function that marriage plays for the state is the disjunction between the *effects* of being married and the *reasons* for getting married. People marry for love, to enjoy sexual relations with each other, to publicly express their desire to live with each other, to maintain a joint household and, possibly, to have children together, or because of social pressure. Marriage, however, also results in a new civil status with a new set of rights and obligations, which for most people is probably only an incidental by-product of the decision to get married. Nevertheless, for the vast majority of people marriage is probably the most important contract they will ever sign in their lives (Eichler, 1988:348).

Writing from a somewhat different perspective, Mohr (1984), a professor at Osgoode Hall Law School at York University, comments that we no longer have a family law, and that this term is a misnomer. We have progressed to a "law of persons," which conforms to our current ideas of independent, autonomous persons. He suggests that at a time when we have begun to realize that this individualistic understanding of law is deeply flawed, it is ironic that we entrench it in our *Charter of Rights and Freedoms*. He concludes as follows:

> Even our new Charter which promises us rights and freedoms and tells us that those can only be limited by the law and by what means the State finds reasonable says nothing about the realities of responsibility and care, the only meaningful way in which rights and freedoms can be expressed. Rights talk and freedom talk is poor family talk. Families do not unite around them, they break up over them (Mohr, 1984:266–267).

Couples deciding to marry often do so without giving careful consideration to the requirements of the marital relationship. Indeed, many couples are not even aware of the contractual or legal requirements of the relationship into which they are about to enter. Unlike most legal contracts, the marriage contract does not provide people with an opportunity to negotiate the terms and carefully consider their obligations before signing on the dotted line. Most people entering into marriage are not informed of their obligations, and are not aware that marriage is not entirely an

individual matter, but that it always involves the state as the "silent" third partner. While marriage is a consensual agreement between the parties that is traditionally viewed as a contract, it is different from other contracts because it confers on the parties a special status prescribed by law. Thus, marriage is a contract based on consent, but it is also institutional in nature. In contrast to other contracts, marriage cannot be ended by the mutual consent of the two parties, but must be dissolved by judicial decree (*Canadian Family Law Guide*, 1991).

A growing proportion of Canadians are choosing not to marry. A 1985 analysis projected that 17 percent of men and 14 percent of women would never get married. In contrast, the figures in 1971 were 10 percent and 8 percent, respectively. The proportion of the population projected to get married declined from 91 percent in 1971 to 85 percent in 1985 (Adams and Nagnur, 1989).

Marriage is legally *understood* to be the "voluntary union for life of one man and one woman to the exclusion of all others" (Payne and Payne, 1994). Whether the parties enter a lifelong union is determined by their intention at the time, regardless of whether they subsequently divorce. Even if same-sex relationships are intended to be lifelong, however, they do not constitute legal marriage at this time. Since marriage is a voluntary union for life, it cannot be imposed on a person without his or her consent. The absence of consent may render a marriage null and void. Common factors that may preclude consent to marriage include the following: unsoundness of mind, or the effects of excessive alcohol and drug consumption; duress, implying the exertion of pressure that induces fear; fraudulent misrepresentation; and error as to the identity of the person being married, or to the nature of the ceremony (Payne and Payne, 1994).

In order to contract a valid marriage, a person must have the **capacity for marriage**, which refers to the legal right to enter the marriage relationship. Four aspects of capacity are age, consanguinity, mental capacity, and monogamy.

■ **Age** At common law, the age at which persons were deemed to have sufficient understanding to consent to marriage was 14 for males and 12 for females. All provinces have raised the effective age at which a marriage can take place, most commonly to 18 without parental consent (19 in Nova Scotia, the Northwest Territories, and the Yukon) and 16 with parental consent, or earlier for a young woman who can provide a physician's certificate that she is either pregnant or the mother of a living child.

■ **Consanguinity** The prohibited degrees of consanguinity (relationship by blood) accepted by most provinces are spelled out in the law. **Incest** is defined as sexual intercourse between persons who are too closely related to marry legally. The 1990 Marriage (Prohibited Degrees) Act provides a codification of the prohibited degrees of consanguinity, affinity, and adoption. Consanguinity involves blood relationships, whereas affinity describes relationships arising out of marriage.

■ **Mental Capacity** A third requirement of marriage is that there must be sufficient mental capacity to give valid consent to the marriage contract.

■ **No Previous Marriage** Finally, the capacity for marriage requires that no previous marriage be still valid. Previous marriages must have been ended by death or divorce (Canadian Family Law Guide, 1991).

Although the Marriage Act (1990) does not define "marriage," we mentioned above that marriage is understood to be between a man and a woman. This definition did not come from legislators but from the British legal case of *Hyde v. Hyde and Womansee* (1866) where Lord Penzance wrote "I conceive that marriage, as understood in Christendom, may for this purpose be defined as the voluntary union for life of one man and one woman, to the exclusion of all others"(as cited in *Halpern v. Canada*, Court of Appeal for Ontario, 2003). As Mohr (1984) foresaw, this definition came into conflict with the understanding of equality as provided in section 15 (1) of the *Canadian Charter of Rights and Freedoms*.

On June 10, 2003, the Court of Appeal for Ontario ruled that the classic formulation of marriage by Lord Penzance breaches section 15(1) of the *Charter of Rights and Freedoms*. The applicants in the case were seven gay and lesbian couples who argued that the 1866 common law definition that dictated that marriage could only be between a man and a woman was discriminatory to homosexual couples by disallowing their right to marriage. The Court of Appeals ruled in their favour, finding that the common law definition did unreasonably violate the Charter of Rights and Freedoms. This ruling followed in the footsteps of previous rulings in some other provinces. However, this ruling had the effect of making the denial of marriage licenses for same sex couples immediately illegal and hence to abruptly change the nature of marriage in Ontario.

It is not clear at this time whether the federal government will draft new legislation regarding marriage or will simply let the court rulings change the nature of marriage. It is undoubtedly the case that the nature of legal marriage is changing in Canada. It is also useful to keep this in perspective: the law and its interpretation is constantly changing. Indeed, it must change in order to stay relevant. In the original case of *Hyde v. Hyde and Womansee* (1866), Lord Penzance's definition was reacting to a case involving polygamy. It was the *many*, rather than *one* man and woman, that Penzance was concerned with defining. The fact is that the sex of the marital partners was not at issue in that case (Eddinger, 2003). So it is somewhat humorous that for the next 137 years this definition became central to our interpretation of marriage. It will also be interesting to see if the original issue of polygamy is revisited with the changing definition of marriage.

Although many people seem alarmed by the prospect of legal homosexual marriage, the actual consequences are unclear. If the federal government changes the statutes, then Canada will join Belgium and the Netherlands in allowing gay marriages. However, many countries such as Switzerland and Germany allow for some form of couple registration. Currently there is a case before the courts in Massachusetts where gay couples are claiming that their children's health is endangered due to the denial of medical support that they would be allowed if married. Groups opposing gay marriages often discuss how recognition of gay marriages would jeopardize the institution of marriage, though it is difficult to understand how homosexual unions could endanger marriage more than do the high cohabitation and divorce rates among heterosexuals. At least one aspect to this dispute is that marriage in North America carries with it the symbol of "legitimacy." Certainly, cohabitations are still viewed as less stable and permanent than marriages and as a failure or refusal to accept the "adult" roles of husband and wife. Marriage legitimizes these relationships in law and in society. To deny a particular type of group this symbol of legitimacy is to keep it from becoming "accepted." So in a very real way this fight over gay marriage is a fight over the symbols of legitimacy and acceptability that heterosexuals enjoy.

Cohabitation and the Law

The increasing popularity of common-law relationships raises the question of their status as compared with legal marriages. The federal government recognizes common-law marriages after a couple has been living together for one year. Each province has its own regulations as to the duration of cohabiting time necessary for a couple to be considered to have a common-law marriage. The recognition of common-law relationship at the federal level is especially important since after that time couple should file income tax as "married" rather than "single." However, matrimonial property acts are governed provincially and thus far there has been a reluctance on the part of courts to extend complete and identical coverage to common-law couples on the grounds that they did not make a conscious decision to enter a contract as do the participants do in marriage.

A **common-law union** is one that has not been formally or legally solemnized, but in which there is a mutual agreement to enter into a marriage-like relationship, consummated by cohabitation as husband and wife and by the mutual assumption of marital duties and obligations. Limited legal recognition of common-law spouses has been noted since 1978, but this primarily includes support obligations rather than the right to matrimonial property. "It doesn't matter if a man and woman live together for 50 years—if they do not marry the only property they are entitled to when they leave is their own property" (Cochrane, 1991:100). Recent legal cases have included settlements with respect to mutual property rights of cohabiting couples, but difficulties collecting on these settlements are common (Eichler, 1988). A *parent* in a common-law relationship is eligible for support and maintenance enforcement if the couple has cohabited for at least one year, during which a child has been born (Ursel, 1993).

Data collected from the 1996 Census indicate that common-law and lone-parent families together constitute over one-quarter (26 percent) of families in Canada, compared to one-fifth (20 percent) in 1986. In the last five years, common-law families increased 28 percent, while lone-parent families increased 19 percent, and married families increased by 1.7 percent. Since 1981, the proportion of married-couple families has declined from 83 percent of all families to 74 percent, and this decline is largely due to substantial increases in both common-law and lone-parent families. Common-law families have increased from 6 percent of all families in 1981, to 12 percent in 1996. Lone-parent families have increased from 11 percent of all families in 1981 to 15 percent in 1996. (Figure 8.1 provides a graphic description of changes in family structure in the last four Census periods). The highest proportion of common-law families was found in Quebec, which had 43 percent of all common-law families in Canada. One couple in four (24 percent) in Quebec lives in a common-law relationship.

For a number of decades the Scandinavian countries have set the pace for the development of changing sexual norms. The recognition of cohabitation as not only a preparation for marriage, but as a substitute for marriage, is one such area.

In the case of cohabitation, the initial tendency was to deny that any legal claim to support could be made. Increasingly, arguments are being advanced in favour of the legal recognition of cohabitation. First, such recognition would protect the community from the burden of supporting those who would otherwise be entitled to social assistance if their relationship breaks up. Second, the changes in family law and social customs reflected in divorce rates have made it increasingly difficult to contrast marriage and cohabitation. The result has been an important narrowing of the gap in terms of the property rights of married couples and cohabitors. Substantial legal recognition of cohabitation has been denied in the area of benefits with regard to the *Immigration Act* and the *Income Tax Act*, but Canadian statutes such as the *Canada Pension Plan*, the *Workers Compensation Act*, the *Family Relations Act* (British Columbia), and the *Succession Law Reform Act* (Ontario) permit cohabitors to make

Figure 8.1 Census Families by Structure

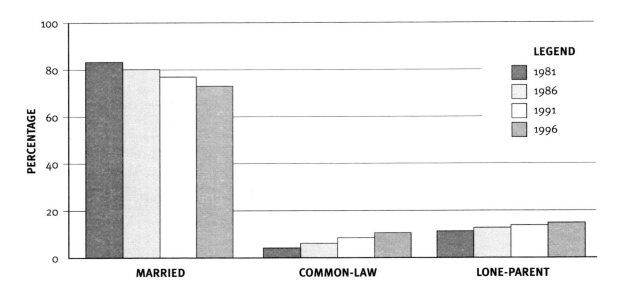

Source: Adapted from the Statistics Canada publications "The Daily," Catalogue 11-001, October 14, 1997, and from "Age, Sex and Marital Status," Catalogue 93-101, 1987.

claims that may be in direct competition with those of a lawful spouse (MacDougall, 1980).

There are three areas of law in which distinctions may be made between legal marriages and common-law unions:

Social Law Social law provides for entitlement to public benefits for those experiencing occupational injuries, and victims of crimes, disasters, or automobile accidents. In most of these areas, the common-law spouse has been fairly well integrated into social legislation. Problems arise when a conflict develops between a legal spouse and a common-law spouse where the husband is not divorced from his wife, or where a claimant cannot prove that she meets the legal criteria of a common-law spouse. Only legal spouses, however, are entitled, upon dissolution of the marriage, to a share in the pension credits accumulated by each of the spouses. It is also not clear whether a person can insure the life of his or her common-law spouse under current Canadian insurance laws (Boivin, 1985).

Matrimonial Law Matrimonial law governs the right to habitation and ownership of the family residence, the obligation to provide economic support, and the division of assets upon the dissolution of the marriage. When a house is used as the principal residence of a married couple, the spouse has the right to live in the residence, even if the other spouse is the sole owner. Upon divorce, the spouse may be able to claim a legal interest in the house. Common-law spouses do not benefit from provisions regarding the principal residence, but must either include the provisions in a domestic contract, or request an order from the court. Spouses are required by law to provide support for each other in accordance with their means. After dissolution of a marriage, spouses must provide support in accordance with need and ability to pay, although alimony judgments are currently rare. In case of death, a portion of the estate may be set aside for the surviving spouse and children, the will notwithstanding. The right to support payments for common-law spouses is recognized only in Ontario, Manitoba, and British Columbia. The division of assets in the case of the dissolution of a common-law relationship may require litigation, whereas the division of assets of a married couple is governed by special legislative provisions in all jurisdictions (Boivin, 1985).

Tax Law Tax legislation also differentiates between married and common-law spouses. The majority of tax provisions do not apply to common-law spouses, with the result that these individuals cannot take advantage of such deductions as the married person's exemption, the transfer of unused deductions, and the spouse's contribution to an RRSP. On the other hand, common-law spouses are not treated as a single economic unit, which results, in some cases, in significant income tax savings. Common-law spouses have recently become eligible for the right to transfer assets from one spouse to the other without tax consequences, and the right to claim deductions for support payments (Boivin, 1985).

One study (*Globe and Mail*, June 18, 1991) found that 58 percent of married couples had less disposable income in 1989 than if they had been cohabiting, while only 29 percent had more disposable income as married rather than cohabiting couples. In 1993 the federal government determined that "individuals are deemed to be married for all tax purposes if they cohabit for a 12-month period or reside together with a child of whom both are parents" (Bala, 1994:275).

Morton (1988) points out that the processes of revising family law in Ontario have resulted in the significant redefinition of the rights and responsibilities of family members regarding property and support. She argues, however, that the position of women (and their dependent children) remains essentially unimproved despite the *ideal* of equality. Both contract equality and state intervention are seen as resulting in the feminization of poverty and the masculinization of wealth.

A much-debated issue is whether legislation governing common-law relationships should be passed. Arguments opposing as well as supporting such legislation have been advanced. Arguments *opposed* to further legislation governing common-law relationships include the following:

- The principle of free choice argues that the state should not interfere in the free choice of persons who decide not to marry specifically to avoid the legal consequences of marriage.

- Some feminists argue that the equality of women will not be achieved without complete autonomy. Identifying common-law relationships with marriage is seen as another means of controlling or dominating women.

- Some people feel that a distinction should be made between those who are prepared to make a more permanent commitment and those who are not. There is a problem with giving legal recognition to a marriage that may last only two years, as opposed to giving no recognition to a common-law relationship that may last 10 or more years. There are also legal problems with determining the duration of common-law relationships.

- Common-law legislation may be perceived as a threat to the preservation of the institution of marriage.

Arguments *supporting* the broader legal recognition of common-law relationships include the following:

- It is unjust to fail to recognize the rights and obligations to support of persons in a relationship that resembles marriage.

- It would be preferable to establish comprehensive legislative policies on common-law relationships rather than to leave such decisions to the courts. The dilemma is how to protect women in common-law relationships without destroying their independence.

- Some jurisdictions make provisions for domestic contracts to govern the various aspects of the relationship of common-law spouses. The problem is that persons who are bound by sentimental attachments shy away from contracts, which may be perceived as reflecting a lack of confidence in the partner—and the result is that women may remain unprotected (Boivin, 1985).

Domestic Contracts

As we have seen, marriage is a contract between two spouses, with the state acting as a silent partner. Because this contract does not meet the needs of every couple, some couples write their own domestic contract. A **domestic contract** is a written legal agreement between an engaged or married couple. It is a variant of the prenuptial agreements brought to this country by early colonists from England, and functions as a supplement to the state contract, helping a couple to clearly specify their expectations, assumptions, and desires before their marriage. In the past, such contracts were primarily economic, and were used where one of the partners had a large estate that was to be disposed of in a particular manner.

Two people who decide to live together without getting married can sign a cohabitation agreement that spells out their support and property rights. If they later decide to get married, their cohabitation agreement automatically becomes a marriage contract, and continues to be binding (The Law Society, 1997). During such relationships the couple may contribute to a joint account, purchase various kinds of property, and generally conduct themselves as a partnership. A domestic contract may be signed to avoid disputes at the dissolution of the relationship.

All provinces require that a domestic contract be recorded in writing, signed by both parties, and witnessed by two others. Each spouse must execute the contract freely and voluntarily, without any coercion on the part of the other spouse. Domestic contracts allow spouses to override legislation that specifies the nature of property division or spousal support. A concern is that individuals may be giving away rights to which they would otherwise be entitled under legislation (King, 1980). The agreement may indicate who has the right to direct the education and moral training of the children, but it cannot override the right to custody of, or access to, children, nor limit the rights to live in and remain in the matrimonial home, even after separation (The Law Society, 1997). Upon marital breakdown, the matrimonial home is subject to equal sharing in most provinces, even when it has been acquired by one spouse prior to the marriage (Morton, 1990).

Most Canadians entering prenuptial contracts do so for two main reasons. First, some wealthy businesspeople with large corporate interests may want to ensure that those interests are protected in case of divorce. Spouses who enter into such prenuptial agreements are abdicating their future claims, but some of these agreements may not hold up in a court of law. Second, some dual-earner couples enter prenuptial contracts to ensure domestic equality (Kurian, 1993).

Contemporary couples who choose to design their own personal marriage contract or prenuptial agreement may include clauses on financial arrangements between the partners and the control of income and expenses, work and career role responsibilities, plans for children, responsibility for household tasks, relationships with relatives, religious considerations, guidelines for sexual fidelity, procedures for changing or dissolving the contract, and more. Even if a couple does not choose to write such a contract, taking the time to discuss the situations normally covered in such an arrangement may be helpful in clarifying the partners' expectations before entering the marital relationship. The most important effect of a personal marriage contract is to define how each partner sees the relationship.

A survey in British Columbia found that the majority of respondents either indicated that personal marriage contracts were a poor idea, or provided only qualified support for such contracts. Only a minority endorsed the idea of marriage contracts for everyone contemplating marriage. Those who agreed with the concept saw it as a useful process in setting out each partner's expectations prior to marriage (Burtch et al., 1985).

The social contexts in which people today make decisions to marry have changed in important ways. Changes in rates of marriage, divorce, and cohabitation reflect changes in the social context of marriage. Barich and Bielby (1996) investigated the relationship of social and cultural beliefs to the marriage expectations of young unmarried adults in 1967 and 1994. They found considerable stability in the rankings of marriage expectations over this period. The same four expectations (amount of love and affection, healthy and happy children, companionship, and emotional security) are ranked high in both periods. They suggest that marital expectations are highly institutionalized and are not strongly influenced by social change. When compared by gender and year, however, changes in the ranking of marital expectations are more substantial among women than among men. Women indicated an increase in the importance of economic security and a decrease in the importance of happy children, whereas men indicated no changes in these expectations. The expectation that love was an important part of marriage achieved the most important ranking for the majority of respondents, despite the social and cultural changes of the past 25 years. Women continue to rank the amount of love and affection higher than men do, but differences in the ranking of economic security have disappeared as a result of the increase in importance, among women, of economic security.

The Transition to Marriage

Researchers often conceptualize the transition to marriage as spanning a duration of time from engagement through the first year of marriage. During this time there are many events that mark the transition from being single to being married, such as the engagement, wedding, and honeymoon. Certainly there is some variation in the experience and occurrence of these marker events for young couples. Some couples may simply decide to elope, or to get married before a justice of the peace. Others may have a small wedding with only immediate family members present. If there is an engagement period, it may be casual and informal, rather than formal and public. This may be particularly true of cohabiting couples. More traditional couples place a greater emphasis on engagement as a formal announcement of their commitment to marry. Frequently, engagement is followed by a large, formal wedding, and a romantic, expensive honeymoon (Benokraitis, 1993).

Hobart (1993a) found evidence of continuing, widespread support for marriage among young people, with more than 90 percent of a national survey indicating they seriously expect to get married. More favourable pro-marriage attitudes were found among Anglophones than among Francophones, and among women than among men. Ambivalence about the loss of freedom and the responsibilities of marriage characterized men more than women, and Francophones more than Anglophones. These favorable attitudes fly in the face of the downward trend in the marriage rate in the 1990s. Marriage rates briefly increased at the turn of this century, but then declined over 6 percent from 2000 to 2003.

An engagement serves several important functions. First, it is an announcement that the couple is no longer in the "marriage market," and that they are no longer available to others. The engagement gives both partners opportunities to become better acquainted with their prospective in-laws, as well as to cement their relationship with each other. As well, it provides both partners with information about the prospective partner's potential or current medical problems. Engagement is often associated with secular or religious premarital counseling (Benokraitis, 1993). Whitehurst and Booth (1980) characterize the engagement period for the female as traditionally one of positive expectancy and hope, as evidenced by the showers of gifts and good wishes. For the male, in contrast, engagement was traditionally seen as a loss of freedom

and independence, and a cutting off of ties that, within marriage, were no longer legitimate. This change was exemplified in the "last fling" of the male stag party.

The Wedding Ceremony

Getting married is a significant critical transition from one social status to another. It is similar to the transition of having a child, or of children leaving home, or of one's spouse dying. Because these transitions represent dramatic changes in family life, they are often marked by ritual activity. These rituals ease the transitions by dealing with the psychic and social implications of the changes involved, and are examples of the rites of passage found in more traditional societies. The symbolism and meaning of many wedding customs and rituals are frequently not understood by the couple or those attending the ceremony. Many of these customs are "echoes of the past—everything from the presence of flowers and a veil, to the old shoes and the rice, to the bridesmaid and the processional" (Seligson, 1974:18). While the original meaning of all these rituals is not always clear, thinking about and discussing the symbolism involved may be of value in deciding which ones to include in one's own wedding. Rituals that are consciously chosen may help make one's own wedding more meaningful.

A wedding may include hundreds of family members and friends, but every wedding must include at least two witnesses. These witnesses affirm that the wedding ceremony involves a public commitment to the marriage contract. In the absence of a licence or written record, the rituals were originally considered essential to make the wedding legal. The word *wedding* comes from *wed*, the Anglo-Saxon word for "pledge," and thus the public ceremony was regarded as a pledge (Chesser, 1980). The presence of family members from both sides, whether or not they ever get together again, demonstrates that marriage creates new social bonds that involve obligations to both sides of the family, and it represents a change from the freedom of courtship to the constraints of the social system.

The oldest and most universal marriage symbol is probably the ring. The Egyptians used wedding rings, as did the ancient Romans and Greeks. The ring generally was used as a seal by which important orders were signed, thus indicating authenticity, and symbolizing the highest form of trust and power. Because most people were right-handed, the left hand was considered inferior, and thus wearing the ring on the left hand was a sign of submission and obedience. One reason for wearing the ring on the fourth finger was the belief that this finger contained a small artery that led straight to the heart, thus symbolizing a pledge of love (Chesser, 1980). Most contemporary couples buy each other wedding rings, suggesting the equality and mutual sharing of modern marriages. Modern ceremonies emphasize that the rings, being circles, symbolize never-ending love, and that, being made of precious metal, they symbolize the significance or worth of the new relationship.

Traditionally, a father gave the bride away to her husband as a symbol of the transfer of ownership of the woman. Likewise, the tradition of the husband carrying the bride across the threshold had its origin in the ownership of daughters by fathers, and symbolized the transfer of ownership. The dowry, or hope chest, was also related to this custom (Chesser, 1980).

Candles or torches traditionally were an important part of wedding ceremonies. In ancient Rome, darkness had normally descended by the time the wedding procession got under way. Torchbearers were used to light the way through the dark city streets as they escorted the wedding party, and the torches symbolized the enduring flame of marriage.

Every culture has developed its own rituals connected with the wedding ceremony (see Box 8.1). In a multicultural society such as Canada, the various ethno-religious groups (Christians, Jews, Buddhists, Muslims, Hindus, and others) each prescribe somewhat different rituals for the wedding ceremony. Many of these rituals are carried over from their culture of origin (Nett, 1993).

The Honeymoon

After the wedding ceremony, many couples will embark on a honeymoon. In North America, the honeymoon is an institutionalized "get-away" for the young, just-married couple. According to Bulcroft, Smein, and Bulcroft (1999), the honeymoon began during the 19th century among upper-class couples who could afford a "wedding tour" often lasting several weeks. The middle class emulated this upper class tour but, having fewer resources, the distance traveled was not as great nor the accommodation as elegant. Destinations during the early 20th century included places such as Niagara Falls and Florida. As travel became more accessible and affordable, more exotic destinations such as Hawaii and Fiji became popular. Currently, there exists a huge commercialization of the honeymoon and travel destinations.

The honeymoon serves to assist the newlyweds in the adjustments they face in moving to the status of a married couple. During the honeymoon, the couple is treated as a couple rather than individuals. Plane reservations, hotel reservations, and dinners all reinforce the couple identity. The newlyweds also may practise the newly legitimized "Mr. and Mrs." status, though this function is de-emphasized for brides keeping their maiden name. Another function of the honeymoon is to reinforce the romantic nature of affection between the partners. For example, hotels and other purveyors of the honeymoon business stress such things as candlelit dinners and heart-shaped hot tubs (Bulcroft et al., 1999).

Box 8.1　　　Cultural Insights: Polish Weddings in Canada

Of the major Polish family transitions (birth, christening, funeral), the wedding was the most festive and elaborate ceremony. In rural areas the feast was often celebrated for two or three days (and nights) with plentiful food, refreshments, and dancing. Inevitably, the period of transition following migration curtailed some of these practices, although one source . . . noted specific Polish customs—the bride's veil being thrown to the bridesmaids, gifts in the form of cash for the young couple, elaborate and plentiful food and refreshments—all being maintained in Canada. Only a few specifically Polish wedding customs and traditions survive to the present, and today, Polish couples generally conform to urban, middle-class practices.

Source: Ishwaran, 1980:54.

The honeymoon also serves as an escape from the attention and focus of family and friends. Though this attention is enjoyed at the wedding ceremony, it is necessary to escape this intense public scrutiny and celebration, as it places stress on the newlywed couple. Finally, the return from the honeymoon serves as a marker for the couple to return to "reality" and to face the challenges of the adjustments and developmental tasks required in marriage.

Adjustments in Marriage

Leaving the single life in favour of marriage involves a significant transition from one social status to another. Young people who have worked hard to achieve independence from parents and family members during adolescence are sometimes rather casual about surrendering this independence for the many responsibilities and duties of married life. Single people's primary responsibilities are to themselves and perhaps their family. Upon marriage, people assume responsibilities not only for themselves, but also for their new spouse—responsibilities that take precedence over other family responsibilities. The transition from independence to interdependence takes place in a number of important areas.

■ **Economics** The economic area is perhaps one of the most difficult adjustments. Individuals who have been free to purchase clothes or cars, go on trips, and pay little attention to budgets must now begin to make long-range plans. In addition to meeting the normal expenses of food, rent, and utilities, which they may or may not have paid before marriage, couples must consider saving up to buy a house or budgeting to start a family.

■ **Leisure** Leisure time pursuits often creates marital conflicts. The desires and interests of one's partner must be taken into consideration, and partners can no longer engage in activities on an unplanned and spontaneous basis. How many leisure time activities should be shared as a couple? How much time can each partner spend with previous friends who remain single and who have more freedom?

■ **Relationships** Marriage also involves fashioning new relationships with parents, and individuals must

make the sometimes difficult transition of moving the primary relationship from parents to spouse. Working out visiting arrangements for special occasions such as Christmas may create problems, especially when long-standing traditions have been established in the families of both spouses.

■ **Children** The arrival of children creates a major transition for both spouses. Children decrease the amount of time available for joint leisure activities, and affect the spontaneity and freedom that a recently married couple experiences. Having children may involve the postponement of a career for the wife, or the "hassle" of making arrangements for satisfactory child care. It certainly involves increased expenditures and responsibilities, and decreased time for the partners as a couple.

There are many other transitions that must be made in order for the marital relationship to be successful and satisfying to both partners. To become accustomed to the habits, food preferences, time schedules, temperature preferences, and other potentially idiosyncratic tendencies of a new mate requires both patience and commitment. Failure to make these transitions is seen in the high divorce rate, particularly among the newly married.

In an examination of how courtship stories told in the first year of marriage are predictive of marital well-being in the third year of marriage, Orbuch et al. (1993) report that only one theme stands out: couples do not generally perceive that wives are initiators in relationship development. In view of the emphasis on romance in our culture, a surprising finding is that having a highly romantic reconstruction of one's courtship does not predict marital well-being. Rather, having a generally positive tone in the relationship without romanticism during courtship is more strongly related to later marital well-being. In fact, the majority of couples do not focus on romantic themes in courtship.

Marriage is a relationship in which two people are bonded together by long-term, repeated interactions, which reduce the risks associated with the uncertainty and opportunism of single life. This bonding process involves three aspects: intimate companionship, child-rearing, and the production of wealth. *Intimate companionship* includes sexual intimacy, but the fundamental desire is for an intimate companion with whom to share all aspects of life. Relationships are also established for the purpose of *child-rearing*. This involves an emotional and physiological bonding of the parents to their children. This shared bond creates an ongoing tie between them. Individuals also join together to *increase their mutual wealth*. This may affect further intimate companionship or child-rearing, or both, either positively or negatively. Intimate companions must make choices between personal goals (e.g., careers) and companionship (emotional or physical bonding) in integrating their wealth production and their companionship. In making choices regarding careers, one or both partners may have to alter personal goals in order to achieve improved companionship or emotional closeness. Similarly, in raising children, parents need to adapt their work patterns in order to provide the most money possible while at the same time providing for direct parental care of the children. This may involve one spouse giving priority to child care while the other concentrates on earning income, at least for a time. Each needs the other if their mutual desires for the children are to be fulfilled (Cornell, 1992).

A study by Allen and Kalish (1984) indicates that the timing of transition to marriage for women is a result of interaction between the relative rewards and costs associated with marriage and other roles. The study showed that women who married at a later age than their contemporaries, for example, gave a higher priority to educational and career goals than to marriage. Women who married late also experienced other alternatives to marriage and "legitimate" sexual relations in that they considered premarital sex and cohabitation more acceptable, and were less likely to believe that marriage was required to legitimize sexual behaviour. Late marriers also experienced greater expectations for an egalitarian marriage with respect to household chores and finances, as well as child care. As well, those who married late were significantly less likely to view marriage as an escape from home, and were more likely to report being able to communicate well with their parents. The authors concluded that the transition to marriage for women is, in part, the result of the attractiveness of alternative roles, in comparison with the rewards and costs of the role of a married woman.

To what extent do marriage preparation programs prepare individuals for the transition to married life? One study of both control and experimental couple groups from 19 Toronto churches of differing religious denominations found that such programs contributed to enhanced marital communication and conflict resolution skills in later marital interaction. Couples who participated in the program reported less conflict regarding interpersonal topics than did control couples. Conflict was more likely to have negative effects on the relationship of control couples, which resulted in their failure to deal realistically with conflict. The control couples showed no improvement in their ability to resolve hypothetical conflict situations, whereas the experimental group showed a steady and significant increase in conflict resolution skills (Bader et al., 1980).

Developmental Tasks in Marriage

As we saw in Chapter 2, the family developmental approach focuses on expectations (norms) as to what family members do to and with each other. What family members do is strongly influenced by what their society and their family expect them to do. A practical application of the developmental approach to the family is found in the discussion of developmental tasks in the beginning marriage. A **developmental task** is one associated with a particular stage in the life of an individual, the successful achievement of which may lead to happiness and success in later stages. One of the best-known attempts to describe the developmental tasks of the beginning marriage is found in Duvall and Miller (1985).

Duvall and Miller discuss eight general developmental tasks of beginning families that may be conflicting, complementary, or both.

1. Finding, furnishing, and settling into their first home. One of the first requirements preceding marriage is to establish where the young couple will live. Finding and furnishing a home on a limited budget, often with unrealistic expectations, may require major lifestyle changes, unless the couple receives significant help from parents or other relatives.

2. Establishing mutually satisfactory ways of supporting themselves. The age and inexperience of the young often conflict with their wants, desires, and needs. Expectations represented in advertising, or even in their own family experiences, accompanied by the ready availability of significant lines of credit, may produce pressures for young couples to live beyond their means. An almost universal solution is for the wife to work, which contributes to more cooperative decisions about how to spend the family income based on joint planning.

3. Allocating responsibilities each partner is willing and able to assume. Traditional couples had clearly established roles that spelled out the duties and privileges of both husband and wife. Today's newly married couples do not have such clear role prescriptions, and they must therefore become involved in the process of negotiating satisfactory joint scripts. Increasingly, the decision of who will do what is not based on clearly established male and female roles, but rather on the basis of relative time and talent, marital power dynamics, personal preference, work schedules, reciprocity, and a sense of fairness.

4. Building foundations for satisfying marital relations. Basic characteristics conducive to high or low levels of marital satisfaction are developed before marriage. The couple needs to build on existing qualities, including such important features as developing effective problem-solving approaches, realistically facing marital conflict and developing constructive conflict-resolution skills, developing functional communication systems through effective communication styles, and establishing mutually satisfactory sexual relations.

5. Controlling fertility and planning a family. Planning a family is not an issue for the couple already expecting at the time of marriage, for those who are already parents when they marry, or for those who voluntarily decide to remain childless. Most couples believe in planned parenthood, and modern contraceptives allow parents to make a conscious choice about parenthood and the timing of the child's arrival. Unplanned pregnancies may precipitate a crisis for the couple, making significant changes necessary in finances, education, career, or other areas. Conversely, infertility may be a source of anguish to couples desiring children, requiring some mental and emotional adjustments on the part of the newly married couple.

6. Starting a family. The first pregnancy contributes to enlarging husband–wife intimacy to include the expected baby. Frequently, the couple role-plays being parents before the baby arrives. Both husbands and wives face new developmental tasks in preparing for the baby's arrival. Prenatal care and counseling assist the couple in these preparations.

7. Interacting with relatives on both sides of the family. The newly married couple finds itself simultaneously in three families: her family of orientation, his family of orientation, and the family of procreation that they are establishing. It is no easy task to shift from the primacy of a child–parent relationship to that of a husband–wife relationship. Each person in the marriage may retain significant emotional attachments to his or her *own* parents, while at the same time feeling threatened by the close relationship of the spouse to his or her parents. This situation may be worsened when parents, whose lives have revolved around their children, exert pressure to remain an important part of their married children's lives and time commitments.

8. Maintaining couple motivation and morale. Marriage requires the establishment of a joint philosophy of life that combines the convictions and values of both partners in a philosophical whole. This philosophy of life is probably not explicit, and it does not require them to take exactly the same position on every issue of life. It does, however, provide basic guidelines and orientations for the major decisions that they confront as a couple.

A number of significant changes take place in a couple's relationship during the first year of marriage, reflecting the realities of living together. Young couples experience the exhilaration of getting married, furnishing their first home, and discovering their firstborn is on the way, as well as the frustrations of efforts to accomplish the developmental tasks that often demand more of them than they are able to give.

Aldous (1996) suggests that the newly married couple must define their relationship not only in terms of developmental tasks or norms, but also in terms of role-making. Increasingly, with husband and wife both employed, they must negotiate their roles by a role-making process. This approach places the emphasis on improvisation rather than on rigidly prescribed norms. While recognizing the influence of general normative guides to behaviour, "role-making" rather than "norm-playing" emphasizes that situational demands determine specific behaviours. Thus, **role-making** is the establishment of marital roles based on a couple's interaction, rather than on normative prescriptions. The role-making approach recognizes that an extensive range of behaviours is regarded as appropriate to a particular role within accepted normative limits. Newly married husbands and wives improvise their behaviours in learning how to complete required tasks. This improvisation is based on personal preference, expressed desires, interests, and power, rather than on social prescriptions. When social prescriptions are changing, the need for role-making is paramount.

The patterns that constitute family structures develop out of a process of habituation rather than out of rigid normative prescriptions. Household responsibilities and decision-making processes are not automatically set by group norms, but arise out of trial-and-error attempts to interact satisfactorily. When satisfactory ways of interacting are found, those patterns tend to become normative and to guide future interactions. Role-making provides greater freedom for personal and couple development, and makes it easier to adapt to change. Role-making also provides each party in the relationship a voice in the final arrangements, and consequently may contribute to building family morale. At the same time, role-making may lead to more disagreements than may following a conventional script; thus, it may also create greater confusion and conflict, and less stable family structures, as a result of the broadened range of family behaviour. The process of role-making requires more negotiating and bargaining than if each spouse were responsible for certain decisions based on prior role scripts.

A factor that has received considerable research attention in the last decades is the concept of marital commitment. Generally, higher levels of commitment are associated with more stable marriages.

Marital Commitment

Commitment is an important dimension of everyday life. It is necessary if you are to pass this course, complete a university degree, get and keep a job, earn a promotion, lose weight, perform well in sports ("He gave 110 percent"), and be successful in relationships. While the importance of goal-setting, persistence, discipline, patience, and stick-to-it-iveness is clearly recognized, the application of these qualities to marriage and family relationships was not clearly addressed by research until the 1970s. Commitment is the cement that holds relationships together. If spouses were not committed, they probably would not put up with some of the difficulties faced in marriage.

Definitions and Meanings

Commitment may have different meanings for different people. One person may be committed to a particular partner or relationship in which they experience companionship, caring, affirmation, self-disclosure, and continuing growth. Another person may be committed to the institution of marriage, but experience little commitment to a partner. Thus, for example, a wife may feel that it is morally wrong to dissolve an abusive relationship in which love, caring and trust are absent, and in which she feels fear of and hate toward her husband. Fehr (1988) asked 172 respondents to rate the central features of commitment. The 12 central attributes, listed in order, were loyalty, responsibility, living up to your word, faithfulness, trust, being there for the other in good times and bad, devotion, reliability, giving your best effort, supportiveness, perseverance, and concern about the other's well-being.

Johnson (1973, 1978, 1985) provided one of the first attempts to apply commitment to the marital relationship. His initial definition differentiated between personal and structural commitment. **Personal commitment** was defined as a personal dedication or determination (often referred to as the "want to" in commitment) to continue or complete a line of action despite adversity or temptations to deviate. **Structural commitment** was defined as events or conditions that constrain an individual (often referred to as the "have to" in commitment) to continue a line of action once it has been initiated, regardless of personal preference. Structural commitment mechanisms include termination procedures, irretrievable investments, social pressures, and available alternatives. Johnson (1985) also referred to **moral commitment**, which was defined as either an internalized personal sense of moral obligation, or an external moral obligation imposed by significant others (the "ought to" of commitment).

In a representative sample of Edmonton residents comprising 179 couples, Goltz (1987) used the concepts of personal and structural commitment developed by Johnson to determine major correlates of marital commitment. The two most powerful predictors of personal commitment were the husband's educational level and the husband's church attendance. Personal commitment increased with an increase in the husband's educational level and with more frequent church attendance. The two most powerful predictors of structural commitment were individualism and the number of times the wife was married. Structural commitment *decreased* as individualism *increased*, and as the number of times the wife was married *increased*. Another variable related to structural commitment was religious preference. Those with a conservative or Catholic religious affiliation experienced higher levels of structural or constraint commitment than did those from mainline churches or those who were unaffiliated with a religion. Thus, individualism and the number of times the wife was married were associated with low structural commitment, while conservative religious affiliation was associated with high structural commitment.

In an investigation of the association between commitment (defined as the perception of costs of leaving a relationship) and of dependency in marriage (measured in terms of income, labour, educational attainment, and occupational prestige), Nock (1995) found that each of these measures of dependence had only modest effects on commitment. By far the strongest component of individual commitment to marriage was the perceived commitment of the spouse.

Lee and Agnew (2003) reviewed 60 studies of marital commitment and found that investments in the relationship accounted for two-thirds of marital commitment. They also reported that marital commitment is a strong predictor of couples' marital stability. Low marital commitment predicted divorce. Sprecher (2002) reports similar findings for a small sample. She found a strong positive relationship between sexual satisfaction and marital commitment, especially for males.

Religion and Marital Commitment

We have seen that religious participation was related to personal marital commitment, and that religious affiliation was related to structural marital commitment. Larson and Goltz (1989) examined the influence of religious homogamy, religious affiliation, and religious participation on personal and structural commitment. Religious homogamy was not a significant predictor of marital commitment. The major reason may be that only 25 percent of the sample were heterogamous. Just as religious homogamy is of decreasing importance in mate choice, it may also be less significant in marriage. On the other hand, the religious differences may have been assimilated through "conversion," or religiously heterogamous couples may already have opted out of their marriage.

Some rather interesting patterns were found between religious affiliation and marital commitment. The lowest levels of structural commitment and highest levels of personal commitment were found among couples who had no religious affiliation. Non-religious couples experienced fewer constraints to remain in their marriage, or fewer barriers to leaving their marriage (given that religion is a powerful barrier). Thus, those non-religious couples who did remain together did so because they had a "good" relationship with a resulting high level of personal commitment. Those without satisfying bonds left the relationship and were no longer in the sample (Larson and Goltz, 1989).

The highest levels of structural commitment and lowest levels of personal commitment were found among husbands of conservative or Catholic religious affiliation. Catholic and conservative husbands were more prepared to stay in the marriage despite the lower levels of personal commitment. The powerful role of religion as a barrier to marital dissolution is thus apparent among conservative husbands, particularly those who are active in the church. They may feel that they have no alternative but to remain in the marriage, responding to either the constraints of religious teachings or to the encouragement of the religious community, or both (Larson and Goltz, 1989).

In a review of the linkages between religion and commitment to marriage, Larson (1989b) pointed out that *structural commitment* was strongly correlated with marital stability. Stable marriages, regardless of the level of satisfaction, were likely to have a high concentration of structural constraints against leaving the marriage, such as unattractive alternatives to the current relationship, strong social pressure from family and friends, and irretrievable investments in the relationship such as time, money, energy, or emotion. On the other hand, *personal commitment* was strongly correlated with marital satisfaction. People who were happy in their marriages were more likely to perceive the marriages as permanent, to invest more of themselves, to give up personal priorities in their partner's interest, and to reject alternative relationships. While correlated, personal commitment and marital satisfaction are distinct concepts (Goltz, 1987; Stanley, 1986).

Larson (1989) suggests that satisfaction is often as volatile as "love." Because disagreement and conflict are a normal part of marriage, satisfaction may be a more fragile correlate of long-term marital growth than may personal commitment. Individuals who are personally dedicated to their marriages will be more steadfast during the rough times, or be impelled toward corrective or enriching actions. Larson and Goltz argue that

> commitment is not the consequence of experiencing a good marriage. Instead, commitment is the individual and relational source of making good (or even weak) marriages better. In this sense, communication is less likely to occur if a couple is uncommitted. Likewise, the resolution of differences (marital adjustment) is less likely to occur if a couple is unable to talk about their differences. Commitment may indeed be the senior variable in the evolution of a strong marriage, from one which is merely "stable" to one that is becoming more "enriching" (1989:397).

Using longitudinal data from a large sample of married persons, Booth et al. (1995) concluded that an increase in religious activity did not improve marital relations, but an increase in marital happiness slightly increased two of five dimensions of religiosity. They concluded that, on the whole, the link between religion and marital quality is reciprocal, but weak.

We have investigated the relationship between commitment and the quality of marriage. In the next section we examine how marital status and gender affect overall marital well-being.

The Impact of Marital Status and Gender on Well-Being

Most people marry with the hope that marriage will bring them a greater sense of fulfillment and happiness. Much research has been devoted to determining how marriage affects individual happiness. An interesting question that has been addressed by this research is,

Who is happier—married or single people? In the minds of many, singlehood is associated with greater freedom, the ability to make your own choices, and not being "tied down," but also with loneliness in later years. In contrast, marriage is associated with responsibilities, a loss of freedom, and being "tied down," but also with having a spouse who *cares*. In addition, we may raise the question whether or not marriage is associated with enhanced well-being in an era when the value of marriage is increasingly questioned or discounted, and when many aspects of marital roles are undergoing rapid change. Two interesting findings with respect to the relationship between marital status and adult well-being have been debated in the research literature: Married people are healthier and happier than the non-married; and marriage tends to have more positive benefits for men than for women. Based on a review of the research literature, Waite (1995:499) concludes as follows: "On average, however, marriage seems to produce substantial benefits for men and women in the form of better health, longer life, more and better sex, greater earnings (at least for men), greater wealth, and better outcomes for children."

The relationship between marital status and well-being was found in a number of important areas. Married people were found to have lower rates of treatment for mental illness and higher levels of psychological well-being (Glenn, 1975; Campbell, 1981; Gove, Hughes and Style, 1983; Gove and Shinn, 1989; Gove, Style and Hughes, 1989; Lee, Seccombe and Shehan, 1991); to experience fewer negative indicators of psychological well-being, such as depression and anxiety (Gove, 1972; Anashensel et al., 1981; Gove and Shinn, 1989); to experience lower rates of early mortality (Gove, 1973; Lillard and Waite, 1995); and to enjoy better physical health than the unmarried (Verbrugge, 1979).

Two major explanations of the positive relationship between marriage and well-being have been advanced. The first is what has been referred to as the "selection" explanation, which argues that healthy, happy people are more likely to get married and stay married than those who are emotionally unstable or in poor physical health. A number of investigators (Renne, 1971; Turner and Gartrell, 1978; Verbrugge, 1979) found evidence that the selection factor does operate, so that people who are less healthy or happy are also less likely to get married or to stay married. In other words, the positive relationship between marriage and well-being exists because healthier people get married, not because marriage makes people healthier. White (1992) argues that age group variations in the relationship between life satisfaction and marital status are congruent with the pattern predicted by the selection hypothesis. Similarly, Mastekaasa (1992) concluded that selection processes make an important contribution to the association between marital status and psychological well-being. Fu and Goldman (1996) found that heavy drug and alcohol use (unhealthy behaviours) and female obesity and short stature for men (physical characteristics) were associated with lower marriage rates.

Other investigators have concluded that this relationship is *not* due to social selection, but that something about marriage *causes* a higher level of well-being.

Lee et al. (1991) agreed that the selection of happier, healthier persons into marriage, and the greater propensity of these persons to remain married, does account for some of the difference between married and unmarried individuals' physical and psychological well-being. However, they found that the effects of the marriage relationship itself on well-being are stronger and more important than selection effects. In a longitudinal sample of young adults over a seven-year period, Horwitz et al. (1996) found that when the effects of premarital levels of depression and alcohol problems were controlled, married people were less depressed and had fewer alcohol problems than people who remained single. While levels of depression and alcohol problems drop among those who remain single, they drop faster among those who get married. Gove et al. (1990) argue that the evidence suggests that the positive relationship between marriage and better mental and physical health is not due to the selection of competent and healthy persons into marriage, but is primarily due to the effect of the marital relationship on individuals. Thus, if the interaction in a marital relationship is positive, the well-being of the spouse is enhanced. In contrast, if such interaction is negative, substantial hurt and anger will be produced, which may be detrimental to the well-being of the individuals involved.

The review of this research has revealed that it provides support for both the social causation and the selection explanations of the reported association between marital status and psychological well-being. It may therefore be wise to conclude that social causation and selection processes may be operating simultaneously.

A second frequent finding is that marriage has more positive benefits for men than for women. These studies suggest that married men reap the benefits of companionship and household labour, but do not suffer declines in occupational rewards. In contrast, married women who do not work outside the home become isolated and powerless; if they do enter the labour force, they suffer from role overload and occupy inferior occupational positions (Rosenfield, 1992). Married women have higher rates of mental illness than do married men, report lower levels of happiness (Gove and Hughes, 1979; Williams, 1988), and experience higher levels of depression (Anashensel et al., 1981). Gove (1972) investigated three plausible explanations for the higher rates of mental illness among women: 1) women may be biologically more susceptible to mental illness; 2) some characteristic of women's generalized sex role makes them more susceptible to mental illness; and 3) something about the roles women occupy in our society may promote mental illness. Because single, divorced, or widowed women tend to have lower rates of mental illness than do men in the same categories, biological and generalized sex roles were rejected as explanations. A greater willingness among women to report illness and a greater ability of women to adopt the sick role because of lesser responsibilities were also rejected as explanations of the sex differences in physical and mental health (Gove and Hughes, 1979). It appears from this research that sex differences in illness are due to the roles of women in our society, and, specifically, to their role in marriage.

Bernard (1972) highlighted the differential effects of marriage for men and women with the concept of "his" and "her" marriages. She argued that, in general, marriage is good for men because married men live longer and are healthier and happier than unmarried men. In contrast, married women are more likely to experience depression and physical illness than are unmarried women. The objectively and subjectively different conditions of men and women were used to explain these differences. Similarly, Marks (1996) found that single women have higher scores on personality characteristics associated with better psychological well-being than do married women.

Based on a sample of more than 2000 married Canadians, Rhyne (1981) supported the finding that men were more "satisfied" than women. Mean levels of satisfaction were higher for men, and a greater percentage of men evaluated their marriages more favourably. More men than women fell into the top 20 percent of an index of marital quality, felt very satisfied with their marriages, graded their marriages as "A," never felt that marriage limited their freedom, and would marry the same person again (differences in the last two categories were not statistically significant). Schumm et al. (1985) found no significant differences in marital satisfaction between husbands and wives. When husbands and wives were compared on a couple-by-couple basis, however, it was found that a minority of women scored much lower than their husbands, while a majority scored slightly higher than their husbands, thus contributing to the lack of significant differences. When a major difference was found in reported marital satisfaction, in over 90 percent of the cases, the more distressed spouse was the wife.

Other researchers have found that while marital status was the most powerful predictor of mental health, it was not marriage per se that predicted positive mental health, but rather the quality of marriage (Gove et al., 1983). Anashensel et al. (1981) found that depression increases as family role obligations, particularly for women, increase. Similarly, Thoits (1986) found that marriage was equally beneficial for men and women, if not more beneficial for women. The role that was the greatest source of disadvantage for women relative to men, however, was employment. Thus, "women's higher distress when employment is combined with marriage and parenthood may reflect role strain rather than less meaning and purpose derived from paid work" (Thoits, 1986:271).

Horwitz et al. (1996) point out that most studies comparing the mental health of men and women use outcomes that rely on internalized symptoms of depression, anxiety, and psycho-physiological disorder far more typical of female than of male outcomes. When measures related to both male and female outcomes of mental health are used, the benefits of marriage accrue to women as well as men. In fact, the results of their research indicate that the major beneficial effects of

getting married may be related to high marital quality between the spouses, rather than to the occupation of certain roles.

Glenn and Weaver (1988), analyzing U.S. national survey data collected during the 1970s and 1980s, concluded that the only statistically significant changes were an increase in happiness for never-married males, and a decrease in happiness for married females. Glenn and Weaver suggested that these data may reflect a weakening of the institution of marriage in American society, and that "in an increasingly individualistic and hedonistic society, an increasingly hedonistic form of marriage is having diminished hedonistic consequences for those who participate in it" (1988:323). In other words, seeking happiness in marriage as an end in itself usually results in diminished happiness.

Greeley (1991), using the same data set as Glenn and Weaver, as well as the 1988 and 1989 American General Social Surveys, contended that the Glenn and Weaver data simply supported the finding that *personal* happiness had declined for women, but that the measure of *marital* happiness showed no changes between the early 1970s and mid-1980s for either men or women. Further, the decline in personal happiness was found primarily among married mothers under age 40, who were facing the cross-pressures of home and work. They were not unhappy with *either* their families *or* their jobs, but they experienced a decline in personal happiness as a result of the pressures of balancing career and family. Research has consistently found that husbands provide little help with housekeeping and child-rearing responsibilities even when wives work full time, resulting in a work overload for the working wife.

In a 40-year longitudinal study of American college men and their wives, Vaillant and Vaillant (1993) found no evidence that marriage was less satisfying for women than for men. In fact, they suggest that their study challenges Bernard's famous statement that there are two marriages in every union—his and hers—and that his is better than hers.

A number of recent Canadian studies address the relationship of marital status to physical and psychological well-being. Trovato and Lauris (1989) used Statistics Canada's Mortality Data Base for four Census periods (1951, 1961, 1971, 1981) to examine the relationship between marital status and death due to cardiovascular diseases and malignant neoplasms. In general, married persons had a lower death rate than the unmarried, and the transition from unmarried to married status generally favoured men more than women. The results for widowed males and single females, however, do not support the conclusion that men benefit more from marriage than do women. Widowed females were found to have a higher general mortality rate as well as higher mortality from cardiovascular disease than widowed males (relative to those who were married), and single males had a higher mortality rate than did single females as a result of cancer, suggesting that marriage would provide more protection for widowed and some single females than for widowed and single males. In a major U.S. study, Lillard and Waite (1995) found that the unmarried face substantially higher risks of dying at an earlier age than the married, but they found no statistically significant differences in marriage advantages between men and women.

Based on data from the 1985 General Social Survey of Canada, White (1992) found that while marital status was related to life satisfaction for males, it was not related to males' subjective or objective health, or to the number of consultations with physicians. Thus, with the exception of life satisfaction, male well-being was not related to marital status. White therefore rejected the conclusion that males benefit more from marriage or suffer more from being single than do females. In contrast, single women experienced higher levels of life satisfaction and subjective health assessments, and had fewer consultations with physicians, than did married women, suggesting that they were better off than married women. White suggested one of the reasons for the different findings between Canada and the United States may be the universal health care program in Canada. Being married in the United States may increase the probability of being covered by a spouse's employee medical benefits package, which may partially account for the increased feelings of physical and psychological well-being among married persons in the United States as compared with widowed, divorced or single people.

Most recently Wu and Hart (2002) researched the hypothesis that a transition from being single to being in any living-together union (marriage or cohabitation) would have beneficial effects on health. Wu and Hart studied a longitudinal panel of over 14 000 people

from the 1998 National Population Health Survey in Canada (Statistics Canada). They found that movement out of marriage and out of a cohabiting relationship had similar detrimental effects on health. They also report the surprising finding that the benefits of staying single over getting married or cohabiting do not seem evident once selection factors and other health causes are controlled. This research clearly proposes that single status has less adverse effects on health than does either married or cohabiting status.

The only conclusion we can reach at this time is that the findings that married people are healthier and happier than the non-married, and that marriage has more positive benefits for men than for women, have been both supported and contradicted by subsequent research. Clearly when we exclude selection variables and other known causes of health, the hypothesis that marriage promotes health becomes more questionable.

SUMMARY

- Marriage laws fall primarily under provincial jurisdiction, but agree in the regulation of important areas such as minimum age at marriage, permissible degrees of consanguinity, mental capacity, and the requirement of monogamy.

- Marriage is a contract between two people based on consent, but it includes the state as a "silent" third partner, so that a marriage cannot be ended without the consent of the state.

- Common-law marriage is increasingly prevalent in Canada, although it does not provide the same privileges and benefits as legal marriage. Three areas of law distinguish legal from common-law marriages: social law, matrimonial law, and tax law.

- In Canada, only heterosexual marriages are regarded as valid, although there is considerable pressure from the gay community to recognize homosexual marriages, partly in order to take advantage of spousal and other benefits.

- Domestic contracts make it possible to override legislation regarding property division or spousal support, but not the right of custody of or access to children, or rights to the matrimonial home.

- Contemporary wedding ceremonies embrace various customs and rituals whose background and meanings are not always clearly understood.

- Leaving the single life in favour of marriage involves a significant transition from one social status to another. This involves changes in the areas of finances, leisure time, relationships with parents and friends, and others.

- Intimate companionship, child-rearing, and the production of wealth tie people together in marriage. The timing of the transition to marriage is a result of interaction between the relative rewards and costs of marriage as compared with alternatives.

- The family developmental approach establishes a number of developmental tasks that must be accomplished in early marriage in order for the marriage to succeed.

- Marital commitment may be expressed toward a partner or toward the institution of marriage. It is most often defined as personal ("want to") commitment, structural or constraint ("have to") commitment, and sometimes in terms of moral ("ought to") commitment.

- Two frequent findings regarding the relationship between marital status and adult well-being are that married people experience higher levels of physical and psychological well-being, and marriage tends to have more positive benefits for men than for women. More recent research suggests that it is not marriage per se that predicts positive mental health, but rather the quality of marriage. The role that is the greatest source of disadvantage for women relative to men is employment. The disadvantage comes from seeking to balance the pressures of careers and families, particularly since men provide little help in household chores and child care, even when their wives are employed full time.

KEY TERMS

Capacity for marriage (171)

Common-law union (173)

Developmental task (180)

Domestic contract (175)

Incest (172)

Moral commitment (182)

Personal commitment (182)

Role-making (182)

Structural commitment (182)

QUESTIONS FOR REVIEW

1. How does the law affect the private decision of two people to cohabit as opposed to getting married?

2. How does the contract of marriage differ from other legal contracts?

3. What are the four elements of capacity that are required to contract a valid marriage? What would be the impact on society of removing any of these requirements?

4. What are personal marriage contracts most often concerned with? What are the benefits and risks of such contracts?

5. Discuss the background and meanings of some of the customs and rituals associated with the wedding ceremony. On the basis of these meanings, which rituals would you retain in your own wedding ceremony?

6. What are the primary developmental tasks of beginning families?

7. What are the differences among personal commitment, structural commitment, and moral commitment? What is the impact of religion on marital commitment?

8. What are the two major areas in which relationships have been found between marital status and adult well-being? What are the two major explanations of the relationship between the two?

QUESTIONS FOR DISCUSSION

1. Why is it that young people who rarely attend church still desire to have their marriage solemnized in the church?

2. Should the state (federal and provincial) be encouraged to vacate the field of marriage legislation? Why or why not?

3. Discuss the consanguinity requirements of Canadian marriage law. Should these requirements be changed?

4. Evaluate the arguments supporting and opposing the legal regulation of common-law marriages.

5. In your opinion, what is the most difficult developmental task that contemporary young people face in early marriage?

6. Does marriage benefit men more than women? Discuss the possible causes and prospective solutions of the position you adopt.

SUGGESTED READINGS

Greeley, Andrew. 1991. *Faithful Attraction: Discovering Intimacy, Love, and Fidelity in American Marriage.* New York: Tom Doherty Associated. This book, an examination of the state of marriage in America today for the lay public, presents an optimistic view of the state of marriage.

Halpern v. Canada (Attorney general)*, (2003-06-10). ONCA C39172; C39174; http://www.canlii.org/on/cas/onca/2003/2003onca10314.html.

Johnson, M. P., J.P. Caughlin, and T.L. Huston. 1999. "The Tripartite Nature of Marital Commitment: Personal, Moral and Structural Reasons to Stay Married," *Journal of Marriage and Family* 61: 160–177. This is a study of the validity and structure of marital commitment. It is the most current work analyzing Johnson's conceptualization of marital commitment.

Payne, Julian D. and Marilyn A. Payne.* 1994. *Introduction to Canadian Family Law.* Scarborough: Carswell. This book is an excellent resource for information regarding the legal status of marriage, cohabitation, domestic partnerships, homosexual partnerships, and other legal information with respect to the family in Canada.

CHAPTER 9

Marital Quality and Communication

After studying this chapter, you should be able to do the following:

- Outline relationships between marital quality and marital stability, and explain how comparison level, and comparison level for alternatives, affect marital stability.
- Summarize the key components of the Lewis and Spanier model of marital quality.
- Outline the impact of children on marital quality and explain the changes that take place in marital satisfaction over the family life span.
- Indicate the impact of the social environment on marital satisfaction.
- Summarize the impact on marital satisfaction of employment condition, gender role attitudes, religion, and health.
- Define *communication*, and describe the four communication styles.
- Explain how levels of self-disclosure are related to quality communication, and describe the differences in communication patterns between distressed and non-distressed couples.
- Distinguish verbal from nonverbal communication, and describe the contribution of each to marital interaction. Indicate the key gender differences in communication.
- Explain the roles of interdependence, ideology, and conflict in traditional, independent, and separate marriages.
- Describe the role of conflict resolution in marital interaction, list four conflict management strategies, and describe five styles of conflict resolution.
- Summarize the seven key areas of marital conflict.
- Define and demonstrate the impact of the sexual revolution on extramarital sexuality.
- Explain how aging is associated with the frequency of sexual relations in marriage for both men and women.
- List the four factors that have been found to be essential in the development of a "vital" marital relationship.

Introduction

Romantic novels or movies often end with the premarital couple, having resolved all their problems, holding hands as the sun sets slowly in the west. The supposition is that they lived "happily ever after." In real life, however, the beginning of marriage often represents a time of conflict and adjustment. Many of these conflicts are related to factors that are not adequately resolved before marriage, or to inadequate reasons for the marriage itself. Couples may get married after a very short acquaintanceship, which has allowed insufficient time for the partners to get to know one another. This is frequently accompanied by a strongly romanticized view of love, which holds that love is sufficient to overcome any obstacle. The objections of parents and friends are sometimes disregarded, and in some cases marriage may even be an escape from an unhappy home situation.

In Chapter 8, we saw that marriage has many institutional dimensions that may or may not make important contributions to marital adjustment and satisfaction. Institutional factors are important, but premarital factors are also important. Indeed, the future adjustment and success of most marriages is often determined in the first few years of marriage. McKie et al. (1983) found that one-fifth of divorcing couples had a marriage duration of less than five years, and nearly half had marriages that lasted less than 10 years.

Marriage is the most intimate of all human relationships. Most couples who marry expect their marriage to be a source of emotional satisfaction, personal security, and continuing growth and fulfillment. Yet, as we will see in Chapter 13, many marriages end in separation and divorce. One of the major predictors of marital stability is marital adjustment and quality of the marriage. Our discussion begins with an examination of the varying relationship between marital quality and marital stability, and how exchange theory may help to explain these relationships. We will present a well-known model of predictors of marital quality. We will then investigate the impact of marital satisfaction, marital communication, and marital conflict on marital quality. The chapter ends with an examination of the relationship of marital sexuality and marital quality.

Marital Quality: Happiness, Adjustment, and Satisfaction

Since the early work on marriage in the 1920s, researchers have been concerned with marital happiness, adjustment, and satisfaction. Indeed, these three measures were treated as separate entities. Marital adjustment was thought to be "how well newly married couples adjusted to life together." Marital satisfaction was thought to be "how satisfied a married couple is with their life together." Marital happiness was defined as "how happy the couple is with their married life." There was a proliferation of questionnaire items produced to measure these three concepts (e.g. Terman, 1938; Locke 1949; Locke and Wallace, 1959).

Researchers were at least intuitively convinced that divorce (which was increasing) would be due to unhappiness in marriage or the failure to adjust to the dyad. Indeed, for quite a few decades these concepts were treated as distinct, and scholars would discuss which was the best predictor of divorce.

In 1976, Graham Spanier tested the notion that measures for marital happiness, marital adjustment, and marital satisfaction are distinct. Spanier (1976) collected items from a huge number of questionnaires and then excluded items that were redundant. He collected responses on these items and then factor analysed them to see if the items measuring marital satisfaction were separable from those for happiness and those for adjustment. He found that these measures were highly intercorrelated and not distinct groupings for happiness and adjustment. He did find a four-dimensional structure, but these dimensions were cohesion, consensus, satisfaction, and affection.

This finding and subsequent reflection led Lewis and Spanier (1979) to argue that all three of these measures (adjustment, satisfaction, and happiness) measure one underlying construct that they called *marital quality*. Marital quality is defined as a spouse's "evaluation of a married couple's relationship" (Lewis and Spanier, 1979:269). Thus, one general and global term "marital quality" now stands for the cluster of concepts attached to adjustment, happiness, and satisfaction. In our discussion that follows, these terms are used interchangeably.

The Lewis and Spanier (1979) work stands as a landmark study of marital quality. It has strongly influenced all subsequent research in this area. The reason that this study has had such an impact is that it formalized and developed the theory and propositions to explain the connection between marital quality and divorce. The theoretical model that Lewis and Spanier developed remains one of the most compelling and complete models in the study of marriage.

Theoretical and measurement refinements to the concept of marital quality have continued. For example, Norton (1983) proposed that marital quality should be a unidimensional construct, that is, measured as one underlying dimension such as "how good is your marriage?" Norton's (1983) argument for a single-dimension measure challenged the popular Dyadic Adjustment Scale (DAS) measure created by

Spanier (1976). Other authors, such as Fincham and Bradbury, (1987) suggested that unidimensional measures of marital quality (Norton) are most appropriate for scientific studies, but multi-dimensional constructs (DAS) are most appropriate for marital diagnostics since they provide greater coverage of marital attitudes and behaviors. This position favouring simple, singular dimension constructs of marital quality is reinforced in recent critical discussions (e.g. Bradbury, Fincham, and Beach, 2000). Likewise, scholars have produced other theoretical models such as that by Karney and Bradbury (1995).

Lewis and Spanier (1979) developed their theoretical model (see Figure 9.1) by reviewing research evidence about the relationship between marital quality and marital stability. As previously noted, the concept of **marital quality** includes the entire range of terms previously used to describe marital satisfaction (happiness, communication, integration, adjustment, and so on). It is defined as the couple's subjective evaluation of their interaction or relationship on a continuum from low to high. **Marital stability** is simply defined in terms of whether a marriage is intact or not. A stable marriage is terminated by the death of one of the spouses, whereas an unstable marriage is terminated by the willful decision of one or both spouses.

As seen in Figure 9.1, Lewis and Spanier identified three major factors that contribute to marital quality. *Premarital variables* such as homogamy, premarital resources, exposure to adequate parental role models, and support for the relationship from significant others are seen as social and personal resources that are related to later marital quality. *Social and economic characteristics* of couples, such as social-economic adequacy, satisfaction with wives' employment, optimal household composition, and embeddedness in the community are identified

as contributing to general satisfaction with lifestyle, and are thus associated with marital quality. Finally, *interpersonal and dyadic factors*, such as positive regard for the spouse, emotional gratification from the relationship (sexual satisfaction is one of the factors included in this category), effectiveness of marital communication, role fit or the absence of role conflict, and the quantity and quality of marital interaction, are identified as rewards from spousal interaction, and are seen as contributing to marital quality.

Marital Quality and Marital Stability: A Research Anomaly

A *research anomaly* is when theoretical expectations do not fit with our observations. We have already noted that early researchers intuitively believed there would be a simple relationship between marital quality and marital stability. It is appealing to think that happy and well-adjusted couples will stay together and that, on the other hand, unhappy, poorly adjusted couples will divorce. However, Lewis and Spanier (1979) acknowledged that our scientific observations do not confirm such a simple view. Table 9.1 shows the anomalous cells as being high quality-unstable marriages and low quality-stable marriages.

For example, Booth and White (1980) studied the correlations of a number of independent variables with the dependent variable "thinking about divorce." They found that high marital quality was sometimes associated with low marital stability, and that low marital quality was sometimes associated with high marital stability (Booth and White, 1980). A specific example of high-quality marriages associated with low stability is newlyweds before the birth of children. Adding to this anomaly is the fact that the period of highest marital

TABLE 9.1   Anomalies in Regard to Marital Quality and Marital Stability

Marital Quality	MARITAL STABILITY	
	LOW	HIGH
Low	Expected	Unexpected anomaly
High	Unexpected anomaly	Expected

Figure 9.1   Marital Quality and Marital Stability

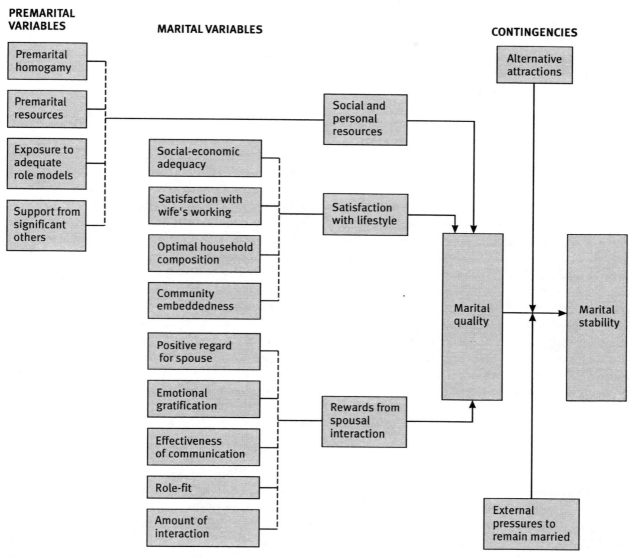

Source: Lewis and Spanier, 1979:289.

quality is experienced between the day of the wedding and the birth of the first child (Spanier and Lewis, 1980; Glenn, 1990). This marital period, however, also has the highest rate of marital dissolution. The fact that about one-third of divorces in the United States occur during the first four years of marriage led Kurdek (1991) to study a sample of newlywed couples about one month after marriage, and again one year later. He found that compared with intact couples, couples who were separated or divorced after one year had fewer years of education, lower incomes, had known each other for a shorter time, and had more children or stepchildren at the time they were married. Demographic factors also predicted decreases in marital quality for intact couples. Those experiencing the least decline were couples in first marriages without children. Those reporting the most decline were those who had experienced premarital pregnancy, remarriage, or who had stepchildren.

On the other hand, low-quality marriages are frequently associated with high stability. Heaton and Albrecht (1991) investigated a number of determinants of stable, unhappy marriages, and found that about seven percent of intact marriages are unhappy, yet stable. The following factors defined unhappy but stable marriages: older age and longer marital duration (the "investment" of many years in a relationship), the belief that marriage is a lifetime commitment, and the consideration of less desirable alternatives to the relationship. It appears that barriers to change or a lack of desirable alternatives are key factors in unhappy but stable marriages. As we shall see later in this chapter, the family life stage literature (Anderson et al., 1983; Lupri and Frideres, 1981; Spanier and Lewis, 1980) indicates that marital satisfaction begins to decline with the birth of the first child, and reaches its lowest point during the child's teenage years. However, the presence of children reduces the probability of marital dissolution (Albrecht and Kunz, 1980; Spanier and Glick, 1981). Similarly, conservative religious affiliation and religious devoutness are negatively associated with marital dissolution (Booth and White, 1980), suggesting that religious constraints may prevent separation or divorce, even when marital quality is low. In contrast, religious heterogamy (associated with less efficiency and more conflict) is associated with a higher likelihood of marital dissolution (Lehrer and Chiswick, 1993).

Why is it that some unhappy marriages remain intact, while some happy marriages break up? *Exchange theory* may help to explain some of these findings. Two important concepts provided by exchange theory are comparison level (CL) and comparison level for alternatives (CLalt). **Comparison level** (CL) is how a person's expected outcomes in a particular relationship compare with his actual outcomes. Thus, a marriage that provides more benefits than a person expected would result in a higher level of marital satisfaction with less probability of dissolution. On the other hand, a marriage that provides fewer benefits than the person expected would be associated with lower levels of marital satisfaction and a greater probability of dissolution. The **comparison level for alternatives** (CLalt) compares the benefits a person receives in the current relationship with the possible benefits that could be derived from an alternative relationship. Thus, a wife

living with an abusive husband may decide to remain in the relationship because her perceived alternatives (for example, raising the children on her own without sufficient income) seem more threatening. Or, a single woman with a fulfilling career may view marriage as far less attractive.

Returning to Figure 9.1 can help us to understand this anomaly. Lewis and Spanier incorporated exchange theory thinking by proposing that although the direct effect of marital quality on marital stability is positive (the higher the quality of the marriage the greater the stability of marriage), this relationship could be changed by alternative attractions or external pressure to remain married. Alternative attractors would include the sex ratio, the number of singles, etc. The external pressures to stay married would include religious institutions, divorce laws and property divisions, and so on. Now we can see that a young person with no religious affiliation, little shared property, surrounded by lots of other single available persons of the opposite sex might be tempted to leave a high-quality marriage. By contrast, the person that shares extensive investments with his or her spouse, is immersed in a religious community supportive of marriage, and has few available alternatives might stay married even if the quality was low. Indeed, White and Booth (1991) studied divorce over the life course and found that younger marrieds are more likely to divorce because of high alternatives and low barriers to divorce versus older couples that have high investments and barriers and few alternatives. Although there remain aspects of this relationship to be further researched, the exchange theory explanation regarding alternative attractors and barriers seems compelling. It also serves to highlight that marriage is dynamic and changes over the life course.

While the impact of courtship, engagement, and early marriage relationships are crucial in determining a couple's marital adjustment, the process of adjustment is not a once-and-for-all achievement. It continues throughout the marriage. Each of the partners changes as the result of differing experiences, and marital relations must constantly take account of these changes. In Figure 9.1, one of the key predictors of satisfaction with lifestyle is optimal household composition. Two related issues that have received consistent and sustained attention by researchers during the last few decades are the effects of children on marital quality, and the relationship between marital quality and the marital career.

Children and Marital Satisfaction

The belief that children enhance marital quality is a frequent assertion of conventional wisdom. Goetting (1986a:105) argued that parenthood has been encouraged through "an elaborate folklore regarding parenthood, which includes beliefs that 1) children improve marriage, 2) childless couples are frustrated and unhappy, and 3) you should not stop with just one child."

A most surprising finding of prior research on marital quality was that children tended to detract from, rather than contribute to, the marital quality of their parents. This finding was confirmed in both the 1980 (Spanier and Lewis, 1980) and 1990 decade reviews (Glenn, 1990) published in the *Journal of Marriage and the Family*. This decline in marital quality may be associated with the decrease in time that the couple has with each other, the stress of child-care arrangements, the economic pressures associated with the child, and, frequently, the loss of the wife's income. On the other hand, Spanier and Lewis reported that research during the 1970s also documented considerable *satisfaction* brought to parents by their children, with some couples reporting that children were frequently their *only* source of satisfaction (Spanier and Lewis, 1980). A number of longitudinal studies, however, questioned the association between transition to parenthood and the decline in marital quality (McHale and Huston, 1985; White and Booth, 1985). The use of a control group of couples who did not have a child during the course of the study allowed a comparison with those who did. Both those who had a child and those who did not experienced a similar decline in marital satisfaction, leading to the conclusion that changes that are attributed to the transition to parenthood may instead be the effects of duration of marriage.

Hill (1988) documented the complex relationship between children and marital satisfaction. She found, first of all, a strong positive relationship between shared leisure time of spouses and marital stability. The presence of children, however, had a negative impact on shared leisure time, with childless couples spending from seven to 10 more hours of leisure time per week together. While the presence of children was associated with a lower probability of divorce or separation, they indirectly contributed to marital dissatisfaction by reducing spousal interaction (represented by shared leisure time).

An interesting study of Canadian never-married undergraduate students measured the level of satisfaction they *expected* to attain in the different stages of family life if they were to marry and have children. Expected satisfaction was found to be lower for both males and females during the child-rearing years. A recovery in expected satisfaction during the post-child-rearing years was found for women, but expected satisfaction continued to decline for men during the post-child-rearing years (McCann et al., 1990).

White et al. (1986) also found that the presence of children had a negative effect on marital interaction, financial satisfaction, and satisfaction with the division of labour, all of which were associated with lower marital happiness. The presence of children was also associated with a more traditional division of labour and with reduced marital satisfaction for wives, but with increased satisfaction for husbands. Preschoolers in particular had a negative effect on marital satisfaction, but there is some evidence that parents of preschoolers delay the dissolution of an unhappy marriage until their children were older. Because the presence of the first child creates a braking effect on divorce, a sample of parents might include a higher proportion of unhappy marriages than might a sample of the childless.

An interesting study of the relationship among maternal employment, marital quality and family size (Rogers, 1996) demonstrated that there are differences between continuously married families with children and mother–stepfather families. Consistent with role strain perspectives, as family demands in the form of the number of children in the household increase, full-time employment of mothers is associated with lower marital quality and higher marital conflict. In contrast, in mother–stepfather families, mothers' full-time employment is associated with lower marital quality and higher marital conflict when the family is small, but with *greater* marital happiness and *less* marital conflict when the family size increases. This may be because employment gets the mother out of the house. The association between full-time employment and parental stress is not limited to Canada, as Box 9.1 illustrates.

Box 9.1   International Insights: Parenting Stress and Marital Quality

A study using a sample of 441 families in Israel examined the impact of roles (mother's employment and household division of labour), children (age composition and number living at home), economic distress and well-being, and duration of marriage on parenting stress and the resulting quality of marriage. The findings suggest that the negative effect of children on their parents' marital quality is largely the result of parenting stress. For both spouses, parenting stress is related to a larger number of children at home and to greater economic pressures or distress.

Source: Lavee et al., 1996.

Family Life Stage and Marital Satisfaction

Another consistent finding of the research on marital quality is the relationship between family life stage and marital satisfaction. Earlier studies have found a consistent decline in marital satisfaction over the family life stage (a linear relationship). One study (Pineo, 1961) characterized this shift in marital satisfaction as the process of "disenchantment." Similarly, in their study of more than 1000 wives in the Detroit area in the 1950s, sociologists Blood and Wolfe (1960) discovered that 52 percent of the wives were very satisfied with their marriages in the first two years, while none were notably dissatisfied. In contrast, after 20 years, only 6 percent were very satisfied, while 21 percent were very dissatisfied—something the authors referred to as "corrosion."

One of the most frequent findings regarding the relationship between family life stage and marital satisfaction is that this relationship is curvilinear, with the highest satisfaction experienced in the newlywed stage and again after the children have left home (Rollins and Feldman, 1970; Anderson et al., 1983). Rollins and Feldman (1970) suggested that the experiences of childbearing and child-rearing have a profound negative effect on marriage, particularly for wives, and that this is primarily the result of a reduction in companionship experiences with their husbands due to child-rearing responsibilities.

The arrival of children in the family requires a primary focus of attention on parental rather than marital roles, with more time and attention focused on the parent–child relationship than on the husband–wife relationship. Medling and McCarrey (1981) examined the relationship between value system similarity of spouses and marital adjustment. They found that the impact of value similarity on marital adjustment over the whole family life stage was minimal and inconsistent. However, they did find a relationship between value similarity and marital adjustment for couples married more than 25 years. They suggested that this may be related to the fact that children have left home and the dyad is once again the nuclear unit of the family. Similarly, in their longitudinal 40-year study of American college men and their wives, Vaillant and Vaillant (1993) found little support for the U-curve of marital satisfaction.

Based on a systematic random sample of couples in Calgary, Lupri and Frideres (1981) set out to determine whether the Canadian data would support the linear or the curvilinear findings regarding the relationship between family life stages and marital satisfaction. Figure 9.2 shows the percentage of husbands and wives who found their marriage very satisfying during each of the seven family life stages used in this study. The stages ranged from couples married fewer than five years with no children, to empty-nesters. The data in Figure 9.2 reveal a curvilinear or U-shaped pattern of marital satisfaction for both husbands and wives over the family life stage.

The curvilinear relationship between family life stage and marital satisfaction was also found in another sample of more than 2000 married Canadians (Rhyne, 1981). Evaluations of overall marital quality were lowest during the child-rearing stages, highest after the children had left home, and second-highest among those with no children. The effects of family life stage on marital quality were greater for women than for men. Gender differences for those at the same stage were important at two stages—as children entered

Figure 9.2 Marital Satisfaction by Family Life Stage

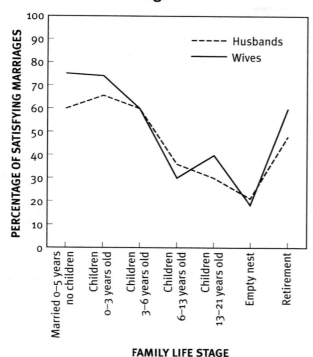

Source: Lupri and Frideres, 1981:289.

adolescence and as they left home—with women being far less satisfied at these stages than were men.

Lupri and Frideres's finding that a higher proportion of childless couples than of couples with children reported happy marriages was also supported by Ramu's (1984) research, which found slightly higher levels of marital happiness among child-free, as compared with parental, couples. Husbands who had children did not differ in marital happiness from those who did not, but wives reported significant differences. Mothers who were gainfully employed, engaged in continuing education, or of low economic status were less satisfied with their marriages than were child-free wives with similar characteristics. Mothers with children indicated, however, that it was not particularly the presence of children that created unhappiness, but rather the failure of spouses to assist in housework and child-rearing. "The non-parents tend to attribute their marital happiness to their child-free status, but the parents often do not directly attribute their marital dissatisfaction to their children" (Ramu, 1984:63).

In addition to optimum household composition, Figure 9.1 identifies enbeddedness in the community as a predictor of marital satisfaction. The next section examines the impact of the social environment on marital satisfaction.

Social Environment and Marital Quality

What is the impact on family relations and on marital satisfaction of a social environment that may not be regarded as conducive to the development of healthy family relations? Krahn et al. (1981) reported the results of a study of family adjustment and satisfaction in Fort McMurray, a rapidly developing resource community in northern Alberta. Such an environment is frequently associated with personal, family, and social problems. Indeed, almost three-quarters (72 percent) of the residents of this community believed that family breakdown was common, and more than one-half (55 percent) believed that marital infidelity was common in the community. The findings, however, indicated that family satisfaction scores were not statistically lower than those of couples living in Edmonton.

A similar study (Felt and Sinclair, 1991) was designed to measure the life satisfaction of people living in the Great Northern Peninsula of Newfoundland, a place of harsh physical beauty but of severely restricted economic opportunity. This region lags behind the rest of Newfoundland and Canada on most important indicators of economic well-being. Contrary to expectations of fairly low levels of life satisfaction, the findings indicated that respondents were just as satisfied as those studied in several other Canadian surveys, and the results were comparable with American and European studies. Analysis of the data indicated that the high level of life satisfaction reflected a logical appraisal of alternative opportunities. Employment opportunities outside the region were perceived by respondents to be restricted to unskilled and semi-skilled work, due to their low level of formal education. Lower wages augmented by unemployment insurance, mortgage-free home ownership, access to family and friends, and enjoyment of outdoor recreational pursuits added to their sense of well-being. Thus, family and general life satisfaction must be seen as dependent on far more than just economic factors or general living conditions. Individuals make a reasonable appraisal of conditions in their current region as compared with alternatives they might experience elsewhere in an urban labour market (Felt and Sinclair, 1991).

Other Determinants of Marital Satisfaction

Employment Conditions There is some evidence that, at the other end of the socioeconomic scale, conditions of employment do affect marital satisfaction. A sample of 85 wives of top-level administrators of Canadian correctional institutions was asked to assess their husbands' responsibilities and marital satisfaction. Those who reported greater infringement of their husbands' jobs on home and family also reported lower levels of overall marital satisfaction (Burke et al., 1980).

Gender Roles The past few decades have witnessed pervasive changes in the ways we view marriage, family life, and gender roles. What is the relationship between gender role attitudes and behaviour, and adjustment in marriage? Lye and Biblarz (1993) found that positive attitudes toward nontraditional family behaviour (egalitarian division of labour, alternatives to marriage, female labour force participation, and more negative attitudes to family life) were associated with lower levels of marital satisfaction than were found among more traditional individuals.

Religion The impact of religious affiliation and participation on marital satisfaction has been widely investigated. Heaton (1984) found that both religious homogamy and church attendance were positively associated with marital satisfaction. Controlling for the effects of homogamy did not change the relationship between church attendance and satisfaction. In contrast, when church attendance was controlled, the relationship between homogamy and satisfaction virtually disappeared, suggesting that religious participation accounts for much of the satisfaction in religiously homogamous marriages. In a study of Catholic marriages, Shehan et al. (1990) also reported that no differences in marital satisfaction between homogamous and heterogamous marriages were found, but that church attendance increased the odds that Catholics described their marriages as happy. In

contrast, Booth et al. (1995), using longitudinal data, found that the link between religion and marital quality was reciprocal, but weak. They found little evidence that an increase in religious activity leads to improved marital quality. Increases in religiosity did not result in enhanced marital happiness or interaction, or in decreased marital conflicts and problems.

Interdependence It is interesting to note that the child begins life wholly dependent on others for all the needs of life. The process of socialization leads to the establishment of independence, which is achieved to a large extent by the time the individual reaches adulthood. Marriage, however, requires the achievement of an *interdependent* relationship. As Ammons and Stinnett suggest, individuation and mutuality must be maintained in a state of dynamic tension. Either extreme is unhealthy. "Thus, individuality and mutuality must coexist harmoniously, forming the warp and woof of an interdependent relationship pattern that encourages both the individual and the relationship to flourish" (1991:195).

Health What is the impact of health on marital quality? The effects of a change in health over a three-year period were investigated with a national sample of married people (Booth and Johnson, 1994). Decrements in health were found to adversely affect marital quality. These effects were greater on the marital quality reported by the *spouses* of persons suffering poorer health than reported by the persons who were suffering such health declines. While it is evident that many factors contribute to marital quality, we must also recognize that the relationship may be reciprocal. In a study of 62 women and 42 men receiving treatment from the Multiple Sclerosis Clinic at the University of Alberta Hospital, Rodgers and Calder (1990) reported that the marital adjustment of individuals, though lower than that of the general population, still made a significant contribution to the positive emotional adjustment of the patients, though the level of their physical disability was not related to their emotional adjustment.

Marital interaction takes many forms and occurs on many different levels. Chapter 8 emphasized that rewarding communication is more likely to take place in a relationship marked by strong commitment than in one marked by weak commitment. Effective communication is a high priority in fulfilling marriages. Lack of communication is frequently cited in reports of couples facing marital problems or breakdown. As can be seen in Figure 9.1, "effectiveness of communication" is a key predictor of rewards from spousal interaction. Research evidence provides strong support for the popular assumption that effective communication is related to marital satisfaction (Noller and Fitzpatrick, 1990). The next section examines the characteristics of communication in marital relationships.

Marital Communication

If you are waiting in any grocery store lineup to pay for your purchases, you might have noticed the various magazine headlines such as "Fourteen Keys to Successful Marital Communication" and "Save Your Marriage; Learn to Communicate." Indeed, the popular press has been mesmerized and captivated by the topic of marital communication. Of course, the effects of marital communication may not be as robust or causal as these periodicals suggest. In this section we examine what social science research tells us about communication in marriage.

The emphasis on **marital communication** is a recent development. While it is regarded as an important dimension in building and maintaining satisfying marital relationships, very few references to the function and importance of marital communication were found in family texts prior to the 1980s. Previous generations, as well as other cultures, placed more emphasis on well-defined roles and responsibilities of husbands and wives, with the result that communication and close relationships were of secondary interest. As marriage changed from predominantly a task and role orientation to companionship and intimacy, the importance of communication became more apparent.

White and Klein (2002) trace the theoretical origins of the study of marital communication to the work of Shannon and Weaver (1949). Since that time the study of human communications has progressed remarkably. Although most studies still use a "sender → receiver" model, several modifications and additions have been made, especially in the area of nonverbal communications, which is one of the most important areas of communications research for the study of marriage.

Early researchers in marriage emphasized the content of what spouses said to each other. However, Mehrabian (1972) reported a series of experiments that led him to estimate that over 80 percent of the emotional affect carried in messages is communicated by nonverbal rather than verbal channels of communication. This finding propelled marital researchers such as Gottman (1979) to investigate the nonverbal aspects of marital communications. Today, our studies of marital communication, both verbal and nonverbal, have evolved to a high level of sophistication.

What impact does communication actually have on marital interaction? Does improving marital communication really contribute to a better marital relationship? Is it possible to have a good relationship without effective communication? These questions reveal a common perception that communication is to be equated with discussing problems and resolving conflicts. Communication, however, also involves just being together, exchanging small talk, touching, and even "the sounds of silence."

Describing Communication Styles

Miller and Miller (1997) suggest that there are four key communication styles that involve particular ways of talking and listening. Talking involves not only *what* you say, or the content, but also *how* you say it, or the style.

Style I: Small Talk and Shop Talk Small talk and shop talk are sociable styles of conversation that people use to connect with one another and to exchange routine information. Small talk is used when exchanging greetings, discussing the news, weather, or sports, joking, or sharing routine information. Small talk builds rapport and keeps an individual "in touch" with others. While small talk is more personal in nature, shop talk, on the other hand, is concerned with task-related matters. It may focus on reporting information, providing facts, passing on messages, or other related issues. Shop talk maintains a system and keeps people informed. Shop talk gathers or gives information, and monitors activities and schedules.

Style II: Control Talk Control talk is a closed style of talking and listening that is not intended to generate information, but rather to assert power and control over others. There are two forms of control talk: *fight talk* and *spite talk*. Fight talk seeks to assert power by attacking others and defending the self. It operates out of a one-up position of power, and uses direct, aggressive, and punitive language. Rather than focusing on the issues, it tends to focus on the person. Spite talk, rather than operating from a one-up position of power, attempts to control from a one-down position, which tends to discount the self, or to approach issues from a position of helplessness or hopelessness based on a long-term lifestyle of low self-esteem that seeks to make others feel sorry for the communicator.

Style III: Search Talk Search talk is concerned with nonroutine matters or complex issues that are not clearly defined. This style explores facts and examines possibilities from a cool and rational perspective. It is tentative in nature, and seeks to explore possible causes, to pose prospective solutions, and to examine various scenarios without making specific commitments. It often suffers from lack of closure.

Style IV: Straight Talk Miller and Miller suggest that straight talk goes to the heart of an issue by disclosing self-information such as feelings and wants, which are typically neglected in other styles of communication. Not only does it focus on one's own experience, but it also tunes in to others and seeks to understand situations from their perspective. This communication style emphasizes connection and collaboration, rather than control and manipulation, and demonstrates commitment to an open process of solving problems and gaining understanding.

The indicators of effective communication in building happy marriages are summarized in Box 9.2.

Components of Quality Communication

Self-disclosure, or transparency, is frequently the focus in studies of communication. Ability and willingness to reveal private thoughts and feelings to one's spouse is an important part of competent marital communication. Marital dissatisfaction is associated with discrepancies between partners in affective disclosure (one partner disclosing more than the other) and with the disclosure of negative rather than positive feelings (Noller and Fitzpatrick, 1990). It is possible, however, to have high levels of disclosure from both partners without having an intimate relationship. In fact, Gilbert (1976) found that a number of studies demonstrated a curvilinear relationship between disclosure and satisfaction, indicating that *both* low self-disclosure and high self-disclosure were associated with lower levels of marital satisfaction. Thus, there is a point at which increased disclosure reduces satisfaction with the relationship, particularly when negative feelings are disclosed. Schumm et al. (1986) reinterpreted Gilbert's curvilinear model in terms of an interaction effect between quantity and quality of self-disclosure. Combinations of high quantity and low quality were found to be detrimental to marital satisfaction, especially for wives. This finding undermines the common notion that the quantity of marital communication is the most important determinant of marital quality. Simply increasing the amount of marital communication does not automatically improve marital satisfaction, which is dependent, among other things, on how

---

Box 9.2 — **Research Insights: Indicators of Effective Communication in a Happy Marriage**

- more positive nonverbal cues
- more agreement and approval
- a higher ratio of agreement to disagreement
- attempts to avoid conflict
- supportive behaviours

- compromises
- consistency in use of nonverbal cues
- less criticism of each other
- a higher ratio of pleasing to displeasing behaviours

Source: Fitzpatrick and Badzinsky (1985:698), as cited in Fitzpatrick (1988c:37).

husbands and wives feel about each other, as well as on the quality of their communication.

A key purpose of research has been to understand the differences in communication patterns between couples in distressed and non-distressed marriages. Schaap et al. (1988) reported that non-distressed couples were more satisfied with the socio-emotional aspects of their relationship, while distressed couples more often experienced destructive communication behaviours and conflict avoidance. Distressed couples experienced more frequent conflict, and spent more time in conflict, even though they disagreed about the same topics as did non-distressed couples. Conflict most often centred on communication, sexuality, and the dispositional characteristics of the partner. Noller and Fitzpatrick (1991) reported that happy couples were more likely to agree, approve, assent, and use laughter or humour. In contrast, unhappy couples were more likely to criticize, disagree, put down, complain, and use excuses and sarcasm.

It is frequently assumed that increasing communication skill levels will automatically increase marital quality. As indicated earlier, Schumm et al. (1986) found that the *quantity* of marital communication is *not* the most important predictor of marital quality. The research of Burleson and Denton (1997) further demonstrates that communication skill levels do not differ as a function of marital distress. In other words, distressed husbands and wives were no less *skilled* than their non-distressed counterparts, but they did express significantly more negative intentions toward each other. "This pattern of results raises the possibility that the negative communication behaviours observed in distressed spouses . . . may result more from ill will than poor skill" (Burleson and Denton, 1997:897). In fact, good communication skills may even intensify marital problems, especially when spouses display negative intentions, motivations, and feelings toward one another.

It is sometimes also presumed that higher-class couples communicate more effectively than do lower-class couples. Aubé and Linden (1991) compared the relationship between communication quality and marital adjustment of Montreal Francophone couples in different socioeconomic categories. They found the level of marital satisfaction and the quality of communication were similar across the different socioeconomic classes in their sample, leading them to conclude that socioeconomic level had little impact on marital satisfaction or communication.

Some people are effective communicators in non-marital relationships, but are ineffective communicators in the marital relationship. Styles of communication (dominant, relaxed, attentive) that predict good communicators in general relationships differ from those styles (friendly, attentive, precise, expressive) that predict good communicators in marital relationships (Honeycutt et al., 1982).

Nonverbal Communication

Communication involves not only *what* is said, but also *how* it is said. What is said may mean many different things, depending on the nonverbal component. **Nonverbal communication** includes facial expression, eye contact, tone of voice, gestures, posture, and general body language. How a person says what is said includes loudness of voice, rate of speaking, and stylistic factors such as dialect or vocabulary. The content of communication provides information, while the nonverbal aspect of communication conveys our emotional meanings and describes the nature of our relationship. Because nonverbal communication represents the emotional aspect of our message, it is frequently more accurate in communicating our feelings than is verbal communication. As mentioned earlier, research has shown that anywhere from 50 percent to 80 percent of our meaning is conveyed by the nonverbal part of our communication. A husband who forgets a luncheon appointment with his wife may apologize and explain that he was extremely pressured to complete a work assignment and that he just forgot. She responds that she understands and is not angry, but when he tries to give her a kiss, she stiffens and turns away from him. Her actions communicate that she really is upset, even though her words say that she is not.

Brehm (1985) summarized three conclusions of the research regarding nonverbal communication:

▪ Nonverbal sensitivity increases as the depth of the relationship or the commitment to the relationship increases. Married couples are more effective in interpreting nonverbal communication than are dating couples.

- Female nonverbal skills are more important in determining satisfaction with the relationship among dating couples and newlyweds, whereas male nonverbal communication skills are more important in distressed married couples. "Thus, it may be that women's nonverbal skills are essential in the development of intimacy in a relationship, while men's abilities to communicate nonverbally are critical for maintaining intimacy within an established relationship" (Brehm, 1985:209).

- There is a *reciprocal* influence between nonverbal communication skills and relationship satisfaction. Poor communication contributes to poor relationships, and poor relationships contribute to poor communication. Individuals may suffer from either a skills deficit or a performance deficit in communication. A person who does not know how to communicate clearly is suffering from a skills deficit, which may be improved by communication training. A person who communicates effectively in other relationships, but not in the marital relationship, is performance deficient. Effective communication involves a basic agreement between the verbal and nonverbal components of our message. To say "I love you" in an indifferent manner or in an angry voice presents conflicting messages.

Gender Differences in Communication

We have already identified a number of gender differences in communication, and in fact research has documented a number of important differences in the way men and women communicate. Men generally talk less than women do, and are not as open about their emotions or feelings. Men are not as likely as women to express feelings such as love, happiness, and sadness (Balswick, 1980). Women are more expressive and sensitive in relationships, and send clearer messages—important skills in effective communication. Wives are much more likely to express emotion (positive or negative) in communication than are their husbands, whereas husbands are more likely to be neutral in their responses (Notarius and Johnson, 1982). Wives are more likely to use emotional appeals or threats in an argument, while husbands are more likely to reason or seek conciliation. Some of these differences may be due to *power* differences between husbands and wives.

Notarius and Johnson (1982) assessed differences in emotional expression between males and females, as well as measuring the relationship between emotional expression and physiological reactivity in persons involved in marital conflict. No differences were found between husbands and wives in their use of positive speech, but wives engaged in less neutral speech and in more negative speech than did their husbands. Husbands had a greater tendency to display increased physiological reactivity to their wives' negative speeches, as measured by galvanic skin responses. "These findings are generally consistent with the sex-role stereotype of the inexpressive male and the expressive female" (Notarius and Johnson, 1982:488).

Other researchers also documented the relationship between negative communication and physiological responses. Gottman and Levenson (1988) reported that men experienced greater physiological responses to stressful stimuli than did women, which may provide biological explanations for understanding differing responses to stress. Women tended to function more effectively than did men in a climate of negative affect, whereas men tended to withdraw emotionally in conflict interactions. Men sought to avoid physiological arousal by withdrawal, avoidance, and rationality. The husband's withdrawal may spur the wife to press the issue, which triggers further withdrawal, further pressing, and so on. This withdrawal-and-pursuit pattern contributes to negative escalation, which is the way major arguments grow out of small things. "The observational studies indicate that wives are more negative, more conflict engaging, more coercive, and use more emotional pressure than their husbands; husbands are more positive, reconciling and pacifying than their wives" (Gottman and Levenson, 1988:198).

A longitudinal study of *non-distressed* couples in the first six years of marriage failed to find the cycle of pursuit by wives and of withdrawal by husbands when facing conflict issues. Observational measures did not indicate such gender differences. In fact, the study found that, rather than just maintaining initial skills, non-distressed couples generally improved in communication and conflict resolution skills with the passage of time. These findings suggest important differences between distressed (clinical) couples and non-distressed (nonclinical) couples in the way they deal with marital conflict (Markman et al., 1993).

Communication and Marriage Types

Fitzpatrick and her colleagues did some of the most creative research relating communication and marital interaction (Noller and Fitzpatrick, 1988; Fitzpatrick, 1988c). They developed an empirical typology of marriage on the basis of three underlying conceptual dimensions: interdependence, ideology, and conflict. *Interdependence* (as opposed to autonomy) assesses the physical, temporal, and psychological connectedness of partners, indicated by the amount of sharing and companionship in marriage as opposed to separation or lack of interaction. *Ideology* is measured in terms of conventional—as compared with nonconventional— beliefs, standards, and values held by individuals regarding relationships and families. Values range on a continuum from stability and predictability to change and uncertainty. *Conflict* engagement or avoidance examines how couples resolve their differences, ranging from avoiding conflict to active engagement (Fitzpatrick, 1988b, 1988c).

Based on the responses of both husbands and wives, three types of marriages were defined (see Table 9.2). The first is the *traditional* marriage, which exhibits *high interdependence*, or high companionship, sharing and interaction. Regular, shared daily timetables and the absence of autonomous physical space in the home encourages companionship. Traditionals also subscribe to *conventional values*, which emphasize stability more than spontaneity. Traditional community customs, such as a woman taking her husband's last name or the rejection of infidelity, are stressed. The communication style of traditionals is nonassertive, but they are willing to engage in *conflict* over serious issues.

The second type is the *independent* marriage, which demonstrates a high level of sharing and companionship (high interdependence), but which asserts *nonconventional values* about relational and family life. Although psychological closeness is regarded as important, separate physical spaces and daily time schedules are maintained. There is a strong belief that marriage should not constrain an individual's freedom in any way. Independents are assertive in their interactions with their spouse, and engage in *conflicts* over a variety of both large and small issues.

The third type is the *separate* marriage, which is *conventional* in marital and family issues, but which simultaneously stresses *individual freedom* (low interdependence) rather than relationship maintenance. Separates have little companionship and sharing in their marriage. Though they may use persuasion, separates *avoid open conflict* with their spouse.

Applying Spanier's adjustment scale to the various marital types led to the conclusion that marital types differ in their levels of marital adjustment. Spouses in the traditional marriage reported the highest levels of adjustment in the satisfaction, consensus, and cohesion scales, and equal levels on the affection scale. Some couples in each of the marital types, however, demonstrated high scores in marital adjustment or satisfaction. "Each of these types may represent functional or workable marriages in that each has achieved a level of marital adjustment that appears to operate without debilitating impasses or blockages" (Fitzpatrick, 1988c:107). This is an important insight in that it points out that different styles of marriage may be suitable for different people, as opposed to the perception that only a traditional or only an independent marriage can possibly bring happiness.

Premarital communication, too, determines later marital satisfaction (Markman, 1981). A longitudinal study measured the relationship between

TABLE 9.2   Communication and Marriage Types

CONVENTIONAL IDEOLOGY		UNCONVENTIONAL IDEOLOGY	
High Conflict	Low Conflict	High Conflict	Low Conflict
High interdependence	*Traditional*	*Independent*	
Low interdependence	*Separate*		

Source: Fitzpatrick, 1988c:77.

communication ratings of couples planning marriage, and their marital satisfaction after one, two-and-a-half, and five-and-a-half years. Positive ratings of interaction at Time 1 (before marriage) were related to higher levels of marital satisfaction five-and-a-half years later. Distressed couples indicated a much less satisfactory communication pattern at Time 1 than did non-distressed couples. Since effective premarital communication is related to later marital satisfaction, does premarital communication training enhance marital communication? Bader et al. (1980) instituted and evaluated a marriage preparation program in Toronto that emphasized the importance of communication patterns and conflict resolution. As compared to a matched control group, couples who participated in the program reported a decrease in conflict over interpersonal topics, an increase in positive conflict resolution, fewer negative effects of conflict on the relationship, and a greater likelihood of seeking assistance in resolving both individual or marital problems.

Communication and conflict are often perceived as the opposite ends of a continuum. The lack of effective communication certainly contributes to marital conflict. But the ability to communicate effectively does not necessarily result in the absence of conflict. The next section examines the role of conflict and its effect on marital adjustment.

Marital Conflict

Many couples, particularly in the beginning stages of marriage, regard conflict in their relationship as a failure that ought to be avoided. But strong marriages and families are not made up of those who never experience conflict; rather, couples learn to deal effectively with, or negotiate, conflict. Indeed, conflict theory approaches marriage as one of the most obvious social groups in which we would expect to find conflict rather than harmony. Living together in a close emotional relationship is bound to result in differences of opinions, conflicting schedules and activities, differing normative expectations, and differing perceptions of situations, as Box 9.3 demonstrates.

Betcher and Macauley (1990) point out seven key areas of marital conflict. Conflicts sometimes arise from *gender* differences. Women are more likely to emphasize expressive qualities, such as developing satisfying interpersonal relationships, while men emphasize instrumental qualities, such as attaining work goals and achieving success. Men and women also have differing understandings of *loyalty*. The husband tends to define loyalty as providing for his family and being faithful to his wife. The wife is more likely to define loyalty as emotional closeness and understanding. *Money* is a frequent source of marital conflict. Partners disagree about how to spend money because they place

---

Box 9.3	Current Insights: The Inevitability of Conflict

He did it again—squished the new toothpaste tube right in the middle. Doesn't he ever listen to anything I say? What does it take... ? Sound familiar?

Most couples act out their own version of the Bickersons at some point every day. True, the radio serial of the feuding husband and wife let us laugh at what was happening in our reality. But fighting between two people who care for each other can very quickly slide from comedy to tragedy, destroying communication, trust, and eventually, the once-previous love.

Take the toothpaste dilemma, or any of life's trivial quibbling points. Instead of saying or doing anything about it—like buying two tubes of toothpaste—they tuck the resentment away to let it fester all out of proportion. Then it becomes something more profound. "I don't think you respect me because I am asking you to do something with the toothpaste, and you just ignore it."

Yet conflict is inevitable, and the most difficult person you struggle with is the one you love the most. Without conflict, change does not happen and if we are not changing and growing, we are standing still. Too many relationships reach that bitter plateau. They co-exist, lead parallel lives, stop talking, quit listening, because they do not use conflict productively.

Source: Morningstar, 1990:B9.

different value on the things money can buy. Marital conflict over *power* may include economic power or decision-making power. The more powerful partner may exercise power through autocratic demands, while the weaker partner may exercise power through manipulation. In egalitarian relationships, conflicts are more likely to be resolved through negotiation or compromise. The role of *sex* in marriage sometimes leads to conflict, including disagreements about its meaning and frequency. Marital partners experience differing needs for *privacy* in terms of space, time, emotions, and property. Failure to understand and respect each other's needs may lead to problems. Finally, although *children* can strengthen a marriage, they may also contribute to marital conflict. This may include disagreements regarding discipline, child care when mothers work, and the involvement (or lack of it) of fathers in child-rearing (Betcher and Macauley, 1990, cited in Benokraitis, 1993).

When conflict does appear in a relationship, it may be handled destructively or constructively. Destructive ways of dealing with conflict involve denial or avoidance. In order to deal constructively with conflict, couples need to recognize that it is a normal experience, and that there are effective means of dealing with disagreements.

Rather than avoiding conflict or denying its existence, couples need to learn proper ways of dealing with conflict. Conflict is not limited to isolated instances that can be resolved and then forgotten, but is, rather, a part of everyday interaction, and a particular conflict situation often continues to affect how other conflicts will be resolved. We tend to develop styles of conflict management that are repeated in different situations and with different individuals.

Conflict Management in Marital Relationships

Chafetz (1980) presented four **conflict management strategies** that are frequently used to secure compliance in a conflict. *Authority* involves the application of institutional norms that support the right of one spouse to make decisions that are binding on the other. This involves the concept of legitimacy. *Control* refers to the ability of one spouse to get the other spouse to comply, regardless of the desires of the other. Control involves the ability to punish, reward, and coerce by using resources (or power) to threaten, bribe, or coerce the other. Control is normally regarded as not legitimate in a marital relationship. *Influence* involves the use of persuasion by superior expertise or knowledge germane to the conflict. Influence is regarded as a legitimate strategy to change the other's mind. *Manipulation* is a nonlegitimate attempt to secure compliance by engaging in behaviours that may result in an unconscious submission on the part of the spouse, who is not aware of being manipulated.

Bell et al. (1982) applied the above formulation in determining how these strategies were used in the marital relationship. For husbands, the most effective strategy was authority, followed by manipulation, with influence being the least effective strategy. For wives, influence was the most effective strategy, followed by authority, control, and manipulation. Contrary to popular belief, husbands used manipulation as frequently as did wives, and far more effectively. Husbands won the majority of conflict situations (88 percent for husbands versus 48 percent for wives). The wife's working experience had a strong influence on her ability to win in conflict situations. Where only the husband was in the labour force, wives won only 25 percent of conflicts, compared to 62 percent where both spouses worked, and 67 percent where only the wife worked. The most frequent strategy choice for both husbands and wives was influence. This may reflect changes in family structure in the direction of greater equality. In a study of 74 French Canadian couples, Sabourin et al. (1991) found that the more likely subjects were to attribute their marital conflicts to global or stable causes and to assign blame for the conflicts to their partners, the more likely they were to report marital dissatisfaction.

Conflict Management Styles

Hocker and Wilmot (1978) identified five different styles of interpersonal conflict management (See Table 9.3). The first style is *competition*, which involves a low degree of cooperation and a high degree of assertiveness. Conflict is viewed as a contest in which the object is to win the fight with little concern about the other person. The emphasis is on dominance or the control of power in the relationship. The second style of conflict management is *avoidance*, which involves a

TABLE 9.3 Styles of Conflict Management

STYLES	COOPERATION	ASSERTIVENESS
Competition	Low	High
Avoidance	Low	Low
Accommodation	High	Low
Compromise	Moderate	Moderate
Collaboration	High	High

low degree of both cooperation and assertiveness. There is little concern for either self or other, but rather for peace at any price. This approach may be dysfunctional or destructive for the marriage, and may lead to the escalation of resentment because the real issues are always avoided rather than resolved. The third style is *accommodation*, which involves a high degree of cooperation and a low degree of assertiveness. This manifests itself in a low degree of concern for self, and a high degree of concern for the other. The accommodator does not avoid conflict but rather tends to give in to the wishes of the partner in order to avoid misunderstanding. *Compromise* involves a moderate degree of cooperation and assertiveness, or of concern for the interests of the self and of the other. The compromiser is willing to engage in conflict, but will moderate his or her position in order to reach a solution that is satisfactory for both spouses. *Collaboration* entails a high degree of cooperation and assertiveness, or a high degree of concern for the self and the other. The collaborator will vigorously pursue his own interests while continuing to demonstrate a genuine concern for the interests of the spouse. In contrast to accommodation or compromise, collaboration involves securing the optimal solution for both parties, and this results in maximum satisfaction for both.

Often, husbands and wives have different styles of conflict resolution. Two collaborators or compromisers may contribute to a stable relationship, whereas two competitors or avoiders would likely create a dysfunctional relationship. It is necessary to recognize our own and our partner's dominant style of conflict resolution

in order to understand what is taking place in conflict situations. It may be necessary to seek to change our style to one that is more effective, or to attempt to use different styles in differing situations in order to reach the optimal solution.

Marital communication and marital conflict resolution are both important for their contributions to marital adjustment. Effective communication differentiates distressed from non-distressed marriages, and effective conflict resolution is correlated with marital adjustment. The issue of marital adjustment, however, is not bounded by its relationship to communication and conflict resolution. Marital adjustment is not achieved during the honeymoon, or even the first year of marriage, but it is a continuing process. Each of the partners changes as the result of differing experiences during the marital life stage, and marital relations must constantly take account of these changes.

Gottman and Levenson (2002) approached styles of conflict management and communication in a slightly different way. Gottman and Levenson argue that young couples during the first seven years of marriage are most likely to get divorced or separated when they employ an emotionally volatile attack-defend conflict style. On the other hand, the couples that practice a low expressive-avoidance style are hypothesized to require a longer trajectory to divorce and separation. Gottman and Levenson's research contained a small longitudinal sample of 21 couples but the detail and internal validity of their work suggests that these two conflict management styles do have different longitudinal consequences.

One of the most important developmental tasks for newly married couples is establishing mutually satisfactory sexual relationships. This developmental task may be somewhat different for those who have experienced premarital sex or cohabitation. Nevertheless, the sexual relationship in marriage requires ongoing adjustment. It is an important area of discussion, to which we now turn.

Marital Interaction and Sexuality

The "sexual revolution" focused a great deal of attention on premarital sexual attitudes and behaviour, and has contributed to a significant increase in public discussion and media presentation of sexual themes over the past several decades. There has been a curious lack of interest, however, in the domain of marital sexuality, and a significant lack of quality research in this area. Greenblat (1983:289) remarked that marital sex "remains more the topic of jokes than of serious scientific investigation." It is only recently that the issue of sexual adjustment in marriage, including its relationship to general marital adjustment, has been addressed.

This section will begin with an examination of marital sexuality in its social and cultural context. This will be followed by a discussion of the nature of marital sexuality, changing patterns of sexual interaction over the life span, and the nature of sexual performance and fulfillment. We will also investigate the issue of extramarital sexuality, which has attracted a growing amount of research.

Marital Sexuality in Social Context

Sexuality, including marital sexuality, must always be seen in terms of its social and cultural context. While the existence of a physiological "sex drive" is widely accepted, it must be recognized that much of sexual behaviour is learned, and that what is regarded as acceptable or unacceptable depends on the particular culture in which it takes place. Reiss (1986) asserts that the importance of sexuality in all societies is based on its bonding power, rather than on its connection to reproduction. Two universal features of sexuality that contribute to its importance are physical pleasure and self-disclosure, and these features are central to all valued human relationships.

Sexuality is linked to three elements of the social structure in all societies, and these elements act as boundary mechanisms around sexual relationships in marriage. They are marital jealousy, gender role power, and beliefs about normality. *Jealousy* is found in some form in all societies, although its intensity may vary from society to society. *Gender role power* is also found in all societies, and since males have greater power than females in most societies, they also possess greater sexual rights. *Beliefs about normality* are an expression of ideology, or the powerful shared beliefs about fundamental human nature that exist in a society. Our sexual ideologies encourage as natural those sexual customs that are viewed as expressing our fundamental

human nature. In our society, sex within heterosexual marriage is seen as natural, whereas homosexuality is typically perceived as unnatural. Also, the prevailing belief is that male and female sexual rights should be equal, resulting in a movement toward greater sexual equality (Reiss, 1986).

Sexuality plays a crucial role in a number of different relationships and situations—premarital, cohabiting, marital, extramarital, postmarital, homosexual, incest, and rape. The key difference between sex in a marital relationship and all other relationships is that it is regarded as legitimate or normative. (See Chapter 1 for an extended discussion of normative definitions.) Sexuality in other relationships has typically been regarded as illegitimate or non-normative, but in recent decades there have been important changes in attitudes toward premarital, cohabiting, and homosexual relationships. Various degrees of physical pleasure and of self-disclosure are experienced in each of these relationships, but their physical and emotional meanings vary with the situation and how the participants define it.

The sexual revolution has affected premarital sexual relationships, but it has also had a major impact on marital sexuality. Whereas at one time it might have been said that sex was "a man's right and a woman's duty," the increase in the premarital sexual experience of females makes for different meanings of sex in marriage. The widespread acceptance of sexual pleasure, not only for men but also for women, and an understanding of the multi-orgasmic capacity of women have created new expectations for sexuality in marriage.

Our meanings of marital sexuality may be described in theatrical terms as sexual "scripts." These scripts set out rules of behaviour. During the 1970s, the sexual script for males emphasized the recreational aspects of sex, and for females, the relational aspects. There has been a convergence in the sexual attitudes and behaviour of males and females, so that the love standard (permissiveness with affection), and the fun standard or recreational standard (permissiveness without affection), have been adopted by increasing numbers of males and females, with greater changes taking place among females. The "recreational" versus "relational" perceptions of men and women, however, often continue to affect relationships.

The Nature of Marital Sexuality

Every known society places marital sexuality within a social and normative context that defines appropriate and inappropriate behaviour. Wide differences are found among societies in what is regarded as normative behaviour, but each society enforces its particular regulations through folkways, mores, laws, or religious controls. In contrast to sex among lower animals, which is exclusively related to reproduction, sex among humans, while including the reproductive function, may also fulfill various other functions, such as pleasure, communication, companionship, and pair bonding.

Among the lower animals, sex is regulated by biological mechanisms related to the *oestrus* cycle, and consequently takes place only periodically for the purpose of reproduction. Sexual responsiveness in animals is directly related to the period of maximum fertility in the female. Among humans, sexual behaviour is clearly related to biological factors such as the sex drive, but it is also affected by psychological and emotional factors. Unlike other species, humans have no period of intense sexual receptivity followed by long periods of sexual disinterest. In contrast, they experience a relatively constant state of potential sexual arousal, in which sexual behaviour is more dependent on learning, values, and social relations than on instincts and biological drives. Since human females are the only mammalian females believed to be capable of intense orgasmic response, the role of pleasure becomes an important function of sexual relations, and this has no necessary connection with reproduction. Because both males and females are in a constant state of sexual receptivity, which is unrelated to the cycle of ovulation, social aspects of communication and pair bonding between males and females become more important (Masters et al., 1986).

Patterns of Sexual Interaction

The research of Alfred Kinsey and his associates, published in the 1940s and 1950s, had a significant impact on both sexual attitudes and behaviour. The Kinsey studies (1948, 1953) were concerned with describing how people behaved sexually, and focused on the frequencies of various sexual behaviours without seeking to make value judgments. Their work was initially severely criticized, but it made available entirely new information and led to a more open discussion and practise of various forms of sexuality. A number of major findings continue to attract contemporary research attention.

One of the key findings of the Kinsey research replicated by subsequent researchers is that there is a reduction in the frequency of sexual relations with the passage of time. Bibby (1995) reports that the proportion of people reporting sexual activity on a weekly or more frequent basis drops from a high of 78 percent of men and 67 percent of women between the ages of 30 and 39 to a low of 22 percent of men and 7 percent of women over the age of 70. Despite this decline, a significant proportion of older people still report sexual activity on a weekly basis. Between the ages of 60 and 70, 30 percent of men and 25 percent of women report sexual activity on a weekly or more frequent basis, while over the age of 70, 22 percent of men and 7 percent of women report weekly sexual activity. A higher proportion of women (66 percent) than men (58 percent) between the ages of 18 and 29 report weekly sexual activity.

Based on the 1988 National Survey of Families and Households, which used a representative sample of more than 7000 American adults, Call et al. (1995) examined the incidence and frequency of marital sex over the life course. The *incidence* of marital sex is high at younger ages (about 96 percent of married respondents age 24 or younger had sex at least once during the previous month), then gradually declines until about age 50 (83 percent of those aged 50 to 54 report having had sex at least once during the previous month), after which sharp reductions are reported (57 percent at ages 65 to 69, and 27 percent at ages 75 or older report having had sex at least once during the previous month).

The *frequency* of sexual intercourse also declines with the age of the respondent. On average, respondents had marital sex 6.3 times a month. Younger respondents reported higher frequencies of marital sex (11.7 times a month at ages 19 to 24, 8.5 times a month at ages 30 to 34) while frequency declines with age (5.5 times a month at ages 50 to 55, 2.4 times a month at ages 65 to 69, and 0.8 times a month at age 75 or older). Cohabiting respondents aged 19 to 39 reported having sex an average of 11 to 13 times a month, which is considerably higher than among married couples.

Age was the variable having the strongest negative impact on the frequency of marital sex. The effects of the aging process continue, even when the effects of illness and poor health are controlled. A frequent explanation for the decline of sexual frequency is habituation, which suggests that the increased accessibility of a partner and predictability of sexual behaviour over time leads to a decreased interest in sex. The current study found that habituation may operate during the first year of marriage (the "honeymoon effect"), but that duration of marriage did not have a significant impact on the frequency of sex after the first year.

The second-largest predictor of sexual frequency was satisfaction in marriage, with unhappy marriages reporting a lower sexual frequency. Work and education did not significantly affect sexual frequency. "The fact that there is not a significant finding for work may mean that couples who want to make time for sex, in fact, do so, despite the obstacles of schedules, fatigue and work-related emotional complications. The DINS dilemma (double income, no sex) may be a myth" (Call et al., 1995:650).

Such background characteristics as sex, race, and region of the country were also not significant in explaining sexual frequency. Of the eight religious groups examined, only being Catholic had a significant (negative) impact on sexual activity. This may be due to the fact that the Catholic religion has traditionally taught that the primary function of sex is reproduction. In contrast, in Canada (Pollara, 1997), Catholics reported more frequent sexual relations (7.4 times per month) than did Protestants (6.6 times per month). Bibby (1995) reports similar findings, with 64 percent of Catholics and 54 percent of Protestants reporting weekly sexual activity. This may be a reflection of a widespread rejection of the teachings of the Catholic Church among Catholics, particularly in Quebec. Similar changes in Quebec are seen in such areas as cohabitation, the use of contraceptives, and church attendance.

A national survey of more than 1400 Canadian adults also examined the frequency of sexual relationships (Pollara, 1997). On average, Canadians reported a higher frequency of sexual relations than did Americans (an average of 7.3 times per month compared with the U.S. average of 6.3 times per month). Similar to the U.S. study, people in common-law relationships have sex more frequently (11.0 times per month) than those in traditional marriages (7.8 times per month). While the U.S. study did not find differences in sexual frequency by region of the country, the Canadian study does. The highest reported levels of sexual frequency are reported in eastern Canada, and gradually decline as we move west (see Figure 9.3). People in the Atlantic provinces and in Quebec report frequencies above the national average of 7.3 (8.3 and 7.8 respectively). As we move west, the frequency of sexual activity declines, from 7.2 in Ontario, to 7.1 in the Prairies, to 6.9 in Alberta, to 6.6 in British Columbia.

Frequency of sexual relations per month also declines with age: age 18 to 24, 8.6 times; 25 to 34, 8.6 times; 35 to 44, 8.0 times; 45 to 54, 7.3 times; 55 to 64, 5.6 times; and 65 and older, 3.5 times. The pattern of sexual frequency also varies by relationship status. The frequency per month is virtually the same for those who are single but in a committed relationship (11.06), as for those who are in a common-law union (10.96). Frequency declines for those who are married (7.78 times per month); those who are married but separated (4.46 times per month); and those who are single and unattached (3.46 times per month). Satisfaction with their sex life is related to respondents' frequency of sex. The highest levels of satisfaction are found in the Atlantic provinces, followed by Quebec, Ontario and the Prairies. Satisfaction is lowest in Alberta and British Columbia.

These figures demonstrate that there is a wide range in the frequency of sexual relations, and that frequency is not necessarily related to satisfaction. Each couple needs to set its own standards and to realize that differences do not necessarily signify sexual dysfunction, but are rather an indication that sexual needs and desires vary from couple to couple.

A sample of 22 men and 55 women at the University of New Brunswick maintained records of three aspects of sexual frequency in cohabiting and marital relationships: sexual initiations, responses to the initiations, and considering initiating but not doing so. Men were found to initiate and to consider initiating sex more frequently than were women, but when the frequency of initiation was controlled, men and women did not differ significantly in their responses to these initiations. Cohabiting individuals, and those who reported higher levels of sexual satisfaction, were more

Figure 9.3   Sexual Frequency by Region (per month)

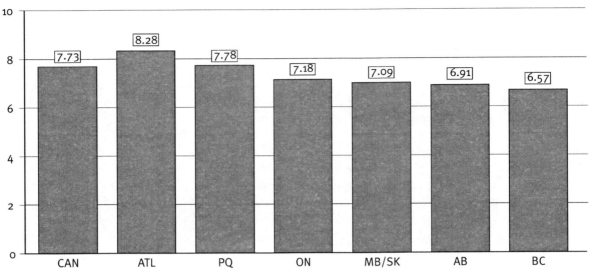

Source: Adapted from Pollara (1997:4).

likely to initiate sex. Gender differences were found, with cohabiting individuals reporting more male initiations, and younger participants who enjoyed greater sexual satisfaction reporting more female initiations (Byers and Heinlein, 1989).

The contemporary shift toward companionship in marriage has highlighted an emphasis on sex as a mutually rewarding experience. As we have seen in previous chapters, there is a growing emphasis on a single standard of sexuality for men and women. Differences in male and female sexuality, however, were highlighted in the Kinsey research, which noted that males reach the peak of their sexual performance somewhere around the age of 16 or 17, whereas females do not reach this point until the age of 28. Jasso (1985) confirmed Kinsey's finding, reporting that women between the ages of 15 and 48 demonstrated an increase in coital frequency, but at a decreasing rate over time. Among men, age had a slight negative effect on coital frequency, so that coital frequency decreased as marital duration increased. Males achieved the peak of their performance quite rapidly, while for females this was a more gradual experience. This finding may help to account for some of the differences between preferred and actual frequencies, but it needs to be balanced by the

understanding that there is a great deal of variation between individuals with respect to sexual interest. Moreover, sexual interest continues well into the elderly years for a large proportion of both men and women.

In their study of 351 couples who had been married for more than 15 years, Lauer and Lauer (1986) developed three principles of sex in a long-term happy marriage:

1. It is possible for couples to have an active and satisfying sex life throughout their entire marriage; neither age nor the number of years they have been married necessarily reduces sexual quality.

2. A long-term satisfying marriage is possible even though one or both fail to experience what they might see as an ideal sexual relationship.

3. The most important issue in sexual satisfaction is not the kind or frequency of sex relations, but rather the extent to which the couple agrees on whatever sexual arrangements are followed.

Extramarital Sexuality

Despite widespread research interest in premarital sexuality, the topic of extramarital sexuality has only recently attracted similar interest. Kinsey's finding that approximately half of married men and one-quarter of married women participate in at least one extramarital affair in their lifetime was met with considerable surprise. Further research has indicated that there may be even more disagreement between attitudes and behaviour with respect to extramarital sexuality than exists with respect to premarital sexuality.

Definition

Extramarital sexuality may include a wide range of activities, from flirtation, kissing, and petting, to coitus with a person other than the spouse. Various terms are used to represent such activities, including extramarital sex, adultery, or infidelity. Current research is rather broad, and seldom specifies the three conditions proposed by Thompson (1983) to clarify the definition of extramarital sexual behaviours. These are 1) relationship sanction (consensual or secretive); 2) nature of relationship (extramarital, extra-cohabiting, extra-multilateral); and 3) nature of behaviour (intercourse, petting, homosexual contact).

Attitudes and Behaviour

Despite a *general* increase in sexual permissiveness since the 1960s, an increase regarding extramarital sexuality is not found (Bibby and Posterski, 1992; Bozinoff and MacIntosh, 1992; Thornton, 1989). An analysis of attitudes toward extramarital sex from 1975 through 1995 indicates that the "idea of having sex with someone other than one's marriage partner has failed to gain acceptance" (Bibby, 1995:74). In fact, in 1975, 22 percent of Canadian adults felt that sex with someone other than the marriage partner was either not wrong at all or only sometimes wrong. In 1995 that figure had dropped to 15 percent. The proportion of those indicating that extramarital sex was always wrong increased from 50 percent in 1975 to 60 percent in 1995.

A recent Gallup poll (Bozinoff and MacIntosh, 1992) found that the vast majority (81 percent) of Canadians considered extramarital affairs wrong. Sixty-four percent believe that extramarital sex is always wrong, while an additional 17 percent believe it is almost always wrong. Only 4 percent think that sexual relations with someone other than the marriage

partner is not wrong at all. In contrast with attitudes toward premarital sex, the strongest disapproval of extramarital sex is found among those between the ages of 18 and 29 (88 percent). Eighty-one percent of those aged 50 and older, and 77 percent of those aged 30 to 49, thought that extramarital affairs were always or almost always wrong. Among high school students, Bibby and Posterski (1992) found that only 10 percent approved of extramarital sex, representing no change from 1984.

A 1997 CTV/Angus Reid Group poll found that half of Canadians (51 percent) believe that having an affair is more acceptable behaviour today than it was 10 years ago, while one-quarter (26 percent) feel that it is less acceptable behaviour, and 19 percent feel that the acceptability of having an affair has not changed.

Incidence surveys of extramarital behaviours, however, indicate that people's behaviour often differs from their expressed attitudes. Thompson (1984) reported that despite the strong disapproval of extramarital relationships by the majority of respondents in the United States, almost half *do* pursue such relations. In contrast, Greeley (1991) reported that the 1988 General Social Survey indicated 86 percent of all sexually active Americans had had only one sexual partner during the previous year, and that a similar study from England reported virtually the same finding. Promiscuity (having more than one sexual partner) was prevalent only among the young (under 24) and unmarried (44 percent for men and 39 percent for women).

The 1989 General Social Survey contained a question regarding the number of sexual partners in the course of a lifetime. When "chastity" was defined as having no more sexual partners than marriage partners since the 18th birthday, 48 percent of married Americans were chaste (65 percent of women and 30 percent of men). "The picture that emerged from these analyses was of sexual experimentation before marriage and of moderately high (and perhaps very high) levels of fidelity after marriage" (Greeley, 1991:17). Blumstein and Schwartz (1983) found that only 26 percent of husbands and 21 percent of wives experienced any form of extramarital involvement since the beginning of their marriage, while 33 percent of male cohabitors and 30 percent of female cohabitors, and 82 percent of gay men and 28 percent of lesbians, experienced sex outside their relationship.

The 1997 CTV/Angus Reid Group poll referred to earlier found that less than one-fifth (18 percent) of adult Canadians report that they have had an affair, compared with 8 in 10 (80 percent) who report that they have not. Those who report being most faithful (or who report not having an affair) are Atlantic Canadians (90 percent), residents of Manitoba/Saskatchewan (90 percent), married Canadians (88 percent), and females (84 percent versus 75 percent among males). One in 10 Canadians (10 percent) report that they would have a one-night stand if their spouse would never find out and there was no chance of contracting a sexually transmitted disease, compared with the majority (86 percent) who would not. The majority of Canadians indicated that if their spouse or partner had an affair, they would "try to work things out," compared with 3 in 10 (29 percent) of Canadians who felt that if their spouse had an affair it would automatically mean the end of their relationship, with no chance of forgiveness. Those who are most likely to try to work things out are British Columbians (72 percent), Albertans (72 percent), Canadians aged 55 and older (72 percent), and those who report having had an affair (81 percent). Rather surprisingly, younger Canadians aged 18 to 34 (38 percent), "single" Canadians (35 percent), and those living in common-law relationships (34 percent) are most likely to indicate that having an affair would automatically end the relationship. It appears that those who are most accepting of *premarital* sex are least accepting of *extramarital* sex.

Impact of Extramarital Sexuality on Marriage

Thompson (1984) distinguished among three kinds of extramarital relationships. These were 1) strongly emotional (in love) but not sexual (intercourse); 2) sexual (intercourse) but not emotional (in love); and 3) emotional (in love) *and* sexual (intercourse). Males were significantly more likely to experience sexual (intercourse only) relationships (31 percent) than were females (16 percent). If the incidence rates for all three kinds of involvement are considered, then female rates (42 percent) were very similar to those of males (46 percent).

Thompson found the evaluation of an extra-dyadic relationship is dependent on its emotional and sexual components. Respondents indicated that sexual relationships that were also emotional were most wrong and most likely to detract from the quality of the primary relationship, while sexual relationships alone were regarded as more wrong and more likely to detract from the primary relationship. Women were more likely than men to have emotional affairs, whereas men were much more likely to have affairs that were only sexual. One study found that 51 percent of males and 72 percent of females reported that the extramarital relationship had some emotional commitment; that is, it was not based on sex alone (Spanier and Margolis, 1983).

When couples are asked about their responses if they found out that a spouse had an affair, men are more likely to be emotionally upset if wives have an affair than are wives when husbands have an affair (Bringle and Buunk, 1991; Shackleford and Buss, 1997). This may be a relatively small problem since Edwards and Booth (1994) found that only about 5 percent of couples found that extramarital affairs had created difficulties in their marriage. Christopher and Sprecher (2000), however, state that there is some disagreement among researchers as to the degree that extramarital affairs pose a problem for marriages.

In contrast to most extramarital relationships, where one or both spouses has intercourse with someone outside the marriage without the partner's knowledge, "swinging," or comarital sex—a form of open marriage—is pursued with the knowledge of the spouse, and usually with the participation of both spouses. Swinging differs from other forms of extramarital sex in that it involves the agreement and participation of both spouses, and avoids the deception that usually accompanies extramarital sex. Blumstein and Schwartz (1983) reported that swinging couples expected their relationship would remain stable and durable. Swinging was seen as a response to sexual boredom, rather than as an acknowledgment that the relationship was intolerable or that it should be brought to an end. They reported, however, that swinging is rather rare.

We have seen that sexuality, including marital sexuality, takes place in a social context. The expression of sexuality among the elderly is, to a large extent, determined by the expectations of society, which says that growing old is incompatible with continuing sexual activity. A number of research studies have investigated the sexual relationships of the elderly.

Sexuality and the Elderly

We have already seen that sexual activity declines with the passage of time. Greeley (1991) reported that the number of people experiencing intercourse at least once a week declined from over 40 percent for those in their twenties to less than 20 percent for those in their seventies. Yet there is evidence that aging does not necessarily mean an end to sexual activity. One study reported that the most common form of erotic activity among those over 80 was touching and caressing without intercourse, followed by masturbation, followed by intercourse. It was also found, however, that 62 percent of the men and 30 percent of the women who were in their eighties and older reported that they still had sexual intercourse (Bretschneider and McCoy, 1988).

Based on data from the 1988 and 1989 General Social Surveys in the United States, Greeley (1991) found that 42 percent of married people in their sixties and 20 percent in their seventies reported very great satisfaction from their sex lives. Also, 20 percent of those over age 60 reported having intercourse at least once a week, while 15 percent of those over age 60 and 10 percent of those over age 70 reported having sex more than once a week. We have already seen that women do not reach their sexual peak until their late forties, and maintain this level into their sixties. Women experience *menopause* (the cessation of menstruation) around the age of 50, but continue to demonstrate sexual interest and ability.

The aging of men is associated with a decline in responsiveness, requiring greater stimulation and time to become aroused, as well as having more difficulty in maintaining an erection. Call et al. (1995) reported that 57 percent of those aged 65 to 69, and 27 percent of those aged 75 or older, reported having had sex at least once during the previous month. They further found that those aged 65 to 69 reported having sex 2.4 times a month, and those aged 75 and older reported having sex 0.8 times a month. The national Canadian survey (Pollara, 1997) found that those aged 65 and older reported that they had sexual relations an average of 3.5 times per month. On the other hand, of those aged 65 and older, 25 percent report that they

did not have sex during the previous month; 21 percent report a frequency of 1–5 times; 11 percent, a frequency of 6–10 times; and 4 percent, a frequency of 11 or more times per month.

We saw at the beginning of this chapter that many factors contribute to effective marital interaction and satisfying family relationships. Every newlywed couple hopes that their marriage will develop into a vital and satisfying relationship. Marital adjustment and satisfaction, however, are not achieved automatically or without effort. The development of a vital marriage is dependent on a number of factors.

Marital Enrichment

Stanley et al. (1995) argue that many of the factors contributing to marital dysfunction are already evident in the premarital relationship, but that effective training programs are available to help couples to prevent divorce and to preserve meaningful relationships. Programs to strengthen couple relationships, such as Relationship Enhancement (Guerney, 1979), Couples Communication (Miller, Miller, Nunnally and Wackman, 1991), and PREP (Prevention and Relationship Enhancement Program) teach partners skills and ground rules for handling conflict and promoting intimacy. A number of longitudinal studies found that communication problems and destructive marital conflict are among the leading risk factors for future divorce and marital distress. Couples who completed the premarital intervention program demonstrated more relationship stability after five-year and 12-year follow-ups, as well as higher relationship quality as measured by better conflict management skills, relationship satisfaction, and lower levels of aggression.

Lauer and Lauer (1986) studied 351 couples who were married a minimum of 15 years. They found four characteristics to be key elements of enduring marriages: friendship or enjoyment in being together; belief in marriage as a long-term commitment; consensus about aims and goals and their philosophy of life; and humour.

A study of couples who were defined as experiencing "vital" marriages found four factors to be essential in the development of such a relationship. Marriage vitality was measured by the degree of satisfaction a person derived from the marriage relationship, the degree of emotional involvement the couple had with each other, the degree to which the couple did things together, and the degree to which they enjoyed living their lives together (Ammons and Stinnett, 1991).

■ **Sex** A majority (86 percent) of respondents reported moderate to very high needs for sexual activity. The need for sex was associated with the need for strong attachments to the spouse, making sex an important component of an overall personal relationship.

■ **Reciprocity** Vital marriage partners expressed high levels of the need to be understanding and supportive, in contrast with the contemporary emphasis on individualism and selfism. Rather than sacrificing one's individuality and the right to personal need gratification, a mutually gratifying relationship resulted in the multiplication of affective rewards for both partners.

■ **Determination and commitment** Developing and sustaining a vital relationship was regarded by these couples as one of their most important life goals. They were strongly committed to their relationship, and were determined to make it work.

■ **Ego strengths** Vital marriage partners had well-developed ego strengths that enabled them to function autonomously in making independent judgments and taking independent actions. High ego strength enabled couples to face stress and conflict while retaining their basic integrity as individuals.

Based on the research conducted by Stinnett and his colleagues (Stinnett and Sauer, 1977; Stinnett, 1979; Stinnett et al., 1982), Schumm (1985) developed a theoretical model to show the underlying or implicit structure of these factors. Six key characteristics of strong relationships were found: expression of appreciation, time together, good communication, a high degree of religious orientation, commitment, and ability to deal with problems and crises in a positive way. The hypothesized relationships among these six variables to each other and to marital strengths is shown in Figure 9.4.- The model suggests that a high degree of religious orientation has a pervasive impact on family strengths. Religious orientation is defined, not in terms of religious denomination or participation, but as an awareness of and commitment to a spiritual lifestyle.

Figure 9.4   A Proposed Model of Marital Strengths

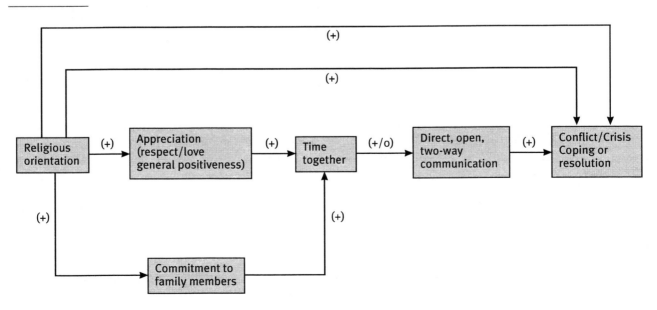

Source: Schumm, 1985:3.

Religious orientation is positively related to appreciation, commitment, time together, and the ability to deal with crises. Commitment and appreciation have a similar impact on time spent together. It is important to note that effective communication is determined by time spent together—it is difficult to communicate when you are separated. Time together is thus a necessary, but perhaps not a sufficient, condition for effective communication. Effective communication contributes to constructive problem-solving and crisis resolution. Effective communication does not prevent couples from quarreling, but assists them in getting their conflict out in the open and enables them to discuss it. Failure to communicate results in the inability to resolve conflicts. Chapter 15 also examines the characteristics of strong marriages and families.

Unstructured interviews with 15 couples who had been married at least 30 years (Robinson and Blanton, 1993) investigated the couples' perception of the qualities that had sustained their relationship in times of closeness and of relational strain. Their analysis suggested the following key elements of enduring marriages: intimacy balanced with autonomy; commitment; communication; congruent perceptions of the relationship; and religious faith.

Robinson and Blanton recognize that their model is very similar to that of Schumm (1985). The key difference is that Schumm sees religious orientation as the "prime mover" that influences all other variables in the model. In contrast, Robinson and Blanton, while recognizing the importance of religious orientation, found that intimacy was the central quality of all enduring marriages. Intimacy in marriage represents a healthy balance between dependency and autonomy. This balance may vary from couple to couple.

Mace (1987) argues that no more than 10 percent of the married population experiences enriching marriages. The achievement of a deeply satisfying and rewarding relationship, he suggests, can take place through three methods: education for marriage, marital therapy, and marriage enrichment. He sees great promise of marital enrichment as a preventive approach, particularly during the first year of marriage.

A variety of marital enrichment programs have been developed, including communication training, behaviour exchange programs, and mixtures of affective training and skills-training programs. The following are the most common goals of these programs:

1. To increase a couple's self-awareness and mutual empathy.
2. To increase awareness of positive characteristics, strengths, and potential as individuals and as a couple.
3. To increase mutual self-disclosure of thoughts and feelings.
4. To increase intimacy.
5. To develop relationship skills in communication, problem-solving, and conflict resolution (Hof et al., 1980).

SUMMARY

- Generally, there is a positive relationship between marital quality and marital stability. Comparison level and comparison level for alternatives have been used to explain the relationship between marital quality and stability.

- Lewis and Spanier (1979) developed the most extensive and widely used model of marital adjustment, which explained the impact of a large number of indicators of marital adjustment or quality on marital stability.

- Marital satisfaction is consistently related to the presence of children and to the family life stage. Children tend to detract from, rather than contribute to, the marital happiness of their parents. The relationship between family life stages and marital happiness is most often found to be curvilinear, with the highest levels of marital satisfaction being reported in the stages before children are born and after they leave home.

- Such other determinants as social environment, employment conditions, gender roles, religion, interdependence, and health also have an impact on marital quality.

- There are four key communication styles, which involve particular ways of talking and listening.

- Self-disclosure, or transparency, is an important component of communication. Communication is improved not so much by an increase in *quantity*, but rather by an increase in *quality*. The negative communication found in distressed couples may be more a matter of ill will than a lack of communication skill. Differences in communication are found between distressed and non-distressed couples, and between males and females. It is possible to be an effective communicator in other relationships while at the same time being an ineffective communicator in the marital relationship.

■ Nonverbal communication is concerned with how the message is transmitted. It conveys emotional meanings, and is frequently more accurate in communicating feelings than is verbal communication. Important differences have been found in the ways in which men and women communicate.

■ Interdependence, ideology, and conflict interact in the determination of traditional, independent, and separate marriages. Each of these styles of marriage is associated with high levels of marital adjustment. Not only is marital communication important for marital satisfaction, but effective *premarital* communication determines later marital satisfaction.

■ The ability to communicate effectively does not necessarily result in the absence of conflict. Seven key areas of conflict have been identified. Conflict may be handled constructively or destructively. Couples apply four conflict management strategies, and five different conflict management styles have been identified.

■ Three elements of the social structure that govern sexual relationships in marriage are jealousy, gender role power, and beliefs about normality.

■ Most married couples experience a reduction in the frequency of sexual relations over time. Males reach the peak of their sexual performance earlier than do women.

■ In contrast to changing attitudes toward premarital sex, attitudes toward extramarital sex have not become more liberal. Conflicting findings are reported with respect to the frequency of extramarital behaviour.

■ Though the frequency of sexual relations declines with age, aging does not necessarily mean the end of sexual activity.

■ Four factors are found to be essential in the development of a "vital" marriage relationship: satisfactory sexual relationships, reciprocity, determination and commitment to make the marriage succeed, and ego strengths.

KEY TERMS

Comparison level (194)
Comparison level for alternatives (194)
Conflict management strategies (205)
Extramarital sexuality (211)
Marital communication (199)
Marital quality (192)
Marital stability (192)
Nonverbal communication (201)
Self-disclosure (200)

QUESTIONS FOR REVIEW

1. What is the relationship between marital quality and marital stability? Explain how comparison level and comparison level for alternatives may help us to understand this relationship.

2. What are the primary determinants of marital adjustment as identified in the Lewis and Spanier model?

3. What is the impact of children on marital quality? Describe the pattern of change in marital quality over the family life stage.

4. Define *communication* and describe its four major components. Review the four styles of communication, and describe gender differences in the use of these styles.

5. What is the effect of the relationship between quantity and quality of communication on marital satisfaction? How do communication patterns differ between distressed and non-distressed marriages, and between males and females?

6. Discuss how nonverbal communication affects verbal communication. What are the main gender differences in communication?

7. List four conflict management strategies, and indicate how husbands and wives use these strategies. Describe the five styles of interpersonal conflict management.

8. How do the three elements of the social structure function as boundary mechanisms around sexual relationships in marriage?

9. Discuss contemporary attitudes and behaviour with respect to extramarital sexuality.

10. List the four factors found to be essential in the development of a "vital" marriage relationship.

QUESTIONS FOR DISCUSSION

1. It would seem logical to assume that high-quality marriages are marked by high stability, and low-quality marriages are marked by low stability. Why are some high-quality marriages marked by low stability, while some low-quality marriages are marked by high stability?

2. According to the family life stage literature, marital satisfaction begins to decline with the birth of the first child and reaches its lowest point during the child's teenage years. However, research also indicates that the presence of children reduces the probability of marital dissolution. Explain this seeming anomaly.

3. It is possible for both partners in a relationship to have high levels of self-disclosure without having an intimate relationship. Why is the quantity of communication not necessarily related to the quality?

4. Discuss the relative effectiveness of the five different styles of interpersonal conflict management. Examine the possible combinations of styles by husbands and wives, and discuss what combinations would be most or least effective. What style of communication do you use most frequently in intimate relationships?

5. Discuss the implications of the finding that although frequency of sexual relationships declines as we move from east to west in Canada, no regional differences are found in the U.S. sample.

6. Discuss the role of sexuality in extramarital and elderly relationships.

SUGGESTED READINGS

Bradbury, T.N., F.D. Fincham, and S.R.H. Beach. 2000. "Research on the Nature and Determinants of Marital Satisfaction: A Decade Review," *Journal of Marriage and Family* 62: 964–980. This is a review of marital quality research over the 1990s and is a clear and concise update of the empirical literature.

Michael, Robert T., John H. Gagnon, Edward O. Laumann, and Gina Kolata. 1994. *Sex in America: A Definitive Survey*. Toronto: Little Brown. This book examines the sexual attitudes and behaviours of more than 3400 randomly selected American males and females—in single, cohabiting, married, divorced, and same-sex relationships—as well as many forms of sexual practices. It provides an overview of up-to-date sexuality in everyday life.

Miller, Sherod and Phyllis A. Miller. 1997. *Core Communication: Skills and Processes*. Littleton: Interpersonal Communication Programs, Inc. An excellent presentation of communication patterns and principles. The book is written from a practical applied perspective, and is very helpful in understanding communication processes.

Schwartz, Pepper. 1994. *Peer Marriage: How Love Between Equals Really Works*. Toronto: The Free Press. This book is a unique and important examination of how love works between men and women who are committed to the principle of defining and establishing equality in marriage. Friendship is seen as the cornerstone of peer marriage, but is not easy to attain, it is argued. However, the benefits of striving toward the goal far outweigh any associated with the traditional norms of inequity.

CHAPTER 10

Work, Marriage, and Family

After studying this chapter, you should be able to do the following:

▪ Describe the prevailing attitudes toward female employment in Canada prior to 1950.
▪ Identify five reasons for the very rapid increase in employment of women in Canada since the 1950s.
▪ Analyze the statistical trends in female participation in the Canadian labour market since 1950.
▪ List four general ways in which employers practised discrimination against women in Canada.
▪ Explain the reasons behind the revolution in the North American family that has taken place over the past 40 years.
▪ Outline the ways in which husbands have responded to the employment of their wives.
▪ Review the ways Canadian society has accommodated the rapid increase in employment of women.
▪ Describe the effects of the wife's employment on performance of domestic work in her home.
▪ Identify the influences that determine what effect a wife's employment has on the quality of her marriage.
▪ Evaluate who has enjoyed the benefits and advantages and who has experienced the costs and disadvantages of the high rates of employment of wives and mothers.

Introduction

Most readers of this chapter grew up during the course of a major revolution that affected great numbers of people—the revolution in the North American family. Since 1960, this revolution has cut the birthrate by 58 percent, seen millions of mothers leave home for paid employment, and caused turmoil in countless marriages. It began with the rising number of women entering the labour force during the late 1950s, and gained momentum as the birth control pill became generally available after 1960. The revolution spread as women, bringing home their own paycheques, felt empowered to press for changes in marital and family relationships.

This chapter is about changes in family and marriage that are linked to women's participation in work

and its consequences. For example, women's work now includes both domestic work—housekeeping and child care—and employment, by which we mean paid work outside the home. On the other hand, feminist scholars (Briskin, 1980) and economists (Hawrylyshyn, 1976; 1977; 1978) have identified unpaid work performed by women as important to the economy of the country (Fox, 1980; Hawrylyshyn, 1976; 1977; 1978) as well as to the smooth functioning of daily life and to the continuation of society. Women's dual work roles add not only to the complexities of women's lives but to the complexity of family interactions.

Researchers have examined domestic work more closely since this revolution began, studying the conditions under which it took place and the effects on women and their families. Meg Luxton's *More than a*

Labour of Love (1980) documented the experience of three generations of women working in their homes in the mining town of Flin Flon, Manitoba. Rosenberg (1987) analyzed the costs of "motherwork" in terms of stress and depression. Recent research has investigated women's feelings of fairness concerning family work (Hawkins, Marshall, and Allen, 1998), the effect of parenthood on division of labour in the home (Sanchez and Thomson, 1997), and the implications of how women's work is defined (Messias et al,1998).

Economists have focused on techniques for estimating the value of human time. Most of these techniques rely upon the valuation of time spent performing non-market work. In 1985, the United Nations General Assembly adopted a resolution calling for recognition of women's contributions to development in the form of unpaid labour in agriculture, food production, reproduction, and household activities. The resolution also calls for the value of these contributions to be measured and reflected in economic statistics such as Gross National Product (GNP). A bill known as the *Unremunerated Work Act* was introduced in the U.S. Congress in 1991. The bill was subsequently passed as the *Counting Unremunerated Work Act* of 1996. The bill requires the Bureau of Labor Statistics to conduct studies of the unpaid labour of men and women, to calculate the monetary value of this labour, and to include that value in calculations of the nation's GNP. No such initiative has yet been launched in Canada.

Most wives and mothers today have remunerated jobs as well as traditional domestic duties. In the 1960s, many women sought careers in response to Friedan's (1963) vision of escape from *The Feminine Mystique*, but more and more, paid work became an economic necessity, as men's incomes began to fall behind the cost of living. Employment has meant empowerment for women, but it has also loaded them with an unfair **double burden**. One burden is the demands of full-time employment in a workplace where women often face exploitation and discrimination. The second is the burden of domestic labour, which most husbands still do not share equally. Identifying the implications of this unfair burden on wives has been a major concern (Fast and Frederick, 1996; Kluwer, Heesink, and Van De Vliert, 1997; Perry-Jenkins, Repetti, and Crouter, 2000).

The first section of this chapter briefly outlines the history of women's employment, and the reasons for its rapid growth since the 1950s. We will describe the obstacles and the exploitation women commonly experience in the workplace. The second section discusses the profound consequences of wives' employment on the daily life of families, including the division of household labour and child care, and women's health. The third section reviews evidence that women's employment has driven the transition from traditional to more egalitarian gender roles (as described in Chapter 6), and discusses the effects of wives' employment on marital relationships. The final section looks at the interactions between women's careers and their families, and the balance of work and family life.

Canadian Women's Labour Force Participation

Historical Background

During the 19th century, single women often worked as domestics. After marriage, they were expected to "keep house" and bear and raise children while the husband financially supported his patriarchal family. But as Coontz argues in *The Way We Never Were* (1992), this idealized pattern was never a reality for most wives, who often spent long hours helping work the farm—planting gardens, raising chickens, preserving food for the winter—or working in the family business. Among homesteading families in western Canada, husbands often left home to work on the railroad or in the mines (or more recently in the "oil patch") to earn needed cash, while their wives and children worked the farm. Wives have always worked, usually very hard—though they were not always paid.

Despite the very significant contributions that wives made to family livelihood, work and family support were seen as primarily the husband's responsibility, as was family decision-making. Historical statistics do show that fathers earned most, if not all, of the cash income. In 1891, only 11.4 percent of women over 10 years of age were employed, comprising 12.6 percent of the labour force (Lowe, 1987). Their numbers tended to grow, however, with the expansion of light industries (such as textile factories), which recruited women because they were a cheap source of semi-skilled or unskilled labour. As can

TABLE 10.1   Labour Force Activity[1] of Females Aged 15 and Over[2]

	1901	1911	1921	1931	1941	1951	1961	1971	1981	1991	1999
% of female population part of labour force	14.4	16.6	17.7	19.4	22.9	24.4	29.3	39.9	47.4	52.6	58.9
Females % of total labour force	14.9	15	17	18.6	20.2	22.3	26.4	32.8	40.4	45.3	45.8

1. Labour force activity includes workers and unemployed seeking a job.
2. Data of 1901 to 1941 are based on female population aged 14 and over and exclude Newfoundland.

Source: Women's History Month 2000, Status of Women Canada, http://www.swc-cfc.gc.ca/dates/whm/2000/stats_e.html (reproduced with the permission of Minister of Public Works and Government Services Canada, 2003.)

be seen in Table 10.1, by 1901 women's participation had increased to 14.4 percent.

Nevertheless, there was a general feeling that paid work was men's work. Working men and their unions had battled for a "family wage" large enough for a husband to adequately support a wife and children. These efforts gave ideological support to the feeling that women should not have to work outside the home. In the middle classes, where there was no need for wives to work, the distinguishing characteristic of femininity was defined as domesticity. Women were to be wives and mothers, responsible for making the home a haven for husbands and children. "Motherhood became the glue that held the family together in the face of... industrialisation" (Wilson, 1991:18).

The First World War (1914–1918) brought women into munitions and other factories in large numbers, and their resulting sense of empowerment strengthened their resolve to gain and exercise the franchise they won in 1918. However, the postwar return to "normalcy," or the status quo, sent many women back to the kitchen so they would not "take jobs away" from the returning soldiers—women were only used as a cheap reserve army of workers to temporarily fill the economic needs of the time. However, this experience of paid employment by women signaled the beginning of

the increasing participation of women in the paid labour force (Wilson, 1996).

Surprisingly, the Great Depression (1929–1939) caused the next wave of female employment. During this economic upheaval, industry wanted to pay only rock-bottom wages, and women were employed more cheaply than were men. The unemployment of millions of fathers brought women into the labour force in even greater numbers than during the First World War. A sharp decline in the birthrate during these years helped to make wives more available for employment (Wilson, 1991). However, women who did work during this time of desperate financial need were "subject to strong negative sanctions because they were seen as responsible both for taking jobs away from men and for a wide range of social problems" (Googins, 1991:89). The economic demands of this period put the issue of welfare on the national agenda (Ursel, 1992).

Severe labour shortages during the Second World War (1939–1945) brought even more women into the labour force, but the end of the war found them at home again. Most women were happy to marry and have children, satisfying the yearnings of men and women alike, long frustrated by the Depression and war years. These interests, together with the adequate family wage levels paid during the postwar boom years, made possible the "golden age" of the traditional family: a breadwinning husband, a stay-at-home wife and mother, three or four children, and a strong family commitment. But during the 1950s, an increasing number of wives became dissatisfied in their traditional role as mother and homemaker. As a result, many women turned to the opportunities and the increased independence found in paid employment (Wilson, 1991). By 1951, female labour force participation had increased to almost 25 percent (see Table 10.1).

Women's Employment since the 1950s

Participation Rate There has been a massive increase in the numbers of women employed since the 1950s. Table 10.1 shows a participation rate in 1950 of 24.4 percent increasing to 58.9 percent in 1999. Indeed the percentage of the female population of working age (15 to 65 years of age) that is employed or actively seeking employment (**female participation rate**) doubled between 1961 and 1996, increasing from 29 percent to 58 percent.

A significant portion of this increase in participation rate was due to the increased employment of mothers with preschool children. During the 1960s and 1970s, the earlier practice of women dropping out of the labour force to bear and raise children declined, and between 1951 and 1971 the increase among women with children was twice as great as the increase among women without children. This change was led by divorced mothers, among whom as many as 43 percent of those with preschool children, and 62 percent of those with older children, were in the labour force as early as 1976 (Statistics Canada, 1980). As well, two-thirds of all female university graduates were in the labour force by 1976, a figure that included a large number of mothers of small children.

However, the upward trend in women's workforce participation rates halted in 1991 (Butlin, 1995), and a very slight decrease in participation can be see between 1991 and 1996. By 1991, few differences remained in the labour force participation rates of men and women. - Table 10.2 documents that for men and women 15–24 there is no real difference in labour force participation in 2002. However, there is a 10 percent difference between men and women 25–44 years. This small difference is attributable to women leaving the labour force to take care of children. The difference between men and women in older cohorts may reflect an older set of norms regarding marriage and work. It is clear from these statistics, however, that women with children (25–44 years) are, for the most part, engaged in the labour force.

Reasons for the Increase Krahn and Lowe (1993) identified five broad categories of influences that have contributed to the rapid rise in employment of women in Canada since the 1950s.

■ **More women available for work** Two very important developments for women were changes in life expectancy and changes in the timing of significant events in their lives (Gee, 1986). There have been dramatic increases in women's "survivorship." The average ages when significant events occur—when women marry, when they have their first and last babies, when their last child leaves home, and when they become widows—have varied considerably since 1831. In our society, there has been a growing tendency for women to delay marriage and to have fewer children (Krahn and Lowe, 1993).

■ **More women completing post-secondary education** Higher educational achievements have raised women's job aspirations, and higher educational qualifications have enabled women to compete more effectively with men for jobs (Krahn and Lowe, 1993). Educational attainment is strongly related to women's employment— the higher her educational level, the more likely it is that she will enter the labour force.

■ **Financial need** The need for earnings has grown as men's real incomes have failed to keep pace with increasing needs and wants. Declining living standards for some families have made a wife's earnings more important. Furthermore, the rising rates of separation and divorce, combined with low or unpaid child-support and alimony payments, have heightened the financial need of many women (Hall, Walker and Acock, 1995; Krahn and Lowe, 1993).

■ **Increase in number of jobs** Job opportunities for women increased significantly as the economy expanded

TABLE 10.2 Age, Gender, and Labour Force Participation Rates

	1998	1999	2000	2001	2002
	(In thousands)				
Labour force	15 417.7	15 721.2	15 999.2	16 246.3	16 689.4
Men	8 380.2	8 534.0	8 649.2	8 769.2	8 989.8
Women	7 037.5	7 187.2	7 350.0	7 477.1	7 699.6
Participation rates	(%)				
15 years and over	65.1	65.6	65.9	66.0	66.9
Men	72.1	72.5	72.5	72.5	73.3
Women	58.4	58.9	59.5	59.7	60.7
15–24 years	61.9	63.5	64.4	64.7	66.3
Men	63.5	65.3	65.9	66.1	67.7
Women	60.2	61.7	62.9	63.3	64.9
25–44 years	85.6	85.8	86.0	86.3	86.8
Men	92.2	92.1	92.1	92.1	92.4
Women	79.0	79.6	80.0	80.4	81.2
45–64 years	47.1	47.8	48.5	48.9	50.3
Men	55.8	56.6	56.9	57.1	58.6
Women	39.2	39.9	40.9	41.5	42.8
65 years and over	6.4	6.2	6.0	6.0	6.7
Men	10.2	9.8	9.5	9.4	10.5
Women	3.5	3.4	3.3	3.4	3.7

Source: Statistics Canada, CANSIM II, table 282-0002.

during the 1960s and 1970s. Moreover, the number of jobs in the service sector increased substantially, and many more part-time jobs were available (Krahn and Lowe, 1993).

■ **Changing attitudes** During the 1950s, women were becoming increasingly dissatisfied with the traditional role of domestic wife and mother (Wilson, 1991). By the late 1950s, even motherhood was becoming less highly regarded. Wives began to find themselves in no-win situations. If a wife chose to be a housewife, she felt apologetic; if she pursued a career, she was neglecting her family. Women were increasingly restless and frustrated, as Friedan (1963) showed in documenting "the problem that has no name."

Women's dissatisfaction with available roles continued to grow. A study by Carisse (1970) of innovative Francophone women showed that many competent, upper-class wives were not very satisfied in their beautiful homes during the early 1960s. She interviewed 150 women judged to be innovators in their fields of action—a union president, a prison director, and a mathematician, among others. These women rejected traditional male–female relationships, and wanted egalitarianism in cross-gender relationships, marriage, and the raising of children.

During the early years of the rapid increase in female labour force participation, public reactions were mixed. Those in favour saw this trend as a further significant step toward the liberation of women, while those opposed saw it as a threat to the stability of marriage, the well-being of children, and the continued willingness of industry to pay a family wage. Attitudes have become more favourable regarding the employment of women, as the traditional stereotypes of women's roles and women's work have weakened and the feminist movement has promoted acceptance of new roles (Krahn and Lowe, 1993).

Striving for Equality

Homemaking and the Courts Household work done by family members often is described as "invisible," since it is done largely by women, within private households, without pay and without social recognition (Eichler, 1988; Wilson, 1996). In developed economies there is a tendency to equate value with money. Consequently unpaid household work often is viewed as being valueless and therefore not even "real" work. As Andre states, "[T]he homemaker's problems begin with the deceptively simple fact that she receives no salary for her work" (Andre, 1981:25).

The legal system, like society in general, has long devalued unpaid work carried out in the household. Until fairly recently, damages for the loss of ability to do unpaid work were seldom considered by the courts. In Canada, the first recognition that unpaid household work has value, and that the value is economic, came in 1885 from Ritchie C.J., who stated in St. Lawrence & Ottawa Wry v. Lett that "the loss of a mother may involve many things which may be regarded as of a pecuniary character."

However, even at a time in legal history when courts were willing to entertain claims for such damages, women could not recover damages because they lacked the property rights that would allow them to sue in their own names. Since a woman's husband was assumed to own and be the main beneficiary of her household work, he could sue for loss of his wife's services, and any award would accrue to him. Even with the advent of property rights for women and the power to sue in their own right, husbands' claims for lost household services continued. The statement "There is no doubt that an economic loss has been experienced by those survivors who were dependent on the housewife services" (Speiser, 1970:196) seems to reflect the prevailing view of the time. A husband's right to recover for loss of a wife's services was even legislated in some jurisdictions.

In contrast, the Canadian legal system has been slow to recognize the economic value of unpaid work such as the household work of family members. For example, in 1983 a plaintiff whose wife had been killed in a hunting accident was awarded only $1500 per year for loss of housekeeping services, even though the deceased wife had performed most of the household work (Agrios).

In Canada, the demise of husbands' claims for loss of their wives' services began with the recent landmark decision by Vancise J.A. in Fobel v. Dean (1991), where the judge viewed the practice of compensating the husband for the loss of his wife's abilities as antiquated, if not sexist. As a result of this decision, financial claims for the loss of unpaid work by spouses is no longer approved.

While men have had the right to sue for loss of household ability, few men file household claims. It has been, and still is, the woman who is primarily responsible for household tasks, but men are responsible for an increasing portion of household tasks. It should be recognized that the loss of the male ability to do household tasks is also a loss.

Gender-Based Inequality The participation rate of women in the labour force is now almost equal to that of men, but do women receive the same treatment in the job market as men, and equal access to the same jobs? Within a work category, do they have equal access to more responsible, better-paying positions? Are they paid the same as men are for work requiring similar levels of training and skill?

Occupational Gender Segregation The tendency to hire men and women for different occupations—**occupational gender segregation**—is a result of the way girls are socialized and educated in our society, and of the way women are treated when they enter the workforce. Though efforts have been made to eliminate the distinctions between "men's work" and "women's work," they are still built into the North American job market. Increasing numbers of women are now employed in the more prestigious, traditionally male-dominated professions. For example, women made up 32 percent of all doctors and dentists in Canada in 1994, as compared to 18 percent in 1982. Women remain the minority of professionals employed in natural sciences, engineering, and mathematics, accounting for only 19 percent of these occupations (Statistics Canada, 1995). A majority of women still work in traditionally female-dominated occupations, accounting for 70 percent of those employed in teaching, nursing and related health occupations, clerical positions, and sales and service occupations (see Table 10.3). This means that men are overrepresented as doctors, dentists, natural scientists, engineers, and mathematicians, and are still underrepresented in traditionally female-dominated occupations (Statistics Canada, 1995).

Many of the occupations in which women predominate—as seamstresses in the clothing industry or cleaning ladies in office buildings, for example—can be described as female job ghettos (Gannagé, 1987;

Peitchinis, 1989). The resulting restricted opportunities, uncertain job security, and low income penalize employed wives and mothers with respect to standard of living, quality of life, and future opportunities. The most visible of these consequences is poverty. Occupational sex segregation contributes substantially to the increasing "feminization of poverty" in Canadian society, in part because women bear the burden of reproduction and provide most of the baby and child care. In so doing, they inevitably sacrifice activities that would qualify them for better jobs, and they are not recompensed for these sacrifices (Krahn and Lowe, 1993).

Gender Segregation within Occupations

Employers within particular occupations have a tendency to hire men for certain types of positions and women for other types of positions, a practice known as **gender segregation within occupations**. In most organizations today, men have the higher-ranking positions, with greater authority, higher pay, and more fringe benefits. This pattern of gender segregation holds true in industry, commerce, government, universities, and hospitals. For example, Canadian women have increased their representation in management and administration positions in business,

TABLE 10.3 Leading Female Occupations in Canada in 1891 and 2001

1891	2001
servant	clerical worker
dressmaker	secretary
teacher	sales clerk
farmer	teacher
seamstress	child care and/or domestic worker
tailoress	nurse
saleswoman	food and beverage server
housekeeper	cashier
laundress	retail food and accommodation manager
milliner	machine operator

Source : United Nations Platform for Action Committee Manitoba, Women and the Economy, http://www.unpac.ca/ca.

from 29 percent in 1982 to 44 percent in 1993, but again women are found at the least responsible and lowest-paying levels (Krahn and Lowe, 1993; Peitchinis, 1989).

Pay Inequality The differential between average earnings of fully employed men and women has declined since 1969, when women's average earnings were only 59 percent of men's earnings (Best, 1995). However, the income level of women is still substantially lower than that of men. In 1993, women working full time, all year, made an average of $28 000 per year, which amounts to 72 percent of the income of their male counterparts (Statistics Canada, 1995). If we look at all women employed, the lower wage level can be attributed in part to their part-time or part-year employment—which is almost twice the rate for men. Thirty-two percent of women work part time, compared to 15 percent of men. A major problem with part-time employment is the lack of employment benefits, such as medical insurance, dental plans, or pension plans. While the principle of equal pay for men and women employed at equal work was enshrined in law throughout Canada by 1991, wage gaps continue to exist.

Sexual Harassment Physical or verbal behaviour that is sexual in nature, is unwanted, and is seen as an implicit or explicit threat to the victim's employment or educational activities is **sexual harassment** (Martin, 1989). While sexual harassment may involve same-sex or opposite-sex persons, typically it involves men harassing women. A 1983 survey by the Canadian Human Rights Commission found that 1.2 million women faced forms of sexual harassment at their places of work (*Globe and Mail*, 1987). Many women do not recognize sexual harassment when it happens, because they have become so used to gender inequality that they accept male domination and female subordination without question (Benokraitis, 1993).

Women's Occupational Mobility Blakely and Harvey (1988) studied economic and educational influences on the occupational mobility of men and women using Canadian Mobility Study data. Of particular interest, they found that paid employment was more vulnerable to economic fluctuations (booms and busts) among women than among men. Women, especially those in the lower social class, were often "last hired and first fired." Discrimination also affects the occupational mobility of women in upper-class positions. Davies-Netzley (1998), in a study of women who attained top executive positions in corporations, believes that "the paucity of women in elite positions has much to do with gender discrimination reinforced by all-male networks and peers' similarities" (352).

FIGURE 10.1   Average Earnings of Full-Year, Full-Time Earners, 2000

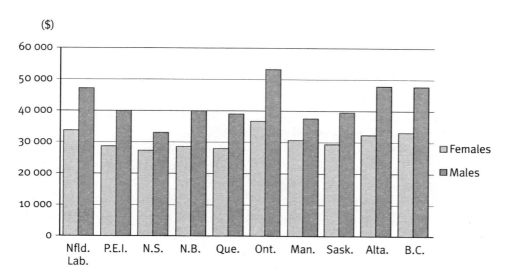

Source: Statistics Canada,
2001 Canada Year Book
(11-402-XPE).

Work and Family Balance

Two or three decades ago researchers examined work satisfaction and family satisfaction as separate and independent constructs. Perry-Jenkins, Repetti, and Crouter (2000) credit the work by Menaghan and Parcel (1990) as foundational to the discussion of work and family during the 1990s. However, most of the work in the area of work-family interface was pioneered by Patricia Voydanoff's book *Work and Family Life* (1987). Furthermore, Tiejde et al (1990) first developed the notion that the balance between work and family life is a critical measurement construct. Since that time researchers such as White (1999) have used this construct to measure the balance between these two areas. Now, much of the research literature discussing the relationship between work and family conceptualizes interconnecting and possibly reciprocal influences between them. One stream of research has been on work–family stress and multiple roles. A second stream has been on social support, in which other members of the workplace or family have a positive effect on employees' health and well-being. Though there has been little integration between these two streams, current researchers are suggesting that relationships between the domains of work and family are complex, and include both conflict and support (Adams, King and King, 1996; Lee and Duxbury, 1998).

Work–Family Stress

A consistent negative relationship is found between all forms of conflict in work–family interaction and a person's job–life satisfaction. For example Hughes et al (1992) report that chronic stress at work is transferred to the home setting. In general, the negative relationship may be stronger for women than for men. Work-to-family conflict, or work interference with family life, tends to hurt job satisfaction the most (Kossek and Ozeki, 1998). Researchers are investigating the interface between people's professional lives and non-work lives (Wallace, 1997), and ways that people can address work and family issues in their personal lives (Kofodimos, 1993; Schnittger and Bird, 1990). (See Box 10.1.)

Men and women think in different ways about integrating family and career. Some women prefer a conventional pattern, in which they maintain primary responsibility for the domestic work. Others follow a role-sharing pattern, in which both spouses pursue a career and share homemaking responsibilities. While these two groups of women show significant differences, they share a common desire to have a spouse who is emotionally supportive and career-oriented (Hallett and Gilbert, 1997).

Women's Work and Childbearing

Raising children has an impact on a woman's career. However, as Figure 10.2 depicts, increasingly women continue to work even with small children. Evidence of the effects of childbearing on the career prospects of wives is found in Usher's (1991) analysis of 1989 survey data from both members of 250 couples in Alberta. The care needs of the child often precipitated a "task–demand crisis" (such as baby tending, which had to be done), which caused the household division of labour to shift toward a more traditional, gender-based pattern. This overburdened the wife in terms of the work she did, but, more importantly, it reduced the perceived legitimacy of her paid employment. The finding regarding effects on parenting and on the children will be discussed in the next chapter.

Other findings agree with the view that parenting is a challenge to a woman's career. Waldron, Weiss, and Hughes (1998) investigated the interacting effects of employment, motherhood, and marriage on the health of women. They state that "current evidence indicates that employment and marriage tend to have beneficial effects of physical health, but the parental role does not" (228). The worst health trends were found in women who were neither married nor employed, and in women who were young when they first gave birth.

"The predominant images of the work and family balance... include those of women who are exhausted by trying to juggle work and family demands, of men who spend more time with their children than previously but still do not evenly divide household chores with their spouse, and of women who opt to leave full-time employment... These images, while attractive because of their graphic qualities, oversimplify the complex interactions of work and family life" (Fouad and Tinsley, 1997:141). For example, White (1999), using a large Canadian sample, found that work-family balance was best for families where the husband assisted with domestic duties.

Box 10.1   Stress—How Dual-Career Couples Handle It

Dual-career couples experience more stress than do other couples, because others expect more of them at work and they expect more of themselves, and dual-career wives are more stressed than are their husbands. Wives tend more to family matters (they phone the sitter more often than their husbands to ask how a child is doing), and they feel more pressure to prove to their bosses and colleagues that they are committed to their work.

Research has identified seven strategies these couples use in coping with stress.

Cognitive restructuring

Our family life is better because both of us are employed. There are more advantages than disadvantages to our lifestyle. My career has made me a better wife/husband.

Delegating

We encourage our children to help out whenever possible, and to be more self-sufficient. We delegate tasks to other family members.

Limiting activities

We cut back on leisure activities, certain community activities, and on the number of outside activities we take on. We're changing our standards of how well household tasks must be done.

Subordinating my career

I'm limiting my involvement on the job—saying "no" sometimes—and reducing the time I spend at work. I'm planning career changes to minimize conflict with family needs.

Compartmentalizing

I separate my work life from family life, so I can concentrate on one area at a time. I make better use of time at work, and plan so major changes at home will not disturb my career goals.

Avoiding responsibility

I postpone certain tasks until they are no longer necessary, and find legitimate excuses to keep from meeting obligations I dislike. I use family responsibilities to justify refusing more career responsibilities.

Using social support

We arrange child care so we can have more time together. We rely on extended family members for support and encouragement, and make friends with other two-career couples.

The coping strategies reported most often by both dual-career spouses were delegating and cognitive restructuring. Generally, wives made more use of coping strategies because they experienced greater stress. In particular, wives more often used delegating (delegating to children is often seen as "wife's work"), cognitive restructuring (career wives more than husbands need to convince themselves that their employment is good for their families) and using social support.

Source: Adapted from Schnittger and Bird, 1990.

Division of Domestic Work

Who Does the Domestic Work? The unprecedented increase in women's paid employment has had a huge impact on Canadian society, particularly on the family. The imbalance in husbands' and wives' performance of domestic work when both are employed full time has led women to speak of the "double day" and "the second shift" in describing their workloads (see Box 10.2). Though there is certainly some movement toward greater equity in the division of household chores between husbands and wives, it has not kept pace with the increasing hours wives spend at paid employment.

Several recent Canadian surveys demonstrate the continuing imbalance in the sharing of domestic work (Frederick, 1995; Harvey et al., 1991; Krahn, 1993; Population Research Laboratory, 1990). A recent study of more than 200 Canadian parents continues to show striking differences between responses from mothers and fathers (Lee and Duxbury, 1998). And, if television images of gender are any indication, there are few changes in gender stereotyping in our culture "to move

Research shows that women spend roughly 15 more hours of paid and unpaid work each week than men, which adds up to an extra month of 24-hour days during the course of a year. Just as there is a "wage gap" between men and women on the job, there is a "leisure gap" between them at home. A study of 600 couples filing for divorce found that the second most common reason women gave for wanting to divorce, after "mental cruelty," was their husbands' neglect of their children or their homes, cited more often than financial problems, infidelity, or physical abuse.

Hochschild observed 52 couples over an eight-year period, and found the wives were more concerned about the conflict between work and family than the husbands were. The wives felt the second shift was their problem, and their husbands agreed. But husbands were affected also, by the resentment their wives felt toward them and by their need to steel themselves against this resentment.

"The second shift" is the wife's problem in part because wives feel more responsible for home and children. They more often keep track of doctors' appointments,

arrange for their children's friends to "come play," and worry about a Halloween costume or a birthday present for a child's school friend. As a result, many more wives than husbands are torn between two kinds of urgency—the need to soothe a child upset when left at day care, and the need to show her boss she is "serious" about her work.

Today, when the two-job family is suffering from a speed-up of work and family life, working mothers are the most affected. Typically, it is they who must rush their children, to see they are dressed, fed and off to day care or school in time to get to work themselves. Thus, mothers are the villains in a process in which they are also the primary victims. Children come to resent their mothers' "hurrying" them, and sometimes rebel. More than the longer hours and the lack of sleep, their children's resentment is the saddest cost to women of the "second shift."

Source: Adapted from Hochschild and Machung, 1989.

FIGURE 10.2   Trends in Dual-Earner and Single-Earner Families with Young Children, Canada, 1976–1999

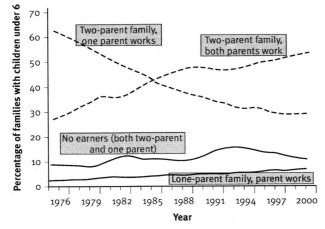

Note: Due to data collection problems, data for 2000 have been omitted.
Source: Labour Force Survey, Public-Use Micro-File; http://socialunion.gc.ca/ecd/2002/b-3.htm.

us in the direction of gender equality in the family or the workplace" (Coltrane and Smith, 1997:345).

Influences on the Division of Domestic Work There are four broad influences on the division of domestic or household work between husbands and wives: traditional role definitions, the stage of the family life cycle, social class differences, and the policies of companies and of nation states.

Traditional Attitudes toward Roles Usher (1991) argues that traditional beliefs about gender roles continue to be supported by two factors: childhood socialization and expectations in many social institutions and organizations. For example, the influence of men's attitudes is seen in a study of the relationship between men's provider-role attitudes (their attitudes about who should support the family) and how much domestic work they actually did (Perry-Jenkins and Crouter, 1990). Based on open-ended interview and questionnaire data from both husbands and wives, the husbands who viewed their wives' incomes as supplementary were classified into three groups: main/secondary providers, ambivalent co-providers, and co-providers. Co-provider husbands acknowledged the importance of their wives' earnings for family well-being, while ambivalent co-provider husbands admitted being dependent on their wives' incomes but contradicted themselves when they talked about provider responsibility. It is no surprise that co-provider husbands did the most domestic work and that main/secondary husbands did the least domestic work. The differences in the figures for proportions of tasks were quite small, given that both spouses were working full time: co-provider husbands did 38 percent of the household tasks reported; ambivalent co-provider husbands did 34 percent, and main/secondary providers did 21 percent. Since both husbands and wives provided information on task performance, these figures are more reliable than data based on single-spouse responses.

For equitable sharing of housework, a change in gender role attitude is necessary in both partners. What are the conditions under which married men are most apt to participate in housework? Based on a recent study by Harpster and Monk-Turner (1998:57), there are four conditions:

- men agree that both partners should share the housework equally if both work full time;

- men are living with women who accept this belief;

- women believe that men are not responsible for being the primary family earner;

- women believe that they are not primarily responsible for housework and child care.

Table 10.4 shows that in 1998, women did 1.629 more hours of unpaid domestic work per day than did males (2.7 hours versus 4.4 hours). Although much of the data that researchers have analyzed in regard to equality of household division of labour is based on hours or time spent in various tasks, some researchers have raised questions about the adequacy of this measurement technique to reflect economic contributions (Ironmonger, 1994; Thoen, 1993). When hours of labour is replaced by the market value of the labour, male contribution is much more equal and sometimes greater. For example, if one were to compare an hour-long plumbing job done by the husband with the same

time unit of house cleaning by the wife, it is clear that in the Canadian marketplace a plumber would be paid at a much higher rate than housecleaners. So debate continues as to the correct and most fair way to compare male and female components of unpaid household labour.

Stage of Family Life Cycle The stage of family life influences domestic work performance, with wives spending less time in domestic work before and after the childbearing years, and husbands spending more time at the beginning and the end of their work careers (Rexroat and Shehan, 1987; Suitor, 1991). Canadian researchers also confirm the increased demands of parenthood: "Parents of younger children need more tangible assistance from their spouses, more practical assistance from friends, and child-care assistance from their employers" (Lee and Duxbury, 1998). Current research suggests that couples are changing employment and housework practices to enable equal division of labour, and intend to incorporate egalitarian ideas in their work choices. But recent studies show that traditional divisions of labour persist. Sanchez and Thomson (1997) found that "the contemporary marital struggles over fatherhood and motherhood seem negotiated principally through couples' choices about wives' employment" (766). The "parenthood effect" is still alive and well, with women's and men's labour allocations shifting toward traditional patterns after the birth of a child. This finding is consistent with multiple bodies of scholarship on the tenacity of domestic work inequality (Coltrane, 1990; Li and Currie, 1992, Lupri and Mills, 1987; Lupri, 1991).

Expectations about Division of Labour Typically, the marital satisfaction of both spouses is greater when the wife is employed, except when the husband has traditional marital role expectations. The mutual influence of who does housework and what people expect in this regard is seen in the Perry-Jenkins and Crouter (1990) study of men's provider-role attitudes. Both co-provider husbands who were highly involved in housework, and husbands who saw their wives as secondary providers and performed few household tasks, reported high levels of marital satisfaction. Men who were highly involved in housework but ambivalent about their wives' paid employment reported low marital satisfaction.

A recent study based on a representative sample of 1700 married couples revealed wives' satisfaction with

TABLE 10.4 Average Time Spent on Activities, by Sex

TYPE OF WORK	MALES (POPULATION[1])	FEMALES (POPULATION[1])
	Hours per day	
Paid work and related activities/unpaid work	7.8	7.8
Unpaid work	2.7	4.4
Household work and related activities	2.4	4.1
Cooking/washing up	0.4	1.1
Housecleaning and laundry	0.3	1.0
Maintenance and repair	0.2	0.1
Other household work	0.4	0.4
Shopping for goods and services	0.7	0.9
Primary child care	0.3	0.6
Civic and volunteer activities	0.3	0.4
Education and related activities	0.5	0.6
Sleep, meals, and other personal activities	10.2	10.6
Free time	6.0	5.6

1. The average number of hours per day spent on the activity for the entire population aged 15 years and over (whether or not the person reported the activity).

Source: Statistics Canada, General Social Survey, 1998. http://www.statcan.ca/english/Pgdb/famil36a.htm.

division of labour. The results showed that levels of satisfaction produced a curvilinear (U-shaped) pattern higher in the earlier and later years, and lower in the middle years (while there were young children at home and their total workload was much heavier than their husbands') (See Figure 10.3). Husbands' satisfaction did not show this changing (curvilinear) pattern. Satisfaction with the division of labour was more important in explaining both marital satisfaction and conflict than was age, educational attainment, or the wife's employment status (Suitor, 1991).

Based on such findings, McHale and Crouter (1992) described two character profiles of couple-partners with strongly negative feelings about their marriages. One profile is wives who have egalitarian sex-role attitudes but do most of the housework and child care. The second profile is husbands who have traditional attitudes but are heavily involved in house-

work and child care. The researchers found that the individuals who fit these profiles voiced more negative feelings about their marriages than did their spouses (who obviously were better off in terms of their expectations), and also more negative feelings than other husbands and wives. This is consistent with earlier research (Bernardo et al., 1987; Gilbert, 1988). Also, when husbands consider themselves inadequate as "breadwinners," there is an increase in depression and in marital conflict and negativity (Crowley, 1998).

It might be expected that increased stress would be experienced by wives who are dissatisfied with carrying a double burden, and by husbands who help with domestic work but feel they should not have to. Ross and Mirowsky (1990) found both of these expectations to be true. Husbands and wives who were both employed and who shared domestic work equally (about 11 percent) had the lowest amount of stress, as measured by

FIGURE 10.3 **Mean Total Hours in Work Week and Weekend Work for Parents Who Are Employed Full Time, by Stage in the Family Life Cycle**

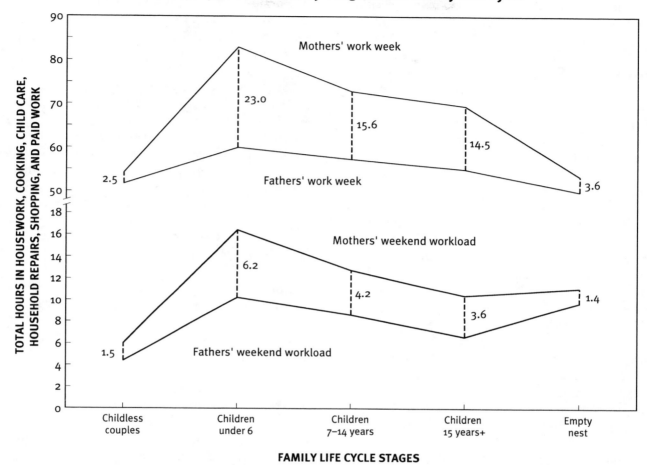

Source: Lupri, 1991: Figure 1.

depression scores. The scores of both partners were equally low, and both were lower than the scores of husbands and wives in traditional marriages where the wife stayed home. Thus, the stresses of two careers and tight family schedules can be minimized if husband and wife equally share the burdens of domestic and paid work. Husbands and wives may deal with potential stresses by working together companionably to minimize stress or by developing ways of coping with it (Krokoff, 1991).

Perceptions of Fairness How satisfied are women with the fairness of the domestic and paid-work sharing arrangements in their marriages? Women may be quite content with an (objectively) unfair sharing arrangement, if they value the outcome, if they compare their situations with those of others who seem worse off, or if they accept justifications for the existing arrangements (Thompson, 1991; Hawkins, Marshall and Allen, 1998). "(F)amily work is about more than getting tasks done: it is also a process by which we explore meanings of gender... there are important personal, interpersonal and familial outcomes dual-earner wives value from their family work, such as feeling appreciated and serving family members" (Hawkins, Marshall and Allen, 1998:256).

The most important factor in creating a sense of fairness for wives was communication from husbands, such as appreciation, sympathy, and mutual decision-making about allocation of tasks.

Vannoy and Philiber (1992) collected data from 452 dual-career households to show the interactions between role attitudes, employment status, and marital quality. The respondents' attitudes were more strongly predictive of their marital quality ratings than were the wives' employment status—and the single most important predictor was the ability to give and receive support.

Where both spouses have the same expectations, and where they each do as the other expects, the possibility of domestic work-related stress and conflict is minimized. Such couples avoid this source of destructive resentment, and their marital satisfaction tends to be high. Couples sharing common expectations with respect to paid and domestic work who cannot achieve these because of economic need or lack of job opportunities often experience frustration and tension, but they tend to agree about the problem, and how they will change things as soon as they can. In other marriages, a partner enjoying an unequal domestic-work arrangement may believe it is right, while the other partner believes it is wrong and feels exploited. This situation may threaten the marriage, especially if the "wronged" partner feels able to get a divorce.

Work–Family Spillover Tension in dual-income families is not only related to the attitudes of the husband and wife, but also to the fit between the marital-role attitudes of husband and wife and to the employment situations in which they find themselves. House et al.'s 1986 study of an American sample found the most stressful combination was a traditionally masculine man with a traditionally feminine wife who had to work to help provide family income.

Gilbert (1988) found that men who worked in environments hostile to their parenting responsibilities, and who were highly competitive and experienced high work demands, reported feeling more tension. Fathers in dual-income families were classified by Gilbert (1988) according to how much housework and child-care responsibility they shared, as traditional, participant (when the husband helped), or role-sharing (when domestic work was shared equally). While the role-sharing husbands typically said they were proud of their wives' employment, their attitudes were also sensitive to outside pressures. While they often wanted to support their wives' career aspirations and to be involved in parenting and household roles, they also wanted to have their own career interests put first.

The benefits from employment usually outweighed the costs for both husbands and wives in most dual-income families. However, satisfaction and dissatisfaction depended on conceptions of the husband and wife roles and degree of success in managing demands on time and effort. The satisfactions that mothers experienced also depended on their husbands' support for their household, maternal, and employee roles. Men's satisfactions depended on their evaluations of the inconveniences they experienced as a result of maternal employment, and the benefits of increased family income (Scarr et al., 1989).

Social Class Maids et al. (1988) looked at the social class differences between husbands and wives with respect to their participation in, their commitment to, and their valuation of home and family activities. Self-report data were obtained from 6000 Anglophone and Francophone workers of both sexes—professional and managerial, clerical and sales, skilled and unskilled. The data showed that while women always reported more participation, commitment, and valuation of home and family activities than men did, the differences were smallest for professional respondents. Managerial and professional men and women were thus more similar in their feelings and their participation in family activities than were people in lower-status occupations.

Policy Self-report data from husbands and wives in Canada, the United States, Sweden, and Norway, collected in the early 1980s, were used to determine whether the different family and work policies of these countries affected how women balanced domestic work and employment (Kalleberg and Rosenfeld, 1990). Only American wives were in the advantageous situation in which more hours of paid work were associated with the performance of less housework. Canadian mothers in the early 1980s appeared to have been the worst off, both in terms of flexible paid-work schedules and help from husbands at home.

Mother's and Father's Employment, Parenting, and Health

Societal Attitudes In important ways, Canadian and other Western societies are not very "child-friendly"—or "parent-friendly" either. Our societal indifference to the availability, adequacy, and affordability of good day care, even though a majority of mothers of preschoolers are now employed, is an example of this. Parents are "on their own" when it comes to working out many provisions for their children, including day care.

While there has been growing societal support for women's participation in the workplace, there has been less support for paid employment for mothers with small children. Gallup surveys found the proportion of Canadians who said the effects of mothers' employment are harmful for young children fell from 59 percent in 1973 to 48 percent in 1988, but increased to 53 percent in 1993 (Neale, 1993; Bozinoff and Turcotte, 1993).

Employment Experiences Studies show that the work situations of mothers and fathers affect their morale, self-confidence, and self-esteem (Kohn and Schooler, 1981), and that their psychological well-being affects their parenting behaviour. Parents with lower levels of self-esteem tend to rate their children's behaviour as negative and to be more punitive, controlling, and rejecting. Mothers who work under difficult conditions show less warmth toward their children, and are more rejecting and punitive (Menaghan and Parcel, 1991; MacEwen and Barling, 1991). Negative work experiences may lower parents' ability to tolerate their children's behaviour. Lowered self-esteem may also cause parents to be more aware of their children's "bad" behaviours and less aware when they are "good," leading to more control and punishment of the child (MacEwen and Barling, 1991). Fathers' parenting behaviour appears to be more vulnerable to these influences than do mothers' (Grimm et al., 1992). The reason may be that men's self-concepts are more influenced by their employment experience than are women's. Grimm et al. argue that employment conditions are increasingly problematic for fathers, while mothers must increasingly obtain full-time employment to fulfill financial obligations. This combination, it is argued, may have increasingly harmful consequences

for their children. Indeed, a father's job insecurity and history of layoffs may affect his children's work beliefs and attitudes. One study found that when a child identified strongly with the father, the father's job insecurity was associated with negative work attitudes and beliefs in the child. This effect was not apparent when the child's identification with the father was low, and was not associated at all with the mother's work history (Barling, Dupre, and Hepburn, 1998).

Employment experience may also benefit parenting relationships. One study found that some workers who learned problem-solving skills on the job made use of these skills in family discussions. Their relationships with their children became more democratic as they came to increasingly value their children's self-direction and problem solving (Crouter, 1984).

Stress and Health Issues Findings examining the relationship between employment and the health and well-being of women have been as inconsistent as women's situations are varied. Many factors have been identified as important, such as the presence of children, type of position, whether the woman wants to work, and level of income.

Feminists emphasize that the stress experienced by employed wives has two distinct sources. The most obvious is *cumulating*—the fact that millions of wives work full time *and* do almost all the domestic work. In addition, there is the *reconciliation* requirement—the need women experience "not only to perform double work but to perform each job well," so that "notwithstanding her paid employment, a woman must be a good housewife, and vice versa" (de Koninck, 1991:239). De Koninck argues that for the vast majority of women, the quantity and quality of work demanded of them is simply beyond their capacities (1991). She maintains this is a hazard to women's health, reflected in the frequency of women's use of medical services and prescription drugs, their fatigue, and their premature aging.

Clearly, outside employment is good for many wives, irrespective of how much help they get from husbands with housework and child care. Studies have found that employed wives experience less depression (Ross and Mirowsky, 1990), commit fewer suicides (Cumming et al., 1975), and have less role strain and parental stress (Guelzow et al., 1991) as compared with stay-at-home housewives. The only group that deviates from this pattern is female executives. In a 1984 study, they were found to suffer more heart attacks, ulcers, and high blood pressure than did their male counterparts (cited in Orr et al., 1985).

A group of researchers recently studied the indirect effects of occupational conditions upon physical health through four interrelated factors: social integration, marital integration, sense of control, and health-risk behaviours (Wickrama, Lorenz, Conger and Matthews, 1997) (See Figure 10.4.) The researchers used an index for health-risk behaviours to measure sleeping and eating habits, exercise, drinking, smoking, and drug use. They found that "occupational quality significantly predicts social integration, marital integration and sense of control for both husbands and wives" and "sense of control significantly reduces health-risk behaviours for both husbands and wives... all these relationships are stronger for husbands than for wives" (1997:369). While social and marital integration were direct deterrents to husbands' health-risk behaviours, only social integration deterred similar behaviours in wives. Thus, the mediating effect of marriage quality was stronger for men than for women, reinforcing earlier research findings that suggest men benefit more from marriage than do women.

Marital Relationships and Work

The wife's employment affects husband–wife relationships for many reasons, but particularly because of the increased power a wife gains with her paycheque. Her cheque reduces her dependence on her husband for support, and her contribution to family income may give her greater influence in decision-making. We note the higher stress levels for such **dual work couples**, and these pressures may result in quiet resentment or ongoing disagreements over who should do which domestic chores. This may lead to heightened conflict—the changing power balance, the strains and disagreements that working spouses feel—with costly consequences with regard to marital satisfaction and marital adjustment.

Figure 10.4   **Model of Relationship between Occupational Quality and Poor Physical Health**

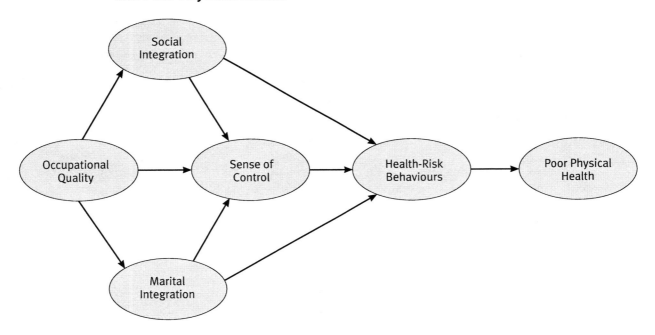

Source: Wickrama et al., 1997.

The Power of Working Wives

"The greater the resources of a wife the more her power" (Pool, 1978:41). Pool's study found that Canadian farm wives who did not have a paying job but who worked on the farm had more influence on family decision-making than did urban women. Among the latter, wives who were employed had more influence than those who were not. This early study showed that wives who made a significant work contribution could influence decision-making even though they did not bring in a paycheque.

Instrumental and Expressive Exchange

Scanzoni (1972), famous for his studies of the changing family, distinguishes between "instrumental role" (concerned with family-support responsibility) and "expressive role" (concerned with family relationships). While the husband's and the wife's roles both involve instrumental and expressive aspects, traditionally the husband's is the more instrumental, and the wife's the more expressive.

The basis of Scanzoni's model in exchange theory is obvious from the diagrams in Figures 10.5A and 10.5B. The better the husband supports his family, the better the wife will do her instrumental domestic work, and the more expressive, grateful, and loving she will be toward her husband. As a result, he will be more expressive and loving toward her, and will then want to provide better support. However, this tends to change, Scanzoni argues, when the husband and wife are both working full time; they may then become co-providers, and equal partners in the relationship. The instrumental and the expressive aspects of the husband's and the wife's roles should become virtually identical. The dynamic of the relationship does not start with the husband's instrumental input, as in the junior-partner pattern, but is influenced by the instrumental occupational behaviours of both wife and husband.

Explanation of Scanzoni's Model

In Scanzoni's (1972) model (see Figures 10.5A and 10.5B), Wd refers to the husband's instrumental duties and Wr to his instrumental rights, and Yd refers to his expressive duties and Yr to his expressive rights. Similarly, Xd and Xr refer to the wife's instrumental rights and duties, and Zd and Zr to her expressive duties and rights.

In junior-partner marriages, the starting point is the effectiveness of the husband's (instrumental) work performance, the line Wd (husband's duty) to Xr (wife's right). If he supports the family well, his wife will be motivated to perform her (instrumental) housekeeping role well (line Xd to Wr). But she will also be more (expressively) appreciative and loving toward him (line Zd to Yr) which will make him more appreciative and loving toward her (Yd to Zr). These feelings will also cause him to work harder (line Y to W) to better support the family, and this in turn will make the wife want to be an even better housewife, and yet more loving toward him. Here, there are two little loops—Wd to Xr, Xd to Wr, and Zd to Yr, Yd to Zr—together with the big loop—W to X to Z to Y—which may cause their relationship to improve, to spiral up. But their relationship may also spiral down: His employment failures may lead to careless housekeeping and cooling affections from her, causing him to cool more toward her and to have less motivation, and fail more at work, leading to increased slovenliness and coolness on the part of the wife, and so on.

As Figure 10.5B shows, in the equal-partner relationship, the roles of husband and wife are analytically identical. In respect to instrumental behaviours, both have duties and rights (lines Wd to Xr and Xd to Wr) and both have occupational and domestic work obligations, though the couple has to decide how to allocate domestic work through negotiation. Likewise, in respect to expressive behaviours, both again have duties and rights (lines Yd to Zr and Zd to Wr) toward each other. Finally, for both husband and wife, the more satisfactorily each performs instrumental obligations, the more positively expressive is the other (the lines W to Y and X to Z). The more positively expressive each feels, the more motivated each is to perform instrumental activities (lines Y to W and Z to X) (Scanzoni, 1972).

Scanzoni assumes that the praiseworthy occupational achievements of either one will elicit more loving responsiveness from the other, and that this will stimulate a more loving response from the first. These feelings, in turn, will motivate a yet more productive (instrumental) work effort. In this relationship, the differences between the husband and wife roles in the junior-partner model simply disappear.

Recently, Sabatelli (1992) found that both husbands and wives reported lower expressive (emotional, nurturant, and affectionate behaviour) levels in families where the wife was employed than in families where she was not. This suggests that, currently at least, a couple's expressive relationship may suffer somewhat when wives are employed.

The Income Factor For women to effectively insist that their husbands do half of the "dirty work,"

they must have power, because few men are willing to do this voluntarily. Her power is reflected in her ability to induce more fair domestic work sharing and to influence family geographical moves to favour her career interests, rather than his career prospects (Scanzoni, 1978). Several recent Canadian studies bear out the validity of this analysis. Harrell (1985), using data from

FIGURE 10.5   A) Marital Interaction in Junior-Partner and Equal-Partner Marriages

Figure A Traditional roles: Husband as provider and wife as junior partner

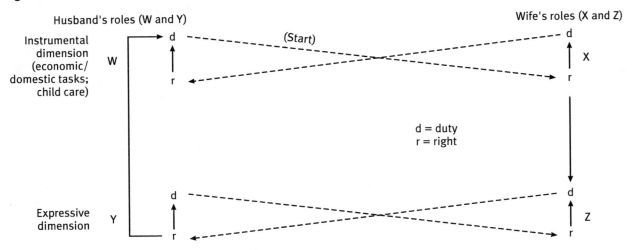

Figure 10.5   B) Marital Interaction in Junior-Partner and Equal-Partner Marriages

Figure B Egalitarian roles: Husband and wife enter as co-providers

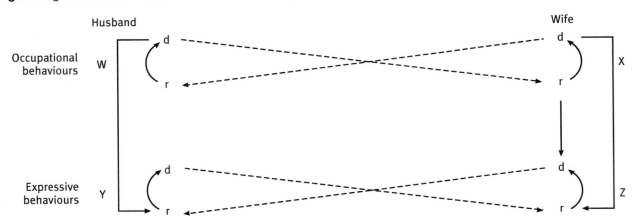

Source: Adapted from Scanzoni, 1972:63, 141.

a random sample of 138 husbands in dual-career households in Edmonton, identified characteristics associated with sharing domestic work. As Scanzoni would predict, the greater the wife's contribution to family income, the more husbands helped out. These more helpful men also had nontraditional views of masculinity, and felt there was little conflict between their work and family life. "Traditionally masculine" men helped out less and reported more conflict between work and home life. Ross and Mirowsky's U.S. research (1990) found that the higher the wife's earnings, the more husbands helped in the home, but the more the husband's own earnings exceeded the wife's, the less the husbands helped in the home.

Marital Quality

In this section, we do not differentiate between marital quality and marital satisfaction, though both terms are used in the research literature we cite. The reason, as noted in Chapter 9, is that the measures used for each have proved to be so similar statistically that "satisfaction," together with "happiness" and "adjustment," are understood to be aspects of marital quality. Most of the research on the effect of wives' employment on marital quality is from the U.S. This research shows that the marital satisfaction and marital conflict experienced by dual-income couples depends on the following: 1) the amount of domestic work that the wife and husband actually perform, 2) their expectations about how much each should perform, and 3) the extent to which they agree on these expectations. Earlier, we discussed the amount of domestic work done; the following section emphasizes research on the expectations of husbands and wives, and the extent to which there is agreement between spouses concerning these expectations.

Marriage and Careers

Career Success

Career Paths and Gender Differences
A British study suggests that men and women are affected differently by factors that influence career success. "When the profile of factors that explain men's career success was applied to women, there was a decrease of about 75 percent in the explained variance of women's career success. Similar figures were found when a female-specific model of career success was applied to men" (Melamed, 1996:237). Two of Melamed's findings in particular are pertinent to our discussion of careers in the context of marriage and family. The first finding is that married men generally earn higher salaries than single men, leading Melamed to conclude that family responsibilities have a positive impact on men's careers by providing a supportive environment and by reinforcing societal gender expectations that the man will act as provider for the family. While previous research suggests that marriage and family responsibilities interfere with women's career advancement, this study found no significant difference between men and women.

The second finding concerns gender distribution within industries. "Men who worked in prosperous industries that offer good salaries and good salary progress opportunities were far more successful than men who worked in less prosperous industries. Women, on the other hand, hardly benefited from such opportunities" (Melamed, 1996:238). Industries with traditionally high female participation, such as service industries, often offer policies regarding work schedules, child care, and breaks in employment that are attractive to women. "Hence, women were more likely to progress in lower paying industries; moreover women also gravitate to these industries as they provide policies that are sensitive to their career paths" (Melamed, 1996:239).

Farber (1996) used a case study approach to investigate the contribution that relational aspects of marriage and family life make to a woman's career development. She considers it necessary to understand individual characteristics, current family interactions, and intergenerational forces that combine to influence a woman's career potential.

Men and women share a common benefit of achieving career aspirations, experiencing lower levels of depression and higher self-esteem than those who do not. While the pressures of blending career and family demands do effect women's health, "paid work may also represent a sense of accomplishment and achievement for women, thereby providing a source of positive mental health at midlife" (Carr, 1997:340).

Meaning and Choices Interviews with a sample of 153 New England wives provided some insight into the meanings of employment for working wives (Potuchek, 1992). The researcher measured three dimensions of attitudes relating to a wife's employment: 1) the importance of her earnings to the family (family support); 2) the importance of her job to the family (job centrality); and 3) the beliefs about who should be the family's financial provider (norms). A high score on financial support meant that the wife believed the family financially needed her earnings. A high score on job centrality meant the wife felt that holding a job was important to herself. A high score on norms meant that the wife believed she should be a family provider. Various combinations of high-low scores on these attitude dimensions suggested there were eight different employment orientations among these wives. The most common type, found among 21 percent of the sample, was **employed homemakers**—housewives who also happened to be employed. They scored low on all three dimensions: financial support, job centrality, and norms. At the opposite extreme were **co-breadwinners**, who scored high on all three dimensions, showing they were as strongly committed to employment as were their husbands (15 percent). Helpers believed that their earnings were financially needed, but that it was not important for them to have a job, and that husbands should be responsible for family support (19 percent).

Women are more apt to work part time than are men. One in four Canadian women works part time, and almost one in three (30 percent) with preschool children works part time (Marshall, 1994; Statistics Canada, 1994a). In 1994 women accounted for 69 percent of the part-time workers in Canada. However, women were not necessarily employed part time by choice. Some 34 percent of woman employed part time said that they would prefer to be working full time (Women in Canada, 1995). The benefits or problems associated with part-time employment have been argued in research. Duffy and Pupo (1993) relate part-time employment to ghettoization, pay inequities, and economic discrimination against women. In contrast many women choose to work part time in order to be able to give more time to their families and to reduce their own level of stress (Fast and Frederick, 1996). Marshall found that a high proportion of mothers

chose to have modified work arrangements. "For example 95 percent of childless women in managerial and professional occupations work full time, compared with 68 percent of women in similar jobs who have preschoolers" (1994:30). Women with children were also found to work more "flex" hours than women without children.

Smith studied the meanings people attach to spouse, parent and worker roles. She found that men and women show gender differences in meaning, reflecting their perception of the costs and benefits associated with a role. Both men and women described positive meanings for their employment role. However, women talked about a negative meaning that men did not mention—that the employment role prevents them from being available to their spouse and children. "(T)his meaning of the work identity for women was accompanied by feelings of inadequacy (as wives and mothers) and guilt and is associated with significantly higher levels of distress" (Smith, 1997:264). Other researchers advocate a further emphasis on personal meaning and identity, stating that the concept of "social role" "fails to give sufficient attention to the political and social nature of the struggle involved in the redefinition of roles" (Clark, Chandler, and Barry, 1996:73)

Future Directions

Research

Barnett (1998) criticizes research in the work and family field by identifying four biases in the current literature: a strong emphasis on conflict, studies done on all-female samples, cross-sectional rather than longitudinal studies, and self-report data. She suggests an "inclusive model for studying work/social system issues" (155). Contextual factors, such as intergenerational effects, social structure, occupational health effects on families, and within-couple effects would be included. Other researchers agree that contextual factors such as these are important in understanding the complex interactions that link social structure, family members and family life, and the stress process (Ali and Avison, 1997; Bowen, 1998).

Recently, health researchers have criticized the division of women's labour into simple categories of paid and unpaid work, because of the complexity and multidimensional nature of women's work. They suggest using time–budget measures that would take into account work performed inside and outside the home, and include women's personal values. "The degree to which the work women do is valued (on the personal, familial and societal levels) may be reflected in the meanings they themselves attribute to their roles and their work at home and in the community" (Messias et al., 1997:313).

Vandenheuvel (1997) investigated women's roles after having a child, and found that a large proportion of women moved in and out of the workplace, following a "mosaic of role sequences" (366). The traditional research approach categorizes women's life course patterns into two groups: labour force participation primary (career track) and family primary (family track). Vandenheuvel found this categorization inaccurate, and recommends a more dynamic conceptualization of women's participation in the labour force.

Remedial Programs and Policies

The Canadian employment picture is now dominated by workers who shoulder major family responsibilities (Lee and Duxbury, 1998). The burdens and costs of female employment at current levels are often excessive, especially for working mothers, in terms of the well-being of the mothers themselves, their children's well-being, and their partner relationships. Many aspects of the employment relationship—including, for example, pension coverage—come into play as women enter the labour force earlier and actively participate longer (Farkas and O'Rand, 1998).

A major need, in the case of married mothers, is for husbands to be unreservedly committed to equal sharing of the double burden. The obstacles to this, even for men committed to egalitarianism, are great; but some significant progress is being made. Ideally, a shortened workday with protections against lost advancement opportunities would permit one parent to always be home with a preschool child, and would help reduce stress and facilitate the sharing of domestic chores.

Of prime importance to all families is the need for Canadian society to value childbearing and parenting enough to invest more heavily in these societal-reproduction activities, as feminists repeatedly emphasize (Maroney and Luxton, 1987). At least three

important measures are required. The first two involve actions by the state, which must provide more adequate maternity or paternity leave, and more and high-quality day care, following patterns already well-established in Europe (Heitlinger, 1987). More adequate maternity and paternity leave provisions will lighten the financial burdens of childbearing on the poor, facilitate better physical and psychological recuperation of new mothers, and result in better care for infants during their first few months. Glass and Riley (1998) found that the length of time available for leave of absence was the most important policy determining whether a woman returns to work after childbirth, along with the policy regarding mandatory overtime, and social support from supervisors and co-workers.

The third and more basic need is for society, and especially employers, to commit to safeguarding the well-being of new mothers, so that these women are spared from paying for their pregnancies through the loss of employment, seniority, or advancement. Such a commitment would necessitate a greater willingness to experiment with various work arrangements. There also need to be changes in the "organizational culture" regarding family demands in general, such as policies concerning family-responsibility leaves. It is also essential that employers encourage their employees to take advantage of these benefits (Lee and Duxbury, 1998). Organizational leaders, often themselves in traditional family structures, need to recognize different family structures and to actively reduce the disadvantages that dual-career families face (Burke, 1997).

Critics might ask, "Can we afford to do this?" Some of us would respond, "In view of the now-apparent costs to families, can we afford not to?"

SUMMARY

- Despite the employment of a large number of women during the First World War, the Great Depression, and the Second World War, a permanent increase in women's participation in the labour force did not begin until the 1950s. The factors that influence a woman's decision to seek paid employment include her age, her marital status, the age of her children, her education, and the family's financial need.

- The rise in the female participation rate can be attributed to the increase in the number of women available for work, the higher educational achievements of women, increased job opportunities for women, increased financial need, and changing attitudes.

- Despite today's high female participation rate, women continue to face gender-based discrimination in the form of occupational sex segregation, gender segregation within occupations, pay inequality, sexual harassment, and restricted occupational mobility. Women in dual-earner marriages face additional problems at home.

- Many men claim to help with the housework, but do very little. However, there are an increasing number of equal-partner relationships, particularly among young working couples, where husbands and wives share housework and child care equally. These tend to be relationships high in quality, satisfaction, and companionability. Marriages between working feminist wives and traditional husbands are often conflict-ridden.

- Five broad influences that affect the division of household work between husbands and wives are as follows: 1) traditional attitudes defining marital roles; 2) the arrival of children; 3) social class differences; 4) the policies of companies and of nation-states; and 5) stage of the family life cycle.

- Having a child may reduce a woman's career advancement and increase her "double burden," because women are raised to see child care as their responsibility; in taking this responsibility more seriously than do men, they become involved in a more traditional role. Even men who share child care with their wives do not share equally. After childbirth, wives' total domestic-plus-employment work hours per week often double in comparison with the increase their husbands experience.

- Fully employed wives experience a transition from the role of "junior partner" to that of "equal partner," with rights and duties similar to those of their husbands. The greater a woman's income, the greater her power in her marriage, and the more her husband helps with the domestic work.

- How fair a wife feels the domestic work-sharing is depends on many influences. There is no consistent evidence that employed wives experience more stress-related symptoms than do those who are not employed, but there may be heightened conflict over the sharing of domestic work in dual-income families.

- Low marital quality and marital satisfaction are often associated with contradictions between the preferences of husbands and wives respecting the wife's employment, and the wife's actual practice.

- Employment under working conditions that are unpleasant may result in harmful parenting behaviours by workers. On the other hand, workers who learn democratic relationship techniques on the job may experience improved parenting skills at home.

KEY TERMS

Co-breadwinner (238)
Double burden (219)
Dual work couples (234)
Employed homemaker (238)
Female participation rate (221)
Gender segregation within occupations (224)
Occupational gender segregation (223)
Sexual harassment (225)

QUESTIONS FOR REVIEW

1. What circumstances contributed to the growth of the perception that men were "breadwinners" and women were "homemakers"?

2. During the past 100 years, when has the labour force participation rate of women been high and when has it been low?

3. Discuss the general factors responsible for the rapid rate of increase in women's employment in Canada in recent decades.

4. What advantages has the increased employment of women brought to wives and husbands? What disadvantages has it brought to each?

5. Describe five forms of gender-based inequality that women face in the labour market today, and how they are used.

6. Evaluate the argument that Canada is denying some women access to employment opportunities. Which women are affected, and how is access being denied to them?

7. What factors influence the effects of wives' employment on marital quality, and on their marital satisfaction and that of their husbands?

QUESTIONS FOR DISCUSSION

1. "A man works from sun to sun, but a woman's work is never done." Evaluate the past and current relevance of this statement for Canadian women.

2. Assess whether the condition of working women in each of the following categories has become better, or

worse, during the past 50 years: a) single women; b) wives with elementary school education; c) university-educated wives; d) lone mothers.

3. Discuss the costs and burdens of women's employment—who pays the most? Be as specific as you can, giving the reasons why you think so.

4. Who gains most from the current employment situation of women in Canada? Why do you think so?

5. What are the circumstances of women today who are experiencing the best and the worst lifestyles—in terms of employment, marriage, motherhood, and so on?

6. Evaluate the argument that the family and work situations of Canadian wives today give them the worst of both worlds and their husbands the best of both worlds.

7. Evaluate the adjustment that Canadian society has made to accommodate high levels of female employment, and discuss whether children have been victims or beneficiaries of these adjustments. What evidence is there to support your position?

8. In view of the evidence presented in this chapter, how do you think the marital quality that your generation will experience will compare with the marital quality of your parents' generation? Why do you think so? What do you think the marital quality of your children's generation will be like?

9. What legislation, programs, or policies (if any) do you think should be enacted or adopted to help families better deal with the high rates of maternal employment

and to improve the well-being of women and their families?

SUGGESTED READINGS

Hattery, Angela. 2000. *Women, Work, and Families: Balancing and Weaving.* Thousand Oaks, CA: Sage Publications. The author uses 30 qualitative interviews in this attempt to understand how women balance family and work.

Hochschild, Arlie, and Anne Machung. 1989. *The Second Shift: Working Parents and the Revolution at Home.* New York: Viking Press. This well-researched study focuses on the problems experienced by American dual-earner couples, particularly the wives. It includes eight case studies, as well as a review of the research literature.

Kofodimos, J. 1993. *Balancing Act: How Managers Can Integrate Successful Careers and Fulfilling Personal Lives.* San Francisco: Jossey-Bass. Finding balance means recognizing assumptions about external criteria of success and coming to a personal definition of what success means. "Mastery orientation" is discussed, including rewards and pitfalls to personal life.

Wilson, Sue J. 1991. *Women, Families and Work.* Toronto: McGraw-Hill Ryerson. This is a well-documented account of the historical roots and current patterns of female employment in Canada from a feminist perspective. Wilson emphasizes the influence female employment has had on the women's movement.

CHAPTER 11

Parenthood, Parent–Child Relationships, and Socialization

After studying this chapter, you should be able to do the following:

- Explain the differences between involuntary childlessness and intentional childlessness.
- Provide an accurate overview of the family situation of children in Canada.
- Explain the major issues in the transition to parenthood, and how the experiences of mothers and fathers differ.
- Identify the characteristics of fathers actually involved in the care of their infant children.
- Describe the paid work situation of young mothers with preschool children.
- Summarize the recent research on the impact of non-parental care on infants under one year of age.
- Describe the different approaches and styles of parenting.
- Summarize the basic effects of parenting on child development.
- Identify the basic characteristics of the parent–adolescent connection.
- Summarize the basic effects of parenting on adolescent attitudes and behaviours.
- Identify the patterns of leaving home, staying at home, and returning to the home among adolescents and young adults.

Introduction

Conception, birth, and parenthood are essential to the survival of every society. When most of us think about having children, however, we don't think of societal survival. Most of us just have children. Research documents that 85 to 90 percent of Canadians are happy with family life (Angus Reid, 1994; Bibby, 1995). A national study by Angus Reid conducted in Canada in 1994 found that 92 percent of parents said that having children has "made me a happier person"—only 3 percent disagreed. About 43 percent of parents considered themselves to be better parents than their parents were, while 33 percent considered their own parents to

have done a better job than they were doing. Eighty percent had good memories of their childhood, and 77 percent said that they had a happy childhood. Even so, 28 percent admitted to having a lot of conflict in their families while growing up.

Despite the evidence that suggests parents are "happy" with parenting, there is also evidence that suggests that parenthood is economically expensive and holds many stressful transitions for both parents and children (e.g., Feeney et al., 2002). In Chapter 14 we review the toll that such stress takes on some families in the form of child and spouse abuse.

In this chapter, we examine why some people choose to have children and others do not (voluntary childlessness). We examine recent demographic and fertility data on children and parents; attitudes and behaviours associated with conception, pregnancy and the birthing of children; the transition to parenthood; parenthood during infancy and early childhood; the connections between parenting and both child development and adolescent development; parental disciplinary techniques and their effects on children; the effects of children and adolescents on parents; and recent evidence on the not-so-empty family nest. Recently, there has been much discussion about gay and lesbian families and parenting. The material in this chapter applies equally well to such families, as the topic of parenting cross-cuts many of the distinctions about family diversity. Indeed, raising children is both a joy and challenge for all types of families.

Childlessness

Involuntary Childlessness

Not all couples who want to are able to have children. **Involuntary childlessness** (Matthews and Martin-Matthews, 1986) refers to couples who have not conceived but have had unprotected sexual intercourse for at least 12 months and have never had a sterilizing operation (cf., United States National Center for Health Statistics, 1982). Based on this definition, U.S. authorities estimate that one in 10 married couples are infertile (1982:1–3). Matthews and Martin-Matthews (1986) point out that the transition to non-parenthood is a difficult experience.

The quest for medical solutions to involuntary childlessness often involves in-depth infertility investigations, innovative drug therapies, and various reproductive technologies including artificial insemination, in vitro fertilization (IVF), or embryo transplants.

Traditional artificial insemination involves the collection of sperm from the husband and implantation of the sperm in the wife's uterus. Alternatively, a married woman and her infertile husband may make application to a sperm bank. (Unmarried single women may also make application for sperm bank services.) The Nobel Sperm Bank in Southern California collects sperm from men of high intelligence and achievement, and couples approved for insemination are not charged a fee. By the fall of 1991, 146 children had been conceived based on impregnations from donors to this sperm bank (*Inside Edition*, 1992). However, most couples do not have access to such services. A Canadian study by Miall (1993) found that most females disapproved of surrogate motherhood (67 percent) as did a majority of men (53 percent). (It is likely, however, that most people would support surrogacy between close friends, as illustrated in Box 11.1.) The number of such births is unknown.

In vitro fertilization (IVF) involves taking eggs from a woman's ovaries, fertilizing them in a petri dish (or test tube) with the sperm from her husband (or another donor), and re-implanting the fertilized eggs in her uterus. So far, approximately 5000 infants have been birthed worldwide through in vitro fertilization, despite only a one-in-10 success rate (Klein, 1989, as reported in Williams, 1992). Between 1975 and 1978, Ontario spent more than $7 million in direct funding to IVF clinics. By the end of 1987, only 207 babies had been born to 130 couples, at a cost of $35 000 per baby (Pappert, 1989, as referred to in a report of the Canadian

---

Box 11.1   Current Issues: Custom-Made by Surrogate

Patti McKern, a close friend of Tina Steward, gave the ultimate gift to her friend: a newborn baby girl. Stewart has diabetes and cannot carry a child. Doctors told Stewart, who had suffered from the age of six with diabetes, that she would go blind and lose 10 to 15 years off her life if she were to carry a child and give birth. Over lunch one day, McKern asked Steward whether she'd ever considered having another woman carry her baby. Doctors took one of Tina's eggs, fertilized it with sperm from her husband and implanted the fertilized egg in McKern's womb. Both sets of parents were present at the implantation. Nine months later, both couples were present in the delivery room. *Comment: In this case, there was no exchange of money. This was merely the gift of a womb for nine months for a friend.*

Source: The Associated Press, 1996.

Advisory Council on the Status of Women, 1991). Bryant (1990) reviewed the new reproductive technologies and concluded that the success rates were too low and the techniques too experimental. She recommended other, less costly programs. The Canadian Advisory Council on the Status of Women funded Bryant's study, and the report, released in 1991, reflects significant reservations about the implications of such technologies for the rights of women:

> In vitro fertilization (IVF), embryo transfer (ET), embryo lavage, gamete intrafallopian transfer (GIFT), and alternative fertilization by donor destabilize the relation between genetic and social parenthood. On the one hand, conceptive technologies may be used to link genetic and social parenthood in ways previously impossible for many infertile women and men. On the other hand, the technologies make it technically feasible to draw a set of new social distinctions: ovum donor, gestational mother, social mother, sperm donor/genetic father, social father. Consequently, a renegotiation of the meanings of maternity and paternity is taking place in the mass media, in our legal system, and in the lives of those affected by the New Reproduction Technologies. (Canadian Advisory Council on the Status of Women, 1991:5).

Canadian research shows that the majority of men and women approve of all these reproductive technologies (Miall, 1993). However, the majority disapprove of surrogate motherhood or surrogacy with a donor embryo. The Miall study also examined attitudes about who should have access to reproductive technologies. Over 90 percent supported access for married couples. In contrast, 72 percent of the men and only 51 percent of the women thought that common-law couples should have access. The majority believed that lesbian and homosexual couples should not have the right to use such technologies.

In a recent Canadian qualitative study of 16 childless couples using IVF technology (Williams, 1992), 13 couples were also simultaneously pursuing the adoption of a child. Williams found that both spouses saw adoption as a last resort, but that wives were much more willing than husbands to consider adoption. The majority of these couples followed what Daly (1986, as cited by Williams, 1992) called the concurrent pattern—trying reproductive technologies while also pursuing adoption. The other three couples followed the *sequential pattern* (Daly, 1986)—exhausting all the technologies before considering adoption. Lipman

(1984) reported that adoptable, healthy, North American-born, newborn children are in short supply in Canada. A similar problem also exists in the United States (Bachrach, 1983). Infertile couples seem to have a strong need to obtain a child of their own.

Daly and Sobol (1992:1994) have analyzed data provided by the adoption coordinators for each of the 10 provinces and the two territories. In 1981, about 3500 infants under one year of age were adopted in Canada, 78 percent through *public* agencies. These infants represented 65 percent of all adoptions in 1981. In 1990, about 1700 infants were adopted, or 60 percent of all adoptions in that year. In contrast with 1981, 59 percent of the adoptions in 1990 were obtained through *private* agencies. These data indicate that there has been a 75-percent decrease in public infant adoptions over the decade, and a sharp increase in private adoptions, out of necessity due to the unavailability of infants.

The demand for adoptable children has varied over the decade. Based on data for seven provinces, the number of applicants for adoptable children was about the same in 1982 and 1990 (more than 9000). Only 30 percent of these applicants were successful in obtaining a child. There is an apparent continuing demand for adoptable children among infertile couples, but a decreasing supply of infants. This is largely due to the fact that more young single women are choosing to keep their babies at birth—an increase from 46 percent in 1981 to 60 percent in 1989. Further, although there has been a decrease in the number of young women choosing an abortion—49 percent in 1981, down to 38 percent in 1989—the choice to have an abortion continues to reduce the population of children available for adoption (Daly and Sobol, 1994:496).

Voluntary Childlessness

Not all couples who *can* have children *want* to have children. **Voluntary childlessness** refers to those couples who initially choose not to have children at all, and who take the steps necessary to preclude pregnancy or childbirth. Some of these couples may eventually change their minds as circumstances change.

Postponed parenthood, in contrast, refers to those who simply choose to have children later. Postponed parenthood is the concept typically used by researchers to describe women who give birth after the age of 30. This view of postponement, however, is influenced by many factors, including the pursuit of higher education, cohabitation, and delayed marriage, as well as the choice to put off parenthood after marriage. In 1980, 31 percent of all married women giving birth were 20 to 24 years of age. In 1990, in contrast, 16.5 percent, or nearly half as many married women in this age cohort, gave birth. There was, however, a small upward trend in 1995—20.5 percent. The percentage of women giving birth at 30 to 34 years of age increased from 20 percent in 1980, to 30 percent in 1990, to 35 percent in 1995. The change was even more dramatic among women 35 or older—5 percent of this group of women gave birth in 1980, compared to 9 percent in 1990, and 12 percent in 1995—a 260-percent increase between 1980 and 1995. This evidence seems to support the postponement hypothesis.

Intentional childlessness (several scholars simply use the term *voluntary childlessness*) is a *committed* choice not to have children. This lifestyle choice is much more widely studied than is postponed parenthood, although there is clearly overlap between the two concepts. A 1980 survey in Quebec indicated that one in 10 couples married between 1971 and 1975 intended to remain childless (Romaniuc, 1984:33). Bloom (1986, as reported in Rao and Balakrishnan, 1988), a demographic researcher in the United States, predicts that childlessness will level off at about 16 in 100 couples. Childless patterns in Canada may eventually be similar to those in the United States. Even so, child-bearing intentions may well be expected to change in future.

Fertility research, which often uses large random samples of the Canadian population and Canadian Census data, also examines childlessness. (The demographic indicator of childlessness is usually "still childless," or the proportion of women still childless in specific age cohorts.) Data from the national fertility survey conducted in 1984 showed that 16 percent of all married women were childless (Rao and Balakrishnan, 1988:188). Of those women married 10 to 14 years, 9 percent were still childless, compared with 4 percent among those married 15 or more years. Using sophisticated statistical procedures (*proportional hazards model analysis*), Rao and Balakrishnan found that

women who married at 22 years of age or later, and who lived in urban areas, obtained 14 or more years of education, had no more than one sibling, were employed, and were married for at least five years, were more likely to remain childless. The most powerful factor in the choice to be childless was the working status of married women. However, the researchers argue that improved child care and maternity leave services will encourage employed married women to have children. A more recent study, using the same database, found that women who attend church services less frequently are more likely to be voluntarily or temporarily childless (Vijaya, 1993).

The intention to remain childless, as well as the decision to postpone the decision, remain issues of concern and debate for Canadian women. Roskies and Carrier (1992) found that unwed, childless career women, aged 35 to 40, were twice as likely to be depressed as were their married colleagues with children (as reported by McGovern, 1993). Life satisfaction was lowest for never-married women; married women without children were more satisfied; and married women with children were the happiest.

A Profile of Canadian Children and Families

The purpose of this section is to examine the 1996 Census data, as well as recent vital statistics, on the characteristics of children and their families. We will also review recent Canadian research that will help explain our fertility attitudes and behaviours.

Demographic Patterns for Children and Youth: Census and Statistics Canada Data

Percentage of Canadian Population In 1994, children aged 0 to 14 years of age represented 20 percent of the Canadian population, while youth represented 14 percent (Canadian Council on Social Development, 1996). One-third of the population was under 25 years of age in 1991, compared to almost half of the population in 1966. The number of children under the age of 15 in 1966 was 6.6 million, *dropping* to 5.4 million by 1986, and then rebounding to 5.7 million in 1991. According to the 1996 Census, there were about 5.9 million children under the age of 15 living in Canada. The upturn is described as a *baby boom echo*, which is now influencing the percentage of children and youth entering the late 1990s (Kerr, Larrivée and Greenhalgh, 1994).

Living Arrangements of Children in Canada

In 1996, 82 percent of children under the age of 15 were living with both parents, and 16 percent were living with one parent. The remaining children (about 122 275, or 2 percent of all children under the age of 15) were living in other situations: with relatives other than one or both of their parents, with non-relatives such as foster parents or single persons, in orphanages, in hospitals or psychiatric institutions, in collective households (such as established by the Hutterites), or in families living outside Canada where their parents were primarily involved in diplomatic services. As indicated in Chapter 1, these living arrangements obviously change as children get older. Seventy-six percent of children 15 to 19 years of age, for example, were living in two-parent households in 1996, and 18 percent in one-parent households. A major shift begins in the early twenties. Young adults aged 20 to 24 are much less likely to still be living at home—43 percent live in two-parent family households, and 19 percent live in one-parent family households (Ross, Scott and Kelley, 1996: 29). While only 1.6 percent of 15- to 19-year-old teens live alone, almost 17 percent of 20- to 24-year-old young people are living alone.

Table 11.1, based on 2001 census data, shows that non-Aboriginal children under 15 years of age predominantly live with two parents (82.5 percent). Results from the first three waves of the National Longitudinal Survey of Children and Youth (1994–1998) suggest that close to 93 percent of these dual parent families include the children's biological parents. Indeed, since the middle of the 1990s we have accumulated data that supports the notion that despite the high divorce rate, children tend to live in relatively stable living arrangements with their biological parents. Table 11.1 also shows that Aboriginal children tend to live with both parents but less frequently than non-Aboriginal children (60.5 percent compared to 82.5 percent). Many more Aboriginal children live in lone parent families than non-Aboriginal children (35.4 percent compared to 16.9 percent).

Some caution is necessary in interpreting the data on child living arrangements. While there is little doubt that lone parent families tend to be more economically disadvantaged than dual parent families, there may be fewer differences in parenting than we would expect. For example, dual parents that both work full time may spend about the same amount of time with their children as working single parents (see Wood, 2003). Indeed, we must be vigilant not to attribute causation to family structure when it is the type of parenting that probably makes the difference to children.

Children's living arrangements vary somewhat by whether the family is rural, suburban, or urban. Table 11.2 shows that rural areas have the greatest number of children residing with two parents for both Aboriginal and non-Aboriginal children. Non-Aboriginal children's

TABLE 11.1   Living Arrangements of Non-Aboriginal and Aboriginal Children Under 15 Years of Age, Canada 2001

	NON-ABORIGINAL	ABORIGINAL
Living with two parents	82.5%	60.5%
Living with a lone parent	16.9%	35.4%
Other living arrangements	0.6%	4%

Source: www12.statcan.ca/English/census01/products/analytic/companion/abor/tables/total/livarrang.cfm#1.

TABLE 11.2 Living Arrangements of Non-Aboriginal and Aboriginal Children Under 15 Years of Age by Census Metropolitan Area (CMA), Urban Non-CMA, and Rural Area, Canada 2001

	NON-ABORIGINAL	ABORIGINAL
Urban CMA		
Living with two parents	81.4%	49.8%
Living with a lone parent	18%	45.6%
Other living arrangement	0.6%	4.6%
Urban non-CMA		
Living with two parents	79.5%	56.9%
Living with a lone parent	19.9%	39.6%
Other living arrangement	0.5%	3.5%
Rural (non-reserve)		
Living with two parents	88.5%	71.4%
Living with a lone parent	10.9%	23.3%
Other living arrangements	0.7%	5.3%

Source: www12.statcan.ca/English/census01/products/analytic/companion/abor/tables/total/livarrang.cfm#1.

living arrangements differ little between suburban (urban non-CMA) and urban (CMA); more Aboriginal children in urban areas reside in lone parent households than do those living in suburban areas.

Vital Statistics

Vital statistics data identify the experiences of individuals each year. Marriages, births, infant deaths, and multiple births are all examples of daily events that are recorded and reported on an annual basis. These events are recorded in each province and then shared with Statistics Canada to provide a yearly profile for Canada. These events are often studied as rates (the number of events per population). From these rates, demographers attempt to address basic questions such as "Is our country growing or shrinking?"

Population growth has long been computed as follows: (Births + Immigration) − (Deaths + Emigration) + Previous Year Population. There are many reasons

why we want to know this information. In general, a growing population offers a native supply of labour and consumers so that a country is less dependent on exporting manufactured goods and less dependent on importing people for labour. Of course the world is far more complex than this reasoning suggests, in terms of trained and skilled labour as well as trade agreements, but the population growth does afford a crude picture.

Table 11.3 shows that Canada has a significantly lower birth rate than does the United States. However, Canada's death rate is lower than the U.S. and it takes in almost double the number of immigrants that the U.S. accommodates. The result is that although the U.S. and other countries may rely on their rates of natural increase (births − deaths), Canada relies heavily on immigration for population growth. If we examine a country such as Sweden we see a very different picture. Sweden has more deaths than births each year. Without substantial immigration such a rate of natural increase would lead to population decline. Indeed, as

TABLE 11.3   Selected Vital Statistics Rates, 2003 (Estimates per 1000 population)

COUNTRY	BIRTHS	DEATHS	MIGRATION
Australia	12.55	7.31	+4.05
Canada	10.99	7.61	+6.01
China	12.96	6.74	-0.23
France	12.54	9.04	+0.66
Germany	8.6	10.34	+2.18
Mexico	21.92	4.97	-2.65
Sweden	9.71	10.58	+1.0
U.S.A.	14.4	8.44	+3.52
United Kingdom	10.99	10.21	+2.2

Source: www.cia.gov/cia/publications/factbook.

most of the developed world experiences an aging population coupled with the preference of young people to have small families, immigration is the only way to maintain either population stability or growth. Sweden, however, has opted to carefully control its rate of immigration and the result is a country on the brink of population decline.

Total Fertility

Simply examining births relative to the total population can lead to some inaccuracies, since the bulk of a population being examined might have an excess of young or elderly that are not available for reproduction. Hence, reporting the number of births relative to the population (crude birth rate) could lead to inaccurate conclusions regarding family size and the reproduction of each fertile woman. In many cases we use a measure called *total fertility*. Total fertility is a measure of the number of live births relative to the number of women that are in the prime reproductive years, usually 15 to 45 years of age.

On the basis of total fertility, Canadian women are significantly lower in fertility than their counterparts in the U.S. (1.52 to 2.08 in 1999). This difference has lead researchers to examine declines in Canadian total fertility. For example, "From 1979 to 1999, the fertility of Canadian women aged 20 to 24 decreased nearly 40 percent, and the fertility among those 25 to 29 declined about 25 percent. In the United States, fertility rates among women in these age groups remained stable" (www.statcan.ca/Daily/English/020703/d020703a.htm).

Many researchers attribute the declining birth rate to the delay of marriage and the later age at marriage. This leaves fewer years for births to occur during a time when women's ability to conceive (fecundity) begins to wane. For instance, the actual number of births to women over 45 years of age nearly doubled between 1991 and 1995, from 99 to 197. Of the 23 657 births in 1995 that occurred before the maternal age of 20, 81 percent were to never-married women. Although there were only 224 births prior to the maternal age of 15, 99 percent were to never-married women. Among never-married mothers, 53 percent gave birth by the age of 24, compared to 14 percent among married mothers. In addition, the data indicate that a large number of children are both conceived and birthed by never-married young women. (We will examine this later in this chapter.) Indeed, in 1995, more than 21 percent of never-married women gave birth after the age of 30, compared with 17 percent in 1990 (Statistics Canada, Live Births, 1995).

Replacement Level

The simplest definition of **replacement level** is the birthrate that must be achieved—to replace males and females who have died—in order to maintain a consistent population level. In 1971, the Canadian fertility rate dropped below the replacement level of 2.1 births per woman, and has remained below replacement level ever since (Ram, 1988). (Due to fetal and infant death rates, the additional 0.1 is the necessary statistical compensation factor to ensure societal continuity.)

The Royal Society of Canada sponsored a colloquium in 1986 to consider Canada's fertility crisis. The results of some of this work were published in proceedings entitled *The Family in Crisis: A Population Crisis?* (Legare et al., 1989). Romaniuc (1989) examined two options for reducing the potential decline in the Canadian population. One was to encourage immigration (immigrants tend to have higher birthrates), and the other was to encourage larger families through economic incentives, or the fostering of pro-family values (also discussed in Chapter 5). Since 1960, the fertility of Quebec women has been lower than that of women in all the other provinces. The government of Quebec became concerned about this pattern, and now offers financial inducements to potential parents on an ascending scale: $500 is paid to parents for the first child, and $1000 is paid in two installments for a second child. A third and each subsequent child garners quarterly payments of $375 for four years, for a total of $6000 (Dumas, 1990).

Transition to Parenthood

We now turn to the process of becoming parents—pregnancy, the transition to parenthood, and parent–infant relationships. Before focusing on the traditional research on parenting, we will first briefly review the unique issues faced by teenagers who give birth and choose to keep their children.

Teenage Parents

In 1995, some 19 277 Canadian teenage women under the age of 20 gave birth to a child, nearly 82 percent of whom were unmarried. However, since that time the rate of teenage pregnancies in Canada has declined. These declines are inversely related to the increasing rates of abortion among women in this age group. Canada has maintained rates about half of what they are in the U.S. The U.S. has some of the highest rates in the world, and relative to other nations Canada remains in the top quarter of the nations in regard to teen births.

Where do teen mothers and their children live? About 57 percent live alone, 8 percent are in common-law relationships (some with the biological father of the child), 32 percent with relatives, and 3 percent with non-relatives (Manning and Smock, 1997). Although undocumented, it is probable that teen mothers are more likely to live with relatives or in common-law relationships than are older unmarried mothers. Indeed, a Canadian study found that after giving birth, most young mothers continued to live with their parents. About one-third were either living common-law or had married the father, while only a minority lived alone (MacDonnell, 1981).

Research on teen mothering is not reassuring. Problematic behaviours prior to giving birth are significantly correlated with maternal unresponsiveness, depression, excessive control, and infant difficulties (Cassidy, Zoccolillo, and Hughes, 1996). Teen fathers, whether live-in or live-apart, were often sources of conflict. Positive and supportive help from the teen mother's mothers, however, seemed to contribute to a reduction of stress (Nitz et al., 1995). The stress of teen parenting is reduced by the support of friends, particularly when there is conflict between the teen parents and their mothers (Richardson et al., 1995).

The Pregnancy Phase

LaRossa (1986:39) reported that when asked what it was like to be an expectant mother, one woman said, "You think that it's all in your womb and then you find out that your whole life is pregnant." Most research in the area of pregnancy uses the familiar "trimesters" used in medicine. The physical changes during these trimesters are also tied to social changes and changes in mobility that restrict social interaction.

The first trimester is often the time when the couple "discovers" that they may become parents. At this time most women do not show external physical signs of pregnancy, so everything may seem the same as before the pregnancy. This is, however, also the time when many women experience the most intense "morning sickness" and this serves to emphasize that they are pregnant. Lastly, this is the time when many primiparous (first birth) women experience miscarriages, so it is a time of some anxiety regarding the pregnancy.

The second trimester is often reported (Cowan and Cowan, 2000) as being the period where the woman experiences the best overall sense of well-being. Sexual intercourse often resumes or increases during this phase. The anxiety regarding the pregnancy often subsides as the woman "shows" externally and begins to experience the movement of the fetus. This movement serves to support her feelings that all is well with the pregnancy.

Increasing physical awkwardness often marks the third and final trimester. Prenatal classes are most often scheduled during the third trimester and further involve the father in the birthing process. Usually the couple will design a birth plan so that decisions about such matters as anesthetics and Caesarean section are not left to a time when neither young parent can focus on the pros and cons involved in these decisions. The third trimester ends with the birth of the child and the entry of the young individual or couple into parenthood.

Most social scientists might emphasize the significance of the pregnancy phase as preparing the young couple for parenthood. This is usually termed "anticipatory socialization." While this is certainly a component of the pregnancy, there is mounting evidence regarding the effect of prenatal marital interaction and later child outcomes. For example, psychologists at the University of Ontario obtained histories of mothers' pregnancies and the postnatal development of their 1300 children up to five years of age (Stott and Langford, 1976; Stott, 1977). Consistent with previous literature, Stott demonstrated that mothers under high levels of stress during pregnancy were significantly more likely to give birth to infants with ill health, neurological dysfunctions, physical defects, and behavioural disturbances. Marital discord during the pregnancy was associated "with a 94-percent above-normal rate of handicap in the child at birth." Stott found that women in stormy marriages ran a 237-percent greater risk of bearing a psychologically or physically damaged child, compared with women in satisfying marriages. There is continuing debate as to the source of these effects. More recently, the significance of the marital behaviours of parents during pregnancy was documented in a longitudinal study of U.S. couples (Howes and Markman, 1989, 1991). These couples were identified in their dating years and tracked through marriage, pregnancy, childbirth, and into the post-preschool years of their children. Based on patterns of communication in the premarital stage, the researchers observed an "interactional signature" characteristic of distressed marriages—the escalation of negative affect and husband withdrawal. Howes and Markman also accurately predicted future attachment insecurities of the infants before their birth, as well as symptoms of resistant and avoidant children in their late preschool years.

Marital Interaction and Transition to Parenthood

One of the best-researched components of the transition to parenthood is the effect it has on the marriage. There are now several decades of research both in Canada and many other countries (especially Australia and the U.S.) replicating the negative effect the transition to parenthood appears to have on marriage. Recently, Feeney et al. (2002) demonstrated similar declines in marital interaction to those noted by Cowan and Cowan (2000) and Belsky and Rovine (1990). Invariably, the transition to parenthood is associated with declines in marital satisfaction and increases in spousal conflict. Although some researchers have noted that not all primiparous couples see declines in marital satisfaction, about 75 percent do reports such declines after the birth.

Several Canadian studies have also focused on pre- and post-birth maternal adjustment. Mothers had more positive feelings about parenthood after birth than during the last month of pregnancy, and were more positive at 16 months postpartum than at the other two measurements, which were taken at one month and three months. In contrast, mothers felt more positively about their relationship with their husbands during pregnancy than at any other time. Negative feelings toward their husbands were most apparent in the first three months (Fleming et al., 1990). Perceived social support, husband involvement in child care, and perceived emotional caring by husbands are significant predictors of maternal adjustment.

Cowan and Cowan (2000) have argued that the reason that couples' relationships decline is because the expectations of shared division of labour are seldom realistic given that the husband most often continues working and the female breastfeeds and cares for the infant. Some have seen these unmet expectations as an "injustice factor"—increased work for mothers and the "back out" by fathers in caring for newborn infants and housework (Kluwer, Heesink, and Van de Vliert, 2002). Johnson and Huston (1998) refer to this trend as "the perils of love," as wives attempt to adapt to the behaviour of their less-involved husbands. This research found the following: "The more wives loved their husbands, the more their preferences changed toward their husbands' preferences, regardless of whether their husbands were more patriarchal or more egalitarian in preferences about the performance of child-care tasks." Cowan and Cowan (1995) have developed prenatal couple interventions to assist the couple in adapting to this transition of roles and expectations.

Parent–Infant Relationships

Even before the baby arrives home, significant elements of bonding such as breast-feeding have begun. Bonding involves both the parent and the infant and should not be looked upon as a one-way street. The transition to parenthood and the characteristics of parent–infant relationships are closely related. In this section, we will briefly summarize mother–infant relationships, the role of fathers, and non-maternal care.

Bonding and Attachment

The area of infant–parent interaction is dominated by the attachment theory approach originating in the work of John Bowlby (1969, 1989). Bolwby defined **attachment** as *behaviours* that represent the need of the infant to attain and maintain proximity and protection with an available and responsive caregiver. Infant attachment to the primary caregiver—typically defined as primarily the infant's mother—is deemed essential to normal, healthy child development (Ainsworth et al.,

1978). Attachment is assumed to occur between the ages of six months and 24 months. Considerable research using stranger-situation experiments demonstrates the degree of infants' biological-psychological attachment to parents. In such experiments, strangers enter a room in which the infant and parents are engaged together in play. *Securely attached* infants head for their mothers, rather than their fathers, in the presence of the stress caused by the appearance of the stranger. If the infant's mother is absent, the infant goes to the father. *Insecurely attached* infants also experience anxiety in the presence of strangers, but seem to either avoid or resist their parents. Most stranger-situation experiments are done in non-home settings. However, a Canadian study (Pederson and Moran, 1995) tested the stranger situation in the mother's home. Attachment patterns—secure, avoidant, and ambivalent—were as evident in the home as in laboratory settings.

Attachment theory has increasingly come under attack from feminist and child researchers (e.g. Hays 1997). There are several dimensions to this critique. The most important dimensions, however, are theoretical and methodological. Theoretically, Bowlby was heavily influenced by the early socio-biological work on imprinting. He argued that a similar mechanism for attachment and modeling might exist in humans and developed the idea of attachment. Since that time, more research has supported the perspective that human infants are more varied in their response than non-human species. The methodological critique has largely focused on whether an infant's anxiety with strangers is really a measure of the strength of attachment or simply a lack of experience. For example, infants with multiple caregivers in daycare fail to exhibit such anxiety and are labeled insecurely attached by attachment theorists while critics argue they simply have a broader range of adaptation than infants who are exclusively reared by mothers.

As you might well imagine, many of the arguments about the infant's "maternal need" and the consequences of "maternal neglect" are framed by attachment theory assumptions. While these assumptions may be correct, they may also be incorrect. At the present time, this remains a contested area in scientific discourse.

The Father Factor

Until the 1980s, there was little research on the role or importance of fathering during infancy. It seems apparent that fathers are becoming more involved with their infants. Involved fathers tend to be more affiliative, caring, nurturant, child-oriented, and affectionate than do uninvolved fathers. They also tend to have higher levels of self-esteem and more satisfying marriages (Levy-Shiff and Israelashvili, 1988; Cowan and Cowan, 1987). Belsky et al. (1996) report that fathers of secure infants were more extraverted and agreeable, had more positive marriages, and had more harmony between their places of work and family life. Together these findings indicate a more engaged, reciprocally playful, and more attached fathering. Fathers seem to perform a special and essential role in infant care and throughout childhood and adolescence (Biller, 1993). (See Box 11.2.)

Non-Parental Care of Young Children

Mothers' Work Situation

Most young mothers now work. The traditional single-earner family is no longer the dominant form in Canada.

Fast and DaPont (1997) report that the percentage of new mothers who have paid work outside the home before the birth of their first child has been continually increasing, from 63 percent in the 1950s to 85 percent in the 1990s. Recent new mothers are also more likely to interrupt paid work for six months or more at the birth of their first child—57 percent now versus 25 percent in the 1950s. Similarly, 1990s mothers typically return to paid work within two years of their first birth, whereas in the 1950s, only 8 percent did so.

Canada provides nationally funded maternity benefit and parental leave plans through unemployment insurance for up to 25 weeks (Symons and McLeod, 1993). This permits mothers to respond to the needs of their infant, their families, and themselves. Mothers are also able to make a decision as to whether to return to work at the end of six months. The evidence indicates that approximately 45 to 50 percent return to work at the end of the six-month period, while others are likely to reenter the workforce within two years.

It is apparent that paid work among mothers in Canada, in its many varying complexities, is a significant dimension of family life.

Child Development and Non-Parental Care

There is continuing disagreement among scholars about the implications of non-parental care on child development, particularly during the first 12 months,

---

Box 11.2   Current Insights: Fathers Are Important

Babies . . . distinguish . . . mother from father as early as . . . three weeks . . . Almost invariably, they make the same distinction, becoming calm in the presence of the mother, aroused and stimulated by the approach of the father . . . Each mother has a distinctive way of cradling her baby, and will cradle him that way nine times out of 10 [says Dr. Kyle Pruett, a professor of psychiatry at Yale University Child Study Center]; [Pruett continues] . . . a given father in 10 tries, [in] contrast, will pick up his baby nine different ways, including upside down. Mothers make more use of toys in playing with their children; fathers are more likely to employ their own bodies as portable, interactive monkey bars and rocking horses . . . 'Even when they are the primary caregivers,' Pruett says, 'fathers do not mother.' . . . When a child confronts a novel situation—a dog, a stranger, a new toy—mothers instinctively move closer, offering the reassurance of their familiar presence; fathers tend to stay back and let the child explore it for herself. Both modes of parenting—the reassuring and the challenging—contribute to a child's emotional growth.

Source: Adler, 1997:73.

but often also including the first three years of life. This is seen as a crucial period in which bonding and attachment between the infant and parents occur. Research notwithstanding, the controversy between traditional and liberal views of child care continues.

Based on several ongoing research projects, it has been found that infants under 12 months of age in day care for more than 20 hours per week are more likely to develop insecure attachments with their mothers and develop heightened aggressiveness and noncompliance during their preschool and early school-age years (Belsky, 1988; Belsky and Rovine, 1988; Belsky, 1990a; Belsky, 1990b; Belsky and Eggebeen, 1991, Bradley et al. 1997). A review of Belsky's work on attachment insecurity among infants, as well as the research of others, concludes that the differences between infants in non-parental care and maternal care are "very small and there is questioning of what it actually means" (Ochiltree, 1994:67). Lamb (1996:338–339), in his review of the effects of non-parental care, concludes that regular exposure to non-parental caregivers "need not have harmful effects on children's development although harmful effects can occur." Lamb argues that "the quality of children's relationships with their parents" is the most important source of influence on children, even when they receive substantial amounts of care outside the home. Indeed, families with moderate to high risk characteristics (such as being more antisocial, negative, depressed) are more likely to have difficulty managing 12- to 24-month-old toddlers when these children experienced 20 or more hours of routine non-maternal care in their first year (Belsky, Woodworth, and Crnic, 1996).

Most mothers work outside the home. Most parents do not use day-care centres. About 68 percent of mothers working part time or full time place their young children with child-sitters, licensed family day-care homes, or relatives (Burke, et al.,1991). Grandparents, followed by aunts or uncles, were the most frequently used relatives. Day-care centres were used by only 8 percent of mothers. Employed mothers use relatives for two reasons: "relatives can be trusted and they are cheaper" (Kuhlthau and Mason, 1996).

Day-care advocates support the availability and accessibility of *licensed* child care for all mothers who are employed—referred to as universal day care (Prentice, 1988). Licensed child care requires trained staff, low staff–child ratios, quality facilities, low turnover rates, and parental involvement. The need for licensed child-care places or spaces is much greater than the number of children needing care. According to Burke et al. (1991), in 1990 there were 1.3 million preschoolers (under the age of six) whose mothers were in the labour force. In the same year, however, there were 321 000 licensed spaces. Just 18 percent of these preschool children were in full-time licensed family day care or day care centres.

Research demonstrates that high-quality day care is particularly beneficial for disadvantaged and high-risk children, and for children in single-parent families. On the other hand, in an era of personal computers, modems, electronic fax machines, and computer networks, the concept of skilled employees working at home now seems uniquely viable. Paid work (including standard benefits of work-site employees) at home seems to be an excellent way of fulfilling child-care and parental needs.

To Work or Not to Work

The June 1992 issue of *Transition* is devoted to the many trade-off issues for stay-at-home and workplace mothers. The title of this focus issue is apt: The Pain of Choice, the Agony of None. A letter by "Tracey," reprinted in *Transition*, illustrates the struggle of many stay-at-home single mothers.

> My son, Skye, is 14 months old. I am a stay-at-home mom, and I am also a welfare recipient. Being a single mom is hard, and staying home to care for my son turned out to be harder than anything else I've ever done.
>
> Of course family and friends help when they can, but am I selfish to think it's not enough? The guilt placed upon me when I decided not to return to my job after Skye was born was not too bad. However, nothing could have prepared me for the loneliness, isolation, lack of motivation and self-esteem, and feeling of loneliness. With winter in full swing the "panic" has begun. The "panic" of losing myself in the task at hand, that task being raising my son in a safe, caring and loving environment.
>
> Luckily, I realize I am trying to do an excellent job of caring for my son, having doubts at times as all mothers do. However, the lack of support, praise for the "job" I do, and not having enough healthy time away from my son (only once every few months) is indeed taking its toll.

Soon I will have to take steps to return to school and/or the workforce, even though this is not my first choice. The financial pressures are just too extensive to put into words. As I've explained, my emotional and mental state doesn't leave much choice as to whether I stay at home or not.

Furthermore, family and friends keep asking me when I'm going to put Skye in day care and get on with "my" life. Breastfeeding was my reply before, but now I just get angry when they ask with sarcasm, "What do you do all day?"

This letter was written to inform, not for sympathy. As well, for those of you who have been lucky to not have had your world turned upside down by one simple loving choice, only my best goes to you when I say to be thankful.

Tracey (*Homebase Magazine*, Spring 1991).

Career women, often late childbearers, must also weigh the pros and cons of their careers and motherhood. Barsky (1992) interviewed several Canadian career women who chose to stay at home until their first and only child was in school. She refers to the career-oriented mothers she talked to as "neohomemakers." A brief version of Diane's story follows.

Prior to conception, Diane, aged 35, put in 12-hour days in her profession. Although she could easily afford a nanny, Diane was reluctant to return to work after her five-month maternity leave—the typical maternity leave is much shorter. She first asked for an extra month of leave, and then considered taking part-time work. Eventually, she realized that what she really wanted to do was stay at home with her daughter until she entered school. Diane is now a committed stay-at-home mom.

Obviously, this story is very different from that of Tracey. Tracey is trying to be a good mother without the necessary financial resources. Diane has the money to get the best child care available, loves her work, but loves being a full-time mother even more. Among these professional women, career and advancement are on hold, and family life takes precedence. Barsky (1992:53) says that these mothers, 30 or more years of age, have "learned from experience that you can have it all, just not all at once."

As Barksky points out, Tracey, and others like her, do not have the same options. Indeed, Riley and Glass (2002) point out that the type of care mothers want and the type that is available are often not congruent.

Socialization of Children and Adolescents

Socialization may be defined as the processes of learning one's culture and acquiring one's personality and personal values throughout the life span. The area of socialization involves the parental modeling of appropriate behaviours, parents' use of various types of discipline to both reward and punish the child's behaviour, and the socialization afforded by interaction with peers. Although much of the socialization literature examines the effects of parents on children, there is also clear evidence that children affect their parents in numerous ways (e.g., Rogers and Hogan, 2003; McBride, Schoppe, and Rane, 2002).

For parents, the first two to three years of raising a child represent a sharp transition from a couple-focus to a parent-focus. Their only parenting knowledge was learned as children in their families of origin, although an increasing number of students and future parents-to-be take parenting classes. Even so, the actual experience of parenting is often uncharted territory.

Quality of Marriage and Child Development

Most children live with their parents. They also live with their parents' *marriage*. Each couple's particular marriage is a model to their children, by intention or default, of what marriage is generally like. Buehler and Gerard (2002) report a strong association between marital conflict and ineffective parenting with the predictable outcome on child maladjustment. Reviews of the research evidence document a strong association between high levels of marital conflict and emotional and behaviour problems among children and adolescents (Reid and Crisafulli, 1990; Gable et al., 1992). More recent research continues to document a strong connection between marital discord, conflict and aggression, and the behaviours of children: child aggression among 5-year-olds, psychological distress, depression, anxiety, distraction, and withdrawal among older children and adolescents (Harrist and Ainslie, 1998; Gordis et al., 1997; Harold et al., 1997; Allen et al., 1996). McNeal et al. (1998) found that marital violence during childhood is a significant predictor of lower levels of psychological well-being and higher levels of relationship violence among young adults. It is also found, however, that frequent church attendance enhances marital quality and co-caregiver (parenting) behaviours (Brody et al., 1994). Couples who are able to resolve their conflicts are seen by their children as more effective role models than are couples who seldom have conflict (Davies et al., 1996). The evidence indicates that mothering is less affected by an unsatisfying marriage than is fathering (Gable et al., 1992).

Parenting and Child Development

Although there are many influences in child development—such as the media, peers, and school—parents seem to be the most salient influence for three reasons. First, parents are much larger and stronger for most of the first two decades of a child's life; the "bulk factor" cannot be ignored in everyday influence. Second, parents are "allocated" the right (if not the requirement) to exercise authority over their children and exact compliance from them. Third, during the critical years of attachment and identification among young children, strong bonds are formed between children and their parents. These bonds supersede most other social bonds in society and, in most cases, remain influential in varying degrees throughout the life span.

Styles of Parenting The typical parent has not taken classes or obtained a degree in parenting. Parents know little of child development, let alone of being parents, outside their own personal experiences as children living with each of their parents, and observing them parent. Even so, there is considerable variation in how parents parent. LeMasters and DeFrain (1989) identified five types of parents. The *parents as martyrs* put the child first in every dimension of their everyday lives. Such parents sacrificed their own needs in the interest of the child's desires. The *parents as pals* were uniquely permissive, allowing their children to do pretty much whatever they liked. The *parents as drill sergeants* were the bosses. Whatever the parent believed to be right was law. The child had to obey with little room for error or questioning of authority. Violation of any kind was punished. The *parents as teachers-counselors* were devoted to guiding their children. Such parents put considerable energy into being informed about the needs of their children, and responding in ways that enhanced their well-being. *The parents as coaches* emphasized the realism of life. To them, children were like members of a team; there were rules and penalties. The winners were disciplined and persistent. The principles, therefore, of competition, assertiveness, and cooperation were emphasized. In real life, most parents are likely to be a little of all of these, depending on their mood and the circumstances, although they tend to specialize in one style more than others.

The four basic styles of parenting that Bronfenbrenner (1961) and Deverieux et al. (1969) identify, based on the variables of support and control, are as follows: discipline, guidance, punishment, and the encouragement of autonomy. **Optimum parenting**, according to their review of the research evidence, involves an ideal (loving, well-thought-out, moderate, prudent) degree of discipline, guidance, punishment, and encouragement of autonomy. In contrast, the extremes of these parenting styles are overprotection, indulgence, authoritarianism, and neglect.

The National Longitudinal Survey of Children and Youth (NLSCY) conducted in Canada, the first phase of which was released in 1996, identified four parenting styles: positive interaction, hostile and ineffective parenting, consistent parenting and aversive parenting. Most of the data and reports on risk factors regarding children were obtained from an adult "person most knowledgeable—PMK," typically the mother. The data show that nearly 4 percent of Canada's children—about 180 000 of them—have or will experience four or more of the following risk factors: single parenthood, having had a teenage parent, being one of four or more children, low income and educational level, low social support, family dysfunction, and depression. As might be expected, girls experienced significantly fewer problems than did boys (Ross et al., 1996; Landy and Tam, 1996). Relative to most studies in both Canada and the United States, these findings are uniquely low. Most research documents a significantly higher proportion of dysfunctional families. The next section provides a brief overview of the impact of parenting attitudes and behaviours on children under the age of 12.

Effects of Parenting on Children

Self-Esteem A major review of the existing research in the United States on the effects of parenting on children (Peterson and Rollins, 1987) documented the positive influence of parental support on the development of social and interpersonal competence in children. Self-esteem, independence, cognitive skills, academic achievement, creativity, self-control, healthy values, and related measures of social competence were apparent attributes of children raised in supportive parental environments. In contrast, the lack of parental support was strongly associated with aggression, emotional and behavioural problems, learning problems, lower levels of moral development, and related indicators of social incompetence in children.

Research in Canada is consistent with these basic findings. The term **scaffolding** is used to refer to parental support in reducing the complexity of a child's task when necessary and removing the support when it is no longer needed. It was found that authoritative parenting (optimum control and warmth) was significantly related to effective scaffolding and to higher levels of mathematical achievement in children (Pratt et al., 1992). Supportive parenting behaviours by both mothers and fathers, as well as husband support of spouse, were significant predictors of child competence (Roberts, 1989). Effective parenting—defined as cohesive, democratic, expressive, organized, intellectual, cultural—continues to be significantly correlated with children's social, psychological, and academic adjustment in both traditional and nontraditional families (Bronstein et al., 1993).

Behavioural Problems Emotional and behavioural problems were examined in the NLSCY Canadian study (Offord and Lipman, 1996). Twenty-four percent of 4- to 11-year-old boys experienced one or more conduct, emotional, or hyperactive disorders. An additional 6 percent of the boys had social relationship problems or were required to repeat a grade. In contrast, only 22 percent of girls experienced one or more of these disorders. In all these families, the very poor were most disadvantaged—nearly 40 percent. In another analysis of this important database (Tremblay et al., 1996), physical aggression (hitting, biting, and kicking) was examined over time. This type of aggression was highest among children under 30 months and decreased in older age groups, decreasing more for girls than for boys. Physical aggression scores were the highest in families with the lowest socioeconomic levels.

Controlling for age and education, MacEwen and Barling (1991) found that working mothers *under stress* were more likely to be rejecting and punishing toward their children. Their children were more likely to have conduct disorders and to have problems with immaturity, irrespective of gender. In a 1988 study, Barling et al. found that inter-role conflict between paid work and mother work is strongly associated with attention and maturity problems among grade-school children.

Several studies have found a higher incidence of problems among the children of divorced, single-mother families, including the following: temper tantrums, fighting, bullying, cheating, lying, and stealing. In response to this evidence, Bank et al. (1993) analyzed data from three longitudinal studies of 252 single-mother, head-of-household families. All these families were encumbered with significant socioeconomic disadvantages. However, three key factors sharply influenced the antisocial behavioural problems of the boys in each sample (kindergarten through grade six): the antisocial qualities of mothers, ineffective discipline by mothers, and inadequate monitoring of child activities.

Physical Punishment Parental punishment or coercion, often called "discipline" in much of the research, is related to the abuse of children. Yelling, verbal threats, the "push-grab-shove trilogy," and slapping or spanking are the most widely used forms of disciplinary action. Mothers are more likely to use a slap or spank, while fathers more often ridiculed their children (Lenton, 1990). Parents are most likely to use the techniques that their own parents used under similar conditions. However, if fathers are unemployed, if family income drops significantly, or if the normative system permits the use of violence, parents tend to use more punitive techniques than their own parents used. In this case, stress is the major cause of increased abuse. A survey published in 1998 (Day et al.), based on a random sample of nearly 3000 respondents, found that

44 percent of the mothers and 31 percent of the fathers said they had spanked during the previous week. Spankings are most common before the age of two. The use of spanking as a punishment decreases significantly when children reach the age of six. Even so, 22 percent of mothers still spank their children at the age of 11, although infrequently. The major findings of this study are these: boys are spanked more frequently than girls; mothers do most of the spanking; Black mothers tend to spank more frequently; mental health, lower educational levels, Fundamentalist religious orientations, and arguing between parent and child are the primary predictors of spanking. A 1995 Gallup Poll found that nearly 85 percent of parents scream and holler at their children, while 65 percent engage in spanking with their bare hands (Associated Press, 1995). And evidence from the National Family Violence survey indicates that more than half of adolescents experience corporal punishment (Straus and Yodanis, 1996).

There is a continuing debate on the role of physical punishment on child outcomes. Since the Steinmetz (1979) review there has been little doubt that physical punishment is associated with child aggression. The problem is that some of this aggression is prosocial aggression such as asking people not to "butt" in line while other parts of the aggression are anti-social aggression such as hitting or pushing. This picture is further complicated by the fact that the same punishment can have different affects depending on the age of the child, the gender of the disciplining parent and the location of the discipline (public versus private). In addition, alternative forms of punishment such as withdrawal of privileges and time out are also associated with increased aggression in children.

The debate has now focused on various forms of parental coercive control over children and the effects of these forms of control on the social and emotional development of children. For example, Straus, Sugarman, and Gils-Sims (1997) demonstrated the first controlled effect for parental use of spanking on the later development of antisocial behaviour in children and subsequent survey data also shows a correlation (McLoyd and Smith, 2002). On the other hand, several studies have shown that spanking is not causally related (see Larzelere, 1996) and some studies have demonstrated positive effects for spanking when used

with reason (Larzelere, Sather, Schneider, Larson, and Pike, 1998). Much of the debate therefore centres on the intensity of physical punishment (harsh to mild) and the effects of moderating variables such as when maternal warmth is present or absent (McLoyd and Smith, 2002). Although the current normative climate in North America allows for parental use of moderate to mild physical discipline, the continuing academic debate will no doubt fuel the fires of ideological arguments in the public and pressure to adopt the "no spanking" approach such as legislated in Sweden.

Parenting and Adolescent Development

The "Parent–Adolescent Connection" The generation gap between parents and their teenagers seems to have shrunk. Family values are a top priority and most teens have strong opinions about moral and social values, although these tend to be more liberal than those of their parents. A 1996 survey, based on a random sample of 1500 teens in the United States, reveals that 9 out of 10 teenagers say their parents are interested in their concerns, and 75 percent say their parents understand their problems. About 94 percent of teens describe their relationship with their mothers as either fairly or very happy; about 80 percent of teens say this about their fathers. Most teens also say that their parents respect them. On a four-point scale, where 4.0 equals "total respect," teens rate their mothers as 3.5, and their fathers as 3.2. Only 12 percent say they have witnessed domestic abuse at home (Hale, 1996).

Do parents and teens perceive things the same way? Recent research continues to document that parents and adolescents give differing reports on parental behaviours (Tein et al, 1994). Parent–child agreement varied from a low of 13 percent to a high of 36 percent. Adolescent "reports" were significantly correlated, as were mother and father reports. The authors conclude that adolescent reports reflect the transition from pre-adolescence to adolescence, amount of stress, and the adolescent's personal characteristics. As may be expected, parents and teens in families with supportive interactions are more likely to grow closer together, work more effectively on resolving problems, and report fewer disagreements (Rueter and Conger, 1995).

In a study by Bibby and Posterski (1992), six out of 10 adolescents said that their families were important, while eight out of 10 put friendship and being loved by their peers at the top of the list. On the enjoyment scale, 93 percent of teens said that they received a high level of enjoyment from their friends; 67 percent said this of their mothers, while only 60 percent were willing to say this of their fathers. Even so, a major study of more than 12 000 junior- and senior high school students, as reported on the Internet, found that adolescents who feel emotionally tied to family or school are less likely to take drugs or engage in other risky behaviour (Udry, 1997). Parents who spend time with and talk to their children, set high standards, and send clear messages to them prevent many forms of risky behaviour.

Effects of Parenting on Adolescents

Self-esteem A unique cross-cultural study in eight countries, including Canada, found that parental nurturance (showing understanding and enjoying talking things over with teens) significantly influenced adolescent self-esteem (Scott and Scott, 1989; Scott et al., 1991). Self-esteem, in turn, was strongly related to satisfaction with friends, satisfaction with school, and academic performance. Parental punitiveness, in contrast, was strongly related to adolescent hostility, which in turn reduced academic performance. (The researchers reported no significant cross-cultural differences.) Familial harmony was strongly related to high self-esteem and low anxiety among the adolescents. Poor interpersonal competence was strongly related to parental protectiveness. Morris et al. (2002) found that negative parenting combined with temperament was related to overall adolescent mental health.

A Canadian study by Avison and McAlpine (1992) also found that if mothers and fathers were perceived to be caring parents, both male and female adolescents experienced a sense of mastery, of feeling loved and affirmed, of self-esteem, and fewer symptoms of depression. Strong mother–daughter bonds were a particularly significant determinant of healthy emotional development among female adolescents. Overprotective fathering was strongly associated with depression.

In a U.S. study of self-esteem in adolescents (Demo et al., 1987), it was found that parents who felt good about their performance in parenting, and their performance in other family roles, liked themselves as parents. Similarly, an adolescent's evaluation of her performance as a teenager was the key issue in her own sense of self-esteem. The single most explicit factor in adolescent self-esteem was effective communication with parents.

Behavioural Problems This section focuses on behavioural problems among adolescents, such as delinquency, drug abuse, running away, and suicide. Emotional and behavioural problems among adolescents are complex and diverse. Explanations are not easy as to why one adolescent commits an act of delinquency while another tries to commit suicide. Even so, social scientists often find similarities and connections.

Delinquency Reichertz and Frankel (1990) compared a clinical and nonclinical sample of families. Adolescents in the 44 clinical families had behaviour problems at home (breaking curfews, disobedience, running away), problems at school (truancy, disruptiveness, achievement problems), and minor delinquency (shoplifting, trespassing, loitering and minor vandalism) and related concerns. Two Canadian authors (Sorenson and Brownfield, 1991), using U.S. data, found that delinquency rates were highest among adolescents who said that they seldom shared their thoughts and feelings—the authors' measure of attachment—with their mothers or fathers.

Hagan and his colleagues studied two types of families: patriarchal—father in paid work and mother primarily responsible for children, and egalitarian—mothers and fathers both employed (Hagan et al., 1987; 1988). The research showed that in patriarchal families, male adolescent delinquency rates were considerably higher than were female rates. In egalitarian families, however, female rates of delinquency were similar to male rates. Adolescents in female-headed households had delinquency rates similar to those in egalitarian families. An earlier study (Hagan et al., 1988) found that unemployed mothers had more control over their daughters' behaviours than they did over their sons'. Employed mothers, however, lost this control and influence, and the gender difference in delinquent behaviour broke down. It seems that the maternal ability to reduce the risk of female delinquency is significantly reduced when mothers are employed.[1] Work overload among mothers and fathers leads to stress and depression, which in turn leads to conflict with children. In response to this stress pattern, adolescents are more likely to engage in problematic behaviours (Galambos et al., 1995).

Substance abuse Peer influence is often found to be a more salient factor in drug use. Hundleby and Mercer (1987), in their study of grade 9 students in Ontario, found that peer influence was essentially twice as significant as parent-and-family influence in the use of drugs. Parental drinking and tobacco use was strongly related to the use of alcohol and tobacco among adolescents. In contrast, parents who were actively involved with, and who exercised some control over the lives of, their children were less likely to have adolescents who used drugs. The major influences of the peer group on adolescent behaviour included peer drug use (the most powerful factor), peer delinquency, low achievement motivation, and lack of religiosity among the adolescent's friends. Health Canada (1987:32) has estimated that "a person with smoking friends was almost seven times more likely to smoke than a person with friends who did not smoke." Van Roosmalen and McDaniel (1992) documented that smoking was learned and reinforced through interacting with others who smoked—a pattern more characteristic of girls. Because girls had fewer friends, the pressure resulting from this smaller group was more intensive. These patterns were reinforced if their mothers and siblings smoked. The "older sibling" who uses substances (alcohol, cigarettes, marijuana) is a significant influence on adolescent substance use in other studies as well (Duncan et al., 1996). Indeed, when both parents and older siblings use such substances, the odds of the younger sibling not doing so are slim.

Mothers seem to have a "lead role"—maternal substance use, more than substance use by fathers, significantly influences substance use among adolescents (Stephenson et al., 1996). High family support and **monitoring** (a measure of control) is significantly related to lower levels of drinking, illicit drug use, deviance, and school misconduct (Barnes and Farrell, 1992; Dishion et al., 1995). Monitoring refers to an accurate knowledge of where the adolescent is at all times. This information was typically held by mothers and given to them by each of their children. Low family support and low monitoring, in contrast, were strongly related to increased adolescent problem behaviours.

Runaways In 1990, there were about 45 000 runaway or missing children *reported* to police departments in Canada (McDonald, 1992). Most (86 percent) of these cases were runaways, about 29 percent of whom had run away more than once. About half the runaways stayed away less than a day, and 77 percent returned in less than a week. The circumstances behind the disappearance of still-missing children remain, of course, unknown. Among formerly missing children who have been found (whether alive or dead), the circumstances included wandering off and getting lost, parental abduction, abduction by strangers, and accidents such as drowning. A 1995 study of 20 505 runaway children using U.S. data (Plass and Hotaling, 1995) reports that 58 percent were girls, 68 percent were 16 to 17 years of age, 74 percent were white, and only 28 percent lived in households with both biological parents present. The most likely destination was a friend's house (60 percent); most episodes lasted less than a week; and nearly 40 percent of children's "families" knew where the runaway was.

One of eight adolescents will run away from home at least once before their eighteenth birthday. Runaways are typically divided into four types. *Short-term runaways* include *crisis escapists*, who spontaneously respond to situational home problems; *casual hedonists*, who are seeking a thrill; and *unhappy runners*, who act in a more deliberate manner in evaluating their circumstances (Brennan et al., 1975, as reported in Young et al., 1983). The fourth type, *long-term runaways*, typically run after extensive plans have been made; they seem to have the necessary skills to survive away from home.

Many runaways are more accurately referred to as "throwaways." In the research, throwaways were more likely to have experienced physical or sexual abuse in their families. Female throwaways were more likely to get involved in prostitution, although boys were sometimes also involved. McCormack et al. (1986) found, in a study of runaways in a Canadian shelter home, that about 46 percent of the adolescents came from intact families, 31 percent from single-parent families, and 23 percent (the balance) from remarried families.

About 67 percent of the runaways had been physically abused; 40 percent, sexually abused. Sexual abuse was more frequent in single-parent and remarried families. McCormack et al. (1986) pointed out that in the single-parent family, the offender was either a stepfather or a live-in boyfriend.

Suicide There are similarities between the causes of running away and of idealizing or attempting suicide. The list includes drug use, sexual problems, loneliness, hopelessness, lack of self-esteem, depression, school-related problems, and significant stress or dissatisfaction in relationships with parents (Choquet et al., 1993; DeMan and Leduc, 1995; Culp et al., 1995; Wagner et al., 1995; Levy et al., 1995; Hollis, 1996). Depression and drug use are typically the most powerful factors.

The most serious "behavioural problem" among youth is the tragedy of actually committing suicide. Leenaars and Lester (1990a) compared suicide rates among Canadian and American adolescents aged 10 to 14 and 15 to 19, for both males and females. Suicide rates (number of suicides per 100 000 population) among teens aged 15 to 19 were five times as high among males as females. Further, older teenagers were nearly nine times more likely to commit suicide than were young teens (10 to 14). Suicide rates among adolescents were significantly higher in Canada than in the United States, particularly after 1977. Canadian suicide rates since 1977 have been mostly in the twenties (per 100 000 population), while U.S. suicide rates have been in the 13–16 range. In a comparative study in Canada and the U.S., Leenaars and Lester (1995) found that parental divorce, childlessness, and unemployment predicted suicide rates among Canadian youth aged 15 to 24. These factors were significant in the U.S. regardless of age. Krull and Trovato (1994) found that parents' divorce had the most significant effect on female suicide in Quebec.

Effects of Children and Adolescents on Parents

Much of this chapter has focused on the influence of parenting on child and adolescent attitudes and behaviours. The impact of children on parents and parenting is a neglected field of study. A pace-setting book by Canadian sociologist Anne-Marie Ambert (1992)

argues that the more a child deviates from the individual child attributes considered "normal" in our society, the more likely it is that parental behaviour will be influenced by their children. If a child is below normal, these more "difficult" children will be more difficult to raise, partly due to the societal expectations held for parents and the inadequate knowledge of how to care for such children. Slow learners, the disabled (such as the blind), the chronically ill, the hyperactive, and children with related characteristics can pose new and unique issues for parents. Children whose attributes are "above normal," such as gifted children and those with a high IQ, will also pose special and unexpected parenting challenges for parents.

As we have seen throughout this chapter, parental support and control are powerful influences in human development. Research has yet to clarify, with precision, how controlling, neglecting, and rejecting parents act when they raise children with "below normal" or "above normal" attributes. Likewise, it is unclear how supportive, responsive, and sensitive parents react to children with attributes that are "non-normal." It may also be emphasized that parents have individual attributes that are an important influence on their own capacities to think and act as parents. Ambert points out that these attributes include their mental and physical health, personalities, coping skills, parenting skills, and multiple other characteristics. Further, societal conditions and organizations will be a significant factor in assisting or hindering parents in performing their responsibilities with regard to child care and development. Ambert's book challenges students of the family to rethink the influence of children and adolescents on parents, and to identify areas of needed research.

The Not-So-Empty Nest

Stage Five of the family career is associated with the "launching" of young adults, typically 18 years of age and older. The purpose of this section is to briefly examine leaving home, staying at home longer, and the processes of returning home.

Leaving the Nest

Marriage has sharply decreased as a reason for leaving home among women, although it remains the *major* reason for leaving home. In contrast, "to obtain independence" has sharply increased as a reason for leaving home among women. In the 25- to 29-year-old age group, the desire for independence and having married, as reasons for leaving home, were equally significant among women. Jobs have decreased as a reason for leaving home for men and women, while schooling as a reason has increased in the youngest age cohorts.

There are also other reasons for home leaving. Mitchell (1996), based on data in the Canadian Youth Foundation Survey, found that family structure is an important aspect of leaving home. Young adults 15 to 24 years of age, living in biological and lone-parent families, are five to six times more likely to remain home for longer periods of time than are youths from stepfamilies. Youths in remarried family environments leave home due to conflict and to achieve independence. Youths from stepfamilies are also less likely to choose marriage or continued schooling. If conflict occurs, youth in lone-parent families follow a similar route. This study also found that females leave home an average of two years earlier than do males. Boyd and Norris (1995) point out that young adults whose parents are divorced tend to live with their mothers; if one parent remarries, young adults are most likely to live with the unmarried parent.

An interesting U.S. study (Thornton et al., 1993) provides several additional insights:

- Although 80 percent of children ages 15 to 23 leave home, the parental home is nevertheless the primary residence for two-thirds of the home leavers. Even among home leavers aged 21 to 23, 40 percent of their time is spent at home.

- After the age of 18, two common forms of non-family living—group quarters and house-mate living—jump sharply, first with transitions to group quarters, which shortly subside, and thereafter to house-mate quarters, ages 19 to 20.

- Young adults seem to fan out in all directions, with 20 percent to 40 percent experiencing marriage, cohabitations, group quarters, living alone, and living with other relatives.

There are considerable in-and-out patterns with respect to going to school, getting jobs, and leaving schools and jobs. These patterns, and many others that are examined in this study, are is significant contrast to

the recent past when marriage was the dominant route out of a parental home. What all this means in terms of home leaving, home staying, and home returning is still unclear.

Even so, research continues to demonstrate that home leaving is difficult for adolescents. Whatever the trauma associated with living with parents throughout the adolescent identity-crisis years, many adolescents and young adults struggle with a new identity crisis when they move away from home. Issues of loneliness, self-esteem, life satisfaction, and related concerns are reopened. Home leaving is a process of disengagement from significant family ties transcending two decades, and the simultaneous "construction of an independent adulthood" (Moore, 1987).

Staying in the Nest Longer

In 1996, according to official Canadian Census data, about 30 percent of all women aged 20 to 24 (24 percent of men), 9 percent aged 25 to 29 (13 percent of men), and 3 percent aged 30 to 34 (5 percent of men) were either still living at, or had returned, home. In single-parent families, males aged 25 to 34 are half again as likely as women in the same age group to stay home (McVey, 1998b).

Delayed home leaving is also an international phenomenon. Since the 1980s, the average age at leaving home has increased in most Western countries of the world, although the variations by country are significant. Among young adults aged 25 to 29, for example, in Greece, Spain, and Italy, 65 percent of men and 44 percent of women are still living with their parents. In contrast, in France, Germany, and the United Kingdom, only 25 percent of men and 11 percent of women were living with their parents (Cordón, 1997). The comparable figures in the U.S. were 20 percent of men and 12 percent of women (Goldscheider, 1997). Explanations include young-adult unemployment (Rossi, 1997), the pursuit of higher levels of education to permit autonomy (Galland, 1997), declining marriage rates in most countries including the U.S. (Monnier and de Guibert-Lantoine, 1996, as reported in Cherlin et al., 1977), and difficult housing situations (van Hekken et al., 1997). The prolonging of co-residence is typically positive, particularly where intergenerational relations are important in the kinship system (van Hekken et al., 1977; Nave-Herz, 1997).

Returning to the Nest

The *Montreal Gazette* (cited in Carson, 1987) ran a story under the headline "The Children are Home Again," while another journal, *The Number News* (*American Demographics*, 1989), ran a story on "boomerang adults." A story in the *Edmonton Journal* (Jimenez, 1992b) likewise reported that "a growing number of adult children are flying back to the family nest." Unfortunately, no evidence is provided. There are a few interesting stories, but no hard facts on how many offspring are moving back home, when they are moving back, what precipitates their "flight home," how long they stay, or how things go for the parents who open their doors. This situation continues to prevail in the social science literature to date.

Most of these news stories refer briefly to the "return," and then reframe the discussion in terms of the "staying at home longer" pattern. It seems self-evident that the same factors that lead young adult children to *remain* at home until their early thirties are reasonable explanations of why other young adults are *returning* to the nest. Job loss, economic impoverishment, marital breakdown, convenient child care, shared expenses, a return to post-secondary education, a wounded spirit from the multiple hard knocks of life, and many other factors seem to be important reasons for returning home. Given current societal conditions, it is probable that there will continue to be late home leaving and increased home returning among young adults.

ENDNOTE

1. It may be emphasized that this research project is not a study of the predictors of delinquent behaviour. It is an explanation of the differences in the incidence of delinquent acts among sons and daughters in families *with delinquent adolescents*. Further, the interpersonal dynamics (e.g., interpersonal equity and justice) of the "egalitarian" and "patriarchal" families are not measured.

SUMMARY

■ About one in 10 couples are involuntarily childless for a variety of reasons. Infertile couples often attempt several reproductive technologies before trying adoption. The intentionally childless may turn out to be simply postponers.

■ Most children under the age of 15 live in two-parent families (82 percent), while about 16 percent live in single-parent families. The remaining two percent live in a variety of settings: with non-Census family relatives, foster families, collective households, hospitals, or orphanages.

■ The majority (70 percent compared to 76 percent in 1990) of births in 1995 occurred to married women, while about 28 percent of births occurred to unmarried women. Nearly all births were single live-born children.

■ Unmarried women obtain about 63 percent of all abortions, compared to 21 percent by married women. Most women who obtain an abortion are doing so for the first time. Women under the age of 25 obtain about 50 percent of all abortions. Most abortions are obtained at under 13 weeks' gestation. Gallup polls in Canada show that the majority of the public support abortion under certain conditions, such as rape. However, only 31 percent support abortion simply on the basis of individual choice.

■ Gallup polls show that the majority of Canadians want to have two or more children. Official statistics, however, show that the actual number of ever-born children is 1.6, considerably less than the ideal and below the replacement level.

■ The transition to parenthood, although a positive experience for many, seems to lead to increased marital dissatisfaction among young mothers, particularly among women who expected more support from their own relatives and their spouses. Involved fathers, in contrast, facilitate stronger marital and parent–infant bonds.

■ The processes of bonding and the beginnings of attachment between mothers and their newborn infants begin in the first few weeks of life.

■ There is an ongoing debate among scholars about the impact of non-parental care on infant development in the first year of life. The quality of family and marital relationships is a salient factor in reducing potential attachment problems among infants in dual-work households.

- Socialization is a lifelong process. It involves three primary dimensions—hierarchical influence, the modes of transmission, and the effects of the person being socialized.
- The nature and quality of marital relationships have both a direct and an indirect effect on the parenting of children and adolescents.
- There are several ways of describing the variety of parenting styles in families. Parenting styles are typically defined by the degree of control and support in parental behaviours.
- Optimal parental support and control is typically strongly related to child and adolescent well-being. Extreme parental support and control, in contrast, tends to undermine child and adolescent well-being, and often results in attitudinal and behavioural problems.
- Although it is often assumed that parents and teens live in two different societies with little connection, the research demonstrates that parent–adolescent bonds are important and largely satisfying.
- Parenting during the adolescent period may have an even more pronounced influence on the self-esteem and behaviours of children, compared with child-rearing in the first decade of a child's life. The need for understanding and support is pronounced. Excessive interference and dominance will exacerbate behavioural problems such as delinquency, substance abuse, running away, and suicide.
- The temperaments and behaviours of children, the unique biological and emotional changes of adolescents, the non-normative characteristics of parents, and the climate of societal conditions together have an influence on the processes of socialization in families.
- Many of the reasons for home leaving have changed. Young adults are staying home longer due to economic and educational pressures. Indeed, it is possible that the rate of return of young adults to the family nest will increase.

KEY TERMS

Attachment (251)
Intentional childlessness (245)
Involuntary childlessness (243)
Monitoring (259)
Optimum parenting (255)
Replacement level (249)
Scaffolding (256)

Socialization (254)
Vital statistics (247)
Voluntary childlessness (244)

QUESTIONS FOR REVIEW

1. What are the major differences among the voluntarily childless?
2. Review the demographic characteristics of children and their families in the 1996 Census.
3. Explain the differing patterns that couples experience in the transition from pregnancy to parenthood.
4. Review the data and issues on bonding, attachment, and non-parental care in the first few years of life.
5. What is the role of the marital relationship in the parenting of children and adolescents?
6. Define optimum parenting and its relationship to parental support and control.
7. Review the basic findings on the influence of parenting on child development.
8. Review the basic findings on the influence of parenting during adolescence.

QUESTIONS FOR DISCUSSION

1. Discuss the inducements by the Quebec government to increase the fertility rate. How might these inducements have influenced the increase in common-law unions in Quebec? Will this be an effective tool in building larger families? What are the political implications?
2. Critically examine the evidence and long-term influence of maternal and marital stress during pregnancy on both fetal and infant development.
3. Why have fathers been so dramatically neglected in the studies of early childhood? In what ways are fathers significant in human development?
4. Evaluate the argument that both parental and infant needs and desires are being inadequately fulfilled by current dual-work paid employment patterns. Evaluate the recent evidence and the various alternative solutions.
5. What are the similarities and differences in parenting issues between childhood and adolescence? How do the effects differ?
6. Under what conditions do children and adolescents have a significant influence on parent development?

SUGGESTED READINGS

Ambert, Anne-Marie. 1997.* Parents, Children, and Adolescents: Interactive Relationships and Development in Context. New York: Haworth Press. This new book, written by a prominent sociologist in Canada, draws on important evidence and resource material from several relevant disciplines. Students will benefit from Ambert's insightful and creative analysis of parent–child issues.

Bibby, Reginald W. and Donald C. Posterski. 1992.* Teen Trends: A Nation in Motion. Toronto: Stoddart. This recent study of more than 3000 15- to 19-year-old teens in Canada is a well-written exposé of how young people think, how they are changing, and what adults should do about it.

Cowan, Carolyn and Phillip Cowan.* 2000. When Partners Become Parents. New York: Erlbaum and Associates. This is an excellent overview of the transition to parenthood by two well-respected Canadian scholars.

Lero, Donna S., and Karen L. Johnson. 1994.* 110 Canadian Statistics on Work and Family. Ottawa: The Canadian Advisory Council on the Status of Women. This publication is full of information culled from many government statistics, research projects funded by government agencies, and published articles on books by Canadian scholars, all of which relate to children, families, and the work world.

Statistics Canada. 1996.* Growing Up in Canada: National Longitudinal Survey of Children and Youth. Catalogue 89-550-MPE. This book is a major report on data collected from 22 831 children, aged from birth to 11 years, and their families. Teachers and principals were a part of this survey. As this is a longitudinal survey, there will be one or more subsequent publications updating the developmental patterns of these children through their teen years.

CHAPTER 12

Aging and Families in Later Life

After studying this chapter, you should be able to do the following:

- Define gerontology, and give examples of four different aspects of gerontology.
- Distinguish between individual and societal aging, list major trends in the number of elderly in the Canadian population, and explain why the elderly are not a homogeneous group.
- Define demographic or population aging, describe the three major factors that determine population aging, and explain the three primary indicators of population aging.
- Explain the impact of the contraction and expansion of the household unit on marital relationships, describe recent changes in living arrangements among Canada's elderly, and review the impact of the family life stage on the happiness of the elderly.
- Summarize the kinship relationships of the elderly among the never-married, the married, the childless, the divorced, the widowed, and the remarried.
- Outline the later-life kinship relationships between parents and adult children, between grandparents and grandchildren, and between siblings.
- Discuss the economic situation and the health of Canadian seniors, describe the impact of physical disabilities on the functioning of seniors, and compare the caregiving contributions of family members to seniors with the contributions of seniors to family members.
- Project the impact of demographic aging on the future experiences and well-being of seniors in our society.

Introduction

Seniors, or the aging, constitute one of the fastest growing segments of the Canadian population. Troll (1971) listed a total of only 16 major studies in the 1960s that were concerned with later-life families. Brubaker (1990), in contrast, found an explosion of research during the 1980s on these families, showing that the study of later-life families has come into vogue. Projections that this group will continue to increase significantly in the next century as a result of the aging of the baby boom generation are attracting increased attention from governments and from those who provide services to the aging. The concern is that the increase in the elderly population will strain medical, social, and other services, and threaten to overload an already stretched social safety net. The fact that people are more likely to live to advanced ages affects the nature of relationships between spouses, as well as those between generations.

This chapter examines the aging population of Canada. The first section provides important background information essential to understanding the later-life family. It includes definitions, demographic information about the elderly, and a discussion of how the changing experiences of life affect them.

The second section examines various kinship relationships experienced by the elderly. The final section investigates caregiving in later-life families.

Understanding Later-Life Families

The term **later-life families** refers to families that are beyond the child-rearing years, and those families with children that have begun to launch them (Brubaker and Roberto, 1993). Following the launching of children, the most significant change faced by individuals is retirement and the movement into the ranks of the elderly. This change is ultimately accompanied by the loss of a spouse, reduced mobility, and deteriorating health.

Definitions

Gerontology is the study of aging. Four aspects of aging are defined. *Chronological aging* refers to how many years we have lived, and determines when we are able to begin school, obtain a driver's licence, marry without the consent of our parents, retire from work, and draw an old-age pension. *Biological aging* refers to physiological changes, including greying hair, balding, wrinkling, and declining strength and dexterity. *Psychological aging* refers to cognitive, intellectual, and emotional changes associated with increasing chronological age. *Social aging* refers to how others, or even various societies, treat people of different ages (Baker, 1988).

Attitudes toward biological or physiological aging differ for males and females. The high value placed on the youthful appearance of women encourages them to spend considerable time and money attempting to appear younger than their chronological age. Some feminists point out that the definition of women in terms of sexuality and fertility makes aging more consequential for them. This leads to a double standard of aging, since an older woman may be taken more seriously in a professional role if she is also attractive. Thus, to be old and female may be a "double jeopardy" because the disadvantages of being a female increase with age (Baker, 1988).

Aging can be defined both from an individual and a societal perspective. From the *individual* perspective, the **elderly** are those who are 65 years of age or older.

The number of Canadians aged 65 and older grew by 50 percent between 1981 and 1995 (from 2.3 million to 3.6 million), compared with an increase of 33 percent among those aged 25 to 44, and 32 percent among those aged 45 to 64. The result is that people aged 65 and older made up 12 percent of the total population in 1995, compared to 8 percent in 1971. By 2041, it is estimated that about 23 percent of the population will be over 65. The 1996 Census metropolitan area with the highest proportion of its population over age 65 was Victoria (18 percent), whereas Oshawa and Calgary, each with 8 percent, had the lowest proportion of elderly people (Lindsay, 1997).

The definition of the elderly as those who are 65 and older is an arbitrary decision, usually related to age at retirement. The establishment of such a chronological age only approximates the threshold of old age. There are wide differences between individuals in terms of the aging process, and some people both feel and look "old" in terms of their biological, psychological, and social functioning long before they reach the chronological age of 65. Others continue to function effectively for many years beyond the time when they are chronologically defined as old.

The 1994 General Social Survey found that 58 percent of men aged 55 and older were retired. The likelihood of retirement increased with age: 14 percent of men aged 55 to 59 were retired, compared to 45 percent aged 60 to 64, and 78 percent aged 65 to 69. The average retirement age for men in the survey was 61.4 years. Retirement age is becoming increasingly varied. In 1989, 19 percent retired at age 65, compared with 10 percent in 1994. This decline is accompanied by an increase in retirement before 65 and after age 65. The largest proportion of retired men left the workforce for health reasons (25 percent) or by personal choice (24 percent). Incentives for early retirement accounted for only 10 percent of men's retirement (Monette, 1996a). In 1989, about half (52 percent) of currently employed Canadians held employer-provided pension plans (55 percent of men and 49 percent of women). Twice the proportion of men (60 percent) as women (30 percent) received a pension from a former employer. This difference helps to account for the higher incidence of low income among elderly women (Lowe, 1992).

In defining the elderly as those who are 65 and older, we must recognize that they are not a homogeneous group. Abu-Laban (1987) pointed out two important differences within this age group. First, families sometimes include two generations of people over the age of 65. Of those over 65, 10 percent also have a parent (or child) who is also over that age. Second, differences in health and availability of family support between those aged 65 to 74 and those aged 75 and older must be recognized.

Table 12.1 shows the marital status of persons 65 years of age and older, by sex, in 2001. A very small percentage were single (e.g., 6.6 percent of men and

TABLE 12.1   Percentage of Males and Females in Marital Status for Elderly Age Group, 2001

AGE GROUP	MARITAL STATUS	MALE	FEMALE
65–69	Never Married	6.6%	5.7%
	Married	76.4	59.8
	Separated	2.8	2.5
	Divorced	8.4	9.1
	Widowed	5.8	23
	Total number	543 825	589 795
70–74	Never Married	6.6	5.8
	Married	75.2	50.3
	Separated	2.5	2
	Divorced	6.1	6.5
	Widowed	9.5	35.3
	Total number	461 780	547 430
75–79	Never Married	6.2	6.1
	Married	72.2	38.1
	Separated	2.2	1.5
	Divorced	4.2	4.4
	Widowed	15.1	49.9
	Total number	338 820	474 850
80–84	Never Married	5.7	6.8
	Married	66.9	24.7
	Separated	2	1.1
	Divorced	2.8	2.8
	Widowed	22.5	64.5
	Total number	192 640	323 495

(Continued)

TABLE 12.1 Continued

AGE GROUP	MARITAL STATUS	MALE	FEMALE
85–89	Never Married	6.2	8.3
	Married	56.7	13.5
	Separated	1.9	0.7
	Divorced	2	1.7
	Widowed	33.2	75.7
	Total number	91 430	190 355
90 & over	Never Married	7.3	9.7
	Married	41.3	5.7
	Separated	1.8	0.4
	Divorced	1.5	1
	Widowed	48.1	83.2
	Total number	34 150	99 970

Source: Census 2001, Statistics Canada, Cat. 95F0407XCB01004.

5.7 percent of women among 65 to 69 years of age). Also, a very small proportion of the population were divorced. Differences in marital status between men and women are most clearly seen in the married and widowed categories. At all age levels, men are much more likely to be married than are women of that age, whereas women are much more likely to be widowed than are men. Thus, almost three-quarters of elderly men are married, whereas almost half of elderly women are widowed.

Historically, there were at least 100 males for every 100 females until after 1951, and women outnumbered men in the Canadian population only among 80-year-olds for the first half of the century. Since 1961, women have outnumbered men in the age groups above 65, and this difference has been increasing. In 1986, the over-65 sex ratio was 72 males for every 100 females (Nett, 1990). In 1996, the sex ratio was 97 (males for every 100 females) for the entire Canadian population, but only 73 for those aged 65 and older. The sex ratio was 84 for those aged 65 to 74, 65 for those aged 75 to 84, and 42 for those aged 85 and over (McVey, 1998). A number of factors may have contributed to these differences between men and women. Men have a lower life expectancy than women, and women tend to marry older men. More opportunities for remarriage are available for widowed men because there are more widows than widowers, and it is more acceptable culturally for men to marry younger women than for women to marry younger men.

Three major transitions are associated with aging. First, aging is associated with less gender differentiation and more similarity in definitions of masculinity and femininity. This results in more egalitarianism in the division of household labour. Second, retirement may be the greatest change in the male gender role; it diminishes the provider role, but also reduces the stress associated with work. The increased amounts of time and proximity associated with retirement may lead to either greater intimacy or greater irritation. The loss of companionship in the workplace may lead to greater dependence on wives, which wives may find excessive. Third, aging is often associated with a decline in health of one or both spouses. If the wife has health problems, the husband may need to assume more household tasks, affecting the division of labour. Thus a wife's illness is often more disruptive to her husband than his illness would be to his wife. The new roles of care-provider and care-recipient often heighten the interdependence and closeness of older spouses, and enable them to continue to live independently (Connidis, 1989b).

Aging may also be defined from a societal perspective. **Demographic** or **population aging** is the process by which an entire population grows older, increasing the proportion of the elderly. In most industrialized societies, there is an increasing proportion of people living to age 65 and into the late seventies and eighties. The United Nations defines an aged population as one in which more than 7 percent is over the age of 65. Demographic aging involves changes throughout the age structure rather than merely an increase in the number of older persons (McDaniel, 1986). From 1981 to 1991, the proportion of Canada's population aged 65 and older increased from 10 percent to 12 percent. The proportion of the population aged less than 15 years, however, *declined* from 23 percent to 21 percent, which also represents an important contribution to the process of demographic aging (Statistics Canada, 1992). In 1881, Canada was "middle-aged," with about 4 percent of its population aged 65 and over. By 1971, it had become an "old" nation, with more than 8 percent of its population in the elderly category (Northcott, 1992b).

Three major factors contribute to population aging. First, increased life expectancy as the result of increased longevity or decreased mortality has only a minor effect because of the ceiling effect of the biological life span. The **biological life span** is the theoretical age limit of the individual, or the age to which he could be expected to live if protected from disease and injury. In our society the life span is about 100 years. Second, the effect of current immigration to Canada is to lower the relative age of the population, since immigration primarily involves younger people. Third, declining fertility makes the most important contribution to an aging population. Demographic aging is one consequence of smaller families and fewer children in Canadian society (McDaniel, 1986).

Gee (1987) reports that for cohorts born between 1900 and 1916, the percentage of ever-married women who remained childless was in the range of 13 to 15 percent. A **cohort** is a group of persons who were born or who married in the same years. Women born between 1902 and 1911 had a childless rate of more than 15 percent, partly because they reached prime childbearing age during the Great Depression. The percentage of ever-married childless women declined among the cohorts born after 1922, with those born between 1922 and 1926 having a childless rate of about 7 percent. These cohorts are the mothers of the baby boom. Canadian women currently under the age of 35 exhibit relatively high rates of childlessness, indicating trends toward increased childlessness, later childbearing, or both (Grindstaff, 1984). Permanent childlessness among today's young women may be in the range of 15 to 20 percent, including both voluntary and involuntary childlessness (Gee, 1987). In 1991, 14 percent (one million) of all families were childless (no children were present, and the woman had never borne any). The woman was still of childbearing age (under 45) in the majority of childless families (79 percent), but the remaining 21 percent of childless families will probably remain so since the woman was above the age of 45 (Statistics Canada, 1993).

This increase in childlessness is accompanied by a significant decrease in fertility among women, from about 6.6 children per woman in the cohorts of 1817 to 1831 to about 1.7 children per woman in the cohorts of 1947 to 1961 (a decrease of about 75 percent). A number of important changes have been identified in Canadian society as contributing to this decline during the past 150 years:

1. significant urbanization, decreasing the utility of children;
2. the development of a skilled labour force, increasing the amount of education required, thereby increasing the costs of child-rearing;
3. increased labour force participation of women, which competes with child-rearing;
4. increasing levels of education, creating an enhanced sense of self that contributes to the willingness to exercise control over one's own life;
5. increasing secularization;
6. increasingly effective modes of contraception (Gee, 1987).

Demographic Developments

Demographic data provide a number of measures of population aging. Table 12.2 presents three indicators of population aging for Canada since 1851 (the time of

TABLE 12.2   Demographic Aging for Canada, 1851–1991

YEAR	MEDIAN AGE	% 65+	TOTAL DEPENDENCY RATIO
1851	17.2	2.7	.909
1861	18.2	3.0	.834
1871	18.8	3.7	.828
1881	20.1	4.1	.749
1891	21.4	4.6	.692
1901	22.7	5.0	.651
1911	23.8	4.7	.603
1921	24.0	4.8	.644
1931	24.8	5.6	.592
1941	27.1	6.7	.526
1951	27.7	7.8	.615
1961	26.3	7.6	.712
1971	26.3	8.1	.604
1981	29.5	9.7	.475
1991	33.5	11.6	.481

Source: David K. Foote. *Canada's Population Outlook: Demographic Futures and Economic Challenges*. Toronto: James Lorimer, p. 9, in McDaniel, 1986:36, and Statistics Canada. 1992. *Age, Sex, and Marital Status*. Ottawa: Catalogue 93-310

the first Census): the median age, the proportion aged 65 and older, and the total dependency ratio. The most commonly used index of aging—the median age—increased steadily from 17.2 in 1851 to 29.5 in 1981, and to 33.5 in 1991. Foote (1982) predicts that the median age of Canada's population will be around 42 years by 2051. The proportion of the population aged 65 and older (Table 12.1, column 2) has also increased steadily over the same period, from less than 3 percent in 1851 to 11 percent in 1986, and to 11.6 percent in 1991. The two periods of most rapid increase were 1931 to 1941 (during the Great Depression, and the associated decline in birthrates and immigration), and 1971 to 1981 (also a period of very low birthrates and low immigration).

The **total dependency ratio** is the ratio of people who are of non-working age (15 years and younger, and 65 years and older) to those who are of working age (15 to 65). This ratio, which is a rough indicator of economic dependency, has been declining over the past century (McDaniel, 1986). It is expected to remain at this low level until about 2010. At that time, when the baby-boom generation begins reaching age 65, the dependency ratio is projected to begin climbing rapidly. By 2030, it is expected to reach the high levels experienced in the 1960s. McDaniel points out, however, that "these ratios have little bearing on actual dependency—many people work who are not yet 18 years old and over age 65; and, conversely, a significant proportion of those aged 18–65 may not work for pay" (1993:7).

A major change, however, is that people aged 65 and older will account for a larger proportion of the dependent population, while those under 15 will account for a smaller proportion. In 1965, 19 percent of the dependent population was aged 65 and older, while 81 percent was under age 15. By 1987, these figures had changed to 34 percent elderly and 66 percent young people. It is projected that by 2030, more than half of the dependent population (55 percent) will be aged 65 and older, while only 45 percent will be under age 15. This shift will have major implications for the funding of social programs, and particularly for medical expenses (Chawla, 1991). In addition, beginning with the 1990s, the fall in the fertility rate which began in 1960 will result in decreased numbers of people between 15 and 65 years of age. This change also has important implications for the financial security of older people, affecting pension plans and health and social services (Termote, 1990).

Impact of Family Structure

One of the inevitable results of aging is that children become more independent and establish their own residences—moving to an apartment, entering a cohabiting relationship, or getting married. This results in a contraction of the household unit that places more emphasis on the marital relationship between the partners. Dyadic interaction, which characterized their relationship before the arrival of children, once again assumes greater importance, since most couples can expect to be two-person households for approximately 15 to 30 years. Couples may need to develop new ways of communication and decision-making. They may also need to establish new ways of communicating with their independent children (Brubaker and Roberto, 1993).

The contraction of the household brings about important changes, but middle-aged and older couples also need to address the resulting changes brought about by the expansion of the family network. When children get married, new relationships need to be established with a son-in-law or daughter-in-law and with their families. In some cases, adult children leave home, but then return again after a few years of independence. This requires a process of readjustment in interaction and decision patterns to accommodate the needs of the parents and the children who have both become more independent while apart. Changing family structure has a significant impact on the patterns of interaction between aging couples. The stage of family life characterized by retirement, caregiving, and negotiating relationships with adult children has received very little attention in research and therapy journals (Brubaker and Roberto, 1993).

Living Arrangements

The 2001 Census reveals that few elderly live in health care facilities or institutions (Table 12.3). The majority of the elderly live in a family with either their spouse or their children. The remaining elderly live outside a family, usually living alone. As Table 12.3 indicates, elderly women are more likely to live alone, in collective households, or outside a family, as compared with men; men are almost twice as likely as women to live as part of a couple. The survivor of an aged couple lives alone as long as possible after the death of a spouse before moving into an institution. Since women are more likely to lose a spouse earlier in life, the living arrangements of elderly men and women are different (Priest, 1993).

Due to low fertility rates and increasing longevity, a growing share of Canada's population is made up of seniors aged 75 and older. In 1991, 4.7 percent of Canadians were aged 75 and older, compared to 3.1 percent in 1971 (Priest and Prasil, 1993). A study of Canada's "older elderly" population (aged 75 and older) found that a major change had occurred in their living arrangements since 1971. A higher proportion were either living alone or in institutions, while the percentage living with others (primarily family) had declined. The proportion of older seniors living in institutions has not changed since the mid-1970s (Priest, 1993). Projections indicate that these trends are likely to continue. **Institutions**, in the context of the elderly, are "establishments providing some level of custody or care, as distinct from other collective dwellings such as hotels or rooming houses where no care is provided" (Priest, 1988:26).

In the five-year period from 1990 to 1995, 23 percent of Canadians aged 60 and older changed their principal residence, compared with almost half (46 percent) of the population aged 15 and older who moved between 1986 and 1991. The majority of Canadians aged 60 and older who moved between 1990 and 1995 settled no more than 50 kilometres from their previous home, while only 10 percent moved more than 200 kilometres. The most frequent reason for moving was the desire for a smaller home. As people become older, a more frequent reason for moving is the desire for social support, such as being closer to family or moving to a seniors' residence (Che-Alford and Stevenson, 1998).

TABLE 12.3   Living Arrangements of Seniors Aged 65 and Over by Sex and Age Group, Canada, 2001

SEX	AGE GROUP	LIVING ALONE	LIVING WITH SPOUSE OR PARTNER (NO CHILDREN)	LIVING WITH CHILDREN	LIVING IN HEALTH CARE INSTITUTION	OTHER LIVING ARRANGEMENTS*	TOTAL
		%					(numbers)
Males	Total 65+	16.0	61.4	13.3	4.9	4.4	1 666 400
	65–74	14.0	64.4	15.4	2.1	4.0	1 008 735
	75–84	18.3	60.7	10.2	6.2	4.6	533 705
	85+	22.7	39.5	8.5	22.6	6.7	123 960
Females	Total 65+	34.8	35.4	12.1	9.2	8.4	2 224 395
	65–74	28.2	48.1	14.1	2.3	7.3	1 135 475
	75–84	42.8	27.7	10.8	9.6	9.2	798 300
	85+	38.5	7.2	8.4	35.4	10.6	290 620

*Includes living with other relatives, e.g., a niece or nephew, or with non-relatives, e.g., a lodger.

Source: Statistics Canada, Census 2001, http://www12.statcan.ca/english/census01/Products/Analytic/companion/fam/ftnt.

"As the population ages, discussion increasingly focuses on how to keep people in the community and out of health-care institutions. But when health fails, the only option may be long-term residential care" (Tully and Mohl, 1995:27). In 1995 elderly women were more likely than men to be residents of health-care institutions. Institutionalized residents were not as healthy as their contemporaries living in households. Three chronic conditions—Alzheimer's disease or other dementia, incontinence, and the effects of stroke—were more common among institutional residents than among household residents (Tully and Mohl, 1995). (See Figure 12.2 later in the chapter.)

The number of older elderly women aged 75 and over who were living alone increased from 26 percent in 1971 to 39 percent in 1993, while the proportion in institutions increased from 14 percent to 18 percent. The number of older elderly men living alone rose from 13 percent to 17 percent between 1971 and 1991, while the proportion living in institutions increased slightly from 9 percent to 10 percent (Priest, 1993). Older elderly men are much more likely than women of the same age to be married and living with their spouse in their own home. In contrast, older elderly women are much more likely to be living alone than are men of the same age. The percentage of older elderly men living in their own home with a spouse increased from 51 percent in 1971 to 58 percent in 1991, while the proportion of older elderly women living in their own home with their spouse increased only slightly, from 18 percent in 1971 to 20 percent in 1991. Research also reveals that the number and percentage of those 75 and older living in someone else's home has decreased during the same period. The proportion of older elderly women living with others declined from 26 percent in 1971 to 12 percent in 1991, while the proportion of older elderly men living with others declined from 17 percent to 8 percent during the same period. This decline suggests that fewer adults now occupy the same dwelling as their elderly parents do. It may also be the result of the increased participation of women in the labour force, which has reduced the likelihood that someone will be at home to look after older parents. Also, rising incomes among the elderly may have enabled more of them to maintain separate living arrangements (Priest, 1993).

Prasil (1993) suggests that there have been considerable changes in the lifestyles of seniors in recent years. Improvements in people's health and longevity, as well as in the quality and variety of services for seniors, have contributed to these changes. Box 12.1 provides a profile of these changes.

Projections indicate that the trend of the elderly toward living alone or in their own home with a spouse will continue. Based on Statistics Canada information, Priest (1993) projects that the proportion of seniors living in institutions will decline from 19 percent in 1981 to 16 percent in 2011 for women, and from 12 percent in 1981 to 10 percent in 2011 for men. At the same time, the proportion of seniors living in their own home with a spouse will increase from 51 percent in 1971 to 60 percent in 2011 for men, and from 18 percent in 1981 to 22 percent in 2011 for women. The proportion of seniors living alone will increase from 13 percent in 1971 to 18 percent in 2011 for men, and from 26 percent in 1971 to 42 percent in 2011 for women. This has important implications for social services to this population. Provisions will need to be made for adequate home care, home security, transportation, and social support to enable elderly people to retain their independence and to delay the necessity of the fuller (and more costly) care of institutions.

Rosenthal (1994) expresses some concern about this shift from an institution-centred long-term care system to one that is community based, in that it may be driven primarily by economic rather than humanitarian reasons. She expresses concern about the fact that care for an older relative is increasingly combined with paid employment on the part of the caregiver, resulting in disturbances in their work, as well as in increased time pressures. This shift may also result in a decrease in available institutional beds. As the number of older elderly increases, the need for institutional beds will increase, particularly for those with severe dementias.

In contrast, a recent national poll finds little support for new national health-care programs for seniors. Given a choice between restoring to the provinces the funding intended for Medicare that was cut by the federal government to help reduce the deficit, or funding new national health-care programs such as a new pharmacare program or a new homecare program, just over 7 in 10 Canadians (71 percent) felt that the government's first priority was to restore health-care funding to the provinces. Of the 27 percent of Canadians who indicated that the government's first priority was to fund new national health-care programs, just over 6 in 10 (61 percent) felt that Ottawa should launch homecare programs first, compared to more than a third (35 percent) who felt that pharmacare programs should be launched first (Angus Reid Group, 1997).

What are the major determinants of the living arrangements of the elderly? Kyriazis and Stelcner

Box 12.1   Research Insights: Lifestyles of the Elderly

Statistics Canada's 1991 Survey on Ageing and Independence provides a profile of the current lifestyles of people aged 75 and over living in private households.

According to the Survey, low incomes and sparse accommodations were more common among senior women aged 75 and over than among men that age. Nonetheless, almost all older women and men were relatively satisfied with their incomes. Many older seniors living at home were limited because of a long-term illness or physical disability. For some, health problems led to feelings of stress or unhappiness. Most older seniors, however, had people in their lives they could rely on for support and perceived their lives as happy. Many older seniors also provided help to others.

Source: Prasil, 1993:26.

(1986) found that the effect of income on living arrangements was not significant for either males or females over 50. The two major determinants of living alone were age and region. The impact of age on living alone was different for men than for women. For men, the odds of living alone increased to age 70 and then declined, whereas for women, the odds of living alone consistently increased with age. The impact of functional incapacity (or the inability to look after basic needs such as meals and laundry) may thus be significant for older males but not for females. Regional differences were also found in the probability of living alone. Both male and female elderly persons living in the eastern provinces and in Quebec were less likely to live alone than were those living in the western provinces. Those living in British Columbia had the highest probability of living alone, perhaps because when they moved to favoured retirement areas, they left their kinfolk behind.

The most powerful predictor of household status of the elderly is fertility, with higher fertility significantly decreasing the probability of living alone. The impact of fertility on the household status of older women was also supported in a previous study (Wister and Burch, 1983), which found that the number of children ever born was the best predictor of the household status of all previously married females (widowed, divorced or separated). Having fewer children was positively associated with the probability of living alone. Other factors positively associated with the higher probability of living alone were education, age, and income.

Marriage appears to act as a deterrent to institutionalization, though this may result in additional strains on the healthy spouse. In 1986, the majority of senior men lived in family households (82 percent of men aged 65 to 74, and 66 percent aged 75 and older). In contrast, only 60 percent of women aged 65 to 74 and 34 percent of women 75 and older lived in family households (Gauthier, 1991).

Family Life Stage and Happiness

As we saw in Chapter 9, the relationship between family life stage and marital satisfaction generally demonstrates a curvilinear pattern. The highest level of satisfaction is found during early marriage before the advent of children in the family. The presence of children is associated with a decline in satisfaction, which continues through the stages with children at home. An increase in satisfaction is experienced at the "empty nest" stage, and satisfaction reaches its second highest level in the retirement stage.

Very little research exists regarding the impact of parent–children relationships on the marital satisfaction of spouses who entered a later-life remarriage. The presence of children, especially stepchildren, had a negative impact on young and middle-aged remarriage quality (White, Booth, and Edwards, 1986). McElhaney (1994) secured data on remarried couples in which at least one spouse was 50 or older at the time of the remarriage. This data failed to find any impact of children on the marital satisfaction of husbands in later-life remarriages. Wives who had satisfying relationships with children, however, were more likely to report higher marital satisfaction (McElhaney, 1994).

In an examination of the pressures and satisfactions experienced with respect to various facets of people's lives, Northcott (1992a) concluded that, in general, older people were less likely to feel stress and more likely to feel satisfied with the various domains of their lives. "In short, the picture one gets of old age is that it is a period of relatively low pressure and relatively high satisfaction, though not without its problems" (Northcott, 1992a:77). Connidis (1987) found that the most positive aspect of older age was the increased freedom and relaxation associated with decreased responsibility. Respondents reported fewer obligations and more time for engaging in chosen pursuits. Women more often mentioned freedom from familial responsibilities, while men emphasized the autonomy of retirement, reflecting the division of labour by sex that is characteristic of this age group.

Keith and Landry (1992) found that older Canadians generally report being healthy and happy. In the 1985 and 1990 General Social Surveys, two-thirds to three-quarters of Canadians aged 55 and older reported being in good or excellent health. Also, more than 90 percent reported being happy or very happy. More than 90 percent of respondents reported that they were satisfied with their relationships with family and friends, current accommodations and jobs, and with their main activities. Health status had an important impact on overall happiness. A greater proportion of the very unhappy than of the very happy reported fair or poor health. Those with physical activity limitations were more likely to report being unhappy. Only 21 percent of the very happy reported activity limitations, compared to 70 percent for the very unhappy, although unhappiness may have led some to exaggerate the limitations they experience. Thus, health and activity limitations appear to be important predictors of general well-being among the elderly.

In a representative sample of 3300 Canadians, Atkinson (1980) found that age was strongly related to overall life satisfaction, with older individuals indicating the highest levels of satisfaction. Despite the fact that income decreases with advancing age, older people still report higher levels of satisfaction. Sixty-one percent of those aged 65 and older were in the lowest income group, but they exhibited the highest levels of satisfaction. Atkinson suggested that this may be the case because the hopes and goals of older people may be more restricted to the present rather than to anticipated future improvements, and because the increased leisure time enjoyed by older individuals may enhance their general satisfaction with life (Atkinson, 1980, cited by Connidis, 1987:456). Box 12.2 reports on the experiences of one couple who have managed to stay together for more than 80 years.

Thus, the highest levels of marital satisfaction are found at the beginning and end of marriage. Several similarities between the newly married and older people are 1) a child-free adult-centred lifestyle; 2) task performance that cuts across traditional gender-role boundaries; 3) more discretionary time to do things together; 4) the necessity to function on a low or reduced income; and 5) a heightened appreciation of their relationship (Abu-Laban, 1987).

One of the most frequent research findings is that health-category variables are strongly associated with the perceived life satisfaction of the elderly. Snider (1980b) reports that self-rated health accounts for the largest proportion of variance in life satisfaction among

---

Box 12.2 Current Insights: Still Sweethearts After 80 Years

Paul and Mary Onessi's marriage has survived two World Wars, the Great Depression and—perhaps more astoundingly—80 years of uncelebrated Valentine's Days.

No flowers, no boxes of chocolates or heart-shaped candies. Not even a romantic picnic at the falls [Niagara Falls] that make their hometown America's "Honeymoon Capital."

Mary Onessi, 93, just shakes her head when asked how she and her 101-year-old husband celebrate February, 14. Like many couples from their generation, the Onessis' relationship is more sensible than sentimental.

"If you have trouble, you go talk about it, argue, and get over it," she said.

In the living room of their tidy apartment hangs [a] plaque given to them on World Marriage Day three years ago, honoring them for being the longest-married couple in the country.

Paul Onessi waves off the accomplishment as if it doesn't merit so much interest. It is the marriages that don't work that get his attention. He thinks there are far too many of those.

"In our family, no one ever wanted to get divorced because no one wanted to tell them," said Laura Cerillo, one of the couple's 28 grandchildren....

Mary Corsaro was 13 and Paul Onessi was 21 when they were married in a small family ceremony in Clymer, Pa., on Aug. 6, 1917.

"I was so young," Mary Onessi said, trying to recall.

She gave birth to their first child a year later. Five more would follow, all born at home....

The children are all parents and grandparents themselves now. The Onessis have seen five of their kids celebrate their 50th wedding anniversaries.

Despite all the modern conveniences that have come along during the past eight decades, the Onessis choose to live relatively simply. They have never gotten a microwave oven, and family members know better than to pick out gifts like pasta- or bread-makers for them.

They did give in to television, though, and are known to bicker over the stations. It's one of the few things left to argue about after so many years together.

Source: The Associated Press, February 14, 1998:4A.

the elderly. Health variables are better predictors of life satisfaction than are activity, socioeconomic status, or social background variables. It is interesting that it is not the objective health status of the elderly, but rather their own subjective evaluation, or attitudes toward health, that predict life satisfaction. Connidis (1987) reports that 10 percent of her sample of elderly liked nothing about their age. These individuals tended to be older (85 and over), to feel that their experiences did not meet their expectations, and to assess their health as poor.

Kinship Relationships in Later Life

Connidis (1989b, 2001) points out that industrialization and modernization have frequently been associated with the breakdown of the traditional family, because of the loss of important family functions and the geographic dispersal of family members, leading to a weakening of the contacts between generations. Recent research, however, has documented high rates of interaction between adult children and their aging parents, as well as mutual support and affection between the generations. Connidis argues that the common belief that the elderly are neglected or abandoned by their families as a result of the emphasis on the nuclear family in our society is a myth. She points out that the modern family has maintained a network of contact and exchange, and provides emotional, social, and practical support for older people. Only a small proportion (5 to 8.5 percent) of all those above age 65 live in institutional settings (Connidis, 1989b, 2001). Other myths contradicted by research are that families treated older people better in the past than they do today, and that less complex societies treat the elderly better than does our own society (Rosenthal, 1987). "Contrary to prevailing myths, only a minority of the elderly experience poor health, institutionalized living, poverty, loneliness, isolation or senility" (McPherson, 1983:12).

More than 50 percent of one sample of Canadian adults indicated that there was at least one person in their extended family who was considered a kin-keeper, and an additional 16 percent said there had been such a person in the past. **Kin-keeping** consists of efforts expended to keep family members in touch with one another. Females are the most frequent kin-keepers, and the succession of this job from one generation to the next descends through the female line. Siblings are most often named as kin-keepers, suggesting that it is ties with siblings and their children that become problematic with aging, particularly after parents die (Rosenthal, 1985). Knowledge of more distant relatives is often forever lost when a grandmother dies.

The Never-Married

The never-married elderly differ from the widowed, divorced, or separated in that they usually have no children or spousal kin in their family network. The never-married elderly in Canada have higher rates of co-residence than do the divorced and widowed, because they are most likely to live with someone who is unrelated. They are more likely to feel lonely, and to receive less emotional, social, and instrumental support from family than are the married. Older single men are more isolated from family than are older single women (Connidis, 1989b, 2001).

The Married

The majority of all Canadians over the age of 65 have been married at some time in their lives. Table 12.1 shows that most men and women over 65 years of age are either still married or were previously married (widowed, separated, or divorced). In old age the majority of males have a spouse, but women increasingly join the widowed category as males predecease their wives.

Being married is associated with a wide range of benefits for older persons. The experiences of retirement, travel, and shared leisure-time activities are important for those who are married, and who have adequate resources. Problems related to health and decreased mobility are easier to endure when shared with a spouse. The availability of companionship and support greatly help people to avoid loneliness and lack of interaction. Retirement also provides the opportunity for them to share more activities around the house (Brubaker, 1990).

According to the 1990 General Social Survey, when married seniors were asked who they would turn to for emotional support, 45 percent of men and

37 percent of women reported that they would turn to their spouse. Married women were more likely to turn to their children (25 percent) or a friend (10 percent) for support than were men (15 percent and 4 percent, respectively.) Elderly women not living with a spouse were more likely to turn to a daughter for emotional support (28 percent), while only 16 percent of the men without spouses would do so. Men were more likely to turn to a friend (24 percent) for support, compared to only 16 percent of women (McDaniel, 1993d).

The Childless

Three primary reasons for being childless in old age are as follows: 1) never marrying; 2) involuntary childlessness in marriage; and 3) voluntary childlessness in marriage. A small number are childless because their child or children predeceased the parents. The childless elderly are more likely to live alone, but are also more likely to have greater economic resources, and thus may be able to engage in other social activities that prevent social isolation. While those with children have more friends and family, those with and without children report similar levels of satisfaction and loneliness in old age (Connidis, 1989b, 2001).

The Divorced

Divorce is currently not common among older individuals, but the rate is increasing. Divorced older women are more likely to turn to family and friends for support and help, while men are more likely to remarry. Divorced older men tend to be the most isolated of all combinations of sex and marital status groups (Connidis, 1989b, 2001).

Divorce may have a significant impact on the financial status of the elderly, especially for women. One study found that divorced men generally had higher incomes than did never-married and widowed men, but divorced women generally had lower incomes than did widowed women. Patterns of social interaction also were affected by divorce, leading to limited contacts and social interaction. The divorced had fewer contacts with family and friends, but divorced women were more likely to maintain such contacts than were divorced men. The divorce of adult children may negatively affect their ability to assist elderly parents because of more limited financial resources; indeed, they sometimes require more assistance from their elderly parents. Divorce may also affect the amount of interaction between grandparents and grandchildren, particularly for paternal grandparents (Brubaker, 1990).

Burch (1990) investigated the remarriage patterns of persons aged 55 to 65 at the time of the 1984 Family History Survey. Relatively few older Canadians (about 8 percent) have experienced remarriage by their 65th birthday. Women are nearly twice as likely as men to experience marriage dissolution through widowhood. Men are more likely than women to remarry following divorce or widowhood—more than half of widowed and divorced women, and about one-third of widowed men, have failed to remarry within 25 years of their marital dissolution. Regional differences in remarriage patterns in Canada were found, with appreciably lower remarriage rates among Quebec residents than among those in the rest of Canada.

Pett et al. (1992) examined the impact of late-life divorce on family rituals. They found that the divorce of older parents was not a single event, but a process that required the constant renegotiation of family celebrations, traditions and ceremonies. While some family rituals were maintained, others were irrevocably changed. The loss of participation by important family kin in these rituals involved not only the divorcing parents, but extended family members. The difficult logistics of including particular family subsystems (for example, parent with new spouse or partner, or a parent alone) were especially challenging during such celebrations as Thanksgiving and Christmas. The perceived disruptiveness of the divorce and the consequent changes in family rituals suggest that the children of divorce must cope with the continuing after-effects of their parents' separation and divorce.

Goldscheider (1990) points out that significant changes will take place among the elderly as a result of the gender revolution, which rests on the growing economic independence of women. This growing independence is associated with a rise in divorce rates, a rise in female employment accompanied by pressures toward greater egalitarianism, and a decline in remarriage. Goldscheider suggests that these changes represent higher risks for men than for women.

The Widowed

Two main features characterize widowhood in contemporary Canadian culture. First, widowhood is sex-selective. Eighty-two percent of the widowed are women, and this proportion is increasing. Factors accounting for this proportion include the differential life expectancy favouring females; the mating gradient, whereby husbands are generally two to three years older than their wives; and the higher remarriage rates for widowers as compared to widows. A second feature of widowhood in Canada is its age-related nature. The average age at widowhood has been steadily increasing in recent decades, resulting in the association of widowhood with the elderly. Most widows in Canada (69 percent) are over age 65. Despite the increase in divorce, death of the spouse will continue to be the typical end to married life of Canadians for the foreseeable future (Martin-Matthews, 1987a).

The current generation of older women may have been more dependent on their husbands' instrumental skills, while older males may have depended on their wives' homemaking and interpersonal skills. Widows are thus more likely to have more interpersonal relationships with kin and neighbours, while widowers are more likely to be more isolated. However, widowers have a distinct advantage in their chances for remarriage (Abu-Laban, 1987).

Considerable debate has focused on whether widowhood is more stressful for men or for women, with conflicting findings. There is no doubt, however, that the experience differs. While widowers have more financial resources than do widows, they also experience higher suicide and mortality rates following bereavement. Widowers are more likely to be more isolated and to experience fewer emotional ties with their families. In contrast, widows enjoy closer relations with their children, and also have a larger group of other widows to provide emotional and social support—but they are more often poor (Martin-Matthews, 1987b; Connidis, 1989b, 2001). Thus, while loneliness is the widow's most frequently identified problem, financial insecurity is the second.

The primary support system of widowed women is their adult children. Significant supportive exchange takes place between them. The widowed aged also engage in exchanges of social support with other extended family members, particularly sisters. In one study, over half of the widows were in regular contact with and exchanged social and emotional support with siblings. Peer relationships with neighbours and friends also provided important emotional support to the widowed, but friendships were the crucial relationship that was most likely to change during bereavement. Because friendship is based on reciprocity and mutual need fulfillment, there may be a decrease in the number of social contacts with friends following the death of a spouse (Martin-Matthews, 1987b).

The Remarried

Remarriage is less likely as a person ages, but a number of older persons do remarry following divorce or the death of a spouse. Older persons who remarry are less homogamous than are younger persons on age and previous marital status (Brubaker, 1990). As described in more detail in Chapter 13, the probability of remarriage in later years is greater for males than for females. The sex differential in life expectancy contributes to the shortage of potential husbands at older ages (Abu-Laban, 1987).

Parent and Adult–Child Relationships

Social bonds among the generations are frequently conceptualized in terms of **solidarity**, which includes cohesion, integration, and support among generations. Rosenthal (1987) identified six dimensions of intergenerational solidarity: structure, association, affect, exchange, consensus, and norms. *Family structure* refers to the number and type of living relatives a person has, including spouse, parents, grandparents, children, and grandchildren. Family structure influences the ability of families to provide intergenerational support to older members.

One important aspect of family structure is geographical proximity, which facilitates or limits association and exchange within the family. *Associational solidarity* involves contact between the generations, including face-to-face contact, telephone calls, and letters, as well as the frequency of contacts and the occasions or reasons for them. *Functional solidarity* includes the exchange of assistance and support between generations, involving services, goods, financial aid, and, socio-emotional support. *Affective solidarity* entails the perceived quality of interaction, including perceived closeness or warmth, understanding, trust, fairness, love, appreciation, and recognition of others. *Consensual solidarity* describes the level of agreement or disagreement of generations on opinions and values. *Normative solidarity* involves the norms or expectations that family members apply to each other and to the family as a group. These different dimensions of solidarity point to the different aspects of social support within the family.

Marcil-Gratton and Légaré (1992) used Statistics Canada's General Social Survey of 1985 to determine if low fertility had any impact on the degree of isolation experienced by today's elderly. No significant differences were found between the childless elderly and those with children in the proportion who were not in daily contact with anybody. Nor were there any significant differences between those with many children (three or more) and those with few children (one or two). The authors concluded that growing isolation for the elderly in the future is not a direct consequence of today's low fertility. Although children played an important role in the lives of their aging parents, they were not the only sources of support for the elderly. "[S]pouseless elderly with few children seem to find the necessary support they need elsewhere, without experiencing greater isolation, and without putting any greater burden on formal services" (Marcil-Gratton and Légaré, 1992:69).

Most older people in Canada (66 to 75 percent) see at least one of their children at least once a week or more, or are in contact with them by phone. The great majority of elderly parents have at least one child living less than an hour's drive away. Children who help their parents more are likely to see them more often. Daughters see their older parents more often than do sons, because daughters provide more help to parents than do sons. Single, divorced, and widowed children see parents more often than do married children, which may reflect their greater freedom, but also their greater needs (Connidis, 1989b, 2001). Older parents both give and receive assistance from their children, but they may receive more than they give. This may be interpreted in an exchange framework, in which children are now repaying the earlier care and nurturing received from their parents. Parents are more likely to

receive health-care assistance from their children as they grow older. Families, rather than nursing homes, provide most services to the elderly. In the absence of a spouse, a daughter or daughter-in-law most frequently provides such services. There is no difference in levels of help with shopping, transportation, household maintenance, emotional support, and service management between daughters who are employed and those who are housewives (Connidis, 1989b, 2001).

However, older parents also supply significant help for their younger children, supporting the finding that while the nuclear family may be geographically isolated, it is not socially isolated from the modified kinship network. Kennedy and Stokes (1982) report that young people who are in the early stages of their lives are most likely to receive extended family support of all types. Higher levels of advice and financial assistance are received by young home owners who are paying high proportions of their income for their residence. This finding supports the hypothesis that young home owners are meeting the rising costs of housing with informal familial support. Regardless of socioeconomic background, the extended family often plays an important role in the purchase of one's own home.

Rosenthal (1987) reported that in a Hamilton sample of 56 men and 63 women, 84 percent of older men and 71 percent of older women with children had *provided* help to children during the year preceding the interview. In contrast, 80 percent of older men and 84 percent of older women had *received* help. The most common form of help was emotional support. While exchange relationships between older parents and their children tend to be reciprocal, some types of aid tend to flow down generational lines, while other types flow upward. Thus, older people were more likely to provide child care, financial assistance, and advice to their children. Children provide more practical assistance, such as help with personal services, household chores, home repairs, and personal care. Exchange was also affected by gender. Women received substantially more financial aid, help with chores, repairs, personal care, and emotional support than did men. Providing help was also related to gender—sons tended to provide financial assistance and advice, while daughters provided services such as caregiving.

Women are more likely to provide care for the elderly than are men. This includes wives caring for husbands, and daughters caring for their mothers. Many middle-aged women today must care for aging parents, while at the same time often caring for children, grandchildren, and a spouse—this group has been termed the "sandwich generation." This experience is also called the **generational squeeze**, affecting women in the middle generation who give significantly more support to family members than they receive. In addition, many women are also in the labour force, leading to the description of middle-aged women as the "caught generation" (Rosenthal, 1987). A recent examination of the likelihood of being "caught in the middle," however, indicates that the risk is not as high as some of the current discussions suggest. While a minority of middle-aged women do provide a significant level of parent care, this is not typical or "normative" for this population. Rosenthal et al. (1989) conclude that most middle-aged women will not be required to provide such support, and most parents will not become burdens to their children. Only a small proportion of women who are providing care to older relatives also have dependent children.

Stull et al. (1994) also argue that this situation may not be as problematic as previously assumed. They found, for example, that employment outside the home was not related to caregiver strain and well-being, suggesting that employment does not lead to added strain for the caregivers, with the exception of an increase in physical strain. They also found that the number of children in the household was actually related to *less* interpersonal strain between the caregiver and the recipient, and to *less* depression and *greater* positive affect. In fact, grandchildren were frequently found to be secondary caregivers, thus relieving the burden for their mother.

The Canadian Aging Research Network conducted a study of 5000 employees over the age of 35 in eight private and public sector organizations. They found that middle-aged Canadians caring for children and elderly parents were absent from work for three or more days at a time more often than were employees having no caregiving responsibilities. The results of such responsibilities were significant job opportunity costs, including fewer business trips, fewer extra projects, and missed job promotions. These opportunity costs were five to seven times greater than in the non-caregiving group. Forty-six percent of respondents reported providing assistance to an elderly relative, and one-quarter reported providing intensive personal elder care an average of nine hours weekly (The Canadian Press, 1993b).

What is the impact of adult sons' current relationships with their mothers and fathers on the sons' psychological distress? Barnett et al. (1992) reported finding equally positive relationships of sons with mothers and fathers. Positive relationships with parents were associated with lower levels of psychological distress than were negative relationships. When both mother and father were alive, the relationship quality with the father was a significant predictor of distress levels, whereas the relationship quality with the mother was not.

A great deal has been written regarding elder abuse, but there is considerable confusion regarding the extent of such abuse. The fundamental problem is how to define elder abuse. Various studies have estimated the incidence of elder abuse to be between 2 and 10 percent. It is impossible to determine if the incidence of elder abuse is increasing. Because the number of older persons is growing, there may be an increase in the absolute number of those abused, yet without a corresponding increase in the rates of abuse (Connidis, 1989b).

Payne and Payne (1994) indicate that financial abuse is the most common abuse of the elderly, and that this is often accompanied by emotional abuse. Financial abuse may include squandering the retirement savings of an elderly parent or grandparent, withholding pension or disability cheques, "jumping the gun" on prospective inheritances, or theft of money or possessions. When elderly persons resist such abuse, the result may be physical abuse.

A 1990 Ryerson Polytechnic University study found that more than one in 25 Canadian seniors were abused financially, physically, emotionally, or, more commonly, through a combination of these. Spouses, children, or caregivers may perpetrate abuse. Theft of money and possessions was involved in at least 60 percent of senior abuse in Canada; an example of such abuse is described in Box 12.3. There are various reasons why seniors do not report instances of abuse: shame that their child would treat them that way; dependence on the abuser and fear of losing further support; fear of

Box 12.3   Current Issues: Anguished Senior Lost Life Savings

"You don't expect anything back: Parents don't expect their kids to support them or anything," the 83-year-old father of two says, his soft voice almost apologetic. "But you don't expect to get robbed either." Bill certainly didn't. And the mistake cost him not just his retirement savings but his relationship with his eldest daughter and her children....

He had made a "gentleman's agreement" to become a 50-50 partner with his eldest daughter on a home. No legal documents, no binding agreement. Just her name on the mortgage. When things went bad, Bill moved out but his daughter stalled on the money. Three years later, when she was selling the house for $300 000, Bill called a lawyer and started court proceedings.

"She was in the process of committing a crime, which maybe she didn't realize, and (I hoped) that this would make her aware of what was happening." But the case dragged on, Bill moved to Vancouver to be near his younger daughter and finally, in November 1989, the then-80-year-old diabetic, emotionally and financially drained, agreed out of court to take $20 000 and go home.

"For an elderly father to take his own daughter—whom he loved unconditionally—to court was probably the hardest thing he ever had to do in his life," says his younger daughter. Few parents are willing to take legal action against a child, some don't realize they have options. And the children take advantage of that.

"We have a whole approach to seniors that automatically makes us question their capability," says [a researcher with the Gerontology Research Centre at Vancouver's Simon Fraser University], who is studying financial abuse of the elderly. "We question the reliability of the information that they give us, we question whether it's valid: it's very easy to be treated as a crazy old coot."

Source: Ramsay, 1993b:H3.

reprisals; a lack of alternatives or fear of being abandoned or sent to a nursing home; a lack of knowledge about their rights; and isolation or lack of ability to communicate (Ramsay, 1993b).

Grandparent Relationships

Almost three-quarters of older people are grandparents, and nearly half are great-grandparents. Becoming a grandparent is frequently the first family role associated with older age, but it is a role for which there are few normative guidelines. Becoming a grandparent at earlier ages is sometimes associated with feelings of discomfort.

The grandparent–grandchild relationship is dependent on the relationship between the older and middle generations, because the middle generation often mediates the grandparent–grandchild relationship. Previous relationships between the middle and older generations may inhibit or encourage contact between the grandparents and the grandchildren. For example, King (2003) found that grandparental divorce is negatively disruptive to the relationship between grandparents and grandchildren. The effect of the disruption was more significant for grandfathers than grandmothers. There is also disruption when an adult child divorces. Parents can expect increased contact with their grandchild(ren) if custody is granted to the adult child. When remarriage occurs, it creates a more complex relationship between grandparents and grandchildren. Research indicates that grandmothers and grandfathers view grandparenthood differently. Grandmothers tend to be more expressive than do grandfathers, while grandfathers tend to be more instrumental (task-oriented) (Brubaker and Roberto, 1993).

The 1990 General Social Survey indicates that 39 percent of grandchildren with a grandparent still living saw at least one of their grandparents once a month or more, 41 percent saw a grandparent less frequently than once a month, and 20 percent had not seen their grandparents in the past 12 months (McDaniel, 1993). Contact with grandparents is primarily determined by geographical distance. The grandparenthood role is quite flexible and ambiguous. Becoming a grandparent is beyond the control of the older generation, since it depends on the child becoming a parent.

Connidis (1989b, 2001) describes three basic styles of grandparenting. In the *companionate* style, grandparents are close to their grandchild(ren), but do not assume the parental role. In the *remote* style of grandparenting, the relationship is less involved, usually because of geographic distance. The *involved* style is characterized by less hesitancy to intrude, less geographical distance, and the frequent assumption of parent-like responsibilities, particularly in a family crisis such as the separation or divorce of the adult child. The companionate style is the most frequent style of grandparenting.

Divorce frequently leads to an increase in contact with grandchildren, sometimes because adult children move closer to, or into, the home of their parents for support. Because mothers more frequently have custody, maternal grandparents usually experience more contact and provide greater assistance following divorce than do paternal grandparents (Connidis, 1989b).

Sibling Relationships

The sibling relationship is the first intimate relationship with a peer, and lasts longer than that between spouses and between parents and children. Siblings have an important impact on each other during childhood and adolescence. They share a common cultural background, early family experiences, and the same genetic pool. Increased rates of divorce and childlessness, and an increase in single (never married) individuals, may enhance the importance of sibling relationships in the future. Smaller families and increased participation in the labour force by women may also increase sibling interaction in later life (Connidis, 1989a).

Goetting (1986b) examined sibling relationships in three successive life stages: childhood and adolescence, early and middle adulthood, and old age. During childhood, the primary tasks of sibling relationships are to provide companionship and emotional support, delegated child caretaking, and aid. During early and middle adulthood, most people establish their families of procreation, with the result that sibling ties become voluntary and less frequent. The most common task of siblingship during this stage relates to cooperation in the care of needy elderly parents. Marital disruption has been found to enhance sibling relationships. The stage of old age is associated with retirement. During this stage, sibling relationships assume increased importance. While older siblings experience less actual contact and

aid, they report greater emotional closeness and compatibility. Much of their interaction is devoted to reminiscing, or discussion of the "good old times" together. During old age, previous sibling rivalries may be resolved.

A third to half of respondents in one study reported seeing siblings at least once a month or more. Sibling interaction is subject to competition from the family of procreation, decreasing with the arrival of children, and increasing when children grow up. Activities with siblings are affected more by geographic distance than are contacts with children and grandchildren. Sibling relationships are based more on voluntary choice and interest than on other primary kin relationships, reflecting shared social activities rather than obligatory assistance (Connidis, 1989b).

A recent study (Connidis and Campbell, 1995) of residents of London, Ontario, who were 55 years of age or older found that gender was the most important predictor of sibling ties. Women's ties with siblings were found to be more involved than those of men. Respondents with sisters *only* were found to be closer to their siblings than were those who had brothers *and* sisters. Women are closer to their brothers *and* their sisters than are men, and are also in more frequent contact with their siblings. The effects of marital status on sibling contacts indicates that singles most frequently maintain contact with both single and married siblings. Emotional closeness has an important impact on sibling contacts, with those who feel closer emotionally to their siblings reporting that they confide in them, talk to them on the phone, and see them in person more often than those who are not as close.

Caregiving in Later-Life Families

As people grow older, contact with other family members is increasingly overshadowed in importance by a growing need for care-receiving, or help with the ongoing necessities of life. Research has consistently found two major factors to be associated with care-receiving as individuals get older: income and health. Those with higher incomes are consistently less likely to require caregiving from other family members. Those in poor health are more likely to require some form of caregiving. We will examine the contributions of each of these factors to the necessity of caregiving in later-life families.

Income and Caregiving

Income of the Elderly On average, seniors have lower incomes than do those under 65. In 1994, the average income of seniors from all sources was just under $19 000, compared with average incomes of $26 000 for people aged 25 to 34, and 55 to 64, and more than $30 000 for those aged 35 to 54. There are some indications, however, that the economic condition of seniors has improved more in recent decades than has that of other Canadians (see Figure 12.1). The average incomes of seniors have risen faster than those of people under the age of 65. In 1994, the average income of seniors was 16 percent higher than in 1981, while there was almost no change in the average income of those aged 15 to 64 in the same period. Women had significantly lower incomes than men.

While the incomes of both senior women and senior men have risen since 1981, the annual income for men in 1994 was 19 percent higher than in 1981, while that for women had only increased by 15 percent during the same period (Lindsay, 1997). The proportion of senior *men* living below the low income cut-off (LICO) declined from 27 percent in 1980 to 11 percent in 1994, while the proportion of senior women living below the LICO declined from 40 percent in 1980 to 26 percent in 1994. The proportion of senior *families*

living below the LICO declined from 19 percent in 1980 to 7 percent in 1994. In 1999, about 8 percent of all seniors were below the LICO cutoff. This is compared with a slight increase in the number of low-income families in the general population, from 12 percent in 1980 to 5 percent in 1994 (Lindsay, 1997).

McDaniel also found that women had lower incomes than men. Despite these economic differences, however, elderly women were remarkably independent. She concluded that older women, despite significantly greater impoverishment than men, greater disability, and greater likelihood of having experienced the disruption and trauma of the death of a spouse were more likely than men to be self-reliant and to maintain social supports. Older women are also more likely to have a network of people on whom they can rely for support, whereas men rely much more heavily on spouses alone (1992:64).

The improving economic situation of seniors is associated with such factors as the maturing of the Canada and Quebec pension plans; full inflation protection of these plans as well as of the Old Age Security and Guaranteed Income Supplements benefits; introduction of Provincial Income Supplements; and increased income from private pensions and investments. Since the early 1970s, the real income of Canadians aged 65 and older has risen faster than that of the rest of the population. (**Real income** refers to income adjusted

Figure 12.1   Fewer Canadian Seniors Are Living in Poverty, 1980–1999*

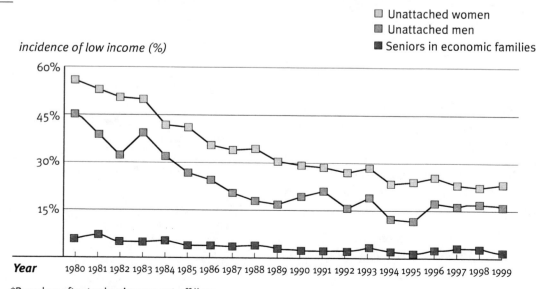

*Based on after-tax low income cut-off lines.

Source: Statistics Canada, www.hc-sc.gc.ca/seniors-aines/pubs/ fed_paper/fedreport3-02-e.htm.

for inflation.) Between 1971 and 1986, average real incomes for unattached women aged 65 and older rose 61 percent, compared with an increase of 28 percent for unattached women below 65. The average real income of unattached men aged 65 and older rose 36 percent during this period, compared to an increase of 13 percent of unattached men below 65. The average real income of elderly families increased 35 percent between 1971 and 1986, compared to 27 percent for families headed by men aged 25 to 64 (Lindsay and Donald, 1988).

The above major improvements in the senior support system have contributed to a significant decline in the level of employment among elderly Canadians in the last three decades. Close to 20 percent of the population aged 65 and older were employed in the late 1950s, whereas by 1986 only 7 percent of the total elderly population were working. Elderly workers made up only 1.5 percent of the total working population in 1986, compared with 4 percent in 1956. This decrease in the proportion of elderly Canadians who are working has taken place despite the abolition of mandatory retirement at age 65 or later under federal jurisdiction as well as under the human rights legislation of most Canadian provinces (Méthot, 1987).

Old Age Security and Guaranteed Income Supplements Old Age Security (OAS) was first introduced in 1927, and was offered to seniors aged 70 and older on the basis of financial need. In 1952, changes to the act allowed pensions to be paid to all individuals aged 70 and older, regardless of need. Starting in 1966, the qualification for OAS benefits was lowered to 65 over a five-year period. At the same time, the Guaranteed Income Supplement (GIS) was added, which provides benefits to seniors with no or little income other than the OAS. In 1975 the Spouse's Allowance (SPA) was added to provide income to OAS pensioners' spouses aged 60 to 64 on an income-tested basis. Most Canadian citizens qualify for the OAS benefits. Starting in 1990, the government has instituted a "clawback" provision for seniors with high personal incomes (Oderkirk, 1996a).

Canada and Quebec Pension Plans The Canada Pension Plan (CPP) and Quebec Pension Plan (QPP) were introduced in 1966, in addition to the OAS, as a second tier of income for seniors. These plans are funded by mandatory contributions from employees, employers, and self-employed people, as well as from interest on the investment of the plan's funds. Since 1987, benefits may begin at age 60, but full benefits are not received until age 65. Benefits received before age 65 are reduced by 0.5 percent for each month between the recipient's current age and 65th birthday. People may also wait beyond age 65 before applying for benefits, and benefits for them are increased by 0.5 percent for each month their age exceeds their 65th birthday. CPP and QPP retirement benefits are equal to 25 percent of average career annual income. Benefits are taxable. Spouses of deceased contributors are eligible to receive a survivor's pension, depending on eligibility rules (Oderkirk, 1996b).

A recent national poll indicated that a substantial majority of Canadians (61 percent) expect to rely significantly on CPP or QPP for financial support during retirement years. Older Canadians were far more likely to indicate that the CPP or QPP will (or currently does) represent an important part of their retirement income (77 percent of those 55 and older, compared with 48 percent of those under 35). A majority (62 percent) responded that they would prefer to see the government increase premiums from workers and employers, versus one in four (26 percent) who would like to see a reduction in the pension benefits that are paid out. There is broad support (69 percent) for maintaining the current pension plan, rather than phasing it out in favour of more incentives for Canadians to save for their own retirement (Angus Reid Group, 1996).

Private Pensions Many employers provide private pension plans for their employees, which may or may not include employee contributions. Employees may also receive benefits from personal savings such as bonds and RRSP investments.

Before the institution of government and private pensions, medical or accident insurance policies, and of subsidized apartments for senior citizens, men and women had to work until they were no longer capable. The elderly who had no savings often depended on their children to look after them, or on the community or charitable organizations (Baker, 1988).

Health and Caregiving

Most seniors, particularly those who live in a private household, indicate that they are in good general health. In 1995, almost three-quarters (73 percent) of those aged 65 and older who were living in private households rather than in institutions said their health was either good (34 percent), very good (27 percent) or excellent (12 percent). Almost one-quarter (21 percent) described their health as fair, and only 6 percent described it as poor (Lindsay, 1997).

Seniors experience more health problems than do the rest of the population (see Figure 12.2). The most common chronic health conditions reported by seniors were arthritis and rheumatism (45 percent), Alzheimer's disease (35 percent), heart disease (27 percent), and high blood pressure (24 percent). Twenty-two percent of seniors reported the effects of a stroke as a chronic health condition (Lindsay, 1997).

One of the most feared diseases often associated with old age is Alzheimer's disease, a form of *dementia* (associated with the mind) or impairment of neurological or mental abilities. It is characterized by slowly progressive and irreversible deterioration of the cognitive functions. Earlier stages affect memory and cognitive abilities such as speech, abstract thought, emotion, and memory. Physical decline follows in the later stages, affecting the ability to take care of oneself and to act clearly and reasonably. Mental and physical decline are eventually fatal, although the progression varies from person to person (Carroll, 1990).

A family in which a member suffers from Alzheimer's disease experiences ambiguous boundaries, in which the sick member is physically present but psychologically absent. Based on stress theory and symbolic interactionism, Boss (1993) concludes that such boundary ambiguity contributes more to the depression and conflict in caregivers than does the severity of the dementia itself. Thus, caregivers must be assisted in "defining the situation" in such a way that they recognize that although they cannot change the physical reality of the disease, they can successfully deal with the reality, both subjectively and objectively (Boss, 1993).

Alzheimer's sufferers typically are unaware of their condition, but an important concern of the elderly is the possibility of sustaining some disability that would affect their ability to look after themselves and to participate in the normal activities of family life. Indeed, Statistics Canada data for 1986 reveal that nearly half (46 percent) of those who are 65 and older, and 82 percent of those aged 85 and older, do have some form of disability. While most elderly people with disabilities are able to live at home and participate in leisure activities, a significant proportion are limited in such

Figure 12.2   Seniors with Chronic Health Conditions

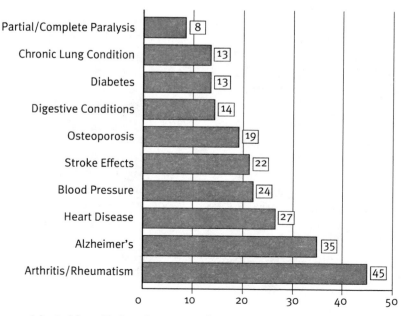

Source: Adapted from Lindsay (1997: 56, 57).

participation because of economic and environmental barriers (Dunn, 1991).

Increasing concern is being expressed regarding health service use by the elderly in view of the continuing escalation of costs. Since the elderly are the most frequent users of the care system, the aging of the population has created growing concern over whether the system is being used by those in most need. Three factors determine health-care use: 1) *predisposing factors*—demographic (for example, age and sex), social structural (for example, ethnicity and education), and attitudes and beliefs; 2) *enabling factors*—family income and health insurance, and availability of community services; and 3) *need factors*—perceived health status and diagnosed conditions. The use of health-care services by older people in Manitoba, including home-care services, physician services, and in-patient hospital services, was measured in 1980 in a random sample of 250 individuals. The need factor was the most important factor in predicting use of both home-care services and in-patient hospital services, but was not significant in predicting the use of physician services. The study concludes that the use of home-care and hospital services is equitable, and that access to existing services is based on need (Chappell and Blandford, 1987).

As we have seen, older people are more likely to suffer from chronic ailments such as arthritis and rheumatism, but the majority of the elderly function well until advanced age without the use of formal support systems. Many of those who are currently in nursing homes simply lack alternative care, and could function in group homes or in their own homes without intensive medical services. The social and health services available to older persons who choose to stay in their own homes are inadequate. There are too few senior-citizen apartments with nursing and homemaker services, and many older people are not informed of government home-care programs (Baker, 1988).

What is the role of kin in meeting the health-care needs of the elderly? Snider showed that in a non-crisis health situation (such as headache, stiff neck, cold), those not living alone were more likely than those living alone to contact their family for assistance. Kin were more likely to be called in the case of a medical crisis (person taken very sick) than in a non-crisis situation. Being female—rather than the number of kin available—was the strongest determinant of whether a

person depended on kin in a health emergency. Kin availability was not significant in determining the health-seeking behaviours of the elderly, leading to the conclusion that kin involvement in providing health-care advice to the elderly is relatively unimportant and has been overestimated (Snider, 1981).

Dependency and Caregiving Connidis (1987) argues that the negative stereotype that equates old age with dependency is inaccurate. The majority of older Canadians are able to function without the aid of community services. Only 9 percent of the older people sampled in London, Ontario, needed the support of any community service. However, two concerns were expressed: 1) with the growing number of older people, the expenditures required to maintain existing programs will escalate, and new services will be needed to meet the growing needs of an older population; and 2) when formal support services are needed, the situation is often crucial, involving multiple needs and limited finances, making such services essential if older people are to remain in the community. Support is also required for such routine needs as household chores, grocery shopping, transportation, and medical care, if older people are to remain relatively independent.

Most Canadians are able to perform most household chores on their own, but advancing age and deteriorating health create an increasing need for assistance, particularly with more difficult tasks. One study showed that the three areas in which seniors were most dependent were yard work, heavy housework, and grocery shopping. Fewer people required aid with less strenuous tasks such as meal preparation, money management, light housework, and personal care, although the need for help with household tasks increased with age and with deteriorating health. An interesting finding was that the proportion of those receiving help exceeded the percentage of those who claimed that they needed it, suggesting that some may have denied their dependency, or that children provided help even when it wasn't needed. While 16 percent of seniors living alone needed help, 21 percent actually received such help. Similar figures were found for grocery shopping (11 percent versus 20 percent) and yard work (39 percent versus 57 percent). Support for older persons came from such sources as children and other relatives, friends and neighbours, and formal support systems such as homemaker services and seniors' centres (Hagey, 1989).

Paletta (1992) found that family members (parents, siblings, children, and other relatives) constituted a substantial proportion of people providing help. Family members contributed 68 percent of financial support, 59 percent of housework, 47 percent of house maintenance, and 36 percent of transportation needs to respondents. Friends also provided significant levels of help, accounting for 62 percent of those providing transportation, 52 percent of those providing house maintenance, and 25 percent of those providing financial help.

Marshall (1987) agrees that most (70 percent to 80 percent) of the assistance received by the elderly does not come from the social service sector, but rather from family, friends, and neighbours. A number of factors, however, contribute to a rather fragile structure in terms of the ability to provide support. Often, there are two generations in retirement rather than only one. However, Shuey and Hardy (2003) found that younger couples tended to focus support on the wife's relatives rather than those of the husband. Also, for young couples the decline in childbearing means that there are fewer children to provide support. About 18 percent of people over the age of 65 have no living children, either because they never married or because they remained childless. A majority of older people do not wish to live with their children and grandchildren. The longer life expectancy of women means that those most in need will be older widows with no husband to care for them. Despite this fragile structure, the family is very willing to provide support to its older members whenever needed.

A number of factors are related to the level of caregiving provided for elderly parents. The amount of assistance increased as the parent's level of activity decreased. The presence of the older person's spouse in the home was associated with a decrease in the amount of help provided. Marital status acted as a competing demand on the helpers' time, with married adult children providing less help than those who were not married. Being employed decreased the amount of help provided by sons, but did not have a significant impact on the amount of help provided by daughters. This may suggest that daughters simply add parental caregiving to their other roles (Stoller, 1983).

Storm et al. (1985) explored how people generally perceived the obligations of various family and non-family members to assist a frail old person with physical care, financial aid, and psychological support. Children were perceived as the primary source of assistance regardless of the type of need. This obligation was seen to be substantially reduced by the lack of financial resources and by geographical distance. The size of the children's families, the need to provide for their education, the need for privacy, and the likelihood that caring for a parent might place strain on a marriage were also perceived as reducing such obligation.

Lee et al. (1994) examined the relationship between location and the extent to which adult children were expected to assist and care for their aging parents. They found that current rural residents have higher filial responsibility expectations than do urban residents, but the overall relationship was not significant. Those who grew up on farms, however, have the highest expectations of help from children, and this relationship was significant.

It is often assumed that caregiving is a one-way experience that is provided by children to parents. The responsibility of caring for parents is often seen as a source of stress and burden for their adult children. This research perspective obscures the other side of the picture, or the impact of adult children's problems on their elderly parents. Based on a 1989 national telephone survey of the non-institutionalized elderly population in Canada, Pillemer and Suitor (1991) concluded that parents whose adult children had mental, physical, or stress-related problems experienced higher levels of depression than did those whose children did not have such problems. The parent's gender, or whether or not the parents and child shared a home, had no effect on this relationship. These findings indicate that certain aspects of parent caregiving affect the psychological well-being of elderly parents. Thus, family caregiving needs to focus attention not only on parents' failing health and dependence, but also on the impact of children's problems and the conflict resulting from them. Children's problems are a more important predictor of distress among the elderly than are marital status or education, but, consistent with other research, the most powerful predictor of distress among the elderly is self-reported health status.

An estimated daily average of 226 000 elderly people were in residential care facilities in 1986 to 1987, compared to 150 000 elderly people in hospitals. A **residential care facility** is defined as a facility with four or more beds which is funded, licensed, or approved by provincial or territorial departments of health or social services. Homes for the aged accounted for seven out of 10 people in residential care, reflecting both the growing number of elderly people and the diminishing tendency for them to live with their adult children. Women made up 70 percent of the residents in homes for the aged. A large majority of residents (77 percent) were 75 years of age or older (Strike, 1989).

The Future of Later-Life Families

As we have seen, the elderly population is expected to increase dramatically as the baby boom generation begins to reach old age, around 2010. By 2030, people aged 65 and older are projected to outnumber dependents under the age of 15 for the first time in Canadian history. These changes have important implications for the costs associated with social programs, and for the ability of the working population (aged 15 to 64) to finance such social expenditures through taxes and social security contributions of the labour force (Burke, 1991).

Within the next 50 years, significant changes in social spending will take place in Canada (see Table 12.4.) Based on current spending levels, it is projected that federal social spending on the elderly will increase from 26 percent in 1980 to 50 percent by 2040. Social spending on the young is projected to drop from 24 percent to 15 percent, and for people aged 15 to 64, from 50 percent to 35 percent (Burke, 1991).

When per capita social spending on education, health care, pensions, unemployment compensation, and family benefits is held constant at 1980 levels, it is projected (see Table 12.4) that, by 2040, pensions (including publicly financed old age, survivors', and permanent sickness pensions) will account for the largest proportion of social expenditures—increasing from 24 percent in 1980 to 38 percent. Health-care expenditures are expected to account for the second largest proportion of the social program budget, increasing from 29 percent to 33 percent of all social spending. Expenditures on other programs are expected to decline as a proportion of all social spending. The largest drop in spending will be in the area of education (from 32 percent in 1980 to 18 percent by 2040), with smaller declines in unemployment and family benefits (Burke, 1991).

TABLE 12.4   Distribution of Social Expenditure, by Program and Age, 1980–2040

	1980 %	2040 PROJECTED %
Major program		
Education	32	18
Health care	29	33
Pensions	24	38
Unemployment	12	9
Family benefits	3	2
Age group		
0–14	24	15
15–64	50	35
65 and over	26	50

Source: OECD. 1988. *Aging Populations: The Social Policy Implications*, in Burke, 1991:7.

A growing number of Canadian citizens are expressing concern over how these increasing social expenditures will be financed. If the level of social benefits increases, as in the past Canadian citizens will be faced with sharp increases in tax burdens. "Canadians will most likely have to choose between increasing tax rates and social security contributions or lower levels of social benefits" (Burke, 1991:8).

Many experts, however, feel that such fears are unrealistic. They point out, for example, that the universality of the Old Age Security pension has already been effectively destroyed by the clawback of benefits from people with more than $50 000 in annual income. The government withdrew its 1985 plan to de-index the basic benefit only after vigorous protests by seniors. The seniors argued that older Canadians who didn't have much education or high-paying jobs have made significant contributions to this society, and that they deserve some return on their investment. "Despite vast changes in seniors' health and life span, many people cling to outdated stereotypes about age and aging: Seniors are frail, apt to be slightly demented and generally aimless, live in expensive nursing homes and are waiting to die" (Ramsay, 1993a:H1). In actuality, seniors continue to make significant contributions to society even after retirement. Seniors are widely involved in volunteer work: churches, hospitals, and charities benefit greatly from the work of those over age 65. Seniors are financially more generous to charities than are those under age 65, despite the squeeze of fixed incomes (Ramsay, 1993a).

The September 1996 issue of *Transition*, published by the Vanier Institute of the Family, addresses the issue of the alarm that is frequently expressed over the greying of Canada, articulated in such harsh suggestions as dismantling social programs and public pensions. A variety of authors address the frequent perception that the sky is falling just because our society is aging.

Glossop (1996) suggests that rather than allowing societal aging and fiscal restraint to pit the interests of different generations against each other, we need to develop effective policies and programs that will continue to sustain intergenerational transfers and commitments. McDaniel (1996) argues that intergenerational transfers have not just benefited the old at the expense of the young. She points out that during the past century, the growth of the ratio of education spending to the GDP has far exceeded the growth of the ratio of public spending on pensions to GDP in Canada. Robertson (1996) suggests that we need to move beyond apocalyptic demography, which concludes that the aging population will significantly drive up health-care costs and result in the collapse of public pension plans. In her view, we need to reject the dependency and independency dichotomy and embrace a moral economy of interdependence that addresses the question of the kind of community or society in which we want to live. Box 12.4 presents a positive discussion of the impact of the greying of Canada.

Box 12.4   Current Issues: Baby Boomers Reach Retirement

What sort of country will the greyer Canada be? Demographics offer no reason for doom and gloom. For the next two to three decades, the baby boomers will be workers, taxpayers, and increasingly savers. Because more Canadians will be savers, more money will be available for capital investment to make our industry more technologically advanced, more competitive, and more productive. Meanwhile, other countries will offer growing markets for the goods and services that these industries produce. And Canada will become less dependent on foreign lenders.

Fears are often expressed about how Canada will cope once the large baby boom generation (those born between 1946 and 1964) reaches its retirement years. Before panic sets in, it should be remembered that even the oldest boomers won't reach 65 until 2012. It should also be remembered that the Canadian workforce by then will have been reinforced by the large echo generation (the children of the baby boom generation). The combination of the echo and the baby bust is larger than the baby boom, so there is little reason to fear a shortage of working-age Canadians during the grey interlude of boomer retirement.

Source: Foote and Stoffman, 1996:15.

Northcott (1992b) argues that the tendency to define population aging as a social "problem" is an alarmist approach that intertwines reality and rhetoric. The application of the "social construction of reality" and the "political economy" perspectives to the study of population aging leads to the conclusion that the population aging "problem" or "crisis" is socially defined or constructed. This definition reflects the dominant interests of service providers and legitimizes their exploitation of seniors at the expense of taxpayers. The crisis definition persists because it serves the needs of powerful interest groups in society.

Schellenberg and Clark (1996) stress that before creating retirement programs for the next century, we need to assess how the characteristics of tomorrow's seniors differ from those of contemporary seniors. A number of key differences are summarized in Box 12.5.

Desjardins and Dumas (1993) clearly recognize that the demographic transition will result in an unprecedented proportion of society being made up of the elderly, and that this will require economic, social, and political adjustments. The ability of society to provide an increasingly older elderly population with the welfare level available to today's elderly may be affected by the growing number and proportion of the elderly. Nevertheless, the researchers suggest that the scenarios of catastrophe need more critical examination. For example,

the age-specific health conditions of the future elderly population may not resemble those observed today. The results of emphasizing preventive approaches in addition to curative approaches may bring about important reductions in the health-care needs of the elderly. There is also an increasing recognition that the health-care needs of the elderly may not require clinical intervention, but may be provided in their usual place of residence.

With respect to the economy, Desjardins and Dumas (1993) argue that important changes are taking place. The pay-as-you-go approach to supporting the retired, in which current wage-earners provide for the needs of retired people, requires adjustment. The reduction in the proportion of wage-earners who are supporting the retired may not remain operational without a thorough rearrangement of policies. Thus, younger generations are being encouraged to subscribe to private retirement savings plans to maintain existing programs such as Old Age Security pension and Guaranteed Income Supplement benefits for the more needy. The moderate labour market participation of women has resulted in a much higher level of poverty for them in retirement. Future generations of elderly women will have contributed to private retirement plans, reducing the pressures on social service agencies. Future increases in productivity and flexible retirement age,

---

Box 12.5   Research Insights: Characteristics of Baby Boom Seniors

Baby boom seniors who will begin to retire about 2013 differ from current seniors in a number of important characteristics:

1. Future seniors are far more likely to enter retirement without a spouse or partner. Seventy percent of current seniors comprised both a husband and a wife when they were between ages 40 and 49. Only 56 percent of families who are currently between 40 and 49 comprise both a husband and a wife.

2. A growing share of households are made up of lone-parent families and individuals living alone. Such families or individuals experience higher levels of poverty and lower levels of social and emotional support.

3. Growing geographical mobility and a smaller number of children suggest that tomorrow's seniors may need to rely on friends and community groups for social and emotional support.

4. The seniors of tomorrow will have a much higher level of education, and will be more likely to have been employed in professional and managerial occupations, so that they will probably have the financial resources to retire early.

5. The increase in women's paid employment will mean that they will make larger contributions to pension plans and will have access to a wider range of retirement income sources.

Source: Schellenberg and Clark, 1996.

which contribute to a reduction in the number of unemployed and an increase in the number of workers, may both reduce pressures on the social safety net.

Nevertheless, the aging of the population, together with continuing budgetary deficits and large accumulated governmental debts (both provincial and federal), as well as rising service costs, raise concerns about our ability to support seniors in the future. The result may well be increases in taxation and reductions in health-care services. There may also be a continued move from facility-based care to community-based care, and from dependence to self-reliance (Northcott, 1992b).

> Given that expenditures on seniors in contemporary welfare states such as Canada... make up a very significant portion of governmental budgets, it is perhaps understandable that governments facing fiscal restraint would attempt to reduce spending on seniors' programs. What is curious is the tendency to "blame the victim." While it is true that seniors are major beneficiaries of governmental programs, and while it is true that population aging may make a bad situation worse, nevertheless... it cannot be argued that population aging caused the current economic difficulties (Northcott, 1992b:88–89).

Despite the fact that most seniors are healthy and happy, some experience major problems. At least one in 25 seniors (4 percent) is abused physically, financially, or emotionally, and these figures are probably conservative. Despite the fact that poverty for seniors dropped between 1980 and 1990, significant numbers (nearly 20 percent) still live below the official poverty line, and this problem is much more serious for single women over the age of 65. The increasing mobility of the younger generation has contributed to the isolation of a growing number of older parents. The shock of retirement by inadequately prepared seniors is a source of significant trauma (Ramsay, 1993a).

By the year 2021, seniors will make up almost a quarter of the population, as baby boomers pass through middle age. "And it will be a different kind of senior—more educated, more aggressive, less likely to accept a seat in the background" (Ramsay, 1993a:H3). These seniors will be able to get what they want from government because of their knowledge of the system, their aggressiveness, their sheer numbers and resulting power.

SUMMARY

■ Gerontology is the study of aging. Four aspects of gerontology are chronological, biological, psychological, and social aging.

■ From an individual perspective, the elderly are those who are 65 years or older. The number of elderly is increasing more rapidly than is the general population. In 1995, the elderly made up about 12 percent of the population.

■ The elderly are not a homogeneous group. At least 10 percent of elderly families include two generations over the age of 65. There are differences in health and availability of support for those aged 65 to 74, and those aged 75 and older. Women make up the majority of Canada's seniors. Senior men are much more likely to be married than are senior women, whereas senior women are much more likely to be widowed than are senior men.

■ Demographic or population aging is the process by which an entire population grows older. Increased life expectancy, immigration, and declining fertility contribute to population aging. The median age, the proportion of the population over the age of 65, and the total dependency ratio are indicators of population aging.

■ Contrary to myth, the elderly are not neglected or abandoned by their families, but maintain a network of contact and exchange. Only a minority of the elderly experience poor health, institutional living, poverty, loneliness, isolation, or senility. Parent/adult–child relationships constitute the most frequent source of contact and support. Sibling relationships assume increased importance in later life, with pairs of sisters maintaining more contact than sister–brother or brother–brother pairs.

■ Income and health are the two most important factors determining the reception of caregiving by the elderly. The economic situation of the elderly has improved over the past decades. Family members (parents, spouse, children, siblings, and other relatives) provide the majority of caregiving to seniors.

■ The elderly population is expected to increase dramatically as the baby boom generation reaches old age, around 2010. This will require changes in patterns of social spending. Most experts feel that fears regarding how such social expenditures will be financed are groundless. Seniors continue to make significant contributions to society even after retirement.

KEY TERMS

Biological life span (269)

Cohort (269)

Demographic or population aging (269)

Elderly (266)

Generational squeeze (280)

Gerontology (266)

Institutions (271)

Kin-keeping (276)

Later-life families (266)

Real income (283)

Residential care facility (288)

Solidarity (278)

Total dependency ratio (270)

QUESTIONS FOR REVIEW

1. Define and outline the four major aspects of gerontology.

2. What is the individual definition of aging? Explain why this definition must recognize that the elderly are not a homogeneous group. What are the three major transitions associated with aging?

3. How is demographic or population aging defined? Describe the relative impact of life expectancy, immigration, and fertility on demographic aging in Canada. What are the major factors contributing to decreased fertility? How do the three indicators of population aging help us to anticipate future population changes?

4. How have the living arrangements of Canada's elderly changed in the past 20 years? What are the major determinants of the living arrangements of the elderly? Explain the impact of the family life stage on the happiness of the elderly.

5. What are the prevailing myths regarding the treatment of the elderly in our society, and what are the realities?

6. Describe kinship relationships among the never-married, the married, the childless, the divorced, the widowed, and the remarried.

7. What is the nature of the relationship between parents and their adult children? What are the key factors that contribute to frequent and meaningful contact? Summarize the mutual relationships that exist between the elderly and their children.

8. Describe sibling relationships in the three successive family life stages: childhood and adolescence, early and middle adulthood, and old age. Describe how gender affects sibling contact.

9. What are the four primary sources of income for seniors? Discuss the changes to senior incomes over the past 50 years, particularly as related to gender.

10. Discuss the two major factors associated with caregiving in later life. What is the impact of these factors on the reception of caregiving?

11. What are the major implications of demographic aging on the future of later-life families?

QUESTIONS FOR DISCUSSION

1. Why do attitudes toward biological or physiological aging differ for males and females? To what extent have these attitudes changed as a result of the influences of the women's liberation movement?

2. Discuss the impact of the contraction and expansion of the household on the process of adjustment for the elderly.

3. What are the impacts of sex, age, and marital status on the living arrangements of the elderly? What are the relative benefits and costs of the elderly living alone versus in an institution?

4. The role of caregiver is frequently associated with negative outcomes. Discuss. How prevalent is the "generational squeeze" in your extended family? What are the implications of the female nature of the caregiver in light of changing gender roles in our society?

5. Discuss the changing nature of retirement income for seniors. What is the impact of gender on retirement income, and how is this changing?

6. Are you aware of elder abuse within your extended family or the families of your friends? Discuss.

7. What are the practical implications of demographic aging on your personal plans for retirement? How would you suggest our government deal with health care and other social service needs of the elderly in view of the demographic changes currently taking place?

SUGGESTED READINGS

Connidis, Ingrid A. 2001.* *Family Ties and Aging.* Thousand Oaks, CA: Sage Publications. This book is an extension of part of a series on individual and population aging in Canada. It provides an excellent synthesis of existing research, and provides original Canadian data on the family ties of older persons as well as U.S. data.

Grollman, Earl A. 1997. *Your Aging Parents: Reflections for Caregivers*. Boston: Beacon Press. Written by a father–daughter team, this book emphasizes the importance of sympathy and understanding with respect to the complex issues of aging. The author discusses the physical changes that accompany aging, as well as the support systems that are available, and the emotions experienced by aging parents and their adult children as they adjust to new relationships.

McDaniel, Susan A. and Carol Strike. 1994.* *Family and Friends*. Statistics Canada Cat. 11-612E, No. 9. Based on the 1990 General Social Survey, Chapter 7 contains valuable resources regarding older Canadians in families.

Monette, Manon. 1996.* *Canada's Changing Retirement Patterns*. Statistics Canada, Catalogue N0. 89-546-XPE. Using the 1994 General Social Survey, Monette examines major topics related to changing retirement patterns, including socio-demographic factors, retirement age, return to work after retirement, and the financial situation of retired persons.

CHAPTER 13

Relationship Endings and New Beginnings

After studying this chapter, you should be able to do the following:

- Describe the changing patterns of relationship endings and new beginnings in Canada.
- Outline the changes in divorce legislation and the effects of these changes.
- Detail some of the various effects of relationship endings and new beginnings on different family members, and their possible causes.
- Describe the composition of different kinds of stepfamilies, and the kinds of problems that they face.
- Explain how having stepchildren in the family can affect quality of family life, quality of remarriage, and the probability that the parents will divorce.
- Explore the legal rights and responsibilities of stepfamily members.
- Describe the incidence of lone-parent families, and the circumstances of these families.

Introduction

The relationship endings considered in this chapter include widowhood, annulment, desertion, separation, and divorce. Relationship endings lead to new beginnings for all involved. These new beginnings may include lone parenting, cohabitation, remarriage, and the new relationships that arise in stepfamilies. Divorce is the ending given the most attention, including the conditions for divorce, its causes, and the consequences for people who divorce and their children. Remarriage and the new relationships that arise in stepfamilies are also given considerable attention. We begin by describing the relative contributions of death and divorce to relationship endings and new beginnings, and the history of divorce and remarriage in Canada. Special attention is paid to the way family relationships change after divorce and remarriage. In the last part of the chapter, we take a closer look at lone-parent families and the circumstances surrounding them.

Widowhood

The reason most marriages end has changed greatly during this century, particularly in the past 25 years. During the 19th century, and as recently as 1921, virtually all marriages ended due to the death of a spouse. In 1960, death still ended 90 percent of marriages, but by 1990, 47 percent of marriages ended in divorce (Gee, 1986, 1987; Lindsay, 1992). Though marriages in earlier times lasted "till death do us part," this did not mean that many lasted a very long time, because early death rates were high for both men and women. Until well into this century, widowed men and women did not remain unmarried for long—their need for a "helpmate" was too great to permit lengthy mourning. Thus, marriage breakup, remarriage, and stepparenting were common experiences during the last century.

With the surge in divorces following changes in Canadian divorce laws in 1968 and 1985, the picture of circumstances leading to remarriage changed, as

Table 13.1 shows (Dumas and Peron, 1992). Prior to 1968, widows and widowers made up the largest proportion of those entering remarriage. Since then, divorced individuals have outnumbered widows and widowers by a growing proportion each year.

There is a radical imbalance in Canada between the numbers of widowed men and women. In 2001, senior widows 65 to 69 years of age outnumbered senior widowers four to one (see Table 12.1 in previous chapter). There are a number of factors that contribute to this imbalance, including the longer life expectancy of women and the tendency for women to marry men older than themselves, while men tend to marry younger women. Widows thus have far fewer chances to remarry than widowers do because they have a smaller pool of possible mates. In fact, the figures for 1985–1987 show us that in the 65–69 age group, men were approximately seven times more likely to remarry than were women of the same age (Norland, 1994).

Another gender difference, again in favour of widowers, is that the interval between the death of the first spouse and the second marriage is shorter for ever-widowed men than for ever-widowed women. One U.S. study found that the average interval between widowhood and remarriage was 3.9 years for men and 6.4 years for women (Wilson and Clarke, 1992). In the first year following the death of a spouse, less than 0.5 percent of women are expected to remarry, while within that same time frame about 3 percent of men have remarried. At five years, fewer than 6 percent of ever-widowed women are expected to remarry, compared to more than 22 percent for men. After 10 years the differences persist, with 11 percent of women and 35 percent of men expected to remarry (Wu, 1995).

TABLE 13.1   Changes in the Prior-Marriage Experience of Newly Married Persons in Canada, 1928–1988

	MALES				FEMALES			
YEAR	SINGLE	WIDOWER	DIVORCED	TOTAL	SINGLE	WIDOW	DIVORCED	TOTAL
1928	67 137	6375	749	74 311	69 085	4487	739	74 311
%	90.4	8.6	1.0	100.0	93.0	6.0	1.0	100.0
1938	83 345	4206	887	88 438	84 876	2773	789	88 438
%	94.2	4.8	1.0	100.0	96.0	3.1	0.9	100.0
1948	111 418	6520	5376	123 314	112 313	6282	4717	123 314
%	90.4	5.3	4.4	100.0	91.1	5.1	3.8	100.0
1958	120 957	5696	4872	131 525	120 312	6228	4985	131 525
%	92.0	4.3	3.7	100.0	91.5	4.7	3.8	100.0
1968	137 309	6352	8105	171 766	136 783	7472	7511	171 766
%	91.6	3.7	4.7	100.0	91.3	4.4	4.4	100.0
1978	131 884	5926	27 713	185 523	134 016	6576	24 931	185 523
%	81.9	3.2	14.9	100.0	83.0	3.5	13.4	100.0
1988	142 956	5372	39 400	187 728	143 943	5709	38 076	187 728
%	76.2	2.9	21.0	100.0	76.7	3.0	20.3	100.0

Source: Statistics Canada; Dumas and Peron, 1992.

Remarriages in Canada involve a divorced person more often than a widowed person for four reasons (Dumas and Peron, 1992):

- More Canadian marriages are now ended by divorce than by death of a partner.

- Two persons enter the "marriage market" from a divorce, but only one from widowhood.

- Those divorced are generally younger than those widowed, and the probability of remarriage declines with age.

- Most of those widowed are older women, who have small chance of remarriage for reasons we have just noted.

Annulment, Desertion, and Separation

Annulment, desertion, and formal separation are not as common now in Canada as they were in the past; however, they are still important in some countries.

Annulment

An **annulment** is a decision by a court of law that a marriage was invalid because of conditions that existed *before* the marriage, so there never was a "real" marriage. All provincial governments set a minimum age for marriage, and all prohibit marriage between certain people. Violation of these conditions gives grounds for annulment. Other grounds include lack of sexual consummation, impotence (but not sterility), and cases in which one party to the marriage consented under duress or coercion. The difference between divorce and annulment is a matter of timing—an annulment is a marriage dissolution on the basis of a condition existing before the marriage; separations and divorces are types of marriage dissolution based on something that happened after the marriage, such as adultery, nonsupport, incompatibility, or cruelty.

Desertion

Desertion is the willful abandonment of spouse and/or children without legal justification. For example, for more than 130 years, white men in the Northwest Territories broke liaisons with Native Canadian women by deserting their wives and children when they left the North (McKie et al., 1983). Desertion is still seen as a "poor man's divorce." Desertion is an ambiguous act because it is not institutionalized and is legally vague in terms of the number of days' absence that constitutes it. If the deserting spouse returns occasionally at unannounced intervals, there is even greater ambiguity. Legislation defining desertion is a provincial responsibility, but while relevant laws exist in all 10 provinces, they are seldom used.

Separation

Separation refers to the situation of two people who are legally married and so cannot remarry, but who no longer share a common household or residence. A *formal* separation is the result of a decision by a court freeing the husband and wife to live apart without being open to the charge of desertion. In societies where divorce was forbidden or greatly discouraged, formal or court-ordered separation was often a permanent solution for incompatible couples.

Almost all the many cases of separation identified by the Census are informal separations—arrangements between husbands and wives who decide to live apart. The courts only become involved if there are disagreements over child-custody or support payments. According to the 1991 Census, 3.7 percent of all married adults (those not single or widowed) reported they were separated.

Since separation is almost always informal, and is usually temporary and often followed in time by divorce, assessing the full extent of marriage breakdown requires combining divorce and separation data (McVey and Robinson, 1981).

Divorce

Divorce is defined as the formal dissolution of a valid marriage by judicial decree. Throughout the last century, marriage was seen as "a divine institution ordained by God," and until 1867 in most of Canada there was no divorce, for any reason. However, in the Maritime provinces, then the most liberal part of the country, divorce was legalized for adultery in the late 1700s; and Nova Scotia permitted divorce for cruelty, as well. After the British North America Act was passed in 1867, divorce became available in Quebec and Ontario, but only if Parliament passed a special act authorizing *each* divorce. The number of these petitions led to the formation of a special Senate divorce committee in the 1880s. A favourable recommendation by this committee required confirmation by both the Senate and the House. The sexual double standard of the time is seen in the fact that divorces were granted to men who proved adultery in their wives, while wives had to prove the husband's desertion or extreme physical or mental cruelty, in addition to adultery, to qualify. Moreover, until 1930, a wife could only sue for divorce in the province where her husband had established permanent residence—if he had deserted, she had to find him first and then take legal action in his home province (McKie et al., 1983).

Divorces were accordingly very rare, averaging only three per year during the early 1870s and 11 per year by 1900. The rate never exceeded two divorces per million population. The law, economic factors, social pressures, and beliefs about the sanctity of marriage all served to lock men and women into their marriages. The restrictions on women were particularly important—as recently as 1900, "wives were not the legal guardians of their children" (McKie et al., 1983:38) and did not have full rights to their property. A wife who left her matrimonial home became propertyless and childless.

The four ways in which divorce rates are calculated are explained in Box 13.1. It is very important to realize that different ways of computing divorce rates lead to differing estimates of divorces. The calculation of the number of divorces in a given year divided by the number of marriages in that year will always inflate the divorce rate. This is because the number of people at risk of getting a divorce (all those currently married) is far greater than the number of people at risk of getting married (usually singles 18 to 30 years of age). Also, some methods of calculation are more useful for cross-cultural comparisons; the crude divorce rate falls

---

Box 13.1   Divorce Rates

Divorce rates are designed to provide information about the probability that couples married in a certain year will divorce. The following four different divorce rates are commonly used, but each one has limitations.

Ever-Married Divorce Rate This is the most accurate statistic. The ever-married divorce rate can only be calculated by waiting until death or divorce ends the last marriage in a marriage cohort (married during a certain year), and then determining the percentage that ended in divorce. The formula is

$$\frac{\text{Number of marriages in cohort}}{\text{Number of divorces in cohort}} \times 1000 = \frac{\text{ever-married}}{\text{divorce rate}}$$

This rate is of historical interest, but it tells us nothing about the *current* incidence of divorce.

Crude Divorce Rate This is the number of divorces per 1000 population, calculated as

$$\frac{\text{number of divorces in given year}}{\text{total population in given year}} \times 1000 = \frac{\text{crude divorce}}{\text{rate}}$$

This rate is optimistically inaccurate, because no children, single, or widowed persons get divorced, so the rate is low. At a time when the proportions of any of these groups in the population are changing, the rate will change, though the rate of married persons divorcing remains unchanged.

Divorces per New Marriages This is calculated as

$$\frac{\text{Number of divorces in given year}}{\text{Number of marriages in given year}} \times 1000 = \frac{\text{divorces per}}{\text{new marriages}}$$

This rate is pessimistically inaccurate, because while all married couples are at risk of divorce, only new marriages are considered in computing the rate, so the actual risk of divorce is much exaggerated.

Refined Divorce Rate This is the number of divorces per 1000 existing marriages in a particular year, calculated as

$$\frac{\text{Number of divorces in given year}}{\text{Number of existing marriages}} \times 1000 = \frac{\text{refined}}{\text{divorce rate}}$$

This rate indicates among all the marriages that are at risk of divorce, what proportion actually divorce. It is the most accurate that can be calculated to give an indication of the divorce-risk of the current married population.

Source: Scanzoni, 1972.

into this category, since it can be calculated from data that is usually collected in most countries. The divorce rate is also very sensitive to demographic booms and busts, however calculated.

Legal Grounds for Divorce

Regulation of marriage is generally a provincial responsibility; however, federal law controls divorce. Important changes were made in the divorce law in 1968 and 1985, as it became clear that many people felt divorce was justified when both husband and wife agreed that their marriage had broken down. The effects that these new divorce laws had on the divorce rate can be seen in Figure 13.1. The 1968 Divorce Act provided two sets of grounds for divorce. *Fault grounds* included adultery and some other sexual behaviours (sodomy, bestiality, and homosexual acts), physical or mental cruelty, and en-

tering into a bigamous marriage. A divorce was granted immediately upon proof that a spouse had offended in one of these ways. *No-fault grounds* for divorce presumed a "permanent marriage breakdown" under a number of conditions: imprisonment or desertion lasting for at least five years, alcohol or narcotic addiction, non-consummation of the marriage, and separation of the couple for at least three years. The separation provision, which required agreement to the divorce by both spouses, but no justification of their decision, was designed to ensure that the marriage had really failed. For example, a husband, who deserted or unilaterally separated from his wife, could also obtain a divorce without the consent of his wife, but only after five years of separation. The 1968 act also required lawyers to discuss reconciliation with their clients; if this appeared to be a possibility, the divorce trial was adjourned to give the couple time to work things out.

Figure 13.1   Divorces per 10 000 Marriages, 1901–1990

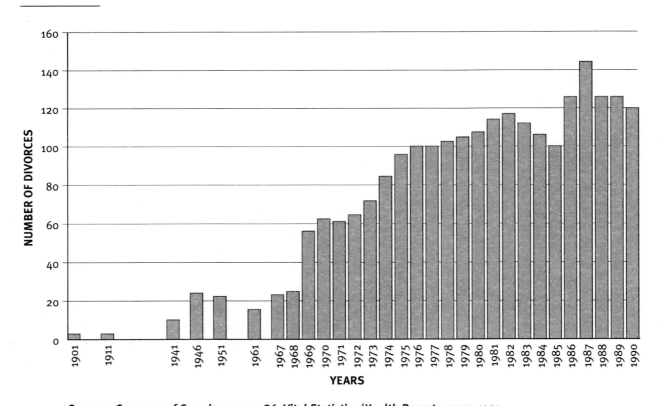

Sources: Censuses of Canada, 1901-1986; Vital Statistics/Health Reports, 1973–1991.

Under the 1985 amendments to the act, which came into effect in 1986, divorce is permitted under the following circumstances: 1) if the couple has lived separately for one year; 2) if a spouse has committed adultery; and 3) if a spouse has treated the other with physical or mental cruelty. Under the first provision, a couple can apply for a divorce at any time after they separate to ensure that the divorce hearing is held soon after one year is ended (which was not possible under the 1968 law). Proof of the last two (fault) conditions results in immediate divorce.

Amendments to the Divorce Act in 1985 resulted in a record 96 200 divorces in 1987. After peaking in 1987, the number of divorces steadily declined, reaching a low of 71 528 in 1996 (Statistics Canada, 1998). A number of factors may explain the decline in divorces across the country by 1996. Given that the incidence of divorce peaks after five or six years of marriage, a national decline in marriages between 1990 and 1991 could be a contributing factor. As well, the increase in cohabitation might suggest that couples who do choose to get married have a greater level of commitment.

Recent Divorce Patterns

The recent pattern for divorce rates has been interesting. Prior to the 1985 liberalization of divorce laws, divorce rates in Canada had started to trend down as in the U.S. Cherlin (1990) notes that divorce rates in the U.S. began declining about 1980. A similar decline started in Canada in 1981 until the more liberal grounds for divorce took effect in 1986 and 1987, giving the divorce rate a temporary bounce (see Table 13.2). From 1986 to 1987 the divorce rate increased by more than 20 percent (Statistics Canada, *The Daily*, Dec. 2, 2002).

TABLE 13.2   Selected Divorce Rates for Canada

YEARS	# OF DIVORCES	RATES PER 100 000 POP.
1921	558	6.4
1941	2462	21.4
1961	6563	36.0
1968[1]	11 343	54.8
1969	26 093	124.2
1981	67 671	271.8
1985[2]	61 980	253.6
1986	78 304	298.8
1987[3]	96 200	362.3
1990	80 998	295.8
1995	77 636	262.2
1997	67 408	224.8

1. Reform of Divorce Laws.
2. Divorce Act ("no fault").
3. Peak year.

Source: Adapted from Ambert, A.M., *Divorce: Facts, Causes and Consequences*, The Vanier Institute of the Family, Table 1, www.vifamily.ca. © 2003.

After 1987 divorce rates resumed a downward trend until 1997.

In 1998 divorce rates once again started to rise, but this time there was no change in divorce laws. The actual rate of change as can be seen in Table 13.3 is modest (2.6 percent and 0.3 percent). The consistency of the trend over the three-year period in Table 13.3 suggests that the years of a declining divorce rate may be over.

One of the questions that many people ask in regard to divorce statistics is not about trends or computational nuances but rather about the risk to their marriage or to their future marriage. This is of course impossible to answer on an individual basis, but we can estimate the risk to marriages based on previous cohorts.

Table 13.4 supplies an estimate for the percentage of marriages divorced by the 30th wedding anniversary (divorce rate per 100). The rate of divorce changes over this 30-year span. In general, the risk of divorce is greatest during the first four years of marriage. The estimated divorce rate for the first year is 5.1 per 1000 marriages, for the second year 17.0 per 1000, for the third year 23.6, and for the fourth year 25.5 per 1000 marriages. After the fourth year the risk begins to decline. Indeed, the risk to those in the early years of marriage is extremely high. For example, in 1999 to 2000 about 60 percent of all divorces were to couples married 15 years or less (Statistics Canada, *The Daily*, December 2, 2002).

TABLE 13.3   Divorces 1998–2000, Canada and Provinces

	1998	1999	1998 to 1999	2000	1999 to 2000
	NUMBER		% CHANGE	NUMBER	% CHANGE
Canada	69 088	70 910	2.6	71 144	0.3
Newfoundland and Labrador	944	892	−5.5	913	2.4
Prince Edward Island	279	291	4.3	272	−6.5
Nova Scotia	1933	1954	1.1	2054	5.1
New Brunswick	1473	1671	13.4	1717	2.8
Quebec	16 916	17 144	1.3	17 054	−0.5
Ontario	25 149	26 088	3.7	26 148	0.2
Manitoba	2443	2572	5.3	2430	−5.5
Saskatchewan	2246	2237	−0.4	2194	−1.9
Alberta	7668	7931	3.4	8176	3.1
British Columbia	9827	9935	1.1	10 017	0.8
Yukon	117	112	−4.3	68	−39.3
Northwest Territories and Nunavut[1]	93	83	−10.8	101	21.7

1. Northwest Territories and Nunavut are combined; prior to 2000 there was no divorce court in the part of the Northwest Territories, which became Nunavut. In 2000, there were 7 divorces in Nunavut.

Source: Statistics Canada, Divorces, *The Daily*, Monday, December 2, 2002, also available in Cat. No. 84F0213XPB.

TABLE 13.4   Total Divorce Rate, by the 30th Wedding Anniversary, Per 100 Marriages

	1998	1999	1998 to 1999	2000	1999 to 2000
			DIFFERENCE		DIFFERENCE
Canada	36.1	37.3	1.2	37.7	0.4
Newfoundland and Labrador	23.2	22.5	−0.7	22.9	0.4
Prince Edward Island	26.4	28.0	1.6	26.9	−1.1
Nova Scotia	28.2	28.2	0.0	30.4	2.2
New Brunswick	26.9	30.4	3.5	31.9	1.5
Quebec	45.2	46.5	1.3	47.4	0.9
Ontario	33.0	34.4	1.4	34.6	0.2
Manitoba	30.1	31.9	1.8	30.3	−1.6
Saskatchewan	31.5	31.7	0.2	31.4	−0.3
Alberta	39.0	40.4	1.4	41.5	1.1
British Columbia	40.0	40.3	0.3	40.6	0.3
Yukon	55.2	51.8	−3.4	33.6	−18.2
Northwest Territories and Nunavut[1]	37.5	34.0	−3.5	40.7	6.7

1. Northwest Territories and Nunavut are combined; prior to 2000 there was no divorce court in the part of the Northwest Territories, which became Nunavut. In 2000, there were 7 divorces in Nunavut.

Source: Statistics Canada, Divorces, *The Daily*, Monday, December 2, 2002, also available in Cat. No. 84F0213XPB.

Reasons for Divorce

While laws provide *legal grounds* for divorce, these are often not the reasons couples get divorced. Ambert (1980) suggests there are *societal* causes, grounded in the kind of society that we have, and *personal* causes relating to the characteristics and situations of people who divorce. In general, it is wise to divide our explanations of divorce into the following two categories:

1. Explanations of the aggregate phenomenon as measured by divorce rates. Such explanations often focus on cross-cultural and regional comparisons to identify the factors that influence the rates.

2. Explanations of the couple phenomenon that focus on why a given couple might get divorced. Such analyses usually include risk factors and interactional factors.

It should be noted that explanations as to a why a couple gets divorced will probably not serve to explain why one country has high divorce rates and another has low divorce rates.

Social causes of divorce include the liberalization of the divorce acts (Abernathy and Arcus, 1977), the social and geographic mobility in a region (Trovato, 1986, 2000), and the normative culture that justifies and promotes divorce as acceptable or desirable (Ambert, 2003). All three of these social causes interact to create a social climate favourable or unfavourable to divorce.

An example of a societal cause of divorce is the rapid increase in public acceptability of divorce since the Second World War. In 1943, only 24 percent of Canadians favoured more liberal divorce laws; 40 years later, strong public sentiment in favour of divorce liberalization led to the passing of the 1985 Divorce Act. More accepting public attitudes result in more liberal divorce laws, which make it possible for more couples to divorce, which then helps to promote further liberalization of public attitudes.

The women's movement has been a relevant societal influence, but the view that it has caused the rapid increase in divorce, often voiced by some anti-feminist groups, is simplistic and misleading (Sevér, 1992). Rather, the women's movement challenged patriarchal power and the subjugation of women in the family. The resulting feelings of empowerment and self-confidence women experienced enabled wives to challenge the family power and domestic work arrangements that feminism insisted were exploitative (Sevér, 1992). Thus, working wives saw divorce as a solution to their family problems more often than did those who were not employed (Hum and Choudhry, 1992). This is clearly a case where the increase in social mobility and opportunity for women is tied to higher divorce.

Trovato (1986) has examined geographic mobility to explain the differences in divorce rates across the provinces (see Table 13.3). He found that there was a significant relationship between interprovincial mobility and divorce. Part of this argument is that moving and changing environments is disruptive and hence related to divorce. There is also the probability that some of these moves are made to escape undesirable relationships and these individuals file for divorce in the new province.

When we examine international divorce rates (Table 13.5), we find that Canada is in the middle range for divorce, while its next-door neighbour, the U.S., is near the top of the range. We would expect two such similar cultures to have about the same divorce rates based on rates of social mobility, geographic mobility, and female employment. Canada, however, accepts many more immigrants relative to its population size than does the U.S., and many of these immigrants are from countries where divorce is not regarded as the norm. Even prior to Canada's increases in immigration, there existed differences in the divorce rates of the 1960s and 1970s. It has been suggested that Canada was a country of more traditional values than the U.S. in terms of institutions such as marriage and family (e.g., Lipset, 1990).

TABLE 13.5 Selected International Divorce Rates, 1999

COUNTRY	DIVORCE RATE PER 1000 PEOPLE	DIVORCE RATE PER 100 MARRIAGES
Belarus	4.3	52.9
Russia	4.3	43.3
United States	4.1	54.8
United Kingdom	2.6	42.6
Sweden	2.4	54.9
Germany	2.3	39.4
Canada	2.28	37
France	2.0	38.3
Yugoslavia	0.9	12
China	0.79	na
Italy	0.6	10.0
Mexico	0.48	na

Source: Americans for Divorce Reform at www.divorcereform.org/gul.html. Reprinted with permission.

Personal and couple causes of divorce include risk factors such as age at marriage, interaction patterns, marital quality (see Chapter 9), and intergenerational transmission of divorce. These personal causes cannot usually explain the aggregate regional or national divorce rates without some tenuous assumptions. For example, it is extremely doubtful that marital interaction and quality declined during the 1970s to cause the extremely high divorce rates of that decade, nor is likely that marital satisfaction is so drastically different in Canada versus the U.S. On the other hand, individuals leave marriages for reasons of personal safety, interaction, and rewards.

Social exchange theory (Lewis and Spanier, 1979) has long predicted that couples that have few barriers and many alternative relationships would be more likely to divorce regardless of how happy they might be. Certainly, survey research such as White and Booth (1990) has supported this hypothesis. South, Trent, and Yang Shen (2001) also found that marriage market considerations tend to keep functioning for marrieds. They reported that married females are more likely to divorce when many men and few women dominate their work situation. Interestingly, the availability of females for married males in the work place showed no similar effect.

Styles of conflict resolution can be seen as an example of a personal cause of divorce. According to Gottman (1994), marital satisfaction and frequency of disagreements are not reliable predictors of divorce. More likely to be associated with divorce are styles of conflict resolution involving stonewalling, contempt, denial, blaming, disrespect, and disengagement (Gottman, 1994; Gottman and Levenson, 2000). However, there is no single reason for divorce that appeared among the top five reasons in all of 10 American studies (Kitson et al., 1985).

For most couples, divorce is less often a *decision* that they make than a *complex process* they go through. A marriage may gradually deteriorate, as for example when traits that previously seemed lovable and good (because they were seen as *complementary*) in time become threatening or gradually less enchanting and appealing. Disillusionment and bitterness may result when a spouse changes too much, and is no longer "lovable" to the other. For reasons such as these, a marriage relationship may slowly deteriorate, or end quite abruptly if it becomes clear one partner is carrying on an affair. Interaction becomes increasingly tense and hostile, and a separation may result.

Despite the fact that this is often a gradual process, social scientists do have some general indicators that assist us in estimating the risks for couples. Age at marriage has long been identified as a risk factor. In addition, the history of a parental divorce is associated with a higher risk of divorce in the marriages of children (Glenn and Kramer, 1987). Teachman (2003) reports a relationship between the timing of first premarital sex in conjunction with cohabitation experience as having an effect on later marital disruption. Although we know a great deal about these risk factors (Teachman, 2002), it is important to remember that as the marriage market and the expectations regarding marriage change, the effects of some of these factors will change. For example, Heaton, Cammack, and Young (2001) note that in Indonesia age at marriage is waning in importance as a predictor of divorce as compared to education level.

Property and Support Settlements

Divorce requires the dividing of *one* into *two*, most obviously with respect to property, but also in respect to the responsibilities, cares, and enjoyment associated with children. These are matters in which the state has an interest, trying to ensure that children are raised to become law-abiding, productive members of society, and that spouses (and children) are not so impoverished by divorce settlements as to become dependent on the state for support. It has been argued that because legislatures and courts have been dominated by men, family law has been much more protective of men's than of women's interests, often resulting in injury to the welfare of women and children (National Council on Welfare, 1990).

Although the federal government makes the laws governing divorce, the responsibility for laws governing division of marital property, as well as child custody and support during *marital separation*, is provincial. Even within the same province there are important variations in practice, because judges interpret laws. Thus "the golden rule of a successful family law practitioner is still: 'Know thy judge,'" according to Payne (1988), a family law lawyer.

Property Settlements Most provinces are common-law jurisdictions, based on English customary or common law. In Quebec, however, which is a civil law jurisdiction, in the absence of more recent laws the courts base their judgments on the Napoleonic Civil Code. As recently as 1970, the Supreme Court of Canada ruled that in the common-law provinces, a wife had no claim on matrimonial property (property acquired during marriage), no matter how hard she had worked to help buy it (see Box 13.2). In Quebec, the Civil Code awarded the wife an equal share in matrimonial property, unless the couple had made an agreement that they would each own property separately, and not have matrimonial property. But the right to administer matrimonial property—to buy, sell, or collect the income from it—belonged to the husband alone (Baker, 1990a).

The obvious injustice of the Supreme Court ruling in the *Murdoch* case led to revisions in matrimonial property laws in all of the provinces by the early 1980s. The transforming assumption on which this Canada-wide legislation is based is that rights to matrimonial property are determined, not by whether either spouse has paid for it, but by their contributions to the marriage, whether or not these produced income. If both husband and wife contributed to the marriage, both may claim an *equal share* of assets they acquired *while married*. A court may order an *unequal* division when this is seen as appropriate. Provincial family laws depend on judicial discretion to ensure equitable divisions in such cases; however, this does involve an adversarial procedure, with lawyers attempting to get the most for their client at the expense of the other spouse (Baker, 1990; Kronby, 1991).

There are variations in provincial laws, particularly with respect to guidelines specifying the conditions under which the court may order an unequal division of business assets. The state has a vested interest in business properties because they are wealth-producing. Division of many small family businesses (a farm, small store, or business partnership) could destroy the business, and thus the wealth, employment, and tax revenues produced by it (McLeod, 1988). Next to ownership of the family home, accumulated pension eligibility is often a couple's most valuable matrimonial asset. While in the past this was lost to the homemaker wife of an employed man, this is no longer the case. A valuation of the pension benefit is made at the time of divorce, and the credits are split between the husband and the wife. If both the husband and the wife have been in the labour force and have acquired pensions, then the total amount of both pensions is calculated and then split equally.

Support for Spouses and Children As with divorce itself, provisions for the support of spouse and children have changed greatly since the passage of the 1968 and 1985 amendments to the Divorce Act. Earlier, only wives could qualify for support (alimony)—but they could only be awarded a "pension for life" (as some judges called it) if they had not contributed to the marriage breakdown through adultery, cruelty, or

---

Box 13.2	The Shocking Murdoch Case

In October 1968, after 25 years of marriage, Irene Murdoch left her husband. She asked for a share of their farm, 480 acres in Alberta. Mrs. Murdoch argued that she had earned a right to the property because during the early years of their marriage, she and her husband had both worked as hired farm hands. With the money earned, they had bought additional acreage, which Mrs. Murdoch had helped to develop and maintain.

The court decided that Mrs. Murdoch had not made a significant financial contribution toward buying any of the properties the couple had acquired during the marriage. It decided, as well, that she had made no relevant contribution in terms of her work. This work, in the opinion of the court, was no more than the effort expected from any rancher's wife. Accordingly it was not enough to give her a right to any of the farm property. In time, the case went to the Supreme Court of Canada, where four out of five of the judges upheld this decision.

Source: Adapted from Baker, 1990:216.

desertion. A wife found guilty of such misconduct lost the custody of her children and the right to any (alimony) support payments.

In the 1970s, provincial legislation was quite explicit in specifying factors judges should consider in ordering support payments during separation, but there was much dissatisfaction with how support needs were met. The 1985 *Divorce Act* corrected this, requiring courts to ignore considerations of marital fault and to make awards on the basis of the economic situations of the spouses and the economic consequences of the marriage and its breakdown for each. Both spouses share the financial costs of child-rearing. Parents are obliged to support a child until age 16, and thereafter if the child is disabled or is otherwise unable to support himself. The child also has a right to support if he wants to attend university or take other training (if the parents can afford this). Judges are also required to consider how long the couple lived together, and the family and support roles each played while married. In addition, judges have deemed it desirable to facilitate the stability of later remarriages, which in practice has meant that many have kept support payments low to help ease the financial burdens of second-marriage families.

A valuable contribution to a marriage that is often overlooked is a spouse's "human capital." This includes things that are difficult to quantify, such as time, effort, and support invested in creating opportunities and potential—the efforts of a doctor's wife who put him through medical school, for example. Since this "capital" cannot be divided, the court may provide substitute compensation through unusually large support payments (Bissett-Johnson, 1988). Only the three prairie provinces allow courts to consider this. Since they also include business assets as matrimonial property, the financial interests of traditional wives, who early decided with their husbands to stay home and raise their children, are well protected. British Columbia is unique in permitting judges to make unequal property awards to either spouse to help her or him become or remain economically self-sufficient (Kronby, 1991; Sloss, 1985). A woman's earning potential shrinks by 1.5 percent each year she is out of the workforce. After divorce, "the sacrifices she has made at home catch up with her . . . . They will often encompass loss of seniority, missed promotions and lack of

access to fringe benefits such as pension plans," wrote Madam Justice Claire L'Heureux-Dubé (Bindman, 1992:A3). Nevertheless, many court decisions are putting increased pressure on younger women to become self-supporting within a fixed period of time, after which alimony payments are ended. Indeed, there is a growing tendency in the courts to award alimony only if the need results from the marriage, rather than from a woman's apparent own job or career choice (Davies, 1988; Baker, 1990).

Many Canadian fathers avoid paying court-ordered support payments following separation or divorce—between 50 and 85 percent of them, according to Steel (1988). In Manitoba, help for divorced mothers was provided by a comprehensive collection system introduced by the province in 1980. Federal and provincial support payments must both be paid through the provincial government, which automatically initiates collection procedures if full payments are not made on time. Many other provinces have adopted the Manitoba model; it is very effective, except where an inadequate number of enforcement staff causes lengthy backlogs (Steel, 1988).

Child Custody and Access

The most significant consequence of divorce, for individuals and for society, is the children's custody arrangements and the way these affect children. **Custody** refers to all the responsibilities and rights with respect to their children that parents are expected by society to exercise. Dilemmas arise because most children have two accessible parents, and the child's welfare is affected by the conditions of access ordered by the court. With respect to divorced parents, there may be a distinction between legal custody and physical custody. **Legal custody** refers to the authority to make the many long-term decisions about how a child is to be raised. **Physical custody** refers to simply being responsible for a child on a day-to-day basis. **Joint custody** describes a situation in which the legal custody of the child is shared equally by both parents. Joint custody does not automatically involve sharing physical custody.

In Canada, custody following divorce is under federal control. The governing principle is simply that custody awards should be based on the best interests of the child, irrespective of the wishes of parents. Because the law depends on judicial discretion to achieve this goal, judges' decisions have reflected the changing attitudes of society. Earlier it was assumed that a mother's care was best for the child, but this is no longer automatically the case. The 1985 Divorce Act does not mention joint custody, but it does permit it, by granting custody to more than one person. For example, a grandparent may be granted shared custody if this would be in the best interests of the child.

Divided custody occurs when a child spends a significant part of the year with each parent, during which time each has the opportunity and responsibility to make important decisions. **Access** refers to the legal right granted to the non-custodial parent to be with the child. While the assumption has long been made that access granted only the right to be with the child, court challenges are now raising the question of whether the non-custodial parent has some additional right to influence the religious upbringing or health care of the child.

Mediation Granting that joint custody may have important benefits, how can it be fairly considered in cases where one parent is opposed? The answer may lie in **mediation**, the process of "resolving conflict through a neutral third party who facilitates communications, helps the parties in conflict define the issues, and works toward the resolution of those issues by assisting the disputants in their own negotiations" (Milne, 1985:4). If one or both members of the couple refuses to participate voluntarily, some would advocate mandatory mediation: the legal requirement that the couple obtain professional help in negotiating their difficulties. The Divorce Act of 1985 contains provision for mediation, and court-based mediation services have now been established in most provinces. This procedure for resolving divorce disputes is usually the least expensive, least embittering for parents, and best for the well-being of the children involved.

Divorcing couples who go through mediation are typically well-satisfied—in one study, between 79 and 91 percent were glad they had tried it, would recommend it to others, and believed it should be mandatory (Donohue, 1991). Further studies show that couples who underwent divorce counselling felt more in control, hopeful, and adjusted, as opposed to those who

hadn't and felt overwhelmed, impotent, and alienated (Conway, 1997). While the issues for mediation might include all the disputed areas arising during a divorce, most court-mandated programs restrict mediation to child custody and visitation issues.

Using data from a large U.S. nationwide survey, Seltzer (1991) studied three aspects of non-custodial fathers' involvement with their children: visiting, economic support, and participating in child-rearing decisions. Many fathers were so little involved with their children that about 40 percent had visited their children, had written or telephoned them, or had participated in a child-rearing decision no more than once during the preceding year, and 53 percent had paid no child support. Fathers who visited did tend to contribute financially and to participate in child-rearing decisions, but such involvement was relatively rare.

The lack of involvement of some fathers is not simply a result of their not caring for their children. A study of a small sample of non-custodial Canadian fathers found that those who were most involved with and attached to their children during the marriage were most likely to lose contact after divorce, while those who were less involved were more likely to remain in contact (Kruk, 1991). Apparently, many fathers who were intensely involved before the divorce could not tolerate a greatly reduced relationship with their children and so cut it off entirely. Doubtless there are other reasons why many non-custodial fathers virtually drop out of their children's lives.

Ahrons (1979, 1994, 1995), objecting to the view of divorce as social disorder and adopting a developmental theory perspective, has suggested that divorce be viewed as a possible stage in family development. A *family*, in the sense of a mother, father and children, does continue to exist after divorce. Ahrons (1979) argued that it should now be seen as a **binuclear family**; that is, a single family having two households (centres), in contrast to single-centred families. Both centres may cooperate in providing for common members. Thus, a binuclear family is found whenever the non-custodial parent is in contact with his or her children.

Stronger relationships within binuclear families have become more necessary with the possibility for divorced parents to share joint custody of their children, as is now becoming increasingly common in Canada. It is often argued that joint custody best ensures the child's welfare (McQueeny, 1984; Mayrand, 1988). Joint custody is often ordered by the courts in the U.S., and fathers' rights groups in Canada maintain the courts should assume that joint custody will be granted unless there are strong reasons not to do so. Women's groups have opposed legislation that would permit courts to impose joint custody on an unwilling parent. They argue that joint custody would grant both parents decision-making authority, while only one parent—usually the mother—would have to live with the consequences. Women argue that joint custody awards do not create *male mothers*, since few fathers would compromise their careers or earning opportunities for the benefit of their children, as many mothers do. However, joint custody would certainly reduce the feelings of powerlessness and bitterness that many divorced fathers now feel, and strengthen the father–child relationship.

With *hostile* couples, however, joint custody may do the children more harm than good. Parents must live with the fact that their children may be living quite a different lifestyle when they are with the other parent (Kennedy, 1990). In its most fully developed form, the binuclear family involves both joint custody and **joint parenting**, with the separated or divorced parents agreeing to share equally the rights and responsibilities of child-rearing, with the rights of neither party superior to the other. Joint parenting can occur without the courts awarding joint legal custody, as long as both parents can come to an agreement. However, if a disagreement arises, only the parent with legal custody has any official control in making decisions about how a child is to be raised.

Joint parenting may encourage the development of constructive, mature, and even friendly ex-spousal relationships. Such relationships could make Ahrons's somewhat wistful conception of really *functional* binuclear family relationships a reality. Indeed, this suggests the possible emergence of a new *extended family-like system* crystallizing out of the remarriage kindred in contemporary society (Furstenberg, 1987). In time, genuine binuclear family relationships may even begin to provide remarried families with a source of support and stability lacking in many of those who are first-married and thus have fewer relatives (Hobart, 1990).

Relationships between Binuclear Family Members and the Remarriage Kindred

Often, former spouses have a continuing relationship only if they have children. If childless, they may split up and never see each other again, though a few continue to be good friends. Some fathers do relinquish all ties with their children, and others maintain only occasional contact. Nevertheless, many divorced couples are inescapably linked by their attachments to their children. At least to the extent that they feel mutual obligation and concern for the development of their children, they must continue to deal with each other. Complicating every aspect of the relationship is the fact that there are no norms specifying how ex-spousal relationships should be patterned—public acceptance of divorce is so recent, and the emotional consequences are so complex and painful, that cultural definitions have not yet evolved (Hobart, 1991; Ahrons and Wallisch, 1987).

A Canadian study provides information on the relationships of remarried parents with their former spouses (Hobart, 1990b). About half the remarried husbands and wives said they had a continuing relationship with their former mate, and about one-quarter said they had a relationship with their current mate's former spouse. It is important for the well-being of the child that cooperative relationships be established between all the parents—natural parents and stepparents.

These data show there are sizable differences between the attitudes of husbands and wives toward their former spouses, but similarities in their attitudes toward the current mate of the former spouse. The reason: these are different kinds of relationships. With the prior spouse one must continue a relationship that led to divorce, while with the prior spouse's new mate, one need only establish a casual new relationship. Here the situations of both former mates are similar. But in their relationships with each other, the divorced couple is sensitive to different issues and has different vested interests. These differences are apparent in their attitudes, seen in Table 13.6. The relationships between current and former wives in an earlier Canadian study were often friendly, but this was never the case when the current wife was the partner in an adulterous affair that broke up the former marriage (Ambert, 1989).

TABLE 13.6   Perceptions of Relationships with Own Former Mates, and with These Persons' Current Mates

	RELATIONSHIP WITH			
	OWN FORMER MATE		MATE'S FORMER MATE	
	HUSBANDS	WIVES	HUSBANDS	WIVES
Positive Aspects				
Friendly	28%	31%	32%	14%
Trusting, communicative	8	12	18	6
Mutual concern for child's welfare	40	34	29	28
Supportive of mutual concerns	12	12	7	14
Necessary, agreeable relationship for the children	7	13	14	28
Appreciation of ex-spouse as good parent	12	3	0	6
Negative Aspects				
Conflicts over custody, visitation, child support	35	45	40	32
Lingering resentment feelings	32	12	10	32
Interference with present marriage plans and relationships	13	7	20	12
Other's unacceptable traits (jealousy, alcoholism)	2	20	0	16
Demanding ex-spouse causing tension	6	7	5	12
All aspects	7	7	13	4

Source: Hobart, 1990b.

With remarriage of the divorced couple, the binuclear family described by Ahrons (1979) expands to what we have called a **remarriage kindred**. The relationship in a binuclear family that appears to be the most influenced by the creation of a remarriage kindred is the one between the nonresident biological parent and the children. In homes where the mother has custody of the children, the remarriage of the father is associated with a decline in contact with the children and a decline in co-parental interaction (Christensen and Rettig, 1995; McKenry et al., 1996). As well, when nonresident fathers remarry or begin cohabiting, they find being a parent less manageable and less satisfying (Christensen and Rettig, 1995; Seltzer and Brandreth, 1994). When it is the resident mother who becomes remarried, there is no effect on the amount of contact with the nonresident father if that contact was casual (i.e., once or twice a month or less). Only fathers who saw their children at least once a week prior to the remarriage experienced a decline in visitation after the mother remarries. Therefore, it is the marital status of the nonresident father, rather than the current marital status of the mother, that has a larger influence on his involvement with his children

(Stephens, 1996). In contrast, remarriage of the custodial mother is strongly associated with a decrease in child support, while remarriage of the nonresident father has no significant effect (Hill, 1992). This is consistent with normative beliefs that stepparents should help support their resident stepchildren, therefore lowering the expected financial obligations of the nonresident father (Ganong, Coleman and Mistina, 1995).

Divorce and remarriage also affect relationships with extended family members. The limited research that has been done on the grandparent–grandchild relationship suggests that this relationship takes on increasing importance as the child moves from nuclear family life, to single-parent family life, to stepfamily life. Grandchildren in stepfamilies report having a significantly closer and more active relationship with their closest grandparent than do grandchildren in nuclear and single-parent families (Kennedy and Kennedy, 1993). This increase in quantity and quality of contact seems to be more likely to occur between the child and the parents of the custodial parent. The reason is twofold: 1) often the custodial parent turns to parents for support and assistance after a divorce, allowing more opportunity for contact between the grandparents and the grandchild or grandchildren; and 2) the parents of the noncustodial parent often experience access difficulties due to the discouragement of contact by their adult ex-child-in-law (Henry, Ceglian, and Ostrander, 1993; Kennedy and Kennedy, 1993; Kruk 1995). This unequal access to grandchildren can have a profound influence on the closeness of the grandparent–grandchild relationship. In Canada in 1995, more than 50 percent of stepfamilies were mother–stepfather families (Statistics Canada, 1996). This could mean that paternal grandparents are at greater risk of losing contact with their grandchildren.

After Divorce, What's Next?

Several years after the divorce, most of those who have been through it say they are happier than they were before (Chiriboga and Catron, 1991; Jekielek, 1998). However, divorce often has a devastating effect on a person's self-image. "Robbed of the [marriage] underpinnings of identity, the individual must confront what remains of selfhood during a time when others may be labeling the self as non-productive, overemotional, a 'bad parent' or 'troubled'" (Chiriboga and Catron, 1991:173). In contrast with a comparison group, Chiriboga and Catron's divorced respondents showed more self-blame and more negative and vulnerable self-images. During the three years between the first and second interviews, respondents' self-images did tend to recover, however, and surviving the divorce experience gave many of them increased self-confidence (Chiriboga and Catron, 1991). Individuals from separated families account for 50 to 80 percent of patients treated by Canadian mental health clinics (Conway, 1998). Stack (1993) found that the suicide rate among the divorced is three to four times higher than among married individuals.

Divorce is usually viewed as a negative, painful experience, but this viewpoint has been challenged for convincing reasons. Escape from a repressive, stifling marriage may be empowering and growth-promoting, especially for wives who are dependent or in an exploitative *marriage cage*. Through divorce a person may realize previously underdeveloped abilities (Sevér, 1992). To confront and successfully deal with a crisis experience such as divorce can be strengthening and confidence-inspiring. Some have reported that their physical and emotional health improved significantly after they were divorced (Huddleston and Hawkings, 1991). Remarriage can also negate some of the negative effects of divorce, and provide some unique benefits. It restores the self-esteem and feelings of well-being, reduces economic and psychological distress, and often provides children abandoned by their non-custodial parents with a helpful, caring substitute (Amato 1987; Coleman and Ganong, 1991; Shapiro, 1996).

Men and women appear to handle divorce differently. A study of 252 divorced Ontario residents (Ambert, 1988b) found that higher proportions of divorced men than women had been hospitalized in a psychiatric ward or received psychiatric treatment. Some 38 percent of the men and 27 percent of the women had received such treatment, and 28 percent of the men but only 5.5 percent of the women had received long-term or repeated treatment. Findings suggest that the post-divorce period is traumatic for men and women, typically more damaging *emotionally* to the husband and *financially* to the wife.

Dating plays an important part in post-separation adjustment, and helps overcome loneliness. Divorced individuals begin dating early, often soon after they separate; this helps them heal the wounds of divorce, particularly the damage to their self-concepts. Evidence of their attractiveness to others helps restore feelings of self-confidence. Older people may find this somewhat difficult because their dating skills are "rusty," and because they are unsure of details such as who pays, and how and when to initiate sexual contact.

Many divorced persons soon enter cohabitation relationships (Dumas and Péron, 1992), and those who remarry often do so after very short dating or engagement periods. Indeed, these couples spend only half as much time in dating and courtship as before their first marriages (O'Flaherty and Eells, 1988), and they rarely do the obvious things that would reduce remarriage problems. For example, one study found that about half did not discuss parenting their prior-marriage children, less than one-quarter talked about financial matters, and 13 percent did not discuss any significant marital issues (Ganong and Coleman, 1989).

As divorce has become increasingly common, the remarriage rate among divorced men and women has fallen, as Figure 13.2 shows, but the decline has been greater for men than for women. Most, if not all, of the decline in the rate of remarriage can be explained by the corresponding increase in cohabitation (Bumpass, Sweet and Cherlin, 1991; Wu and Balakrishnan, 1994). A 1990 Statistics Canada survey found that among divorced persons aged 30 to 39, 62 percent of the men and 41 percent of the women were cohabiting (living common-law), and among those divorced aged 40 to 49 years, these figures were 46 percent for men and 28 percent for women (Dumas and Péron, 1992). According to research by Bumpass, Sweet, and Cherlin (1991), cohabitation is even more prevalent among divorced and separated individuals than it is among those who have never been married. They have also found evidence that although cohabitation unions in general tend to be short-lived, the cohabiting unions of the previously married are significantly longer in duration than are those among never-married individuals.

Especially when children are involved, cohabitation may be the equivalent of engagement in earlier times (Wineberg and McCarthy, 1998). About half of all currently married stepfamilies began as a cohabiting relationship (Bumpass, Raley and Sweet, 1995). Cohabitation, however, is not necessarily a prelude to marriage, but is seen by many previously married individuals as an alternative family arrangement. Compared to never-married cohabitors, previously married cohabitors are almost twice as likely to expect not to get married to anyone in the future (Wu and Balakrishnan, 1994). This could be an indication that cohabitation is substituting for remarriage for a large proportion of those who have experienced marital disruption.

It is estimated that in Canada in 1995, 10 percent of all couples with children were stepfamilies. Slightly more than half of these approximately 430 000 families consisted of couples who were currently married, while the rest were cohabiting (common-law) couples (Statistics Canada 1996). Many children, therefore, gain a stepparent through cohabitation, rather than through remarriage. As well, given that a significant number of cohabiting couples eventually marry, it can be limiting to view the stepfamily as forming only after a legal marriage. "Analyses that limit the definition of stepfamilies to married couples misclassify a significant proportion of families, and underestimate both the prevalence and the duration of stepfamily experience" (Bumpass, Raley, and Sweet, 1995:426). Restricting the definition of stepfamilies to married couples also ignores other two-parent family forms with children that are prevented from being recognized through legal marriage, such as gay and lesbian parents with a same-sex partner.

All women are disadvantaged in their chances to remarry in comparison with men. Age is also an influence: for both men and women, the probability of remarriage after divorce declines with age. More specifically, using 1984 to 1986 data, Adams and Nagnur (1988) were able to predict the probability that divorced Canadian men and women would remarry, for each year of age. Their most noteworthy finding is the sharp decline in the probability that a divorced woman will remarry after age 35 (Adams and Nagnur, 1988). There is no such sharp decline for men.

A recent study by Sweeney (1997) found that for women experiencing divorce at relatively younger ages, good socioeconomic prospects have a negative impact on remarriage. The opposite is true for relatively older women, where a positive relationship exists between socioeconomic prospects and remarriage. These results imply that younger women with good socioeconomic prospects can afford to stay single and engage in a more

Figure 13.2 Marriage Rates by Age for Divorced Men and Women, Canada, 1965–1967, 1975–1977, and 1985–1987

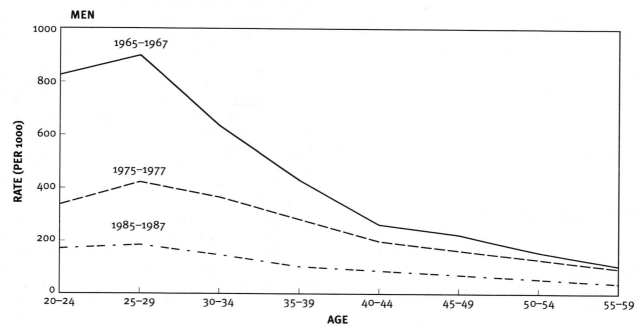

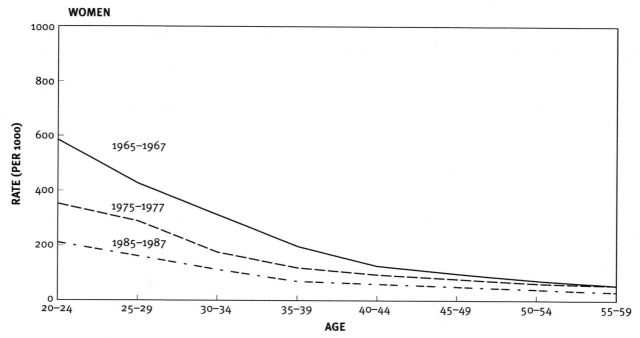

Source: Dumas and Péron, 1992.

lengthy search for a new partner, while for older women, higher socioeconomic prospects increase their attractiveness in the dating pool, giving them an increased advantage.

It is interesting to note that the age of the youngest child seems to have more influence on remarriage probabilities than does the total number of children. In a recent study, women who had a youngest child under the age of six were about 37 percent less likely to remarry than were women with no children. For men, having a youngest child between the ages of 13 and 17 years was associated with a 34-percent reduction in the likelihood of remarriage, compared to men with no children. No significant effects were found for the number of children (Sweeney, 1997).

Remarriage and Stepfamilies

The simplest form of remarriage involves a couple in which one or both members was married before, but had no children. Whether or not such couples eventually have children, in terms of their kinship relationships they are *structurally* like first-married couples. However, family life is more difficult in stepfamilies in which there are prior-marriage children. The rest of this section deals primarily with stepfamilies created through remarriage. These families experience the most difficulties because the mix of children is a major source of tension and conflict. The simplest type of stepfamily is the **stepfather family**, in which only the wife has prior-marriage children. The **stepmother family** is one in which only the husband has a prior-marriage child. The difficulties stepmothers may experience are described later in this chapter. A **complex stepfamily** is one in which both the remarried husband and wife have prior-marriage children. This type of family has more potential problems, particularly for the mother, because of the "mix" of children. Who the children are living with does not play a role in determining the type of stepfamily. Figure 13.3 shows the 1995 breakdown of stepfamilies by type in Canada.

The belief that the stepfamily will behave as a nuclear family is often the most persistent and perplexing unrealistic expectation of stepfamilies. The myth of instant love that leads stepparents to believe there should be immediate feelings of love and affection for a stepchild can, when the myth is not fulfilled, lead to feelings of guilt and denial, and ambivalent or

Figure 13.3   Stepfamilies by Type in Canada, 1995

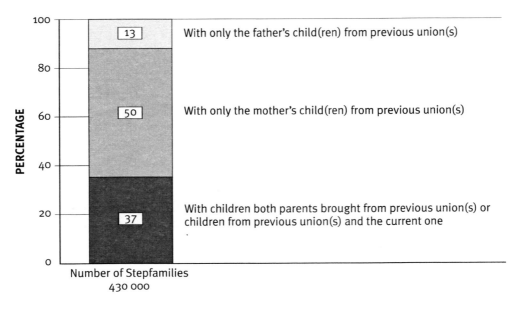

Source: Statistics Canada, *The Daily*, June 19, 1996.

overcompensating behaviours, all of which can inhibit the natural development of the stepparent–stepchild bond (Ganong and Coleman, 1997). Pill (1990) found that one or both partners in 41 percent of the responding stepfamilies said they entered remarried life expecting their stepfamily members would become as closely bonded as in first-married families. Seventy-five percent of the respondents found their expectations were not fulfilled. One-third of the respondents described living in a stepfamily as requiring continual and deliberate effort, and most were unprepared for these demands.

Visher and Visher (1990) have outlined six major dynamics to which the stepfamily must respond in order to be successful:

1. Members must accept the losses associated with this family transition and let go of the past.

2. Members must realize that their new family form is going to be different from a first-marriage family, and develop realistic expectations that are not based on an attempt to duplicate a nuclear family.

3. A strong and unified couple leads the stepfamily. They work together and support each other in household decisions.

4. New family rituals are established that develop positive shared memories and feelings of belonging.

5. Members realize that positive step-relations are not automatic, and understand that these relationships must be cultivated over a period of time that may vary depending on a number of factors.

6. It is particularly important for the couple to create a parenting coalition, so that all the adults who are involved act to support each other in establishing discipline and setting limits, regardless of whose children they are raising.

Parenting and Parent–Child Relationships after Remarriage

One of the most important role strain predictors for the biological parent in the stepfamily is dealing with competition between the new spouse and the children. For the stepparent, the strongest predictor of role strain is low clarity on stepparenting expectations (Saint-Jacques, 1995). The relationship between stepparents and their stepchildren can be a difficult one to negotiate. Pauline I. Erera-Weatherley (1996) identified five stepparenting styles that have been adopted by stepparents in her research:

- biological parent

- super good step-mom

- detached stepparent

- uncertain stepparent

- friendship

These various stepparenting styles have been observed in other studies as well (Coleman and Ganong, 1997; Cooksey and Fondell, 1996; Marsiglio, 1992; Mekos et al., 1996). The process of adopting a particular stepparenting style seems to be ongoing. Stepparents often attempt various parenting styles before finding one that seems to work best, and over time, as the relationship between stepparents and stepchildren changes, the stepparenting style often changes as well (Erara-Weatherley, 1996).

Society does not provide clear norms specifying parental authority and disciplinary role of stepparents relative to stepchildren. These are frequent and serious sources of stress between the two parents in stepfamilies. Society often views a stepfather's discipline as less justifiable and excusable than a biological father's discipline (Claxton-Oldfield, 1992). Children often challenge a stepparent's authority as well— "You're not my *real* parent. I don't have to do what you say." One important issue is trust: Does the mother trust the stepfather to discipline her children fairly? Do adolescent stepchildren trust the wisdom and justice of their stepparents? Do they believe these parents discipline their own children with equal consistency and severity (Fowler, 1993; Benokraitis, 1993)?

The majority of studies on child abuse in stepfamilies suggest greater risks to children, especially in regard to the sexual abuse of girls. It should be stressed that this does not mean all children in stepfamilies are at risk. Rather, "[t]he factors that increase risk in stepfamilies likely include the same factors that put other children at risk, plus some individual and group characteristics that are more common in stepfamilies, and also a general lack of understanding and training for parental care and a morality which stresses the needs of children" (Giles-Sims, 1997:227).

Research has shown that stepmothers experience more difficulty raising stepchildren than their own biological children, and that this increased difficulty is more likely to occur for stepmothers than stepfathers (MacDonald and DeMaris, 1996). There are a number of reasons stepmothers may have more negative attitudes than stepfathers toward stepchildren. First, due to current custody trends, often the man must consider the consequences of becoming a stepfather when courting a lone mother, while a woman considering marrying a divorced father often has little reason to think about the problems she may experience as a stepmother. Second, due to the gendered division of labour in the home, both visiting and live-in children often increase the housework loads for stepmothers. Contrary to her expectations, Ambert (1989) found that husbands do not increase their help to their wives when their prior-marriage children visit. As well, the father is often reluctant to act in ways that might spoil the visit, and so fails to discipline his children when needed. This leaves the stepmother to deal with conflicts involving the husband's visiting children. Very few stepmothers express satisfaction with this role or their performance of it (Coleman and Ganong, 1997). These issues are sources of frequent conflict within the remarried couple (Fowler, 1993). The resulting spousal conflict increases the stepmother's dislike of her stepchildren.

The Stepsibling Subsystem

The relationships between siblings, half-siblings, and stepsiblings are another piece to the stepfamily puzzle that has been largely neglected in research. In an exploratory study on the stepsibling subsystem, Ganong and Coleman (1993) found great diversity in the amount of contact between stepsiblings: 10 percent had no contact, 50 percent were together a "few days each year," 13 percent were together "a few days each month," and 25 percent were together "most of the time." Fifty-seven percent of the children in this study identified problems with their stepsiblings, such as having to share resources like parental attention and space. Despite these problems, the majority rated their stepsibling relationship as better than average. This could be due to such things as low expectations for the relationship, compensation for feelings of guilt about

jealousy, denial, or even a sincere effort to get along with stepsiblings in order to please their parent. It appears the stepsibling relationship is neither inherently positive nor inherently negative. Stepsiblings are fought with less, taught less and helped less often than siblings. Overall, half-siblings were responded to more positively than were stepsiblings. In fact, several children in the study objected to the terms half-brother and half-sister because they did not distinguish between siblings and half-siblings. The findings of this exploratory study seem to indicate that the presence of stepsiblings is more of a problem for the parents than for the children (Ganong and Coleman, 1993).

The majority of children in a stepfamily subsystem report having contact with their stepsibling(s) or half-sibling(s) in adulthood. However, contact was significantly less frequent than it was with full siblings. The longer the child lived with a stepparent, the more likely contact was maintained in adulthood with stepsibling(s) or half-sibling(s). Children with *only* stepsiblings or half-siblings had more frequent contact with them in adulthood than did those who had both full *and* stepsiblings or half-siblings, indicating a possible substitution effect (White and Riedmann, 1992).

Quality of Marital and Family Life in Stepfamilies

The circumstances of stepfamilies probably make them particularly vulnerable to conflict in two areas, in comparison with first-married families. One is child-rearing, because when there are prior-marriage children, the natural parent may object to how the stepparent deals with them (Fowler, 1993). Heightened conflict may also be expected over financial issues, because the available money must often provide for more children than in most first-marriage families. Hobart (1991) confirmed both of these expectations.

A review by Coleman and Ganong (1991b) concluded there were few differences in the marital satisfaction of first and subsequent marriages. An important distinction may be drawn between *stepfamily* satisfaction and *marital* satisfaction, and some studies have found that the two do not go together. A study of a small sample of stepfamilies (Pill, 1990) found that in comparison with first-marriage families, stepfamilies had high levels of *adaptability* and much lower levels of family *cohesiveness*. Both these characteristics were associated with satisfaction with the stepfamily, but not with marital satisfaction.

The presence of prior-marriage children in the home appears to have differing effects on marital intimacy for each spouse. For the biological parent, the presence of their prior-marriage children in the household is associated with greater feelings of marital intimacy. Stepparents, on the other hand, experience more marital intimacy when the stepchildren are not residing in the home, and less when they are (Gold et al., 1993). In contrast, a Canadian study of 109 stepparents in Quebec found that both stepmothers and stepfathers reported more positive experiences with in-living than with out-living stepchildren—both stepparents said they were closer emotionally to in-living stepchildren. As a result, stepmothers of in-living stepchildren reported more positive effects on their marriage than those having out-living stepchildren. This is further support of a distinction between marital satisfaction and stepfamily satisfaction. In the end, however, many stepparents reported their marriages would be happier and more harmonious without stepchildren (Ambert, 1986).

Fine and Kurdek (1995) have shown in their research that the quality of the stepparent–stepchild relationship has a greater impact on perceived marital quality than does the quality of the biological parent–child relationship. They argue that because the stepparent develops a relationship with the spouse and stepchild concurrently, the marital subsystem and the stepparent–stepchild subsystem are more closely linked. In addition, while stepparents may be able to attribute difficulties with their stepchild to action (or inaction) on the part of the biological parent, "biological parents, because of their shared history and the relatively stable relationship with their child, are less likely to attribute the source of these problems to the stepparent" (Fine and Kurdek, 1995:221) The result is that marital intimacy and marital quality are more negatively influenced by the presence of prior-marriage children for the stepparent than for the biological parent. This can be problematic, because most biological parents perceive their relationship with their children to be more positive than the relationships stepparents report having with their stepchildren (Fine et al., 1993).

U.S. research evidence shows that the divorce rate for remarried couples is higher, but not very much higher, than that of first-married couples, and also that a divorce occurs sooner after a remarriage than after a first marriage (Clarke and Wilson, 1994; Martin and Bumpass, 1989). Booth and Edwards (1992) suggest that to justify and initiate a divorce, previously divorced individuals may not require as disturbing a decline in marital satisfaction as may first-marriage individuals. It has also been found that although more remarriages than first marriages end in divorce early on in the relationship, as time passes the divorce rates for these two groups converge (Clarke and Wilson, 1997).

Research by Wineberg (1992) has shown that the presence of school-age, prior-marriage children increases the risk of marital dissolution, whereas the presence of preschool-age children at the time of remarriage does not have any negative effects on marital stability. This could reflect the easier time younger children have adjusting to stepfamilies, implying that the adjustment problems of older children have negative consequences for marital stability. The research shows that the birth of a "shared child" after remarriage helps to bring step-children closer together. Wineberg (1992) found that the positive effects were still significant after 10 years.

The Effects of Relationship Endings and New Beginnings on Children

Hundreds of studies have assessed the effects of divorce on children. Children are the most frequent victims of family breakup and any accompanying hostility and bitterness, because they are the most vulnerable members of a family. When badly hurt, children may suffer for the rest of their lives. Damage to children is a burden to the state as well, in terms of the social and financial costs of dealing with emotionally disturbed children and the ineffective and perhaps dangerous adults they may become.

There is some good news to be noted, however. Sevér (1992) identifies half a dozen Canadian studies conducted between 1955 and 1980 that found either no negative effects or no *lasting* negative effects of divorce for children. Some benefits of divorce were reported, including findings that children of divorce are more empathic and independent, have more egalitarian attitudes, and have closer relationships with their mothers (though their relationships with their fathers often suffer) when compared with children in two-parent families. Sevér also emphasizes the resilience of children in coping with events.

Although most children from divorced families and stepfamilies do not experience adjustment problems (Emery and Forehand, in Hetherington et al., 1998), there is a consensus among researchers that children, adolescents, and adults from these types of families have an increased risk of developing problems in adjustment when compared to those from two-parent, non-divorced families (Hetherington et al., 1998). Children raised in lone-parent families are often socially and economically disadvantaged (Parsons, 1990), and some problems of children of divorce reflect lower-class influences, because divorce reduces many middle-class mothers and children to lower-class circumstances.

Preschool children of divorce are the most frightened—fearful both parents will abandon them. They are often afraid to be alone, and troubled by nightmares. They often regress and wet the bed; some want to be put in diapers (Fassel, 1991; Stirtzinger and Cholvat, 1991). Elementary school-age children are troubled about economic insecurity. The boys in particular have more behavioural and emotional problems—heightened aggression, anxiety, emotional dependency, and a tendency to withdraw—possibly due to the absence of the father. Elementary school girls, on the other hand, show no distinctive problems (Benokraitis, 1993). Once they become adolescents, girls and boys who were under the age of seven when their parents divorced are three times more likely to be in psychological counselling, and are suspended or expelled from school at five times the rate of children from intact families (cited in Benokraitis, 1993). Among a random sample of 1519 Montreal high school and college students, those from divorced homes were the most disadvantaged in respect to mental health, self-esteem, school performance, and confidence in their future prospects. Less disadvantaged in these respects were those with widowed parents, while children from intact homes were least disadvantaged, most happy, and most secure (Saucier and Ambert, 1986).

The total disruptive consequences of divorce for children reflected in U.S. statistics are staggering. A study combining the findings from 92 studies of children of divorced parents concluded that such children suffer in respect to academic achievement, conduct, psychological adjustment, self-esteem, and social relations (Amato and Keith, 1991b). It has also been found that parental loss, be it through divorce, separation, or death, is the "single most powerful predictor of adult psychopathology" (Bolgar, 1995:143).

Often the children of divorce do not outgrow their earlier problems. As adults, many avoid intimacy because they fear abandonment. They often get little enjoyment from life, reporting low levels of satisfaction with leisure activities, friendships, and family life, and low levels of happiness (Glenn, 1991). Amato and Keith identified the statistically significant findings from 37 studies based on a total of 81 000 respondents. They concluded that "adults who experienced parental divorce exhibited lower levels of well-being than did adults whose parents were continuously married" (1991a: 43), because of depression, low educational attainment, low income and occupational prestige, impaired physical health, unhappy marriage, and more frequent divorce. Adult men (children of divorced parents) had more educational problems than did women, while adult women (children of divorced parents) were more likely than men to end up getting divorced as a result of their own parents' divorce.

Wallerstein (1992) completed a 10-year follow-up study of 60 divorced families, chosen because their divorce outcomes were predicted to be favourable. They were middle-class, mostly university-educated families, with children doing well in school and parents in good mental and emotional health. But over the years the researchers were "stunned" by their findings. Many families, even 18 months after the divorce, were still in crisis. Five years after the divorce, 37 percent of the children were depressed, were unable to concentrate in school, had trouble making friends, and had a wide range of behavioural problems. Only one-third were clearly doing well. By 10 years after the divorce, 41 percent were "doing poorly," entering adulthood as "worried, underachieving, self-depreciating, and sometimes angry young men and women," and 14 percent had uneven patterns of adjustment (p.164).

While earlier research found that pre-teen girls adjusted well to parental divorce, Wallerstein's study found a "sleeper effect" that appeared when girls experienced serious love relationships—they were immobilized by *fear of commitment*. Having seen how the good relationships of their parents could "blow up," they became fearful of betrayal, of committing to a relationship that could go painfully bad, when they experienced a possible love relationship (Wallerstein, 1992). Girls, like boys, are thus vulnerable to being seriously hurt by divorce, but the effects show up later and in different ways. Wallerstein also found that children of divorce are overburdened by feeling responsible for a troubled, needy, or depressed parent, or by being assigned a parenting role that the disturbed parent needed the child to play (Wallerstein, 1985; Wallerstein and Blakeslee, 1989).

Amato (1993) used findings from more than 80 studies to determine the reasons for the severe problems that children of divorce experience. He found that "the strongest and most consistent support" was obtained for the explanation that *parental conflict* causes the children's difficulties. Amato's basic conclusion is supported by findings from many studies that children in families where there is a great deal of parental conflict often experience emotional problems, whether or not there is a divorce (Demo and Acock, 1991). Such conflict also contributed indirectly to children's poor adjustment by making their mothers less warm and empathic, thus damaging the mother–child relationship (Kline et al., 1991). Longitudinal studies in Great Britain and the U.S. have found that among children, especially boys, achievement and behavioural problems often existed well before their parents separated when there was much marital conflict in the home (Cherlin et al., 1991).

Some of the adjustment problems associated with remarriage include increased substance abuse among girls (Needle et al., 1990), greater delinquency among boys (Pagani et al., 1998), and higher rates of suicide for both genders (Rubenstein et al., 1998).

Hetherington, Bridges, and Insabella (1998) outline five basic perspectives found in the literature that explain the adjustment problems of children in stepfamilies:

■ **Individual risk and vulnerability:** It has been argued that certain personal characteristics (i.e., antisocial behaviour, depression) of parents and children are present before certain family transitions occur, and that the presence of these personal characteristics increases their risk of exposure to these transitions and makes them more vulnerable to the associated adverse effects.

■ **Family composition:** This view adheres to the concept of the nuclear family and argues that any family structure that deviates from this norm (two biological parents and their offspring) will be problematic for children.

■ **Stress:** The emphasis here is on the changes involved in marital transition—such as the renegotiations of family roles and relationships—that can cause practical problems and stress. These, in turn, have a negative impact on the well-being of parents and their children.

■ **Parental distress:** This perspective argues that it's not the stressors themselves that influence children's adjustment, but the way the parents respond to the stressors. In other words, if the parent is not coping adequately with the stressors, he or she will experience parental distress and diminished well-being, and it is this negative response by the parent that has an effect on the children's adjustment.

■ **Disrupted family process:** The argument behind this view is that the efforts of children to adapt to their new family situations can be supported or undermined by changes in family relationships. Disruptions in family processes such as discipline, child-rearing practices, parent–child relationships, and problem-solving strategies lead to adjustment problems in children. If there is continuity in these family processes from one family form to another, then the previously mentioned risk factors (individual characteristics, family composition, stress, and parental distress) are less likely to have a negative effect on children's adjustment.

A two-year longitudinal study of 57 American stepfather families found that longer intervals between divorce and remarriage of the custodial mother were associated with lower levels of social competence in children for a period after the remarriage. The reason: increased time in a lone-parent family made adjustment to the stepfamily more difficult. In addition, children whose custodial mother cohabited before remarriage appeared to be more socially competent throughout the first two years after remarriage, and experienced fewer negative family relationships (Montgomery et al., 1992). The most probable reason was that these children had become accustomed to the stepparent during the cohabitation period.

Children's attitudes appear to be influenced by the divorce of their parents and subsequent remarriages. Children who experience their mother's remarriage are more likely to endorse premarital sex and cohabitation than are children from intact, divorced, or widowed family homes. As well, while children of divorced parents experience a reduced enthusiasm for marriage, children who experience their mother's divorce and remarriage have similar attitudes toward marriage to children from intact non-divorced families (Axinn and Thornton, 1996).

While the mass of evidence shows that experience in remarried families often has negative consequences, this is not always the case. A recent study, which confirmed earlier findings, found that although children in stepfamilies had experienced the most structural family changes, they did not show the lowest general well-being. In fact, their sense of well-being was comparable to that of children in stable intact families and significantly greater than that of children in divorced or single-parent families. Even more dramatic, children in stepfamilies generally scored better on physical and psychological well-being than did children from conflict-ridden intact families (Spruijt and de Goede, 1997). Experiences dealing with new step-relatives seem to lead to increased flexibility and the development of improved interpersonal skills. As well, children in stepfamilies have a larger potential kin network with which to develop positive relationships, and may also benefit from having a stepparent who is more objective than their biological parent (Coleman and Ganong, 1991).

Stepfamilies from a Legal Perspective

Cherlin (1978) described stepfamilies as institutionally incomplete, because society does not provide clear role definitions as to how step-relatives should deal with each other. As we shall see in the following discussion, the lack of consensus on the legal rights and responsibilities of step-relatives support this assertion. (Box 13.3 reviews the legal perspective.) In fact, in many cases no legal rights or responsibilities exist, and

if they do they are restricted to stepfamilies in which the stepparent and the custodial biological parent are legally married and the stepchildren are under the age of 18 and living with them (Fine and Fine, 1992; Mason and Mauldon, 1996; Redman 1991). This specific distinction could marginalize cohabiting stepfamilies and the stepparent–nonresident-stepchild relationship by not providing equally needed norms and role definitions.

Stepparents are rarely required by law to financially support their stepchildren. In 1997, only 10 states required support by stepparents for residential minor stepchildren. An additional eight states required only that stepparents provide support where the resident children would otherwise be impoverished. The remaining states have no requirements for stepparents to support their stepchildren, even if these children live with them. In addition, every state recognizes that the stepparent is free from any obligations of support if co-residence with the child is terminated (Mahoney, 1997). Although there are exceptions, the general rule is that the stepparent voluntarily takes upon himself or herself the role of parent ("in loco parentis" or "in the place of parent") and the relationship can be terminated at will, usually after the divorce from the natural parent (Fine and Fine, 1992; Mahoney, 1997; Redman, 1991).

With regard to inheritance, the only way stepchildren can inherit from a stepparent is if they are named in the stepparent's will. The stepparent must be very specific in naming the stepchild. For example, if the stepparent designates an inheritance to a group of people without naming them specifically, such as "for my children," the courts will not recognize stepchildren as belonging to this category. When there is no will, the state inheritance laws determine the distribution of the deceased's property. In this case, stepchildren have no claim on any inheritance, even if they were dependent upon the stepparent at the time of death (Fine and Fine, 1992; Mahoney, 1997).

With few exceptions, after the dissolution of the remarriage the custody of the children remains with the biological parent. Only a handful of states allow stepparents to pursue visitation rights (Fine and Fine, 1992; Mason and Mauldon, 1996). Custody may also become an issue after the death of the custodial biological parent. In this situation, the courts normally feel it is in the best interest of the children that they be

Box 13.3 — The Canadian Legal Perspective

The legal rights and responsibilities of stepfamilies in Canada are very similar to those in the U.S. Some believe that the laws in Canada are even more progressive than in the U.S., while others would argue that we still have a long way to go before a consistent countrywide policy can be agreed upon. In 1997, the Manitoba Court of Appeal denied an appeal to Sharon Chartier regarding the decision that her estranged husband did not have to pay child support for the daughter she had from a previous relationship. The couple was married in June 1991, and separated the following spring in May 1992. Ms. Chartier argued that her estranged husband should be responsible for the child until she reaches the age of majority. A Court of Queen's Bench judge argued that Mr. Chartier never adopted the child, so he was not liable to pay child support. In another province, Ms. Chartier's argument might have received a different response. Alberta and Saskatchewan courts have ruled that stepparents have an obligation to their stepchildren that cannot be dismissed upon divorce. Ontario would have ruled in her favour as well, if she could prove that her husband assumed a "settled intent" to treat the stepchild as his own. In British Columbia, on the other hand, she would not have been able to win her case. In 1996, the B.C. Supreme Court ruled that stepparents were not responsible for financial maintenance of their stepchildren. Until a case is decided in the Supreme Court of Canada and a national precedent is set, the provinces will continue to vary in their judgments and make the rules however they see fit.

Source: *The Globe and Mail*, July 13, 1997.

placed with the non-custodial biological parent. This holds true even if the deceased custodian appointed the stepparent as legal guardian in a will, and the stepparent has been "in loco parentis" for an extended period. In situations in which the biological non-custodial parent is not in the picture, or deemed an "unfit" parent, the likelihood of the stepparent receiving custody is increased. However, they may still have to compete with other third-party requests for guardianship, such as those made by grandparents or other relatives (Mahoney, 1997).

The only case in which the relationship between a stepparent and stepchild can legally resemble that of a biological parent–child relationship is that of formal adoption of the stepchild by the stepparent. Before this can occur, the stepparent must be willing to accept the legal responsibilities of this new relationship, the residential parent must agree to this change in parental status, the nonresident parent must relinquish all parental claims to the child, and the child, if old enough, must consent. Generally, the nonresident parent does not want to give up parental rights voluntarily, and thus prevents stepchild adoption. The residential parent and the stepparent can initiate legal proceedings to have the parental rights of the nonresident parent involuntarily relinquished. However, as long as the nonresident parent has played an active role in the child's life and he or she is not deemed an "unfit" parent, the courts will be reluctant to sever the nonresident parent's relationship with the child. This holds true even if the nonresident parent has failed to pay court-ordered child support (Ganong et al., 1998; Mahoney, 1997).

For the most part, stepparents (Mahoney, 1997) do not adopt their stepchildren. In general, stepfamilies do not contemplate adoption when the nonresident parent has a relationship with the children. Financial concerns such as the loss of child support from the nonresident parent, the requirement of continued financial commitment to the child even in the event of a divorce, and the actual legal costs of adopting all serve as barriers to stepchild adoption. Surprisingly, the lack of legal relationships between step-relatives is not a motivating factor for most families considering stepchild adoption. The desire to resemble a nuclear family, and the belief that adoption would normalize and cement the stepfamily, are main considerations. As well, stepparents and stepchildren, more than any other family members, contemplate adoption (Ganong et al., 1998); it appears that the family members with the most ambiguous relationships are the most likely to desire to change their family structure to one with more clearly defined roles and norms.

Lone-Parent Families

Not all divorced or widowed individuals remarry. Some take on the difficult task of raising their children alone. Even individuals who do remarry usually spend some time as a lone parent. The causes of lone parenthood have changed greatly during the past five decades, as Figure 13.4 shows. In 1941, 85 percent of parents were single because of the death of their spouse. By 1986, this had fallen to less than 30 percent, with the steady increase in divorces and in unwed parenthood. The almost one million lone-parent families in 1991 represented 14 percent of all families, almost twice the 8 percent reported in 1961. Due mainly to high maternal mortality rates, in 1941, 26 percent of lone-parent fathers headed families, compared with 17 percent in 1981. The percentage of lone-parent families headed by fathers is again on the rise, reaching 19 percent in 1991, because courts are more often giving custody of children to fathers.

A recent Canadian study details the financial situation of lone-parent families. In Chapter 5 we saw that the LICO (low income cut-off) is the income figure below which families of a certain size spend 20 percent more of their total income on food, shelter and clothing than the average family of that size. In 1990, 56 percent of lone-parent families had incomes below the LICO. They made up almost half (47 percent) of all low-income families. Among the more than one million children living in low-income families in 1990, 43 percent were in lone-parent families. Almost all children living with two parents (93 percent) were in above-LICO families (Odekirk, 1992).

An important reason for the intensity of poverty in many lone-parent families is that women head more than four out of five of these families. Most are young women who are less well educated than other women their age. One study showed that 7 percent of lone mothers, but virtually no lone fathers, were under 25 years of

Figure 13.4   **Lone-Parent Families by Cause, 1941–1986**

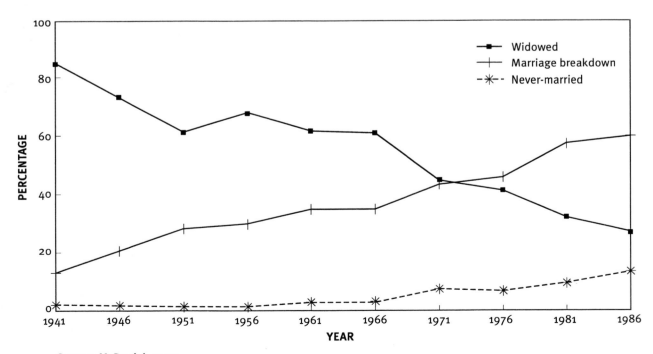

Source: McDaniel, 1990.

age, and that 26 percent of lone mothers were graduates of some post-secondary program, compared to 41 percent of lone fathers (Odekirk and Lochhead, 1992).

There are major differences in income between lone mothers and lone fathers (Odekirk and Lochhead, 1992). Three times as many lone mothers as lone fathers (45 percent versus 13 percent) have below-LICO incomes.

A longitudinal study of 5875 divorced men and women, based on their tax file information from 1982 to 1986, found that in the first year of divorce, women's family income dropped by about half, and men's dropped by about one-quarter. When adjusted on the basis of family size during the first year, women's incomes were found to *drop* by 40 percent, while men's incomes *increased* slightly. The percentage of women living in poverty increased from 16 percent in the last pre-divorce year to 40 percent in the first post-divorce year, while for men the increase was only from 14 percent to 17 percent (Finnie, 1993). The differences in post-divorce incomes between men and women in Canada are not quite as large as those reported for the U.S., but the consequences for the lifestyle of women are probably similar (though mitigated somewhat by better Canadian health-care services and social safety nets).

Lone-Mother Families

Family History Survey data suggest it is very probable that a large minority of the current generation will experience lone parenthood because of unmarried motherhood, separation or divorce, or widowhood. However, far from being a permanent condition for men or women, it is often sequential, with marriage followed by divorce, and often remarriage and divorce again, as family cycle and family power theorists point out (Pool and Moore, 1986). Out of all female lone-parent families, never-married mothers are the most likely to end their lone-parenting phase through marriage (97.4 percent) compared to divorced or separated lone parents (77.4 percent), and widowed lone parents (59.3 percent) (Lindsay, 1992).

Many lone mothers, because they are often ill-educated, have few work skills, and must often care for preschool children, are unable to earn sufficiently more than government social assistance payments to cover the costs of day care. In Edmonton in 1990, for example, a single mother with two children, working 40 hours a week at the minimum wage, would earn $2000 less than she would receive in social assistance. She would have to work 91 hours a week to earn a poverty-line income level (Engman, 1990:A1).

Mothers lose other important resources, besides income, following divorce. The most significant is probably the sharp fall in bank credit that many divorced women experience. Loss of employee benefits, such as paid dental care, may also result (Pain, 1988).

Statistics Canada found that lone mothers experienced more sleep problems (34 percent versus 22 percent) and pain and discomfort feelings (24 percent versus 17 percent) than mothers with spouses (McGovern, 1993).

On the other hand, it must be emphasized that while these losses are painful and make life difficult, some women, particularly those who have escaped from abusive or overbearing husbands, experience strong feelings of *empowerment* after divorce. These feelings are enhanced by the finding that they are able to deal effectively with the much more difficult financial and physical circumstances in which they find themselves (Sevér, 1992).

Lone-Father Families

A 1993 study using recent, nationally representative data showed that there was a preschool child in more than 30 percent of lone-father families, as compared with more than 45 percent of lone-mother families. Contrary to the myth that almost all the children in the custody of their fathers are sons, about 44 percent of the children in American lone-father families were girls (Meyer and Garasky, 1993). It is often argued that children of divorce do best when they are in the custody of their same-sex parent, and some small-sample studies have supported this conclusion. However, an analysis of 1988 representative U.S. data from almost 8000 eighth graders living in lone-parent homes used 35 indicators of psychological, social, and academic adjustment, and found no evidence that the adjustment of children living with same-sex parents was any better than that of children living with opposite-sex parents (Downey and Powell, 1993).

More Canadian lone fathers had jobs (71 percent) than did lone mothers (52 percent), but both had lower employment rates than married parents, among whom 65 percent of mothers and 87 percent of fathers were employed. There were dramatic differences in average family incomes in 1991, with lone mothers reporting annual incomes of $22 000, lone fathers, $37 000, and two-parent families, $57 000. Since these families had averages of 2.6, 2.5 and 3.9 members, respectively, the per capita family income was $14 600 for lone-father families—almost twice the $8460 figure for lone mothers. These fathers had slightly more income per capita than two-parent families. (Two-parent families have slightly lower per capita incomes than lone-parent families because there are 1.4 more family members.) Lone fathers are thus quite able to support their children financially.

Though men head almost one-fifth of all lone-parent families, there have been very few studies of them, perhaps because the rarity of lone fathers makes them harder to locate, or because they seem less vulnerable than lone mothers. In a British study, loneliness and depression were reported "all the time" or "occasionally" by more than two-thirds of a sample of lone fathers, because of "the never-ending succession of days filled with work and evenings and weekends filled with chores" (George and Wilding, 1972; quoted in O'Brien, 1980:116). When interviewed after more than three years of separation, more than half were still upset (O'Brien, 1980). However, few reported financial problems.

SUMMARY

- The major cause of marital dissolution is now divorce, rather than death. As divorce has become easier, divorce rates have increased, whereas annulment, desertion, and formal separation have become rare in Canada.
- In Canada's early years, in some areas there were no legal grounds for divorce. Now, simply the wish of both to divorce after being separated for one year is legal grounds for divorce.
- Rights to matrimonial property in Canada after divorce are currently determined by contributions to the marriage, regardless of whether these contributions produced income. Both husband and wife may claim an equal share of assets they acquired while married if they contributed to the marriage. A court may order an unequal division when this is seen as appropriate.
- Both parents are obliged to support a child until age 16, and thereafter if the child is disabled or is otherwise unable to support himself or herself. The child also has a right to support if he or she wants to attend university or take other training (if the parents can afford this).
- Divorce rates are explained by aggregate factors, whereas a couple's divorce is explained by personal factors and couple interaction.
- Canada is in the middle range for divorce rates; the U.S. has one of the highest divorce rates in the world.
- Mediation usually works well to promote amicable settlements of custody issues. Although often opposed by women's groups, joint custody and co-parenting arrangements appear to best promote the adjustment of parents after divorce, and to best ensure the normal development of their children.
- Ahrons argues that a family, in the sense of a mother, father, and children, does continue to exist after divorce. However, it should now be seen as a binuclear family with two households, in contrast to a common household. When these households are further expanded through remarriage, a remarriage kindred develops.
- It is not uncommon for former spouses to have a relationship with their ex-spouse's new partner, although these relationships are commonly centred on the children.
- Remarriage of the nonresident father is associated with a decline in contact with his children, while remarriage of the custodial mother has little influence on contact. However, remarriage of the custodial mother is associated with a decrease in child support, while remarriage of the nonresident father has no significant financial effect.
- Most, if not all, of the decline in the rate of remarriage can be explained by the corresponding increase in cohabitation. Compared to never-married cohabitors, previously married cohabitors are almost twice as likely to expect not to get married to anyone in the future. However, about half of all currently married stepfamilies began with a cohabiting relationship.
- Research indicates that stepmothers have more difficulty dealing with stepchildren than stepfathers do. It also appears that the presence of stepsiblings is more of a problem for the parents than for the children. While the presence of stepchildren in remarried families may have adverse effects on the quality of family life, it does not have such effects on the couple's marriage adjustment.

- Although most children from divorced families and stepfamilies do not experience adjustment problems, there is a consensus among researchers that children, adolescents, and adults from these types of families have an increased *risk* of developing problems in adjustment when compared to individuals from two-parent, non-divorced families.

- There is a lack of consensus on the legal rights and responsibilities of step-relatives. In many cases, no legal rights or responsibilities exist, and if they do they are restricted to stepfamilies in which the stepparent and the custodial biological parent are legally married and the stepchildren are under the age of 18 and living with them.

- About one-fifth of lone parents are lone fathers. Lone fathers are more likely than lone mothers to be employed, and are less likely to have incomes below the LICO.

KEY TERMS

Access (306)

Annulment (296)

Binuclear Family (306)

Complex Stepfamily (312)

Custody (305)

Desertion (296)

Divided Custody (306)

Divorce (296)

Joint Custody (305)

Joint Parenting (307)

Legal Custody (305)

Mediation (306)

Physical Custody (305)

Remarriage Kindred (308)

Separation (296)

Stepfather Family (312)

Stepmother Family (312)

QUESTIONS FOR REVIEW

1. What changes have there been in divorce legislation during the past 30 years, and what have been the major effects of these changes?

2. What were the relative contributions of death, annulment, separation, and divorce to marriage dissolution 50 years ago, and what are their contributions today?

3. How do boys and girls react to their parents' divorce? To their remarriage? How does age affect these reactions?

4. Describe the various ways in which Cherlin's concept of "incomplete institutionalization" is relevant to stepfamilies.

5. How do stepchildren affect the quality of family life and of marriage in stepfamilies?

6. What is the difference in the way we compute the crude divorce rate and the divorce rate per 1000 marriages?

QUESTIONS FOR DISCUSSION

1. If you were given the job of proposing changes in divorce legislation to minimize the damage to children, what changes would you advocate?

2. Given the arguments for the beneficial and the destructive consequences of relatively easy no-fault divorce, do you think the current provisions are appropriate and justified, or should they be changed? If so, how?

3. What are the potential strengths, and serious vulnerabilities, of stepfamilies?

4. How realistic do you think it is to believe that the remarriage kindred might evolve into a supportive kin network, which can help out divorced parents, stepparents, and stepchildren? What developments might realistically improve the chances?

5. In what ways are the issues facing cohabiting stepfamilies and first-marriage stepfamilies different from remarriage stepfamilies? What issues do they have in common?

SUGGESTED READINGS

Ahrons, Constance. 2001. *Divorce and Remarriage: The Children Speak Out.* NY: HaperCollins. This is a follow up to the sample first analysed in the 1989 Ahrons and Rodgers study. It has statements from the children of divorce as to how divorce and family reorganization affected them.

Conway, John F. 1997.* *The Canadian Family in Crisis.* Toronto: James Lorimer and Company Ltd. Conway looks at families past, present, and future. He considers the implications of divorce, the impact of social changes on men, women and children, and suggests how these issues might be better addressed through family policy. Well-written, provocative, and insightful, this modern look at today's family is a must-read for anyone in sociology, family studies, or politics.

Kelley, P. 1995. *Developing Healthy Stepfamilies*. Binghamton, NY: Harrington Park. Kelly objects to the deficit view of stepfamilies and avoids comparing stepfamilies to first-marriage families. Instead, she takes us into the lives of 20 healthy stepfamilies to help us identify healthy stepfamily functioning based on the unique characteristics of these types of families.

Thompson, Ross A. and Paul R. Amato. 1999. *The Post-Divorce Family*. California: Sage Publishers. This is a multidisciplinary approach to the consequences of divorce for children, the parents' responsibilities after divorce, nonresident parenting, and the societal effects of high divorce rates. The book is analytical and thought-provoking.

CHAPTER 14

Family Stress, Crises, and Abuse

After studying this chapter, you should be able to do the following:

- Explain why some families cope well with crises, and some do not.
- List the various theories that explain mistreatment of family members.
- Outline the incidence rates of mistreatment of wives, husbands, children and elders.
- Review the effects of physical and sexual assault on children.
- Explain how the treatment that a woman experiences from an abusive husband tends to "lock her in" to this relationship.
- List some similarities and some differences between abusers of elders and abusers of women and children.

Introduction

"When *home* is where the *hurt* is," reads a poster in Edmonton subway stations, "family violence can be stopped." One of the great tragedies of our time is that our homes, where we hope for love, caring, and understanding, are the very places where many Canadians are most at risk of physical and emotional harm. In this chapter, we try to understand families in trouble—families that must attempt to respond, adapt, and cope when hit by tragedy or disaster. We try to understand families in which violence, physical and sexual abuse of children, spouses, and elders—and sometimes kin-murder—take place. First, we focus on the positive aspects of the family, how it seeks to cope and sustain its members in the face of adversity. We then turn to the abusive, violent, at times murderous, families—we ask who the victims are and why, and what becomes of them. We give greater emphasis to the negative aspects of families, because many of the family catastrophes of earlier times, such as premature death or natural catastrophe, are now less common,

and because abusive and violent families seem to be increasing in number.

Family Stress and Catastrophes

Family stress is "a state which arises from an actual or perceived *imbalance* between demand (e.g., challenge, threat) and capacity (e.g., resources, coping) in the family's functioning. It is characterized by a *nonspecific* demand for adjustment or adaptive behaviour. When this imbalance is due to demands exceeding resources, this is a state of *hyperstress*" (McCubbin and Patterson, 1983:10) [Emphasis added]. Hill (1949) devised the famous ABCX Family Crisis Model to provide a *conceptual* answer to this question: Why do some families respond well to stress, even thrive on it, while others collapse? It is a simple model: "A (the stressor event) interacting with B (the family's crisis-meeting resources) interacting with C (the definition the family makes of the event) produce X (the crisis)" (Hill, 1958:141). Since Hill's pioneering work various researchers such as McCubbin and Patterson (1983) and most recently Patterson (2002) have linked how families cope with stress and the resiliency of the family.

There are many possible stressors (factor A in the model). Hill classified them in terms of how they would affect families:

- **New members** additions to the family structure such as a (wanted or not wanted) baby, a grandparent, a divorced son
- **Family dismemberment** changes in family structure resulting from death
- **Deliberate changes in family structure** desertion or divorce
- **Demoralization in the family** alcoholism, substance abuse, criminal activity

To this list we add:

- **Sudden change in status** significant changes in income level
- **Natural catastrophe** earthquakes, hurricanes, fires, and so on, damaging or destroying the family home or other possessions

The B factor in the model, *family's crisis-meeting resources*, refers to the ability of the family to prevent the stressor from creating a crisis or breakdown. Two very important resources are *family integration* and *family adaptability*. The first refers to the bonds of unity running through family life, among which common interests, affection, and a sense of economic interdependence are perhaps the most important. *Family adaptability* refers simply to its ability to change when circumstances make this advantageous. Other family resources include agreement about the family role structure, and the willingness to subordinate personal desires to family goals (Hill, 1958).

The C factor in the ABCX model—the family's *definition* of the crisis event—is as important as both integration and adaptability. As social psychologist W. I. Thomas said, "If people perceive a situation as real, it is real in its consequences." The definition of the crisis may overestimate or underestimate the stressor, in both cases to the disadvantage of the family. The meaning it gives to the stressor reflects the family's values and its earlier experience in dealing with change and meeting crises. The stress the family experiences thus reflects its concern that its resources may not be equal to these demands. Where this concern is valid and resources are inadequate, crisis (the X factor) results,

and the family is to some degree disrupted, disorganized, or incapacitated. If its resources are adequate to the stressor, the family copes, thus preventing a crisis.

The Hill model has been expanded to the **double ABCX crisis model**, seen in Figure 14.1, to take account of the fact that the ability to cope depends on family circumstances *when the stressor is experienced*. Since virtually all families experience prior strains and hardships, any new stressor creates a *pile-up of stresses* (AA in the model), imposing new demands on the family resources. Family coping may be assisted by obtaining *new resources*, perhaps including additional personal resources, social support, family cohesion, and adaptability (BB in the model). But the family may also lose some preexisting resources while trying to cope. Family coping is also influenced by the family's *perception* of the demand pile-up (CC in the model). Does the family see this as a challenge or a catastrophe (McCubbin and Patterson, 1983)?

If the family does deal relatively satisfactorily with the stressor(s), as families usually do, it will find itself *adjusting* and *adapting*. Adjustment may involve modifying its coping strategies so as to avoid the stressor by ignoring or eliminating it. Adjusting serves to preserve the family structure in the face of the stressor. Adaptation is an assimilating strategy, and involves trying to make appropriate changes in family relationships and interaction patterns, and thus in its very structure. Such an approach requires restructuring the family in terms of its roles, rules, goals, and interaction patterns, to better cope with the situation (McCubbin and Patterson, 1983:19–23).

Researchers (McCubbin and McCubbin, 1987; 1989; 1993) have confirmed that strong families do adapt much more successfully to stress than do weak families. Strong families are able to work together to solve problems, and do so democratically. Members of these families delegate responsibilities, respect and love each other, and share values—all factors which encourage family cohesion and support in times of stress. Members of weak families are more prone to blame each other in difficult situations, do not help each other out, do not share their troubles, and resist compromising with other members. As a result, weak families have less flexibility and fewer resources for dealing with stress, and do so less effectively.

Figure 14.1   The Double ABCX Model of Family Strains

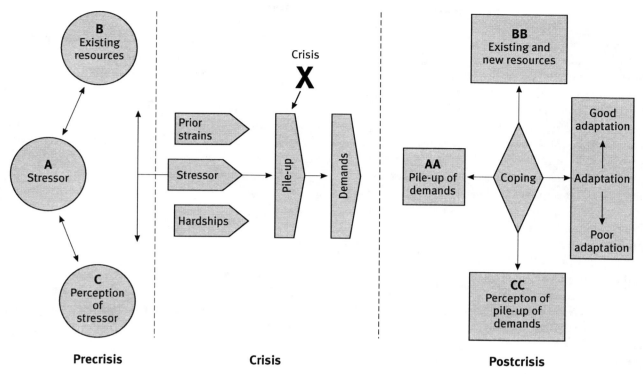

Source: Adapted from Hill, 1958, and McCubbin and McCubbin, 1983.

Social support has been found to be one of the strongest predictors of successful problem-solving for individuals and families (Sarason et al., 1990). Conger and Conger (2002) report that marital support and coping skills are linked to overcoming economic adversity among rural families. Some families establish broad informal support systems consisting of friends and extended families (Antonucci, 1991; Holahan and Moos, 1983), whereas other families, who value their privacy, develop a more tightly knit support system, asking for help only in extreme circumstances. The key to effective support does not appear to be the frequency with which families ask for help, but their belief that a request for assistance will result in the care and support that is needed (Antonucci, 1991). Seccombe (2002) argues that while attention to national economic policies can enhance family resilience, those policies must both increase family resiliency and reduce the conditions that put families and children at risk.

Abuse within the Family

We have described the family as the group to which people first look for understanding, assistance, and support. But what if "the family *is* where the hurt is?" What if family love is "terrifying love" (Walker, 1989), or no love at all, only abuse and violence? Such family life is the experience of many Canadians, and it is to these most tragic of destructive families that we now turn. The central theme is *abuse*, a short word that covers terrible deeds and often produces terrible consequences. We shall describe the abuse experienced by wives, husbands, children, and the elderly, but first we must consider causes. Why is there abuse of family loved ones?

Theories and Reasons

The following section will present the most accepted theories that try to explain abuse or domestic violence. Each theory provides insight into reasons for family violence, yet taken alone none fully explains why it happens.

Feminist Theory Feminist explanations hold that wife-battering is a consequence of **patriarchy**, the system of family decision-making in which the father has supreme authority. Patriarchal societies assume that women are to be dominated by men, forcefully if necessary. Violence against women is just one of many ways of keeping women subjugated in patriarchal societies (Campbell, 1992). Historical evidence supports these assertions (Pleck, 1987) and studies demonstrate the relationship between violence against women and patriarchal social structures (Baron and Straus, 1987). Ethnographic studies also provide support (Campbell, 1992). Interestingly, there is little wife abuse in societies having female economic work groups, which tend to empower women (Kalmuss and Straus, 1982).

Feminists explain the perpetuation of patriarchy by emphasizing gender differences in socialization, which train boys to be assertive and aggressive, and women to be passive, accepting, and dependent. Patriarchy is thus "a product of how women and how men have been socialized in relations of dominance and subordination" (Smith and Burstyn, 1987:3).

Social Stratification Theory It is common, particularly in the wife-abuse literature, to argue that abusive treatment is found among couples in all categories of people: religious, racial, ethnic, and social. Sociologists have wanted to emphasize this in order to avoid charges of stereotyping particular races or social classes. And it is true that some abuse is found in all populations. There are many indications, however, that domestic violence is more common in young, lower-income families than in higher-income families (Conway, 1990; McKenry, Julian and Gavazzi, 1995; Rodgers, 1994). Although some cases of domestic violence exist in higher-income families, the high rates of severe individual and social problems in poor families provide an explanation for increased rates of hostility and abuse in these families. This is particularly true of the *underclass* in poverty ghettos. The explanation for the class difference in violence is that individuals in the middle or upper classes have been socialized through increased education and resources to deal with anger, frustration, and marital disputes through verbal mediation and communication

(McKenry et al., 1995). Societal norms in middle and upper classes frown on physical aggression, and middle-class men have often learned to inhibit their aggressive tendencies—they stand to lose more if they act violently. These norms may not exist for those in the lower-income bracket, and in fact the contrary may be true—individuals in a lower-class family are more likely to have seen violence tolerated or rewarded during their own childhood (Gelles and Conte, 1990).

Young and immature married or cohabiting couples, who often have lower-class origins, have elevated violence rates (Rodgers, 1994). Similarly, child physical and sexual abuse is more frequent in the families of young parents or single parents; these parents are often socially isolated and experiencing financial stress and conflict (Conway, 1990; Finkelhor, Moore, and Straus, 1996).

Psychological Theories Psychology makes two contributions to the understanding of abusive family relations. The first, the *frustration–aggression hypothesis*, predicts that frustrated persons often respond aggressively (Dollard et al., 1939, cf. Kesner, Julian and McKenry, 1997). When these individuals are unable to vent their hostility on the source of the frustration, they may direct it at an accessible substitute target (Julian and McKenry, 1993). Poverty, unemployment, and economic stress are powerful sources of frustration, and the frustration–aggression hypothesis thus provides an explanatory link between economic hardship and violence in the home.

The second psychological theory predicts that certain kinds of deviant personalities will be more violence-prone than others. This has been demonstrated by many studies (McKenry et al., 1995; O'Leary, 1993). Berger (1980a), reviewing the literature on parental characteristics of abusing families, reports high rates of behavioural and social deviance, personality disorders, and neurotic (though rarely psychotic) symptoms. Such parents are often found to be narcissistic, rigid, compulsive, anxious, hostile, and depressed, and to have low self-esteem, poor impulse control, and poor empathic ability (Berger, 1980a).

Social Exchange Theories From an *exchange theory* perspective, family members will be violent toward each other if the benefits of violence outweigh the costs (Gelles, 1983; Leonard, 1996). Combined with assertions from *social control theory*, *social exchange theory* posits that all people will act violently in the absence of effective social controls. If there are no legal ramifications for violent behaviours, or if the perpetrator does not expect to be condemned, continued violent acts are likely to occur (Dutton et al., 1990). This premise is supported by findings that batterers believe there are no negative sanctions (Carmody and Williams, 1987), and that spousal abuse is seldom reported due to the victim's attitude that reporting is useless because no negative consequences are likely to occur (Rodgers, 1994). Gelles (1983) believes that the isolation and privacy of the contemporary nuclear family enables family members to be violent without cost. Ethnographic studies give some support to this theory (Campbell, 1992).

The Abusive Family System Perspective

Many research studies have found that abusive individuals were abused as children. One of the most frequent findings is that violent adults grew up in violent homes, where they often experienced violence themselves, and witnessed attacks on other children or violence between their parents (Gelles, 1979; Lackey and Williams, 1995; Okun, 1986; Rodgers, 1994). Supporting evidence for this comes from the 1993 Violence Against Women Survey, which indicated that abused women were three times more likely than non-abused women to have an abusive father-in-law. Fifty-five percent of women whose partner had witnessed violence while growing up reported being abused by their partner more than once. These findings suggest the existence of an **abusive family system**, a family system that produces abusive individuals who create new abusive families when they marry. This theme is consistent with intergenerational family systems theory, which posits that patterns within families are *transgenerational*, passed on from generation to generation (Barnett and Fagan, 1993; Bowen, 1978).

Human Ecology Perspective Human ecology is a relatively new field that views individuals within their near and farther environments. As such, this perspective views issues from a multifactoral, biopsychosocial framework. A human ecology model considers the interactions among the biological, psychological,

sociocultural, and familial systems in individuals' lives to gain understanding of an issue or problem (Bulboz and Sontag, 1993).

From the preceding discussions, it is obvious that domestic violence is a complex phenomenon arising from the interaction of multiple variables. Attempts to find a single cause for violent behaviour are reductionistic and inaccurate (Johnson, 1996; McKenry et al., 1995). The interaction of societal, economic, cultural, political, psychological, historical, familial, and biological factors may predispose certain individuals to violent behaviour. Summarized, the most salient predictors for perpetrators of family violence include the following: biological/psychological factors, such as hormonal imbalance, psychological maladaption, or cognitive/affective dysfunction; familial factors, including history of child abuse (possibly intergenerational), demography, financial strain, and conflictual family patterns; and social factors, such as cultural and political views on traditional roles and violence, lack of sanctions, social inequalities, and glorification of violence through the media. These factors may produce a medium ripe for domestic violence. From a human ecology perspective, none of these factors alone predict violence—it is the interaction of all the systems in an individual's life that predict and explain behaviours (McKenry et al., 1995).

Domestic Violence in Canada

There are a variety of forms of domestic violence in Canada. These include physical, emotional, psychological, verbal, and sexual abuse. While many of the predictors and outcomes of these various forms of violence may overlap, some specific factors are involved in each situation. The following sections of the chapter will identify some forms of domestic violence, and highlight what researchers tell us about the incidence, predictors, and outcomes of the abuse.

Physical Violence against Wives

Based on the 1993 Violence Against Women Survey, 29 percent—or approximately 2.7 million—of women married or living common-law had been physically or sexually abused by their partner at some point in the relationship. Some 312 000 women experienced abuse in the year prior to the study (Rodgers, 1994). Of women whose spouse assaulted them, two-thirds indicated that the abuse occurred on more than one occasion. Statistics Canada reports that women are beaten an average of 35 to 40 times before they go to the police (*Edmonton Journal*, 1992a), and the same figure has been reported in the U.S. (Jaffe and Burris, 1982). Canadian Urban Victimization Survey data show that 16 percent of women who reported any spousal assault also said they were assaulted repeatedly during the preceding year (Solicitor General of Canada, 1985).

Given the serious nature of wife abuse, and the frequency and intensity at which it occurs, it is reasonable to assume that many of these women have feared for their lives. In the 1993 survey, 13 percent—or 130 000 women—currently in abusive situations indicated they had at some point been afraid their partner would kill them. Forty-five percent of women who had left an abusive partner said they had feared their spouse would take their lives.

Most people in Canada believe that pregnant women should receive special consideration. Thus, it is particularly horrifying that abusive husbands beat their pregnant wives. Statistics Canada reports that in 1992, half of women physically assaulted by their partners were assaulted during pregnancy (*Edmonton Journal*, 1992a). The 1993 survey indicated that for 40 percent of women, the abuse began during pregnancy (Rodgers, 1994). Among a sample of 435 battered women collected in Denver, no less than 52 percent were beaten during the third trimester of their pregnancy (Walker, 1984).

Violence against wives has not always been seen as important and is underreported both by police and by the women themselves. Reasons cited for not reporting the violence include (in order) fears that the incident was too minor, desire to keep the incident private, not wanting help or not wanting to get the courts involved, fear of partner, belief that the police could do nothing, shame and embarrassment, and not wanting the spouse to be arrested (Rodgers, 1994).

Many studies in Canada and the U.S. have found a pattern in the characteristics of abusive families. Violence against wives is inversely associated with level of income and educational attainment, and is more frequent in young families (Grandin and Lupri, 1997; Grandin et al., 1997). Women aged 19 to 34 are four times as likely to experience violence as those aged 45 to 64. Unemployed husbands are more often violent than those employed full time or part time (DeKeseredy and Hinch, 1991; Johnson, 1996; Rodgers, 1994).

Sexuality in Abusive Relationships and Marital Rape

It is not surprising that women in abusive relationships report significantly lower levels of intimacy and compatibility in their marriages. To date, little research has been conducted to explore issues of sexuality in abusive relationships. In a recent U.S. study of women in both violent and nonviolent distressed marriages, women in abusive relationships demonstrated more traditional sex-role ideology, negative disposition toward sex, stronger avoidance of sex, and lower levels of sexual assertiveness, arousability, and satisfaction than non-abused women. Despite the negative attitudes toward sex, women in abusive relationships reported significantly higher frequency of intercourse with their spouses (Apt and Hurlburt, 1993). Whether the negative attitudes toward sex were influential in the incidence of abuse, or resulting *from* the abuse, is unclear. What does seem evident, however, is that sex for women in abusive relationships is most likely forced. In its extreme, forced sexual interaction in a marriage is marital rape.

Wives who are raped often suffer other forms of violence as well. Estimates of the proportions of battered wives who are also raped by their husbands range from 18 percent to 41 percent (Thorne-Finch, 1992). One study found that 59 percent of 91 wives having abusive husbands had been raped by them, and that all had experienced more extreme physical violence (Shields and Hanneke, 1983). Many violent men explain that after physically abusing their wives, they feel guilty and want to "make up" through the physical intimacy of sexual intercourse, which is often forced. The more credible explanation is that marital rape is simply another way that men assert control over women.

Effects of Abuse on Women

The effects of violence on abused women fit a pattern described by psychologists as the battered *woman syndrome*. Distinguishing characteristics of this pattern include anxiety, affective disorders, cognitive disorders, cognitive distortions including dissociation and memory loss, disruption of interpersonal relationships, and psycho-physiological disturbances (Walker, 1984). Approximately one-quarter of abused women turn to alcohol or drugs to cope with the situation (Barnett and Fagan, 1993; Rodgers, 1994). A very important component is "learned helplessness," a concept coined by experimental psychologists to describe how some animals, when traumatized, simply give up and do not try to do anything to improve their situations. Some abused wives of violent husbands do the same thing. Women, more than men, are predisposed to learned helplessness in our society because they are more often raised to be passive and dependent. Wives who escape from abusive relationships demonstrate fewer symptoms of learned helplessness than wives who remain in such relationships (Campbell, Miller, Cardwell and Belknap, 1994; Walker, 1988). Women who had removed themselves from the abusive situation demonstrated relatively healthy psychosocial function, and had discovered creative ways to cope with the abuse, to minimize the violent situations, and eventually, to leave the relationship (Campbell et al., 1994).

Some women learn helplessness in childhood, while others learn it in abusive adult relationships. *Childhood* learned helplessness has been more significant in explaining why women stay in abusive relationships. Factors associated with childhood learned helplessness include being battered in the home, being sexually molested or assaulted, having rigidly traditional parents, and having health problems. Factors associated with *adult relationship* learned helplessness include experiencing many violent incidents, pathological jealousy and possessiveness in the husband, experiencing sexual assault and "kinky" sex, murder threats by the husband, and "psychological torture" in the form of isolation, sleep or food deprivation, verbal humiliation, and murder threats (Johnson, 1995; Walker, 1988).

The majority of women in abusive relationships do, in fact, leave the abuser. Many leave and return an average of five times before they permanently terminate the relationship (Campbell et al., 1994; Rodgers, 1994; Ulrich, 1991). For those who do not leave, however, the most haunting question is this:

"Why do wives stay and take it—why don't they just leave their husbands?" There is no simple answer to this question; many factors are involved. Information regarding why they stay in the relationship is difficult to obtain, because few women in violent relationships participate in studies. Researchers have speculated that because there is more frequent abuse in families experiencing economic stress, wives are probably more fearful of leaving their husbands when they doubt they can support themselves. Johnson's (1995) explanation of patriarchal terrorism indicates that women in these types of relationships may be completely controlled—economically subordinate, dominated by threats of physical violence to themselves or their children, isolated from any external social supports, and so psychologically damaged they do not have the self-confidence to believe they could make it on their own. Another deterrent is the desire to avoid shaming their families, their husbands, and themselves by taking action that would bring their abusive families to public attention. Thus, some abused wives continue to suffer in silence.

Walker (1979) has proposed a *cycle theory of violence*—a derivation of psychological theory—which helps explain why battered wives do not leave. There are three distinct phases. In the first, *tension building*, there is increasing friction and hostility between the partners. During this period, the wife tries to placate her husband, but gradually increasing fearfulness makes her pull back from him. The eventual result, in phase two, is the husband's *uncontrollable discharge of aggression*, often physical, which may injure the wife but does drain off the built-up tension. This is followed by the third *loving contrition* phase, in which the husband feels remorse, shows kindness, gives his wife gifts, and promises "never again"—after which the cycle begins again. The second, violent phase thus leads to the husband's being contrite, kind, and generous, and to the restoration of a "good" relationship between wife and husband, so that the violence phase is followed by one rewarding to the wife. Data provided by 435 battered wives in Denver strongly supported this cycle theory, with the additional finding, however, that as abusive relationships persisted over longer periods, the violent husbands were less and less loving and contrite after a violent incident (Walker, 1984).

Causes of Wife Abuse

The most consistent and general finding is that abusive people were raised in abusive homes (Thorne-Finch, 1992), but this fails to explain why men are more abusive than women. Feminist theory points to gender socialization and gender relationships, as noted earlier. Most boys are taught to be "tough" and sometimes to fight. Hitting is a sign of toughness, and swaggering, aggressive masculinity ("machismo") is valued in some European and Latin societies. The finding that assault rates are higher in the impoverished lower classes points to the role of deprivation. Violence against wives is often a reaction to the frustration and hardship these families experience. Figure 14.2 suggests an association with patriarchy, since there is a strong relationship between marital power and marital violence, with the rates of both husband- as well as wife-beating highest in husband-dominant families.

Kesner, Julian, and McKenry (1997) found that the greatest predictors of male violence to his female intimate partner include the following: 1) perceived deficiency in love and caring from their mother while growing up; 2) lower self-esteem; 3) perception of less relationship support; 4) perceptions of low relationship autonomy (issues surrounding freedom, personal choices and decision-making; 5) number of recent life stressors. From an *attachment theory perspective*, each of these are linked to the perpetrator's insecurity resulting from poor attachment to his mother during childhood. The most salient of these predictors—low perceived relationship support from his female partner—may be linked to his own insecurities and inability to form secure attachments in his adult life.

From an ecological perspective, violence is probably due to the interactions of multiple biological, psychological, familial, and social variables. Two studies assessed male violence from a combined perspective, and found the most salient predictors from each domain included the following:

■ family income and relationship quality on the social domain;

■ increased levels of testosterone and alcohol use on the biological domain;

■ increased levels of stress and depression and lowered self-esteem on the affective domain;

■ history of violence during childhood on the familial domain (Johnson, 1996; McKenry et al., 1995).

Stopping Wife Battering

The prevalence and the horror of wife assault raises the following question: Can society not find ways of stopping it? Society's attitude that family privacy should be respected has perhaps made it possible for the state to

Figure 14.2   The Relationship between Marital Violence and Marital Power

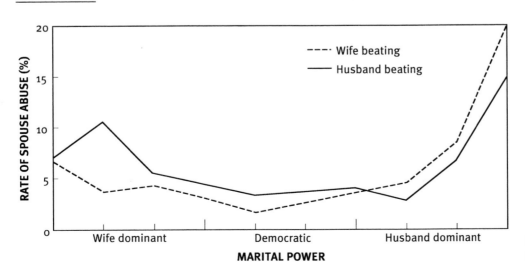

Source: Straus, Gelles, and Steinmetz, 1980:194.

be too casual in its attitude toward male violence. Moreover, the approaches of treatment therapists have been too limited and narrow—the majority of abusers have not undergone treatment (Thorne-Finch, 1992). Thorne-Finch argues, "What is really needed is substantially increasing treatment availability, utilizing the school system to improve communication and nonviolent conflict resolution skills, pressuring the private sector to end its abuse of women, and examining how best to end the creation of violent men" (1992:189).

Although the most effective means of deterring current offenders is criminal sanctions, Lackey and Williams (1995) suggest efforts need to be directed toward stopping the intergenerational cycle. From a *social bonding framework* (Hirschi, 1969), these authors tested the probability that men from abusive childhood histories who develop strong attachments to and receive negative sanctions from significant others (partner, friends, and relatives) are more likely to be nonviolent in their adult relationships. Their findings support this hypothesis. Other studies have demonstrated the importance of strong social support in helping abusive individuals to manage their abusive tendencies and form positive, healthy intimate relationships (Dutton, Webb and Ryan, 1993; Jack, Dutton, Webb and Ryan, 1995; Runtz and Schallow, 1997). The research suggests intergenerational patterns can be broken, and that efforts to provide social support to assist individuals from abusive family histories to develop strong adult attachments may help to stop recurring family violence.

The Role of Alcohol

The relationship between alcohol use and violent behaviour is well-established in the literature (Julian and McKenry, 1993). Past studies indicate that alcohol consumption has been reported in 6 to 85 percent of domestic violence cases (Kantor and Straus, 1987). Although the role of alcohol in violent behaviour is not clearly understood, alcohol use is thought to combine with psychological and biochemical factors to produce violence (Johnson, 1996). It is believed that increased alcohol use, or chronic use of alcohol, may cause acute pharmacological effects that lead to organic brain damage or illness associated with violent behaviour.

In a study of maritally violent versus nonviolent men, significantly more of the batterers drank more often and in greater amounts than their nonviolent counterparts. The results of the study provided support for many assumptions regarding substance abuse and violent behaviour (Barnett and Fagan, 1993). As distress and depression increase, so does alcohol consumption. The alcohol, for whatever reason, acts as a "disinhibitor." Thus, where an individual may otherwise be able to control and mediate his anxiety and hostility when sober, alcohol removes these natural inhibitors, and the anger and hostility are acted out upon another, resulting in violence (Barnett and Fagan, 1993). Most batterers assaulted their partners while they were drunk, and heavy drinkers (five or more drinks at a time) were six times more likely to abuse than were those who never drank (Gorney, 1989; Barnett and Fagan, 1993).

Although many women who are abused consume alcohol, most do so following the incident. The alcohol consumption for these women is believed to be a coping mechanism used in the aftermath of abuse, rather than a contributor to the beating (Barnett and Fagan, 1993). Thus, alcohol not only increases the incidence of abuse, but is also used as a coping mechanism in dealing with abuse. In both cases, the alcohol tended to serve as an excuse, a target to attribute blame, and a reason for not seeking other support and developing alternative, more positive and useful coping strategies.

Husband Abuse

Inevitably, when family violence is so common, some husbands will be victims of abuse. In some marriages, the wife is stronger, more dominant or aggressive, more frustrated, or under greater stress than is her husband. In fact, wife-to-husband assault is more prevalent than husband-to-wife, but because injurious wife assault is more frequent than injurious husband abuse, it is less often discussed (Grandin and Lupri, 1997). A Canadian study indicated the rates of minor violence were 18.3 percent for husband-to-wife violence, and 25.3 percent for wife-to-husband. Severe violence rates were 9.9 percent for husband-to-wife compared to 15.5 percent for wife-to-husband (Grandin, Lupri, and Brinkerhoff, 1997). In a smaller Calgary study conducted in 1997, similar

On March 9, 1977, in Danville, Michigan, Francine Hughes, aged 30, poured gasoline around the bed in which her husband slept and set it on fire. Then she went to the office of the County Sheriff with her three children and turned herself in. She was charged with first-degree murder. But during the trial the jury heard about her 12 years of brutalization by her husband. On the day when she finally killed him, he had repeatedly beaten Francine, terrorized the children, forced her to clean up food and garbage he deliberately dumped out, smeared food on her face and hair, torn up her college course books, threatened to wreck her car to stop her attending classes, and finally raped her before falling asleep, half drunk.

The jury heard of her repeated, unsuccessful attempts to get help from welfare agencies and the police—and decided that she was not guilty.

Source: Adapted from Conway, 1990:149.

results were found. In this study, 13.2 percent of the females inflicted physical violence against their spouse, compared to a husband-to-wife rate of 10.3 percent. Although this study did not separate minor and severe abuse, the results indicate that the incidence of wife-to-husband violence is greater (Grandin and Lupri, 1997).

Wife-to-husband psychological abuse is also more prevalent. Women are almost twice as likely as men to abuse verbally and psychologically (23.5 percent versus 13.2 percent). The long-term ramifications of psychological abuse can be equally devastating and cannot be ignored (Grandin and Lupri, 1997).

What is perplexing is why the incidence of husband abuse is greater. It has been speculated that wives may fight back against their husbands and defend themselves. They may also hit first in an attempt to regain a sense of power or to try to alter the family pattern and stop the violence. Women in distressed or dysfunctional family patterns may be more distressed than their husbands, and lash out either physically or verbally (Ben-David, 1993). Whatever the reason, the seriousness of wife-to-husband abuse can no longer be ignored.

In any case, many men feel that when their wives hit them they are justified in hitting back. Some do so, often much harder. Wives usually suffer more in the ensuing fight. The evidence leaves no doubt that women are more often injured by men than men are by women, because men are typically bigger, stronger, and more aggressive (Rodgers, 1994).

Spousal Murder The most extreme form of domestic violence is murder. In fact, spousal murder is the most common type of murder in Canada. In an analysis of the 10 756 murders committed in Canada between 1961 and 1990 where the suspect was known (but not necessarily convicted), Silverman and Kennedy (1993) found that 2911 (27 percent of the total) were spousal murders. Wife murder is the most prevalent—in almost three-fourths of the spousal homicides (73 percent), the husband killed the wife. Of all murdered women, husbands killed almost half (49 percent). Intimate partners kill approximately 70 Canadian men each year (Duhaime, 1996). Several recent cases have shown that persistent, violent abuse was the motive for these women to kill their husbands (see Box 14.1). Only 10 percent of murdered men were killed by their wives. More than twice as many men (12 percent) as women (5 percent) kill their spouses after separation or divorce.

Domestic Violence among Gays and Lesbians

Until recently, domestic violence in the gay and lesbian community had not been addressed in research or social policy. It had been believed that gays and lesbians were less violent than their heterosexual counterparts. This myth is now being dispelled—domestic violence in same-sex couples occurs at approximately the same rate as violence in opposite-sex couples.

The incidence of physical violence in same-sex relationships is estimated at between 22 and 46 percent. Incorporating verbal and psychological abuse, the incidence is estimated at 73 to 76 percent (Elliot, 1996;

Lei et al., 1991). Reasons for the abusive behaviour are similar to those identified in heterosexual partners, with particular emphasis on the need for one partner to control the other (Elliot, 1996). Farley (1996) reported that predictors of violence by the perpetrator include past history of child abuse, secondary (self-) abusive behaviours, including alcohol or multiple substance abuse, and mental health diagnoses.

Interestingly, individuals in same-sex violent relationships tend to stay in the relationship for similar reasons to those attributed to battered women. However, for individuals in this population, an additional factor makes it difficult for the victim to break away. That factor has been identified as "blackmail," in which the perpetrator threatens to "come out" regarding their relationship, making it public knowledge. For some, this may have devastating ramifications for their employment and family lives. In addition, social support for gay and lesbian couples in abusive situations is limited. Gay and lesbian domestic violence has not yet been recognized by public policy as a societal issue requiring attention and funding (Elliot, 1996).

Child Neglect and Abuse

Children are the potential victims most at risk in families because they are most vulnerable, and in abusive families the strongest members victimize the weakest (Finkelhor, 1983). Small children, usually under six years of age, suffer the most injurious and even deadly forms of abuse (Propper, 1990). Children are vulnerable to neglect, to incestuous sexual abuse, and to sexual abuse by non-family members. Children also suffer from witnessing violence between their parents (Markward, 1997). The incidence of these events, and the characteristics of neglectful and abusive parents and of neglected and abused children, are discussed in this section.

Child Neglect

Definitions of **child neglect** vary, but they involve a broad range of parental behaviours, including inadequate supervision leading to accidental harm to the child, and failure to care for a child by providing adequate food, clothing, shelter, or personal cleanliness. Equally damaging is *emotional* neglect, which involves decreased parent–child interactions, leaving children alone too much, and providing too little caring and love. When interaction occurs, it is generally withdrawn, sullen, and unpredictable. While parents are generally unresponsive, episodes of violence or rage may be used to control the children's behaviour. Parents in these families leave their children to fend for themselves and demonstrate little interest in their child's life (Gaudin, Polansky, Kilpatrick and Shelton, 1996).

Families who demonstrate neglect are likely to be extremely poor, predominantly single-parent families, and have a larger number of children that typically may be sired by more than one father (Gaudin et al., 1996). A study of those treated in the Toronto Hospital for Sick Children found neglected children more often came from impoverished families, multi-problem families, and those having very young parents, many of them single mothers. Children of mothers who were themselves children (aged 13 to 16) were particularly at risk of neglect. Functioning within the family tends to be conflictual, with decreased positive communication, problem-solving, and conflict resolution skills, decreased affection for each other, and decreased verbal and nonverbal expression of feelings. Much neglect, however, and particularly those forms not likely to come to official attention, is the result of parents having too little concern, interest, time, or energy for their children (Watters et al., 1986).

As with the other forms of child maltreatment and family violence, alcohol again plays a role. In alcoholic families, less attention and support is available for the children. These families tend to be disorganized and to be focused on the alcoholic parent demonstrating a general breakdown of parental protectiveness (Miller, Downs, and Testa, 1993). Children in these families are often unattended when their parents are unavailable due to drunkenness, and left to fend for themselves.

Whatever the reason for the neglect, children suffer greatly psychologically, socially, and emotionally from a lack of care and love. Efforts need to be taken by communities and societies to better identify the problem and to find ways of dealing with the neglect to allow all children access to the attention and care they deserve.

The most thorough investigation of both child abuse and maltreatment in Canada is the Canadian Incidence Study of Reported Child Abuse and Neglect.

The researchers were especially careful to substantiate reported cases, making this one of the most accurate assessments to date. In 1998, there were 12.5 investigated cases of child abuse or maltreatment for every 1000 Canadian children. Thirty-three percent of these cases were found to be unsubstantiated and 22 percent were suspicious but unconfirmed. Forty percent of these cases involved neglect (Figure 14.3 show the major forms of neglect). Clearly lack of parental supervision is the major form of neglect. Almost a third of these cases were physical abuse; Figure 14.4 shows that the vast majority of these substantiated cases involved inappropriate use of physical punishment.

Verbal and Physical Abuse of Children

Physical child abuse and child neglect are the most frequent forms of mistreatment that children experience. Abusive treatment may include both physical and verbal abuse. Verbal abuse is an extremely serious form of mistreatment because words define a child and shape the child's self-concept. Harmful words can psychologically destroy a child. However, because there are no procedures for estimating the incidence of emotional or verbal abuse of children, we note only that it must be much more common than physical assault. Only the rare parent has never thoughtlessly or unjustifiably yelled at his or her child, making the child feel stupid

Figure 14.3   Forms of Substantiated Neglect

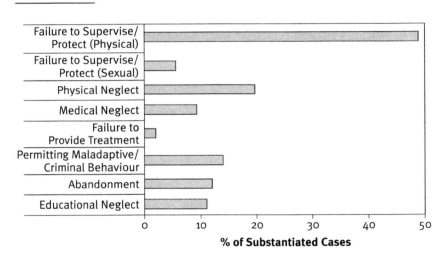

Source: *Canadian Incidence of Reported Child Abuse and Neglect: Final Report,* and *Child Maltreatment in Canada: Selected Results from the Canadian Incidence Study of Reported Child Abuse and Neglect,* Child Maltreatment Division, Health Canada, 2001.

Figure 14.4   Forms of Substantiated Physical Abuse

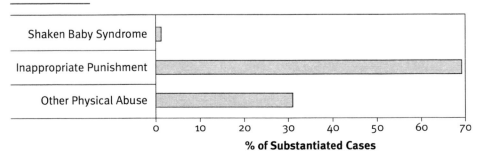

Source: *Canadian Incidence of Reported Child Abuse and Neglect: Final Report,* and *Child Maltreatment in Canada: Selected Results from the Canadian Incidence Study of Reported Child Abuse and Neglect,* Child Maltreatment Division, Health Canada, 2001.

or clumsy. While the occasional verbal lashing may not cause permanent damage, repeated, unjustified verbal abuse may leave a child scarred for life.

Nonverbal mistreatment of a child includes both physical and sexual abuse. **Physical abuse** is defined as any non-accidental physical injury sustained by a child, resulting from acts of commission or omission by a parent, guardian, or other adult in the parental role. In addition to physical injury, however, such abuse may damage the child's self-feelings, because the action says more loudly than words, "You are so bad that you deserve this treatment." Severe physical assault may cause lasting trauma, increased aggressiveness, inability to express emotions, nightmares, or lifelong recurrent depression and neuroses. Those who have not themselves been abused but have witnessed abuse tend to be more aggressive, have difficulties in school, withdraw from social situations, oppose parental authority, and have difficulties sleeping (Markward, 1997). Tragically, child abuse perpetuates the cycle of violence, as the assaulted child often becomes an abusing parent (Merrill, Herzig and Milner, 1996).

Incidence of Violent Abuse There is no clear evidence as to whether physical child abuse is increasing. One indication of increase is a 1982 Canadian Gallup poll finding that only 11 percent of respondents admitted to personal awareness of a serious case of child abuse; by 1988 this figure was 14 percent. Most published discussions dismiss this apparent increase, arguing that it is the *awareness* of child abuse that has increased. Conway (1990) believes this may not be true, since despite almost universal condemnation, systematic detection programs, and legal sanctions, reports of abuse continue to increase. He also suggests that *family stressors* causing parents to abuse children may be more characteristic of some new family forms. Certainly raising children is more difficult in families having only one parent, or families in which both parents have full-time employment, than in families with a traditional stay-at-home mother and working father. In the U.S., an increase from 2.5 million abused or neglected children in 1990 to 2.7 million in 1991 was explained in terms of the prolonged recession. In fact, the American Child Abuse Prevention Centre reported that three or four children die each day, most of them under one year of age, half due to neglect and the

remainder to abuse (*Edmonton Journal*, 1992c). In Canada, abuse is often linked to family and spousal violence. Figure 14.5 demonstrates that almost 60 percent of substantiated cases of child maltreatment are due to exposure to spousal and family violence.

Causes of Violence against Children What do we know about the causes of violence against children? Research evidence suggests there are three categories of causes: societal sources, family structures, and personality characteristics. Societal sources include prevalent economic conditions and the available social "safety net" provisions, which jointly affect the levels of stress that families experience. Research findings show child assault rates are elevated in poor and large families (Conway, 1990; Finkelhor et al., 1996; Sigler, 1989; Burgess and Youngblade, 1988), but not because poor parents are violence-prone. As noted earlier, poor families are more abusive because they lack the resources for coping with problems that would be less devastating if money were less tight, or if societal support programs were available before stress reached dangerous levels. With the increase in poverty, unemployment, and financial insecurity during the late 1980s and early 1990s, children likely suffered more than in previous decades. This suffering may affect their behaviour as parents.

Figure 14.5   Abuse Linked to Family and Spousal Violence

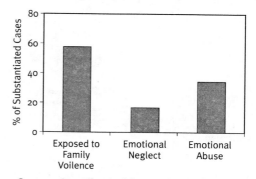

Source: *Canadian Incidence of Reported Child Abuse and Neglect: Final Report*, and *Child Maltreatment in Canada: Selected Results from the Canadian Incidence Study of Reported Child Abuse and Neglect*, Child Maltreatment Division, Health Canada, 2001.

There is more child abuse in stepfamilies and lone-parent families than in once-married, two-parent families (Burgess and Garbarino, 1983; Finkelhor et al., 1996). Stepchildren are particularly at risk, because the affection that two natural parents feel for their often-frustrating children is lacking.

Abusive parents are often reported to have experienced abuse as children, which gave them the coping strategies and the parenting behaviours seen in their own abusive behaviour (Sigler, 1989; Burgess and Youngblade, 1988; Burgess and Garbarino, 1983). While abusing parents are not psychotic, they show high rates of psychiatric and neurotic problems, and of behavioural and social deviance. Many studies have found these parents to be narcissistic, immature, rigid, compulsive, anxious, lacking in empathy and hostile, with low self-esteem and poor control of their impulses (Berger, 1980a).

Abuse of alcohol or other substances was found to be a significant predictor of child abuse. Second only to a history of abuse in childhood, the use of alcohol is related to general family dysfunction, and consequent abuse or neglect of the children (McGaha and Leoni, 1995; Merrill et al., 1996).

Gelles has tried to illustrate the interrelationships of psychological and social influences on child abuse in the diagram seen in Figure 14.6. The diagram indicates that the child's characteristics have some influence on the likelihood of abuse: parents are more prone to abuse particular kinds of children. Unwanted children are

Figure 14.6   A Social Psychological Model of Child Abuse

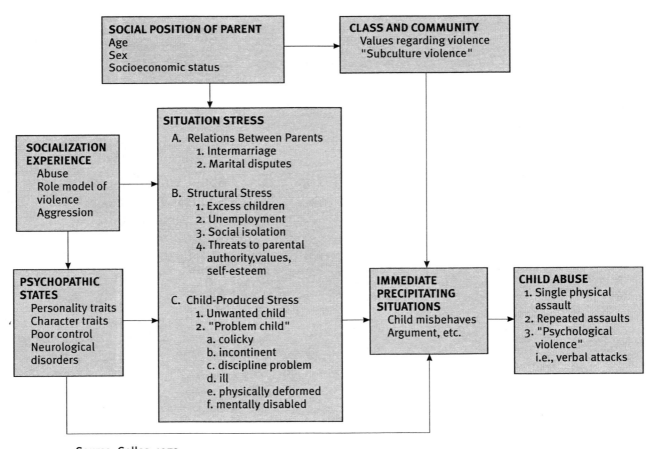

Source: Gelles, 1973.

automatically more vulnerable, irrespective of any other characteristics. Others are stigmatized from birth, crushing the expectations of hopeful parents—those who are physically deformed, mentally disabled, with physical problems, sick, colicky, incontinent. Some are "problem children"—rebellious, dishonest, sneaky—who often become that way because of harsh parental treatment, only to suffer abuse thereafter because their parents don't like them.

A hopeful note comes from Herrenkohl et al. (1983), who show that experiencing such treatment as a child does not inevitably lead to abusive parenting. They describe the case of a woman who was emotionally abused and abandoned by her mother and raped by her stepfather. She was able to become a good mother through the support of a very loving husband, and membership in a supportive religious group. Social support, finding a loving and successful intimate relationship, and learning positive coping strategies have been noted as a means of breaking the abusive cycle (Feinauer, Callahan and Hilton, 1996; Runtz and Schallow, 1997).

Sexual Abuse of Children

There are different forms of child sexual abuse, all of them damaging to the child and capable of causing a family crisis when the abuse becomes known. **Incest** refers to sexual intercourse between family members who are closely related. **Rape** in the family/child context refers to sexual intercourse forced on a child by a stepparent, stepsibling, other non-blood relative, or common-law (cohabiting) member of the family. **Abusive sexual touching** may involve the abuser touching the child or forcing the child to touch him or her. **Sexual exposure** includes both forced exposure of the child to the abuser (and others) and exposure of the abuser to the child. A convenient distinction can be made between *contact* and *noncontact* forms of child sexual abuse.

Researchers generally agree on the following: 1) the incidence of sexual abuse of children in families is higher than was once generally believed; 2) girls are more often victimized than boys, because the abusers are more often heterosexual men, and perhaps because girls tend to be more passive; and 3) fathers, stepfathers, and male cohabitors are the most frequent abusers (Levesque, 1994; Tierney and Corwin, 1983; Thomilison et al., 1991; Wellman, 1993), with 30 percent of the reports of incest involving assaults on girls by their brothers (Ennew, 1986). Figure 14.7 show the forms of sexual abuse for substantiated cases investigated in 1998.

Influences on Sexual Abuse of Children There are many reasons for the high rates of child sexual abuse; the defenselessness of children, and particularly of girls, and the presence of a stepfather or male cohabitor in the home are the most important. Children of unwed or working mothers are at increased risk from cohabitors and family members (Finkelhor and Baron, 1986; Rosenzweig, 1985). Children and adolescents with histories of

Figure 14.7 Forms of Substantiated Sexual Abuse

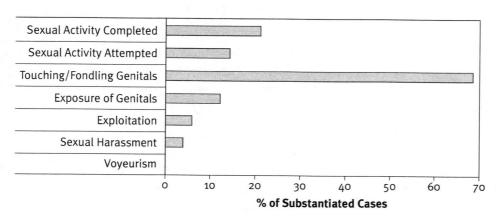

Source: *Canadian Incidence of Reported Child Abuse and Neglect: Final Report,* and *Child Maltreatment in Canada: Selected Results from the Canadian Incidence Study of Reported Child Abuse and Neglect,* Child Maltreatment Division, Health Canada, 2001.

prior victimization are also at increased risk for subsequent abuse (Boney-McCoy and Finkelhor, 1995). Public attitudes are also involved. For example, only 16 percent of respondents in a U.S. survey said that seduction of a 14-year-old girl by a 14-year-old boy was child sexual abuse, and only 34 percent said that seduction of a 14-year-old girl by a 24-year-old man was child sexual abuse (Best, 1990). Some sexually abusing fathers claim they believe that parental rights over children include sexual access to the child's body, and that parents are particularly sensitive teachers of sexual activity (Ennew, 1986).

Research literature shows that child molesters often have a number of common characteristics, including arrested development, immaturity, hormonal abnormalities, heightened sexual arousal to children, relevant early childhood conditioning, difficulty relating to adult women, inadequate social skills, and sexual anxiety (Araji and Finkelhor, 1986). Briggs and Hawkins (1996) found that 93 percent of the child molesters in their sample had been sexually abused in childhood.

Contrary to past beliefs, abuse by a female perpetrator is not less severe, but equal to that inflicted by a male. Females tend to be caretakers more often, and abuse children who are an average of 3.3 years younger than themselves. For children who believe that their caretaker is someone they can trust and who should provide warmth and security, this violation of trust leads to significant negative psychosocial adjustment in both childhood and adulthood (Rudin, Zalewski, and Bodmer-Turner, 1995).

Children at the highest risk of sexual abuse are daughters of actively dating single mothers who bring their male friends home. The most important predictor of childhood sexual abuse, Finkelhor (1984) found, was the presence of a stepfather; this more than doubled the probability that a girl would be abused, even in middle-class homes. The chances a girl would be sexually abused by her stepfather were one out of six, over six times the probability of abuse by her biological father (one out of 40). Other predictors of abuse risk were having a mother who was hostile to questions or behaviour relating to sex, and who was a high-school dropout. Children who had a poor relationship with their mothers, who had never lived apart from their mothers, received no physical affection from their fathers, had few close friends during childhood, and came from poor homes were also at elevated risk. Finkelhor reports that for children in his study who experienced none of these risk factors, there were no reports of sexual abuse. Among children with five or more of these risk factors, 66 percent had been sexually abused (1984).

The relationship among family functioning, the incidence of child sexual abuse, and adjustment has received considerable attention in the literature. Families in which sexual abuse is evident tend to demonstrate poor family functioning. Long and Jackson (1994) found disorganized patterns of functioning to be overrepresented in these families. Disorganized families are characterized by decreased levels of stability, order, and belongingness, and tend to display poor interpersonal relationship and personal growth dimensions. Partners in these families tend to be younger, less educated, and to have more children living at home; husbands and wives report few friends and confidants, low levels of social interaction, and above-average levels of depression. A high prevalence of marital breakdown and psychopathology among parents of victimized children has been noted (Beitchman et al., 1991). Interestingly, regardless of the relationship of the perpetrator to the victim, families demonstrating stronger patterns of family functioning provided greater social support for the victim, contributing to decreased maladjustment and psychopathy (Ray and Jackson, 1997).

Fleming, Mullen, and Bammer (1997) indicate the following to be the four most significant factors predicting child sexual abuse: 1) physical abuse in the family; 2) having a mentally ill or deceased mother; 3) not having someone to confide in; and 4) being socially isolated, usually due to the poor economic status of the family. Where the perpetrator of the child sexual abuse was a family member, having an alcoholic father was added to this list (Fleming et al., 1997). Poor family functioning and less stable family structure have been noted as predictors of both the incidence of child sexual abuse and consequent maladjustment of the victim (Beitchman et al., 1991; Jackson and Long, 1994; Ray and Jackson, 1997).

Short-Term Effects of Abuse on Children

Physical, psychological, and sexual abuse of children often has devastating effects on victims' psychosocial functioning and development in both the short and long term. Short-term effects, occurring within two years of the abuse, have been summarized by Downs (1993) to include fear, anger and hostility, guilt and shame, depression, low self-esteem and poor self-image, physical and somatic complaints, sexual behaviour disturbances, and poor social functioning. Among adolescents, commonly reported sequelae include sexual dissatisfaction, promiscuity, homosexuality, and increased risk for revictimization (Beitchman et al., 1991; Beitchman et al., 1992; Boney-McCoy and Finkelhor, 1995; Mennen and Meadow, 1994).

Sexual abuse may have varying effects on its victims. In attempts to find a means of coping with the abuse, children often develop destructive adjustments and coping mechanisms. Finkelhor and Browne (1988) identified four of these:

1. Traumatic sexualization This occurs when a child's sexual feelings and attitudes are distorted, and can happen 1) when the children are rewarded with affection, privileges, gifts, and so on, for sexual behaviour that is inappropriate to their level of development; 2) when parts of a child's anatomy are given distorted importance and meaning during sexual abuse experiences; and 3) when affectionate and sexual activity becomes associated with fearful events. **Traumatic sexualization** can lead children to acquire inappropriate repertoires of sexual behaviour, distorted sexual self-concepts, and bizarre emotional meanings for sexual activities.

2. Betrayal These feelings result from experiences when a parent or other person on whom a child is vitally dependent has manipulated or caused the child harm. A child may experience betrayal not only by the abuser, but also by parents who are unable or unwilling to protect or to believe the child.

3. Powerlessness Also known as *disempowerment*, this refers to the process by which the child's will, wishes, and feelings of capability are negated, as when children are repeatedly handled sexually against their will. The experience of powerlessness is reinforced when children find attempts to halt the abuse are useless, when they are unable to make adults understand or believe what is happening. This is exacerbated when children

realize their weakness and dependency means they are trapped and cannot escape the continuing abuse.

4. Stigmatization This includes all the negative feelings—being bad, feeling shame or guilt—that are communicated to the child about the sexual abuse experience, and which then may become incorporated into the child's self-concept. These feelings may be communicated by the abuser's words, or by the abuser's furtiveness and insistence on secrecy. They may also be reinforced by attitudes expressed in the family or community that the abusive activity is deviant, wrong, or sinful (Finkelhor and Browne, 1986).

A review of 45 studies by Kendall-Tackett and colleagues (1993) that compared sexually abused and non-abused children found that abused children consistently had more symptoms of distorted development, such as sexualized behaviour, particularly promiscuity, general behaviour problems, poor self-esteem, acute fears, and neurotic symptoms. A recent Canadian study found similar symptoms displayed by their sample as well as significant levels of self-blame and externalizing behaviours (Ligezinska et al., 1996). To this list of symptoms, Friedrich, Jaworski, Huxsahl, and Bengtson (1997) added an increased display of dissociative disorders, including forgetfulness, shifts in attention, variable sense of identity, daydreaming, amnesiac periods (trance-like states) and marked changes in behaviours and functioning, impulsivity, lying, and age-inappropriate sexuality. Females, more than males, tend to show greater levels of difficulties, specifically increased degrees of depression and anxiety and decreased self-esteem (Mennen and Meadow, 1994).

Increased numbers of symptoms were associated with abuse by a relative, frequent and long duration of the victimization, forceful sexual abuse, and sexual penetration (Beitchman et al., 1991). Increased symptoms were also associated with lack of maternal support at the time of disclosure and "a victim's negative outlook or coping style" (Kendall-Tackett et al., 1993:171). No clear effects of the age at which a child experienced abuse were apparent. A study of 156 abused children found that two-thirds had been coerced through threats or violence, often by family abusers. The level of the violence determined the child's level of distress more often than did the type of sex experienced or the duration of the abuse (Gomes-Schwartz et al., 1990). Higher levels of distress seemed to be associated with penetration, forceful non-father assault, (Mennen and Meadow, 1995), and prior history of physical or sexual victimization (Boney-McCoy and Finkelhor, 1995).

Dealing with child sexual abuse poses a number of dilemmas. Where the abuser is the father, other family members often become angry at the victim for disclosing the abuse, and the victim often feels guilt, and regrets disclosing. Fear of retaliation, of disrupting the family, or of losing economic support or a home may also hinder disclosure (Lamb and Edgar-Smith, 1994). The process of investigation is often upsetting, particularly to young children, and often there is debate over whether removal of the child from its family may actually do the child more harm than good. The impossibility of confidently distinguishing between the effects on the child of the abuse experience, and the effects of investigation and treatment, complicates these decisions (Gomes-Schwartz, 1990). Some of the issues relating to investigation and persecution are discussed in Knudsen and Miller (1991).

Long-Term Effects: Adult Survivors of Child Abuse

Studies have identified numerous problems with the psychosocial adjustment of individuals who have suffered from childhood physical, psychological, or sexual abuse. Many of these symptoms overlap; others are specific to the type of abuse experienced. Silverman, Reinherz, and Giaconia (1996) reported that 80 percent of their sample of young adults who had experienced childhood physical or sexual abuse demonstrated significant impairment in functioning, including depressive symptomology, anxiety, psychiatric disorders, post-traumatic stress symptomology, emotional-behavioural problems, suicidal ideation, and suicide attempts. Adults who grew up experiencing physical abuse tend to demonstrate lower levels of tolerance, resulting in distrusting, suspicious, fault-finding, resentful, and prejudiced attitudes. These individuals often have difficulties forming interpersonal relationships with others, tend to be less sociable or more withdrawn, and demonstrate lower levels of self-esteem. In forming adult relationships, abused individuals often

misinterpret the dynamics of the relationship, and more often experience higher rates of conflict and aggression, and report less support from their intimate partners. Survivors of childhood abuse tend to internalize problems or blame them on outside factors or their spouse (Varia, Abian, and Dass, 1996).

Because sexual abuse often goes hand in hand with physical abuse, victims of child physical abuse experience many of the same difficulties as do victims of child sexual abuse (Rodriguez, Ryan, Van de Kemp, and Fay, 1997). However, survivors of child sexual abuse also show some specific psychological and emotional maladaptations in adult life. These adults have demonstrated higher levels of addiction, neuroticism, and lower levels of socialization (Peters, Maltzman, and Villone, 1994). An increased risk for drug abuse and consequent contraction of AIDS from contaminated needles has also been noted (*The Health Quarterly*, 1993). For a woman, the degree of maladaptation is heightened when her childhood involved both child sexual abuse and alcoholism within the family (Yama, Fogas, Teegarden, and Hastings, 1993). Sexual dysfunction, including gender identity fragility, homophobia, sexual desire disorder, and sexual addiction, is prevalent in both male and female survivors of child sexual abuse (Meyers, 1989; Schwartz, 1994). In female survivors, the degree of sexual dysfunction is related to the duration of the abuse and the degree to which family dysfunction was present. Sexual dysfunction in males tends to be associated more with adverse family relationships and insecure attachment than with the sexual victimization (Kinzl, Traweger, and Biebl, 1995).

For adult survivors of child sexual abuse, powerlessness and stigmatization translate into the development of psychopathologies, including guilt, social isolation, and feelings of inability to control one's life (Draucker, 1995). Stigmatization in victims of sexual abuse has been identified as being associated with maladjustment and psychopathy due to the shame and attribution of blame upon themselves (Feiring, Taska, and Lewis, 1996). For victims who minimize the childhood experience and avoid confronting the memories, poor psychosocial adjustment in adult life has been noted. These individuals tend to be more withdrawn, blame themselves for adult relational problems, demonstrate lower levels of self-control and tolerance, and have the most difficulty forming adult relationships and managing the relationships they do form (Feinhauer, Callahan, and Hilton, 1996; Varia, Abian, and Dass, 1996).

It has been suggested that individuals who experience maltreatment as children are at higher risk of becoming abusive or neglectful parents (Merrill, Hervig, and Milner, 1996; Faller, 1989). Survivors of abuse tend to demonstrate increased degrees of anger, hostility, and aggressiveness to conflictual situations, decreased support in the spousal relationship, less confidence and consistency in behaviours, and consequent lower levels of parenting skills (Cole, Power and Smith, 1992; Dutton et al., 1993; Jack et al., 1995; Peters, Maltzman, and Mallone, 1994). However, studies assessing the degree of intergenerational transmission of abuse are equivocal, with percentages ranging from 18 to 70 percent. It seems that a history of child abuse, combined with low income, low education, and the lack of a support network, may be the greatest predictor for intergenerational transmission of abuse (Gelles and Conte, 1990).

The development of eating disorders and alcoholism has been identified as a possible outcome for those with histories of child sexual abuse. Recent literature in the eating disorder field suggests that the association may be indirect rather than direct. Child sexual abuse and child physical abuse may lead to traumatic symptomology, and the eating disorder response may be a function of the traumatic distress rather than a direct symptom of the abuse (Bryam, Wagner, and Waller, 1995; Schaaf and McCanne, 1994; Waller, 1994). It has also been suggested that an abusive family environment may lead to the development of borderline personality disorder, of which bulimia is often a symptom (Byram et al., 1995; Kern and Hastings 1995; Wonderlich, Wilsnack, Wilsnack, and Harris, 1996). A strong relationship between the development of alcoholism, particularly for women, and a history of abuse has been noted (Miller, Downs, and Testa, 1993).

How adults survive their childhood abuse is dependent on the development of coping strategies, the degree of social support available to them, and family functioning. Resiliency has been demonstrated to be associated with blame—those who blame the perpetrator display the lowest levels of symptomology; those who blame themselves or fate display higher levels of traumatic symptoms and maladjustment (Feinhauer and Stuart, 1996). Victims experiencing high levels of guilt and shame exhibit poorer social adjustment than individuals who recall the abuse with anger or disgust (Long and Jackson, 1993). Survivors who avoid confronting the memories tend to be more withdrawn, blame themselves for adult relational problems, have lower levels of tolerance and self-control, and have difficulties forming adult relationships (Varia et al., 1996). Victims who focus on the past, de-emphasize the central role of self, and place greater emphasis on others tend to experience greater maladjustment as adults (Klein and Janoff-Bulman, 1996). Social support, particularly from a non-abusive parent and support-oriented family environment, may allow the abused individuals to form positive coping strategies (Ray and Jackson, 1997; Runtz and Schallow, 1997). Four predictors of adult adjustment have been identified, including 1) disclosing and discussing the child sexual abuse, 2) positive reframing of the experience, 3) refusing to dwell on the experience, and 4) access to strong social support from family or an intimate partner (Himelein and McElrath, 1996; Feinauer et al., 1996).

Child-Killing

The ultimate form of parental abuse of a child is to kill the child. A total of 620 children were killed by their parents in Canada between 1961 and 1990, 6 percent of all the murders compiled during this period. They fell into two classes: infanticide and child murder.

Infanticide is the killing of a baby under one year of age. These cases most often involve an immature, unwed teenage mother who is pregnant and does not want the baby. Often she hides her pregnancy and then kills the baby, not knowing what else to do. One study showed these women often felt no remorse because they were just disposing of a "problem." Their most frequent occupation was given as "student" (Silverman and Kennedy, 1993).

Immature, incompetent parents, overwhelmed by frustration with their children or other life stressors, may kill children past infancy. Unable to find other sources of stress relief, these parents may have "taken it out" on their children, accidentally killing them. Children were killed more often by their fathers (52 percent) than by their mothers (48 percent). Younger children were more at risk; 84 percent of the victims were pre-teens. For younger children, however, mothers were more often the killer; of the victims under two years of age, 12 percent were killed by fathers and 43 percent by mothers. It has been suggested that children die at the hands of their parents because they are *substitute* targets for their parents' aggression (Silverman and Kennedy, 1993).

Abuse and Neglect of the Elderly

Mistreatment of the elderly is broadly similar to mistreatment of children, since in both cases the victims are typically vulnerable, and are often both dependent on, and sources of frustration to, their abusers. Like children, the elderly are vulnerable to neglect, physical abuse, psychological abuse, and financial exploitation.

Neglect includes both active and passive refusal of service. The first involves refusing to satisfy caretaking obligations, including providing food and health-related services, as well as abandonment. Passive refusal involves failure to fulfill caretaking obligations because of inadequate knowledge, laziness, or infirmity. In the following discussion, the term *mistreatment* will be used to refer to both abuse and neglect.

Inevitably, elder mistreatment is covert. It seldom takes place in public, and probably only the most severe cases ever come to public attention. Accordingly, there are no grounds for making authoritative, empirically based estimates of the frequency of elder abuse. The *World at Six* CBC newscast reported "100 000 elderly Canadians are regularly abused, many in their own homes" (February 7, 1993), but neither the basis nor the source of this estimate were given. The actual frequency is probably high.

Those elderly people who are most often abused have a predictable pattern of characteristics. Victims are often very old. Female victims outnumber male victims two to one, partly because of their longevity, but also because women are seen as more vulnerable. Having physical or mental disabilities, which increase victims' dependence on their caregivers, is also associated with abuse, partly because such conditions increase the work and the frustration of caregivers (Podnieks et al.,

1989). Old people can be very demanding, abusive, uncooperative, and unreasonable. The frustration of people caring for them month after month, and perhaps year after year, without relief is understandable, though this does not justify abuse.

The characteristics of people who abuse the elderly also fit a pattern. Many studies have found that more than 80 percent of the abusers are related to the victim (McDonald et al., 1991). Most often the abusers are spouses, daughters, or daughters-in-law (Philips, 1986; Bristowe and Collins, 1989). The first abuse episode may be triggered by a crisis, and the resulting guilt simply increases the stress level of the caretaker and the likelihood of further abuse (Vadasz, 1988). A cross-Canada study found the abuser's relationship to the victim was associated with the type of abuse. Material abusers were more often distant relatives not providing care, while those chronically, verbally, and physically abusive were more often spouses (Podnieks et al., 1989).

Alcohol consumption is also implicated in abuse of the elderly. A British Columbia study found that 88 percent of the abusive caregivers use alcohol, as compared with only 30 percent of those not abusive. Moreover, frequent alcohol use was associated with more frequent and more severe verbal and physical abuse (Bristowe and Collins, 1989). Abusive caretakers were also often reported to have more psychological or emotional problems (79 percent) than were non-abusive caretakers (29 percent) (Pillemer, 1986).

SUMMARY

- Families respond differently to internal and external stressors. Strong families cope effectively with crises, while weak families are prone to ascribing blame.

- Theorists point out that domestic violence is a complex phenomenon arising from the interaction of multiple variables.

- The incidence of wife abuse is very high, and includes wife murder, which is the most frequent form of homicide. Wives often stay with their abusing husbands partly due to "learned helplessness," which causes them to give up trying to improve their situations, and partly because they get caught up in a cycle of violence that rewards the acceptance of abuse with contrition.

- Incidence figures for wife-to-husband violence are higher than those for husband-to-wife violence, probably reflecting the frustrations of disempowered wives. Husbands may see their wives' violence as justifying their own violent responses.

- The most damaging form of family violence is child abuse, because of its lifelong consequences. Child abuse is most prevalent in families in which parents were themselves abused, are impoverished, or lack adequate social support.

- Girls are the most frequent victims of sexual abuse in families, particularly by male cohabitors and stepfathers. Such abused children may experience traumatic sexualization, feelings of betrayal by parents, disempowerment, and stigmatization.

- The incidence of child neglect, including both physical and emotional neglect, may be as high as incidence of child abuse. Like child abuse, child neglect in the family is hidden from public view. Physical neglect is more characteristic of poor families, but emotional neglect is more widely encountered.

- Victims of elder abuse are most often women and the very old, who may experience physical, emotional, or material abuse. Relatives who are caring for the elderly, particularly daughters and spouses, inflict abuse most often. Elder abuse also takes place in nursing homes, commonly in the form of overrestraint and verbal abuse.

- There are reasons for believing that family abuse may soon begin to decline, with the increase in influences favouring normative husband–wife egalitarianism.

KEY TERMS

Abusive family system (329)

Abusive sexual touching (339)

Child neglect (335)

Double ABCX crisis model (326)

Family stress (325)

Incest (339)

Patriarchy (328)

Physical abuse (337)

Rape (339)

Sexual exposure (339)

Traumatic sexualization (341)

QUESTIONS FOR REVIEW

1. What are the components of Hill's family crisis model?

2. What kinds of family problems are not covered by Hill's model?

3. What are some of the differences between families that tend to have the most problems, and those that have the fewest problems?

4. When is child murder by parents just an extension of parental abuse of children, and when is this not the case?

5. What is meant by "learned helplessness," and how is this concept relevant to understanding violence in families?

6. What is meant by the "cycle of violence," and what does this concept help us to understand?

7. What kinds of family violence are better understood in terms of "perpetuation of violence," and what kinds are not?

8. Who most often abuses elders, and what forms does this abuse take?

QUESTIONS FOR DISCUSSION

1. Discuss the significance of patriarchy in understanding the abuse of family members by one another.

2. In what ways are the abuse of wives, husbands, children, and elders similar, and in what ways are they different?

3. What would be the characteristics of a society that had minimal abuse of family members?

4. Which of the various influences identified in Gelles's diagram of the causes of family violence are probably the most significant?

5. Do you believe that relationships in families will get significantly better or significantly worse in your lifetime? Why?

6. How will changes now taking place in the roles of adult men and women probably affect the amount and kinds of mistreatment that people may experience at the hands of other family members?

SUGGESTED READINGS

McDonald, P. Lynn, Joseph P. Hornick, Gerald B. Robertson, and Jean E. Wallace. 1991.* *Elder Abuse and Neglect in Canada*. Toronto: Butterworths. The prevalence of elder abuse and neglect, characteristics of victims and abusers, and theories seeking to explain elder abuse are discussed in the first two chapters. The remaining chapters describe legal safeguards, special protection legislation, relevant programs and services for elders, together with an assessment of future prospects.

Thorne-Finch, Ron. 1992.* *Ending the Silence: The Origins and Treatment of Male Violence Against Women*. Toronto: University of Toronto Press. This Canadian work first examines the extent of male battering, emotional abuse, sexual harassment and assault, and femicide (woman killing), and then discusses the reasons for male violence, traditional and recent treatment programs, how men's responses tend to reinforce the status quo, and the prospects for change.

Trocme, N., B. MacLaurin, B. Fallon, J. Daciul, D. Billingsley, M. Tourigny, M. Mayer, J. Wright, K. Barter, G. Burford, J. Hornick, R. Sullivan, and B. McKenzie. 2001.* *Canadian Incidence Study of Reported Child Abuse and Neglect*: Final Report. Health Canada. This report provides some of the best information available on actual confirmed cases of child abuse and neglect. The report is currently available as a PDF file at http://www.hc-sc.gc.ca/pphb-dgspsp/publicat/cisfr-ecirf/.

CHAPTER 15

Family Trends and Family Policy in the 21st Century

After studying this chapter, you should be able to do the following: .

■ Distinguish between and explain the four ways that family scholars interpret the patterns and trends in families.
■ Define and explain the importance of family policy.
■ Define and explain the three types of preventive social services.
■ Review the variety of prevention-oriented actions to strengthen families that have been recommended by councils and professionals involved in family study, policy, or services.

Introduction

We have now traversed much of the knowledge and information available about Canadian marriages and families. In this last chapter it is important to regain a larger perspective on this material. The purpose of this chapter is twofold. First, we will present several differing scholarly interpretations of the trends in marriage and family life. Many descriptive phrases have been used in interpreting the evidence, such as pessimistic, optimistic, progressive, objective, traditional, liberal, radical, rethinking, ambivalent, concerned, and others. These perspectives lead us to form opinions as to what should be done to assist families and children. Thus, the second section examines family policy issues, the many actions that have been recommended to improve individual and family well-being, and the various ways in which governments, educational institutions, and private organizations are attempting to shape the future of families.

What the Patterns and Trends Mean

This section examines the variety of scholarly interpretations of what is now happening to marriage and family life. There are many organizations, lobbying groups, and concerned citizens actively involved in promoting or opposing programs, policies, and practices related to sexual, marital, and family life. Attitudes toward current trends and patterns include despair, pessimism, neutrality, optimism, and outspoken advocacy for radical new ideas. Scholars likewise reflect some degree of either pessimism or uncertainty. Four different, if not competing, scholarly views are briefly described below. Each perspective is presented as fairly as possible without detailed critique.

The "Demise of the Family" Perspective

There are many negative phrases used to describe the condition of the contemporary family, including decay and disintegration, or more modest phrases such as decline or disturbing the (family) nest. With the beginning of the 20th century, a number of prominent sociologists, as well as family scholars, predicted the disintegration of the family. Pitirim Sorokin, the founder of the first sociology department at Harvard University in 1930, believed that a strong and healthy family was the core of a strong society. Sorokin predicted the future of family life long before the evidence was available: "[T]he family as a sacred union of husband and wife, of parents and children, will continue to disintegrate. Divorces and separations will increase until any profound difference between socially sanctioned marriage and illicit sex-relationship disappears . . . ever increasing divorce, licentiousness, sexual anarchy, promiscuity, sexual perversions, and illicit sex adventures outside of marriage." (Sorokin, 1957 [reprinted, 1985:700]). He argued that "*homo sapiens* is replaced by *homo sexualis* packed with genital, anal, oral, and cutaneous libidos" (Sorokin, 1956:9, 13, 17, 88). Sexual licence, he argued, leads to demoralization—venereal disease, neuroses and psychoses, and urban centres that are jungles of crime and promiscuity. Pleasure replaces responsibility as children are neglected, their care turned over to the state.

Zimmerman (1947), as reported in Chapter 4, likewise identifies the family in contemporary North American society as an *atomistic family* characterized by rampant individualism—a family system that cannot rear children capable of maintaining an orderly society. High rates of divorce, drug abuse, crime, child neglect and abuse, and delinquent problems among children and youth have systematically destroyed societies in the past and they are doing so again. The destructive significance of individualism in family decay is also emphasized in the work of historian Christopher Lasch (1977, 1978).

Several distinguished scholars of the nineties, with less colourful rhetoric, are now emphasizing concerns about family well-being based on empirical evidence. David Popenoe, a sociologist at Rutgers University, simply argues that the term "family decline" is the "best fit" for the many changes that have taken place in family life (1990). In his earlier book (1988), Popenoe assesses the Swedish welfare state, considered by many to be a model society, and concludes that the concept of "familism" has little relevance to everyday life there. Sweden has the lowest marital rates, highest rates of cohabitation, highest divorce rates, and the largest proportion of single-person households of any industrialized society. The family in Sweden, according to Popenoe, exists only as a practical arrangement for meeting selected social needs. Popenoe argues that these patterns are applicable to all advanced societies as individual rights increasingly replace the principle of familism.

In a more recent paper, Popenoe summarizes the empirical evidence over the past 30 years and concludes that the family in the U.S. is also in unambiguous decline (Popenoe, 1993a). Given the scope of Popenoe's thesis, the paper's editor requested a response from several scholars. A demographer agreed with the thesis and issued a plea for greater attention to the empirical evidence (Glenn, 1993). However, Stacey, a feminist, argued that the family idealized by Popenoe is no longer needed or desirable (Stacey, 1993).

The authors of four recent books ably defend the "demise of the family" thesis (Biller, 1993; Blankenhorn, 1995; Popenoe, Elshtain, and Blankenhorn, 1996; Popenoe, 1996; Whitehead, 1997). The details in each of these works, as well as in many chapters in books and articles in refereed journals, cannot be casually ignored. Glenn (1996), a demographer in the family field, has been tracking changes since the early 1970s. In his view, the "weakening of the ideal of marital permanence" is the crucial reason for the decline in marital success, accompanied by a decline of a sense of duty, the feeling that an individual can, and deserves to, "have it all." Marriage is no longer a social institution with rights and duties—it is a personal relationship. Gallagher believes that the U.S. has been "systematically privatizing the responsibilities of marriages . . . while . . . extending the rights of marriage to the unmarried . . . and transferring the costs of nonmarriage to the general public (1996:239). She also contends that "no-fault divorce" is really *unilateral divorce* "because it only takes one person to divorce, at any time and for any reason." All of these eminent, not to mention controversial, scholars have much of importance to say. The thesis advocated in their many works is articulate, based on reasoned empirical evidence, and important. Even so, a significant minority of scholars hold the family-decline school of thought.

The Adjustment Perspective

The adjustment school of thought is represented by scholars ranging from those who see contemporary family patterns as contextual and faddish to those who view various family changes as permanent alterations. Scholars in the first category believe that social institutions such as the family change very slowly, and that much of the "seeming change" is most accurately classified as "social process." Larson (1970), for example, analyzed the booming communal movement in the sixties and concluded that group marriage and communes would become a significant alternative lifestyle in North America. Within a few years, however, more than 90 percent of those who entered communes had left and re-entered mainstream social life with only modest shifts in values. Such evidence encourages more intensive scrutiny in making projections. The adjustment-oriented perspective accepts the significance of the dilemmas and crises now associated with various changes in family life. However, these scholars expect change to slow and modify sufficiently for people to re-establish who they are, and to find order and meaning within the new forms and functions of families. This optimistic perspective is represented in several important works (Bane, 1976; Schroeder, 1989; Blankenhorn et al., 1991; Coontz, 1992). Most people marry. The majority stay married. Most people still desire children and care for them with concern and affection. Those who leave marriage want to remarry and the majority do, typically within five years. When divorce ends a marriage, most people experience grief and distress. Few people divorce twice. Bumpass (1990: 491) illustrates the adjustment perspective well:

> In the midst of all this disruption and changing role behaviour, why hasn't the family disappeared? Why does anyone bother to form families with children? . . . The answer seems obvious . . . . Intimacy with a partner in the context of commitment provides unique aspects of meaning and social support[;] . . . the majority of us continue to find family roles intrinsically and uniquely rewarding.

Three highly visible and significant new family forms emerged in the 1970s: single-parent families, dual-work and dual-career families, and remarried families. The traditional single-breadwinner, two-parent, two or more children, never-divorced family is now a minority family form (Eichler, 1988). The adjustment school of thought assumes that these new family forms will, with time, increasingly work more effectively than they seem to be working now. A recent critique of the Popenoe thesis concerning the decline of the institution of the family in both Sweden and the U.S. (Houseknecht and Sastry, 1966) concluded that the hypothesis was overextended. The evidence seems, in their view, to more accurately reflect processes of adjustment than processes of demise.

The Rethinking Perspective

The rethinking school of thought includes scholars who emphasize the salience and necessity of family changes. The troublesome aspects of family change are acknowledged, but priority is assigned to the long-term virtues of reformulated family lifestyles and the construction of new meanings in intimacy. It is argued that current changes in the family, while temporarily problematic, will in the longer term result in a more equitable and healthy family system. Two basic types of emphasis are reflected among those who hold a rethinking view.

The moderate feminist orientation challenges traditional interpretations of family patterns and changes, and strongly supports continuing and necessary changes in family attitudes and behaviours (Eichler, 1988; McDaniel, 1989b; McDaniel, 1993a). This view emphasizes the role of patriarchal family models in enabling and perpetuating the following:

1. domestic and societal inequities in male and female roles;
2. the idealization of antiquated models of the family and the rejection of a diversity of families;
3. domestic violence;
4. the blaming of women for rape;
5. opposition to non-parental child care;
6. opposition to divorce;
7. opposition to sexual behaviour outside marriage;
8. opposition to abortion;
9. the maintenance of a heterosexist bias;
10. opposition to sex education without more instruction;
11. and the rejection of the rights of gay men and lesbian women to establish marriages and form families.

The feminist movement is also openly committed to influencing how students evaluate and interpret what is happening to families. From the feminist perspective, teaching is a political activity, including topics, methods, emphases, and guest speakers (Allen and Baber, 1992).

A second type of rethinking, much more radical in tone and substance, emphasizes the significance of the current evidence for new ways of theorizing about families. Scanzoni et al. (1989) believe the evidence on family patterns and trends reflects pervasive changes in the nature and meaning of relationships. While the everyday person still uses terms such as *marriage, family, single-parent families, remarried families*, and so on, Scanzoni et al. suggest that it is time for academics to use different language. The concept of "the family as a social institution" is discarded in the interest of a new concept—*sexually based primary relationships*, or SBPRs. The nuclear family and the married couple are redefined as two minor examples of many types of sexually based relationships. It is argued that the family is, or eventually will be, simply an alternative form of *close relationship* that includes sexual activity. The theoretical model developed in this work examined the commonalities and differences in the conditions of entry, exit, re-entry, transitions, and the evolution of new structures of intimacy.

In reacting to these ideas, Goltz and Larson (1991) argued that this model was uniquely speculative because much of the empirical research to date must be radically reinterpreted. Mental, emotional, and behavioural outcomes in children and adults as a result of relationship trauma (such as depression, aggression, regression, loneliness, separation, divorce, suicide, death, and adultery) have long been defined as problematic. But Scanzoni et al. (1989) define these patterns as progressive, an assumption that most scholars would consider absurd. Goltz and Larson also pointed out that this model ignores a basic fact—most individuals *continue* to seek enduring and fulfilling intimacy within the social institutions of marriage and family relationships. As documented in earlier chapters, however, the ways in which people enter these institutions is changing.

In a more recent article, Scanzoni and Marsiglio (1993) emphasize that "the family," as widely defined in structural-functionalist theoretical models, is one of many alternative lifestyles. It is now argued, based on the outline of a *new action theory*, that individuals of the 1990s are "struggling to make the conditions of their lives better through creating fresh arrangements" (p.108). Erotic friends, whether straight or gay, seek the same rights as married couples and their children. These authors further argue that public policies must acknowledge "the dynamic aspects of persons' struggles to find meaning in, and promote their well-being through, the primary group activities that they perceive as being family" (Scanzoni and Marsiglio, 1993:128).

A Canadian sociologist, in rethinking why scholars seem to cling to traditional views of the Standard North American Family (SNAF), argues that our family models are so deeply ingrained that we are insensitive to new ways of thinking (Smith, 1993). Smith argues that the SNAF is an *ideological code*, not unlike a genetic code. This means that people and scholars who think about families regularly use the SNAF code as a lens through which everything is viewed. Smith says, "[The standard North American family ideological code] is a constant generator of procedures for selecting syntax, categories and vocabulary in the writing of texts and the production of talk and for interpreting sentences, written or spoken, ordered by it. An ideological code can generate the same order in widely different settings of talk or writing—legislative, social scientific, popular writing, administrative, television advertising, and whatever" (Smith, 1993:52). For Smith, the SNAF code for family is "mother." She further argues that "SNAF-infected" thinking influences data collection in the Census, the presentation of data, and almost all scholarly research on sexuality, marriage, and family life in Canadian society.

Conservative or traditional perspectives of family life are defined, by most rethinking interpreters of family change, as obstructing the need to redraw the configurations of social groups that will facilitate new forms of self-fulfillment and companionship. Aspects of the rethinking view of the family, particularly the work of Scanzoni et al. (1989), are considered too extreme, and are rejected by most family scholars.

The "Don't Know" Perspective

The "don't know" perspective may be considered the safest perspective for a scholar, because predictions are often wrong. This school of thought tends to reflect significant uncertainty about the *implications* of what is now happening to marriages and families. One recent study, for example, documented that prolonged exposure to pornography significantly lowered the valuation of marriage, reduced the desire to have children, and promoted the acceptance of male dominance and female servitude (Zillman and Bryant, 1988). The prolonged consumption of pornography also facilitated greater approval of premarital sex, marital infidelity, promiscuity, and the attitude that sexual repression posed a health risk to society. Even so, these authors refused to *directly* comment on the findings. The majority of scholars in this school of thought, however, openly reflect on their concerns about what the data seems to mean for individual and family well-being. Even so, there is disagreement on which family changes are problematic and which promote family health. A brief summary follows of selected issues that we are classifying as "don't know" interpretations.

Escalating Individualism Coontz (1992:3) reports a study of morality in the U.S. in which it was found that 25 percent of the respondents admitted that they would abandon their entire family if they were to win $10 million. Coontz says that "a large number of people are evidently willing to do the same thing for free, judging from the astonishing statistics on how few non-custodial fathers spend time with their children after divorce." This theme is consistent with the widely held view that the individual has become more salient in daily life than the family unit. In a special issue of the *Journal of Family Issues* (Glenn, 1987), several well-known scholars were invited to submit their opinions on the "state of the family." Most argued that the welfare of marriage, and of children in particular, is being undermined by individualistic attitudes and behaviours.

Priority of Individual Rights As documented in Chapter 8, individual rights have largely replaced the concept of family law in Canada. A female adolescent is free to obtain an abortion without consulting with or obtaining the approval of her parents. Likewise, an adult woman may obtain an abortion without consulting or obtaining the approval of her spouse or partner. Yankelovich (1981) has been doing national

studies of attitudes and behaviours in the United States for several decades. His 1981 book summarizes many of his findings in detail, and he concludes that 80 percent of the public are what he calls "changers," or weak-to-strong "formers." The characteristics of these respondents reflect a strong need for self-fulfillment and personal discovery. These needs outweigh concerns about significant others, such as spouses or children. Self-fulfillment means having everything, or the "*big ands*": a career *and* marriage *and* children *and* sexual freedom *and* autonomy *and* being liberal *and* having money *and* choosing nonconformity *and* insisting on social justice *and* enjoying city life *and* enjoying country living *and* simplicity *and* graciousness *and* reading *and* good friends . . . *and* . . . *and* . . . Yankelovich hopes that people will eventually adopt an ethic of commitment—working hard at building stronger relationships. This may be an overly optimistic conclusion, because it seems as though the needs of spouses and children have become far less important than the needs and rights of the individual.

Increasing Complexities of Family A third theme in changing family values is the increased complexity of family life. Bumpass (1990) argues that the interests of parents and children in the preservation of marriage often differ. Children are virtually powerless, as parents act in their own self-interest. A recent book by Furstenberg and Cherlin (1991), called *Divided Families*, emphasizes that family life has simply become more variable and less predictable for children. In the authors' view, it is clear that children are expected to cope with family flux, many ambiguous relationships (particularly in the context of divorce and remarriage), and a "thinner form of kinship." Due to ongoing changes in family structure, it is argued, both children and adults are related to more and more people, to each of whom they owe less and less. Fine (1992) also affirms this view of contemporary family life. He documents that mothers and fathers are increasingly unsure of what it means to be mothers and fathers. These concerns are accelerated in stepfamilies and single-parent families. Multiple roles provide conflicting and confusing messages to children. Fine also believes that parents have significantly less influence as socialization agents in the lives of their children. He argues that parents simply do not spend enough time with their children to have a marked influence on their values. Fine believes that schools and culture, as represented in television and other media, are more powerful influences in human development than are parents.

Coupled with the changing role of parents is the ever-increasing impact of technology on the family. White (2003) identifies five major areas of impact for computer technology on the family. These areas of impact are education, communication, home management, recreation, and home offices. Certainly the impact of Internet resources for education and information about home management and health is obvious. It is much less obvious how the Internet serves to enhance communications between family members and even foment dating relationships. Although we have all seen the impact of computer games as a source of recreation, the computer also provides solitary games and interaction with unseen others. The advent of the home office makes possible parental supervision of children along with work tasks. In addition, the Internet provides children with uncensored access to materials and information forbidden to previous generations; parents now face new challenges for monitoring their children's access to this material. All of these changes provide challenges for families that were previously unanticipated.

Disconnection between Childbearing and Marriage There is a fourth theme in the "don't know" school of thought. There seems to be a plausible connection between a) delayed marriage, cohabitation, and relatively uninhibited sexual experience, and b) changing family values. As McDaniel (1989a) aptly points out, there is no longer a clear connection between childbearing and marriage. Giving birth to a child, McDaniel argues, is no longer a significant route to marriage; at least it is not as salient as it once was. Furthermore, conception is no longer an automatic route to childbearing. Abortion has become the post-conception contraceptive. Whatever one's perspective on the morality of abortion, reproductive choice is a clear example of self-interest, as opposed to the interest of others. Furthermore, sexual behaviour itself is no longer exclusively a function of marriage. Sexual activity is increasingly a matter of self-gratification and short-term affection, quite independent of commitment. The traditional objections to living together

without the permission or approval of the church or government are a natural outcome of uninhibited premarital sexual activity. Further, as Bumpass (1990) has emphasized, cohabitation is conceptualized as an important way to "try out marriage" before marrying. Although the virtues of a trial marriage are widely held, the scholarly evidence continues to question these supposed benefits. Divorce rates are half again as high among those who cohabited before marriage as among those who did not cohabit (for example, Booth and Johnson, 1988). Traditional family values have long been synonymous with commitment, fidelity, and permanence. These values are still idealized by most who eventually marry. In contrast, sexual behaviour without commitment, affection without commitment, childbearing without commitment, and living together without commitment seem to undermine the family values that many still idealize. In addition, self-interest now precludes the voluntary pledge to stay together for the sake of children. The mechanisms by which many couples enter marriage seem to have changed rather markedly. Even so, the value of eventually marrying and becoming a family is still widely professed.

Each of these *competing* views, despite their glaring differences in interpreting the evidence, has merit in helping us understand the implications of family change. Although each perspective has differing implications for family policy, it seems clear that unambiguous policies need to be established in the long-term interest of individual and family well-being. Certain elements of all these interpretations of the "state of family" imply important policy initiatives that most family scholars can support. The next section focuses on family policy issues and various alternative actions recommended by family scholars.

Family Policy Issues
The Nature and Importance of Family Policy

In 1987, Moen and Schorr argued that government interest and concern about families was largely rhetorical. They reported that government publications and policy initiatives used catchy phrases such as "preserving," "rehabilitating," "reuniting," and "strengthening" families, when the focus was really on individuals.

Moen and Schorr further argued that family concerns were really afterthoughts in government enactments. Social insurance, for example, was designed for the individual. Its goals were to provide economic security and to encourage retirement. As it turned out, social insurance also helped families. In general, government programs for dependent spouses, mothers, and children were secondary concerns. It was also argued that families occasionally get help because their needs coincide with other national interests. Housing programs, for example, are designed as economy boosters. A fringe benefit is that families who need affordable housing may get it. Almost all programs are corrective in thrust, rather than preventive, and often occur so late that little substantive help results.

Establishing a policy or policies for families, however, is not a simple matter. Garbarino (1985) raises several key questions that policy makers should consider:

- Where shall we set the minimum standard of care for children?

- Will we allow poverty to determine basic life prospects for our children?

- Are we willing to compromise family privacy to prevent child mortality, morbidity (illness), and pathology?

- Do we have the will to implement preventive family support systems?

- Do we have the fiscal capacity and moral commitment for a comprehensive preventive program for children?

In elaborating the complexities and implications of each policy question, he argues that both families and the community should have "joint custody" of children; or, put another way, the family should have custody and the community should have visiting rights (a basic right to know what is going on with its children). While the need for policy action is evident, these questions demand careful attention. Doyle (1983) suggests that governments have an aversion to comprehensive approaches and are reticent about explicitly stating policy goals and objectives about families.

Even so, policy is the cornerstone of every goal-oriented organization. Policy reflects the basic guidelines for action and non-action. It defines the basic rules in the formulation of specific programs, and sets the parameters for the evaluation of all proposals. Without a set of general policy objectives—regardless of the level of government (federal, provincial or local)—programs, legislation, and services will be without direction. According to Zimmerman (1988), family policy is different from social policy in that it focuses on families instead of individuals. The following definition of **family policy** is partly based on the thoughts of Moen and Schorr (1987) and Zimmerman (1988):

> A policy for families is a widely agreed-on set of objectives for the well-being of children and families, the establishment of which shall guide and rationalize programs, services, and all derivative policies.

There are four reasons why Canada is still without a national family policy (Lero and Kyle, 1991):

1. Canada is a country of diverse values. Attempts to achieve a national policy are based on the premise that there are shared goals.

2. The historical division between federal and provincial jurisdiction undermines the achievement of a federal policy.

3. Canadians largely consider family life to be a private matter. Parents are to assume full responsibility for their children.

4. It is assumed that government should not get involved in family life unless serious problems are evident.

The continued absence of an effective federal family policy, of concrete family policies in every province, and of community-level family policies continues to reinforce a piecemeal set of ideas about ways of promoting family and child well-being. Furthermore, government programs have a marked influence on families, directly or indirectly, with or without family policies (Schottland, 1967; Chilman et al., 1988). The importance and strength of this impact in many domains and dimensions of family life, whether positive or negative, is apparent in several recent publications (Zimmerman, 1988—welfare, suicide, teen birthrates, mental disability, and the elderly disabled; Kahn and Kammerman, 1988—child support; Wilcox and Uyeda, 1988—mental health; Chilman, 1988—family finances; Nichols, 1988—family law).

Likewise, the programs and policies of employers have major consequences for families. Hiring and firing, promotions and transfers, training and retraining, benefits programs, retirement programs, commuter time, flex-time and job sharing, compressed work weeks, and related practices—all affect family life and well-being. The corporate enterprise must be subject to government legislation and regulation in the interest of family well-being. Indeed, the very absence of such programs, laws, practices or policies, by intention or default (the failure to act or to even consider whether action is important), *is action.*

Types of Preventive Services

A brief fictional story (see Box 15.1) illustrates the meaning of a preventive approach to social services. Until the mid-1980s, most services were almost exclusively remedial. Mace (1983) reported, for example, that nearly 96 percent of health-care costs were for diagnosis and treatment, and less than 4 percent were for prevention. Things have now changed. In the media, in pamphlets in doctors' offices, and in government-sponsored regulations, the focus in health care has shifted to the control of unhealthy behaviours and lifestyles (such as quitting smoking, encouraging healthy diets, and reducing stress). It is obvious that similar principles apply to societal conditions, family concerns, family pathologies, and dysfunctional family relationship traditions or patterns. We seem to wait until families are in serious trouble before intervening.

Three levels of prevention are typically defined (L'Abate, 1983). **Primary prevention** involves intervening "before it happens." Premarital and pre-parent preparation, marital and family enrichment, and child and parenting enrichment programs, as well as societal policies and legislation designed to either enhance the quality of life or reduce conditions that impugn or weaken family life, are all examples of primary prevention. **Secondary prevention** involves programs designed to intervene "before things get worse." Marriage and family counselling, divorce counselling, preparation for remarriage programs, and courses on coping skills and dealing with stress are examples of secondary prevention. Laws that resist quick and simple solutions to family problems while also providing effective and reasonable grounds for ending and exiting degrading or abusive relationships, are also examples. Programs designed to reduce problems at a secondary level often produce other problems. Attempting to reduce teen pregnancy by encouraging the use of contraceptives, for example, also seems to encourage casual sexuality.

The third type of prevention is called **tertiary prevention** ("before it is too late"). Programs that seek to prevent sexual abuse, where evidence of serious problems exists, are examples of tertiary prevention (Conte, 1988). Such programs include teaching young children what abuse is, and teaching assertive skills for escaping or resisting such abuse. Preventing child sexual abuse involves the deterrence and treatment of perpetrators, and the protection of victim groups. This is the most difficult type of prevention both because it

---

Box 15.1   **Current Insights: The Origins of Preventive Caregiving**

The breathtaking viewpoint high in the mountains attracted thousands of people annually. Tourists would often go to the very edge to gaze over the immense valley. Children, in particular, would often take risks at this special spot. Sometimes children would lose their footing and fall to the rocks several hundred feet below. Some were seriously injured; others were killed. With the passage of time, the community got together and spent a lot of money on ambulances. They put the ambulances at the bottom of the mountain so that when people fell, help would be readily available. The community and its ambulances cared for the injured and buried the dead. As a result of community initiatives, it was eventually decided to build a fence around the edge of the mountaintop to prevent people from falling off. In doing so, the casualties went down, and so did the expenses.

Source: Unknown.

is seldom possible to intervene in time, and because the technology of detection and control still remains ineffective. Based on current screening knowledge, intervention services would have to be provided to five or more families that didn't need the service for every one family that did (McMurtry, 1985).

Family Policies and Actions for the 21st Century

Unfortunately, despite frequent attempts by various levels of government to establish family-friendly policies, very little has been achieved. In addition, there continue to be significant disagreements and controversies about what programs and policies should be enacted (Baker, 1994; Pratt, 1995). Baker's outstanding cross-cultural review and analysis on family policies is a must-read. Much can be learned from other countries. Professional organizations in Canada—namely the Vanier Institute of the Family, a national organization, and the B.C. Council for the Family, a provincial organization—have a long-standing commitment to meet the needs of families. Research is funded, projects to assist families are established, and multiple publications provide frequent information to professionals involved in family study and services. Professional organizations in the U.S. have also been active in searching for ways to strengthen families, including the National Council on Family Relations (NCFR), an international organization of family specialists. There are no federal family policies in Canada that *directly* relate to families. Quebec is the only province in which the government has established a set of coherent measures specifically to facilitate the well-being of families and, insofar as is possible, has implemented them, making necessary adjustments between 1987 and 1994 (Le Bourdais and Marcil-Gratton, 1994). Quebec programs are specifically intended to correct negative demographic trends in family matters, and to help Quebec families achieve social equity.

Bronfenbrenner (1990), a prominent child development and family scholar, has developed a "policy grid" in the interest of children. He identifies what we consider to be an important set of priorities for all children and families:

1. In order to develop, a child requires participation, on a regular basis over an extended period, with one or more persons with whom the child develops a strong mutual emotional attachment, and who is committed to the child's well-being and development for life. (*Authors' comment:* There is disagreement with the seeming "equivocation" in this first statement. Based on compelling evidence, the phrase "one or more persons" should be replaced by "a mother *and father*" . . . who "are" committed to the child's well-being and development for life (Popenoe, 1996; Blankenhorn, 1995). Bronfenbrenner is, of course, justified in asserting that a committed single parent *can* fulfill this high calling.)

2. The establishment of interaction conditions of strong mutual attachment enhances the young child's responsiveness to other features of the physical, social, and symbolic environment. These activities accelerate the child's psychological growth.

3. The establishment and maintenance of emotional attachment between caregiver and child depends on the involvement of another adult, a *third party* (such as a grandparent), who assists and expresses admiration and affection for the person caring for the child.

4. The effective functioning of child-rearing processes requires establishing patterns of exchange, communication, mutual accommodation, and mutual trust between the principal settings in which children and their parents live their lives. In our society, these settings are the home, child-care programs, the school, and the parents' places of work.

5. The effective functioning of child-rearing processes requires public policies and practices that support child-rearing activities, not only on the part of parents, caregivers, teachers, and other professional personnel, but also relatives, friends, co-workers, and communities, and the major economic, social, and political institutions of the entire society.

Bronfenbrenner believes the major criteria of any program established in the interest of families should be straightforward: Is the parent–child bond strengthened, and is the well-being of the child enhanced?

Family policy is now a major focus among scholars who study family relationships. As indicated above, there are a diversity of policy views not unlike the four perspectives identified earlier in this chapter. Priority actions often reflect ideological biases: humanistic, conservative, liberal, Marxist, feminist, and related perspectives. Our goal is to summarize what the literature has to say about policy initiatives in the interest of family well-being. Many of the proposals are either impossible to fund, or out of touch with values of the public. Obviously, whether left, right, or centrist, the proposals vary in both feasibility and acceptability.

Preparing for Marriage and Parenthood

Many clergy, although not all, are increasingly refusing to perform weddings unless the couple consents to several premarital counselling sessions or classes. Clergy are not alone. Tiesel and Olson (1992) advocate government-sponsored premarital and pre-parenting programs. Their proposals include the following:

1. All couples would be required to enroll in free premarital programs.
2. Funding for these programs would be derived from licence fees based on the income of the applicants.
3. Leaders of the programs would be certified family life educators.
4. Annual couple check-ups would be offered at approved centres or clinics.
5. At-risk couples would be referred to counselling services. Health insurance companies could insure the benefits of these programs; alternatively, the cost of such programs could be a deductible expense on income tax returns.

A premarital preparation program called Prepare, developed by Dr. David Olson, has been widely used throughout North America. Research has demonstrated its value in improving marriage and sharply reducing the possibility of divorce—nearly 90 percent of couples who enrol in Prepare and Enrich programs stay together. The British Columbia Council on the Family provides a booklet on marriage to every couple who obtains a marriage licence. Currently, pre-parenting programs are not as widely used, although the B.C. Council is one of the few in Canada that offer such programs. Their focus gives couples exactly what they need: an understanding of pregnancy realities, and the transitional issues to parenthood from a marital dyad to a family triad. These programs are deemed absolutely essential (Cowan and Cowan, 1995). Most parent-training programs occur after one or more children have "arrived" who have various developmental, learning, or behavioural problems (Thompson et al., 1993). The typical parent-training program tends to focus on *secondary prevention* with pregnant teenagers

and adolescent parents at risk. Cowan and Cowan (1995) clearly examine the similarities and differences of "typical" married couples and their transitions to parenthood, compared to high-risk couples dealing with trauma (e.g., the impoverished, adolescent mothers). There are many ideas to consider in developing a useful pre-parenting class.

Strengthening Marriages and Preventing Divorce

Numerous programs have been established to strengthen marriage, many of which are follow-up programs for couples who have been through premarital enrichment programs. Enrich is the companion program to Prepare, and is widely used. PREP (the Prevention and Relationship Enhancement Program) is designed to teach partner skills, rules for handling conflict, and promotion of intimacy (Stanley et al., 1995). There are many other nationally known marital enrichment programs, including Marriage Encounter, Retrouvaille, and ACME. These programs all provide an important service in our society, although they are less successful than the effort portends. Marital therapy and counselling are major industries, and will likely continue to be a major part of the "relationship landscape." As documented in the research by Gottman (1994), complaining and criticizing, contempt, defensiveness, and stonewalling are staples in marital conflict. As individuals get into marriage without the individual and relational skills, insights, or commitments to resolve salient differences, they will likely maintain the high divorce rates.

Popenoe, Elshtain, and Blankenhorn (1996: 308–314) believe that the real source of the problem is that the social institution of marriage has undergone a radical shift in values. Marriage has historically been "the seed-bed of civic virtue—for protecting child well-being, turning children into good citizens, and fostering good behaviour among adults." The solution, therefore, in their view, is to:

■ reclaim the ideals of marital permanence;

■ model excellence in marriage;

■ limit child-bearing to within the marital bond;

■ have a father and mother who stay together and whose relationship reflects mutual sharing and comfort to each other and for each of their children;

■ resolve that parents will increase the amount of time they spend raising their children.

Their specific goals are spelled out in detail for religious leaders, civic leaders, employers, human service professionals, counsellors and therapists, family law attorneys and judges, and any and every other source of influence on the nature and meaning of marriage. Obviously, this is quite a different vision from that held by those of the rethinking perspective, who advocate new relationship forms and resist irrelevant and out-of-date solutions.

Promoting Domestic Equality As reported in earlier chapters, fathers are significantly under-involved in domestic duties in dual-earner households. Both liberal and conservative scholars would probably agree that equality, justice, and mutual involvement in domestic responsibilities should be "natural" where both parents are engaged in paid employment. The essence of affection, caring, commitment, and bonding in marriage relationships requires everyday equity. Garbarino (1988) argues that the foundation of a caring society (and caring families) rests on whether men will adopt feminine ways of exercising power and service to others. Men, he says, must learn that active, caring involvement in the care of children is an investment that pays large dividends. As indicated above, educational institutions, the media, religious organizations, government, and related agencies of influence need to teach and reinforce caring involvement, equality, respect, and justice between dual-earner fathers and mothers (Popenoe, 1988; Lero and Kyle, 1991), as well as between working partners with spouses who are traditional homemakers without income, a pension, or recognition for unpaid domestic work (McDaniel, 1990b, 1992a).

Reducing Family Violence

Marital Violence Policy experts agree that spousal violence must be eradicated. Conway (1990) believes that charges should be automatically laid against husbands who batter their wives, independent of the wishes of the victim. Accused husbands should be arrested—under certain circumstances, held without bail—and on conviction sentenced to participate in treatment programs. In this way, wives and children would be able to remain in their homes in safety. It is argued that educational institutions, the media,

religious organizations, government, and related agencies of influence need to teach and reinforce equality, respect, and justice between men and women. However, as Scott (1988, as reported in Conway, 1990:155) has demonstrated, men who batter often struggle with "depression, alcohol dependency, loneliness, insecurity and paranoia." These characteristics are often related to having been reared in impoverished dysfunctional families. Policies that eradicate poverty and the conditions that foster dysfunctional child-rearing will go a long way toward reducing family violence. However, it must be emphasized that family violence occurs at all socioeconomic levels, regardless of education, occupation, or religious affiliation. Other actions often emphasized in policy research include the following:

- improving and expanding emergency shelters
- using the media to disseminate information about the rights of women and sources of help
- removing violence from media programming
- establishing violence crisis centres
- providing professional training for staff who work with victims of violence
- educating against violence in religious organizations and schools at all levels (Larson, 1980)

Child Protection The physical and sexual abuse of children cannot be tolerated. Intervention should be prompt and just (Barnhorst and Walter, 1991). Barnhorst and Walter emphasize, however, that many children in Canada are also at risk due to inadequate care and neglect. The definition of these terms, as they point out, is inadequate. Legislation in most of Canada places considerable discretion in the hands of social workers. Intervention, when it is essential, may occur far too quickly, too slowly, or not at all. Laws on child protection, it is argued (Barnhorst and Walter, 1991; Bala et al., 1991), should do three things: 1) if possible, keep children with their families; 2) if removal of children is necessary, maintain contact between the parent and child; and 3) if reunification of the parent and child is not possible, find a new *stable* and permanent foster family location for the child.

Such laws are now limited to the provinces of Alberta and Ontario (Barnhorst and Walter, 1991;

Bala et al., 1991). Policies often emphasize the improvement of assistance to families before child abuse or neglect occurs (such as emergency counselling and homemaker services, parent day-out programs, and crisis nursery centres), early detection, trauma teams at local hospitals, wider dissemination of information to the public, and professional training in detection in social work, counselling, and nursing (Larson, 1980).

Developing Family-Friendly Work Policies
These policies assist mothers and fathers, as single parents and as married partners, in caring more effectively for their children.

Parental Leave Both Canada and the U.S. lag behind many European countries in the provision of maternity leave programs. Sweden has the most progressive plan in the world: 12 months' parental leave at 90 percent of previous wage, as well as the rights to a reduced workday until a child reaches the age of eight (see also Baker, 1995;173–177). In sharp contrast, maternity benefits in the United States are limited to 12 weeks of *unpaid* leave from one's place of employment. In Canada, under provisions of the *Unemployment Insurance Act*, eligible workers may obtain regular unemployment, sickness, maternity, or parental benefits. Maternity benefits are paid for 15 weeks, plus 10 weeks of parental leave at 57-percent wage replacement; however, depending on the province, up to 18 weeks of unpaid maternity leave is also available (Baker, 1995:161–162,166–167). Adoptive parents are eligible as well. The legislation also requires that all pension, health, and disability benefits are continued during the leave, and also provides for reassignment to a different job if the working conditions are hazardous (Skrypnek and Fast, 1996:798).

Reduced Work Hours Parents need more time with their children. The importance of flexible work schedules is emphasized. These should be flexible enough for parents to begin work and finish work at different times, which would enable one parent to be with the children until they leave for school, while the other parent would be able to be home by the time they return from school. Other options include part-time employment, or sharing one full-time job

with another employee, *without the loss of job benefits or career advancement*. Part-time work is widely available today, but few employers provide any employee benefits for part-time workers. Such measures are not family-friendly (Lero and Kyle, 1991; Eichler, 1988; Bronfenbrenner, 1990; Fuchs, 1990; Mellman et al., 1990).

Day Care The need for high-quality day care for parents who are working, pursuing an education, or taking part in retraining programs is widely emphasized. High-quality day care typically means publicly funded and licensed according to rigid standards—professionally trained and well-paid staff, low staff–child ratios, excellent facilities, and parent involvement. The need for a comprehensive and fully funded national, universally accessible day-care policy is often emphasized. Most scholars are also concerned about the low salaries paid to day-care workers, which often mean high turnover rates and a lower level of professionalism. A variety of child-care programs is recommended, including licensed family-care homes, drop-in centres, and before- and after-school programs for the many children whose parents do not have flex-time employment. On-site day care is also urged, for mothers in particular, at their place of employment. There is some resistance to private day care due to the absence of adequate standards (Lero and Kyle, 1991; Eichler, 1988; Conway, 1990; McDaniel, 1990). We argued in Chapter 11 that high-quality, subsidized day care is essential for single parents (mothers in particular), families in poverty, and dysfunctional families. Universal day care may be unrealistic. Policy attention must be given to reduced work hours, attractive parental leave policies, and homemaker subsidies, to permit young parents to be with their newborn children for the first few years of their lives. See Baker (1995; Chapter 6) for an excellent review and analysis of child-care delivery.

Working from Home More and more Canadians are working from home due to technological advances such as personal computers, modems, and fax machines—a phenomenon referred to as telework (Nadwodny, 1996). According to the 1991 Census, 743 000 people worked at home in non-agricultural occupations, about half of whom were women. About one-third were self-employed, while the rest worked for employers off-site. Most of the women—40 percent—worked part time. Seventy percent had a regular daytime schedule; 20 percent had an irregular schedule. "At home" employees tend to have lower levels of education and to earn less than do on-site employees.

Benefit Innovations One new option for working mothers is on-site day care. This means that parents can take their babies to work with them and care for them, as needed, during the day. One recent study (Secret, Sprang, and Bradford, 1998), conducted at a university where day care is available on campus for university employees, found positive attitudes toward the staff, facilities, and the concept. There were no negative effects on employee performance on the job. This concept is not limited to universities. Case studies of various benefits programs provided by 11 Canadian corporations for parents with newborn children have been positively evaluated (Johnson, 1994). The employers supported the concept due to improvements in the following: recruitment, retention of employees, employee morale, reduced absenteeism, and increased productivity. Employees had more time for their children, flexibility in work interruptions, on-site child care, location of worksite within the residential community in which the parent(s) lived, as well as job sharing and part-time work options. Unions were also enthusiastic about members' job flexibility and job security, and the maintenance of benefits.

Other benefit innovations suggested by family scholars include "personal days" off for taking children to the dentist or doctor and related necessities, employer-funded homemaker services for children in need of special care, flexibility in choosing benefits (e.g., dental insurance versus life insurance), and complementary benefits for dual-work couples instead of overlapping benefit packages (Eichler, 1988; Lero and Kyle, 1991).

Economic Equality There are two major concerns that underlie this aspect of the public support of families: pay equity and affirmative action. Pay equity refers to equal pay for work of equal value. Men and women with the same education and training for a particular job should receive equal pay. Women often earn less; mothers, considerably less. The maternal burden would be lowered if mothers were to earn an equitable wage for the hours they work. Affirmative action proposals, in contrast, are designed to enable qualified women to obtain positions in traditional male occupations. The federal government passed an employment equity law in 1986 to be fully implemented within two years. The purpose of this legislation was to eliminate discriminatory employment barriers against women (as well as Native people, the disabled, and visible minorities). Companies doing business with the federal government are required to fulfill the terms of the law. Both McDaniel (1990) and Conway (1990) strongly support pay equity and affirmative action programs for women. It should be noted, however, that affirmative action is considered "reverse discrimination" by a substantial number of scholars and politicians.

Policies for Low-Income Families As has been emphasized in several chapters, poverty is a major source of child-rearing problems in families. This section focuses on policy-related actions to improve the financial condition of impoverished single-parent and two-parent families.

Financial Assistance The universal family allowance plan, long a staple in Canada, was eliminated in 1993 (Baker, 1995:73, 129–131). The government now only assists parents with dependent children whose net income is below $25 921. The solution, according to Fuchs (1991), is that the money should simply be transferred from high-income households to low-income households. This solution is widely advocated among Canadian economists, although with uncertainty and the belief that more research is essential. Another suggestion is that the federal government provide jobs to the unemployed. Public jobs programs provide income to needy families while completing various public works projects (Levitan et al., 1988). McDaniel (1992) points out that homemakers have no pensions (other than old age security), no severance pay upon job completion or loss (divorce or "retirement"), and little social recognition for their services. Women are also active caregivers for the elderly, without social or financial support (McDaniel, 1990). A 1980 review of action priorities in reducing poverty conducted by professionals working with the financially impoverished (Larson, 1980) led to several recommendations, including the following:

- equal pay for equal work
- subsidized child-care services
- financial incentives to work by enabling welfare recipients to retain a larger proportion of their earnings.

Guaranteed Annual Income The most dramatic and still widely debated policy is to ensure that all families have a minimum level of annual income, employment notwithstanding. Eichler (1988), for example, suggested that the program be set up for every *individual*. Those earning an income above this minimum guaranteed amount would be taxed at normal rates. This policy would eradicate poverty among individuals and families, child poverty, and the poverty of lone mothers following divorce. The elimination of poverty would in turn reduce family breakdown and the incidence of dysfunctional families (Eichler, 1988; Conway, 1990). Critics argue that such a program would further weaken the individual's desire to work, and increase the burden on taxpayers. Others question whether a policy directed toward individuals, as opposed to families, might not further weaken family ties.

Single Motherhood McDaniel (1993c) warns, in an era of debt reduction and balanced budgets, of policy apartheid against single mothers. Eichler (1993) argues for a model of social responsibility for non–co-resident fathers toward all of their children. Two principles are emphasized: 1) all fathers should be financially responsible for their children whether they live with them or not, regardless of any other living situation the father might be in, and 2) lone parents should automatically be paid a minimum amount of financial support from public funds and the balance from the nonresident fathers. Dooley (1995), an economist, argues that the best answer is to simply increase child-support payments from the non-custodial parent, given the obvious evidence that the non-custodial parent (almost always the father) earns significantly higher levels of income. Indeed, several economists did a lot of empirical digging for answers to the dilemma of poverty among lone-parent families. Phipps (1995) strongly recommended restoring the family allowance program to lone-parent families, but at a much higher level: $1000 to $1500 per child per year. Given the current situation, the smaller subsidy would cost a total of about $5 billion per year.

Five other economists also participated in this research assessment (Richards and Watson, 1995). Baker (1996), the author of the important book *Canadian Family Policies*, points out that "employability" is not the solution to the "single-parent family–poverty connection." The employability focus permits the government to do the following: ignore the absence of jobs that provide a living wage, ignore the need for improving income security, and deny that caring for one's children is real work. The search for answers continues. Dooley (1993), using Canadian income data for mothers working and mothers on welfare, has documented the fact that welfare benefits do not decrease lone-mother employment.

Well-Family Clinics Conway (1990) suggests that clinics be located in local schools to assist low-income families in several ways, such as providing breakfast and lunch programs, family-life education programs, sexual and birth control counselling, basic health care, and assistance to troubled families.

Policies for the Aging Policy priorities in the early 1980s emphasized the need for community housing for seniors, income subsidies, and support services to elders in their own homes, such as Meals on Wheels and household assistance (Larson, 1980). Reverse mortgages have been offered to older individuals as a way of helping them to receive a monthly income based on their home equity. The poverty rates among elderly women are double those of elderly men. The life-long dependence of women on men, often as homemakers, leaves many elderly women with only old age pension income. There are serious inequities that elderly women face after their spouses die. Most pension programs reduce the payment to the widow even though she will outlive her spouse by an average of a decade. Concerns over the Canada Pension Plan tend to focus on the demographic issues in funding, rather than on the inadequacy of the pension schemes or the increasing needs of the elderly for an adequate income throughout their lifetime (McDaniel, 1987, 1990; Gee and McDaniel, 1991). The need for caregiving for elders is increasing. Existing policies are contradictory or ambivalent, often based on principles several decades out of date. Current government policies are demanding more of adult children, primarily women, who increasingly have less time and energy to give. Many Canadian scholars continue to urge policy action (Gee and McDaniel, 1992; McDaniel, 1993b; McDaniel and Gee, 1993; McDaniel and McKinnon, 1993; Baker, 1995, 1996).

Policies: A Diversity of Issues and Views

A number of priority actions recommended by Canadian and U.S. scholars with an interest in family policy have been summarized. We have not highlighted policies about which there is often controversy. Feminist scholars, for example, strongly advocate a woman's right to obtain an abortion without regulation (often referred to as reproductive choice) and universal day care. Conservative scholars, in contrast, advocate programs such as abstinence education, adoption planning for women with an unwanted pregnancy, and economic subsidies for young mothers to stay at home with their children. Despite their diversity (liberal, conservative, controversial), the goal of these and related policies is to a) affirm the physical, emotional, and relational well-being of individuals, marriages, and families (two-parent, lone-parent, stepparent) throughout our society, and b) reduce, and hopefully eliminate, the unnecessary and unjustified trauma created by poverty, dysfunctionality, discrimination, and uncaring governments, organizations, and communities. The proposed policies and the methods to implement them, however, are often only reasonable suggestions that need careful evaluation. We believe that the policy grid recommended by Bronfenbrenner (1990) to the United Nations on behalf of children is important in evaluating proposed actions.

There are also other considerations that require careful review in a society such as ours. Many of the recommended actions, however important, involve moral and political sensitivities. Environment, trade, human rights, parent rights, child rights, and sexual rights have become battlegrounds in many societies. Well-schooled lobby groups compete *for* their own pet policies and programs, and *against* groups or policies

that may undermine their own particular goals. Further, some of the proposed actions themselves will involve significant financial expenditures at a time when the national debt is at unprecedented levels. Other proposals, in the view of some, will undermine freedom of speech. Even if the majority of people support such policies, others may define implementation of certain policies as censorship. These are the realities of modern society. Even so, divorce laws (partner rights, child rights), marriage laws (age at marriage, bigamy, licence procedures), and child abuse laws were established to improve individual and family well-being. These laws, while seeming to limit certain individual freedoms, promote a responsibility and a freedom that liberates and enhances well-being. It is reasonable to also argue—the complexities of modern society notwithstanding—that new policies, programs, and laws may need to be implemented to reduce dysfunctionality in families and reaffirm individual and family well-being. Cooperative efforts among all levels of government (federal, provincial, municipal), organizations (business, social service, educational, legal, and religious institutions), and local communities (private agencies, leagues, churches) would be an important step toward this basic goal.

Global Families and a Multicultural Society

The changes and challenges that the Canadian family faces are not isolated from worldwide changes. Today, families in Canada represent a diverse array of cultures, traditions, languages, and beliefs. The obvious causes of this diversity are the higher rates of immigration into Canada, economic migration, and Canada's continuing role as a protector of political refugees fleeing oppression. There are, however, equally important causes that are much less obvious. For example, without changes in the immigration system it is doubtful that the "visibility" of today's immigrants and cultures would be so pronounced. Furthermore, the continuing low fertility of Canada-born citizens creates a need for immigration to address the problem of reproduction and population growth. And finally, Canada's tolerant and welcoming policy of multiculturalism is rare amongst the developed nations of the world, many of whom insist on assimilation. The policy of multiculturalism in Canada has also given renewed vigour to those groups that had all but assimilated and now want to recover their cultural roots, such as immigrants from eastern Europe and Asia.

The challenges that these vast social changes imply are far reaching. Not only do we now live in a society with many cultures, but many of these subcultures within the larger culture of Canada are evolving in ways that differ from the culture of origin. Once social groups have immigrated to Canada they may try to maintain their culture of origin which they see as frozen in the time at which they emigrated. In reality, their culture of origin continues to evolve on a different trajectory, so that sometimes the cultures preserved in Canada represent more traditional forms than are found in the countries of origin. This provides a conservative challenge to social change in dating and marriage customs for the subsequent generations. This might be a more conservative focus than young people might find in their parents' country of origin.

Another challenge is that cultural symbols become ambiguous and vague. For example, in traditional western societies, black attire was associated with death and mourning, but for other cultures such as Chinese the appropriate colour would be different. The confusion of cultural symbols is of course reduced by the presence of mass media throughout the world as it attempts to standardize mass culture into a "global village."

Yet another challenge to today's families is that they must not only learn to live with diversity between families, but also within families. Many of us think about an Indian-Canadian family as different from a Coast Salish-Canadian family and both of those as different from a German Mennonite-Canadian family. These are all example of diversity between families; this variance in diversity is a natural consequence of tolerance and multiculturalism. Today, there is the growth of diversity within families and this requires a very personal form of tolerance. The causes of this diversity within families are the more individualized voluntary mate selection in Canada and the increasing tolerance of young people regarding race, religion, and culture. For example, one of the authors of this book comes from a blended family that mixed Jewish and Protestant religions; the children went on to contract inter-racial and cross-cultural marriages. As a result, the diversity we see all around us is increasingly within our own families as well as between families. As individuals, our children and our children's children can be expected to marry across the many characteristics of diversity found in our society. Such a development can only serve to further secure Canada as a tolerant society.

There are many other challenges as families change within a changing Canada. These include the role of filial piety, the role of arranged marriages, and the challenge to marriage customs such as monogamy. Many of these changes will be played out against compelling issues such as fertility, child discipline, intergenerational economic responsibility, and cohabitation as a replacement for marriage. Despite all of these changes and issues, history has taught us that the family will change, adapt, and survive. There is no other form of social group that has such an emotional and primordial hold on its members. There is no other social group that can do what the family does best, which is to recreate society from generation to generation while incorporating the best of humanity: joy, love, kindness, care, trust, and, most of all, loyalty.

SUMMARY

- Despite growing concerns about marriage and family life, much is known about the characteristics of strong marriages and families. These principles are essential building blocks in facilitating family well-being.

- Social scientists do not agree on what is happening to families in our society. Some believe the family as we know it is declining into disintegration, while others feel families are adjusting to the changes with only minor difficulty. Still others believe that the changes, while difficult, will ultimately create new and alternative ways of fulfilling individual and interpersonal sexual and intimacy needs. The fourth group of family specialists is concerned about what is happening, but is not sure of the outcome. There is agreement on the importance of preventive family policy and programs.

- Recent priority actions in affirming the needs of husbands, fathers, wives, mothers, and children are emphasized. Important steps need to be taken in facilitating interpersonal caring, equality, and justice in families.

KEY TERMS

Family policy (353)
Primary prevention (354)
Secondary prevention (354)
Tertiary prevention (354)

QUESTIONS FOR REVIEW

1. Distinguish between the demise, adjustment, rethinking, and "don't know" views of family change.
2. Define the three types of preventive services for families.
3. Define *family policy*, and specify several guidelines in policy-making.
4. How is the policy of multiculturalism related to globalization?
5. Policy addressing the work–family interface is often aimed at employers. Why?
6. What is a "guaranteed annual income" policy?

QUESTIONS FOR DISCUSSION

1. Given what you have read about changing families, how would you interpret these patterns? Which of the four models would you choose as your own? Do you have another view? What evidence would you use to defend your view?
2. A large number of recommended actions, programs, and policies have been identified to facilitate individual and family well-being. If you were assigned the task of choosing five specific actions, which ones would you consider most important?
3. What are the tradeoffs between pro-natalist policies to increase fertility and multicultural policies and immigration?
4. Can you imagine policies that might promote individual well-being at the expense of family well-being and vice versa? Which should have priority, the welfare of the social group of the family or the welfare of the individual?

SUGGESTED READINGS

Baker, Maureen. 1996.* *Canadian Family Policies: Cross-National Comparisons*. Toronto: University of Toronto Press. This book is an excellent and thorough examination of issues in family policy in Canada, the U.S., and six other major countries. It is a must-read book for anyone concerned about the well-being of families.

Johnson, Laura C., and Dick Barnhorst (eds.). 1991.* *Children, Families and Public Policy in the 90s*. Toronto: Thompson Educational Publishing. An excellent review of issues and policies in financial assistance, child care, balancing concerns between home and work, and support networks for families in Canada.

Popenoe, David. 1996. *Life Without Father: Compelling New Evidence that Fatherhood and Marriage are Indispensable for the Good of Children and Society*. New York: The Free Press (Martin Kessler Books). This book is an excellent example of the "demise of the family" approach. Anyone seriously interested in issues affecting families in our society should carefully examine this work.

Glossary

ABCX crisis model is Hill's family crisis model, in which A is the stressor event, B is the family's crisis-meeting resources, and C is the definition the family places on the event, which produce X, the crisis as the family experiences it.

Access rights are the rights to spend time with his or her child granted by a court of law to a non-custodial parent following a divorce.

Acculturation refers to the process of incorporating aspects of other cultures into one's own culture.

Affinal kin are people to whom we are related "by marriage" or affinity.

Agape or altruistic love, is a generous, unselfish giving of oneself. The agapic lover is kind, caring, and sensitive to the other's needs, without making demands for the self.

AIDS (Acquired Immune Deficiency Syndrome) causes a weakening of the body's ability to fight disease. People who contract AIDS become susceptible to other infections, to which healthy people are virtually immune.

AmerNative Canadians Aboriginal families in Quebec.

Androgyny among both women and men, is defined as being both instrumental *and* expressive, both assertive *and* yielding, both masculine *and* feminine, depending on the situational appropriateness of these various behaviours.

Annulment is the dissolution of a marriage because of a decision by a court of law that the conditions for a *valid* marriage did not exist when the marriage took place.

Arranged marriages are those where the parents of the participants exercise complete control of the selection of the marriage partner.

Atomistic family refers to Zimmerman's conception of the family form in which family authority is minimal, individualism is supreme, divorce is easy and frequent, and the birth rate is low.

Attachment refers to behaviours that represent the need of an infant to attain and maintain proximity and protection with an available and responsive caregiver.

Autonomous marriages are those where the participants themselves have free choice in their selection of a marriage partner.

Avunculocal residence is the practice in which following marriage, the couple lives in the band or village of the groom's mother's brother.

Battered woman syndrome refers to Walker's description of the effects that repeated violence has on abused women, including anxiety, affective and cognitive disorders, cognitive distortions, disruption of interpersonal relationships, and so on.

Bilateral descent is the system of tracing descent in which kinship is acknowledged to others related through both the father's and the mother's lines.

Bilocal residence is the practice in which after marriage, the couple may go to live in the household, band, or village of either the groom's father or the bride's mother.

Binuclear family is a family consisting of children and their parents who live in two households (centres) because the parents are divorced.

Bisexual refers to a person who is sexually attracted to people of either sex.

Bride capture is the practice of obtaining a wife by capturing her from a neighbouring band or village.

Bride exchange is the practice in which two bands exchange women to provide wives for the men of each band.

Bride price refers to goods given to the bride's family by the groom's family when the bride and groom are married.

Bride service is service or work performed by the prospective groom for the family of the bride-to-be, which "pays" the bride's family for losing her when she marries.

Capacity for marriage refers to the legal right to enter the marriage relationship, and includes age, consanguinity, mental capacity, and monogamy.

Cenogamy is the form of marriage in which two or more men collectively marry two or more women.

Census family is a now-married couple (with or without never-married sons and/or daughters of either or both spouses), a couple living common-law (with or without never-married sons and/or daughters of either or both partners), or a lone parent of any marital status, with at least one never-married son or daughter living in the same dwelling.

Child abuse is the physical or mental injury, sexual abuse, or maltreatment of a child under the age of 18 years.

Child neglect refers to a broad range of inadequate parental behaviours, ranging from inadequate supervision leading to accidental harm to the child, to failure to care for the child in terms of food, clothing, shelter, or personal cleanliness.

Child support refers to monetary payments by the non-custodial parent to help pay child-rearing expenses incurred by the custodial parent.

Cohabitation is the sharing of a household by an adult man and woman who are living together as husband and wife without a legal marriage.

Cohort is a group of persons who were born or who married in the same year.

Common-law union is a cohabiting relationship that has not been formally or legally solemnized but in which there is mutual agreement to live in a marriage-like" union, and which has lasted at least one year (Canada).

Companionate (mature) love includes physical attraction and emotional attachment, but also involves a realistic assessment of the partner and of the relationship, resulting in both intimacy and commitment.

Comparison level for alternatives or (CL_{alt}) compares the benefits a person receives in the present relationship with the possible benefits that could be derived from an alternative relationship.

Comparison level or (CL) is how a person's outcomes in a particular relationship compare with his or her expected outcomes.

Complex stepfamily is a stepfamily in which the married couple have one or more children of their own, as well as prior-marriage children.

Conceptual approach is a set of assumptions, concepts, and statements about human phenomena.

Conflict management strategies are ways used to secure compliance in a conflict by exercising authority, control, influence, or manipulation.

Conflict Tactics Scale the scale of items Strauss devised for measuring the level of verbal/physical violence characteristic of spousal and parent-child conflict in a family.

Conjugal family is the small family unit that places greater emphasis on the marriage (conjugal) bond between husband and wife than on the bond between blood relatives.

Consanguineal kin are genetic or blood-line kin.

Contactful communication is high in disclosure of feelings, and is also open to explore the other's experience.

Control variable is a variable, based on conceptual assumptions or a review of literature, that is expected to modify or clarify the relationships between predictor and dependent variables.

Controlling communication is closed, but of high disclosure (free expression of intentions, emotions, or feelings).

Conventional communication is closed (minimizing the other's experience) and low in disclosure (avoiding issues or personal feelings).

Coparenting is an agreement between separated/divorced parents that they will share the rights and responsibilities of child-rearing equally.

Correlation is a statistic, which varies between -1.00 and +1.00, that measures the positive or negative strength of the relationship between two variables.

Courtship consists of "going together" activities and interaction that enable couples to explore deeper levels of interpersonal intimacy and commitment in order to determine if marriage is feasible and desirable for them.

Custody refers to having primary responsibility for the welfare and upbringing of a child.

Cycle Theory of Violence is Walker's model of wife abuse, involving a *tension building* phase, an *uncontrollable aggression* phase, and a *loving contrition* phase in which the aggressor expresses remorse.

Date rape is the situation in which a woman is forced by her partner to engage in unwanted sexual activities while on a date.

Dating continuum consists of various identifiable dating stages from least serious to most serious (casual dating, frequent dating, steady dating, and engagement).

Dating consists of "going together" activities and interaction that enable couples to develop personal interests in each other and to explore varying levels of interpersonal intimacy and commitment.

Demographic or population aging is the process by which an entire population grows older, involving an increase in the proportion of the elderly.

Demography is the study of the age and sex composition of a population, and the processes responsible for this composition.

Dependent variable is a variable (attribute, thought, feeling, behaviour, and so on) that a researcher wants to understand or explain.

Desertion is the wilful abandonment of spouse and/or children without legal justification.

Developmental task is a set of critical expectations in the marriage or family career that must be successfully fulfilled in order to make an effective transition to the next stage or phase of the relationship.

Developmental tasks are tasks that are associated with a particular stage in the life of an individual, whose successful achievement leads to happiness and success in later stages.

Divided custody occurs when a child spends a significant portion of the year with each parent, so that each is for a time responsible for the welfare and upbringing of the child.

Divorce faults are offences such as adultery or cruelty committed by a husband or wife that justify divorce.

Divorce rate is the number of recorded divorces per 100 000 population (or another population unit, such as 1000 or 10 000) in a calendar year.

Divorce is the formal dissolution of a valid marriage by judicial decree.

Domestic contract a written legal agreement between a man and a woman who are already married or who are planning to marry.

Domestic family is Zimmerman's conception of the family form in which the rights of the individual and the rights of the family are in creative balance, thus enabling civilization to flourish.

Double ABCX crisis model expands the ABCX model by focusing on the family circumstances *when the stressor is experienced*. Prior strains and pressures create a pile-up of stresses and the family therefore requires new resources in coping.

Double descent is the practice in which kinship is recognized through both the father's line of fathers and the mother's line of mothers.

Double standard asserts that premarital sexual intercourse is more acceptable for males than for females.

Dower property is a portion of the husband's property that will become the property of the wife if she is divorced or widowed.

Dowry is the money, goods, or property that in some traditional societies a bride is required to bring to her marriage.

Dual-career marriage is a marriage in which both the husband and the wife actively pursue professional, business, or scholarly careers.

Dual-work couples are husbands and wives who both work full-time but who do not define their jobs as careers.

Enculturation refers to the process by which one learns one's own culture.

Endogamy requires a person to select a marriage partner from certain acceptable groups, despite the absence of formal regulations.

Equal partner marriages are marriages in which working wives see themselves as co-providers.

Eros or love of beauty, is marked by an irrational and powerful attraction to the physical appearance of the other.

Exogamy requires a person to select a marriage partner from outside certain prohibited groups, despite the absence of formal regulations.

Experience hypothesis of cohabitation suggests that the experience of premarital cohabitation affects the participants' attitudes and beliefs about marriage and relationships.

Explanation is a reliable answer or reason for why individuals or groups of individuals feel, think, or behave the way they do.

Extended family is a family in which two or more generations live together or close to each other.

Extramarital sexuality may include a wide range of activities, from flirtation, kissing and petting, to coitus with a person other than the spouse.

Family dismemberment refers to changes in family structure resulting from death.

Family life career is the stages of the family life span defined by *changes* in the presence or absence of children, family size, and the age composition of the child(ren) and parent(s).

Family of orientation is the family into which we are born.

Family of procreation is the family in which we bear and rear our own children.

Family policy is a widely held set of objectives for the well-being of children and families, the establishment of which shall guide and rationalize programs, services, and all derivative policies.

Family stress is a state that arises from an actual or perceived imbalance between the threat or challenge a family experiences and the capacity or resources of the family for coping with this.

Female infanticide is the practice of killing female infants to control the number of females able to birth children.

Fraternal polyandry is when a woman that marries a man automatically also marries his brothers.

Functional prerequisite is a societal need that must be fulfilled in order for a society to survive.

Gender egalitarianism   is the belief that men and women should share rights, duties, responsibilities, and decision-making power equally in marriage.

Gender identity   is the primary identification of an individual with one sex or the other, or the personal sense of being either male or female.

Gender role   is the culturally defined set of characteristics and behaviours that are considered sex-appropriate in a particular society or those cultural aspects of behaviour in which males and females differ.

Gender segregation within occupations   is the tendency to restrict women to lower, less well-paying levels within an occupation.

Generational squeeze   refers to women in the middle generation who give significantly more support to family members than they receive.

Genetic relatives   are people who are related because they share one or more common ancestors; "blood" relatives.

Gerontology   is the study of aging, including chronological, biological, psychological, and social aging.

Great transformation   is Shorter's conception that during the 18th century in Europe there occurred a transformation in mate selection, mother–infant, and other relationships, with a shift from *survival* to *sentiment* as the determining influence.

Habitant family   a 17–18th century rural French Canadian family which emphasized close ties with multitudes of relatives.

Heider's Balance Theory   is the theory predicting that in triadic relationships, balance exists when all the relationships are positive, or when two people like each other but both dislike the third person. Imbalance exists when one person likes the other two, but these two both dislike each other. This theory is relevant to many stepfamily relationships.

Heterogamy   is the tendency of persons to select mates with different social or personal characteristics.

Hierarchical influence   refers to the ways that the structure and process of social influence in human development is systematically organized at differing phases or time periods throughout the life span.

Homogamy   (assortative matching) is the tendency of persons to select mates with similar social or personal characteristics, despite the absence of formal requirements.

Homosexual   is a person who is sexually attracted to a person of the same sex.

Household   is a person or group of persons who occupy the same dwelling and do not have a usual place of residence elsewhere in Canada.

Hypergamy   refers to the situation in which a woman marries up in terms of age or other factors such as social class, socioeconomic status, education, and intelligence.

Hypothesis   is a proposition that uses the actual indicators available in the data collected to test the conceptual approach.

Illegitimacy   refers to child bearing outside the bonds of wedlock.

Impartible inheritance   is the inheritance of family property by only a single surviving member, typically either the oldest or youngest son.

Incest   refers to sexual intercourse between genetically-related parents, or between siblings.

Inclusive definitions   a family is each individual's interpretation of who their "kin" really are.

Infanticide   is the culturally prescribed or permitted practice of killing some babies.

Informal separation   is an arrangement between a husband and wife to live apart (without the involvement of a court of law).

Institutions   in the context of the elderly, are establishments providing some level of custody or care, as distinct from other collective dwellings such as hotels or rooming houses where no care is provided.

Intentional childlessness   is the condition of a woman and/or couple ideologically opposed to having children under any circumstances and who takes what it is believed to be permanent steps to prohibit pregnancy or childbirth.

Interval variable   is the mathematically measurable difference between the categories in a variable, the distance between each category being equal.

Intimacy   is the close relationship between two people that is characterized by interdependence, need fulfilment, and emotional attachment.

Involuntary childlessness   is the condition of a woman and/or couple desiring to have children who has had unprotected sexual intercourse for at least 12 months, and who has never had a sterilizing operation.

Joint custody   is the formal provision by a court of law providing that both divorced parents share equally the responsibility for the welfare and the upbringing of a child.

Joint family   is a group of male heirs who, together with their wives and children, inhabit a common household in which the eldest male exercises authority.

Joint parenting   separated and divorced parents agree to share the rights and responsibilities of child-rearing equally, with the rights of neither part superior to the other.

Judicial separation is the decision by a court of law freeing a husband and wife to live apart, immune to the charge of *desertion*, though yet legally married and so unable to remarry.

Junior partner marriages are marriages in which wives are employed, but see their husbands as the main provider.

Kindred refers to a network of persons who are related through common ancestry, adoption, or marriage. Kindreds are recognized and have significance primarily in westernized societies.

Kin-keeping consists of efforts expended to keep family members in touch with one another.

Kinship system is the social unit composed of people who are seen as relatives of each other, and thus as having rights and duties with respect to each other.

Later-life families include families that are beyond the child-rearing years, and those families with children that have begun to launch them.

Legal custody refers to the authority to make the many long-term decisions about how a child is to be raised.

Legal definition of marriage marriage is limited to a legal relationship between one man and one woman.

Levirate is the practice whereby if a man dies, one of his brothers becomes husband to his wife and father to his children.

Low income cut-off (LICO) is the family income figure, adjusted for family size, at which a family spends 58.5 percent of total family income for food, clothing, and shelter. This is the "poverty line," and families with incomes below this figure are officially poor.

Ludus or playful love, treats love as a game in which one does not become too involved. The obsessive passion is not for the partner, but for the game of love itself.

Mania or obsessive love, was called by the Greeks "the madness from the gods." Sleep, hunger, and the normal experiences of life are replaced by obsessive thoughts of the beloved.

Marital quality is defined as a couple's subjective evaluation of their interaction or relationship on a continuum from low to high, and refers to the adjustment, satisfaction, and happiness that characterize a couple's relationship.

Marital stability indicates whether a marriage is intact or not.

Marriage is a normatively defined relationship between at least one man and at least one woman, established with the intentions of permanence; and a sexually-based bond where children may be conceived.

Matrifocal family is the family form in which the head of the family is a woman, typically a mother and/or grandmother of other family members.

Matrilineal descent is the practice of tracing descent only through the line of mothers (through the mother, the mother's mother, the mother's mother's mother, and so on).

Matrilocal residence is the practice in which after marriage, the couple goes to live with the bride's mother's band or village.

Matripatrilocal residence is the practice in which after marriage, the couple first lives in the household or band of the bride's mother until they have a child, after which they move to the household or band of the groom's father.

Mediation is the process of resolving conflict with the assistance of a neutral third party.

Modified extended family refers to a family system in which separate households of related individuals are tied to a wider system through bonds of affection, obligation, and exchange of goods and services.

Monitoring is a measure of control, including an accurate knowledge of where the adolescent is at all times.

Monogamy is a marital relationship in which a person is married to only one other spouse (at a time).

Moral commitment is defined as either an internalized personal sense of moral obligation, or an external moral obligation which is imposed by significant others (the "ought to" of commitment) to remain in a relationship.

Neolocal residence is the practice under which after marriage, the couple establishes a residence that is separate from the residences of both the bride's and groom's parents.

Network interference refers to the attempts of family members or friends to influence the dating choices of individuals.

No-fault divorce is the process for legally dissolving a marriage without need to establish guilt for the marriage breakdown.

Nominal variable is a variable that contains two or more categories that are qualitatively different, where the differences cannot be determined mathematically.

Nonfraternal polyandry is a form of marriage in which the husbands and fathers are not related by blood.

Nonprobability sample is a sample drawn from a population where the characteristics of this population are not known.

Nonverbal communication includes facial expression, eye contact, tone of voice, gestures, posture, and general body language.

Normative definition of marriage Marriage is a relationship between at least one man and at least one woman, established with the intentions of permanence; marriage is also the primary sexually-based bond in which the reproduction of children is expected to occur.

Nuclear family is a family unit composed of both a mother and a father who have one or more children.

Nurturant care is the provision of the basic emotional and social needs of human beings.

Objectivity is a value-free way of obtaining knowledge about phenomena without biasing the information itself or the way in which it is obtained.

Occupational gender segregation is the practice of assigning unpleasant, ill-paid, and/or unskilled occupations to women, and more pleasant, better-paid, more-skilled occupations to men.

Operationalization refers to how a variable is measured.

Optimum parenting is a style of parenting that uses ideal levels of support (love, encouragement) and control (permissiveness, restrictiveness) in responding to a child's needs and desires.

Ordinal variable is a variable difference between two or more categories that can be rank ordered.

Partible inheritance is the practice of dividing family property among surviving members of a family.

Patriarchy is the patterning of family relationships in which the eldest male—usually the father—holds authority over all family members.

Patrilineal descent is the practice of tracing descent only through the line of fathers (father, father's father, father's father's father, and so on).

Patrilocal residence is the practice in which after marriage, the couple go to live with the groom's father's band or village.

Patrinominal is the practice whereby children acquire the surname of their father.

Pedi-focal family all those involved in the nurturance and support of an identified child, regardless of household membership (where the child lives).

Personal commitment is a personal dedication or determination (often referred to as the "want to" in commitment) to continue or complete a line of action despite adversity or temptations to deviate.

Personal marriage contracts are written agreements between married partners that spell out the duties and obligations of each partner to the other and to the relationship.

Physical abuse refers to any non-accidental physical injury sustained by a family member resulting from acts of omission or commission by another family member. Such abuse of children is the most common.

Physical custody refers to having responsibility for the welfare of a child on a day-by-day basis.

Polyandry is the marriage practice in which one woman may be married to two or more men at the same time.

Polygamy is the marriage practice in which either the husband or the wife has two or more mates at the same time.

Polygynadry is the marriage practice in which both men and women have plural spouses.

Polygyny is the marriage practice in which one man may be married to two or more women at the same time.

Pragma or realistic love, is "love with a shopping list," or love based on a careful evaluation of one's own "marketability" compared with the good and bad points of the partner.

Predictor variable is a variable, based on conceptual assumptions or a review of literature, that a researcher uses to help understand or explain a dependent variable.

Primary prevention refers to intervention programs and services in place to enhance individual and family well-being and reduce the likelihood of family problems occuring.

Primogeniture is the traditional practice in which the oldest son inherits the property and noble title (if any).

Principle of least interest asserts that the person *least* interested in continuing the relationship has the most power or control in the relationship.

Probability sample is the equal chance of each individual (or household) member of a known population of being drawn if a subsample is drawn from that population.

Propositions are statements that predict the connection between two or more concepts in a study of human phenomena.

Qualitative research is data obtained, without the use of standardized questions or measures, through open-ended interviews in which individuals report their own experiences. Data analysis typically identifies patterns and commonalities in the experiences of those participating in the study.

Quantitative research is data obtained using standarized questions or measures designed to test specific assumptions or hypotheses. Data analysis typically focuses on frequencies and statistical patterns among the variables in the data collected.

Rape in the family context refers to sexual intercourse forced on a child by a stepparent, stepsibling, other non-blood relative, or common-law (cohabiting) member of the family.

Real income refers to income adjusted for inflation.

Reference set is a set of persons, defined by an individual, as the most significant others in that individual's life at a particular point in time.

Reliability indicates the degree to which the indicator being used to measure a concept is a dependable measure of the concept each time the concept is used in other research studies.

Remarriage kindred is the network of persons sharing current *and* prior marriage family ties, including current marriage and former marriage husbands, wives, children, grandparents, and other relatives.

Replacement level is the level at which new births compensate for deaths in a society.

Replicability ensures that methods used in data collection can be accurately duplicated in follow-up research; in this way, findings can be confirmed or disconfirmed.

Role-making is the establishment of marital roles based on a couple's interaction, rather than on normative prescriptions.

Romantic love involves a strong physical and emotional attraction to another person, frequently leading to their idealization.

Sati is the practice in India where a widow throws herself on the funeral pyre of her dead husband and so burns herself to death.

Scaffolding is parental support that reduces the complexity of a child's task when necessary and removes support when it is no longer needed.

Secondary prevention refers to programs and services designed to intervene before family problems get worse.

Segmented labour market is a *divided* labour market that recruits some kinds of labour (such as minorities and disadvantaged persons) for one part of the market and other kinds of labour (such as historically favoured groups of persons) for another part of the market.

Self disclosure is the revelation of private thoughts and feelings to another person.

Separation occurs when a couple that is legally married, and so cannot remarry, no longer shares a common household or residence.

Sex ratio refers to the number of males for every 100 females in a particular population.

Sex-dimorphic cognitive abilities refers to differing cognitive abilities between males and females (for example, higher verbal ability in females or visual-spatial abilities in males).

Sexual harassment is physical or verbal behaviour that is sexual in nature, is unwanted, and is seen as an implicit or explicit threat to the victim's employment or educational activities.

Sexual orientation is defined as erotic responsiveness to one sex or the other (homo-, hetero-, or bi-sexual).

Sexual socialization includes both informal instruction with respect to sex provided by parents and peers, as well as formal programs of instruction through religious education in churches or the school system.

Sexually transmitted diseases are diseases that can only be transmitted by various forms of sexual contact.

Significance test assesses the probability that the results of any research were obtained by chance.

Sister exchange is the practice whereby a man obtains a bride by giving his sister as wife to one of his bride's male relatives.

Situational definitions *see* pedi-focal definition of family.

Social identity is derived from names (surnames and first names) that individuals are assigned at birth.

Social institution is a social organization or group considered by the *majority* of persons in a society to perform essential functions in the maintenance of individual and societal well-being.

Social networks in the context of the elderly, refers to relations among households and kin.

Social process is a recurring attitudinal or behavioural pattern that seems to reflect real change in the short term but which in the long term tends to reflect cycles.

Social role refers to expectations that society and one's family have for the social categories that individuals occupy.

Social status is the value or social worth assigned to the social position that individuals occupy.

Socialization refers to the processes of learning one's culture, personality, and personal values throughout the life span.

Solidarity in the context of the elderly, refers to social bonds among the generations, including cohesion, integration, and support.

Sororal polygyny is the form of polygyny in which a man's multiple wives are sisters.

Sororate is the rule favouring the marriage of a widower to a sister of his wife if she cannot bear children or if she dies young.

Stem family is a household consisting of elderly parents and a single (typically married) son who has been selected to work the family farm or business and who will inherit it.

Stepfamily is a family in which the husband and/or wife has a child from a prior relationship.

Stepfather family is the family formed when a prior-married mother remarries.

Stepmother family is the family formed when a prior-married father remarries.

Step-parent family is the family formed when a prior-married father and a prior-married mother marry each other.

Storge or companionate love, is a "slow-burning" relationship that is rarely hectic or urgent. It comes gradually with the passage of time and the enjoyment of shared activities.

Structural commitment is defined as events or conditions that constrain an individual (often referred to as the "have to" in commitment) to continue a line of action once it has been initiated, regardless of personal preference.

Temperament is a relatively stable biological or emotional characteristic of infants at birth considered to be an indicator of personality.

Tertiary prevention refers to programs and services designed to try to reduce widespread family problems before all hope of intervention is lost.

Test of significance is a statistic that assesses the probability that correlational results were obtained by chance.

Theoretical framework a set of low level and middle range theories that are united in sharing common assumptions and concepts.

Theory consists of propositions that have been empirically verified (they are found to be valid, reliable, and statistically significant) in multiple studies conducted, under differing conditions, in differing places, at differing times, by independent researchers.

Total dependency ratio is the ratio of people who are of non-working age (under age 15 and 65 years and over) to those who are of working age (15 to 65).

Total Fertility Rate is the number of children that 1000 women would have in a specific year if throughout their lifetimes they bore children equal to the age-specific birth rates of the population for the given year.

Transitional double standard accepts the right of males to engage in premarital intercourse, but suggests that females may do so only if they are in love or engaged.

Transsexual is a person who persistently feels an incongruity between his or her biological sex and gender identity, or who feels she or he has been "born in the wrong body," and who expresses a compulsion to become a person of the other sex.

Transvestite is a person who obtains sexual pleasure from dressing like the other sex, but does not usually want a permanent change of anatomy or appearance.

Traumatic sexualization is the distortion of a child's sexual feelings, attitudes, and behaviours that may result from sexual abuse.

Trustee family is Zimmerman's conception of the family form in which the rights and privileges of the individual are completely subordinate to the authority of the family, typically exercised by the oldest male.

Ultimogeniture is the traditional practice whereby the youngest son inherits family property and noble title (if any).

Unilineal descent is the practice of tracing descent through a single parental line only, either through the line of fathers or through the line of mothers.

Universal definition is a definition that can be used to identify the most common and most widely accepted marriage or family form (or any other institution group or phenomena) in every known society.

Validity signifies that the indicator being used to measure a concept is an *accurate* measure of that concept.

Vital statistics are the experiences of individuals officially recorded as they occur, including abortions, births, deaths, divorces, marriages, and related data of official interest.

Voluntary childlessness is the condition of a woman and/or couple who chooses, at least for the present, not to have children and who takes the necessary steps to prohibit pregnancy or childbirth.

Bibliography

Note: Asterisks indicate material drawing on Canadian research.

Abella, Rosalie S. 1981.* "Economic Adjustment on Marriage Breakdown Support," *Family Law Review*, 4:1–10.

Abernathy, Thomas and Margaret Arcus, 1977.* "The Law and Divorce in Canada," *The Family Coordinator*, 26: 409–413.

Abma, Joyce, Anne Driscoll and Kristin Moore. 1998. "Young Women's Degree of Control Over First Intercourse: An Exploratory Analysis," *Family Planning Perspectives*, 30(1):12–18.

Abu-Laban, Sharon M. 1987.* "The Family Life of Older Canadians," in Victor W. Marshall (ed.). *Aging in Canada*. Don Mills: Fitzhenry and Whiteside.

Abu-Laban, Sharon McIrvin and Baha Abu-Laban. 1994.* "Culture, Society, and Change," in William A. Meloff and W. David Pierce (eds). *An Introduction to Sociology*. Scarborough: Nelson Canada. Pp. 47–73.

Adams, G.A., L.A. King and D.W. King. 1996.* "Relationships of Job and Family Involvement, Family Social Support, and Work–Family Conflict with Job and Life Satisfaction," *Journal of Applied Psychology*, 81(4):411–420.

Adams, Gerald R. and Gordon Munro. 1979.* "Portrait of the North American Runaway: A Critical Review," *Journal of Youth and Adolescence*, 8:359–373.

Adams, O. B. and D. N. Nagnur. 1988.* *Marriage, Divorce and Mortality: A Life Table Analysis for Canada and Regions, 1980–1982*. Catalogue No. 84–536E. Ottawa: Supply and Services Canada.

Adams, Owen and Dhruva Nagnur. 1989.* "Marrying and Divorcing: A Status Report for Canada," *Canadian Social Trends*, 13:24–27.

Adams, Owen, and Dhruva Nagnur. 1990*. "Marrying and Divorcing: A Status Report for Canada," in Craig McKie and Keith Thompson (eds.). *Canadian Social Trends*. Toronto: Thompson Educational Publishing.

Adams, Owen. 1988.* "Divorce Rates in Canada," *Canadian Social Trends*, Winter, 1988:18–21.

Adams, Owen. 1990.* "Divorce Rates in Canada," in Craig McKie and Keith Thompson, (eds.). *Canadian Social Trends*. Toronto: Thompson Educational Publishing.

Adamson, Nancy, Linda Briskin and Margaret McPhail. 1988.* *Feminist Organizing for Change, The Contemporary Women's Movement in Canada*. Toronto: Oxford University Press.

Adler, Jerry. 1997. "It's a Wise Father Who Knows... His Child," *Newsweek*, Special Issue: Your Child, From Birth to Three, Spring/Summer:73.

Agnew, Robert and Sandra Huguley. 1989. "Adolescent Violence Toward Parents," *Journal of Marriage and the Family*, 51:699–711.

Ahmed, N. et al. 1986. "South Asian Families in the United States: Pakistani, Bangladeshi, and Native Canadian Muslims," in B. Asswad and B. Bilge, (eds.) *Family and Gender Among American Muslims*. Philadelphia: Temple University Press. Pp. 155–172.

Ahrons, Constance R. 1979. "The Binuclear Family: Two Households, One Family," *Alternative Lifestyles*, 2:499–515.

Ahrons, Constance R. 1980. "Redefining the Divorced Family: A Conceptual Framework for Postdivorce Family System Reorganization," *Social Work*, 25:427–441.

Ahrons, Constance R. 1981. "The Continuing Coparental Relationship Between Divorced Spouses," *American Journal of Orthopsychiatry*, 51:415–428.

Ahrons, Constance R. 1983. "Predictors of Paternal Involvement Postdivorce: Mothers' and Fathers' Perceptions," *Journal of Divorce*, 6:55–69.

Ahrons, Constance R. 1994. *The Good Divorce: Keeping Your Family Together When Your Marriage Comes Apart*. NY: HarperCollins.

Ahrons, Constance R. 1995. *Making Divorce Work*. NY: Guilford Publications.

Ahrons, Constance R. and Lynn Wallisch 1987. "The Relationship Between Former Spouses," in D. Perlman and S. Duck (eds.). *Intimate Relationships*. Newbury Park: Sage.

Ahrons, Constance R. and Roy H. Rodgers.* 1987. *Divorced Families: A Multidisciplinary Developmental View*. New York: W.W. Norton.

Ainsworth, M.D.S., M.C. Blehar, E. Waters and S. Wall. 1978. *Patterns of Attachment: A Psychological Study of the Strange Situation*. Hillsdale: Lawrence Erlbaum.

Al-Haj, Majid. 1995. "Kinship and Modernization in Developing Societies: The Emergence of Instrumentalized Kinship," *Journal of Comparative Family Studies*, 26(3):311–328.

Al-Nouri, Qais N. 1995. "University Modernizing Effects on Libyan Family and Culture," *Journal of Comparative Family Studies*, 26(3):329–347.

Alberta Area Survey. 1987.* Unpublished data. Edmonton: Population Research Laboratory, University of Alberta.

Alberta Government, Personnel Administration Office. 1991.* *Balancing Work and Family, Survey Results.* Edmonton: Personnel Administration Office, Alberta Government.

Albrecht, Stan L. and Philip R. Kunz. 1980. "The Decision to Divorce: A Social Exchange Perspective," *Journal of Divorce,* 3:319–337.

Aldous, Joan. 1996. *Family Careers: Rethinking the Developmental Perspective.* Thousand Oaks: Sage Publications.

Ali, J. and W.R. Avison 1997.* "Employment Transitions and Psychological Distress: The Contrasting Experiences of Single and Married Mothers," *Journal of Health and Social Behavior,* 38(December):345–362.

Allen, Joseph P., Stuart T. Hauser, Thomas G. Bell and Charlene Eickholt. 1996. "The Connection of Observed Hostile Family Conflict to Adolescents Developing Autonomy and Relatedness with Parents," *Development and Psychopathology,* 8(2):425–442.

Allen, Katherine R. 1988. "Integrating a Feminist Perspective into Family Studies Courses," *Family Relations,* 37:29–35.

Allen, Katherine R. 1995. "Opening the Classroom Closet: Sexual Orientation and Self-disclosure," *Family Relations,* 44(2):136–141.

Allen, Katherine R. and Kristine M. Baber. 1992. "Starting a Revolution in Family Life Education: A Feminist Vision," *Family Relations,* 41:378–384.

Allen, Suzanne M. and Richard A. Kalish, 1984. "Professional Women and Marriage," *Journal of Marriage and the Family,* 46:375–382.

Aloni, Shulamit. 1984. "Israel: Up the Down Escalator," in Robin Morgan (ed.). *Sisterhood is Powerful.* Garden City: Anchor Press/Doubleday.

Alpert, H. (ed.) 1988. *We Are Everywhere: Writings By and About Lesbian Parents.* Freedom, CA: Crossing Press.

Alsdurf, Phylis and James M. Alsdurf. 1988. "Wife Abuse and Scripture," in Ann L. Horton and Judith A. Williamson (eds.). *Abuse and Religion: When Praying Isn't Enough.* Lexington: Lexington Books.

Amato, Paul R. 1987. "Family Processes in One-Parent, Stepparent and Intact Families: The Child's Point of View," *Journal of Marriage and the Family,* 49:327–337.

Amato, Paul R. 1991. "The 'Child of Divorce' as a Person Prototype: Bias in the Recall of Information About Children in Divorced Families," *Journal of Marriage and the Family,* 53:59–60.

Amato, Paul R. 1993. "Children's Adjustment to Divorce: Theories, Hypotheses and Empirical Support," *Journal of Marriage and the Family,* 55:23–28.

Amato, Paul R. and Bruce Keith. 1991b. "Parental Divorce and the Well-Being of Children," *Psychological Bulletin,* 110:26–46.

Ambert, A.M. 2003. *Divorce: Facts, Causes and Consequences,* The Vanier Institute of the Family's website at www.vifamily.ca.

Ambert, Anne-Marie and Maureen Baker. 1984.* "Marriage Dissolution: Structural and Ideological Changes," in Maureen Baker (ed.). *The Family.* Toronto: McGraw-Hill Ryerson.

Ambert, Anne-Marie. 1980.* *Divorce in Canada,* Don Mills: Academic Press.

Ambert, Anne-Marie. 1983.* "Separated Women and Remarriage Behavior: A Comparison of Financially Secure Women and Financially Insecure Women," *Journal of Divorce,* 6:43–54.

Ambert, Anne-Marie. 1985.* "The Effect of Divorce on Women's Attitude Toward Feminism," *Sociological Focus,* 18:265–272.

Ambert, Anne-Marie. 1986.* "Being a Stepparent: Live-in and Visiting Stepchildren," *Journal of Marriage and the Family,* 48:795–804.

Ambert, Anne-Marie. 1988. "Relationship with Ex-in-Laws After Divorce," *Journal of Marriage and the Family,* 50:679–686.

Ambert, Anne-Marie. 1988a.* "Relationship Between Ex-Spouses: Individual and Dyadic Perspectives," *Journal of Social and Personal Relationships,* 5:327–346.

Ambert, Anne-Marie. 1988b.* "Trajectory of Treatment for Emotional Problems Among Divorced/Remarried Persons: An Exploratory Study." Keynote address at the Conference on Family, State and Society at Crossroads, University of Saskatchewan, March 17.

Ambert, Anne-Marie. 1989.* *Ex-Spouses and New Spouses: A Study of Relationships.* Greenwich: JAI Press.

Ambert, Anne-Marie. 1990.* "Marriage Dissolution: Structural and Ideological Changes," in Maureen Baker (ed.). *Families: Changing Trends in Canada.* Toronto: McGraw-Hill Ryerson. Chapter 15.

Ambert, Anne-Marie. 1992.* The Effect of Children on Parents. New York: Haworth Press.

Ambert, Anne-Marie. 1997.* *Parents, Children, and Adolescents: Interactive Relationships and Development in Context.* New York: Haworth Press.

Ambert, Anne-Marie. 2001.* *Families in the New Millennium.* Boston, MA: Allyn & Bacon.

American Demographics, Inc. 1989. "Focus... on the Boomerang Adults," *The Number News,* July 6:6.

Ames, Lynda J., Alana B. Atchison and D. Thomas Rose. 1995. "Love, Lust and Fear: Safer Sex Decision Making Among Gay Men," *Journal of Homosexuality,* 30:53–73.

Ammons, Paul and Nick Stinnett. 1991. "The Vital Marriage: A Closer Look," in Jean E. Veevers. *Continuity and Change in Marriage and Family*. Toronto: Holt, Rinehart and Winston of Canada.

Anashensel, Carol S., Ralph R. Frerichs and Virginia A. Clark. 1981. "Family Roles and Sex Differences in Depression," *Journal of Health and Social Behavior*, 22:379–393.

Anderson, Alan.* 1985. *Ethnic Identity Retention in Francophone Communities in Saskatchewan: A Sociological Survey*. Saskatchewan: University of Saskatchewan.

Anderson, Kristin L. 1997. "Gender, Status, and Domestic Violence: An Integration of Feminist and Family Violence Approaches," *Journal of Marriage and the Family*, 59(3):655–669.

Anderson, M. M. and M.J. Lynam. 1987. "The Meaning of Work for Immigrant Women in the Lower Echelons of the Canadian Labour Force," *Canadian Ethnic Studies*, 19(20):67–90.

Anderson, Stephen A., Candyce S. Russell and Walter R. Schumm. 1983. "Perceived Marital Quality and Family Life-Cycle Categories: A Further Analysis," *Journal of Marriage and the Family*, 45:127–139.

André, R. 1998. *Homemakers: The Forgotten Workers*. Chicago: University of Chicago Press.

Andry, Carl F. 1981. *Paul and the Early Christians*. Washington: University Press of America.

Angus Reid Group. 1994.* *The State of the Family in Canada*.

Angus Reid Group. 1996.* *Public Attitudes on Specific Gay Rights Issues*. www.angusreid.com/pressrel/gayrights.html.

Angus Reid Group. 1996.* *Canadians' Views on the Canada Pension Plan*. www.angusreid.com/pressrel.

Angus Reid Group. 1997.* *Canadians' Views on Health Care Funding Priorities*. www.angusreid.com/pressrel.

Antonucci, Tony C., Hiroko Akiyama and Jennifer E. Lansford. 1998. "Negative Effects of Close Relations."

Apt, C. and D. Hurlbert. 1993. "The Sexuality of Women in Physically Abusive Marriages: A Comparative Study," *Journal of Family Violence*, 8(1):57–69.

Aquilino, William S. 1990. "The Likelihood of Parent– Adult Child Coresidence: Effects of Family Structure and Parental Characteristics," *Journal of Marriage and the Family*, 52:405–419.

Araji, Sharon and David Finkelhor. 1986. "Abusers: A Review of the Research," in David Finkelhor (ed.). *Sourcebook on Child Sexual Abuse*. Beverly Hills: Sage.

Aries, Philippe. 1962. *Centuries of Childhood: A Social History of Family Life*. New York: Vintage Books.

Armstrong, Pat and Hugh Armstrong. 1984.* *The Double Ghetto, Canadian Women and their Segregated Work* (second edition). Toronto: McClelland and Stewart.

Arnsberg, C. M., and S. T. Kimball. 1940. *Family and Community in Ireland*. Cambridge: Harvard University Press.

Assh, S. Donna and E. Sandra Byers. 1990.* "Effects of Behavioural Exchanges and Cognitions on the Relationship Satisfaction of Dating and Married Persons," *Canadian Journal of Behavioural Science*, 22:223–235.

Associated Press. 1995. "Majority of Parents Spank, Scream at Their Children," Gallup Poll, December 10.

Associated Press. 1996. "Birth Rate Leaps for Girls 10 to 14," *Register Guard*, May 11.

Associated Press. 1997. "Abortion Rate Continues Decline." A press release from The Centers of Disease Control and Prevention, December 5.

Associated Press. 1998. "Septuplets Finally Under One Roof." "Hospital Asks Parents to Take Babies Home," March 2.

Associated Press. 1998. "Still Sweethearts after 80 years," *Register Guard*, February 14:4A.

Astrachan, A. 1986. *How Men Feel: Their Response to Women's Demands for Equality and Power*. New York: Anchor Press/Doubleday.

Atkin, David J., Jay Moorman and Carolyn A. Lin. 1991. "Ready for Prime Time: Network Series Devoted to Working Women in the 1980s," *Sex Roles*, 25:677–685.

Atkinson, Maxine P. and Becky L. Glass. 1985. "Marital Age Heterogamy and Homogamy, 1900 to 1980," *Journal of Marriage and the Family*, 47:685–691.

Atkinson, Tom. 1980.* "Perceptions on the Quality of Life," *Perspectives Canada III*. Ottawa: Supply and Services Canada, 277–292.

Aubé, Nicole and Wolfgang Linden. 1991.* "Marital Disturbance, Quality of Communication and Socioeconomic Status," *Canadian Journal of Behavioural Science*, 23:125–132.

Auerswald, E. H. 1980. "Drug Use and Families — in the Context of Twentieth Century Science," in B. G. Ellis (ed.). *Drug Abuse from the Family Perspective*. Rockville: National Institute of Drug Abuse.

Avison, William R. and Donna D. McAlpine. 1992.* "Gender Differences in Symptoms of Depression Among Adolescents," *Journal of Health and Social Behaviour*, 33:77–96.

Axinn, William G. and Arland Thornton. 1996. "The Influence of Parents' Marital Dissolutions on Children's Attitudes Toward Family Formation," *Demography*, 33(1):66–81.

Bachofen, J. J. 1961. *Das Mutterrecht*. Stuttgart: Krais and Hoffman.

Bachrach, C.A. 1983.* "Adoption as a Means of Family Formation: Data from the National Survey of Family Growth," *Journal of Marriage and the Family*, 45: 859–865.

Bader, Edward, Gisele Microys, Carole Sinclair, Elizabeth Willett and Brenda Conway. 1980.* "Do Marriage Preparation

Programs Really Work? A Canadian Experiment," *Journal of Marriage and Family Therapy*, 6:171–179.

Badgley, A. W. 1984.* *Report of the Federal Committee on Sexual Offenses against Children and Youth*. Ottawa: Federal Departments of Justice and Health and Welfare.

Bagley, C., F. Bolitho and L. Bertrand. 1997.* "Sexual Assault in School, Mental Health and Suicidal Behaviors in Adolescent Women in Canada," *Adolescence*, 32(126):361–366.

Bailey, Roger C. and Nathaniel A. Vietor. 1996. "A Religious Female Who Engages in Casual Sex: Evidence of a Boomerang Effect," *Social Behavior and Personality*, 24(3):215–220.

Baker, Hugh D. R. 1979. *Chinese Family and Kinship*. New York: Columbia University Press.

Baker, Maureen (ed.). 1984.* *The Family: Changing Trends in Canada*. Toronto: McGraw-Hill Ryerson.

Baker, Maureen (ed.). 1990a.* *Families: Changing Trends in Canada* (second edition). Toronto: McGraw-Hill Ryerson.

Baker, Maureen and J. I. Hans Bakker. 1980.* "The Double-Bind of the Middle-Class Male: Men's Liberation and the Male Sex Role," *Journal of Comparative Family Studies*, 11:547–561.

Baker, Maureen. 1985.* *What Will Tomorrow Bring?: A Study of the Aspirations of Adolescent Women*. Ottawa: Canadian Advisory Council on the Status of Women.

Baker, Maureen. 1988.* *Aging in Canadian Society*. Toronto: McGraw-Hill Ryerson.

Baker, Maureen. 1990b.* "Introduction: Theories, Methods, and Concerns in Family Sociology," in Maureen Baker 1990. *Families: Changing Trends in Canada* (second edition). Toronto: McGraw-Hill Ryerson.Chapter 1.

Baker, Maureen. 1994a.* "Thinking About Families: Trends and Policies," in Baker, Maureen (ed.). Canada's Changing Families: Challenges to Public Policy. Ottawa: The Vanier Institute of the Family. Chapter 1.

Baker, Maureen. 1994b.* "The Effectiveness of Family and Social Policies," in Baker, Maureen (ed.). 1994.* *Canada's Changing Families: Challenges to Public Policy*. Ottawa: The Vanier Institute of the Family. Chapter 10.

Baker, Maureen. 1995.* *Canadian Family Policies: Cross-National Comparisons*. Toronto: University of Toronto Press.

Baker, Maureen. 1996.* "Social Assistance and the Employability of Mothers: Two Models from Cross-National Research," *Canadian Journal of Sociology*, 21(4):483–503.

Bala, Nicholas, Joseph P. Hornic and Robin Vogl (eds.). 1991.* *Canadian Child Welfare Law: Children, Families and the State*. Toronto: Thompson Educational Publishing.

Bala, Nicholas. 1994.* "Canada: Growing Recognition of the Realities of Family Life," *University of Louisville Journal of Family Law*, 32:269–80.

Balakrishnan, T. R., Evelyne Lapierre-Adamcyk and Karol J. Krotki. 1988b.* "Attitudes Towards Abortion in Canada," *Canadian Studies in Population*, 15:201–215.

Balakrishnan, T. R., K. Vaninadha Rao, Evelyne Lapierre-Adamcyk and Karol Krotki. 1987.* "A Hazard Model Analysis of the Covariates of Marriage Dissolution in Canada," *Demography*, 24:395–406.

Balakrishnan, T. R., K. Vaninadha Rao, Karol Krotki and Evelyne Lapierre-Adamcyk. 1985.* "Age at First Birth and Lifetime Fertility," *Journal of Biosocial Science*, 20:167–174.

Balakrishnan, T. R., Karol Krotki and Evelyne Lapierre-Adamcyk. 1985.* "Contraceptive Use in Canada," *Family Planning Perspectives*, 17:209–215.

Balakrishnan, T.R., Evelyne Lapierre-Adamcyk, and Karol K. Krotki. 1993.* *Family and Childbearing in Canada*. Toronto: University of Toronto Press.

Baldwin, J. D. and J. I. Baldwin. 1986. *Behavior Principles in Everyday Life* (second edition). Englewood Cliffs: Prentice-Hall.

Baldwin, Mark W. and Beverley Fehr. 1995.* "On the Instability of Attachment Style Ratings," *Personal Relationships*, 2:247–267.

Balkwell, Carolyn and Jack Balswick. 1981. "Subsistence Economy, Family Structure and the Status of the Elderly," *Journal of Marriage and the Family*, 43:423–429.

Balswick, Jack. 1980. "Explaining Inexpressive Males: A Reply to L'Abate," *Family Relations*, 29:231–233.

Balswick, Jack and Charles W. Peek. 1971. "The Inexpressive Male: A Tragedy of American Society," *The Family Coordinator*, 20:363–368.

Bandura, Alfred. 1977. *Social Learning Theory*. Englewood Cliffs: Prentice-Hall.

Bandura, Alfred. 1986. *Social Foundations of Thought and Action: A Social Cognitive Theory*. Englewood Cliffs: Prentice-Hall.

Bane, Mary J. 1976. *Here to Stay: American Families in the Twentieth Century*. New York: Basic Books.

Bank, Lew, Marion S. Forgatch, Gerald R. Patterson and Rebecca A. Fetrow. 1993. "Parenting Practices of Single Mothers: Mediators of Negative Contextual Factors," *Journal of Marriage and the Family*, 55(2):371–384.

Barbara, Augustin. 1989. *Marriage Across Frontiers*. Clevedon: Multilingual Matters, Ltd.

Barber, Brian K. and Darwin L. Thomas. 1986. "Dimensions of Fathers' and Mothers' Supportive Behavior: The Case for Physical Affection," *Journal of Marriage and the Family*, 48:783–794.

Barich, Rachel R. and Denise D. Bielby. 1996. "Rethinking Marriage: Change and Stability in Expectations, 1967–1994," *Journal of Family Issues*, 17:139–169.

Barling, J., K.E. Dupre and C.G. Hepburn. 1998.* "Effects of Parents' Job Insecurity on Children's Work Beliefs and Attitudes," *Journal of Applied Psychology*, 83(1):112–118.

Barling, Julian. 1990. *Employment, Stress and Family Functioning*. Chichester, England: John Wiley.

Barling, Julian, Clive Fullagar and Jenifer Marchl-Dingle. 1988.* "Employment Commitment as a Moderator of the Maternal Employment Status/Child Behavior Relationship," *Journal of Organizational Behavior*, 9:113–122.

Barnes, G. M., and M. P. Farrell. 1992. "Parental Support and Control as Predictors of Adolescent Drinking, Delinquency, and Related Problem Behaviors," *Journal of Marriage and the Family*, 54:763–776.

Barnes, Gordon E., Leonard Greenwood and Reena Sommer. 1991.* "Courtship Violence in a Canadian Sample of Male College Students," *Family Relations*, 40:37–44.

Barnett, R.C. 1998. "Toward a Review and Reconceptualization of the Work/Family Literature," *Genetic, Social and General Psychology Monographs*, 124(2):125–182.

Barnett, Rosalind C., Nancy L. Marshall and Joseph H. Pleck. 1992. "Adult Son–Parent Relationships and Their Association with Sons' Psychological Distress," *Journal of Family Issues*, 13:505–525.

Barnett, Rosalind C., Nancy L. Marshall and Joseph H. Pleck. 1992. "Adult Son–Parent Relationships and Their Association with Sons' Psychological Distress," *Journal of Family Issues*, 13:505–525.

Barnett, O. and R. Fagan. 1993. "Alcohol Use in Male Spouse Abusers and Their Female Partners," *Journal of Family Violence*, 8(1):1–25.

Barnhorst, Dick and Bernd Walter. 1991.* "Child Protection Legislation in Canada," in Nicholas Bala, Joseph P. Hornic and Robin Vogl (eds.). *Canadian Child Welfare Law: Children, Families and the State*. Toronto: Thompson Educational Publishing. 17–32.

Baron, Larry and Murray A. Strauss. 1987. "Legitimate Violence, Violent Attitudes and Rape: A Test of the Cultural Spillover Theory," *Annual of the New York Academy of Sciences*, 528:79–110.

Barrett, C. K. 1968. *A Commentary on the First Epistle to the Corinthians*. San Francisco: Harper and Row.

Barry, Herbert, Margaret K. Bacon and Ervin L. Child. 1957. "A Cross-Cultural Survey of Some Sex Differences in Socialization," *Journal of Abnormal and Social Psychology*, 55:327–332.

Barsky, Lesley. 1992.* "Our Families Come First: Why More Mothers are Choosing to Stay at Home," *Chatelaine*, February: 49–53,102.

Basran, G.S. 1993.* "Indo-Canadian Families: Historical Constraints and Contemporary Contradictions," *Journal of Comparative Family Studies*, 24 (3):339–352.

Baumrind, D. 1971. "Current Patterns of Parental Authority," *Developmental Psychology Monographs*, 4:1–103.

Baumrind, Diana. 1996. "The Discipline Controversy Revisited," *Family Relations*, 45(4):405–414.

Bayer, Alan E. 1981. "The Psychoanalyti-++----***c Frame of Reference in Family Study," in F. Ivan Nye and Felix M. Berardo, (eds.). *Emerging Conceptual Frameworks in Family Analysis*. New York: Praeger, Chapter 7.

Beaujot, Roderic P. and Kevin McQuillan. 1986.* "The Social Effects of Demographic Change: Canada 1851–1981," *Journal of Canadian Studies*, 21:57–69.

Beaujot, Roderic, et al. 1994.* "Self-Employment Among Immigrants: A Test of Blocked Mobility Hypothesis," *Canadian Studies in Population*, 21(2):81–94.

Becker, G.S. 1981. *A Treatise on the Family*. Cambridge, MA: Harvard University Press.

Beebe, Steven A and John T. Masterson. 1986. *Family Talk: Interpersonal Communication in the Family*. New York: Random House.

Beer, W.R. (ed.). 1988. *Relative Strangers: Studies of Stepfamily Processes*. New York: Bowman and Littlefield.

Beitchman, J., K. Zucker, J. Hood, G. daCosta and D. Akman. 1991. "A Review of the Short-Term Effects of Child Sexual Abuse," *Child Abuse and Neglect*, 151:537–556.

Beitchman, J., K. Zucker, J. Hood, G. daCosta, D. Akman and E. Cassavia. 1992. "A Review of the Long-Term Effects of Child Sexual Abuse," *Child Abuse and Neglect*, 16:101–118.

Bell, Alan P. and Martin S. Weinberg. 1978. *Homosexualities: A Study of Diversity Among Men and Women*. New York: Simon and Schuster.

Bell, Alan P., Martin S. Weinberg and Sue K. Hammersmith. 1981. *Sexual Preference—Its Development in Men and Women*. Bloomington: Indiana University Press.

Bell, David C., Janet S. Chafetz and Lori H. Horn. 1982. "Marital Conflict Resolution," *Journal of Family Issues*, 3:111–132.

Bell, Norman W. and Ezra F. Vogel. 1960. *A Modern Introduction to the Family*. New York: The Free Press.

Bellah, Robert et al. 1985. *Habits of the Heart: Individualism and Commitment in American Life*. Berkeley: University of California Press.

Belsky, J. 1990b. "Developmental Risks Associated with Infant Day Care: Attachment Insecurity, Noncompliance and Aggression?" in S. Chehrazi (ed.). *Balancing Work and Parenting: Psychological and Developmental Implications of Day Care*. New York: American Psychiatric Press. Pp. 37–68.

Belsky, J. and D. Eggebeen. 1991. "Early and Extensive Maternal Employment/Child Care and 4- to 6-year-olds' Socioemotional Development," *Journal of Marriage and the Family*, 53(1):157–167.

Belsky, J., B. Gillstrap and M. Rovine. 1984. "The Pennsylvania Infant and Family Project. 1: Stability and change in mother–infant and father–infant in a family setting at one, three, and nine months," *Child Development*, 55:692–705.

Belsky, Jay and Michael J. Rovine. 1988. "Nonmaternal Care in the First Year of Life and the Security of Infant– Parent Attachment," *Child Development*, 59:157–167.

Belsky, Laurence Steinberg., and Patricia Draper. 1991. "Childhood Experiences, Interpersonal Development, and Reproductive Strategy: An Evolutionary Theory of Socialization." *Child Development*, 62:647–670.

Belsky, Jay, Sharon Woodworth and Keith Crnic. 1996. "Trouble in the Second Year: Three Questions about Family Interaction," *Child Development*, 67(2):556–578.

Belsky, Jay. 1988. "The 'Effects' of Infant Day Care Reconsidered," *Early Childhood Quarterly*, 3:235–272.

Belsky, Jay. 1990. "Developmental Risks Associated with Infant Day Care: Attachment Insecurity, Noncompliance and Aggression." in S. Chehraz (ed.). *Psychosocial Issues in Day Care*. Washington: American Psychiatric Press, 37–68.

Bem, Sandra L. 1975. "Sex-Role Adaptability: One Consequence of Psychological Androgyny," *Journal of Personality and Social Psychology*, 31:634–643.

Ben-David, S. 1993. "The Two Facets of Female Violence: The Public and the Domestic Domains," *Journal of Family Violence*, 8(4):345–359.

Ben-Rafael, Eliezer. 1997. *The Kibbutz at Century's End*. New York: State University of New York Press.

Benin, Mary Holland and Debra A. Edwards. 1990. "Adolescents' Chores: The Difference between Dual- and Single-Earner Families," *Journal of Marriage and the Family*, 52:361–373.

Benokraitis, Nijole V. 1993. *Marriages and Families: Changes, Choices and Constraints*. Englewood Cliffs: Prentice-Hall.

Benson-von der Ohe, Elizabeth. 1987. *First and Second Marriages*. New York: Praeger.

Bergen, Elizabeth. 1991. "The Economic Context of Labor Allocation," *Journal of Family Issues*, 12:140–157.

Berger, Audrey M. 1980a. "The Child Abusing Family I: Methodological Issues and Parent-Related Characteristics of Abusing Families," *American Journal of Family Therapy*, 8:53–66.

Berger, Audrey M. 1980b. "The Child Abusing Family II: Child and Child-Rearing Variables, Environmental Factors and Typologies of Abusing Families," *American Journal of Family Therapy*, 8:52–68.

Bernard, Jessie. 1973. "My Four Revolutions: An Autobiographical History of the ASA," in J. Huber (ed.). *Changing Women in a Changing Society*. University of Chicago Press, 11–29.

Bernard, Jessie. 1972. *The Future of Marriage*. New York: Bantam Books.

Bernardes, Jon. 1993. "Responsibilities in Studying Postmodern Families," *Journal of Family Issues*, 14(1):35–49.

Bernardo, D.H., C.L. Shehan and G.R. Leslie. 1987. "A Residue of Tradition: Jobs, Careers and Spouses' Time in Housework," *Journal of Marriage and the Family*, 49:381–390.

Bernstein, Anne C. 1997. "Stepfamilies from Siblings' Perspectives," *Marriage and Family Review*, 26(1/2): 153–175.

Berry, J. 1986. "The Acculturation Process and Refugee Behavior," in C. Williams and J. Westermeyer (eds.). *Refugee Mental Health in Resettlement Countries*. Washington: Hemisphere Publishing Corporation. Pp. 25–37.

Best, Joel. 1990. *Threatened Children: Rhetoric and Concern About Child-Victims*. Chicago: University of Chicago Press.

Best, Pamela. 1995. "Women, Men and Work," *Canadian Social Trends*, (Spring):30–34.

Betcher, William and Robie Macauley. 1990. *The Seven Basic Quarrels of Marriage*. New York: Villard Books.

Bettor, Laura, Susan S. Hendrick and Clyde Hendrick. 1995. "Gender and Sexual Standards in Dating Relationships," *Personal Relationships*, 2(4):359–369.

Bharat, Shalini. 1995. "Attitudes and Sex-Role Perceptions Among Working Couples in India," *Journal of Comparative Family Studies*, 26(3):371–388.

Bhargava, Gura. 1984.* "Advertising for Mates Among South Asia in North America: A Study of Autonomy and Arrangement in Mate-Seeking," unpublished paper.

Bhargava, Gura. 1988.* "Seeking Immigration Through Matrimonial Alliance: A Study of Advertisements in an Ethnic Weekly," *Journal of Comparative Family Studies*, 19:245–249.

Bianchi, S. M. 1990. "America's Children: Mixed Prospects," *Population Bulletin*, 45:3–41.

Bibby, Reginald and Donald C. Posterski. 1985.* *The Emerging Generation: An Inside Look at Canada's Teenagers*. Toronto: Irwin Publishing.

Bibby, Reginald W. 1995.* *The Bibby Report: Social Trends Canadian Style*. Toronto: Stoddart.

Bibby, Reginald W. 1997.* "The Persistence of Christian Religious Identification in Canada," *Canadian Social Trends*, 44:24–28.

Bibby, Reginald W. and Donald C. Posterski, 1992.* *Teen Trends: A Nation in Motion*. Toronto: Stoddart.

Bieber, Irving et al. 1962. *Homosexuality: A Psychoanalytic Study*. New York: Random House.

Biller, Henry B. 1993. *Fathers and Families: Paternal Factors in Child Development*. Westport, Connecticut: Auburn House.

Bindman, Stephen, 1992.* "Court Rejects 'Sink or Swim' Alimony: Ex-husband Must Keep Paying," *Edmonton Journal*, December 19:A3.

Bindman, Stephen. 1993.* "Top Court Rules Against Gay Man," *Edmonton Journal*, February 26:A3.

Bissett-Johnson, Alastair. 1988.* "Family Law—Judicial Variation of Final Global Settlements: Pelech v. Pelech, Caron v. Caron, Richardson v. Richardson," *Canadian Bar Review*, 67:153–167.

Blakely, John H. and Edward B. Harvey. 1988.* "Market and Non-Market Effects on Male and Female Occupational Status Attainment," *Canadian Review of Sociology and Anthropology*, 25:23–40.

Bland, Roger and Helene Orn. 1986.* "Family Violence and Psychiatric Disorder," *Canadian Journal of Psychiatry*, 31:129–137.

Blankenhorn, D., S. Bayme and J. Elshtain (eds.). 1991. *Rebuilding the Nest: A New Commitment to the American Family*. Milwaukee: Family Service America.

Blankenhorn, David. 1995. *Fatherless America: Confronting Our Most Urgent Social Problem*. New York: Basic Books.

Blau, Peter M. 1964. *Exchange and Power in Social Life*. New York: Wiley.

Block, Jeanne H. 1983. "Differential Premises Arising from Differential Socialization of the Sexes: Some Conjectures," *Child Development*, 54:1335–1354.

Blood, Robert O. and Donald M. Wolfe. 1960. *Husbands and Wives*. New York: The Free Press.

Bloom, D. E. 1986. "The Labour Market Consequences of Delayed Childbearing," paper presented at the American Statistical Association meetings, Chicago.

Blumberg, Rae Lesser with Maria Pilar Garcia. 1977. "The Political Economy of the Mother–Child Family," in Luis Lenero-Otero (ed.). *Beyond the Nuclear Family Model*. Beverly Hills: Sage.

Blumstein, Philip and Pepper Schwartz. 1983. *American Couples: Money, Work, Sex*. New York: William Morrow. Chapter 9.

Boeringer, S.B., C.L. Shehan and R.L. Akers. 1991. "Social Context and Social Learning in Sexual Coercion and Aggression: Assessing the Contribution of Fraternal Membership," *Family Relations*, 40(1):58–64.

Bohannan, Paul. 1970. *Divorce and After*. Garden City: Doubleday.

Boivin, Suzanne P. 1985.* "To Marry or Not to Marry? A Study of the Legal Situation of Common Law Spouses in Canadian Law," in Elizabeth Sloss. (ed.). *Family Law in Canada: New Directions*. Ottawa: Canadian Advisory Council on the Status of Women.

Bolgar, R., H. Zweig-Frank, and J. Paris. 1995. "Childhood Antecedents of Interpersonal Problems in Young Adult Children of Divorce," *Journal for the American Academy of Child and Adolescent Psychiatry*, 34 (2):143–151.

Boney-McCoy, S. and D. Finkelhor. 1995. "Prior Victimization: A Risk Factor for Childhood Sexual Abuse and for PTSD-Related Symptomatology among Sexually Abused Youth," *Child Abuse and Neglect*, 19(12):1401–1421.

Booth, Alan (ed.). Contemporary Families: Looking Forward, Looking Back. Minneapolis: National Council in *Family Relations*.

Booth Alan and David Johnson. 1988. "Premarital Cohabitation and Marital Success," *Journal of Family Issues*, 9:255–272.

Booth, Alan and David Johnson. 1988. "Premarital Cohabitation and Marital Success," *Journal of Family Issues*, 9:255–272.

Booth, Alan and David R. Johnson. 1994. "Declining Health and Marital Quality," *Journal of Marriage and the Family*, 56:218–223.

Booth, Alan and John N. Edwards. 1992. "Starting Over: Why Remarriages are More Unstable," *Journal of Family Issues*, 13(2):179–194.

Booth, Alan and Lynn White. 1980. "Thinking About Divorce," *Journal of Marriage and the Family*, 42:605–616.

Booth, Alan, David R. Johnson, Ann Branaman and Alan Sica. 1995. "Belief and Behavior: Does Religion Matter in Today's Marriage?" *Journal of Marriage and the Family*, 57:661–71.

Booth, Alan. 1977. "Wife's Employment and Husband's Stress: A Replication and Refutation," *Journal of Marriage and Family*, 39:645–650.

Bosga, Marion B., John B.F. de Wit, Ernest M.M de Vroome, Hans Howeling, Winfred Schop and Theo G.M. Sandfort. "Differences of Perception of Risk with Steady and Non-steady Partners Among Homosexual Men," *AIDS Education and Prevention*, 7:103–115.

Boss, Pauline G. 1993. "The Reconstruction of Family Life with Alzheimer's Disease," in Boss et al. (eds.). *Sourcebook of Family Theories and Methods*. New York: Plenum Press.

Boss, Pauline G., William J. Doherty, Ralph LaRossa, Walter R. Schumm and Suzanne K. Steinmetz (eds.). 1993. *Sourcebook of Family Theories and Methods: A Contextual Approach*. New York: Plenum Press.

Boswell, John. 1988. *The Kindness of Strangers: The Abandonment of Children in Western Europe from Late Antiquity to the Renaissance*. New York: Pantheon Books.

Botev, Nikolai. 1994. "Where East Meets West: Ethnic Intermarriage in the Former Yugoslavia, 1962 to 1989," *American Sociological Review*, 59:461–480.

Bouchard, G. (1987). "Sur la reproduction en milieu rural: Systeme ouvert et systeme clos." *Reserches Sociographiques* 28, 229–252.

Bouchard, G. (1992). "Les migrations de reallocation comme strategie de reproduction familiale en terrroir neuf." In R. Bonnain, G. Bouchard, and J. Goy (Eds.), *Transmettre, Heriter, Succeder: La Reproduction familiale en milieu rural France-Quebec XVIIIe-XXe Siecles*. Lyon: Presses Universitaires de Lyon.

Bouchard, Thomas J. Jr., David T. Lykken, Matthew McGue, Nancy L. Aegal and Auke Tellegen. 1990. "Sources of Human Psychological Differences: The Minnesota Study of Twins Reared Apart," *Science*, 250:223–228.

Bould, Sally. 1993. "Familial Caretaking: A Middle-Range Definition of Family in the Context of Social Policy," *Journal of Family Issues*, 14(1):133–151.

Bourbeau, Robert and Jacques Légaré. 1982.* *Evolution de la mortalité au Canada et au Québec 1831–1931*. Montreal: University of Montreal Press.

Bowen, G.L. 1998. "Effects of Leader Support in the Work Unit on the Relationship between Work Spillover and Family Adaptation," *Journal of Family and Economic Issues*, 19(1):25–52.

Bowker, Lee H. 1983. *Beating Wife Beating*. Lexington: Lexington Books.

Bowker, Lee H. 1988. "Religious Victims and Their Religious Leaders: Services Delivered to One Thousand Battered Women by the Clergy," in Anne L. Horton and Judith A Williamson (eds.). *Abuse and Religion: When Praying Isn't Enough*, Lexington: Lexington Books.

Bowlby, John. 1969. *Attachment and Loss: Volume 1. Attachment* (second edition). New York: Basic Books.

Bowlby, John. 1989. "The Role of Attachment in Personality Development and Psychopathology," in Stanley I. Greenspan and George H. Pollock (eds.). *The Course of Life: Volume I. Infancy*. Madison: International Universities Press, 229–270.

Bowman, Henry A. and Graham B. Spanier. 1978. *Modern Marriage*. New York: McGraw-Hill.

Bowman, Madonne E. and Constance R. Ahrons. 1985. "Impact of Legal Custody Status on Father's Parenting Post-divorce," *Journal of Marriage and the Family*, 47:481–488.

Boyd, M. (1990).* "Immigrant Women: Language and Socio-Economic Inequalities and Policy Issues," in S. Halli, et al. (eds.). *Ethnic Demography: Canadian Immigrant, Racial and Cultural Variations*. Ottawa: Carleton University Press.

Boyd, M. (1991).* "Immigration and Living Arrangements: Elderly Women in Canada," *International Migration Review*, 25(1):4–7.

Boyd, Monica and Edward T. Pryor. 1989a.* "The Cluttered Nest: The Living Arrangements of Young Canadian Adults," *Canadian Journal of Sociology*, 14: 461–477.

Boyd, Monica, and Doug Norris. 1995.* "Leaving the Nest? The Impact on Family Structure," *Canadian Social Trends*, Autumn:14–17.

Boyd, Monica and Edward T. Pryor. 1989b.* "Young Adults Living in their Parents' Homes," *Canadian Social Trends*, Summer:17–20.

Boyd, Monica. 1975.* "English-Canadian and French-Canadian Attitudes Toward Women: Results of the Canadian Gallup Polls," *Journal of Comparative Family Studies*, 6:153–170.

Boyd, Monica. 1983.* "The Social Demography of Divorce in Canada," in K. Ishwaran (ed.). *Marriage and Divorce in Canada*. Toronto: Methuen.

Boyd, Monica. 1984.* *Canadian Attitudes Toward Women: Thirty Years of Change*. Ottawa: Women's Bureau, Labour Canada.

Bozinoff, Lorne and André Turcotte. 1992b.* "Support for Legalization of Abortion Is Increasing," *The Gallup Report*, October 19.

Bozinoff, Lorne and André Turcotte. 1993.* "Canadians Split Over Effects of Working Moms," *The Gallup Report*, January:1–2. Toronto: Gallup Canada, Inc.

Bozinoff, Lorne and Peter MacIntosh. 1991.* "Majority of Canadians Believe Two-Child Family Ideal," *The Gallup Report*, April 22.

Bozinoff, Lorne and Peter MacIntosh. 1992.* "70% Believe Premarital Sex is Not Wrong," *The Gallup Report*, August 27:1–3.

Bozinoff, Lorne and Peter MacIntosh. 1992.* "Majority Opposes Same Sex Marriages." Toronto: *The Gallup Report*, May 21, 1992.

Bozon, Michel. 1990. "Women and Age Difference Between Spouses: Domination by Consent, II," *Population*, 45:565–602.

Bozon, Michel. 1991. "Women and the Age Gap Between Spouses: An Accepted Domination?" *Population*, 3:113–148.

Bradburn, Norman. 1969. *The Structure of Psychological Well-Being*. Chicago: Aldine.

Bradburn, Norman and David Caplovitz. 1965. *Reports on Happiness*. Chicago: Aldine.

Bradbury, T.N., F.D. Fincham, and S.R.H. Beach. 2000. "Research on the Nature and Determinants of Marital Satisfaction: A Decade Review." *Journal of Marriage and the Family* 62: 964–980.

Bradley, A. and J. Wood. 1996. "How Do Children Tell? Disclosure Process in Child Sexual Abuse," *Child Abuse and Neglect*, 2(9):881–891.

Bradley, R. H., L. Whiteside-Mansell, J. A. Brisby, and B. M. Caldwell. 1997. "Parents' Socioemotional Investment in Children, *Journal of Marriage and the Family*, 59:77–90.

Bradshaw, John. 1988. *The Family*. Deerfield Beach: Health Communications Inc.

Bradshaw, John. 1990. *Homecoming*. New York: Bantam Books.

Brand, Eulalee and W. Glenn Clingempeel. 1987. "Interdependencies of Marital and Stepparent–Stepchild Relationships and Children's Psychological Adjustment: Research Findings and Clinical Implications," *Family Relations*, 36:140–145.

Brannon, Robert. 1976. "The Male Sex Role: Our Culture's Blueprint of Manhood and What It's Done for Us Lately," in Deborah S. David and Robert Brannon. 1976. *The Forty-Nine Percent Majority: The Male Sex Role*. Reading: Addison-Wesley.

Brehm, Sharon S. 1985. *Intimate Relationships*. New York: Random House.

Brehm, Sharon S. 1992. *Intimate Relationships* (second edition). New York: Random House.

Brennan, T., F. Blanchard, D. Hulzinga and D. Elliot. 1975. *Final Report: The Incidence and Nature of Runaway Behavior*. Boulder: Behavioral Research and Evaluation Corporation.

Bretherton, Inge. 1993. "Theoretical Contributions from *Developmental Psychology*," in Pauline G. Boss, William G. Doherty, Ralph LaRossa, Walter R. Schumm and Suzanne K. Steinmetz (eds.). *Sourcebook of Family Theories and Methods*: A Contextual Approach. New York: Plenum Press. Chapter 12.

Bretl, Daniel J. and Joanne Cantor. 1988. "The Portrayal of Men and Women in U.S. Television Commercials: A Recent Content Analysis and Trends Over 15 Years," *Sex Roles*, 18:595–609.

Bretschneider, Judy G. and Norma L. McCoy. 1988. "Sexual Interest and Behavior in Healthy 80- to 102-year olds," *Archives of Sexual Behavior*, 17:109–129.

Brewster, Karin, Elizabeth C. Cooksey, David K. Guilkey and Ronald R. Rindfuss. 1998. "The Changing Impact of Religion on the Sexual and Contraceptive Behavior of Adolescent Women in the United States," *Journal of Marriage and the Family*, 60(2):493–504.

Briggs, Freda and Russell M.F. Hawkins. 1996. "Low Socioeconomic Status Children are Disadvantaged in the Provision of School-based Child Protection Programmes," *British Journal of Social Work* 26(5):667–678.

Bringle, R.G. and B.P. Buunk. 1991. "Extradyadic Relationships and Sexual Jealousy." In K. McKinney and Susan Sprecher (Eds.) *Sexuality in Close Relationships* (pp. 135–153). Hillsdale,NJ: Erlbaum.

Bringle, Robert G. 1995. "Sexual Jealousy in the Relationships of Homosexual and Heterosexual Men: 1980 and 1992," *Personal Relationships*, 2:313–325.

Brinkerhoff, Merlin and Eugen Lupri. 1988.* "Interspousal Violence," *Canadian Journal of Sociology*, 13: 407–434.

Brinkerhoff, Merlin B. 1977.* "Women Who Want to Work in a Man's World: A Study of the Influence of Structural Factors in Role Innovativeness," *Canadian Journal of Sociology*, 2:283–303.

Brinkerhoff, Merlin B. and Marlene MacKie. 1985.* "Religion and Gender: A Comparison of Canadian and American Student Attitudes," *Journal of Marriage and the Family*, 47:415–429.

Briskin, Linda. 1980.* "Domestic Labour: A Methodological Discussion," in Bonnie Fox (ed.). *Hidden in the Household: Women's Domestic Labour Under Capitalism*. Toronto: The Women's Press.

Bristowe, E., and J.B. Collins. 1989.* "Family Mediated Abuse of Noninstitutionalized Frail Elderly Men and Women Living in British Columbia," *Journal of Elder Abuse and Neglect*, 1:45–64.

Broderick, Carlfred. 1979. *Marriage and the Family*. Englewood Cliffs: Prentice-Hall.

Broderick, Carlfred and James Smith. 1979. "The General Systems Approach to the Family," in Wesley R. Burr, Reuben Hill, F. Ivan Nye and Ira L. Reiss (eds.). *Contemporary Theories about the Family*, Volume II. New York: The Free Press. Chapter 3.

Broderick, Carlfred B. 1993. *Understanding Family Process: Basics of Family Systems Theory*. Newbury Park: Sage.

Brody, Gene H., Zolinda Stoneman, Douglas Flor and Chris McCrary. 1994. "Religion's Role in Organizing Family Relationships: Family Process in Rural, Two-Parent African American Families," *Journal of Marriage and the Family*, 56(4):878–888.

Brody, Hugh. 1971.* *Indians on Skid Row*. Ottawa: Northern Science Research Group, Department of Indian Affairs and Northern Development.

Bronfenbrenner, U. 1989. "Ecological Systems Theory," in R. Vasta (ed.), *Annals of Child Development*, 6:187–249.

Bronfenbrenner, Urie. 1961. "Toward a Theoretical Model for the Analysis of Parent–Child Relationships in a Social Context," in J.C. Glidewell (ed.). *Parental Attitudes and Child Behavior*. Springfield: Charles C. Thomas.

Bronfenbrenner, Urie. 1979. *The Ecology of Human Development*. Cambridge: Harvard University Press.

Bronfenbrenner, Urie. 1990. "Discovering What Families Do," in David Blankenhorn, Steven Bayme and Jean Bethke Elstain (eds.). *Rebuilding the Nest: A New Commitment to the American Family*. Milwaukee: Family Service America, 27–38.

Bronstein, Phyllis, JoAnna Clauson, Miriam Frankel Stoll and Craig L. Abrams. 1993. "Parenting Behavior and Children's Social, Psychological, and Academic Adjustment in Diverse Family Structures," *Family Relations*, 42(3):268–276.

Brooks, A. 1985. "Stepchildren on Panel Tell Parents How It Is," *New York Times*, January 13:B5.

Brown, David and Charles Hobart. 1988.* "Effects of Prior-Marriage Children on Adjustment in Remarriage: A Canadian Study," *Journal of Comparative Family Studies*, 19:381–396.

Brown, Prudence and Roger Manela. 1978. "Changing Family Roles: Women and Divorce," *Journal of Divorce*, 1:315–360.

Brown, Susan L. and Alan Booth. 1996.* "Cohabitation Versus Marriage: A Comparison of Relationship Quality," *Journal of Marriage and the Family*, 58:668–678.

Brubaker, Timothy. 1990. "Families in Later Life: A Burgeoning Research Area," *Journal of Marriage and the Family*, 52:959–981.

Brubaker, Timothy H. (ed.). 1992. *U.S. Families: Present and Future* (special issue of *Family Relations*), 41:378–439.

Brubaker, Timothy H. and Karen A. Roberto. 1993. "Family Life Education for the Later Years," *Family Relations*, 42:212–221.

Bryam, V., H. Wagner and G. Waller. 1995. "Sexual Abuse and Body Image Distortion," *Child Abuse and Neglect*, 19(4):507–510.

Bryant, Heather. 1990.* *The Infertility Dilemma: Reproductive Technologies and Prevention*. Ottawa: Canadian Advisory Council on the Status of Women.

Bubolz, Margaret M. and M. Suzanne Sontag. 1993. "Human Ecology Theory," in Boss, Pauline G., William J. Doherty, Ralph LaRossa, Walter R. Schumm, and Suzanne K. Steinmetz (eds). *Sourcebook of Family Theories and Methods: A Contextual Approach*. New York: Plenum Press. Pp. 419–448.

Bubolz, Margaret M. and Suzanne Sontag. 1993. "Human Ecology Theory," in Pauline G. Boss, William G. Doherty, Ralph LaRossa, Walter R. Schumm and Suzanne K. Steinmetz (eds.). *Sourcebook of Family Theories and Methods: A Contextual Approach*. New York: Plenum Press, Chapter 17.

Buehler, Cheryl and Jean M. Gerard (2002). "Marital conflict, ineffective parenting, and children's and adolescent's maladjustment." *Journal of Marriage and Family* 64, 78–92.

Bulcroft, K., L. Smeins, and R. Bulcroft.* 1999. *Romancing the Honeymoon*. Thousand Oaks, CA: Sage Publications.

Bulcroft, Richard and James M. White. 1997. "Family Research Methods and Levels of Analysis," *Family Science Review*, 10:2–19.

Bumpass, Larry L. 1990. "What's Happening to the American Family? Interactions between Demographic and Institutional Change," *Demography*, 27:483–498.

Bumpass, Larry L. and James A. Sweet. 1989. "National Estimates of Cohabitation," *Demography*, 26:615–625.

Bumpass, Larry L., James A. Sweet and Andrew Cherlin. 1991. "The Role of Cohabitation in Declining Rates of Marriage," *Journal of Marriage and the Family*, 53(November):913–927.

Bumpass, Larry L., R. Kelly Raley and James A. Sweet. 1995. "The Changing Character of Stepfamilies: Implications of Cohabitation and Nonmarital Childbearing," *Demography*, 25(3):425–436.

Burch, Thomas K. 1990.* "Remarriage of Older Canadians," *Research on Aging*, 12:546–559.

Burgess, Robert L. and James Garbarino. 1983. "Doing What Comes Naturally? An Evolutionary Perspective on Child Abuse," in David Finkelhor, Richard J. Gelles, Gerald T. Hotaling and Murray A. Strauss (eds.). *The Dark Side of Families: Current Family Violence Research*. Beverly Hills: Sage.

Burgess, Robert L. and Lise M. Youngblade. 1988. "Social Incompetence and the Intergenerational Transmission of Abusive Parental Practices," in Gerald T. Hotaling, David Finkelhor, John T. Kirkpatrick, and Murray A. Straus. (eds.). *Family Abuse and Its Consequences: New Directions in Research*. Newbury Park: Sage.

Burgoyne, Jacqueline and David Clark. 1984. *Making a Go of It: A Study of Stepfamilies in Sheffield*. London: Routledge and Kegan Paul.

Burke, Mary A. 1991.* "Implications of an Aging Society," *Canadian Social Trends*, 20:6–8.

Burke, Mary Anne, Susan Crompton, Allison Jones and Katherine Nessner. 1991.* "Caring for Children," *Canadian Social Trends*, Autumn:12–15.

Burke, R. J. 1997. "Alternative Family Structures: A Career Advantage?" *Psychological Reports*, 81:812–814.

Burke, Ronald J. and Tamara Weir. 1976. "Relationship of Wives' Employment Status to Husband, Wife and Pair Satisfaction and Performance," *Journal of Marriage and the Family*, 38:279–287.

Burke, Ronald J., Tamara Weir and Richard E. Duwors. 1980.* "Perceived Type A Behaviour of Husbands and Wives' Satisfaction and Well-Being," *Journal of Occupational Behaviour*, 1:139–150.

Burleson, Brant R. and Wayne H. Denton. 1997. "The Relationship Between Communication Skill and Marital Satisfaction: Some Moderating Effects," *Journal of Marriage and the Family*, 59:884–902.

Burns, C. 1985. Stepmotherhood: *How to Survive Without Feeling Frustrated, Left-Out, or Wicked*. New York: Harper and Row.

Burr, W., R. Hill, F.I. Nye and I.L. Reiss (eds.). 1979. *Contemporary Theories About the Family, Volume 1*. New York: The Free Press.

Burr, Wesley R., Geoffrey K. Leigh, Randall D. Day and John Constantine. 1979. "Symbolic Interaction and the Family," in Wesley R. Burr, Reuben Hill, F. Ivan Nye and Ira L. Reiss (eds.). *Contemporary Theories about the Family, Volume II*. New York: The Free Press, Chapter 2.

Burr, Wesley R., Reuben Hill, F. Ivan Nye and Ira L. Reiss (eds.). 1979. *Contemporary Theories about the Family, Volume II*. New York: The Free Press.

Burstyn, Varda and Dorothy Smith. 1985* *Women, Class, Family and the State*. Toronto: Garamond Press.

Burtch, Brian E., Andy Wachtel and Carol P. LaPrairie. 1985.* "Marriage Preparation, Separation, Conciliation and Divorce: Findings From the Public Images of Law Study," *Canadian Journal of Family Law*, 4:369–384.

Bush, Malcolm. 1988. *Families in Distress*. Berkeley: University of California Press.

Butlin, G. 1995.* "Adult Women's Participation Rate at a Standstill," *Perspectives*, Autumn, 231–246.

Byers, E. Sandra and Larry Heinlein. 1989.* "Predicting Initiations and Refusal of Sexual Activities in Married and Cohabiting Heterosexual Couples," *The Journal of Sex Research*, 26:210–231.

Byles, J.A. 1980a.* "Family Violence in Hamilton," *Canada's Mental Health*, 28:4–6.

Byles, John A. 1980b.* "Adolescent Girls in Need of Protection," *American Journal of Orthopsychiatry*, 50:264–278.

Caldwell, J.C. and P. Caldwell. 1990. "High Fertility in the Sub-Saharan Africa," *Scientific American*, 262(5):118–125.

Call, Vaughn, Susan Sprecher and Pepper Schwartz. 1995. "The Incidence and Frequency of Marital Sex in a National Sample," *Journal of Marriage and the Family*, 57:639–652.

Cameron, A. 1980. "The Battered Woman: Why Does She Stay?" *The Feminist Connection*, 10:12.

Cameron, Paul. 1985. "Homosexual Molestation of Children/Sexual Intervention of Teacher and Pupil," *Psychological Reports*, 57:1227–1235.

Campbell, A. 1981. *The Sense of Well-Being in America: Recent Patterns and Trends*. New York: McGraw-Hill.

Campbell, A., P.E. Converse and W.L. Robers. 1976. *The Quality of American Life*. New York: Russell Sage Foundation.

Campbell, J., P. Miller, M. Cardwell and A. Belknap. 1994. "Relationship Status of Battered Women Over Time," *Journal of Family Violence*, 9:99–111.

Campbell, J.C., 1992. "Battered Women and Their Children," *Annual Review Nursing Research*, 10:77–94.

Campbell, Jacquelyn C. 1992. "Wife Battering: Cultural Contexts Versus Western Social Sciences," in Dorothy Ayers Counts, Judith K. Brown and Jacquelyn C. Campbell (eds.). *Sanctions and Sanctuary, Cultural Perspectives on the Beating of Wives*. Boulder: Westview Press.

Campbell, Marian L. and Phyllis Moen. 1992.* "Job–Family Role Strain Among Employed Single Mothers of Preschoolers," *Family Relations*, 41:205–211.

Canada Employment and Immigration Advisory Council. 1991.* Symposium on Immigrant Settlement and Integration. Toronto.

Canadian Advisory Council on the Status of Women. 1991.* *Brief to the Royal Commission on New Reproductive Technologies*. March: No. 91–L–174. Ottawa.

Canadian Advisory Council on the Status of Women. 1991.* *Male Violence Against Women: The Brutal Face of Inequality*. Publication No. 910S-175. Ottawa.

Canadian Council on Social Development and Native Women's Association of Canada. 1991.* *Voices of Aboriginal Women*. Ottawa.

Canadian Family Law Guide. 1991.* Don Mills: CCH Canadian Limited.

Canetto, Silvia Sara. 1996. "What is a Normal Family? Common Assumptions and Current Evidence," *The Journal of Primary Prevention*, 17(1):31–46.

Carasco, Emily F. 1986. "Native Children: Have Child Welfare Laws Broken the Circle?" *Canadian Journal of Family Law*, 5:111–138.

Carisse, Colette. 1970.* "Family Values of Innovative Women: Perspective for the Future," unpublished paper delivered at the Seventh World Congress of Sociology, Varna, Bulgaria, September 1970.

Carmody, Dianne C. and Kirk Williams. 1987. "Wife Assault and the Perceptions of Sanctions," *Violence and Victims*, 2:25–38.

Carr, D. 1997. "The Fulfillment of Career Dreams at Midlife: Does It Matter for Women's Mental Health?" *Journal of Health and Social Behavior*, 38(December):331–344.

Carrier, J.M. 1980. "Homosexual Behavior in Cross-Cultural Perspective," in Judd Marmor (ed.). *Homosexual Behavior: A Modern Reappraisal*. New York: Basic Books.

Carroll, David L. 1990. *When Your Loved One Has Alzheimer's*. New York: Harper and Row.

Carson, Susan. 1987.* "The Children are Home Again," *The Montreal Gazette*, August 31: Living Section.

Carter, D. Bruce (ed.). 1987. *Current Conceptions of Sex Roles and Sex Typing*. New York: Praeger.

Cassidy, Beverly, Mark Zoccolillo and Susan Hughes. 1996.* "Psychopathology in Adolescent Mothers and Its Effects on Mother–Infant Interactions: A Pilot Study," *Canadian Journal of Psychiatry*, 41(6):379–384.

Cassidy, M. and G. Lee. 1989. "The Study of Polyandry: A Critique and Synthesis," *Journal of Comparative Family Studies*, 20(1):1–12.

Cate, Rodney M., Edgar Long, Jeffrey J. Angera and Kirsten K. Draper. 1993. "Sexual Intercourse and Relationship Development," *Family Relations*, 42(2):158–164.

Census of Canada, 1608–1876. 1878.* Volume 5, Tables A and F. Ottawa: Maclean, Rogers and Co.

Census of Canada, 1890–1891. 1893.* Volume 1, Volume 2, Ottawa: The King's Printer.

Census of Canada, 1901, 1911, 1921, 1931, 1941, 1951, 1961, 1966, 1971, 1981. Ottawa: The King's/Queen's Printer.

Chadwick-Jones, J.K. 1976. *Social Exchange Theory*. New York: Academic Press.

Chafetz, Janet S. 1999. "Varieties of Gender Theory in Sociology." In J.S. Chafetz (Ed.) *Handbook of the Sociology of Gender*. Pp. 3–23. New York: Kluwer Academic/ Plenum Publishing.

Chafetz, Janet S. 1997. "Feminist Theory and Sociology." *Annual Review of Sociology* 23, 97–120.

Chafetz, Janet S. 1980. "Conflict Resolution in Marriage," *Journal of Family Issues*, 1:397–421.

Chafetz, Janet Saltzman and Jacqueline Hagan. 1996. "The Gender Division of Labor and Family Change in Industrial Societies: A Theoretical Accounting," *Journal of Comparative Family Studies*, 27(2):187–219.

Chalifoux, J. 1980. "Secondary Marriage and Levels of Seniority Among the Abisi (Piti), Nigeria," *Journal of Comparative Family Studies*, 11(3):335–344.

Chandwani, Ashok. 1993a.* "Prime Victims of Injustice: Minority Women's Concerns Important," *Edmonton Journal*, March 8:A9.

Chandwani, Ashok. 1993b.* "Safe Haven is Overdue," *Edmonton Journal*, March 21:A11.

Chang, Jui-Shan. 1996. "What Do Education and Work Mean? Education, Nonfamilial Work/living Experiences and Premarital Sex for Women in Taiwan," *Journal of Comparative Family Studies*, 27(1,Spring):13–40.

Chao, Paul. 1977. *Women Under Communism: Family in Russia and China*. Bayside: General Hall.

Chappell, Neena L. and Audrey A. Blandford. 1987.* "Health Service Utilization by Elderly Persons," *Canadian Journal of Sociology*, 12:195–215.

Charles, Enid. 1948.* *The Changing Size of the Family in Canada*. Ottawa: The King's Printer.

Charon, Joel M. 1979. *Symbolic Interactionism* (second edition). Englewood Cliffs: Prentice-Hall.

Chawla, Raj. 1991.* "Dependency Ratios," *Canadian Social Trends*, 20:3–5.

Che-Alford, Janet and Kathryn Stevenson. 1998.* "Older Canadians on the Move," *Canadian Social Trends*, 48:15–18.

Cheal, David J. 1987.* "'Showing Them You Love Them': Gift Giving and the Dialectic of Intimacy," *The Sociological Review*, 35:150–169.

Cheal, David. 1991.* *Family and the State of Theory*. Toronto: Harvester Wheatsheaf.

Cheal, David. 1993.* "Unity and Difference in Postmodern Families," *Journal of Family Issues*, 14(1):5–19.

Cherlin, A.J. 1976. *Economics, Social Roles and Marital Separation*. Baltimore: Department of Social Relations, Johns Hopkins University.

Cherlin, A.J., F.F. Furstenberg Jr., P.L. Chase-Lansdale, K.E. Kiernan, P. K. Robins, D.R. Morrison and J.O. Teitler. 1991. "Longitudinal Studies of Effects of Divorce on Children in Great Britain and the United States," *Science*, June 7:1386–1389.

Cherlin, Andrew. 1978. "Remarriage as an Incomplete Institution," *American Journal of Sociology*, 84:634–650.

Cherlin, Andrew. 1981. *Marriage, Divorce, Remarriage: Changing Patterns in the Postwar United States*. Cambridge: Harvard University Press.

Cherlin, Andrew and James McCarthy. 1985. "Remarried Couple Households: Data from the June 1980 Current Population Survey," *Journal of Marriage and the Family*, 47:23–30.

Cherlin, Andrew J. and Frank F. Furstenberg, Jr. 1994. "Stepfamilies in the United States: A Reconsideration," *Annual Review of Sociology*, 20:359–381.

Cherlin, Andrew J. and McCarthy. 1985. "Remarried couple households: Data from the June 1980 Current Population Survey," *Journal of Marriage and the Family*, 47:23–30.

Cherlin, Andrew J., Eugenia Scabini and Givovanna Rossi. 1997. "Delayed Home Leaving in Europe and the United States," *Journal of Family Issues*, 18(6):572–575.

Chesser, Barbara J. 1980. "Analysis of Wedding Rituals: An Attempt to Make Weddings More Meaningful," *Family Relations*, 29:204–209.

Chilman, Catherine S. 1988. "Public Policies and Families in Financial Trouble," in Catherine S. Chilman, Fred M. Cox and Elam W. Nunnally (eds.). *Employment and Economic Problems: Families in Trouble Series*, Volume I. Beverly Hills: Sage, Chapter 10.

Chilman, Catherine S., Fred M. Cox and Elam W. Nunnally, (eds.). 1988. *Employment and Economic Problems: Families in Trouble Series*, Volume I. Beverly Hills: Sage.

Chiriboga, David A. and Linda S. Catron and Associates. 1991. *Divorce: Crisis, Challenge or Relief?* New York: New York University Press.

Choi, Jai-Seuk. 1978."Comparative Study on the Traditional Families in Korea, Japan and China," in Reuben Hill and Rene Konig (eds.). *Families in East and West*. Paris: Mouton, 202– 210.

Choquet, Marie, Viviane Kovess and Nathalie Poutignat. 1993.* "Suicidal Thoughts Among Adolescents: An Intercultural Approach," *Adolescence*, 28(111):649–659.

Chotalia, S. P. 1994. "Immigrant Women and the Law," *Law Now*, 19:16–19.

Chowdhury, Fakhrul and Frank Trovato. 1994.* "The Role and Status of Women and the Timing of Marriage in Five Asian Countries," *Journal of Comparative Family Studies*, 25:143–157.

Christensen, Donna Hendrickson and Kathryn D. Rettig. 1995. "The Relationship of Remarriage to Post-Divorce Co-Parenting," *Journal of Divorce and Remarriage*, 24(1/2):73–88.

Christopher, F. Scott and Rodney M. Cate. 1985. "Anticipated Influences on Sexual Decision-Making for First Intercourse," *Family Relationships*, 34:265–270.

Christopher, F. Scott, Laura A. Owens and Heidi L. Stecker. 1993. "Exploring the Darkside of Courtship: A Test of a Model Male Premarital Sexual Aggressiveness," *Journal of Marriage and the Family*, 55:469–479.

Christopher, F. Scott, Mary Madura, Lori Weaver. 1998. "Premarital Sexual Aggressors: A Multivariate Analysis of Social, Relational, and Individual Variables," *Journal of Marriage and the Family*, 60(1):56–69.

Christopher, F. Scott and Susan Sprecher. 2000. "Sexuality in Marriage, Dating, and Other Relationships: A Decade Review." *Journal of Marriage and the Family* 62: 999–1017.

Cicirelli, Victor G. 1994. "Sibling Relationships in Cross-Cultural Perspective," *Journal of Marriage and the Family*, 56(1):7–20.

Cicone, Michael V. and Diane N. Ruble. 1978. "Beliefs about Males," *Journal of Social Issues*, 34:5–16.

Clark, H., J. Chandler and J. Barry. 1996. "Work Psychology, Women and Stress: Silence, Identity and the Boundaries of Conventional Wisdom," *Work Psychology, Women and Stress*, 3(2):65–77.

Clark, Mary T. (ed.). 1984. *Augustine of Hippo, Selected Writings*. New York: Paulist Press.

Clark, R. 1973. *Ellen Swallow*. Chicago: Follett.

Clarke, Edith. 1957. *My Mother Who Fathered Me*. London: George Allen and Unwin.

Clarke, Sally Cunningham, and Barbara Foley Wilson. 1994. "The Relative Stability of Remarriages: A Cohort Approach Using Vital Statistics," *Family Relations*, 43(July):305–310.

Clarke-Stewart, A. 1987. "Predicting *Child Development* from Child Care Forms and Features: The Chicago Study," in D.A. Phillips (ed.). *Quality in Child Care: What Does Research Tell Us?* Washington: National Association for the Education of Young Children, 21–41.

Claxton-Oldfield, Stephen. 1992. "Perceptions of Stepfathers: Disciplinary and Affectionate Behavior," *Journal of Family Issues*, 13(3):378–389.

Clingempeel, W. Glenn, Eulalee Brand and Richare Levoli. 1984. "Stepparent–Stepchild Relationships in Stepmother and Stepfather Families: A Multi-Method Study," *Family Relations*, 33:465–473.

CNN. 1996. "House Votes to Bar Gay Marriages Under Federal Law," Internet: U.S. News Story Page.

Cochrane, Michael. 1991.* *The Everyday Guide to Canadian Law*. Scarborough: Prentice-Hall Canada.

Cohen, Erminie, J, the Honourable. 1997.* *Sounding the Alarm: Poverty in Canada*. Source unknown.

Cohen, Laurie L. and R. Lance Shotland. 1996. "Timing of First Sexual Intercourse in a Relationship: Expectations, Experiences, and Perceptions of Others," *The Journal of Sex Research*, 33(4):291–299.

Cohen, M. 1995.* "Paid Work," in Pierson, Ruth Roach and Marjorie Griffin Cohen. *Canadian Women's Issues: Volume II - Bold Visions*. Toronto, ON: James Lorimer and Company Publishers.

Cohen, Shaughnessy. 1984.* "Family Law in Canada," in Maureen Baker (ed.). *The Family: Changing Trends in Canada*. Toronto: McGraw-Hill Ryerson.

Colasanto, D. and J. Shriver. 1989. "Problems Plague Even Happily Wed," *Star Tribune*, May 2:1E.

Cole, P., T. Power and K.D. Smith. 1992. "Parenting Difficulties among Adult Survivors of Father–Daughter Incest," *Child Abuse and Neglect*, 16:239–249.

Coleman M. and L.H. Ganong. 1991. "Remarriage and Step-family Research in the 1980s," in A. Booth (ed.). *Contemporary Families: Looking Forward, Looking Back*. Minneapolis: National Council on Family Relations.

Coleman, Marilyn and Lawrence H. Ganong. 1991. "Remarriage and Stepfamilies: What About the Children?" *Family and Conciliation Courts Review*, 29(4):405–412.

Coleman, Marilyn and Lawrence H. Ganong. 1997. "Stepfamilies from the Stepfamily's Perspective," *Marriage and Family Review*, 26(1/2):107–121.

Collier, Jane, Michelle Z. Rosaldo and Sylvia Yanagisako. 1982. "Is There a Family? New Anthropological Views," in Barrie Thorne and Marilyn Yalom (eds.). *Rethinking the Family: Some Feminist Questions*. New York: Longman, Chapter 2.

Collins, G. 1985. "Remarriage: Bigger Ready-Made Families," *New York Times*, July 21:A14.

Collins, Jock. (1993). "Immigrant Families in Australia," *Journal of Comparative Family Studies*, 24(3):291–313.

Coltrane, S. and M. Adams. 1997. "Work–Family Imagery and Gender Stereotypes: Television and the Reproduction of Difference," *Journal of Vocational Behavior*, 50:323–347.

Coltrane, Scott. 1990. "Birth Timing and the Division of Labor in Dual-Earner Families," *Journal of Family Issues*, 11:157–118.

Coltrane, Scott and Masako Ishii-Kuntz. 1992. "Men's Housework: A Life Course Perspective," *Journal of Marriage and the Family*, 54 (1):43–58.

Conger Rand D. and Katherine J. Conger. 2002. "Resilience in Midwestern Families: Selected Findings from the First Decade of a Prospective Longitudinal Study." *Journal of Marriage and Family* 64: 361–373.

Conklin, George H. 1988. "The Influence of Economic Development on Patterns of Conjugal Power and Extended Family Residence in India," *Journal of Comparative Family Studies*, 19:187–206.

Connidis, Ingrid A. 1987.* "Life in Older Age: The View From the Top," in Victor W. Marshall (ed.). *Aging in Canada: Social Perspectives* (second edition). Markham: Fitzhenry and Whiteside.

Connidis, Ingrid A. 1989a.* "Contact Between Siblings in Later Life," *Canadian Journal of Sociology*, 14:429–442.

Connidis, Ingrid A. 2001. *Family Ties and Aging*. Thousand Oaks, CA: Sage Publications.

Connidis, Ingrid A. 1989b.* *Family Ties and Aging*. Toronto: Butterworths.

Connidis, Ingrid A. and Lori D. Campbell. 1995.* "Closeness, Confiding, and Contact Among Siblings in Middle and Late Adulthood," *Journal of Family Issues*, 16:722–745.

Connolly, Jennifer A. and Anne M. Johnson. 1996.* "Adolescents' Romantic Relationships and the Structure and Quality of Their Close Interpersonal Ties," *Personal Relationships*, 3:185–195.

Conte, Jon. 1988. "Research on the Prevention of Sexual Abuse of Children," in Gerald Hotaling et al. (eds.). *Coping with Family Violence: Research and Policy Perspectives*. Newbury Park: Sage, 300–309.

Conway, John F. 1990.* *The Canadian Family in Crisis*, Toronto: James Lorimer.

Cook, J. and J. Fonow. 1986. "Knowledge and Women's Interest: Issues of Epistemology and Methodology in Feminist Sociological Research," *Sociological Inquiry*, 56:2–29.

Cook, Karen S. and Richard M. Emerson. 1978. "Power, Equity and Commitment in Exchange Networks," *American Sociological Review*, 43:721–739.

Cooksey, Elizabeth C. and Michelle M. Fondell. 1996. "Spending Time with His Kids: Effects of Family Structure on Fathers' and Children's Lives," *Journal of Marriage and the Family*, 58(August):693–707.

Coontz, Stephanie. 1992. *The Way We Never Were: American Families and the Nostalgia Trap*. New York: Basic Books.

Corbett, D. 1997.* *Canada's Immigration Policy: A Critique*. Toronto: University of Toronto Press.

Cordón, Juan Antonio Fernández. 1997. "Youth Residential Independence and Autonomy: A Comparative Study," *Journal of Family Issues*, 18(6):576–607.

Corey, M., 1990. "When a Family Falls Apart: For Adult Children the Trauma Can Be Long-Lasting," *Baltimore Sun*, November 15, 1F, 2F.

Cornell, Arthur B. Jr. 1992.* "When Two Become One and Then Come Undone: An Organizational Approach to Marriage and Its Implications for Divorce Law," *Family Law Quarterly*, 26:103–139.

Cornille, T.A., D.R. Boronto, M.F. Barnes and P.K. Hall. 1996. "Dealing with Family Distress in Schools," *The Journal of Contemporary Human Services*, 77(7):435–445.

Corwin, Laura, A. 1977. "Caste and Class and the Love Marriage: Social Change in India," *Journal of Marriage and the Family*, 39:823–831.

Coser, Rose L. (ed.). 1964. *The Family: Its Structure and Functions*. New York: St. Martin's Press.

Counts, Dorothy Ayers, Judith K. Brown and Jacquelyn C. Campbell (eds.). 1992. *Sanctions and Sanctuary, Cultural Perspectives on the Beating of Wives*. Boulder: Westview Press.

Covell, Katherine and Rona Abramovitch. 1987. "Understanding Emotion in the Family: Children's and Parents' Attributions of Happiness, Sadness and Anger," *Child Development*, 58:985–991.

Coverman, Shelley and Joseph Sheley. 1986. "Change in Men's Housework and Child-Care Time," *Journal of Marriage and the Family*, 48:1965–1975.

Cowan, Carolyn P. and Phillip A. Cowan. 2000. *When Partners Become Parents*. New York: Erlbaum and Associates.

Cowan, Carolyn P. and Phillip A. Cowan. 1995. "Interventions to Ease the Transition to Parenthood: Why They Are Needed and What They Can Do," *Family Relations*, 44(4):412–423.

Cowan, Carolyn Pape and P.A. Cowan. 1987. "Men's Involvement in Parenthood: Identifying the Antecedents and Understanding the Barriers," in Phyllis W. Berman and Frank A. Pederson (eds.). *Men's Transitions to Parenthood: Longitudinal Studies of Early Family Experience*. Hillsdale: Lawrence Erlbaum, 145–174.

Cox, Bob. 1991.* "Date Rape Surveys Show Women Seen as 'Fair Game,'" *The Edmonton Journal*, April 16:A4.

Cox, Bob. 1992b.* "Campbell Offers Protection for Gays, Lesbians: Same-Sex Union Not Recognized," *The Edmonton Journal*, December 11:A3.

Coyne, Andrew. 1995.* "How Far Do We Take Gay Rights?" *Saturday Night*, (December):66,68–69.

Coysh, William S., Janet R. Johnston, Jeanne M. Tschann, Judith S. Wallerstein and Marsh Kline. 1989. "Parental Postdivorce Adjustment in Joint and Sole Physical Custody Families," *Journal of Family Issues*, 10:52–71.

Craig, Steve. 1992. *Men, Masculinity and the Media*. Newbury Park: Sage.

Crawford, Isiaah, and Elizabeth Solliday. 1996. "The Attitudes of Undergraduate College Students Toward Gay Parenting," *Journal of Homosexuality*, 30(4):63–77.

Crawford, M. and J. Marecek. 1989. "Psychology Reconstructs the Female: 1968–1988," *Psychology of Women Quarterly*, 13:147–165.

Crawley, Judith L. 1991.* *Giving Birth is Just the Beginning: Women Speak about Mothering*. Montreal; Book Project.

Cregheur, Alain and Mary Sue Devereaux. 1991.* "Canada's Children," *Canadian Social Trends*, Summer:2–5.

Crissman, Lawrence. 1991. "Chinese Immigrant Families in Australia: A Variety of Experiences," *Journal of Comparative Family Studies*, 22(1):25–37.

Crosbie-Burnett, Margaret and Edith A. Lewis. 1993. "Theoretical Contributions from Social, Cognitive, and Behavioral Psychology," in Pauline G. Boss, William G. Doherty, Ralph LaRossa, Walter R. Schumm and Suzanne K. Steinmetz (eds.). *Sourcebook of Family Theories and Methods: A Contextual Approach*. New York: Plenum Press, Chapter 21.

Crosbie-Burnett, Margaret and Edith A. Lewis. 1993. "Use of African-American Structures and Functioning to Address the Challenges of European-American Post-Divorce Families," *Family Relations*, 42(3):243–248.

Crosby, John F. and Nancy L. Jose. 1983. "Death: Family Adjustment to Loss," in Charles R. Figley and Hamilton I. McCubbin (eds.). *Stress and the Family*, Vol. 2. New York: Brunner and Mazel.

Crouter, A.C. 1984. "Participative Work as an Influence on Human Development," *Journal of Applied Developmental Psychology*, 5:71–90.

Crowley, M.S. 1998. "Men's Self-Perceived Adequacy as the Family Breadwinner: Implications for Their Psychological, Marital, and Work–Family Well-Being," *Journal of Family and Economic Issues*, 19(1):7–23.

Culp, Anne McDonald, Mary M. Clyman and Rex E. Culp. 1995. "Adolescent Depressed Mood, Reports of Suicide Attempts, and Asking for Help," *Adolescence*, 30(120):827–837.

Cumming, Elaine, Charles Lazer and Lynne Chisholm. 1975.* "Suicide as an Index of Role Strain Among Employed and Not Employed Married Women in British Columbia," *Canadian Review of Sociology and Anthropology*, 12:462–470.

Cummings, E.M., D. Vogel, J.S. Cummings and M. El-Sheikh. 1989. "Children's Responses to Different Forms of Expression of Anger between Adults," *Child Development*, 60:1392–1404.

Curran, Delores. 1985. *Stress and the Healthy Family*. Minneapolis: Winston Press.

Cushman, Linda F., Debra Kalmuss and Pearila B. Namerow. 1993. "Placing an Infant for Adoption: The Experiences of Young Birthmothers," *Social Work: Journal of the National Association of Social Workers*, 38(3):264–272.

Dagenais, D. 2000. *La Fin De La Famille Moderne. Signification Des Transformations Contemporaines De La Famille*. Quebec City: Presses de l' Universite Laval.

Dalhouse, Marie and James S. Frideres. 1996.* "Intergenerational Congruency: The Role of the Family in Political Attitudes of Youth," *Journal of Family Issues*, 17(2):227–248.

Daly, Kerry J. 1986.* *Reshaped Parenthood Identity: The Case of Infertile Couples Who Adopt*, unpublished manuscript, University of Guelph, Ontario.

Daly, Kerry J. 1993.* "Reshaping Fatherhood: Finding the Models," *Journal of Family Issues*, 14(4):510–530.

Daly, Kerry J. 1996.* "Spending Time with the Kids: Meanings of Family Time for Fathers," *Family Relations*, 45(4):466–476.

Daly, Kerry J. and Michael P. Sobol. 1992.* *Adoption as an Alternative for Infertile Couples: Prospects and Trends*. No. 210E. Ottawa: Royal Commission on New Reproductive Technologies.

Dasgupta, Sathl. 1992. "Conjugal Roles and Social Networks in Indian Immigrant Families: Bott revised," *Journal of Comparative Family Studies*, 23(3):465–480.

Data Releases. 1995.* *Health Reports*, Vol. 7, No. 1.

David, Deborah H. and Robert Brannon. 1976. *The Forty-Nine Percent Majority: The Male Sex Role. Reading*: Addison-Wesley.

Davies, Christine. 1988.* "Divorce and the Older Woman in Canada," 1988. *National Family Law Program*, Vol. 1:A4–1 to A-4–14. The Federation of Law Societies of Canada and the Canadian Bar Association.

Davies, Patrick T., Robin L. Myers and E. Mark Cummings. 1996. "Responses of Children and Adolescents to Marital Conflict Scenarios as a Function of the Emotionality of Conflict Endings," *Merrill-Palmer Quarterly*, 42(1):1–21.

Davies-Netzley, S.A. 1998. "Women Above the Glass Ceiling," *Gender and Society*, 12(3):339–355.

Davis, Kingsley and Wilbert E. Moore. 1945. "Some Principles of Stratification," *American Sociological Review*, 10:242–249.

Davis, Nanciellen. 1985.* *Ethnicity and Ethnic Group Persistence in an Acadian Village in the Maritimes Canada*. New York: AMS Press.

Day, Randal D. and Stephen J. Bahr. 1986. "Income Changes Following Divorce and Remarriage," *Journal of Divorce*, 9:75–87.

Day, Randal D., Gary W. Peterson and Coleen McCracken. 1998. "Predicting Spanking of Younger and Older Children by Mothers and Fathers," *Journal of Marriage and the Family*, 60(1):79–94.

de Koninck, Maria. 1991.* "Double Work and Women's Health," in Jean Veevers (ed.). *Continuity and Change in Marriage and Family*. Toronto: Holt, Rinehart and Winston.

de Man, A.F., L. Labreche-Gauthier and C.P. Leduc. 1991.* "Parental Control and Anomie in French-Canadian Adolescents," *Psychological Reports*, 69:199–200.

de Pomerai, Ralph. 1930. *Marriage: Past, Present and Future*. London: Constable.

de Ruyter, Barbara. 1976.* "Ethnic Differentials in Age at First Marriage, Canada, 1971," *Journal of Comparative Family Studies*, 7:159–166.

de Vaux, Roland. 1965. *Ancient Israel*. Volume 1: Social Institutions. Toronto: McGraw-Hill.

Deal, James E. and Karen S. Wampler. 1986. "Dating Violence: The Primacy of Previous Experience," *Journal of Social and Personal Relationships*, 3:457–471.

Deane, Herbert A. 1963. *The Political and Social Ideas of St. Augustine*. New York: Columbia University Press.

DeKeseredy, Walter. 1994.* "Addressing the Complexities of Woman Abuse in Dating: A Response to Gartner and Fox," *Canadian Journal of Sociology*, 19:75–80.

DeKeseredy, Walter and Katharine Kelley. 1995.* "Sexual Abuse in Canadian University and College Dating Relationships: The Contribution of Male Peer Support," *Journal of Family Violence*, 10:41–53.

DeKeseredy, Walter and Katharine Kelly. 1993.* "The Incidence and Prevalence of Woman Abuse in Canadian University and College Dating Relationships," *Canadian Journal of Sociology*, 18:137–159.

DeKeseredy, Walter S. 1988a.* "Woman Abuse in Dating Relationships: A Critical Evaluation of Research and Theory," *International Journal of Sociology of the Family*, 18:70–96.

DeKeseredy, Walter S. 1988b.* *Woman Abuse in Dating Relationships: The Role of Male Peer Support*. Toronto: Canadian Scholars' Press Inc.

DeKeseredy, Walter S. and Ronald Hinch. 1991.* *Woman Abuse, Sociological Perspectives*. Toronto: Thompson Educational Publishing.

DeKeseredy, Walter. 1990.* "Woman Abuse in Dating Relationships: The Contribution of Male Peer Support," *Sociological Inquiry*, 60:236–43.

DeKeseredy, Walter. 1994.* "Addressing the Complexities of Woman Abuse in Dating: A Response to Gartner and Fox," *Canadian Journal of Sociology*, 19: 75–80.

DeMan, A.F. and C.P. Leduc. 1995.* "Suicidal Ideation in High School Students: Depression and Other Correlates," *Journal of Clinical Psychology*, 51(2):173–181.

DeMaris, Alfred and K. Vaninadha Rao. 1992. "Premarital Cohabitation and Subsequent Marital Stability in the United States: A Reassessment," *Journal of Marriage and the Family*, 54:178–190.

DeMaris, Alfred and K. Vaninadha Rao. 1992. "Premarital Cohabitation and Subsequent Marital Stability in the United States: A Reassessment," *Journal of Marriage and the Family*, 54:178–190.

DeMaris, Alfred and William MacDonald. 1993. "Premarital Cohabitation and Marital Instability: A Test of the Unconventionality Hypothesis," *Journal of Marriage and the Family*, 55:399–407.

Demo, D.H. and A.C. Acock. 1991. "The Impact of Divorce on Children," in A. Booth (ed.). *Contemporary Families: Looking Forward, Looking Backward*. Minneapolis: National Council on Family Relations.

Demo, David H. 1992. "Parent–Child Relations: Assessing Recent Changes," *Journal of Marriage and the Family*, 54:104–117.

Demo, David H., Stephen A. Small and Ritch C. Savin-Williams. 1987. "*Family Relations* and the Self-Esteem of Adolescents and their Parents," *Journal of Marriage and the Family*, 49:705–715.

Demos, Vasilikie. 1994. "Marital Choice, Gender and the Reproduction of Greek Ethnicity," in V. Demos and M. Texler Segal (eds.). *Ethnic Women: A Multiple Status Reality*. New York: General Hall Inc. Pp. 82–94.

Desjardins, Bertrand and Jean Dumas. 1993.* *Population Aging and the Elderly*. Catalogue 91–533E. Ottawa: Statistics Canada.

Devadoss, T.S. 1979. *Hindu Family and Marriage: A Study of Social Institutions in India*. Madras: University of Madras Press.

Devereux, Mary Sue. 1990.* "Marital Status," in Craig McKie and Keith Thompson (eds.). *Canadian Social Trends*. Toronto: Thompson Educational Publishing.

Deverieux, Everett C. 1970. "Socialization in Cross-Cultural Perspective: Comparative Study of England, Germany and the United States," in Reuben Hill and R. Konig (eds.). *Families in East and West*. Netherlands: Mouton and Co.

Deverieux, Everett C., Urie Bronfenbrenner and R.R. Rodgers. 1969. "Child-Rearing in England and the United States: A Cross-National Comparison," *Journal of Marriage and the Family*, 31:257–270.

Dhruvarajan, Vanaja. 1988.* "Religious Ideology and Inter-Personal Relationships within the Family," *Journal of Comparative Family Studies*, 19:273–286.

Dhruvarajan, Vanaja. 1993.* Ethnic Cultural Retention and Transmission Among First Generation Hindu Asian Native Canadians in a Canadian Prairie City. *Journal of Comparative Family Studies*, 224(1):63–80.

Dion, Karen K. 1995.* "Delayed Parenthood and Women's Expectations about the Transition to Parenthood," *International Journal of Behavioral Development*, 18 (2):315–333.

Dion, Karen K. and Kenneth L. Dion, 1991.* "Psychological Individualism and Romantic Love," *Journal of Social Behavior and Personality*, 6:17–33.

Dion, Karen K. and Kenneth L. Dion. 1993.* "Individualistic and Collectivistic Perspectives on Gender and the Cultural Context of Love and Intimacy," *Journal of Family Issues*, 49:53–69.

Dion, Karen K. and Kenneth L. Dion. 1996.* "Cultural Perspectives on Romantic Love," *Personal Relationships*, 3:5–17.

Dishion, Thomas J., Deborah Capaldi, Kathleen M. Spracklen and Fuzhong Li. 1995. "Peer Rcology of Male Adolescent Drug Use," *Development and Psychopathology*, 7:803–824.

Dittus, Patricia J., James Jaccard, and Vivian V. Gordon. 1997. "The Impact of African American fathers on Adolescent Sexual Behavior," *Journal of Youth and Adolescence*, 26(4):445–465.

Dobash, R.E. and R.P. Dobash. 1980. "Wife Beating: Patriarchy and Violence Against Wives," in Open University (eds.). *Conflict in the Family*. Milton Keynes: Open University.

Dobson, James C. 1998. *October Newsletter of Focus on the Family*, October:2.

Dodoo, F. Nii-Amoo. 1998. "Marriage Type and Reproductive Decisions: A Comparative Study in Sub-Saharan Africa," *Journal of Marriage and the Family*, 60(1):232–242.

Doherty, R. LaRossa, W.R. Schumm, and S.K. Steinmetz (eds.), *Sourcebook of Family Theories and Methods*. New York: Plenum Press.

Doherty, W.J., P.G. Boss, R. LaRossa, W.R. Schumm and S.K. Steinmetz. 1993. "Family Theories and Methods: A Contextual Approach," in P.G. Boss et al., *Sourcebook of family theories and methods: A contextual approach*. New York: Plenum. Pp. 3–30.

Dollard, J., L. W. Doob, et al. 1939. *Frustration and Aggression*. New Haven: Yale University Press.

Domingo, Lita J. and Elizabeth M. King. 1992. "The Role of the Family in the Process of Entry to Marriage in Asia," in Ellza Berquó and Peter Xenos. *Family Systems and Cultural Change*. Oxford: Clarendon Press. Pp. 87–107.

Donohue, William A. 1991. *Communication, Marital Dispute and Divorce Mediation*. Hillsdale: Lawrence Erlbaum.

Dooley, Martin D. 1991.* "The Demography of Child Poverty in Canada, 1973–1986," *Canadian Studies in Population*, 18:53–74.

Dooley, Martin D. 1993.* "Recent Changes in the Economic Welfare of Lone Mother Families in Canada: The Roles of Market Work, Earnings and Transfers," in Joe Hudson and Burt Gallaway (eds.). *Single Parent Families: Perspectives on Research and Policy*. Toronto: Thompson Educational Publishing. Chapter 7.

Dooley, Martin D. 1995.* "Lone-Mother Families and Social Assistance Policy in Canada," in Richards, John and William G. Watson (eds). 1995. *Family Matters: New Policies for Divorce, Lone Mothers, and Child Poverty*. Ottawa: C.D. Howe Institute. Pp. 35–98.

Dosman, Edgar J. 1972.* *Indians: The Urban Dilemma*. Toronto: McClelland and Stewart.

Dosser, David A. Jr., Jack O. Balswick and Charles F. Halverson. 1986. "Male Inexpressiveness and Relationships," *Journal of Social and Personal Relations*, 3:241–258.

Downey, Douglas B. and Brian Powell. 1993. "Do Children in Single-Parent Households Fare Better Living with Same-Sex Parents?" *Journal of Marriage and the Family*, 55:55–71.

Downey, Maureen. 1992.* "Under Pressure to be Pretty," *The Edmonton Journal*, July 26:F2.

Downs, W.R. 1993. "Developmental Considerations for the Effects of Childhood Sexual Abuse," *Journal of Interpersonal Violence*, 8:331–345.

Doyle, Robert. 1983.* "The Making, or Unmasking, of Social Policy for the Family," in *Changing Structures of Families: Adaptation or Fragmentation*. Ottawa: Family Service Canada, 47–68.

Drachman, D. et al. 1996. "Migration and Resettlement Experiences of Dominican and Korean Families," *Families in Society: The Journal of Contemporary Human Services*, 77(10):626–638.

Draucker, C. 1995. "A Coping Model for Adult Survivors of Childhood Sexual Abuse," *Journal of Interpersonal Violence*, 10(2):159–175.

Duberman, L. 1975. *The Reconstituted Family: A Study of Remarried Couples and their Children*, Chicago: Nelson-Hall.

Duffy, Ann and Norene Pupo. 1993. *The Part-Time Paradox Connecting Gender, Work and Family*. Toronto: McClelland & Stewart.

Dumas, Jean. 1991.* *Report on the Demographic Situation in Canada 1991*, Catalogue No. 910209E. Ottawa: Statistics Canada.

Dumas, Jean and Alain Bélanger. 1997.* *Report on the Demographic Situation in Canada 1996*, Statistics Canada Catalogue 91–209–XPE.

Dumas, Jean and Yolande Lavoie. 1992.* *Report of the Demographic Situation in Canada 1992: Current Demographic Analysis*, Catalogue 91–209E. Ottawa: Statistics Canada.

Dumas, Jean and Yves Peron. 1992.* *Marriage and Conjugal Life in Canada: Current Demographic Analysis*, Statistics Canada, Catalogue 91–534E.

Dumas, Jean and Yves Péron. 1992.* *Marriage and Conjugal Life in Canada*, Ottawa: Minister of Industry, Science and Technology.

Dumas, Jean and Yves Péron. 1994. *Marriage and Conjugal Life in Canada*. Ottawa: Minister of Industry.

Duncan, Terry E., Susan C. Duncan and Hyman Hops. 1996. "The Role of Parents and Older Siblings in Predicting Adolescent Substance Use: Modeling Development via Structural Equation Latent Growth Methodology," *Journal of Family Psychology*, 10(2):158–172.

Dunn, Peter A. 1991.* "Seniors with Disabilities," *Canadian Social Trends*, 20:14–16.

Dunning, R.W. 1959.* *Social and Economic Change Among the Northern Ojibwa*. Toronto: University of Toronto Press.

Dupuis, Dave. 1998. "What Influences Peoples' Plans to Have Children?" *Canadian Social Trends*, 48:2–5.

Durkheim, Emile. 1960. *The Division of Labor in Society*. New York: The Free Press.

Dutton, D.G., A.N. Webb and L. Ryan. 1994.* "Gender Differences in Anger: Anxiety Reactions to Witnessing Dyadic Family Conflict," *Canadian Journal of Behavioural Science*, 26(3):353–363.

Dutton, Donald G. 1986a.* "The Outcome of Court-Mandated Treatment for Wife Assault: A Quasi-Experimental Evaluation," *Violence and Victims*, 1:163–175.

Dutton, Donald G. 1986b.* "Wife Assaulters' Explanations for Assault: The Neutralization of Self-punishment," *Canadian Journal of Behavioural Science*, 18:381–390.

Dutton, Donald G., Stephen D. Hart, Leslie W. Kennedy and Kirk R. Williams. 1990.* "Arrest and the Reduction of Repeat Wife Assault," in E. Buzawa (ed.). *Domestic Violence*. Newbury Park: Sage.

Duvall, Evelyn M. and Brent C. Miller. 1985. *Marriage and Family Development* (sixth Edition). New York: Harper and Row.

East, Patricia L. 1996. "Do Adolescent Pregnancy and Childbearing Affect Younger Siblings?" *Family Plannine Perspectives*, 28(4):148–153.

Ebomoyi, E.W., N.E. Bissonette and O.M. Ukaga. 1998. "Campus Courtship Behaviour and Fear of Human Immunodeficiency Virus Infection by University Students," *Journal of the National Medical Association*, 90:395–399.

Economic Council of Canada. 1992.* *The New Face of Poverty, Income Security Needs of Canadian Families.*

Catalogue No. EC22–186/1992E. Ottawa: Supply and Services Canada.

Eddinger, Elizabeth. Personal communication, July 3, 2003.

Edleson, Jeffrey L. 1990. "Judging the Success Of Interventions With Men Who Batter," in Douglas J. Besharov (ed.). *Family Violence: Research and Public Policy Issues*. Washington: The AEI Press.

Edmonton Journal, 1990.* "Survey Unveils Which Women are Most Stressed Out," May 24:B9.

Edmonton Journal. 1992a.* "Violence and the Canadian Family: The Facts," December 5:A3.

Edmonton Journal. 1992b.* "What Happened to the Family: Changes are Radical, But It Survives," November 8:A1.

Edmonton Journal. 1992c.* "Experts Blame Recession for Hike in Child Abuse," December 20:D11.

Edmonton Journal. 1992.* "Average Mother Older as Birth Rate Rises Again," March 31:A3.

Edwards, P. 1986. "Smoking: A Feminist Issue," *Health Sharing*, Summer:8–12.

Eekelaar, John and Sanford W. Katz (eds.). 1980.* *Marriage and Cohabitation in Contemporary Societies*. Toronto: Butterworths.

Ehrhardt, Anke A. and Heino F.L. Meyer-Bahlberg. 1981. "Effects of Prenatal Sex Hormones on Gender-Related Behavior," *Science*, 211:1312–1318.

Ehrhardt, Anke A., Christiana Nöstliner, Heino F.L. Meyer-Bahlurg, Theresa M. Exner, Rhoda S. Gruen, Sandra L. Yingling, Jack M. Gorman, Wafaa El-Sadr and Stephan J. Sorrell. 1995. "Sexual Risk Behavior Among Women with Injected Drug Use Histories," *Journal of Psychology and Human Sexuality*, 7(1–2):99–119.

Eichler, Margrit. 1983.* *Families in Canada Today: Recent Changes and their Policy Consequences*. Toronto: Gage.

Eichler, Margrit. 1988.* *Families in Canada Today: Recent Changes and their Policy Consequences*. Toronto: Gage.

Eichler, Margrit. 1993.* "Lone-Parent Families: An Instable Category in Search of Stable Policies," in Joe Hudson and Burt Galaway (eds.). *Single Parent Families: Perspectives on Research and Policy*. Toronto: Thompson Educational Publishing, Chapter 9.

Einstein, Elizabeth. 1979. "Stepfamily Lives," *Human Behavior*, 8:62–68.

Elder, G.H. Jr., A. Caspi and G. Downery. 1986. "Problem Behavior and Family Relationships: A Multi-generational Analysis," in A. Sorensen, F. Weinert, and L. Sherrod (eds.). *Human Development and the Life Course: Multidisciplinary Perspectives*. Hillsdale: Lawrence Erlbaum.

Elias, Marilyn. 1989. "Parents' Divorce Affects Sex Lives of Collegians," *USA Today*, November 8:D1.

Elliot, P. 1996. "Shattering Illusions: Same-Sex Domestic Violence," *Journal of Gay and Lesbian Social Services*, 4(1):1–8.

Ellis, H. Havelock. 1937. *Sex in Relationship to Society*. New York: Random House.

Emery, R.E. 1982. "Interparental Conflict and the Children of Discord and Divorce," *Psychological Bulletin*, 92:310–330.

Engman, Kathleen. 1990.* "Raising Family a 91-Hour Job at Basic Wage: Welfare Pays Single Mom More— Study," *Edmonton Journal*, July 15:A1.

Ennew, Judith. 1986. *The Sexual Exploitation of Children*. Cambridge: Polity Press.

Erera-Weatherley, Pauline I. 1996. "On Becoming a Stepparent: Factors Associated with the Adoption of Alternative Stepparenting Styles," *Journal of Divorce and Remarriage*, 25(3/4):155–174.

Erikson, Erik H. 1963. *Childhood and Society* (second edition). New York: Norton.

Erikson, Erik H. 1982. *The Life Cycle Completed: A Review*. New York: W. W. Norton.

Erlanger, Howard S. 1974. "Social Class Differences in Parents' Use of Physical Punishment," in Suzanne K. Steinmetz and Murray A. Straus (eds.). *Violence in the Family*. New York: Dodd, Mead and Co.

Errington, Jane. 1988.* "Pioneers and Suffragists," in Sandra Burt, Lorraine Code and Lindsay Dorner (eds.). *Changing Patterns: Women in Canada*. Toronto: McClelland and Stewart.

Espiritu, Yen, Le. 1997. *Asian American Women and Men*. California: Sage Publications.

Eversley, David. 1983. "The Family and Housing Policy: The Interaction of the Family, the Household and the Housing Market," in *The Family, British Society for Population Studies*, Occasional Paper No. 31. London: Office of Population Censuses and Surveys, 82–95.

Fabes, Richard A. and Erik E. Filsinger. 1988. "Odour Communication and Parent–Child Interaction," in Erik E. Filsinger (ed.). *Biosocial Perspectives on the Family*. Newbury Park: Sage, Chapter 4.

Fagan, Jeffrey. 1988. "Desistance from Family Violence: Deterrence and Dissuasion," in M. Tonry and L. Ohlin (eds.). *Crime and Justice: An Annual Review of Research*. Chicago: University of Chicago Press.

Fagan, Jeffrey. 1990. "Contributions of Research on Criminal Justice Policy on Wife Assault," in Douglas J. Besharov (ed.). *Family Violence: Research and Public Policy Issues*. Washington: The AEI Press.

Faller, K. 1989. "Why Sexual Abuse? An Exploration of the Intergenerational Hypothesis," *Child Abuse and Neglect*, 13:543–548.

Faller, K.C. 1989. "Characteristics of a Clinical Sample of Sexually Abused Children: How Boy and Girl Victims Differ," *Child Abuse and Neglect*, 13:281–291.

Farber, R. S. 1996. "An Integrated Perspective on Women's Career Development Within a Family," *American Journal of Family Therapy*, 24(4):329–342.

Farkas, J. I. and A. M. O'Rand. 1998. "The Pension Mix for Women in Middle and Late Life: The Changing Employment Relationship," *Social Forces*, 76(3):1007–32.

Farley, N. 1996. "A Survey of Factors Contributing to Gay and Lesbian Domestic Violence," *Journal of Gay and Lesbian Social Services*, 4(1):35–42.

Farrington, Keith and Ely Chertok. 1993. "Social Conflict Theories of the Family," in Pauline G. Boss, William G. Doherty, Ralph LaRossa, Walter R. Schumm and Suzanne K. Steinmetz (eds.). *Sourcebook of Family Theories and Methods*: A Contextual Approach. New York: Plenum Press, Chapter 15.

Fassel, D. 1991. *Growing Up Divorced: A Road to Healing for Children of Divorce*. New York: Pocket Books.

Fast, J. and J. Frederick. 1996.* "Working Arrangements and Time Stress. *Canadian Social Trends*, 43(Winter):14–19.

Fast, Janet and Moreno Da Pont. 1997.* "Changes in Women's Work Continuity," *Canadian Social Trends*, Autumn:2–7.

Faulder, Liane and Marina Jimenez. 1992.* "Tilting the Playing Field," *The Edmonton Journal*, November 21:D1, D2.

Faulder, Liane. 1992.* "Teenage Girls and their Crisis of Self-Confidence," *The Edmonton Journal*, November 21:A1, A9.

Federico, J. 1979. "The Marital Termination Period of the Divorce Adjustment Process," *Journal of Divorce*, 3:93–106.

Feeney, Judith. 2002. *Becoming Parents: Exploring the Bonds between Mothers, Fathers, and Their Infants*. New York: Cambridge University Press.

Fehr, Beverley. 1988.* "Prototype Analysis of the Concepts of Love and Commitment," *Journal of Personality and Social Psychology*, 55:557–579.

Fehr, Beverley. 1994.* "Prototype-Based Assessment of Laypeople's Views of Love," *Personal Relationships*, 1:309–331.

Feinhauer, L. and D. Stuart. 1996. "Blame and Resilience in Women Sexually Abused as Children," *The American Journal of Family Therapy*, 24(1):31–40.

Feinhauer, L., H. Callahan and H.G. Hilton. 1996. "Positive Intimate Relationships Decrease Depression in Sexually Abused Women," *The American Journal of Family Therapy*, 24(2):99–105.

Feiring, C., L. Taska and M. Lewis. 1996. "A Process Model for Understanding Adaptation to Sexual Abuse: The Role of Shame in Defining Stigmatization," *Child Abuse and Neglect*, 20(8):767–782.

Feldman, Harold. 1971. "The Effects of Children on the Family," in Andree Michel (ed.). *Issues of Employed Women in Europe and America*. Leiden, Netherlands: E.G. Brill.

Felmlee, Diane H. 1984. "A Dynamic Analysis of Women's Employment Exits," *Demography*, 21:171–183.

Felt, Lawrence F. and Peter R. Sinclair. 1991.* "Home Sweet Home!: Dimensions and Determinants of Life Satisfaction in an Underprivileged Region," *Canadian Journal of Sociology*, 16:1–21.

Fengler, Alfred P. 1974. "Romantic Love in Courtship: Divergent Paths of Male and Female Students," *Journal of Comparative Family Studies*, 5:134–139.

Ferree, Myra M. 1990. "Beyond Separate Spheres: Feminism and Family Research," *Journal of Marriage and the Family*, 52:866–884.

Ferreiro, Beverly W. 1990. "Presumption of Joint Custody: A Family Policy Dilemma," *Family Relations*, 39:420–426.

Figley, Charles R. 1983. "Catastrophes: An Overview of Family Reactions," in Charles R. Figley and Hamilton I. McCubbin (eds.). *Stress and the Family, Vol. 2: Coping With Catastrophe*. New York: Brunner and Mazel.

Filsinger, Erik E. 1988. (ed.). *Biosocial Perspectives on the Family*. Newbury Park: Sage.

Fine, Mark A. 1986. "Perceptions of Stepparents: Variation in Stereotypes as a Function of Current Family Structure," *Journal of Marriage and the Family*, 48:537–543.

Fine, Mark A. 1992. "Families in the United States: Their Current and Future Prospects," *Family Relations*, 41:430–435.

Fine, Mark A. 1993. "Current Approaches to Understanding Family Diversity: An Overview of the Special Issue," *Family Relations*, 42(3):235–237.

Fine, Mark A. and Lawrence A. Kurdek. 1995. "Relation Between Marital Quality and (Step)parent–Child Relationship Quality for Parents and Stepparents in Stepfamilies," *Journal of Family Psychology*, 9(2):216–223.

Fine, Mark A., and David R. Fine. 1992. "Recent Changes in Laws Affecting Stepfamilies: Suggestions for Legal Reform," *Family Relations*, 41(July):334–340.

Fine, Mark A., Patricia Voydanoff and Brenda W. Donnelly. 1993. "Relations Between Parental Control and Warmth and Child Well-Being in Stepfamilies," *Journal of Family Psychology*, 7(2):222–232.

Finkelhor, D., D. Moore, S. Hamby and M. Straus. 1997. "Sexually Abused Children in a National Survey of Parents: Methodological Issues," *Child Abuse and Neglect*, 21(1):1–9.

Finkelhor, David. 1979. *Sexually Victimized Children*. New York: The Free Press.

Finkelhor, David. 1983. "Common Features of Family Abuse," in David Finkelhor, Richard J. Gelles, Gerald T. Hotaling and Murray A. Straus (eds.). *The Dark Side of Families: Current Family Violence Research*. Beverly Hills: Sage.

Finkelhor, David. 1984. *Child Sexual Abuse*. New York: The Free Press.

Finkelhor, David and Angela Browne. 1988. "Assessing the Long-Term Impact of Child Sexual Abuse: A Review and Conceptualization," in Gerald T. Hotaling, David Finkelhor, John T. Kirkpatrick and Murray A. Straus (eds.). *Family Abuse and Its Consequences: New Directions in Research*. Newbury Park: Sage.

Finkelhor, David and Kersti Yllo, 1983. "Rape in Marriage: A Sociological View," in David Finkelhor, Richard J. Gelles, Gerald T. Hotaling and Murray A. Straus (eds.). *The Dark Side of Families: Current Family Violence Research*. Beverly Hills: Sage.

Finkelhor, David and Larry Baron. 1986. "High-Risk Children," in David Finkelhor (ed.). *Source Book on Child Sexual Abuse*. Beverly Hills: Sage.

Finnie, Ross. 1993.* "Women, Men and the Economic Consequences of Divorce: Evidence from Canadian Longitudinal Data," *Canadian Review of Sociology and Anthropology*, 30:204–241.

Firestone, S. 1970. *The Dialectic of Sex*. New York: William Morrow.

Fischbach, R. and B. Herbert. 1997. "Domestic Violence and Mental Health: Correlates and Conundrums Within and Across Cultures," *Social Sciences and Medicine*, 45(8):1161–1176.

Fischer, Doug. 1993. "Poverty Spending Criticized; UN Report Chides Canada," *Edmonton Journal*, May 29:A1.

Fitzpatrick, Mary Anne. 1988a. "Approaches to Marital Interaction," in Patricia Noller and Mary A. Fitzpatrick. *Perspectives on Marital Interaction*. Philadelphia: Multilingual Matters Ltd., 1–28.

Fitzpatrick, Mary Anne. 1988b. "A Typological Approach to Marital Interaction," in Patricia Noller and Mary A. Fitzpatrick. *Perspectives in Marital Interaction*. Philadelphia: Multilingual Matters Ltd., 98–120.

Fitzpatrick, Mary Anne. 1988c. *Between Husbands and Wives: Communication in Marriage*. Newbury Park: Sage.

Fitzpatrick, Mary Anne and D. Badzinsky. 1985. "All in the Family: Communication in Kin Relationships," in M.L. Knapp and G.R. Miller (eds.). *Handbook of Interpersonal Communication*. Beverly Hills: Sage.

Fleischmann K. 1974. "Marriage by Contract: Defining the Terms of Relationship," *Family Law Quarterly*, 8:44.

Fleming, Alison S., Gordon L. Flett, Diane N. Ruble and Vicki Van Wagner. 1990.* "Adjustment in First-time

Mothers: Changes in Mood and Mood Content During the Early Postpartum Months," *Developmental Psychology*, 26:137–143.

Fleming, Jillian, Paul Mullen and Gabriele Bammer. 1997. "A Study of Potential Risk Factors for Sexual Abuse in Childhood," *Child Abuse and Neglect* 21(1):49–58.

Flewelling, Robert L. and Karl E. Bauman. 1990. "Family Structure as a Predictor of Initial Substance Use and Sexual Intercourse in Early Adolescence," *Journal of Marriage and the Family*, 52:171–181.

Focus. 1993.* "Immigrant Women: Overcoming Abuse in a New Country," Winter: 1.

Follingstad, Diane R., Shannon Wright, Shirley Lloyd and Jeri A. Sebastion. 1991. "Sex Differences in Motivations and Effects in Dating Violence," *Family Relations*, 40:51–57.

Foo, Louise and Gayla Margolin. "A Multivariate Investigation of Dating Aggression," *Journal of Family Violence*, 10:351–377.

Foote, David K. 1982.* *Canada's Population Outlook: Demographic Futures and Economic Challenges*. Toronto: James Lorimer.

Foote, David K. and Daniel Stoffman. 1996.* "The Grey Interlude," *Transition*, September:14–15.

Ford, Clellan S. and Frank A. Beach. 1951. *Patterns of Sexual Behaviour*. New York: Harper and Row.

Ford, David A. 1991. "Preventing and Provoking Wife Battery through Criminal Sanctions: A Look at the Risks," in Dean D. Knudsen and JoAnn L. Miller (eds.). *Abused and Battered, Social and Legal Responses to Family Violence*. New York: Aldine de Gruyter.

Ford, David and François Nault. 1996. "Changing Fertility Patterns, 1974 to 1994," *Health Reports*, Vol. 8, No. 3:39–46.

Ford, Donna Y. 1994. "An Exploration of Perceptions of Alternative Family Structures Among University Students," *Family Relations*, 43(1):68–73.

Forste, Renata and Koray Tanfer. 1996. "Sexual Exclusivity Among Dating, Cohabiting, and Married Women," *Journal of Marriage and the Family*, 58(1):33–47.

Fortin, Gerald. 1968.* "Woman's Role in the Evolution of Agriculture in Quebec," in *The Family in the Evolution of Agriculture*. Ottawa: The Vanier Institute of the Family.

Foster, E. Michael, Damon Jones and Saul D. Hoffman. 1998. "The Economic Impact of Nonmarital Childbearing: How Are Older, Single Mothers Faring?" *Journal of Marriage and the Family*, 60(1):163–174.

Fouad, N.A. and H.E.A. Tinsley. 1997. "Work–Family Balance," *Journal of Vocational Behavior*, 50(2):141–144.

Fowler, Nancy Ann. 1993.* "Stages Through Which a Stepmom Passes in Developing a Mutually Suitable Relationship With Her Stepdaughter," unpublished Master of Education thesis, University of Alberta, Edmonton.

Fox, Bonnie. 1980.* "Women's Double Work Day: Twentieth-Century Changes in the Reproduction of Daily Life," in Fox, Bonnie. (ed.). *Hidden in the Household*. Toronto: Women's Press.

Fox, Greer, L. 1980. "The Mother–Adolescent Daughter Relationship as a Sexual Socialization Structure: A Research Review," *Family Relations*, 29:21–28.

Fox, Greer L. and Judith K. Inazu. 1980. "Patterns and Outcomes of Mother–Daughter Communication About Sexuality," *Journal of Social Issues*, 36:7–29.

Fraiberg, Selma. 1977. *Every Child's Birthright: In Defense of Mothering*. New York: Basic Books.

Francis, Lesley. 1990.* "Growing Pains," *The Edmonton Journal*, December 8:B8.

Francis, Lesley. 1992.* "Teens Happy to Hang Out but They Don't Date," *The Edmonton Journal*, April 27:A1, A2.

Frank, Jeffrey. 1996.* "15 Years of AIDS in Canada," *Canadian Social Trends*, 41:4–10.

Frankel, B. Gail and David J. DeWit. 1989.* "Geographic Distance and Intergenerational Contact: An Empirical Examination of the Relationship," *Journal of Aging Studies*, 3:139–162.

Franklin, Cynthia, Darlene Grant, Jacqueline Corcoran, Pamela O'Dell Miller and Linda Bultman. 1997. "Effectiveness of Prevention Programs for Adolescent Pregnancy: A Meta-Analysis," *Journal of Marriage and the Family*, 59(3):551–567.

Frederick, J. 1995.* *As Time Goes By: Time Use of Canadians*. Ottawa: Statistics Canada.

Freud, Sigmund. 1965. *New Introductory Lectures on Psychoanalysis*. New York: W.W. Norton.

Frideres, James S. 1974.* *Canada's Indians: Contemporary Conflicts*. Scarborough: Prentice-Hall Canada.

Frideres, James S. 1993.* *Native Peoples in Canada, Contemporary Conflicts*. (fourth edition). Scarborough: Prentice-Hall Canada.

Friedan, Betty. 1963. *The Feminine Mystique*. New York: W.W. Norton.

Friedan, Betty. 1981. *The Second Stage*. New York: Summit Books.

Friedrich, W., T. Jaworski, J. Huxsahl and B. Bengtson. 1997. "Dissociative and Sexual Behaviors in Children and Adolescents with Sexual Abuse and Psychiatric Histories," *Journal of Interpersonal Violence*, 12(2):155–171.

Fromm, Erich. 1956. *The Art of Loving*. New York: Harper.

Frum, David. 1995.* "How Far Do We Take Gay Rights?" *Saturday Night* (December):67, 69–70, 72–73.

Fu, Haishan and Noreen Goldman. 1996. "Incorporating Health into Models of Marriage Choice: Demographic and Sociological Perspectives," *Journal of Marriage and the Family*, 58:740–758.

Fuchs, Victor R. 1991. "Are Americans Under-Investing in their Children?" *Society*, 28(6):14–22.

Fulton, E. Kaye. 1993.* "Babies Having Babies: Teenage Mothers Face a Bleak Future," *Maclean's*, February 22:32–33.

Fulton. 1993. "When Young Girls Have Babies." *Maclean's*, pp 32–33.

Furstenberg, Frank F. Jr. 1987. "The New Extended Family: The Experience of Parents and Children after Remarriage," in Kay Pasley and Marilyn Ihinger-Tallman (eds.). *Remarriage and Stepparenting: Current Research and Theory*. New York: Guilford Press. (Chapter 16.)

Furstenberg, Frank F. Jr. and Andrew J. Cherlin. 1991. *Divided Families: What Happens to Children When Parents Part?* Cambridge: Harvard University Press.

Furstenberg, Frank F. Jr. and Graham B. Spanier. 1984. *Recycling the Family: Remarriage After Divorce*. Beverly Hills: Sage.

Furstenberg, Frank F. Jr., S. Philip Morgan and Paul D. Allison. 1987. "Paternal Participation and Children's Well-Being After Marital Dissolution," *American Sociological Review*, 52:695–701.

Health Quarterly. 1992. Public Broadcasting System, January 5, 1993.

Gable, Sara, Jay Belsky and Keith Crnic. 1992. "Marriage, Parenting and *Child Development*: Progress and Prospects," *Journal of Family Psychology*, 5:276–295.

Gaffield, Chad. 1982.* "Schooling, The Economy and Rural Society in Ninteenth-Century Ontario," in Joy Parr (ed.). *Childhood and Family in Canadian History*. Toronto: McClelland and Stewart.

Gaffield, Chad. 1990.* "The Social and Economic Origins of Contemporary Families," in Maureen Baker (ed.). *Families: Changing Trends in Canada* (second edition). Toronto: McGraw-Hill Ryerson, Chapter 2.

Galambos, Nancy L. and David M. Almeida. 1992.* "Does Parent–Adolescent Conflict Increase in Early Adolescence?" *Journal of Marriage and the Family*, 54:737–747.

Galambos, Nancy L., Heather A. Sears, David M. Almeida and Giselle C. Kolaric. 1995.* "Parents' Work Overload and Problem Behavior in Young Adolescents," *Journal of Research on Adolescence*, 5(2):201–223.

Gallagher, Maggie. 1996. "Re-creating Marriage," in Popenoe, David, Jean Bethke Elshtain and David Blankenhorn. *Promises to Keep: Decline and Renewal of Marriage in America*. Lanham, Maryland: Rowman and Littlefield. Chapter 10.

Galland, Oliver. 1997. "Leaving Home and Family Relations in France," *Journal of Family Issues*, 18(6):645–670.

Galligan, Richard. 1982. "Innovative Techniques in Studying Marriage and the Family: Siren or Rose?" *Journal of Marriage and the Family*, 44:875–888.

Gallup Report. 1988a. October 2.

Gallup Report. 1988b. October 13.

Gallup Report. 1988c. November 3.

Gannagé, Charlene. 1987.* "A World of Difference: The Case of Women Workers in a Canadian Garment Factory," in Heather Jon Maroney and Meg Luxton (eds.). *Feminism and Political Economy, Women's Work, Women's Struggles*. Toronto: Methuen.

Ganong, Lawrence and Marilyn Coleman. 1993. "An Exploratory Study of Stepsibling Subsystems," *Journal of Divorce and Remarriage*, 19(3/4):125–141.

Ganong, Lawrence H. and Marilyn Coleman. 1988. "Do Mutual Children Cement Bonds in Stepfamilies?" *Journal of Marriage and the Family*, 50:699–708.

Ganong, Lawrence H. and Marilyn Coleman. 1989. "Preparing for Remarriage: Anticipating the Issues, Seeking Solutions," *Family Relations*, 38:28–33.

Ganong, Lawrence H. and Marilyn Coleman. 1997. "How Society Views Stepfamilies," *Marriage and Family Review*, 26(1/2):85–106.

Ganong, Lawrence H., Marilyn Coleman and Deborah Mistina. 1995. "Normative Beliefs About Parents' and Stepparents' Financial Obligations to Children Following Divorce and Remarriage," *Family Relations*, 44(July):306–315.

Ganong, Lawrence, Marilyn Coleman, Mark Fine and Annette Kusgen McDaniel. 1998. "Issues in Contemplating Stepchild Adoption," *Family Relations*, 47(1):63–71.

Garbarino, J., and D. Sherman. 1980. "High-Risk Neighborhoods and High-Risk Families: The Human Ecology of Child Maltreatment," *Child Development*, 51:188–198.

Garbarino, James. 1985. "The Role of Social Policy in the Health and Welfare of Young Children," *Journal of Child Care*, 3:1–13.

Garbarino, James. 1988. *The Future as if It Really Mattered*. Longmont: Bookmakers Guild.

Garbarino, James. 1989. "Plenary Presentation," in *A Symposium About Families, Volume I. Speakers' Papers*. Regina: Government of Saskatchewan, 28–43.

Garbarino, James, Cynthia Schellenbach and Janet Sebes. 1986b. *Troubled Youth, Troubled Families: Understanding Families At-Risk for Adolescent Maltreatment*. New York: Aldine.

Garbarino, James, Edna Guttmann and Janis Seeley. 1986a. *The Psychologically Battered Child*. San Francisco: Jossey-Bass.

Garbarino, James, Frances M. Stott and the Faculty of the Erikson Institute. 1989. *What Children Can Tell Us: Eliciting, Interpreting and Evaluating Information from Children*. San Francisco: Jossey-Bass.

Garenne, M. and E. van de Walle. 1989. "Polygyny and Fertility Among the Sereer of Senegal," *Population Studies*, 43:267–283.

Garfinkel, Irwin and Donald Oellerich. 1989. "Noncustodial Fathers' Ability to Pay Child Support," *Demography*, 26:219–233.

Garigue, Philippe. 1960.* "The French Canadian Family," in Mason Wade (ed.). *Canadian Dualism—La dualité canadienne*. Toronto: University of Toronto Press.

Garigue, Philippe. 1980.* "French Canadian Kinship and Family Life," in K. Ishwaran (ed.). *Canadian Families: Ethnic Variations*. Toronto: McGraw-Hill Ryerson.

Gartrell, Nanette, Jean Hamilton, Amy Banks, Dee Mosbacher, Nancy Reed, Caroline H. Sparks and Holly Bishop. 1996. "The National Lesbian Family Study: 1. Interviews with prospective mothers," *American Journal of Orthopsychiatry*, 66(2):272–281.

Gaskell, Jane. 1983.* "The Reproduction of Family Life: Perspectives of Male and Female Adolescents," *British Journal of Sociology of Education*, 4:19–38.

Gaudin, J., N. Polansky, A. Kilpatrick and P. Shilton. 1996. "Family Functioning in Neglectful Families," *Child Abuse and Neglect*, 20(4):363–377.

Gecas, Viktor and Monica Seff. 1990. "Families and Adolescents: A Review of the 1980s," *Journal of Marriage and the Family*, 52:941–958.

Gee, E.M. 1986.* "The Life Course of Canadian Women: An Historical and Demographic Analysis," *Social Indicators Research*, 18:263–283.

Gee, Ellen M. 1982.* "Marriage in Ninteenth Century Canada," *Canadian Review of Sociology and Anthropology*, 19:311–325.

Gee, Ellen M. 1987.* "Historical Change in the Family Life Course of Canadian Men and Women," in Victor W. Marshall (ed.). *Aging In Canada*. Markham: Fitzhenry and Whiteside.

Gee, Ellen M. and Susan A. McDaniel. 1991.* "Pension Politics and Challenges: Retirement Policy Implications," *Canadian Public Policy — Analyse de Politiques*, 17:456–472.

Gee, Ellen M. and Susan A. McDaniel. 1992.* "Social Policy for an Aging Society," *Journal of Canadian Studies*, 27:3.

Gee, Ellen M.T. 1980.* "Female Marriage Patterns in Canada: Changes and Differentials," *Journal of Comparative Family Studies*, 11:457–473.

Gelles, R. and J. Conte. 1990. "Domestic Violence and Sexual Abuse of Children: A Review of Research in the Eighties," *Journal of Marriage and the Family*, 52:1045–1058.

Gelles, R.J. and J.R. Conte. 1991. "Domestic Violence and Sexual Abuse of Children," in Alan Booth (ed.). Contemporary Families: Looking Forward, Looking Back. Minneapolis: National Council on Family Relations, 326–340.

Gelles, Richard. 1979. *Family Violence*. London: Sage.

Gelles, Richard. 1983. "An Exchange/Social Theory," in David Finkelhor, Richard J. Gelles, Gerald T. Hotaling and Murray J. Straus (eds.). *The Dark Side of Families*. Beverly Hills: Sage.

Gelles, Richard J. 1973. "Child Abuse as Psychopathology: A Sociological Critique and Reformulation," *American Journal of Orthopsychiatry*, 43: 611–621.

Gelles, Richard J. and Murray A. Straus. 1988. *Intimate Violence*. New York, Simon and Schuster.

Gentleman, Jane F. and Evelyn Park. 1994.* "Age Differences of Married and Divorcing Couples," *Health Reports*, 6:225–240.

Gentleman, Jane F. and Evelyn Park. 1997. "Divorce in the 1990s," *Health Reports*, Vol. 9, No. 2:53–58.

Genuis, Stephen. 1991.* *Risky Sex*. Edmonton: KEG Publishing.

George, V. and P. Wilding. 1972. *Motherless Families*. London: Routledge and Kegan Paul.

Gerin, L. (1932). "The French-Canadian Family: It's Strengths and Weaknesses." *Revue Trimestrielle Canadienne* 19, 37–63. In M. Rioux and Y. Martin (Eds./ Trans.) (1964). *French Canadian Society*. Ottawa: Carleton Library No. 18/ McClelland and Stewart.

Gerstel, N. 1987. "Divorce and Stigma," *Social Problems*, 34:172–186.

Gfellner, Barbara M. 1990.* "Culture and Consistency in Ideal and Actual Child-Rearing Practices: A Study of Canadian Indian and White Parents," *Journal of Comparative Family Studies*, 21:413–423.

Ghalam, Nancy Zukewich. 1996.* "Living with Relatives," *Canadian Social Trends*, Autumn:20–24.

Gibbs, N. 1991. "The Clamor on Campus: When is it Rape?" *Time*, June 3:48–54.

Gibbs, Nancy. 1993. "How Should We Teach Our Children About Sex?" *Time*. May 24:50–56.

Gies, Frances and Joseph Gies. 1987. *Marriage and the Family in the Middle Ages*. New York: Harper and Row.

Gil, David G. 1970. *Violence Against Children*. Cambridge: Harvard University Press.

Gilbert, Lucia A. 1988. *Sharing It All: The Rewards and Struggles of Two-Career Families*. New York: Plenum Press.

Gilbert, Shirley L. 1976. "Self-Disclosure, Intimacy and Communication in Families," *The Family Coordinator*, 25:221–231.

Giles-Sims, J. and M. Crosbie-Burnet. 1989. "Adolescent Power in Stepfather Families: A Test of Normative-Resource Theory," *Journal of Marriage and the Family*, 51:165–178.

Giles-Sims, Jean. 1997. "Current Knowledge About Child Abuse in Stepfamilies," *Marriage and Family Review*, 26(3/4):215–230.

Gill, Dhara S. and Bennett Mathews. 1995. "Changes in the Breadwinner Role: Punjabi Families in Transition," *Journal of Comparative Family Studies*, 26(2):255–263.

Gilligan, Carol. 1982. *In a Different Voice: Psychological Theory and Women's Development*. Cambridge: Harvard University Press.

Gillmore, Mary Rogers, Steven M. Lewis, Mary Jane Lohr, Michael S. Spencer and Rachelle D. White. 1997. "Repeat Pregnancies Among Adolescent Mothers," *Journal of Marriage and the Family*, 59(3):536–550.

Gilmour, R. and S. Duck (eds.). 1986. *The Emerging Field of Personal Relationships*. Hillsdale: Lawrence Erlbaum.

Givens, Benjamin P. and Charles Hirschman. 1994. "Modernization and Consanguineous Marriage in Iran," *Journal of Marriage and the Family*, 56(4):820–834.

Glaser, B.G. 1978. *Theoretical Sensitivity*. Hill Valley: Sociology Press.

Glass, J. and L. Riley. 1998. "Family Responsive Policies and Employee Retention Following Childbirth," *Social Forces*, 76(4):1401–1435.

Glass, Jennifer. 1992. "Housewives and Employed Wives: Demographic and Attitudinal Change, 1972–1986," *Journal of Marriage and the Family*, 54:559–569.

Glenn, E.N. 1983. "Split Household, Small Producer and Dual Wage Earner: An Analysis of Chinese-American Family Strategies," *Journal of Marriage and the Family*, 45:35–46.

Glenn, N.D. 1991. "Qualitative Research on Marital Quality in the 1980s," in A. Booth (ed.). *Contemporary Families: Looking Forward, Looking Backward*. Minneapolis: National Council on *Family Relations*.

Glenn, N.D. and K.B. Kramer. 1987. "The Marriages and Divorces of Children of Divorce," *Journal of Marriage and the Family*, 49:811–825.

Glenn, Norval. 1991. "The Recent Trend in Marital Success in the United States," *Journal of Marriage and the Family*, 53:261–270.

Glenn, Norval. 1993. "A Plea for Objective Assessment of the Notion of Family Decline," *Journal of Marriage and the Family*, 55:542–544.

Glenn, Norval D. (ed.). 1987. "The State of the American Family," special issue of *Journal of Family Issues*, 7:347–476.

Glenn, Norval D. 1975. "The Contribution of Marriage to the Psychological Well-Being of Males and Females," *Journal of Marriage and the Family*, 37:594–600.

Glenn, Norval D. 1990. "Quantitative Research on Marital Quality in the 1980s: A Critical Review," *Journal of Marriage and the Family*, 52:818–831.

Glenn, Norval D. 1996. "Values, Attitudes, and the State of American Marriage," in Popenoe, David, Jean Bethke Elshtain, and David Blankenhorn. *Promises to Keep: Decline and Renewal of Marriage in America*. Lanham, Maryland: Rowman and Littlefield, pp. 15–33.

Glenn, Norval D. 1997a. "A Critique of Twenty Family and Marriage and the Family Textbooks," *Family Relations*, 46(3):197–208.

Glenn, Norval D. 1997b. "A Response to Cherlin, Scanzoni and Skolnick: Further Discussion Of Balance, Accuracy, Fairness, Coverage, And Bias In Family Textbooks," *Family Relations*, 46(3):223–226.

Glenn, Norval D. and Charles N. Weaver. 1988. "The Changing Relationship of Marital Status to Reported Happiness," *Journal of Marriage and the Family*, 50:317–324.

Glick, Paul C. 1988. "Fifty Years of Family Demography: A Record of Social Change," *Journal of Marriage and the Family*, 50:861–873.

Glick, Paul and Sung-Ling Lin. 1987. "Remarriage After Divorce, Recent Changes and Demographic Variations," *Sociological Perspectives*, 30:162–179.

Glick, Paul C. and Sung-Ling Lin. 1986. "More Young Adults are Living with Their Parents: Who are They?" *Journal of Marriage and the Family*, 48:107–112.

Globe and Mail. 1980.* October 23.

Globe and Mail. 1987.* "Report on Business," 16 March, 1987.

Globe and Mail. 1992.* March 13:A7, in Bibby and Posterski. *Teen Trends: A Nation in Motion*. Toronto: Stoddart.

Globe and Mail. 1997.* "Stepparents in Child-Support Limbo," July 15, 1997.

Glossop, Robert. 1996.* "Perspectives: Of Mutual Benefit," *Transition*, September:4, 13.

Goetting Ann. 1986a. "Parental Satisfaction: A Review of Research," *Journal of Family Issues*, 7:83–109.

Goetting Ann. 1986b. "The Developmental Tasks of Siblingship Over the Life Cycle," *Journal of Marriage and the Family*, 48:703–714.

Goetting, Ann. 1979. "The Normative Integration of the Former Spouse Relationship," *Journal of Divorce*, 2:395–413.

Goetting, Ann. 1982. "The Six Stations of Remarriage: Developmental Tasks of Remarriage After Divorce," *Family Relations*, 31:222–231.

Goetting, Ann. 1986. "Parental Satisfaction: A Review of Research," *Journal of Family Issues*, 7:83–109.

Gold, Dolores and David Andres. 1978.* "Developmental Comparisons between Ten-Year-Old Children with Employed and Nonemployed Mothers," *Child Development*, 49:75–84.

Gold, Joshua M., Donald L. Bubenzer and John D. West. 1993. "The Presence of Children and Blended Family Marital Intimacy," *Journal of Divorce and Remarriage*, 19(3/4):97–108.

Goldner, Virginia. 1993. "Application: Feminist Theories," in Pauline G. Boss, William G. Doherty, Ralph LaRossa, Walter R. Schumm and Suzanne K. Steinmetz (eds.). *Sourcebook of Family Theories and Methods: A Contextual Approach*. New York: Plenum Press, 623–626.

Goldscheider, Frances K. 1990. "The Aging of the Gender Revolution," *Research on Aging*, 12:531–545.

Goldscheider, Frances. 1997. "Recent Changes in U.S. Young Adult Living Arrangements in Comparative Perspective," *Journal of Family Issues*, 18(6):708–724.

Goldstein, Jay and Alexander Segall. 1991.* "Ethnic Intermarriage and Ethnic Identity," in Jean E. Veevers. *Continuity and Change in Marriage and Family*. Toronto: Holt, Rinehart and Winston of Canada.

Goldstein, Lauren Heim, Marissa L. Diener and Sarah C. Mangelsdorf. 1996. "Maternal Characteristics and Social Support Across the Transition to Motherhood: Associations with Maternal Behavior," *Journal of Family Psychology*, 10(1):60–71.

Goltz, J. Walter. 1987.* "Correlates of Marital Commitment," unpublished doctoral dissertation, Edmonton, The University of Alberta.

Goltz, J. Walter and Lyle E. Larson. 1991.* "Religiosity, Marital Commitment and Individualism," *Family Perspective*, 25:201–219.

Gomes-Schwartz, Beverly, Johnathan M. Horowitz and Albert P. Cardarelli. 1990. *Child Sexual Abuse, The Initial Effects*. Newbury Park: Sage.

Goode, William J. 1959. "The Theoretical Importance of Love," *American Sociological Review*, 24:38–47.

Goode, William J. 1964. *The Family*. Englewood Cliffs: Prentice-Hall.

Goode, William J. 1970. *World Revolution and Family Patterns*. New York: The Free Press.

Goode, William. 1956. *World Revolution and the Family*. New York: The Free Press.

Goodstein, Laurie and Marjorie Connelly. 1998. "Teen-Age Poll Finds a Turn to the Traditional," *The New York Times*, April 30:A20.

Googins, B. K. 1991. *Work/family Conflicts: Private Lives—Public Responses*. New York, NY: Auburn House.

Gordis, Elana B., Gayla Margolin and Richard S. John. 1997. "Marital Aggression, Observed Parental Hostility, and Child Behavior During Triadic Family Interaction," *Journal of Family Psychology*, 11(1):76–89.

Gordon, L. 1979. "The Struggle for Reproductive Freedom: Three Stages of Feminism," in Z.R. Eisenstein (ed.), *Capitalist Patriarchy and the Case for Socialist Feminism*. New York: Monthly Review Press. Pp. 107–136.

Gore, M.S. 1968. *Urbanization and Family Change*. Bombay: Popular Prakashan.

Gorlick, Carolyne. 1987.* "Economic Stress, Social Support and Female Single Parents," unpublished paper.

Gorney, B., 1989. "Domestic Violence and Chemical Dependency: Dual Problems, Dual Interventions," *Journal of Psychoactive Drugs*, 21(2):229–238.

Gottman, John M. 1979. *Marital Interaction: Empirical Investigations*. New York: Academic Press.

Gottman, John M. and Robert W. Levenson. 1988. "The Social Psychophysiology of Marriage," in Patricia Noller and Mary A. Fitzpatrick. *Perspectives on Marital Interaction*. Philadelphia: Multilingual Matters Ltd., 182–200.

Gottman, John M. and Robert W. Levenson. 2002. "A Two-factor Model for Predicting When a Couple Will Divorce: Exploratory Analyses Using 14 year Longitudinal Data." *Family Process* 41: 83–96.

Gottman, John Mordechai. 1994. *What Predicts Divorce? The Relationship between Marital Processes and Marital Outcomes*. New Jersey: Lawrence Erlbaum Associates.

Gottman, John, Howard Markman and Cliff Notarius. 1977. "The Topography of Marital Conflict: A Sequential Analysis of Verbal and Nonverbal Behavior," *Journal of Marriage and the Family*, 39:461–477.

Gough, E. Kathleen. 1960. "Is the Family Universal: The Nayar Case," in Norman Bell and Ezra Vogel (eds.). *A Modern Introduction to the Family*. New York: The Free Press, 76–92.

Gove, Walter R. 1972. "The Relationship Between *Sex Roles*, Marital Roles and Mental Illness," *Social Forces*, 51:34–44.

Gove, Walter R. 1973. "Sex, Marital Status, and Mortality," *American Journal of Sociology*, 79:45–67.

Gove, Walter R. and Hee-Choon Shin. 1989. "The Psychological Well-Being of Divorced and Widowed Men and Women," *Journal of Family Issues*, 10:122–144.

Gove, Walter R. and Jeanette F. Tudor. 1972. "Adult Sex Roles and Mental Illness," *American Journal of Sociology*, 78:814–816, 831.

Gove, Walter R. and Michael Hughes. 1979. "Possible Causes of the Apparent Sex Differences in Physical Health: An Empirical Investigation," *American Sociological Review*, 44:126–146.

Gove, Walter R., Carolyn Briggs Styles and Michael Hughes. 1990. "The Effect of Marriage on the Well-Being of Adults," *Journal of Family Issues*, 11:4–35.

Gove, Walter R., Michael Hughes and Carolyn B. Style. 1983. "Does Marriage Have Positive Effects on the Psychological Well-Being of the Individual?" *Journal of Health and Social Behavior*, 24:122–131.

Gove, Walter R. 1973. "Sex, Marital Status and Mortality," *American Journal of Sociology*, 79:45–67.

Grandin, E. and E. Lupri. 1997.* "Intimate Violence in Canada and the United States: A Cross-National Comparison," *Journal of Family Violence*, 12(4):417–448.

Grandin, E., E. Lupri and M. Brinkerhoff. 1997.* "Couple Violence and Psychological Distress," *Canadian Journal of Public Health*, 88(3).

Gray, Ellen. 1988. "The Link Between Child Abuse and Juvenile Delinquency: What We Know and Recommendations for Policy and Research," in Gerald T. Hotaling, David Finkelhor, John T. Kirkpatrick and Murray A. Straus (eds.). *Family Abuse and its Consequences: New Directions in Research*. Newbury Park: Sage.

Gray, Heather M. and Vangie Foshee. 1997. "Adolescent Dating Violence: Differences Between One-Sided and Mutually Violent Profiles," *Journal of Interpersonal Violence*, 12:126–141.

Greeley, Andrew W. 1989. "The Declining Morale of Women," *Sociology and Social Research*, 73:53–58.

Greeley, Andrew W. 1991. *Faithful Attraction: Discovering Intimacy, Love and Fidelity in American Marriage*. New York: Tom Doherty Associates.

Green, B.L. and D.T. Kenrick. 1994. "The Attractiveness of Gender-typed Traits at Different Relationship Levels: Androgynous Characteristics May be Desirable After All." *Personality and Social Psychology Bulletin* 20:244–253.

Greenblat, C. S. 1983. "The Salience of Sexuality in the Early Years of Marriage," *Journal of Marriage and the Family*, 45:289–299.

Greene, Barbara. 1991.* *Canada's Children: Investing in Our Future*. Ottawa: Supply and Services Canada.

Greenspan, Stanley I. and George H. Pollock. 1989. *The Course of Life: Volume I. Infancy*. Madison: International Universities Press.

Griffith, Janet D. and Helen P. Koo. 1984. "Childlessness and Marital Stability in Remarriages," *Journal of Marriage and the Family*, 46:577–585.

Grimm, Karen, Catherine Huddleston and Maureen Perry-Jenkins. 1992. "Work Conditions, Self-Esteem and Parents' Perceptions of Parenting in Dual-Earner Families," presented at the 1992 National Council on Family Relations Annual Conference, Orlando, Florida, November, 1992.

Grindstaff, Carl F. 1984. "Catching Up: The Fertility of Women Over 30 Years of Age, Canada in the 1970s and Early 1980s." *Canadian Studies in Population*, 11 (2):95–109.

Grosheide, F.W. 1954. *Commentary on the First Epistle to the Corinthians*. London: N.T.C.

Gruber, J.E. 1990. "Methodological Problems and Policy Implications in Sexual Harassment Research," *Population Research and Policy Review*, 9:235–254.

Grunebaum, H. 1997. "Thinking about Romantic Love," *Journal of Marital and Family Therapy*, 23:295–307.

Grusec, Joan E. and Leon Kuczynski. 1980.* "Direction of Effect in Socialization: A Comparison of the Parent's versus the Child's Behavior as Determinants of Disciplinary Techniques," *Developmental Psychology*, 16:1–9.

Guberman, Connie and Margie Wolfe (eds.). 1985. *No Safe Place: Violence Against Women and Children*. Toronto: Women's Press.

Gubrium, Jaber F. and James A. Holstein. 1990.* *What is a Family?* Toronto: Mayfield Publishing Company.

Guelzow, Maureen G., Gloria W. Bird and Elizabeth H. Koball. 1991. "An Exploratory Path Analysis of the Stress Process for Dual-Career Men and Women," *Journal of Marriage and the Family*, 53:151–164.

Guerney, B.G. 1977. *Relationship Enhancement*. San Francisco: Jossey-Bass.

Guidubaldi, John, Joseph D. Perry, and Bonnie K. Nastasi. 1987. "Growing Up in a Divorced Family: Initial and Long-Term Perspectives on Children's Adjustment," *Applied Social Psychology Annual*, 7:202–237; as reported in David Popenoe. 1996. *Life Without Father: Compelling New Evidence that Fatherhood and Marriage are Indispensable for the Good of Children and Society*. New York: (Martin Kessler Books) The Free Press.

Gunter, B. G. 1977. "Notes on Divorce Filing as Role Behavior," *Journal of Marriage and the Family*, 39:95–97.

Gupta, Giri Raj. 1976. "Love and Arranged Marriage and the Indian Social Structure," *Journal of Comparative Family Studies*, 8:175–186.

Guttman, Herta A. 1977.* "The New Androgyny: Therapy of 'Liberated' Couples," *Canadian Psychiatric Association Journal*, 22:225–230.

Gwanfogbe, Philomina N., Walter R. Schumm, Meredith Smith and James L. Furrow. 1997. "Polygyny and Marital Life Satisfaction: An Exploratory Study from Rural Cameroon," *Journal of Comparative Family Studies*, 28(1):55–71.

Haddad, Tony and Lawrence Lam. 1988.* "Canadian Families—Men's Involvement in Family Work: A Case Study of Immigrant Men in Toronto," *International Journal of Comparative Sociology*, 29(Sept/Dec): 269–281.

Haddad, Tony and Lawrence Lam. 1994.* "The Impact of Migration on the Sexual Division of Family Work: A Case Study of Italian Immigrant Couples," *Journal of Comparative Family Studies*, 25(2):167–182.

Haddad, Y. and Smith J. 1996. "Islamic Values Among American Muslims," in, Asswad, B. and B. Bilge (eds.). *Family and Gender Among American Muslims*. Philadelphia: Temple University Press. Pp. 19–40.

Hagan, John, John Simpson and A.R. Gillis. 1987.* "Class in the Household: A Power-Control Theory of Gender and Delinquency," *American Journal of Sociology*, 92:788–816.

Hagan, John, John Simpson and A.R. Gillis. 1988.* "Feminist Scholarship, Relational and Instrumental Control and a Power-Control Theory of Gender and Delinquency," *British Journal of Sociology*, 39:301–336.

Hagestad, G.O. 1981. "Problems and Promises in the Social Psychology of Inter-Generational Relations," in R. Fogel, E. Hatfield, S. Kiesler and J. March (eds.). *Stability and Change in the Family*. New York: Academic Press.

Hagey, Janet. 1989.* "Help Around the House: Support for Older Canadians," *Canadian Social Trends*, 14:22–24.

Hagey, N. Janet, Gilles Larocque and Catherine McBride. 1989a.* *Highlights of Aboriginal Conditions, 1981–2001, Part 1, Demographic Trends*. Ottawa: Indian and Northern Affairs Canada.

Hagey, N. Janet, Gilles Larocque and Catherine McBride. 1989b.* *Highlights of Aboriginal Conditions, 1981–2001, Part 2, Social Conditions*. Ottawa: Indian and Northern Affairs Canada.

Hagey, N. Janet, Gilles Larocque and Catherine McBride. 1989c.* *Highlights of Aboriginal Conditions, 1981–2001, Part 3, Economic Conditions*. Ottawa: Indian and Northern Affairs Canada.

Hale, Diane. 1996. "How Teenagers See Things," *Parade Magazine*, August 18.

Hall, David R. and John Z. Zhao. 1995.* "Cohabitation and Divorce in Canada: Testing the Selectivity Hypothesis," *Journal of Marriage and the Family*, 57:421–427.

Hall, Elizabeth. 1986. "New Directions for the Kinsey Institute," *Psychology Today*, June:33–9.

Hall, James A. 1987. "Parent–Adolescent Conflict: An Empirical Review," *Adolescence*, 22:767–789.

Hall, Leslie D., Alexis J. Walker and Alan D. Acock. 1995. "Gender and Family Work in One-Parent Households," *Journal of Marriage and the Family*, 57(3):685–692.

Hallett, M. B. and L.A. Gilbert. 1997. "Variables Differentiating University Women Considering Role-sharing and Conventional Dual-career Marriages," *Journal of Vocational Behavior*, 50:308–322.

Halli, S.S. and Zachary Zimmer. 1991.* "Common Law Union as a Differentiating Factor in the Failure of Marriage in Canada, 1984," *Social Indicators Research*, 24:329–345.

Halpern v. Canada (Attorney general), (2003-06-10) ONCA C39172; C39174; Source: http://www.canlii.org/on/cas/onca/2003/2003onca10314.html

Hanley, M. Joan and Patrick O'Neill, 1997.* "Violence and Commitment: A Study of Dating Couples," *Journal of Interpersonal Violence*, 12:685–703.

Hanson, Marci J. and Eleanor W. Lynch. 1992. "Family Diversity: Implications for Policy and Practice," *Topics in Early Childhood Special Education*, 12(3):283–306.Hare, Douglas R.A. 1993. Matthew. Louisville: John Know Press.

Harold, Gordon T., Frank D. Fincham, Lori N. Osborne and Rand D. Conger. 1997. "Mom and Dad Are at It Again: Adolescent Perceptions of Marital Conflict and Adolescent Psychological Distress," *Developmental Psychology*, 33(2):333–350.

Harpez, Beth. 1999. "Rise in Unsafe Sex Seen Among Gays," Associated Press, January 31. Published in *Eugene Register Guard*:1A,12A.

Harpster, P. and E. Monk-Turner. 1998. "Why Men Do Housework: A Test of Gender Production and the Relative Resources Model," *Sociological Focus*, 31(1):45–59.

Harrell, W. Andrew. 1985.* "Husband's Involvement in Housework: The Effects of Relative Earning Power and Masculine Orientation," presented at the California State Psychological Association Meetings, San Francisco.

Harrell, W. Andrew. 1986.* "Do Liberated Women Drive Their Husbands to Drink?" *International Journal of Addictions*, 21:385–391.

Harrell, W. Andrew. 1990.* "Husband's Masculinity, Wife's Power and Marital Conflict," *Social Behavior and Personality*, 18:207–216.

Harrist, Amanda and Ricardo C. Ainslie. 1998. "Marital Discord and Child Behavior Problems: Parent–Child Relationship Quality and Child Interpersonal Awareness as Mediators," *Journal of Family Issues*, 19(2):140–163.

Hartley, Ruth E. 1959. "Sex Role Concepts Among Elementary School Age Girls," *Journal of Marriage and the Family*, 21:59–64.

Hartman, A. 1990. "Family Ties," *Social Work*, 35:195–196.

Hartman, Moshe and Harriet Hartman. 1983. "Sex-Role Attitudes of Mormons Versus Non-Mormons in Utah," *Journal of Marriage and the Family*, 45:897–902.

Hartman, M. and H. Hartman. 1986. "International Migration and Household Conflict," *Journal of Comparative Family Studies*, 17(1-Spring):131–138.

Hartzler, Phil. 1993. "Traditional Values of Family Overtaken," *The Edmonton Journal*, March 5:A15.

Hartzman, Carole. 1991.* *Not Yet Canadians: The Latin American Immigrant Experience in Nova Scotia*. Nova Scotia: International Education Centre.

Harvey, Andrew S., Katherine Marshall and Judith A. Frederick. 1991.* *Where Time Goes*. Catalogue No. 11–612E No. 4. Ottawa: Ministry of Industry, Science and Technology.

Harvey, C.D. and H.M. Bahr. 1974. "Widowhood Morale and Affiliation," *Journal of Marriage and the Family*, 36:97–106.

Hattery, Angela. 2000. *Women, Work, and Families: Balancing and Weaving*. Thousand Oaks, CA: Sage Publications.

Hawkins, A.J., C.M. Marshall, and S.M. Allen. 1998. "The Orientation Toward Domestic Labor Questionnaire: Exploring Dual-Earner Wives' Sense of Fairness about Family Work," *Journal of Family Psychology*, 12(2):244–258.

Hawkins, Michele J. and Cathleen Gray. 1995. "Gender Differences of Reported Safer Sex Behaviors Within a Random Sample of College Students," *Psychological Reports*, 77:963–968.

Hawrylyshyn, Oli. 1976.* "The Value of Household Services: A Survey of Empirical Estimates," *Review of Income and Wealth*, Series 22, No. 2, June 1976.

Hawrylyshyn, Oli. 1977.* "Towards a Definition of Non-Market Activities," *Review of Income and Wealth*, Series 23, No. 1, March 1977.

Hawrylyshyn, Oli. 1978.* "The Economic Nature and Value of Volunteer Activity in Canada," *Social Indicators Research*, Vol. 5.

Hays, Sharon. 1997. "The Fallacious Assumptions and Unrealistic Prescriptions of Attachment Theory: A Comment on 'Parents' Socioemotional Investment in Children,'" *Journal of Marriage and the Family*, 60 (3):782–790.

Health and Welfare Canada. 1987.* *Active Health Report*. Ottawa: Health and Welfare.

Health and Welfare Canada. 1993.* *Quarterly Surveillance Update: AIDS In Canada*. Ottawa: HIV/AIDS Division.

Health Canada. 1998a.* "AIDS." www.hc-sc.gc.ca/aids.htm

Health Canada. 1998b.* "Sexually Transmitted Disease Surveillance in Canada." www.hc-sc.gc.hpb/lcdc

Health Canada. 1998c.* "HIV and AIDS in Canada." www.hc-sc.gc.ca/hpb/lcdc

Health Division, Vital Statistics and Disease Registries Section. 1989.* *Life Tables, Canada and Provinces, 1985–1987*. Statistics Canada. Ottawa, Supplies and Services Canada.

Health Reports. 1991.* Births, 1989, Supplement No. 14. Catalogue No. 82–003S14. Ottawa: Statistics Canada.

Health Reports. 1991.* Supplement No. 16. Catalogue 82–003516. Ottawa: Statistics Canada, 10,11.

Health Reports. 1992.* Births, 1990, Supplement No. 14. Catalogue No. 82–003S14. Ottawa: Statistics Canada.

Health Reports. 1992.* Divorce, 1990, Supplement No. 17. Catalogue No. 82–003S16. Ottawa: Statistics Canada.

Health Reports. 1992.* Marriages, 1990, Supplement No. 16. Catalogue No. 82–003S16. Ottawa: Statistics Canada.

Health Reports. July 1990.* Volume 2, No. 1. Catalogue No. 82–003. Ottawa: Supply and Services Canada.

Heaton, Tim B. 1984. "Religious Homogamy and Marital Satisfaction Reconsidered," *Journal of Marriage and the Family*, 46:729–733.

Heaton, Tim B. 1991.* "Religious Group Characteristics, Endogamy and Interfaith Marriages," *Social Analysis*, 51:363–376.

Heaton, Tim B. 1996. "Socioeconomic and Familial Status of Women Associated with Age at First Marriage in Three Islamic Societies," *Journal of Comparative Family Studies*, 27(1):41–58.

Heaton, Tim B. and Stan L. Albrecht. 1991. "Stable Unhappy Marriages," *Journal of Marriage and the Family*, 53:747–758.

Heaton, Tim B., Mark Cammack and Larry Young. 2001. "Why is the Divorce Rate Declining in Indonesia?" *Journal of Marriage and Family* 63, 480–490.

Heer, David M. 1971.* "The Trend of Interfaith Marriages in Canada: 1922–1957," in K. Ishwaran (ed.). *The Canadian Family*. Toronto: Holt, Rinehart and Winston of Canada.

Heer, David M. and Charles A. Hubay. 1976.* "The Trend of Interfaith Marriages in Canada, 1922–1972," in K. Ishwaren (ed.). *The Canadian Family: Revised*. Toronto: Holt, Rinehart and Winston of Canada.

Heer, David M., Robert W. Hodge and Marcus Felson. 1985. "The Cluttered Nest: Evidence that Young Adults are More Likely to Live at Home Now Than in the Recent Past," *Sociology and Social Research*, 69:436–441.

Hegar, Rebecca L. and Geoffrey L. Greif. 1991. "Abduction of Children by their Parents: A Survey of the Problem," *Social Work*, 36:421–426.

Heider, Fritz. 1958. *The Psychology of Interpersonal Relations*. New York: Wiley.

Heitlinger, Alena. 1987.* "Maternity Leaves, Protective Legislation and Sex Equality: Eastern European and Canadian Perspectives," in Heather Jon Maroney and Meg Luxton (eds.). *Feminism and Political Economy, Women's Work, Women's Struggles*. Toronto: Methuen.

Hendrick, Clyde and Susan Hendrick. 1983. *Liking, Loving and Relating*. Monterey: Brooks/Cole Publishing Company.

Hendrick, Clyde, Susan Hendrick, Franklin H. Foote and Michelle J. Slapion-Foote. 1984. "Do Men and Women Love Differently?" *Journal of Social and Personal Relationships*, 1:177–195.

Hendy, H.M., Weiner, K., Bakerofskie, J., Eggen, D., Gustitus, C., & McLeod, K. 2003. "Comparison of Six Models for Violent Romantic Relationships in College Men and Women." *Journal of Interpersonal Violence* 18:645–665.

Henripin, J. 1972.* *Trends and Factors of Fertility in Canada, 1961 Census Monograph*. Ottawa: Statistics Canada.

Henry, Carolyn S, Cindi Penor Ceglian and Diane L. Ostrander. 1993. "The Transition to Stepgrandparenthood," *Journal of Divorce and Remarriage*, 19(3/4):24–44.

Henry, Jules. 1971. *Pathways to Madness*. Chicago: Random House.

Henshaw, Stanley K. and Kathryn Kost. 1996. "Abortion Patients in 1994–1995: Characteristics and Contraceptive Use," *Family Planning Perspectives*, 28(4):140–147, 158.

Hensley, Wayne. 1996. "The Effect of a Ludus Love Style on Sexual Experience," *Social Behavior and Personality*, 24(3):205–212.

Henton, June, Rodney Cate, James Koval, Sally Lloyd and Scott Christopher. 1983. "Romance and Violence in Dating Relationships," *Journal of Family Issues*, 4:467–482.

Herold, Edward S. 1984.* *Sexual Behaviour of Canadian Young People*. Markham: Fitzhenry and Whiteside.

Herold, Edward S. and Marilyn S. Goodwin. 1981a.* "Premarital Sexual Guilt and Contraceptive Attitudes and Behaviour," *Family Relations*, 30:247–253.

Herrenkohl, Ellen C., Roy C. Herrenkohl and Lori J. Toedter. 1983. "Perspectives on the Intergenerational Transmission of Abuse," in David Finkelhor, Richard J. Gelles, Gerald T. Hotaling and Murray A. Strauss (eds.). *The Dark Side of Families: Current Family Violence Research*. Beverly Hills: Sage.

Hetherington, E.M., Martha Cox and Roger Cox. 1978. "The Aftermath of Divorce," in J.H. Stevens and M. Matthews (eds.). *Mother/Child Relationships, Father/Child Relationships*. Washington: National Association for the Education of Young Children.

Hetherington, E. Mavis. 1981. "Children and Divorce," in R. Henderson (ed.). *Parent–Child Interaction: Theory, Research and Prospect*. New York: Academic Press.

Hetherington, E. Mavis and Kathleen A. Camara. 1985. "Families in Transition: The Processes of Dissolution and Reconstitution," *Review of Child Development Research*, 7:398–439.

Hetherington, E. Mavis, Margaret Bridges and Glendessa M. Insabella. 1998. "What Matters? What Does Not? Five Perspectives on the Association Between Marital Transitions and Children's Adjustment," *Social Behavior and Personality*, 53(2):167–184.

Hetherington, E. Mavis, Martha Cox and Roger Cox. 1981. "Divorce and Remarriage," paper presented at the meeting of the Society for Research in Child Development, Boston, April 1981.

Hetherington, E. Mavis, Martha Cox and Roger Cox. 1982. "Effects of Divorce on Parents and Children," in Michael Lamb, (ed.). *Nontraditional Families: Parenting and Child Development*, Hillsdale, N.J.: Lawrence Erlbaum.

Hetherington, E. Mavis, Martha Cox and Roger Cox. 1985. "Long-Term Effects of Divorce and Remarriage and the Adjustment of Children," *Journal of American Academy of Child Psychiatry*, 24:518–530.

Hicks, Mary W. and Marilyn Platt. 1970. "Marital Happiness and Stability: A Review of the Research in the Sixties," *Journal of Marriage and the Family*, 32:553–574.

Higginson, Joanna Gregson. 1998. "Competitive Parenting: The Culture of Teen Mothers," *Journal of Marriage and the Family*, 60(1):135–149.

Hill, C.T., Z. Rubin and L.A. Peplau. 1976. "Breakups Before Marriage: The End of 103 Affairs," *Journal of Social Issues*, 32:147–168.

Hill, Martha S. 1988. "Marital Stability and Spouses' Shared Time," *Journal of Family Issues*, 9:427–451.

Hill, Martha S. 1992. "The Role of Economic Resources and Remarriage in Financial Assistance for Children of Divorce," *Journal of Family Issues*, 13(2):158–178.

Hill, R. 1949. *Families Under Stress*. New York: Harper and Row.

Hill, R. 1958. "Generic Features of Families Under Stress," *Social Casework*, 49:139–150.

Hill, Reuben and Donald A. Hansen. 1960. "The Identification of Conceptual Frameworks Utilized in Family Study," *Marriage and Family Living*, 22: 299–311.

Hill, Reuben and Roy H. Rodgers. 1964. "The Developmental Approach," in Harold T. Christensen (ed.). *Handbook of Marriage and the Family*. Chicago: Rand McNally, 171–211.

Himelein, M. and J.A. McElrath. 1996. "Resilient Child Sexual Abuse Survivors: Cognitive Coping and Illusion," *Child Abuse and Neglect*, 20(8):747–758.

Hirschi, T. 1969. *The Causes of Delinquency*. Berkeley: The University of California Press.

Ho, Fung Chu and Ronald C. Johnson. 1990. "Inter-Ethnic and Intra-Ethnic Marriage and Divorce in Hawaii," *Social Biology*, 37:44–51.

Hobart, Charles W. 1958.* "The Incidence of Romanticism During Courtship," *Social Forces*, 36:362–367.

Hobart, Charles W. 1965.* "Eskimo Education in Residential Schools in the Mackenzie District." Unpublished report for the Department of Indian Affairs and Northern Resources.

Hobart, Charles W. 1972.* "Sexual Permissiveness in Young English and French Canadians," *Journal of Marriage and the Family*, 34:292–303.

Hobart, Charles W. 1974.* "The Social Context of Morality Standards Among Anglophone Canadian Students," *Journal of Comparative Family Studies*, 5:26–40.

Hobart, Charles W. 1976.* "Youth and Sex Expression," in K. Ishwaran (ed.). *The Canadian Family*. Toronto: Holt, Rinehart and Winston, 418–436.

Hobart, Charles W. 1981.* "Sources of Egalitarianism in Young Unmarried Canadians," *Canadian Journal of Sociology*, 6:261–282.

Hobart, Charles W. 1984.* "Changing Profession and Practice of Sexual Standards: A Study of Young Anglophone and Francophone Canadians," *Journal of Comparative Family Studies*, 15:231–255.

Hobart, Charles W. 1988.* "The Family System in Remarriage: An Exploratory Study," *Journal of Marriage and the Family*, 50:649–661.

Hobart, Charles W. 1988.* "Perceptions of Parent-Child Relationships in Nuclear and Remarried Families," *Family Relations*, 37:175–182.

Hobart, Charles W. 1988.* "Premarital Sexuality," in G. N. Ramu (ed.). *Marriage and the Family in Canada*. Scarborough: Prentice-Hall Canada.

Hobart, Charles W. 1988.* "Relationships in Remarried Families," *Canadian Journal of Sociology*, 13:261–292.

Hobart, Charles W. 1989a.* "Experiences of Remarried Families," *Journal of Divorce*, 13:121–144.

Hobart, Charles W. 1989b.* "Structural Variations in Remarried Families: An Exploratory Study," *International Journal of Sociology of the Family*, 19:89–115.

Hobart, Charles W. 1990a.* "Premarital Sexual Standards Among Canadian Students at the End of the Eighties," unpublished manuscript, Edmonton.

Hobart, Charles W. 1990b.* "Relationships Between the Formerly Married," *Journal of Divorce and Remarriage*, 14:1–25.

Hobart, Charles W. 1991.* "Conflict in Remarriages," *Journal of Divorce and Remarriage*, 15:69–85.

Hobart, Charles W. 1993a.* "Interest in Marriage Among Canadian Students at the End of the Eighties," *Journal of Comparative Family Studies*, 24:45–61.

Hobart, Charles W. 1993b.* "Sexual Behaviour," in G. N. Ramu (ed.). *Marriage and the Family in Canada Today (second edition)*. Scarborough: Prentice-Hall Canada.

Hobart, Charles W. and Frank Grigel. 1990.* "Premarital Sex among Canadian Students at the End of the Eighties," unpublished manuscript, Edmonton.

Hobart, Charles W. and Frank Grigel. 1992.* "Cohabitation Among Canadian Students at the End of the Eighties," *Journal of Comparative Family Studies*, 23:311–337.

Hochschild, Arlie and Anne Machung. 1989. *The Second Shift: Working Parents and the Revolution at Home*. New York: Viking Press.

Hocker, Joyce L. and William W. Wilmot. 1978. *Interpersonal Conflict*. Dubuque: William C. Brown.

Hodge, Robert D., D. A. Andrews and D. Robinson. 1990.* "Patterns of Child and Parenting Problems Within Six Family Types," *Canadian Journal of Behavioural Science*, 22:99–109.

Hof, Larry M., Norman Epstein and William R. Miller. 1980. "Integrating Attitudinal and Behavioral Change in Marital Enrichment," *Family Relations*, 29:241–8.

Holahan, Charles J. and Rudolf H. Moos. 1983. "The Quality of Social Support: Measures of Family and Work Relationships," *British Journal of Clinical Psychology*, 22(3):157–162.

Hollis, Chris. 1996. "Depression, Family Environment, and Adolescent Suicidal Behavior," *Journal of the American Academy of Child and Adolescent Psychiatry*, 35(5):622–630.

Holstein, James A. and Jaber F. Gubrium. 1995. "Deprivatization and the Construction of Domestic Life," *Journal of Marriage and the Family*, 57(4):894–908.

Holubitsky, Jeff. 1993.* "Condomnation," *The Edmonton Journal*, January 18:E1.

Holy Bible, Revised Standard Version. 1952. New York: Thomas Nelson and Sons.

Holy, L. (1996). *Anthropological Perspectives of Kinship*. Chicago: Pluto Press

Holy, L. (1996). *Anthropological Perspectives of Kinship*. Chicago: Pluto Press

Homans, George. 1950. *The Human Group*. New York: Harcourt Brace.

Honeycutt, James M., Charmaine Wilson and Christine Parker. 1982. "Effects of Sex and Degrees of Happiness On Perceived Styles of Communication In and Out of the Marital Relationship," *Journal of Marriage and the Family*, 44:395–406.

Hook, N. and B. Paolucci. 1970. "The Family as an Ecosystem," *Journal of Home Economics*, 62:315–318.

Horna, Jarmila and Eugen Lupri. 1987.* "Father's Participation in Work, Family Life and Leisure: A Canadian Experience," in Charlie Lewis and Margaret O'Brien (eds.). *Reassessing Fatherhood: New Observations on Fathers and the Modern Family*. London: Sage, 54–73.

Hornung, C. A. and B. C. McCullough. 1981. "Status Relationships and Dual-Employment Marriages: Consequences for Psychological Well-Being," *Journal of Marriage and the Family*, 43:125–141.

Horton, Anne L., Melany M. Wilkins and Wendy Wright. 1988. "Women Who Ended Abuse: What Religious Leaders and Religion Did For These Victims," in Anne L. Horton and Judith A. Williamson (eds.). *Abuse and Religion: When Praying Isn't Enough*. Lexington: Lexington Books.

Hortuung, C.A. and B.C. McCullough. 1981. "Status Relationships and Dual-Employment Marriages: Consequences for Psychological Well-Being," *Journal of Marriage and the Family*, 43:125–141.

Horwitz, Allan V., Helene R. White and Sandra Howell-White. 1996. "Becoming Married and Mental Health: A Longitudinal Study of a Cohort of Young Adults," *Journal of Marriage and the Family*, 58:895–907.

Hotaling, Gerald T., David Finkelhor, John T Kirkpatrick and Murray A. Straus (eds.). 1988. *Family Abuse and Its Consequences: New Directions in Research*. Newbury Park: Sage.

House of Commons. 1987.* *Sharing the Responsibility: Report of the Special Committee on Child Care*. Ottawa: Queen's Printer.

House, J. S., V. Strecher, H. L. Metzner and C.A. Robbins. 1986. "Occupational Stress and Health Among Men and Women in the Tecumseh Community Health Study," *Journal of Health and Social Behavior*, 27:62–77.

Houseknecht, Sharon K. and Jaya Satry. 1996. "Family 'Decline' and Child Well-Being: A Comparative Assessment," *Journal of Marriage and the Family*, 58(3):726–739.

Houts, Renate M., Elliott Robins, and Ted Huston. 1996. "Compatibility and the Development of Premarital Relationships," *Journal of Marriage and the Family*, 58:7–20.

Howes, P.W. and H.J. Markman, 1991. "Longitudinal Relations between Premarital and Prebirth Adult Interaction and Subsequent Parent–Child Attachment," Department of Psychology, University of Denver.

Howes, P.W. and H.J. Markman. 1989. "Marital Quality and Child Functioning: A Longitudinal Investigation," *Child Development*, 60:1044–1051.

Huber, Joan and Glenna Spitze. 1980. "Considering Divorce: An Expansion of Becker's Theory of Marital Instability," *American Journal of Sociology*, 86:75–89.

Huddleston, Richard J. and Lucille Hawkings. 1991.* "A Comparison of Physical and Emotional Health After Divorce in a Canadian and United States' Sample," *Journal of Divorce and Remarriage*, 15:193–207.

Hudson, Joe and Burt Galaway (eds). 1993.* *Single Parent Families: Perspectives on Research and Policy*. Toronto: Thompson Educational Publishing.

Hum, Derek P.J. and Saud Choudhry. 1992.* "Income, Work and Marital Dissolution: Canadian Experimental Evidence," *Journal of Comparative Family Studies*, 23:249–264.

Hundleby, John D. and G. William Mercer. 1987.* "Family and Friends as Social Environments and their Relationship to Young Adolescents' Use of Alcohol, Tobacco and Marijuana," *Journal of Marriage and the Family*, 49:151–164.

Hunt, David. 1970. *Parents and Children in History: The Psychology of Family Life in Early Modern France*. New York: Basic Books.

Huston, Ted L., Susan M. McHale and Ann C. Crouter. 1986. "When the Honeymoon's Over: Changes in the Marriage Relationship over the First Year," in R. Gilmour and S. Duck (eds.). *The Emerging Field of Personal Relationships*. Hillsdale: Lawrence Erlbaum.

Hutchinson, S. 1986. "Grounded Theory: The Method," in P.L. Munhall and C.J. Oiler (eds.). *Nursing Research: A Qualitative Perspective*. Norwalk: Century Crofts, 111–130.

Hutter, Mark. 1997. "Immigrant Families in the City," in Mark Hutter (ed.). *The Family Experience: A Reader in Cultural Diversity*, second edition. Massachusetts: Allen and Bacon Inc. Pp. 89–96.

Hynie, Michaela, John E. Lydon and Ali Taradesh. 1997. "Commitment, Intimacy, and Women's Perception of Premarital Sex and Contraceptive Readiness," *Psychology of Women Quarterly*, 21:447–464.

Ihinger-Tallman, M. and K. Pasley, 1987. *Remarriage*. Beverly Hills: Sage.

Ingoldsby, Bron B. 1995. "Marital Structure," in Bron B. Ingoldsby and Suzanna Smith (eds). *Families in Multicultural Perspective*. New York: Guilford Press. Pp. 117–137.

Ingoldsby, Bron B. and Suzanna Smith (eds). 1995. *Families in Multicultural Perspective*. New York: Guilford Press.

Inkeles, Alex and David Smith. 1974. *Becoming Modern: Individual Change in Six Developing Countries*. Cambridge, Mass: Harvard University Press.

Inside Edition. 1992. A Special Program on Reproductive Technologies aired on the National Broadcasting Network, January 6th.

Ironmonger, Duncan. 1994. *The Value of Care and Nurture Provided by Unpaid Household Work*. Family Matters 37, 46–51.

Irving, Howard H., Michael Benjamin and Nicolas Trocme. 1984.* "Shared Parenting: An Empirical Analysis Utilizing a Large Data Base," *Family Process*, 23:561–569.

Isaac, Susan V., Roger C. Bailey and Walter L. Isaac. 1995. "Perceptions of Religious and Nonreligious Targets Who Participate in Premarital Sex," *Social Behavior and Personality*, 23(3):229–234.

Isaacs, Maria Beth and George H. Leon. 1988. "Remarriage and Its Alternatives Following Divorce: Mother and Child Adjustment," *Journal of Marital and Family Therapy*, 14:163–173.

Ishwaran, K. (ed.). 1971.* *The Canadian Family*. Toronto: Holt, Rinehart and Winston of Canada.

Ishwaran, K. (ed.). 1976.* *The Canadian Family: Revised*. Toronto: Holt, Rinehart and Winston of Canada.

Ishwaran, K. 1980.* *Canadian Families: Ethnic Variations*. Toronto: McGraw-Hill Ryerson Limited.

Ishwaran, K. 1982.* "Interdependence of the Elementary and Extended Family," in John S. Augustine (ed.). *The Indian Family in Transition*. New Delhi: Vikas Publishing.

Jabbra, Nancy. 1991.* "Household and Family Among Lebanese Immigrants in Nova Scotia: Continuity, Change and Adaptation," *Journal of Comparative Family Studies*, 22(1):39–56.

Jaccard, James, Patricia J. Dittus and Vivian V. Gordon. 1996. "Maternal Correlates of Adolescent Sexual Behavior and Contraceptive Behavior," *Family Planning Perspectives*, 28(4):159–165, 185.

Jack, L., D. Dutton and A. Webb. 1995.* "Effects of Early Abuse on Adult Affective Reactions to Exposure to Dyadic Conflict," *Canadian Journal of Behavioural Science*, 27:484–500.

Jacobs, Joanne. 1993. "New Feminism Just Too Limiting," *The Edmonton Journal*, March 28:A9.

Jaffe, P. and C.A. Burris. 1982.* *An Integrated Response to Wife Assault: A Community Model*. Ottawa: Research Report of the Solicitor General of Canada.

Jamieson, Kathleen. 1978.* *Indian Women and the Law in Canada: Citizens Minus*. Ottawa: Advisory Council on the Status of Women.

Jamieson, Kathleen. 1986.* "Sex Discrimination and the Indian Act," in J. Rick Ponting (ed.). *Arduous Journey: Canadian Indians and Decolonization*. Toronto: McClelland and Stewart.

Jang, D., D. Lee and R. Morello-Frosch. 1991. "Domestic Violence in the Immigrant and Refugee Community: Responding to the Needs of Immigrant Women," *Response*, 13(4):2–7.

Janus, Samuel S. and Cynthia L. Janus. 1993. *The Janus Report on Sexual Behavior*. Toronto: Wiley.

Jasso, Guillermina. 1985. "Marital Coital Frequency and the Passage of Time: Estimating the Separate Effects of Spouses' Ages and Marital Duration, Birth and Marriage Cohorts and Period Influences," *American Sociological Review*, 50:224–241.

Jensen-Campbell, L.A., W.G. Graziano, and S.G. West. 1995. Dominance, Prosocial Orientation an Female Preferences: Do Nice Guys Finish Last?" *Journal of Personality and Social Psychology* 68:427–440.

Jimenez, Marina. 1992a.* "Many Indo-Canadians Follow Age-Old Custom," *The Edmonton Journal*, July 26:B3.

Jimenez, Marina. 1992b.* "Nest Gets Cluttered When Adult Kids Come Home," *The Edmonton Journal*, July 20:A1–A2.

Johnson, Elizabeth M. and Ted L. Huston. 1998. "The Perils of Love, or Why Wives Adapt to Husbands During the Transition to Parenthood," *Journal of Marriage and the Family*, 60(1):195–204.

Johnson, H. 1988.* "Wife Abuse," *Canadian Social Trends*. Spring:17–22.

Johnson, H. 1996. "Violence and Biology: A Review of the Literature," Families in Society: *The Journal of Contemporary Human Services*, 77(1):3–18.

Johnson, Laura C. 1994.* *Changing Families, Changing Workplaces: Case Studies of Policies and Programs in Canadian Workplaces*. Ottawa: Women's Bureau, Human Resources Development Canada.

Johnson, Laura C. and Dick Barnhorst (eds.). 1991. *Children, Families and Public Policy in the 90s*. Toronto: Thompson Educational Publishing.

Johnson, M. 1995. "Patriarchal Terrorism and Common Couple Violence: Two Forms of Violence Against Women," *Journal of Marriage and the Family*, 57:283–294.

Johnson, Michael P. 1973. "Commitment: A Conceptual Structure and Empirical Application," *Sociological Quarterly*, 14:395–406.

Johnson, Michael P. 1978. "Personal and Structural Commitment: Sources of Consistency in the Development of Relationships," unpublished manuscript, Pennsylvania.

Johnson, Michael P. 1985. "Commitment, Cohesion, Investment, Barriers, Alternatives, Constraint: Why Do People Stay Together When They Really Don't Want To?" unpublished manuscript, Pennsylvania.

Johnson, Michael P. and Leigh Leslie. 1982. "Couple Involvement and Network Structure: A Test of the Dyadic Withdrawal Hypothesis," *Social Psychology Quarterly*, 45:34–43.

Johnson, Michael P. and Robert M. Milardo. 1984. "Network Interference in Pair Relationships: A Social Psychological Recasting of Sclater's Theory of Social Regression," *Journal of Marriage and the Family*, 46:893–899.

Johnson, P.J. (2000). "Ethnic Differences In Self-Employment Among A Group Of Recent Immigrants." *Journal of Small Business Management* 38:78–86.

Johnson, P.J. (1998). "Performance of household tasks by Vietnamese and Lao refugees: Tradition and change." *Journal of Family Issues* 19:245–273.

Johnson, P.J. 1990*. "Experiencing Unemployment: A Comparison Of Refugee And Canadian Resident Families," *Family Perspective*, 24(2):159–174.

Johnson, P.J. 1989*. "Resources For Coping With Economic Distress: The Situation Of Unemployed Southeast Asian Refugees," *Lifestyles: Family and Economic Issues*, 10(1):18–43.

Johnson, P.J. 1988*. "Consequences Of Economic Distress: The Experiences Of Unemployed Southeast Asian Refugees." *Journal of Consumer Studies and Home Economics*, 12:257–275.

Johnston, Charlotte. 1991.* "Predicting Mothers' and Fathers' Perceptions of Child Behaviour Problems," *Canadian Journal of Behavioural Science*, 23:349–357.

Jones, F.L. 1996. "Convergence and Divergence in Ethnic Divorce Patterns: A Research Note," *Journal of Marriage and the Family*, 58:213–218.

Jones, Warren H., Mary E. Chernovitz and Robert O. Hansson. 1978. "The Enigma of Androgyny: Differential Implications for Males and Females?" *Journal of Consulting and Clinical Psychology*, 46:298–313.

Jorgensen, Stephen R. and Alberta C. Johnson. 1980. "Correlates of Divorce Liberality," *Journal of Marriage and the Family*, 42:617–626.

Jorgensen, Stephen R., Susan L. King and Barbara A. Torry. 1980. "Dyadic and Social Network Influences on Adolescent Exposure to Pregnancy Risk," *Journal of Marriage and the Family*, 42:141–155.

Journal of Marriage and the Family, 1995, 57(4). A special methodological issue on paradigms, design, measures and analysis in doing family research.

Julian, T. and P. McKenry. 1993. "Mediators of Male Violence Toward Female Intimates," *Journal of Family Violence*, 8(1):39–56.

Kahn, Alfred J. and Shelia B. Kammerman (eds.). 1988. *Child Support: From Debt Collection to Social Policy.* Beverly Hills: Sage.

Kahn, Alice. 1992. "Teens Warm to Chastity in Sex Ed," *The Edmonton Journal*, February 16:H7.

Kalb, Claudia. 1997. "How Old Is Too Old?" *Newsweek*, May 5:64.

Kalisch, Philip and Beatrice J. Kalisch. 1984. "Sex-Role Stereotyping of Nurses and Physicians on Prime-Time Television," *Sex Roles*, 10:533–553.

Kalleberg, Arne L. and Rachael A. Rosenfeld. 1990. "Work in the Family and in the Labor Market: A Cross-National, Reciprocal Analysis," *Journal of Marriage and the Family*, 52:331–346.

Kallman, Frederick J. 1952. "Comparative Twin Study in the Genetic Aspects of Male Homosexuality," *Journal of Nervous and Mental Disease*, 115:283–298.

Kalmijn, Matthijs. 1991. "Shifting Boundaries: Trends in Religious and Educational Homogamy," *American Sociological Review*, 56:786–800.

Kalmuss, Debra S. and Murray A. Straus. 1982. "Wife's Marital Dependency and Wife Abuse," *Journal of Marriage and the Family*, 44:277–286.

Kanin, Eugene J., K.R. Davidson and S.R. Sheck. 1970. "A Research Note on Male–Female Differentials in the Experience of Heterosexual Love," *The Journal of Sex Research*, 6:64–72.

Kantor, D. and W. Lehr. 1975. *Inside the Family*. New York: Jossey-Bass.

Kantor, G. and M. Straus. 1987. "The Drunken Bum Theory of Wife Abuse," *Journal of Social Problems*, 34:213–230.

Kantrowitz, B. with T. Barrett, K. Springen, M. Hager, L. Wright, G. Carroll and D. Rosenberg. 1991. "Striking a Nerve," *Newsweek*, October 21:34–40.

Kapinus, C.A. and Johnson, M.P. 2003. "The Utility Of Family Life Cycle As A Theoretical And Empirical Tool—Commitment And Family Life-Cycle-Stage," *Journal of Family Issues*, 24:155–184.

Kapur, Primilla. 1973. *Love, Marriage and Sex*. Delhi: Vikas Publishing.

Karney, B.R. and T.N. Bradbury. 1995. "The Longitudinal Course of Marital Quality and Stability: A Review of Theory, Method and Research," *Psychological Bulletin*, 118:3–34.

Katz, Sanford N. 1984. "Introductory Comments on Joint Custody," in *Seeking Solomon's Wisdom*. New Orleans: Loyola University School of Law.

Kaufman, Debra R. 1990. "Engendering Family Theory: Toward a Feminist-Interpretive Framework," in Jetse Sprey (ed.). *Fashioning Family Theory: New Approaches.* Newbury Park: Sage, Chapter 5.

Kawash, George and Lorene Kozeluk. 1990.* "Self-Esteem in Early Adolescence as a Function of Position within Olson's Circumplex Model of Marital and Family Systems," *Social Behavior and Personality*, 18:189–196.

Keefe, S.E., and A.M. Padilla. 1987. *Chicano Ethnicity*. Albuquerque: University of New Mexico Press.

Keith, Julie and Laura Landry. 1992.* "Well-Being of Older Canadians," *Canadian Social Trends*, 25:16–17.

Kelley, Katherine D. 1994.* "The Politics of Data," *Canadian Journal of Sociology*, 19:81–85.

Kelley, Katharine D. and Walter DeKeseredy. 1994.* "Women's Fear of Crime and Abuse and University Dating Relationships," *Violence and Victims*, 9:17–30.

Kemper, Theodore D. 1978. *A Social Interactional Theory of Emotions*. New York: Wiley.

Kendall-Tackett, Kathleen A., Linda Meyer Williams and David Finkelhor. 1993. "Impact of Sexual Abuse on Children: A Review and Synthesis of Recent Empirical Studies," *Psychological Bulletin*, 113:164–180.

Kennedy, Gregory and C.E. Kennedy. 1993. "Grandparents: A Special Resource for Children in Stepfamilies," *Journal of Divorce and Remarriage*, 19(3/4):45–68.

Kennedy, Janice. 1990.* "Two Parents, Two Homes," *Edmonton Journal*, July 30:C1.

Kennedy, Leslie W. and Dennis K. Stokes. 1982.* "Extended Family Support and the High Cost of Housing," *Journal of Marriage and the Family*, 44:311–318.

Kennedy, Leslie W. and Donald G. Dutton. 1989.* "The Incidence of Wife Assault in Alberta," *Canadian Journal of Behavioural Science*, 21:40–54.

Kennedy, Leslie W., David R. Ford, Michael D. Smith and Donald G. Dutton. 1989.* "Knowledge of Spouse Abuse in the Community: A Comparison Across Locations," unpublished paper.

Kenny, Eoin. 1993.* "Mothers Who Work Growing in Number," *Edmonton Journal*, March 3:A3.

Kerckhoff, A. C. and Davis, K. E. 1962. "Value Consensus and Need Complementarity in Mate Selection," *American Sociological Review*, 27:295–303.

Kern, J. and T. Hastings. 1995. "Differential Family Environments of Bulimics and Victims of Childhood Sexual Abuse: Achievement Orientation," *Journal of Clinical Psychology*, 51(4):499–506.

Kerr, Don, Daniel Larrivée and Patricia Greenhalgh. 1994.* *Children and Youth: An Overview*. Statistics Canada Catalogue No. 96–320E.

Kersten, Karen K. and Lawrence K. Kersten. 1991.* "A Historical Perspective on Intimate Relationships," in Jean E. Veevers (ed.). *Continuity and Change in Marriage and Family*. Toronto: Holt, Rinehart and Winston of Canada.

Kesner, J., T. Julian, and P. McKenry. 1997. "Application of Attachment Theory to Male Violence Toward Female Intimates," *Journal of Family Violence*, 12(2):211–228.

Kibria, N. 1993.* *Family Tightrope: The Changing Lives of Vietnamese Americans*. Princeton: Princeton University Press.

Kibria, N. 1994, "Household Structure and Family Ideologies: The Dynamics of Immigrant Economic Adaptation Among Vietnamese Refugees," *Social Problems*, 41:81–96.

Kidder, Louse H. and Charles Judd. 1986. *Research Methods in Social Relations*, Fifth Ed. New York: Harcourt.

Kim, Kwang Chung and Won Moo Hurh. 1988. "The Burden of Double Roles: Korean Wives in the USA," *Ethnic and Racial Studies*, 11(2):151–167.

Kincaid, Pat J. 1982.* *The Omitted Reality: Husband–Wife Violence in Ontario and Policy Implications for Education*. Maple: Publishing and Printing Services.

King, Alan J.C., Richard P. Beazley, Wendy K. Warren, Catherine A. Hankins, Alan S. Robertson and Joyce L. Roberts. 1988.* *Canada Youth and Aids Study*. Ottawa: Health and Welfare Canada.

King, Lynn. 1980.* *What Every Woman Should Know About Marriage, Separation and Divorce*. Toronto: James Lorimer.

King, Valarie (2003). "The Legacy Of A Grandparent's Divorce: Consequences For Ties Between Grandparents And Grandchildren," *Journal of Marriage and Family* 65, 170–183.

Kingsbury, Nancy and John Scanzoni. 1993. "Structural Functionalism," in Pauline G. Boss, William G. Doherty, Ralph LaRossa, Walter R. Schumm and Suzanne K. Steinmetz (eds.). *Sourcebook of Family Theories and Methods: A Contextual Approach*. New York: Plenum Press, Chapter 9.

Kingsbury, Nancy M. and Robert B. Minda. 1988.* "An Analysis of Three Expected Intimate Relationship States: Commitment, Maintenance and Termination," *Journal of Social and Personal Relations*, 5:405–422.

Kinnaird, Keri L. and Meg Gerrard. 1986. "Premarital Sexual Behaviour and Attitudes Toward Marriage and Divorce among Young Women as a Function of Their Mothers' Marital Status," *Journal of Marriage and the Family*, 48:757–765.

Kinsey, Alfred C., Wardell B. Pomeroy and Clyde E. Martin. 1948. *Sexual Behavior in the Human Male*. Philadelphia: Saunders.

Kinsey, Alfred C., Wardell B. Pomeroy, Clyde E. Martin and Paul H. Gebhard. 1953. *Sexual Behavior in the Human Female*. Philadelphia: Saunders.

Kinzel, Cliff. 1989.* *Edmonton Area Series Report No. 65: All Alberta Study 1989*. Population Research Laboratory, Edmonton: University of Alberta.

Kinzl, J., B. Mangweth, C. Traweger and W. Biebl. 1996. "Sexual Dysfunction in Males: Significance of Adverse Childhood Experiences," *Child Abuse and Neglect*, 20(8):759–766.

Kinzl, J., C. Traweger and W. Biebl. 1995. "Sexual Dysfunctions: Relationship to Childhood Sexual Abuse and Early Family Experiences in a Nonclinical Sample," *Child Abuse and Neglect*, 19(7):785–792.

Kitson, G., K. Barri and M. Roach. 1985. "Who Divorces and Why: A Review," *Journal of Family Issues*, 6:255–293.

Klein, David M. and James M. White. 1996.* *Family Theories: An Introduction*. Thousand Oaks, CA: Sage Publications.

Klein, R.D. 1989. *The Exploitation of a Desire: Women's Experiences with In Vitro Fertilization*. Geelong, Australia: Deakin University Press.

Klein, I. and R. Janoff-Bulman. 1996. "Trauma History and Personal Narratives: Some Clues to Coping Among Survivors of Child Abuse," *Child Abuse and Neglect*, 20(1):45–54.

Kline, Marsha, Janet R. Johnston and Jeanne M. Tschann. 1991. "The Long Shadow of Marital Conflict: A Model of Children's Postdivorce Adjustment," *Journal of Marriage and the Family*, 53:297–309.

Klomegah, Roger. 1997. "Socio-Economic Characteristics of Ghanaian Women in Polygynous Marriages," *Journal of Comparative Family Studies*, 28(1):73–88.

Kluwer, Esther S., Jose A.M. Heesink and Evert Van de Vliet. (2002). "The Division Of Labor Across The Transition To Parenthood: A Justice Perspective," *Journal of Marriage and Family* 64:930–943.

Kluwer, Esther S., Jose A.M. Heesink and Evert Van de Vliert. 1997. "The Marital Dynamics of Conflict over the Division of Labor," *Journal of Marriage and the Family*, 59(3):635–653.

Knapp, M.L. and G.R. Miller (eds.). 1985. *Handbook of Interpersonal Communication*. Beverly Hills: Sage.

Knox, David and Kenneth Wilson. 1981. "Dating Behaviours of University Students," *Family Relations*, 30:255–258.

Knox, David and Michael J. Sporakowski. 1968. "Attitudes of College Students Toward Love," *Journal of Marriage and the Family*, 30:638–642.

Knudsen, Dean D. and JoAnn L. Miller. (eds.). 1991. *Abused and Battered: Social and Legal Responses to Family Violence*. New York: Aldine de Gruyter.

Kofodimos, J., 1993. *Balancing Act: How Managers Can Integrate Successful Careers and Fulfilling Personal Lives*. San Francisco: Jossey-Bass.

Kohlberg, Lawrence. 1966. "A Cognitive-Developmental Analysis of Children's Sex-Role Concepts and Attitudes," in Eleanor E. Maccoby (ed.). *The Development of Sex Differences*. Stanford: Stanford University Press.

Kohn, M.L. and C. Schooler. 1981. "Job Conditions and Personality: A Longitudinal Assessment of their Reciprocal Effects," *American Journal of Sociology*, 87:1257–1286.

Korman, Sheila K. 1983. "Nontraditional Dating Behaviour: Date-Initiation and Date Expense-Sharing Among Feminists and Nonfeminists," *Family Relations*, 32:575–581.

Kossek, E.E. and C. Ozeki. 1998. "Work–Family Conflict, Policies, and the Job–Life Satisfaction Relationship: A Review and Directions for Organizational Behavior–Human Resources Research," *Journal of Applied Psychology*, 83(2):139–149.

Kourvetaris, George. 1997. *Studies on Greek Americans*. New York: Columbia University Press.

Kozol, Jonathan. 1990. "The New Untouchables," *Newsweek, Special Edition: The 21st Century Family*, Winter/Spring:48–49, 52–53.

Krahn, Harvey and Graham S. Lowe. 1993.* *Work, Industry and Canadian Society*. Toronto: Nelson Canada.

Krahn, Harvey, John Gartrell and Lyle Larson. 1981.* "The Quality of Family Life in a Resource Community," *Canadian Journal of Sociology*, 6:307–324.

Krahn, Harvey. 1993.* "Work and Employment: Measurement Issues for the 1990s," in the Discussion Paper series. Edmonton: Population Research Laboratory, University of Alberta.

Kressel, K., M. Lopez-Morillas, J. Weinglass and M. Deutsch. 1979. "Professional Intervention in Divorce: The Views of Lawyers, Psychotherapists and Clergy," in G. Levinger and O. Moles (eds.). *Divorce and Separation*. New York: Basic Books.

Krishnan, P. and Karol J. Krotki. 1976.* *Growth of Alberta Families Study*. Edmonton: Population Research Laboratory, University of Alberta.

Krishnan, V. 1995.* "Effect of Housing Tenure on Fertility," *Sociological Spectrum*, 15(2):117–129.

Krishnan, Vijaya. 1998.* "Premarital Cohabitation and Marital Disruption," *Journal of Divorce and Remarriage*, 28:157–170.

Krokoff, Lowell J. 1991. "Job Distress is No Laughing Matter in Marriage, Or Is It?" *Journal of Social and Personal Relationships*, 8:5–25.

Kronby, Malcolm C. 1991.* *Canadian Family Law* (fifth edition). Don Mills: Stoddard.

Kruk, Edward. 1991.* "Discontinuity Between Pre- and Post-Divorce Father–Child Relationships: New Evidence Regarding Paternal Disengagement," *Journal of Divorce*, 16:195–227.

Kruk, Edward. 1995.* "Grandparent–Grandchild Contact Loss: Findings from a Study of 'Grandparent Rights' Members," *Canadian Journal on Aging*, 14(4):737–754.

Krull, Catherine, and Frank Trovato. 1994.* "The Quiet Revolution and the Sex Differential in Quebec's Suicide Rates," *Social Forces*, 72(4):1121–1147.

Krupinski, J. et al. 1977. "The Impact of Contemporary Society on the Migrant Family," in Rachelle Banchevska (ed.). *The Family in Australia*. Melbourne: Victoria Family Council.

Ku, Leighton, Freya L. Sonenstein, Laura D. Lindberg, Carol H. Bradner, Scott Boggess and Joseph H. Pleck. 1998. "Understanding Changes in Sexual Activity Among Young Metropolitan Men: 1979–1995," *Family Planning Perspectives*, 30(6):256–262.

Kubler-Ross, E. 1969.* *On Death and Dying*. New York: Macmillan.

Kuhlthau, Karen, and Karen Oppeneim Mason. 1996. "Market Child Care versus Care by Relatives: Choices Made by Employed and Nonemployed Mothers," *Journal of Family Issues*, 17(4):561–578.

Kuppersmith, J. 1994. "The Double Bind of Personal Striving: Ethnic Working Class Women in Psychotherapy," in V. Demos and M. Texler Segal (eds.). *Ethnic Women: A Multiple Status Reality*. New York: General Hall Inc. Pp. 82–94.

Kurdek, Lawrence A. 1990. "Effects of Child Age on the Marital Quality and Psychological Distress of Newly Married Mothers and Stepfathers," *Journal of Marriage and the Family*, 52:81–85.

Kurdek, Lawrence A. 1991. "Marital Stability and Changes in Marital Quality in Newly Wed Couples: A Test of the Contextual Model," *Journal of Social and Personal Relationships*, 8:27–48.

Kurdek, Lawrence A. 1991. "The Relationship Between Reported Wellbeing and Divorce History, Availability of a Proximate Adult and Gender," *Journal of Marriage and the Family*, 53:71–78.

Kurdek, Lawrence A. 1994. "Areas of Conflict for Gay, Lesbian, and Heterosexual Couples: What Couples Argue about Influences Relationship Satisfaction," *Journal of Marriage and the Family*, 56:923–934.

Kurdek, Lawrence A. 1996. "The Deterioration of Relationship Quality for Gay and Lesbian Cohabiting Couples: A Five-Year Prospective Longitudinal Study," *Personal Relationships*, 3:417–440.

Kurian, G. and Ghosh, R. 1983.* "Child-Rearing in Transition in Native Canadian Immigration Families in Canada," in G. Kurian and R.P. Srivastava (eds.). *Overseas Native Canadians: A Study in Adaptation*. New Delhi: Vikas Publishing House. Pp. 128–138.

Kurian, George. 1986. "Dynamics of Youth Attitudes in South Asian Families," *International Journal of Contemporary Sociology*, 23(1,2):69–85.

Kurian, George. 1982. "A Review of Marriage and Adjustment in Indian Families," in John S. Augustine (ed.). *The Indian Family in Transition*. New Delhi: Vikas Publishing.

Kurian, George. 1993.* "Marital Patterns in Canada," in G. N. Ramu. *Marriage and the Family in Canada Today*, (second edition). Scarborough: Prentice-Hall Canada.

Kyriazis, Natalie and Morton Stelcner. 1986.* "A Logit Analysis of Living Arrangements in Canada: A Comparison of the Young and the Aging," *Journal of Comparative Family Studies*, 17:389–402.

L'Abate, Luciano. 1983. "Prevention as a Profession: Toward a New Conceptual Frame of Reference," in David R. Mace (ed.). *Prevention in Family Services: Approaches to Family Wellness*. Newbury Park: Sage, 49–62.

Labour Canada. 1988.* *Women in the Labour Force, 1986–1987 Edition*. Ottawa: Minister of Supplies and Services.

Lackey, C. and K. Williams. 1995. "Social Bonding and the Cessation of Partner Violence Across Generations," *Journal of Marriage and the Family*, 57:295–305.

Lackey, Pat N. 1989. "Adults' Attitudes about Assignment of Household Chores to Male and Female Children," *Sex Roles*, 20:271–281.

LaFrenier, P., D. Dubeau and M. Bigras. 1989.* "Marital Relations and Childhood Behaviour Problems," paper presented at the Society for Research in Child Development, Kanas City.

Lamb, Michael E. 1996.* "Effects of Nonparental Child Care on Child Development: An Update," *Canadian Journal of Psychiatry*, 41:330–342.

Lamb, S. and S. Edgar-Lamb. 1994. "Aspects of Disclosure: Mediators of Outcome of Childhood Sexual Abuse," *Journal of Interpersonal Violence*, 9(3):307–326.

Landy, Sarah and Kwok Kwan Tam. 1996. "Yes, Parenting Does Make a Difference to the Development of Children in Canada," *National Longitudinal Survey of Children and Youth*. Statistics Canada: Catalogue No. 89–550–MPE: 103–118.

Lane, Katherine E. and Patricia Gwartney-Gibbs. 1985. "Violence in the Context of Dating and Sex," *Journal of Family Issues*, 6:45–59.

Laner, M.R. and N.A. Ventrone. 1998. "Egalitarian Daters/Traditionalist Dates," *Journal of Family Issues*, 19:468–477.

Langford, Nanci. 1998.* "Immigrant Couples' Coping Strategies." Unpublished. Edmonton: Department of Human Ecology, University of Alberta.

Lansden, Pamela. 1992. "Going Home Alone, Too," *Newsweek*, December 28:7.

LaPierre-Adamcyk, E., LeBourdais, C. and Marcil-Gratton, N. (2003). "French Canadian Families." In J. Ponzetti et al. (Eds.) *International Encyclopedia of Marriage and Family* (Vol. 2). New York: MacMillan Reference, 697–702.

LaPrairie, Carol. 1991.* "Native Women and Crime: A Theoretical Model," in Samuel W. Corrigan. (ed.). *Readings in Aboriginal Studies, Volume 1, Human Services*. Brandon: Bearpaw Publishing.

Laroche, Michel et al. 1996. "An Empirical Study of Multidimensional Ethnic Change: The Case of the French Canadians in Quebec," *Journal of Cross-Cultural Psychology*, 27(1):114–131.

LaRossa, Ralph. 1986. *Becoming a Parent*. Beverly Hills: Sage.

LaRossa, Ralph and Donald C. Retzes. 1993. "Symbolic Interactionism and Family Studies," in Pauline G. Boss, William G. Doherty, Ralph LaRossa, Walter R. Schumm and Suzanne K. Steinmetz (eds.). *Sourcebook of Family Theories and Methods: A Contextual Approach*. New York: Plenum Press, Chapter 6.

Larson, Lyle E. 1970.* "The Family in Contemporary Society and Emerging Family Patterns," in *Day Care—A Resource for the Contemporary Family*. Ottawa: The Vanier Institute of the Family.

Larson, Lyle E. 1974a. "An Examination of the Salience Hierarchy during Adolescence: The Influence of the Family," *Adolescence*, 9:317–332.

Larson, Lyle E. 1974b. "System and Subsystem Perception of Family Roles," *Journal of Marriage and the Family*, 36:123–138.

Larson, Lyle E. 1976a.* "Toward a Conceptual Model of Heterosexual Love," in Lyle E. Larson (ed.). *The Canadian Family in Comparative Perspective*. Scarborough: Prentice-Hall Canada.

Larson, Lyle E. 1976b.* *The Canadian Family in Comparative Perspective*. Scarborough: Prentice-Hall Canada.

Larson, Lyle E. 1980.* "Issues in Family Life, 1977–1980," unpublished paper based on data collected in the 1980 Edmonton Area Survey.

Larson, Lyle E. 1980.* *Improving Family Services in the City of Edmonton*. Edmonton: Office of the Mayor.

Larson, Lyle E. 1984.* "Marital Breakdown in Canada: A Sociological Analysis?" in Joseph A. Buijs (ed.). *Christian Marriage Today. Growth or Breakdown? Interdisciplinary Essays*. New York: The Edwin Mellen Press, 35–69.

Larson, Lyle E. 1987.* "Interpersonal Perception in Marriage: A Research Note," *Canadian Association of the Study of Families Newsletter*, 4:3–7.

Larson, Lyle E. 1989.* "Family Policies, Community Context and Preventative Services to Families," in *Symposium About Families: Volume 1, Speakers' Papers*. Regina: Government of Saskatchewan, 78–96.

Larson, Lyle E. 1989b.* "Religiosity and Marital Commitment: 'Until Death Do Us Part' Revisited," *Family Science Review*, 2:285–302.

Larson, Lyle E. and Brenda Munro. 1985.* "Religious Intermarriage in Canada, 1974–1982," *International Journal of Sociology of the Family*, 15:31–49.

Larson, Lyle E. and Brenda Munro. 1990.* "Religious Intermarriage in Canada in the 1980s," *Journal of Comparative Family Studies*, 21:239–250.

Larson, Lyle E. and J. Walter Goltz. 1993.* "Family Values, Religion and Individualistic Attitudes," unpublished paper, Edmonton.

Larson, Lyle E. and J. Walter Goltz.* 1989. "Religious Participation and Marital Commitment," *Review of Religious Research*, 30:387–400.

Larzelere, Robert E. (1996). "A Review Of The Outcomes Of Parental Use Of Non-Abusive Or Customary Physical Punishment," *Pediatrics*, 98:824–831.

Larzelere, Robert E., Sather, P., Schneider, W. Larson, D. and Pike, P. (1998). "Punishment Enhances Reasoning's Effectiveness As A Disciplinary Response To Toddlers," *Journal of Marriage and Family*, 60:388–403.

Lasch, Christopher. 1977. *Haven in a Heartless World: The Family Besieged*. New York: Basic Books.

Lasch, Christopher. 1978. *The Culture of Narcissism: American Life in an Age of Diminishing Expectations*. New York: W. W. Norton.

Laslett, Peter. 1979. *The World We Have Lost*. London: Methuen.

Lauer, Jeanette C. and Robert H. Lauer. 1986. *'Til Death Do Us Part: How Couples Stay Together*. New York: The Haworth Press.

Laumann, Edward O., John H. Gagnon, Robert T. Michael and Stuart Michaels. 1994. *The Social Organization of Sexuality: Sexual Practices in the United States*. Chicago: University of Chicago Press.

Lavee, Yoav, Shlomo Sharlin and Ruth Katz. 1996. "The Effect of Parenting Stress on Marital Quality," *Journal of Family Issues*, 17:114–135.

Lawrance, Kelli-an, David J. Taylor, Sandra E. Byers. 1996. "Differences in Men's and Women's Global, Sexual, and Ideal-Sexual Expressiveness and Instrumentality," *Sex Roles*, 34:337–357.

Layland vs. Ontario.* (Minister of Consumer and Commercial Relations) 1993. 104 Dominion Law Reporter (4th) 214.

Layman, Richard. 1990. *Child Abuse*. Detroit: Omnigraphics, Inc.

Le, B, and Agnew, C.R. 2003. "Commitment And Its Theorized Determinants: A Meta-Analysis Of The Investment Model." *Personal Relationships* 10:37–57.

Le Bourdais, Céline and Nicole Marcil-Gratton. 1994.* "Quebec's Pro-active Approach to Family Policy: 'Thinking and acting family,'" in Baker, Maureen (ed.). *Canada's Changing Families: Challenges to Public Policy*. Ottawa: The Vanier Institute of the Family. Chapter 8.

LeBlanc, Marc, Pierre McDuff, Pierre Charlebois, Claude Gagnon, Serge Larrivee and Richard E. Tremblay. 1991.* "Social and Psychological Consequences, at 10 Years Old, of an Earlier Onset of Self-Reported Delinquency," *Psychiatry*, 54:133–147.

Lee, C.M. and L. Duxbury. 1998. "Employed Parents, Support from Partners, Employers, and Friends," *Journal of Social Psychology*, 138(3):303–322.

Lee, G. 1982. *Family Structure and Interaction: A Comparative Analysis*. Minneapolis: University of Minnesota Press.

Lee, Gary R. 1984. "Status of the Elderly: Economic and Family Antecedents," *Journal of Marriage and the Family*, 46:267–275.

Lee, Gary R. 1988. "The Feasibility of an Integration," in Erik E. Filsinger (ed.), *Biosocial Perspectives on the Family*. Newbury Park: Sage, Chapter 7.

Lee, Gary R. 1996. "Economies and Families: A Further Investigation of the Curvilinear Hypothesis," *Journal of Comparative Family Studies*, 27(2):353–372.

Lee, Gary R., Karen Seccombe and Constance L. Shehan. 1991. "Marital Status and Personal Happiness: An Analysis of Trend Data," *Journal of Marriage and the Family*, 53:839–844.

Lee, Gary R., Karen Seccombe and Constance L. Shehan. 1991. "Marital Status and Personal Happiness: An Analysis of Trend Data," *Journal of Marriage and the Family*, 53:839–44.

Lee, Gary R., Raymond T. Coward and Julie K. Netzer. 1994. "Residential Differences in Filial Responsibility Expectations Among Older Persons," *Rural Sociology*, 59:100–109.

Lee, Grant and Marvin J. Westwood. 1996. "Cross-cultural Adjustment Issues Faced by Immigrant Professionals," *Journal of Employment Counseling*, 33(1):29–42.

Lee, John A. 1973.* *The Colours of Love.* Toronto: New Press.

Lee, John A. 1974.* "The Styles of Loving," *Psychology Today*, October: 43–51.

Lee, John A. 1975.* "The Romantic Heresy," *Canadian Review of Sociology and Anthropology*, 12:514–528.

Lee, John A. 1977.* "A Typology of Styles of Loving," *Personality and Social Psychology Bulletin*, 3:173–182.

Lee, John A. 1988.* "Love Styles," in Robert J Sternberg and Michael L. Barnes (eds.). *The Psychology of Love.* New Haven: Yale University Press.

Leenaars, Antoon A. and David Lester. 1990a.* "Suicide in Adolescents: A Comparison of Canada and the United States," *Psychological Reports*, 67:867–873.

Leenaars, Antoon A. and David Lester. 1990b.* "A Comparision of Rates and Patterns of Suicide in Canada and the United States, 1960–1988," unpublished paper, Windsor, Ontario.

Leenaars, Antoon A. and David Lester. 1995.* "The Changing Suicide Pattern in Canadian Adolescents and Youth, Compared to Their American Counterparts," *Adolescence*, 30(119):539–547.

Leenaars, Antoon A. and G. Domino. 1990.* "A Comparison of Community Attitudes Towards Suicide in Canada and the United States," unpublished paper, Windsor, Ontario.

Légaré, Jacques, T.R. Balakrishnan and Roderic P. Beaujot (eds.). 1989.* *The Family in Crisis: A Population Crisis?* Ottawa: Lowe-Martin Company.

Lehrer, Evelyn L. and Carmel U. Chiswick. 1993. "Religion as a Determinant of Marital Stability," *Demography*, 30:385–404.

Leibowitz, Lila. 1978. *Females, Males, Families: A Biosocial Approach.* North Scityate: Duxbury Press.

Leik, Robert K. and S.A. Leik. 1977. "Transition to Interpersonal Commitment," in R. L. Hamblin and J. Kunkle (eds.). *Behavioral Theory in Sociology.* New Brunswick: Transaction Books.

LeMasters, E.E. and John DeFrain. 1989. *Parents in Contemporary America: A Sympathetic View* (fifth edition). Belmont: Wadsworth.

Lempers, J. and D. Clark-Lempers. 1997. "Economic Hardship, Family Relationships, and Adolescent Distress: An Evaluation of a Stress–Distress Mediation Model on Mother–Daughter and Mother–Son Dyads,"*Adolescence*, 32(126):339–356.

Lenton, Rhonda L. 1990.* "Techniques of Child Discipline and Abuse by Parents," *Canadian Review of Sociology and Anthropology*, 27:157–185.

Leonard, E. 1996. "A Social Exchange Explanation of Childhood Sexual Abuse Accommodation Syndrome," *Journal of Interpersonal Violence*, 11(1):107–117.

LePlay, F. (1871). *L'Organisation de la Famille, Selon le Vrai Modele Signale par l'Historie de Toutes les Races et de Tous les Temps.* Paris: Tequi.

Lero, Donna S. and Irene Kyle. 1991.* "Work, Families and Child Care in Ontario," in Laura C. Johnson and Dick Barnhorst (eds.). *Children, Families and Public Policy in the 1990s.* Toronto: Thompson Educational Publishing, 25–72.

Lero, Donna S. and Karen L. Johnson. 1994. *110 Canadian Statistics on Work and Family.* Ottawa: The Canadian Advisory Council on the Status of Women.

Lero, Donna S., Alan R. Pence, Margot Shields, Lois M. Brockman and Hillel Goelman. 1992.* *Canadian National Child Care Study: Introductory Report.* Catalogue 89–526E. Ottawa: Statistics Canada.

Leslie, Gerald R. and Sheila K. Korman. 1985. *The Family in Social Context.* New York: Oxford University Press.

Leslie, Leigh A., Ted L. Huston and Michael P. Johnson. 1986. "Parental Reactions to Dating Relationships: Do They Make a Difference?" *Journal of Marriage and the Family*, 48:57–66.

Levant, Ronald F., Susan C. Slattery and Jane E. Loiselle. 1987. "Fathers' Involvement in Household and Child Care with School-Aged Daughters," *Family Relations*, 36:152–157.

Levesque, R.J. 1994. "Sex Differences in the Experience of Child Sexual Victimization," *Journal of Family Violence*, 9(4):357–369.

Levin, Irene and Jan Trost. 1992. "Understanding the Concept of Family," *Family Relations*, 41:19–26.

Levine, Nancy E. and Walter H. Sangree. 1980. "Conclusion: Asian and African Systems of Polyandry," *Journal of Comparative Family Studies*, 11:385–410.

Levinger, George. 1966. "Systematic Distortion in Spouses' Reports of Preferred and Actual Sexual Behaviour," *Sociometry*, 29:291–299.

Levinger, George. 1979. "A Social Exchange View on the Dissolution of Pair Relationships," in R.L. Burgess and T.L. Huston (eds.). *Social Exchange in Developing Relationships.* New York: Academic Press.

Levinson, D. 1981. "Physical Punishment of Children and Wifebeating in Cross-Cultural Perspective," *Child Abuse and Neglect*, 5:193–195.

Levitan, Sar A., Richard S. Belous and Frank Gallo. 1988. *What's Happening to the American Family: Tensions, Hopes and Realities* (revised edition). Baltimore: Johns Hopkins University Press.

Levy, Samantha R., Gregory L. Jurkovic and Anthony Spirito. 1995. "A Multisystems Analysis of Adolescent Suicide Attempters," *Journal of Abnormal Psychology*, 23(2):221–234.

Levy-Shiff, Rachel and R. Israelashvili. 1988. "Antecedents of Fathering: Some Further Exploration," *Developmental Psychology*, 24:434–440.

Lewin, Bo. 1982. "Unmarried Cohabitation: A Marriage Form in a Changing Society," *Journal of Marriage and the Family*, 44:763–773.

Lewis, Robert A. and Graham B. Spanier. 1979. "Theorizing About the Quality and Stability of Marriage," in Wesley R. Burr, Reuben Hill, F. Ivan Nye and Ira L. Reiss. *Contemporary Theories About the Family*. New York: The Free Press.

Li, Peter S. and Dawn Currie. 1992.* "Gender Differences in Work Interruptions as Unequal Effects of Marriage and Childrearing: Findings from a Canadian National Survey," *Journal of Comparative Family Studies*, 23:217–229.

Lichter, Daniel T. 1990. "Delayed Marriage, Marital Homogamy, and the Mate Selection Process Among White Women," *Social Science Quarterly*, 71:802–811.

Lichter, Daniel T., Robert N. Anderson, and Mark D. Hayward. 1995. "Marriage Markets and Marital Choice," *Journal of Family Issues*, 16:412–431.

Ligezinska, M., P. Firestone, I. Manion, J. McIntyre, R. Ensom and G. Wells. 1996.* "Children's Emotional and Behavioural Reactions Following the Disclosure of Extrafamilial Sexual Abuse: Initial Effects," *Child Abuse and Neglect*, 20(2):111–125.

Lillard, Lee A. and Linda J. Waite. 1995. "'Til Death Do Us Part: Marital Disruption and Mortality," *American Journal of Sociology*, 100:1131–1156.

Lillard, L.A., M.J. Brien and L.J. Waite. 1995. "Premarital Cohabitation and Subsequent Marital Dissolution: a Matter of Self-selection?" *Demography*, 32(3):437–457.

Lindsay, Colin and Shelley Donald. 1988.* "Income of Canada's Seniors," *Canadian Social Trends*, 10:20–25.

Lindsay, Colin. 1992.* *Lone-Parent Families in Canada*. Catalogue No. 89–522E. Ottawa: Supply and Services Canada.

Lindsay, Colin. 1997. *A Portrait of Seniors in Canada*. Statistics Canada, Catalogue No. 89–519–XPE.

Linton, Ralph. 1939. "Marquesan Culture," in Abram Kardiner. *The Individual and His Society*. New York: Columbia University Press.

Linton, Ralph. 1959. "The Natural History of the Family," in Ruth N. Anshen (ed.). *The Family: Its Function and Destiny*. New York: Harper and Row.

Lipman, M. 1984.* "Adoption in Canada: Two Decades in Review," in P. Sachdev (ed.). *Adoption: Current Issues and Trends*. Toronto: Butterworths.

Lipset, Seymour M. 1990. *Continental Divide: The Values and Institutions of the United States and Canada*. London: Routledge.

Livingstone, D.W. and Meg Luxton. 1989.* "Gender Consciousness at Work: Modification of the Male Breadwinner Norm Among Steelworkers and Their Spouses," *Canadian Review of Sociology and Anthropology*, 26:240–275.

Lloyd, Sally A. 1991. "The Darkside of Courtship: Violence and Sexual Exploitation," *Family Relations*, 40:14–20.

Lloyd, Sally A. and Rodney M. Cate. 1985. "The Developmental Course of Conflict in Dissolution of Premarital Relationships," *Journal of Social and Personal Relationships*, 2:179–194.

Lloyd, Sally A., Rodney M. Cate and June M. Henton. 1984. "Predicting Premarital Stability: A Methodological Refinement," *Journal of Marriage and the Family*, 46:71–76.

Locke, H.J. 1947. "Predicting Marital Adjustment By Comparing Divorced And Happily Married Group," *American Sociological Review*, 12:187–191.

Locke, H.J. and Wallace, K.M. 1959. "Short Marital Adjustment And Prediction Tests: Their Reliability And Validity," *Marriage and Family Living*, 21:251–255.

Long, Edgar C.J., Rodney M. Cate, Del A. Fehsenfeld and Kimberly M. Williams. 1996. "A Longitudinal Assessment of a Measure of Premarital Sexual Conflict," *Family Relations*, 45(3):302–308.

Long, P. and J. Jackson. 1993. "Initial Emotional Response to Childhood Sexual Abuse: Emotion Profiles of Victims and Relationship to Later Adjustment," *Journal of Family Violence*, 8(2):167–181.

Long, P. and J. Jackson. 1994. "Childhood Sexual Abuse: An Examination of Family Functioning," *Journal of Interpersonal Violence*, 9(2):270–277.

Lopata, H.Z. 1970. "The Social Involvement of American Widows," *American Behavioural Scientist*, 14:41–57.

Lopata, Helena Z. (ed.). 1987. *Widows* (Volume II). Durham: Duke University Press.

Lorber, Judith and Susan A. Farrell. 1991. *The Social Construction of Gender*. Newbury Park: Sage.

Lord, Cathy. 1992.* "Woman Says She Begged For Life as Ex-Lover Beat Her With Hammer," *Edmonton Journal*, January 20:B3.

Los Angeles Times. 1996. "Birth Rates for Teens, Unmarried Women Fall." Press release by National Center for Health Statistics, October 5.

Losh-Hesselbart, Susan. 1987. "Development of Gender Roles," in Marvin B. Sussman and Suzanne K. Steinmetz (Eds.). *Handbook of Marriage and the Family*. New York: Plenum Press.

Lovdal, Lynn. 1989. "Sex Role Messages in Television Commercials: An Update," *Sex Roles*, 21:715–724.

Lowe, Graham S. 1987.* *Women in the Administrative Revolution: The Feminization of Clerical Work*. Toronto: University of Toronto Press.

Lowe, Graham S. 1992.* "Canadians and Retirement," *Canadian Social Trends*, 26:18–21.

Lowe, Graham S. and Harvey Krahn. 1985.* "Where Wives Work: The Relative Effects of Situational and Attitudinal Factors," *Canadian Journal of Sociology*, 10:1–22.

Lund, Mary. 1985. "The Development of Investment and Commitment Scales for Predicting Continuity of Personal Relationships," *Journal of Social and Personal Relationships*, 2:3–23.

Lupri, Eugen. 1989.* "Male Violence in the Home," *Canadian Social Trends*, Autumn:19–21.

Lupri, Eugen. 1990.* "Hidden in the Home: The Dialectics of Conjugal Violence: The Case of Canada," English version of "Harmonie und Aggression: Uber die Dialektik ehrlicher Gewalt," *Kolner Zeitschrift fur Soziologie und Sozialpsychologie*, 42:479–501.

Lupri, Eugen. 1990a.* "Male Violence in the Home," in C. McKie and K. Thompson (eds.). *Canadian Social Trends*. Toronto: Thompson Educational Publishing.

Lupri, Eugen. 1991.* "Fathers in Transition: The Case of Dual-Earner Families in Canada," in Jean E. Veevers (ed.) *Continuity and Change in Marriage and Family*. Toronto: Holt Rinehart and Winston.

Lupri, Eugen. 1993.* "The Dark Side of Family Life: The Case of Wife Abuse," in M. Featherstone (ed.). *The Future of Adult Life*.

Lupri, Eugen and Donald L. Mills. 1987.* "The Household Division of Labour in Young Dual-Earner Couples: The Case of Canada," *International Review of Sociology*, New Series, No. 2:33–54.

Lupri, Eugen and James Frideres. 1981.* "The Quality of Marriage and the Passage of Time: Marital Satisfaction over the Family Life Cycle," *Canadian Journal of Sociology*, 6:283–305.

Luster, Tom and Stephen A. Small. 1994. "Factors Associated with Sexual Risk-Taking Behaviors Among Adolescents," *Journal of Marriage and the Family*, 56(3):622–632.

Lutz, Patricia. 1983. "The Stepfamily: An Adolescent Perspective," *Family Relations*, 32:367–375.

Luxton, Meg. 1980.* *More than a Labour of Love, Three Generations of Women's Working in the Home*. Toronto: Women's Press.

Lye, Diane N. and Timothy J. Biblarz. "The Effects of Attitudes Toward Family Life and Gender Roles on Marital Satisfaction," *Journal of Family Issues*, 14:157–188.

Lytton, Hugh and David M. Romney. 1991.* "Parents' Differential Socialization of Boys and Girls: A Meta-Analysis," *Psychological Bulletin*, 109:267–296.

Maccoby, Eleanor E. and Carol N. Jacklin. 1974. *The Psychology of Sex Differences*. Stanford: Stanford University Press.

MacDonald, William L. and Alfred DeMaris. 1996. "Parenting Stepchildren and Biological Children: The Effects of Stepparent's Gender and New Biological Children," *Journal of Family Issues*, 17(1):5–25.

MacDougall, Don. 1980.* "Policy and Social Factors Affecting the Legal Recognition of Cohabitation Without Formal Marriage," in John M. Eekelaar and Sanford M. Katz (eds.). *Marriage and Cohabitation in Contemporary Societies*. Toronto: Butterworths, 313–322.

Mace, David R. (ed.). 1983. *Prevention in Family Services: Approaches to Family Wellness*. Newbury Park: Sage.

Mace, David R. 1987. "Three Ways of Helping Married Couples," *Journal of Marital and Family Therapy*, 13:179–185.

MacEwen, Karyl E. and Julian Barling. 1991.* "Effects of Maternal Employment Experiences on Children's Behavior via Mood, Cognitive Difficulties and Parenting Behavior," *Journal of Marriage and the Family*, 53:635–644.

MacIver, Robert. 1964. *Social Causation*. New York: Harper & Row.

MacKenzie, Betsy. 1990.* "Therapeutic Abortion in Canada," in Craig McKie and Keith Thompson (eds.). *Canadian Social Trends*. Toronto: Thompson Educational Publishing.

Mackie, Marlene. 1991.* *Gender Relations in Canada: Further Explorations*. Toronto: Butterworths.

MacLeod, Linda. 1987.* *Battered But Not Beaten… Preventing Wife Battering in Canada*. Ottawa: Canadian Advisory Council on the Status of Women.

Madill, H.M., E.S.G. Brintnell, D. MacNab, L.L. Stewin and G.W. Fitzsimmons. 1988. "The Delicate Balance: Working and Family Roles," *International Journal for the Advancement of Counseling*, 11:219–230.

Maglin, Nan Bauer and Nancy Schneidewind. 1989. *Women and Stepfamilies: Voices of Anger and Love*, Philadelphia: Temple University Press.

Mahoney, Margaret M. 1997. "Stepfamilies from a Legal Perspective," *Marriage and Family Review*, 26(3/4): 231–247.

Makepeace, James M. 1981. "Courtship Violence Among College Students," *Family Relations*, 30:97–102.

Makepeace, James M. 1986. "Gender Differences in Courtship Violence Victimization," *Family Relations*, 35:383–388.

Malhotra, A. and Tsui, A. 1999. "Work and Marriage: Mother–Daughter Similarities in Sri Lanka," *Journal of Comparative Family Studies*, 30:219–241.

Malinowski, Bronislaw. 1929. *The Sexual Life of Savages*. New York: Harcourt, Brace and World.

Man, Guida. 1995.* "The Experience of Women in Chinese Immigrant Families: An Inquiry into Institutional and Organizational," *Asian and Pacific Migration Journal*, 4(2-3):303–323.

Mandell, Nancy and Ann Duffy (eds.). 1988.* *Reconstructing the Canadian Family: Feminist Perspectives*. Toronto: Butterworths.

Maneker, Jerry S. and Robert P. Rankin. 1993. "Religious Homogamy and Marital Duration Among Those Who Filed for Divorce in California, 1966–1971," *Journal of Divorce and Remarriage*, 19:233–247.

Manning, Wendy D. and Pamela J. Smock. 1997. "Children's Living Arrangements in Unmarried-Mother Families," *Journal of Family Issues*, 18(5):526–544.

Maracle, Brian. 1992.* *Crazywater*. Toronto: Viking Press.

Marcil-Gratton, Nicole and Jacques Légaré. 1992.* "Will Reduced Fertility Lead to Greater Isolation in Old Age for Tomorrow's Elderly?" *Canadian Journal on Aging*, 11:54–71.

Maret, Elizabeth and Barbara Finlay. 1984. "The Distribution of Household Labor Among Women in Dual-Earner Families," *Journal of Marriage and the Family*, 46:357–364.

Marin, Peter. 1983. "A Revolution's Broken Promises," *Psychology Today*, July:50–57.

Markman, Howard J. 1981. "Prediction of Marital Distress: A 5–Year Follow-up," *Journal of Consulting and Clinical Psychology*, 49:722–760.

Markman, Howard J., Louise Silvern, Mari Clements and Shelley Kraft-Hanak. 1993. "Men and Women Dealing with Conflict in Heterosexual Relationships," *Journal of Social Issues*, 49(3):107–125.

Marks, Nadine F. 1996. "Flying Solo at Mid-Life: Gender, Marital Status, and Psychological Well-Being," *Journal of Marriage and the Family*, 58:917–932.

Marks, Stephen R. 1995. "The Art of Professing and Holding Back in a Course on Gender," *Family Relations*, 44(2):142–148.

Markward, M. 1997. "The Impact of Domestic Violence on Children," *Families in Society: The Journal of Contemporary Human Services*, 78(1):66–70.

Marmor, Judd (ed.). 1980. *Homosexual Behavior: A Modern Reappraisal*. New York: Basic Books.

Maroney, Heather J. and Meg Luxton. 1987.* "From Feminism and Political Economy to Feminist Political Economy," in Heather J. Maroney and Meg Luxton (eds.). *Feminism and Political Economy: Women's Work, Women's Struggles*. Toronto: Methuen, Chapter 1.

Maroney, Heather Jon and Meg Luxton. 1987.* "Editors' Introduction," in Maroney, Heather Jon and Meg Luxton (eds.). *Feminism and Political Economy: Women's Work, Women's Struggles*. Toronto: Methuen.

Maroney, Heather Jon and Meg Luxton. 1987.* *Feminism and Political Economy, Women's Work, Women's Struggles*. Toronto: Methuen.

Marshall, Katherine. 1987.* "Women in Male-Dominated Professions," *Canadian Social Trends*, Winter:7–11.

Marshall, K. 1993. "Dual Earners: Who's Responsible for Housework?" *Canadian Social Trends*, Winter:11–14.

Marshall, K. 1994. "Balancing Work and Family Responsibilities," *Perspectives*, Spring, 1994.

Marshall, Victor W. 1980.* *Aging in Canada: Social Perspectives*. Don Mills: Fitzhenry and Whiteside.

Marshall, Victor W. 1987.* *Aging in Canada: Social Perspectives*. (second edition). Markham: Fitzhenry and Whiteside.

Marsiglio, William. 1992. "Stepfathers with Minor Children Living at Home: Parenting Perceptions and Relationship Quality," *Journal of Family Issues*, 13(2):195–214.

Martin, Karen. 1993.* *Searching for a Reason: How Parents Cope with a SIDS Death*, unpublished report, Department of Sociology, University of Alberta.

Martin, S.E. 1989. "Sexual Harassment: The Link Joining Gender Stratification, Sexuality and Women's Economic Status," in J. Freeman. (ed.). *Women: A Feminist Perspective* (fourth edition). Mountain View: Mayfield.

Martin, T.C. and L.L. Bumpass. 1989. "Recent Trends in Marital Disruption," *Demography*, 26:37–51. (Chapter 16.)

Martin-Matthews, Anne. 1987a.* "Support Systems of Widows in Canada," in H. Z. Lopata (ed.). *Widows: Volume II*. Durham: Duke University Press.

Martin-Matthews, Anne. 1987b.* "Widowhood as an Expectable Life Event," in Victor W. Marshall. *Aging in Canada: Social Perspectives* (second edition). Markham: Fitzhenry and Whiteside.

Maslow, Abraham. 1968. *Toward a Psychology of Being*. New York: Van Nostrand.

Mason, Mary Ann and Jane Mauldon. 1996. "The New Stepfamily Requires a New Public Policy," *Journal of Social Issues*, 52(3):11–27.

Mastekaasa, Arne. 1992. "Marriage and Psychological Well-Being: Some Evidence on Selection into Marriage," *Journal of Marriage and the Family*, 58:740–758.

Masten, A.S., N. Garmezy, A. Tellegen, D.S. Pellegrini, K. Larkin and A. Larsen. 1988. "Competence and Stress in School Children: The Moderating Effects of Individual and Family Characteristics," *Journal of Child Psychology and Psychiatry*, 29:745–764.

Masters, William H., Virginia E. Johnson and Robert C. Kolodny. 1986. *Masters and Johnson on Sex and Human Loving*. Boston: Little, Brown and Company.

Matthews, Ralph and Anne Martin-Matthews. 1986.* "Infertility and Involuntary Childlessness: The Transition to Nonparenthood," *Journal of Marriage and the Family*, 48:641–649.

Matthews, Victor H. and Don C. Benjamin. 1993. *Social World of Ancient Israel*. Peabody: Hendrickson Publishers, Inc.

Mattlessich, Paul and Reuben Hill. 1987. "Life Cycle and Family Development," in Marvin B. Sussman and Suzanne K. Steinmetz (eds.). *Handbook of Marriage and the Family*. New York: Plenum Press, Chapter 17.

May, Rollo. 1969. *Love and Will*. New York: W.W. Norton.

Mayrand, Armand. 1988.* "La garde conjointe, rééquilibrage de l'authorité parentale," *The Canadian Bar Review*, 67:193–228.

Maziade, Michel, Hugues Bernier, Jacques Thivierge and Robert Cote. 1987.* "The Relationship Between Family Functioning and Demographic Characteristics in an Epidemiological Study," *Canadian Journal of Psychiatry*, 32:526–533.

Mc Bride, Brent A., Schoppe, Sarah J. and Rane, Thomas R. (2002). "Child Characteristics, Parenting Strss, And Parental Involvement: Father Versus Mothers," *Journal of Marriage and Family*, 64:998–1011.

McCall, Marnie L., Joseph P. Hornick and Jean E. Wallace. 1988.* *The Process and Economic Consequences of Marriage Breakdown*. Calgary: Canadian Research Institute for Law and the Family.

McCann, Stewart J.H., Leonard L. Stewin and Robert H. Short. 1990.* *Psychological Reports*, 66:1187–1194.

McCarthy, J.F. 1978. "A Comparison of the Probability of Dissolution of First and Second Marriages," *Demography*, 15:345–359.

McCord, Joan. 1988. "Parental Aggressiveness and Physical Punishment in Long Term Perspective," in Gerald T. Hotaling, David Finkelhor, John T. Kirkpatrick and Murray A. Straus (eds.). *Family Abuse and Its Consequences: New Directions in Research*. Newbury Park: Sage.

McCormack, Arlene, Ann Wolbert Burgess and Peter Gaccione. 1986.* "Influence of Family Structure and Financial Stability on Physical and Sexual Abuse among a Runaway Population," *International Journal of Sociology of the Family*, 16:251–262.

McCubbin, H.I. and J.M. Patterson. 1983. "The Family Stress Process: The Double ABCX Model of Adjustment and Adaptation," in H.I. McCubbin, M.B. Sussman and J.M. Patterson (eds.). *Social Stress and the Family: Advances and Developments in Family Stress Theory and Research*. New York: Haworth Press.

McCubbin, Hamilton I. and Joan M. Patterson. 1983. "Family Transitions: Adaptation to Stress," in Hamilton I. McCubbin and Charles R. Figley (eds.). *Stress and the Family, Vol. 1: Coping with Normative Transitions*. New York: Brunner and Mazel.

McCubbin, M.A. and H.I. McCubbin. 1983. "The Role of Family Meanings Inadaptation to Chronic Illness and Disability," in Danielson, C.B., B. Hamel-Bissell and P. Winstead-Fry (eds.). 1993. *Families, Health and Illness; Perspectives on Coping and Intervention*. St. Louis: C.V. Mosby.

McCubbin, Marilyn A. and Charles R. Figley. 1983. *Stress and the Family, Vol. 1. Coping with Normative Transitions*. New York: Brunner and Mazel.

McCubbin, Marilyn A. and Hamilton I. McCubbin. 1987. "Family Stress Theory and Assessment," in Hamilton I. McCubbin and Anne I. Thompson (eds.). *Family Assessment Inventories for Research and Practice*. Madison: University of Wisconsin Press.

McCubbin, Marilyn A. and Hamilton I. McCubbin. 1989. "Theoretical Orientations to Family Stress and Coping," in Charles Figley (ed.). *Treating Families Under Stress*. New York: Brunner and Mazel.

McDaniel, Susan A. 1989b.* "An Alternative to the Family in Crisis Model," in Jacques Légaré, T.R. Balakrishnan and Roderic P. Beaujot (eds.). *The Family in Crisis: A Population Crisis?* Ottawa: The Royal Society of Canada, 439–451.

McDaniel, Susan A. 1986.* *Canada's Aging Population*. Toronto: Butterworths.

McDaniel, Susan A. 1987.* "Demographic Aging as a Guiding Paradigm in Canada's Welfare State," *Canadian Public Policy — Analyse de Politiques*, 13:330–336.

McDaniel, Susan A. 1989a.* "Reconceptualizing the Nuptiality/Fertility Relationship in Canada in a New Age," *Canadian Studies in Population*, 16:163–185.

McDaniel, Susan A. 1990a.* *Families Today: Change, Diversity and Challenge*. Edmonton: Government of Alberta.

McDaniel, Susan A. 1990b.* *Towards Family Policies in Canada with Women in Mind*, No. 17 in *Feminist Perspectives*. Ottawa: Canadian Research Institute for the Advancement of Women.

McDaniel, Susan A. 1992a.* "Life Rhythms and Caring: Aging, Family and the State," 23rd Annual Sorokin Lecture. Saskatoon: University of Saskatchewan.

McDaniel, Susan A. 1992b.* "Women and Family in the Later Years: Findings from the 1990 General Social Survey," *Canadian Woman Studies*, 12:62–64.

McDaniel, Susan A. 1993.* "Bridges and Frontiers: Families, Women and Work in an Aging Canada." Research Discussion Paper No. 96, Population Research Laboratory, University of Alberta.

McDaniel, Susan A. 1993a.* "Families, Feminism and the State: Canada in the 1990s," in L. Samuelson and B. Marshall (eds.). *Social Problems: Thinking Critically*. Toronto: Garamond.

McDaniel, Susan A. 1993b.* "Caring and Sharing: Demographic Aging, Family and the State," in Jon Hendricks and Carolyn Rosenthal (eds.). *The Remainder of Their Days: The Impact of Public Policy on Older Families.* Toronto: Garland Press.

McDaniel, Susan A. 1993c.* "Single Parenthood: Policy Apartheid in Canada," in Hudson, Joe and Burt Galaway (eds.). *Single Parent Families: Perspectives in Research and Policy.* Toronto: Thompson Educational Publishing, Chapter 12.

McDaniel, Susan A. 1993d.* "Emotional Support and Family Contacts of Older Canadians," *Canadian Social Trends,* 28:30–33.

McDaniel, Susan A. 1996.* "At the Heart of Social Solidarity," *Transition,* September:9–11.

McDaniel, Susan A. and Allison L. McKinnon. 1993.* "Gender Differences in Informal Support and Coping Among Elders: Findings from Canada's 1985 and 1990 General Social Surveys," *Journal of Women and Aging,* 5:2.

McDaniel, Susan A. and Ellen M. Gee. 1993.* "Social Policies Regarding Caregiving to Elders: Canadian Contradictions," *Journal of Aging and Social Policy,* 5:1–2.

McDonald, P. Lynn, Joseph P. Hornick, Gerald B. Robertson and Jean E. Wallace. 1991.* *Elder Abuse and Neglect in Canada.* Toronto: Butterworths.

McDonald, Ryan J. 1991.* "Canada's Off-Reserve Aboriginal Population," *Canadian Social Trends,* 23:208. Catalogue No. 11–00E.

McDonald, Ryan J. 1992.* "Missing Children," *Canadian Social Trends,* Spring:2–5.

McElhaney, Lori J. 1994. "The Relationship Between Marital Quality and Children in Later Life Remarriages: An Exploratory Study." Working Paper #94–09, Population Research Institute, The Pennsylvania State University.

McGaha, Johnny E. and Edward L. Leoni. 1995. "Family Violence, Abuse, and Related Family Issues of Incarcerated Delinquents with Alcoholic Parents Compared to Those With Non-alcoholic Parents," *Adolescence,* 30(118):473–482.

McGinnis, Sandra L. 2003. "Cohabiting, Dating, and Perceived Costs of Marriage: A Model of Marriage Entry," *Journal of Marriage and Family,* 65:105–116.

McGoldrick, Monica and Elizabeth Carter. 1982. "The Family Life Cycle," in Froma Walsh (ed.). *Normal Family Processes.* New York: The Guilford Press.

McGovern, Celeste. 1993a.* "The High Cost of Cheap Divorce," *Alberta Report,* January 18:28–29.

McGovern, Celeste. 1993b.* "To Bear or Not to Bear," *Alberta Report,* January 4:24–25.

McHale, Susan M. and Ann C. Crouter. 1992. "You Can't Always Get What You Want: Incongruence Between Sex-Role Attitudes and Family Work Roles and Its Implications for Marriage," *Journal of Marriage and the Family,* 54:537–547.

McHale, Susan M. and Ted L. Huston. 1985. "The Effect of the Transition to Parenthood on the Marriage Relationship: A Longitudinal Study," *Journal of Family Issues,* 6:409–434.

McIntyre, Jennie. 1981. "The Structure-Functional Approach to Family Study," in F. Ivan Nye and Felix Berardo (eds.). *Emerging Conceptual Frameworks in Family Analysis.* New York: Praeger, Chapter 3.

McKenry, P., T. Julian and S. Gavazzi. 1995. "Toward a Biopsychosocial Model of Domestic Violence," *Journal of Marriage and the Family,* 57:307–320.

McKenry, Patrick C., Mary W. McKelvey, Diana Leigh and Linda Wark. 1996. "Nonresidential Father Involvement: A Comparison of Divorced, Separated, Never Married, and Remarried Fathers," *Journal of Divorce and Remarriage,* 25(3/4):1–13.

McKern, Patti. 1996. Associated Press. "Surrogate Carries Baby for Friend Who Is Unable," *Eugene Register Guard,* February 13, 1996:3C.

McKie, Craig. 1986.* "Common Law: Living Together as Husband and Wife Without Marriage," *Canadian Social Trends,* Autumn:39–41.

McKie, D.C., B. Prentice and P. Reed. 1983.* *Divorce: Law and the Family in Canada.* Ottawa: Supply and Services Canada.

McKinnon, Allison L. 1991.* "AIDS: Knowledge, Attitudes and Behaviours in Alberta," *Canadian Social Trends,* 23:25.

McKinnon, Allison L. and David Odynak. 1991.* *Elder Care, Employees and Employers: Some Canadian Evidence.* Discussion paper prepared for the Demographic Review Secretariat, Health and Welfare Canada. Edmonton: Population Research Laboratory, University of Alberta.

McLanahan, Sara and Karen Booth. 1991. "Mother-Only Families," in Alan Booth (ed.). *Contemporary Families: Looking Forward, Looking Back.* Minneapolis: National Council on Family Relations, 405–428.

McLaren, Angus. 1978.* "Birth Control and Abortion in Canada, 1870–1930," *Canadian Historical Review,* 59:319–340.

McLeod, James B. 1988.* "Unequal Distribution of Family Property: Valuation of Property," *1988 National Family Law Program,* Vol. 2:D-1–153. The Federation of Law Societies of Canada and the Canadian Bar Association.

Mc Loyd, Vonnie C. and Julia Smith (2002). "Physical Discipline And Behavior Problems In African American, European American, And Hispanic Children: Emotional Support As A Moderator." *Journal of Marriage and Family* 64:40–53.

McMurtry, Steven. 1985. "Secondary Prevention of Child Maltreatment: A Review," *Social Work*, January–February:42–48.

McNeal, Cosandra and Paul R. Amato. 1998. "Parents' Marital Violence: Long-Term Consequences for Children," *Journal of Family Issues*, 19(2):123–139.

McNeece, C. Aaron. 1995. "Family Social Work Practice: From Therapy to Policy," *Journal of Family Social Work*, 1(1):3–17.

McPherson, Barry D. 1983.* Aging as a Social Process. Toronto: Butterworths.

McQueeny, Jane. 1984. "Joint Custody: A Paradigm of Tomorrow's Family?" in *Seeking Solomon's Wisdom*. New Orleans: Loyola University School of Law.

McVey Jr., Wayne W. and Warren E. Kalbach. 1995. *Canadian Population*. Toronto: Nelson Canada.

McVey Jr., Wayne W. 1997.* Special data preparations by the author and provided to the authors of this textbook.

McVey, Wayne. 1998. "Population by Single Years of Age, Showing Sex, for Canada, Provinces, and Census Metropolitan Areas: 1996," Statcan 6.1 (prepared by Demografics, Ltd.).

McVey, Wayne and Warren Kalbach, 1993.* *Canadian Population*, Toronto: Nelson Canada.

McVey, Wayne W. 1998b. Special data preparations by the author provided to the authors of this textbook.

McVey, Wayne W. Jr. and Barrie W. Robinson. 1981.* "Separation in Canada: New Insights Concerning Marital Dissolution," *Canadian Journal of Sociology*, 6:353–366.

McVey, Wayne W. Jr. and Barrie W. Robinson. 1985.* "The Relative Contributions of Death and Divorce to Marital Dissolution in Canada and the United States," *Journal of Comparative Family Studies*, 16:93–109.

Mead, Margaret. 1975. *Male and Female*. New York: William Morrow.

Medling, James M. and Michael McCarrey. 1981.* "Marital Adjustment over Segments of the Family Life Cycle: The Issue of Spouses' Value Similarity," *Journal of Marriage and the Family*, 43:195–203.

Meissner, Martin, Elizabeth W. Humphreys, Scott M. Meiss and William J. Scheu. 1975.* "No Exit for Wives: Sexual Division of Labour and the Cumulation of Household Demands," *Canadian Review of Sociology and Anthropology*, 12:424–439.

Mekos, Debra, E. Mavis Hetherington and David Reiss. 1996. "Sibling Differences in Problem Behavior and Parental Treatment in Nondivorced and Remarried Families," *Child Development*, 67:2148–2165.

Melamed, T. 1996. *Career Success: An Assessment of a Gender Specific Model*.

Mellman, Mark, Edward Lazarus and Allan Rivlin. 1990. "Family Time, Family Values," in David Blankenhorn, Steven Bayme and Jean Bethke Elshtain. *Rebuilding the Nest: A New Commitment to the American Family*. Milwaukee: Family Service America, 73–92.

Menaghan, Elizabeth G. and Toby L. Parcel. 1991. "Parental Employment and Family Life," in Alan Booth (ed.). *Contemporary Families: Looking Forward, Looking Back*. Minneapolis: National Council on Family Relations, 361–380.

Menaghan, G. and T.L. Parcel. 1991. "Determining Children's Home Environments: The Impact of Maternal Characteristics and Current Occupational and Family Conditions," *Journal of Marriage and the Family*, 53:417–431.

Mendes da Costa, Derek. 1978.* "Domestic Contracts in Ontario," *Canadian Journal of Family Law*, 1:232–253.

Mendes, H. 1975. *Parental Experiences of Single Fathers*, unpublished PhD thesis, University of California at Los Angeles.

Mennen, F. and D. Meadow. 1995. "Depression, Anxiety, and Self-Esteem in Sexually Abused Children," *Families in Society: The Journal of Contemporary Human Services*, February:74–81.

Mennen, F. and D. Meadow. 1995. "The Relationship of Abuse Characteristics to Symptoms in Sexually Abused Girls," *Journal of Interpersonal Violence*, 10(3):259–274.

Merrill, L., L. Hervig and J. Milner. 1996. "Childhood Parenting Experiences, Intimate Partner Conflict Resolution, and Adult Risk for Child Physical Abuse," *Child Abuse and Neglect*, 20(11):1065–1996.

Messias, D.K.H., E. Im, A. Page, H. Regev, J. Spiers, L. Yoder and A. Meleis. 1997. "Defining and Redefining Work: Implications for Women's Health," *Gender and Society*, 11(3):296–323.

Messinger, Lillian. 1976. "Remarriages Between Divorced People and Children from Previous Marriages: A Proposal for Preparation for Remarriage," *Journal of Marriage and Family Counseling*, 2:193–200.

Messinger, Lillian. 1984. *Remarriage, A Family Affair*. New York: Plenum Press.

Meston, Cindy M., Paul D. Trapnell and Boris B. Gorzalka. 1996. "Ethnic and Gender Differences in Sexual Behavior Between Asian and Non-Asian University Students," *Archives of Sexual Behavior*, 25(1):33–72.

Méthot, Suzanne. 1987.* "Employment Patterns of Elderly Canadians," *Canadian Social Trends*, Autumn 1987:7–11.

Meyer, Daniel R. and Steven Garasky. 1993. "Custodial Fathers: Myths, Realities and Child Support Policy," *Journal of Marriage and the Family*, 55:73–89.

Meyers, M.F. 1989. "Men Sexually Assaulted as Adults and Sexually Abused as Boys," *Archives of Sexual Behaviour*, 18(3):203–215.

Miall, Charlene E. 1993. "The Regulation of Reproduction: The Relevance of Public Opinion for Legislative Policy Formation," *International Journal of Law and the Family*, 7(1):18–39.

Michael, Robert T. 1988. "Why Did the U.S. Divorce Rate Double Within a Decade?" *Research in Population Economics*, 6:367–399.

Michael, Robert T., John H. Gagnon, Edward O. Laumann and Gina Kolata. 1994. *Sex in America*. Toronto: Little, Brown and Company.

Michelson, William. 1985. *From Sun to Sun: Daily Obligations and Community Structure in the Lives of Employed Women and Their Families*. Totowa: Rowman and Allanheld.

Miedema, B. and N. Nason-Clark. 1989. "Second Class Status: An Analysis of the Lived Experiences of Immigrant Women in Fredericton," *Canadian Ethnic Studies*, 21(2): 63–73.

Millar, Wayne J., Surinder Wadhera and Stanley K. Henshaw. 1997.* "Repeat Abortions in Canada, 1975–1993," *Family Planning Perspectives*, 29(1):20–24.

Miller, B., W. Downs and M. Testa. 1993. "Interrelationships between Victimization and Women's Alcohol Use," *Journal of Studies on Alcohol*, Supplement No. 11:109–117.

Miller, Barbara Diane. 1992. "Wife-Beating in India: Variations on a Theme," in Dorothy Ayers Counts, Judith K. Brown and Jacquelyn C. Campbell (eds.). *Sanctions and Sanctuary, Cultural Perspectives on the Beating of Wives*. Boulder: Westview Press.

Miller, Brent C. and C. Raymond Bingham. 1989. "Family Configuration in Relation to the Sexual Behaviour of Female Adolescents," *Journal of Marriage and the Family*, 51:499–506.

Miller, Kim S., Beth A. Kotchick, Shannon Dorsey, Res Forehand and Anissa Y. Ham. 1998. "Family Communication about Sex: What Are Parents Saying and Are Their Adolescents Listening?" *Family Planning Perspectives*, 30(5):218–222,235.

Miller L.C., B.A. Bettencourt, S.C. DeBro, and V. Hoffman. 1993. "Negotiating Safer Sex: Interpersonal Dynamics," in J. Pryor and G. Reeder (eds.). *The Social Psychology of AIDS Infection*. Hillsdale: Erlbaum. Pp. 85–123.

Miller, Rita S. 1978. "The Social Construction and Reconstruction of Physiological Events: Acquiring the Pregnancy Identity," *Studies in Symbolic Interaction*, 1:181–204.

Miller, S., P. Miller, E. Nunnally and D. Wackman. 1991. *Talking and Listening Together*. Littleton: Interpersonal Communication Programs.

Miller, Sherod and Phyllis A. Miller. 1997. *Core Communication: Skills and Processes*. Littleton: Interpersonal Communication Programs, Inc.

Milne, Ann L. 1985. "Mediation or Therapy — Which Is It?" in Sarah C. Grebe (ed.). *Divorce and Family Mediation*. Rockville: Aspen.

Min, P. G. "Korean Immigrant Wives' Overwork," *Korean Journal of Population and Development*, 21(1):23–36.

Minuchin, P. 1985. "Families and Individual Development: Provocations from the Field of Family Therapy," *Child Development*, 56:289–302.

Mirabelli, Alan. 1997.* "The Fence at the Edge of the Cliff: Approaching Family Policy in Canada," *Transition*, March:10–13.

Mirowsky, John and Catherine E. Ross. 1987. "Belief in Innate Sex Roles: Sex Stratification versus Interpersonal Influence in Marriage," *Journal of Marriage and the Family*, 49:527–540.

Mischel, Walter. 1966. "A Social-Learning View of Sex Differences in Behaviour," in Eleanor E. Maccoby (ed.). *The Development of Sex Differences*. Stanford: Stanford University Press.

Mitchell, Barbara A. 1994.* "Family Structure and Leaving the Nest: A Social Resource Perspective," *Sociological Perspectives*, 37(4):651–671.

Mitchell, Barbara A., Andrew V. Wister and Thomas K. Burch. 1989.* "The Family Environment and Leaving the Parental Home," *Journal of Marriage and the Family*, 51:605–613.

Mitic, Wayne. 1990.* "Parental versus Peer Influence on Adolescent's Alcohol Consumption," *Psychological Reports*, 67:1273–1274.

Moberly, Elizabeth R. 1983. *Psychogenesis: The Early Development of Gender Identity*. London: Routledge and Kegan Paul Ltd.

Moen, Phyllis and Alvin L. Schorr. 1987. "Families and Social Policy," in Marvin B. Sussman and Suzanne K. Steinmetz (eds.). *Handbook of Marriage and the Family*. New York: Plenum Press, Chapter 28.

Moen, Phyllis, Donna Dempster-McClain. 1987. "Employed Parents: Role Strain, Work Time and Preferences for Working Less," *Journal of Marriage and the Family*, 49:579–590.

Mohr, J.W. 1984.* "The Future of the Family, the Law and the State," *Canadian Journal of Family Law*, 4:261–273.

Monette, Manon. 1996a.* "Retirement in the '90s: Retired Men in Canada," *Canadian Social Trends*, 42:8–11.

Monette, Manon. 1996b.* *Canada's Changing Retirement Patterns*. Statistics Canada: Minister of Industry.

Money, John. 1986. *Lovemaps*. New York: Irvington Publishers.

Money, John. 1987. "Homosexual Gender Identity and Psychoneuroendocrinology," *Social Behavior and Personality*, 42:384–399.

Money, John and Anke A. Ehrhardt. 1974. *Man and Woman, Boy and Girl*. New York: Mentor.

Monnier, A. and C. de Guibert-Lantoine. 1996. "La Conjoncture Démographique: L'Europe et les Pays Developpe's d'Outre-Mer," *Population*, 51:1005–1030.

Montgomery, Barbara M. 1981. "The Form and Function of Quality Communication in Marriage," *Family Relations*, 30:21–30.

Montgomery, Jason. 1981.* *Family Crisis as Process*. Washington: University Press of America.

Montgomery, Marilyn J. and Edward R. Anderson. 1992. "Patterns of Courtship for Remarriage: Implications for Child Adjustment and Parent–Child Relations," *Journal of Marriage and the Family*, 54:686–698.

Montgomery, Marilyn J. and Gwendolyn T. Sorell. 1997. "Differences in Love Attitudes Across Family Life Stages," *Family Relations*, 46:55–61.

Moody, Fred. 1990. "Divorce: Sometimes a Bad Notion," *Utne Reader*, 42:70–78.

Mooney, Linda and Sarah Brabant. 1987. "Two Martinis and a Rested Woman: 'Liberation' in the Sunday Comics," *Sex Roles*, 17:409–420.

Moore, Barrington. 1960. "Thoughts on the Future of the Family," in Maurice R. Stein, Arthur J. Vidich and David M. White (eds.). *Identity and Anxiety*, Glencoe: The Free Press.

Moore, DeWayne. 1987. "Parent–Adolescent Separation: The Construction of Adulthood by Late Adolescents," *Developmental Psychology*, 23:298–307.

Moore, Kristin A., Brent C. Miller, Dana Glei and Donna Ruane Morrison. 1995. *Adolescent Sex, Contraception, and Childbearing: A Review of Recent Research*. Washington, DC: Child Trends, Inc.

Moore, Kristin A., James L. Peterson and Frank F. Furstenberg. 1986. "Parental Attitudes and the Occurrence of Early Sexual Activity," *Journal of Marriage and the Family*, 48:777–782.

Moore, K.A., C.W. Nord and J.L. Peterson. 1989. "Nonvoluntary Sexual Activity Among Adolescents," *Family Planning Perspectives*, 21(3):110–114.

Moore, Maureen. 1988.* "Female Lone Parenthood: The Duration of Episodes," *Canadian Social Trends*, Autumn:40–42.

Moore, Maureen. 1989.* "Female Lone Parenting Over the Life Course," *Canadian Journal of Sociology*, 14:335–351.

Moore, Maureen. 1990.* "Women Parenting Alone," in Craig McKie and Keith Thompson (eds.). *Canadian Social Trends*. Toronto: Thompson Educational Publishing.

Moore, Samuel (translator). 1967. *The Communist Manifesto* (authored by Karl Marx and Fredrick Engels in 1849). Baltimore: Penguin.

Moorman, Jeanne E. and Donald J. Hernandez. 1989. "Married-Couple Families with Step, Adopted and Biological Children," *Demography*, 26:267–277.

Moos, R.H. and B.S. Moos. 1981. *Family Environment Scale Manual*. Palo Alto: Consulting Psychologists Press.

Morawski, J.G. 1987. "The Troubled Quest for Masculinity, Femininity and Androgyny," in Philip Shaver and Clyde Hendrick. *Sex and Gender*. Newbury Park: Sage.

Moreaux, Colette. 1971.* "The French-Canadian Family," in K. Ishwaran (ed.). *The Canadian Family: A Book of Readings*. Toronto: Holt, Rinehart and Winston.

Morgan, Lewis Henry. 1877. *Ancient Society*. New York: Holt Rinehart and Winston.

Mori, George A. 1987.* "Religious Affiliation in Canada," *Canadian Social Trends*, Autumn, 1987:12–16.

Morningstar, Lasha. 1987.* "Custom-Made by Surrogate," *Edmonton Journal*, March 8:B1.

Morningstar, Lasha. 1990.* "The Joy of Fighting," *The Edmonton Journal*, May 24:B9.

Morris, A.S., Silk, J., Steinberg, L., Sessa, F., Avenevoli, S. and Essex, M. 2002. "Temperamental Vulnerability And Negative Parenting As Interacting Predictors Of Child Adjustment." *Journal of Marriage and Family* 64:461–471.

Morris, Leon. 1974. *The First Epistle of Paul to the Corinthians*. Grand Rapids: Eerdmans Publishing Company

Morrison, Richard J. and Jillian Oderkirk. 1991.* *Canadian Social Trends*. 21:15–20.

Morton, Mary E. 1988.* "Dividing the Wealth, Sharing the Poverty: The (Re)formation of 'Family' Law in Ontario," *Canadian Review of Sociology and Anthropology*, 25:254–275.

Morton, Mildred. 1990.* "Controversies Within Family Law," in Maureen Baker (ed.). *Families: Changing Trends in Canada* (second edition). Toronto: McGraw-Hill Ryerson.

Mosher, William D. and Christine A. Bachrach. 1996. "Understanding U.S. Fertility: Continuity and Change in the National Survey of Family Growth, 1985–1995," *Family Planning Perspectives*, 28(1):4–12.

Moss, Barry F. and Andrew I. Schwebel. 1993. "Defining Intimacy in Romantic Relationships," *Family Relations*, 42:31–37.

Moysa, Marilyn. 1992.* "Women Still Do Most Housework, Childcare," *Edmonton Journal*, August 19:A5.

Muir, Karen. 1988. *The Strongest Part of the Family: A Study of Lao Refugee Women in Columbus, Ohio*. New York: AMS Press.

Munro, Brenda and G.R. Adams. 1978.* "Love American Style: A Test of Role Structure Theory on Changes in Attitudes Towards Love," *Human Relations*, 31:215–228.

Murdock, George P. 1949. *Social Structure*. New York: The Free Press.

Murstein, B. 1974. *Love, Sex and Marriage Through the Ages*. New York: Springer.

Murstein, Bernard I. 1980. "Mate Selection in the 1970s," *Journal of Marriage and the Family*, 42:777–792.

Murstein, Bernard I. 1986. *Paths to Marriage*. Beverly Hills: Sage.

Murstein, Bernard I. 1987. "A Clarification And Extension Of The SVR Theory Of Dyadic Pairing." *Journal of Marriage and the Family* 49:929–933.

Murstein, Bernard I., Mary Cerreto and Marcia G. MacDonald. 1977. "A Theory and Investigation of the Effect of Exchange-Orientation on Marriage and Friendship," *Journal of Marriage and the Family*, 39:543–548.

The Law Society of Upper Canada. 1997.* "Domestic Contracts (Marriage and Cohabitation). The Internet: Tape #375.

"The World at Six," CBC news broadcast, February 7, 1993.

Nadwodny, Richard. 1996.* "Canadians Working at Home," *Canadian Social Trends*, Spring:16–20.

Naidoo, Josephine C. and J. Campbell Davis. 1988.* "Canadian South Asian Women in Transition: A Dualistic View of Life," *Journal of Comparative Family Studies*, 19:311–328.

Nakamura, Alice, Masao Nakamura and Dallas Cullen. 1979.* *Employment and Earnings of Married Females*. Ottawa: Minister of Supplies and Services.

National Council on Welfare. 1988.* *Poverty Profile 1988*. Ottawa: Supply and Services Canada.

National Council on Welfare. 1990.* *Women and Poverty Revisited*. Ottawa: Supply and Services Canada.

National Council on Welfare. 1992.* *Poverty Profile, 1980–1990*. Ottawa: Supply and Services Canada.

National Council on Welfare. 1993.* *Poverty Profile Update for 1991*. Ottawa: Statistics Canada.

National Institute of Child Health and Human Development: The NICHD Early Child Care Research Network. 1997. "Familial Factors Associated with the Characteristics of Nonmaternal Care for Infants," *Journal of Marriage and the Family*, 59(2):389–408.

Native Canadian and Northern Affairs Canada. 1993. *The Incidence of Family Poverty on Canadian Native Canadian Reserves*. Ottawa: Minister of Supply and Services Canada.

Native Consultant Services. 1985.* *Crisis Centre Needs Assessment Project, Nova Scotia Native Women's Association, Final Report*. Truro, Nova Soctia.

Nave-Herz, Rosemarie. 1997. "Still in the Nest: The Family and Young Adults in Germany," *Journal of Family Issues*, 18(6):671–689.

Neale, Deborah. 1993.* "Women and Work: Changing Gender Role Attitudes in Alberta," *Population Research Laboratory Survey Highlights*,12:1–4.

Needle, Richard H., S. Susan Su and William J. Doherty. 1990. "Divorce, Remarriage and Adolescent Substance Use: A Prospective Longitudinal Study," *Journal of Marriage and the Family*, 52:157–169.

Nelson, Geoffrey. 1982.* "Coping with the Loss of Father: Family Reaction to Death or Divorce," *Journal of Family Issues*, 3:41–60.

Nett, Emily M. 1981.* "Canadian Families in Social-Historical Perspective," *Canadian Journal of Sociology*, 6:239–260.

Nett, Emily. 1990.* "The Family and Aging," in Maureen Baker (ed.). *The Family: Changing Trends in Canada*. Toronto: McGraw-Hill Ryerson.

Nett, Emily. 1993. *Canadian Families: Past and Present*, Second Edition. Toronto: Harcourt, Brace and Company, Canada.

Nett, Emily M. 1988.* *Canadian Families Past and Present*. Toronto: Butterworths.

Newcomb, Michael B. 1986. "Cohabitation, Marriage and Divorce Among Adolescents and Young Adults," *Journal of Social and Personal Relationships*, 3:473–494.

Newcomb, Michael B. and Peter M. Bentler. 1980. "Cohabitation Before Marriage: A Comparison of Married Couples Who Did and Did Not Cohabit," *Alternative Lifestyles*, 3:65–85.

Newcomer, Susan F. and J. Richard Udry. 1987. "Parental Marital Status Effects on Adolescent Sexual Behaviour," *Journal of Marriage and the Family*, 49:235–240.

Ney, P.G. 1986.* "Does Verbal Abuse Leave Deeper Scars: A Study of Children and Parents," *Canadian Journal of Psychiatry*, 32:371–378.

Ng, Edward. 1992.* "Children and Elderly People: Sharing Public Income Resources," *Canadian Social Trends*, 25:12–15.

Nichols, Margaret J. 1988. "Family Law Policies and Programs: Too Little, Too Late?" in Elam W. Nunnally, Catherine S. Chilman and Fred M. Cox (eds.). *Troubled Relationships: Families in Trouble Series*, Volume III. Beverly Hills: Sage, Chapter 12.

Nilsson Schönnesson, Lena and Ulrich Clement. 1995. "Sexual Attitudinal Conflict and Sexual Behavior Changes Among Homosexual HIV-positive Men," *Journal of Psychology and Human Sexuality*, 7(1–2):41–58.

Nimkoff, M.F. 1965. "Types of Families," in M.F. Nimkoff (ed.). *Comparative Family Systems*. Boston: Houghton Mifflin.

Nitz, Katherine, Robert D. Ketterlinus and Linda J. Brandt. 1995. "The Role of Stress, Social Support, and Family

Environment in Adolescent Mothers' Parenting," *Journal of Adolescent Research*, 10(3):358–382.

Noble, Robert C. 1991. "There Is No Safe Sex," *Newsweek*, April 1:8.

Nock, Steven L. 1995. "A Comparison of Marriages and Cohabiting Relationships," *Journal of Family Issues*, 16:53–76.

Nock, Steven L. 1995. "Commitment and Dependency in Marriage," *Journal of Marriage and the Family*, 57:503–514.

Noh, Samuel and William Avison. 1996.* "Asian Immigrants and the Stress Process," *Journal of Health and Social Behavior*, 37(June):192–206.

Noivo, E. 1993.* "Ethnic Families and the Social Injuries of Class, Migration, Gender, Generation, and Minority Group Status," *Canadian Ethnic Studies*, 25(3):68–75.

Noller, Patricia and Mary A. Fitzpatrick. 1988. *Perspectives on Marital Interaction*. Philadelphia: Multilingual Matters Ltd.

Noller, Patricia and Mary A. Fitzpatrick. 1990. "Marital Communication in the Eighties," *Journal of Marriage and the Family*, 52:832–843.

Noller, Patricia and Mary A. Fitzpatrick. 1991. "Marital Communication in the Eighties," in A. Booth (ed.). *Contemporary Families: Looking Forward, Looking Back*. Minneapolis: National Council on Family Relationships.

Norland, J.A. 1994.* *Focus on Canada: Profile of Canada's Seniors*. Statistics Canada and Prentice-Hall Canada Inc. Catalogue No. 96–312E.

Northcott, Herbert C. 1984.* "Widowhood and Remarriage Trends in Canada 1956 to 1981," *Canadian Journal on Aging*, 3:63–78.

Northcott, Herbert C. 1992a.* "The Best Years of Your Life," *Canadian Journal on Aging*, 1:72–78.

Northcott, Herbert C. 1992b.* *Aging in Alberta: Rhetoric and Reality*. Calgary: Detselig Enterprises Ltd.

Notarius, Clifford and Jennifer S. Johnson. 1982. "Emotional Expression in Husbands and Wives," *Journal of Marriage and the Family*, 44:483–489.

Nye, F. Ivan. 1979. "Choice, Exchange, and the Family," in Wesley R. Burr, Reuben Hill, F. Ivan Nye and Ira L. Reiss (eds.). 1979. *Contemporary Theories about the Family, Volume II*. New York: The Free Press, Chapter 1.

O'Brien, Margaret. 1980. "Lone Fathers: Transition from Married to Separated State," *Journal of Comparative Family Studies*, 11:115–128.

O'Flaherty, K.M. and Laura Workman Eells. 1988. "Courtship Behavior of the Remarried," *Journal of Marriage and the Family*, 50:499–506.

O'Hara, P. 1994. "Canadian Law, Immigrants and Cultural Conflicts," *Law Now*, 19:7–9.

O'Leary, K.D. 1993. "Through a Psychological Lens: Personality Traits, Personality Disorders and Levels of Violence," in Gelles, R.J. and D.R. Loseke (eds.). *Current Controversies on Family Violence*. Newbury Park, CA: Sage. Pp. 7–30.

O'Neil, John. 1997.* "Issues in the Health Policy for Indigenous Peoples in Canada," *Australian Journal of Public Health*, 19(6):559–567.

O'Neill, W.L. (ed.). 1972.* *Women At Work*. Toronto: Burns and MacEachern.

Oakley, Ann. 1985. *Sex, Gender and Society*. New York: Harper and Row.

Ochiltree, Gay. 1994. *Effects of Child Care on Young Children: Forty Years of Research*. Australian Institute of Family Studies Early Childhood Study Paper No. 5.

Odekirk, Jillian and Clarence Lochhead. 1992.* "Lone Parenthood: Gender Differences," *Canadian Social Trends*, 27:16–19.

Odekirk, Jillian. 1992.* "Parents and Children Living with Low Incomes," *Canadian Social Trends*, 27:11–15.

Oderkirk, Jillian. 1994. "Marriage in Canada: Changing Beliefs and Behaviours 1600–1990," *Canadian Social Trends*, 33:2–7.

Oderkirk, Jillian. 1996a.* "Old Age Security," *Canadian Social Trends*, 40:3–7.

Oderkirk, Jillian. 1996b.* "Canada and Quebec Pension Plans," *Canadian Social Trends*, 40:8–15.

Offord, David R. and Ellen L. Lipman. 1996. "Emotional and Behavioural Problems," *National Longitudinal Survey of Children and Youth*. Statistics Canada: Catalogue No. 89–550–MPE:119–126.

Ogburn, W.F. and M.F. Nimkoff. 1955. *Technology and the Changing Family*. New York: Houghton Mifflin Co.

Okun, Lewis. 1986. *Woman Abuse: Facts Replacing Myths*. Albany: State University of New York Press.

Oliver, D. 1955. *A Solomon Island Society*. Cambridge, MA: Harvard University Press.

Olson, David H. and Meredith Kilmer Hanson (eds.). 1990. *2001: Preparing Families for the Future*. Minneapolis: National Council on Family Relations.

Olson, David H., D.H. Sprenkle and C.S. Russell. 1979. "Circumplex Model of Marital and Family Systems: I. Cohesion and Adaptability Dimensions, Family Types, and Clinical Applications," *Family Process*, 18:3–28.

Oommen, T.K. 1982. "The Urban Family in Transition," in John S. Augustine (ed.). *The Indian Family in Transition*. New Delhi: Vikas Publishing.

Orbuch, Terry, Joseph Veroff and Diane Holmberg. 1993. "Becoming a Married Couple: The Emergence of Meaning in the First Years of Marriage," *Journal of Marriage and the Family*, 55:815–826.

Orr, Fay, Lori Cohen and Barbara Henker. 1985.* "The High Price of Having It All," *Alberta Report*, July 1:12–17.

Osiek, Carolyn and David L. Balch. 1997. *Families in the New Testament World*. Louisville: Westminster John Knox Press.

Osmond, Marie W. 1987. "Radical-Critical Theories," in Marvin B. Sussman and Suzanne K. Steinmetz (eds.), *Handbook of Marriage and the Family*. New York: Plenum Press, Chapter 5.

Osmond, Marie W. and Charles M. Grigg. 1978. "Correlates of Poverty: The Interaction of Individual and Family Characteristics," *Social Forces*, 56:1099–1120.

Osmond, Marie Withers and Barrie Thorne. 1993. "Feminist Theories: The Social Construction of Gender in Families in Society," in Pauline G. Boss, William G. Doherty, Ralph LaRossa, Walter R. Schumm and Suzanne K. Steinmetz (eds.). *Sourcebook of Family Theories and Methods: A Contextual Approach*. New York: Plenum Press, Chapter 23.

Osofsky, Joy D. and Howard J. Osofsky. 1972. "Androgyny as a Lifestyle," *The Family Coordinator*, 21:411–418.

Pagani, Linda, Richard E. Tremblay, Frank Vitaro, Margaret Kerr and Pierre McDuff. 1998. "The Impact of Family Transition on the Development of Delinquency in Adolescent Boys: A Nine-Year Longitudinal Study," *Journal of Child Psychology and Psychiatry*, 39(4):489–499.

Page, Faith. 1993.* "I Dream People Will Help Needy Children," *Edmonton Journal*, February 24:A13.

Pagelow, Mildred D. and Pam Johnson. 1988. "Abuse in the American Family: The Role of Religion," in Anne L. Horton and Judith A. Williamson (eds.). *Abuse and Religion: When Praying Isn't Enough*. Lexington: Lexington Books.

Pain, Beverly. 1988.* "Resource Reallocation Following Separation/Divorce," unpublished paper delivered at the Conference on Family, State and Society at Crossroads, University of Saskatchewan, March 17.

Painton, Priscilla. 1993. "The Shrinking Ten Percent," *Time*, April 26:33–35.

Paletta, Anna. 1992.* "Today's Extended Families," *Canadian Social Trends*, 27:26–28.

Pam, Alvin and Judith Pearson. 1996. "When Marriage Ends in a Love Triangle: Jealousy, Family Polarization, Effects on Children," *Journal of Divorce and Remarriage*, 25(3/4):175–199.

Pankhurst, Jerry G. and Sharon K. Houseknecht. 1983. "The Family, Politics, and Religion in the 1980s: In Fear of the New Individualism," *Journal of Family Issues*, 4:5–34.

Pappert, Ann. 1989.* *The Reproductive Revolution*. Toronto: Atkinson Foundation.

Parish, Thomas S. and Bruno M. Kappes. 1980. "Impact of Father Loss on the Family," *Social Behavior and Personality*, 8:107–112.

Parliament, Jo-Anne B. 1990.* "Women Employed Outside the Home," in Craig McKie and Keith Thompson (eds.). *Canadian Social Trends*. Toronto: Thompson Educational Publishing.

Parr, Joy. 1982.* "Introduction," in Joy Parr (ed.). *Childhood and Family in Canadian History*. Toronto: McClelland and Stewart.

Parsons, Marianne D. 1990.* "Lone Parent Canadian Families and the Socioeconomic Achievements of Children as Adults," *Journal of Comparative Family Studies*, 21:353–367.

Parsons, Talcott and Robert F. Bales. 1955. *Family, Socialization and Interaction Process*. New York: The Free Press.

Partida, Jorge. 1996. "The Effects of Immigration on Children in the Mexican-American Community," *Child and Adolescent Social Work Journal*, 13(3):241–254.

Pask, E. Diane. 1988.* "Pension Division Across Canada: New Developments," *1988 National Family Law Program*, 2:D-5–1 to D-5–32, The Federation of Law Societies of Canada and the Canadian Bar Association.

Pask, E. Diane and Marnie L. McCall. 1989.* *How Much and Why? Economic Implications of Marriage Breakdown: Spousal and Child Support*. Calgary: Canadian Research Institute for Law and Family.

Patterson, Gerald R. 1982. *Coercive Family Process*. Eugene: Castalia.

Patterson, Gerald R. 1988. "Stress: A Change Agent for Family Process," in N. Garmezy and M. Rutter (eds.). *Stress, Coping, and Development in Children*. New York: Johns Hopkins Press.

Patterson, Joan M. 2002. "Integrating Family Resilience And Family Stress Theory," *Journal of Marriage and Family*, 64:349–360.

Patterson, J.M. 1993. "The Role of Family Meanings in Adaptation to Chronic Illness and Disability," in Turnbul A.P., J.M. Patterson, S.K. Behr, D.L. Murphy. J.G. Marquis and M. J. Blue-Banning (eds.). *Cognitive Coping, Families, and Disability*. Baltimore: Paul H. Brookes. Pp. 221–238.

Patterson, Joan M. and Hamilton I. McCubbin. 1983. "Chronic Illness: Family Stress and Coping," in Charles R. Figley and Hamilton I. McCubbin (eds.). *Stress and the Family, Vol. II, Coping With Catastrophe*. New York: Brunner and Mazel.

Payne, Julien D. 1988.* "A Practitioner's Guide to Spousal Support in Divorce Proceedings," *1988 National Family*

Law Program, Vol. 1:A1–42. The Federation of Law Societies of Canada and the Canadian Bar Association.

Payne, Julien D. and Marilyn A. Payne. 1994.* Introduction to Canadian Family Law. Scarborough: Carswell.

Pearlin, Leonard I. and Joyce S. Johnson. 1977. Marital Status, Life-Strains and Depression," American Sociological Review, 42:704–715.

Pederson, David R. and Greg Moran. 1995.* "A Categorical Description of Infant–Mother Relationships in the Home and Its Relation to Q-Sort Measures of Infant–Mother Interaction," Monographs of the Society for Research in Child Development, 60(2–3):111–132.

Pedraza, Silvia. 1991. "Women and Migration: the Social Consequences of Gender," Annual Review of Sociology, 17:303–325.

Peek, Charles W., Nancy J. Bell, Terry Waldren and Gwendolyn T. Sorel. 1988. "Patterns of Functioning in Families of Remarried and First-Married Couples," Journal of Marriage and the Family, 50:699–708.

Peitchinis, Stephen G. 1989.* Women at Work: Discrimination and Response. Toronto: McClelland and Stewart.

Pemberton, Kim. 1992.* "Man Defends 10–Year 'Marriage' to Daughter," The Edmonton Journal, November 22:A3.

Peplau, Letitia A., Charles T. Hill, and Zick Rubin. 1993. "Sex-Role Attitudes in Dating and Marriage: A 15–year Follow-up of the Boston Couples Study," Journal of Social Issues, 49:31–52.

Peplau, Letitia A., Zick Rubin, and Charles T. Hill. 1977. "Sexual Intimacy in Dating Relationships," Journal of Social Issues, 33:86–109.

Perdue, Leo G. 1997. Families in Ancient Israel. Louisville: Westminster John Knox Press.

Perlman, D. 1983.* "The Premarital Sexual Standards of Canadians," in K. Ishwaran (ed.). Marriage and Divorce in Canada. Toronto: Methuen.

Perry-Jenkins, Maureen and Ann C. Crouter. 1990. "Men's Provider-Role Attitudes," Journal of Family Issues, 11:136–156.

Perry-Jenkins, M., Repetti, R. and Crouter, A. 2000. "Work and Family in the 1990s," Journal of Marriage and the Family 62:981–998.

Personal Communication with the Nova Scotia Native Women's Association, March 31, 1993.

Pérusse, Daniel. 1994.* "Mate Choice in Modern Societies," Human Nature, 5:255–278.

Peters, John. 1980.* "High School Dating: Implications for Equality," International Journal of Comparative Sociology, 21:109–118.

Peters, John. 1995. "Canadian Families into the Year 2000," International Journal of Sociology of the Family, 25(1):63–79.

Peters, John F. 1985.* "Adolescents as Socialization Agents to Parents," Adolescence, 80:921–933.

Peters, John F. 1987.* "Youth, Family and Employment," Adolescence, 22:465–473.

Peters, John F. 1991.* "Parental Contributions to Adolescents' Possessions and Educational Expenses: Gender Differences," Adolescence, 26:649–657.

Peters, K., I. Maltzman and K. Villone. 1994. "Childhood Abuse of Parents of Alcohol and Other Drug Misusing Adolescents," The International Journal of the Addictions, 29(10):1259–1268.

Petersen, Anne C. 1987. "Those Gangly Years," Psychology Today, September:28–34.

Petersen, Larry R. and Gregory V. Donnenwerth. 1997. "Sexularization and the Influence of Religion on Beliefs about Premarital Sex," Social Forces, 75(3):1071–1088.

Peterson, Gary W. and Boyd C. Rollins. 1987. "Parent–Child Socialization," in Marvin B. Sussman, and Suzanne K. Steinmetz (eds.). Handbook of Marriage and the Family. New York: Plenum Press, 471–508.

Peterson, Richard R. and Kathleen Gerson. 1992. "Determinants of Responsibility for Child Care Arrangements Among Dual-Earner Couples," Journal of Marriage and the Family, 54:527–536.

Pett, Marjorie A., Nancy Lang and Anita Gander. 1992. "Late-Life Divorce: Its Impact on Family Rituals," Journal of Family Issues, 13:526–552.

Philips, L.R. 1986. "Theoretical Explanations of Elder Abuse: Competing Hypotheses and Unresolved Issues," in K.A. Pillemer and R.S. Wolf (eds.). Elder Abuse: Conflict in the Family. Dover: Auburn House Publishing Co.

Phinney, J. 1989. "Stages of Ethnic Identity Development in Minority Group Adolescents," Journal of Early Adolescence, 9(1,2):34–49.

Phinney, J. et al. 1996. "Ethnic and American Identity as Predictors of Self-Esteem Among African American, Latino, and White Adolescents," Journal of Youth and Adolescence, 26(2):165–185.

Phipps, Shelley A. 1995.* "Taking Care of Our Children: Tax and Transfer Options for Canada," in Richards, John and William G. Watson (eds.) 1995. Family Matters: New Policies for Divorce, Lone Mothers, and Child Poverty. Ottawa: C.D. Howe Institute. Pp. 186–211.

Piccinino, Linda J. and William D. Mosher. 1998. "Trends in Contraceptive Use in the United States, 1982–1995," Family Planning Perspectives, 30:4–10.

Picot, Garnett and John Myles. 1996.* "Children in Low-income Families," Canadian Social Trends, Autumn: 15–19.

Piddington, Ralph. 1971.* "A Study of French-Canadian Kinship," in K. Ishwaran (ed.). The Canadian Family: A Book of Readings. Toronto: Holt, Rinehart and Winston.

Pike, Robert. 1975.* "Legal Access and the Incidence of Divorce in Canada: A Sociohistorical Analysis," *Canadian Review of Sociology and Anthropology*, 12:115–133.

Pill, Cynthia. 1990. "Stepfamilies: Redefining the Family," *Family Relations*, 39:186–193.

Pillemer, K. 1986. "Risk Factors in Elder Abuse: Results from a Case-Control Study," in K.A. Pillemer and R.S. Wolf (eds.). *Elder Abuse: Conflict in the Family*. Dover: Auburn House Publishing Co.

Pillemer, K. and D. Finkelhor. 1988. "The Prevalence of Elder Abuse: A Random Sample Survey," *The Gerontologist*, 28:51–57.

Pillemer, K. and D.W. Moore. 1989. "Abuse of Patients in Nursing Homes: Findings from a Survey of Staff," *The Gerontologist*, 29:314–320.

Pillemer, Karl and J. Jill Suitor. 1991.* "Will I Ever Escape My Child's Problems? Effects of Adult Children's Problems on Elderly Parents," *Journal of Marriage and the Family*, 53:585–594.

Pineo, Peter C. 1961.* "Disenchantment in the Later Years of Marriage," *Marriage and Family Living*, 23:3–11.

Piotrkowski, Chaya S., Robert N. Rapoport and Rhona Rapoport. 1987. "Families and Work," in Sussman, Marvin B. and Suzanne K. Steinmetz (eds.). *Handbook of Marriage and the Family*. New York: Plenum Press, 251–283.

Plass, P.S. and G.T. Hotaling. 1995. "The Intergenerational Transmission of Running Away: Childhood Experiences of the Parents of Runaways," *Journal of Youth and Adolescence*, 24(3):335–348.

Pleck, Elizabeth. 1987. *Domestic Tyranny: The Making of Social Policy Against Family Violence from Colonial Times to the Present*. New York: Oxford University Press.

Pleck, Joseph. 1980. *The Myth of Masculinity*. Cambridge: Harvard University Press.

Podnieks, E., K. Pillemer, J. Nicholson, J. Shillington and A. Frizzell. 1989.* *National Survey on Abuse of the Elderly in Canada: Preliminary Findings*. Toronto: Office of Research and Innovation, Ryerson Polytechnical Institute.

Pollara. 1997.* "Canada Speaks," *National Poll on Sexual Relations*. Toronto: Pollara.

Pollock, A. 1998. "College Women's Definitions of and Experiences with Social Power," *Psychological Reports*, 82:717–718.

Pollock, Frederick and Frederik W. Maitland. 1911. *The History of English Law Before the Time of Edward I, Volume 1*. Cambridge: Cambridge University Press.

Pommer, Dave. 1992.* "The Business of Love," *The Calgary Herald*, cited in *The Edmonton Journal*, August:F6.

Ponting, J. Rick. 1986.* "Assessing a Generation of Change," in J. Rick Ponting (ed.). *Arduous Journey: Canadian Indians and Decolonization*. Toronto: McClelland and Stewart.

Pool, Ian. 1978.* "Changes in Canadian Female Labour Force Participation and Some Possible Implications for Conjugal Power," *Journal of Comparative Family Studies*, 9:41–52.

Pool, Ian and Maureen Moore. 1986.* *Lone Parenthood: Characteristics and Determinants*, Ottawa: Supply and Services Canada.

Popenoe, David. 1988. *Disturbing the Nest: Family Change and Decline in Modern Societies*. New York: Aldine De Gruyter.

Popenoe, David. 1993a. "American Family Decline, 1960–1990: A Review and Appraisal," *Journal of Marriage and the Family*, 55:527–542.

Popenoe, David. 1996a. *Life Without Father: Compelling New Evidence that Fatherhood and Marriage are Indispensable for the Good of Children and Society*. New York: (Martin Kessler Books) The Free Press.

Popenoe, David. 1996b. "Modern Marriage: Revising the Cultural Script," in Popenoe, David, Jean Bethke Elshtain, and David Blankenhorn (eds). 1996. *Promises to Keep: Decline and Renewal of Marriage in America*. London, England: Rowman and Littlefield Publishers. Chapter 11.

Popenoe, David B. 1990. "Family Decline in America," in David Blankenhorn, Steven Bayme and Jean Bethke Elshtain. *Rebuilding the Nest: A New Commitment to the American Family*. Milwaukee: Family Service America, 39–51.

Popenoe, David, Jean Bethke Elshtain, and David Blankenhorn (eds). 1996. "Marriage in America: A Report to the Nation," in *Promises to Keep: Decline and Renewal of Marriage in America*. London, England: Rowman and Littlefield Publishers. Chapter 13.

Population Research Laboratory. 1990.* *Survey Highlights No.1: The PRL 1989 Alberta Survey—Changing Family Issues*. Edmonton Department of Sociology, University of Alberta, May.

Potuchek, Jean L. 1992. "Employed Wives' Orientations to Breadwinning: A Gender Theory Analysis," *Journal of Marriage and the Family*, 54:548–558.

Prasil, Sandrine. 1993.* "Seniors 75+: Lifestyles," *Canadian Social Trends*, 30:26–29.

Pratt, Clara C., 1995. "Family Professionals and Family Policy: Strategies for Influence," *Family Relations*, 44(1):56–62.

Pratt, Michael W., David Green, Judith MacVicar and Marie Bountrogianni. 1992.* "The Mathematical Parent: Parental Scaffolding, Parenting Style and Learning Outcomes in Long-Division Mathematics Homework," *Journal of Applied Developmental Psychology*, 13:17–34.

Premier's Council in Support of Alberta Families. 1992.* *Alberta Families Today*. Edmonton, Alberta.

Premier's Council in Support of Alberta Families. 1992.* *Alberta Families Today*. Edmonton.

Prentice, Alison, Paula Bourne, Gail C. Brandt, Beth Light, Wendy Mitchinson and Naomi Black. 1988.* *Canadian Women: A History*. Toronto: Harcourt, Brace, Jovanovich.

Prentice, Susan. 1988.* "The 'Mainstreaming' of Day-care," *Resources for Feminist Research*, 17:59–63.

Preston, J. (ed.). 1992. *A Member of the Family*. New York: Dutton.

Price, Sharon J. and Patrick C. McHenry, 1988. *Divorce*. Newbury Park: Sage.

Priest, Gordon E. 1988.* "Living Arrangements of Canada's 'Older Elderly' Population," *Canadian Social Trends*, 10:26–30.

Priest, Gordon E. 1993.* "Seniors 75+: Living Arrangements," *Canadian Social Trends*, 30:24–25.

Priest, Gordon E. and Sandrine Prasil. 1993. "Seniors 75+: Living Arrangements and Lifestyles," *Canadian Social Trends*, 30:23.

Propper, Alice. 1990.* "Patterns of Family Violence," in Maureen Baker (ed.). *The Family, Changing Trends in Canada*. Toronto: McGraw-Hill Ryerson.

Proulx, Jocelyn and David Koulack. 1987.* "The Effect of Parental Divorce on Parent–Adolescent Separation," *Journal of Youth and Adolescence*, 16:473–480.

Putman, F. and P. Trickett. 1993. "Child Sexual Abuse: A Model of Chronic Trauma," *Psychiatry*, 56:82–95.

Quebec Native Women's Association. 1996. *Our Families: A World to Discover*. Montreal: Quebec Native Women Incorporation.

Queen, S., R. Habenstein, and J. Quadagno. 1985. *The Family in Various Cultures*. New York: Harper and Row.

Queen, Stuart A. and Robert W. Habenstein. 1974. *The Family in Various Cultures*. Philadelphia: J.B. Lippincott.

Quinn, Sally. 1992. "The Feminist Betrayal," *The Washington Post*, January 19.

Radcliffe-Brown, A.R. 1959. *African Systems of Kinship and Marriage*. New York: Oxford University Press.

Rak, Diana S. and Linda M. McMullen. 1987.* "Sex-Role Stereotyping in Television Commercials," *Canadian Journal of Behavioural Science*, 19:25–39.

Ram, Bali. 1988.* "Reproduction: The Canadian Family in Transition," *Journal of Biosocial Science*, 20:19–30.

Ram, Bali. 1990.* *Current Demographic Analysis: New Trends in the Family*. Catalogue No. 91-535E. Ottawa: Supply and Services Canada.

Ramsay, Joan. 1993a.* "Prime Time: Aging in the Nineties," *The Edmonton Journal*, January 23:H1, H3. (Ch14)

Ramsay, Joan. 1993b.* "Family Ties Trap Abused Seniors," *The Edmonton Journal*, January 23:H3.

Ramu, G.N. (ed.). 1993.* *Marriage and the Family in Canada Today* (second edition). Scarborough: Prentice-Hall Canada.

Ramu, G.N. 1977. *Family and Caste in Urban India: A Case Study*. New Delhi: Vikas Publishing.

Ramu, G.N. 1988. "Marital Roles and Power: Perceptions and Reality in an Urban Setting," *Journal of Comparative Family Studies*, 19:207–228.

Ramu, G.N. 1993.* "Courtship and Mate Selection," in G.N. Ramu (ed.). *Marriage and the Family in Canada Today* (second edition). Scarborough: Prentice-Hall Canada.

Rao, K. Vaninadha and T.R. Balakrishnan. 1988.* "Recent Trends and Sociodemographic Covariates of Childlessness in Canada," *Canadian Studies in Population*, 15:181–200.

Rao, P. Venkata and V. Sudarsen. 1978. "Continuity and Change in Marital Choice: A Note on Matrimonial Advertisements in South India," *Social Action*, 28:1.

Rapoport, Rhona. 1962. "Normal Crisis, Family Structure and Mental Health," *Family Process*, 2:68–80.

Rapoport, Rhona. 1964. "The Transition From Engagement to Marriage," *Acta Sociologica*, 8:36–55.

Rapoport, Rhona and Robert Rapoport. 1964. "New Light on the Honeymoon," *Human Relations*, 17:35–56.

Rapoport, Rhona and Robert Rapoport. 1975. "Men, Women and Equity," *The Family Coordinator*, 24:421–432.

Ravanera, Zenaida R., Fernando Rajulton and Thomas K. Burch. 1992.* "A Cohort Analysis of Home-Leaving in Canada, 1910–1975," Discussion Paper No. 92–3. Waterloo, Ontario: Population Studies Centre, University of Western Ontario.

Ravanera, Zenaida R., Fernando Rajulton and Thomas K. Burch. 1995.* "A Cohort Analysis of Home-Leaving in Canada, 1910–1975," *Journal of Comparative Family Studies*, 27(2):179–193.

Ray, K.C. and J. Jackson. 1997. "Family Environment and Childhood Sexual Victimization," *Journal of Interpersonal Violence*, 12(1):3–17.

Razin, E. and A. Langlois.* 1995. "Immigrant and Ethnic Entrepreneurs in Canadian and American Metropolitan Areas: A Comparative Perspective," in Laprerriere, A. et al. (eds.). *Immigration and Ethnicity in Canada*. Montreal: Association for Canadian Studies. Pp. 127–144.

Redman, Michael R. 1991. "Supporting Children in Blended Families," *Family Law Quarterly*, 25(1):83–94.

Redmond, Marcia A. 1985. "Attitudes of Adolescent Males Toward Adolescent Pregnancy and Fatherhood," *Family Relations*, 34:337–342.

Registrar General of Census. 1983. *1981 Census of India Publications*. New Delhi: Ministry of Home Office.

Reichertz, Diane and Harvy Frankel. 1990.* "Family Environments and Problematic Adolescents: Toward an Empirically Based Typology," *Community Alternatives: International Journal of Family Care*, 2:51–74.

Reid, W.J. and A. Crisafulli. 1990. "Marital Discord and Child Behavior Problems: A Meta-Analysis," *Journal of Abnormal Psychology*, 18:105–117.

Reiss, David, E. Mavis Hetherington, Robert Plomin, George W. Howe, Samuel J. Simmens, Sandra H. Henderson, Thomas J. O'Connor, Danielle A. Bussell, Edward R. Anderson and Tracy Law. 1995. "Genetic Questions for Environmental Studies: Differential Parenting and Psychopathology in Adolescence," *Archives of General Psychiatry*, 52(11):925–936.

Reiss, Ira. 1981. "Some Observations on Ideology and Sexuality in America," *Journal of Marriage and the Family*, 43:271–283.

Reiss, Ira L. 1960. "Toward a Sociology of the Heterosexual Love Relationship," *Marriage and Family Living*, 22:130–145.

Reiss, Ira L. 1965. "The Universality of the Family: A Conceptual Analysis," *Journal of Marriage and the Family*, 27:443–453.

Reiss, Ira L. 1967. *The Social Context of Premarital Sexual Permissiveness*. New York: Holt, Rinehart and Winston.

Reiss, Ira L. 1980. *Family Systems in America* (third edition). New York: Holt, Rinehart and Winston.

Reiss, Ira L. 1986. "A Sociological Journey into Sexuality," *Journal of Marriage and the Family*, 48:233–242.

Reiss, Ira L. and Brent C. Miller. 1979. "Heterosexual Permissiveness: A Theoretical Analysis," in W. Burr, R. Hill, F.I. Nye and I.L. Reiss (eds.). *Contemporary Theories About the Family*, Volume 1. New York: The Free Press, 57–100.

Rempel, Judith. 1985.* "Childless Elderly: What Are They Missing?" *Journal of Marriage and the Family*, 47:343–348.

Renne, Karen S. 1971. "Health and Marital Experience in an Urban Population," *Journal of Marriage and the Family*, 33:338–350.

Rexroat, Cynthia and Constance Shehan. 1987. "The Family Life Cycle and Spouses' Time in Housework," *Journal of Marriage and the Family*, 49:737–750.

Rhyne, Darla. 1981.* "Bases of Marital Satisfaction Among Men and Women," *Journal of Marriage and the Family*, 43:941–955.

Rice, Rodger and Ann Annis. 1992. *A Survey of Abuse in the Christian Reformed Church*. Grand Rapids: Social Research Center, Calvin College.

Rich, A. 1980. "Compulsory Heterosexuality and Lesbian Existence," in C.R. Stimpson and E.S. Person (eds). *Women: Sex and Sexuality*. Chicago: University of Chicago Press. Pp. 62–91.

Richard, Madeline A. 1991.* *Ethnic Groups and Marital Choices*. Vancouver: University of British Columbia Press.

Richards, John and William G. Watson (eds.). 1995.* *Family Matters: New Policies for Divorce, Lone Mothers, and Child Poverty*. Ottawa: C.D. Howe Institute.

Richardson, Rhonda A., Nancy E. Barbour and Donald L. Bubenzer. 1995. "Peer Relationships as a Source of Support for Adolescent Mothers," *Journal of Adolescent Research*, 10(2):278–290.

Riggs, David S. and Marie B. Caulfield. 1997. "Expected Consequences of Male Violence Against Their Female Dating Partners," *Journal of Interpersonal Violence*, 12:229–240.

Riley, Nancy E. 1994. "Interwoven Lives: Parents, Marriage, and Guanxi in China," *Journal of Marriage and the Family*, 56(4):791–803.

Riordan, Robert. 1994.* "Two by Two? Sex Ratios of Unattached Canadians," *Canadian Social Trends*, 32:26–29.

Risman, Barbara J., Charles T. Hill, Zick Rubin and Letitia A. Peplau. 1981. "Living Together in College: Implications for Courtship," *Journal of Marriage and the Family*, 43:77–83.

Roberts, Alexander and James Donaldson (eds.). 1886. *The Ante-Nicene Fathers*. Buffalo: The Christian Literature Co.

Roberts, George W. and Sonja A. Sinclair. 1978. *Women in Jamaica: Patterns of Reproduction and Family*. Millwood, New York: KTO Press.

Roberts, William I. 1987.* "Two Career Families: Demographic Variables, Parenting and Competence in Young Children," *Canadian Journal of Behavioural Science*, 19:347–356.

Roberts, William L. 1989.* "Parents' Stressful Life Events and Social Networks: Relations with Parenting and Children's Competence," *Canadian Journal of Behavioural Science*, 21:132–146.

Robertson, Ann. 1996.* "Beyond Apocalyptic Demography," *Transition*, September:12–13.

Robinson, Linda C. and Priscilla W. Blanton. 1993. "Marital Strengths in Enduring Marriages," *Family Relations*, 42:38–45.

Robson, Bonnie. 1979.* *My Parents Are Divorced, Too: What Teenagers Experience and How They Cope*, Toronto: Dorset Publishing.

Rodgers, Jennifer and Peter Calder. 1990.* "Marital Adjustment: A Valuable Resource for the Emotional Health of Individuals With Multiple Sclerosis," *Rehabilitation Counseling Bulletin*, 34:24–32.

Rodgers, Karen. 1994.* "Wife Assault in Canada." *Canadian Social Trends*: Statistics Canada. Catalogue 11–008E.

Rodgers, Roy H. 1973. *Family Interaction and Transaction: The Developmental Approach.* Englewood Cliffs: Prentice-Hall.

Rodgers, Roy H. 1987. "Postmarital Reorganization of *Family Relationships*: A Propositional Theory," in Daniel Perlman and Steve Duck. (eds.). *Intimate Relationships: Development, Dynamics and Deterioration*, Newbury Park: Sage.

Rodgers, Roy H. and James M. White. 1993.* "Family Development Theory," in Pauline G. Boss, William G. Doherty, Ralph LaRossa, Walter R. Schumm and Suzanne K. Steinmetz (eds.). *Sourcebook of Family Theories and Methods*: A Contextual Approach. New York: Plenum Press, Chapter 10.

Rodriguez, N., S. Ryan, H. Van de Kemp and D. Foy. 1997. "Posttraumatic Stress Disorder in Adult Female Survivors of Childhood Sexual Abuse: A Comparison Study," *Journal of Consulting and Clinical Psychology*, 65(1):53–59.

Rogers, Carl R. 1972. *Becoming Partners: Marriage and its Alternatives.* New York: Delacorte Press.

Rogers, Michelle L. and Dennis P. Hogan (2002). "Family Life With Children With Disabilities: The Key Role Of Rehabilitation," *Journal of Marriage and the Family*, 65:818–834.

Rogers, Stacy J. 1996. "Mothers' Work Hours and Marital Quality: Variations by Family Structure and Family Size," *Journal of Marriage and the Family*, 58:606–617.

Rollins, Boyd C. and Darwin L. Thomas. 1979. "Parental Support, Power and Control Techniques in the Socialization of Children," in Wesley R. Burr, Reuben Hill, F. Ivan Nye and Ira L. Reiss (eds.). *Contemporary Theories about the Family: Research-Based Theories*, Volume I. New York: The Free Press.

Romaniuc, A. 1984.* "Fertility in Canada: From Baby-Boom to Baby Bust," *Current Demographic Analysis*. Catalogue No. 91–524 Occasional. Ottawa: Statistics Canada.

Romaniuc, Anatole. 1989.* "Fertility in Canada: A Long View," in Jacques Légaré, T.R. Balakrishnan and Roderic P. Beaujot (ed.). *The Family in Crisis: A Population Crisis?* Ottawa: Lowe-Martin Company, 252–270.

Rordorf, Willy. 1969. "Marriage in the New Testament and in the Early Church," *Journal of Ecclesiastical History*, 20:193–210.

Rosenberg, Harriet. 1987.* "Motherwork, Stress and Depression: The Costs of Privatized Social Reproduction," in Heather Jon Maroney and Meg Luxton (eds.). *Feminism and Political Economy, Women's Work, Women's Struggles.* Toronto: Methuen.

Rosenblatt, Paul C. 1974. "Cross-Cultural Perspective on Attraction," in Ted R. Huston (ed.). *Foundations of Interpersonal Attraction.* New York: Academic Press.

Rosenblatt, Paul C. 1977. "Needed Research on Commitment in Marriage," in George Levinger and Harold L. Rausch (eds.). *Close Relationships: Perspectives on the Meaning of Intimacy.* Amherst: University of Massachusetts Press.

Rosenfield, S. 1992. "The Costs of Sharing: Wives' Employment and Husbands' Mental Health," *Journal of Health and Social Behavior*, 33:213–226.

Rosenthal, Carolyn J. 1985.* "Kinkeeping in the Familial Division of Labor," *Journal of Marriage and the Family*, 47:965–974.

Rosenthal, Carolyn J. 1987.* "Aging and Intergenerational Relations in Canada," in Victor W. Marshall. *Aging in Canada: Social Perspectives* (second edition). Markham: Fitzhenry and Whiteside.

Rosenthal, Carolyn J. 1994.* "Long-Term Care Reform and 'Family' Care: A Worrisome Combination," *Canadian Journal on Aging*, 13:419–422.

Rosenthal, Carolyn J. and Victor W. Marshall. 1986.* "The Head of the Family: Social Meaning and Structural Variability," *Canadian Journal of Sociology*, 11:183–198.

Rosenthal, Carolyn J., Sarah H. Matthews and Victor W. Marshall. 1989.* "Is Parent Care Normative? The Experience of a Sample of Middle-Aged Women," *Research on Aging*, 11:244–260.

Rosenthal, D.A. 1984. "Intergenerational Conflict and Culture: A Study of Immigrant Adolescents and Nonimmigrant Adolescents and Their Parents," *Genetic Psychology Monographs*, 109:53–75.

Rosenthal, D. A. and S. S. Feldman. 1992. "The Nature and Stability of Ethnic Identity in Chinese Youth: Effects of Length of Residence in Two Cultural Contexts," *Journal of Cross-Cultural Psychology.* 23:214–227.

Rosenzweig, Herschel D. 1985. "Sexual Abuse: Practical Implications of Knowledge," in Eli H. Newberger and Richard Bourne (eds.). *Unhappy Families: Clinical and Research Perspectives on Family Violence.* Littleton: PSG Publishing Co.

Rosin, M.B. 1987. *Stepfathering: Stepfather's Advice on Creating a New Family.* New York: Simon and Schuster.

Roskies, Ethel and Sylvie Carrier. 1992.* "Marriage and Children for Professional Women: Asset or Liability?" paper presented at the American Psychological Association/NIOSH conference, Washington, D.C., November 1992.

Ross, Aileen D. 1961. *The Hindu Family in its Urban Setting.* Toronto: University of Toronto Press.

Ross, Catherine E. and John Mirowsky. 1990. "Women, Work and Family: Changing Gender Roles and Psychological Well-Being," in Maureen T. Hallinan David M. Klein and Jennifer Glass (eds.). *Change in Societal Institutions.* New York: Plenum Press.

Ross, Catherine E., John Mirowsky and Karen Goldsteen. 1991. "The Impact of the Family on Health," in Alan Booth (ed.). *Contemporary Families: Looking Forward, Looking Back*. Minneapolis: National Council on Family Relations, 341–360.

Ross, David et al. 1996.* *Child Poverty: What Are the Consequences?* Ottawa: Centre for International Statistics.

Ross, David P., Katherine Scott and Mark A. Kelly. 1996.* *Growing Up in Canada: National Longitudinal Survey of Children and Youth*. Catalogue No. 89–550–MPE, No.1, Statistics Canada and Human Resources Development Canada:15–45.

Ross, H.L. and I.V. Sawhill. 1975. *Time of Transition: The Growth of Families Headed by Women*. Washington, D.C.: The Urban Institute.

Ross, Hildy and Heather Taylor. 1989.* "Do Boys Prefer Daddy or His Physical Style of Play?" *Sex Roles*, 20:23–34.

Rossi, A. 1977. "A Biosocial Perspective on Parenting," *Daedalus*, 106:1–30.

Rossi, A. 1984. "Gender and Parenthood," *American Sociological Review*, 49:1–19.

Rothberg, Barbara and Dana L. Weinstein. 1966. "A Primer on Lesbian and Gay Families," *Journal of Gay and Lesbian Social Services*, 4(2):55–68.

Roxburgh, Susan. 1997.* "The Effect of Children on the Mental Health of Women in the Paid Labor Force," *Journal of Family Issues*, 18(3):270–289.

Royal Commission on Aboriginal Peoples. 1996.* *Canada's Aboriginal Population, 1981–1991*. Canada: Canada Housing and Mortgage Corporation.

Rubenstein, Judith L., Antonia Halton, Linda Kasten, Carol Rubin and Gerald Stechler. 1998. "Suicidal Behavior in Adolescents: Stress and Protection in Different Family Contexts," *American Journal of Orthopsychiatry*, 68(2):274–284.

Rubin, R.T., J.M. Reinisch and R.F. Haskett. 1981. "Postnatal Gonadal Steroid Effects on Human Behaviour," *Science*, 211:1218–1324.

Rubin, Roger H. 1985. "Premarital Sex," in Harold Feldman and Margaret Feldman. *Current Controversies in Marriage and Family*. Beverly Hills: Sage.

Rubin, Zick, Letitia A. Peplau and Charles T. Hill. 1981. "Loving and Leaving: Sex Differences in Romantic Attachments," *Sex Roles*, 7:821–835.

Ruddick, Sara. 1982. "Maternal Thinking," in Barrie Thorne and Marilyn Yalom (eds.). *Rethinking the Family: Some Feminist Questions*. New York: Longman, 76–94.

Rudin, M., C. Zalewski, and J. Bodmer-Turner. 1995. "Characteristics of Child Sexual Abuse Victims According to Perpetrator Gender," *Child Abuse and Neglect*, 19(8):963–973.

Rueter, Martha A. and Rand D. Conger. 1995. "Antecedents of Parent–Adolescent Disagreements," *Journal of Marriage and the Family*, 57(2):435–448.

Runtz, M. and J. Schallow. 1997. "Social Support and Coping Strategies as Mediators of Adult Adjustment Following Childhood Maltreatment," *Child Abuse and Neglect*, 21(2):211–226.

Russel, Diana. 1980. "The Prevalence and Impact of Marital Rape in San Francisco," Paper presented at the annual meeting of the American Sociological Association, New York.

Russel, Diana. 1982. *Rape in Marriage*. New York: Macmillan.

Ryan, K.M. 1995. "Do Courtship-Violent Men Have Characteristics Associated with a 'Battering Personality'?" *Journal of Family Violence*, 10:99–120.

Ryan, Michael. 1996. "Family Is What You Make It," *Parade Magazine*, May 12:4–5.

Sabatelli, Ronald M. 1992. "The Impact of the Employment Status of Wives and Parenthood on the Marital Exchange Relationship," presented at the 1992 National Council on Family Relations Annual Conference, Orlando, Florida, November 1992.

Sabatelli, Ronald M. and Constance L. Shehan. 1993. "Exchange and Resource Theories," in Pauline G. Boss, William G. Doherty, Ralph LaRossa, Walter R. Schumm and Suzanne K. Steinmetz (eds.). *Sourcebook of Family Theories and Methods: A Contextual Approach*. New York: Plenum Press, Chapter 16.

Sabourin, Stéphane, Yvan Loussier and John Wright. 1991.* "The Effects of Measurement Strategy on Attributions for Marital Problems and Behaviors," *Journal of Applied Social Psychology*. 21:734–746.

Sadker, Myra and David Sadker. 1985. "Sexism in the Schoolroom of the 80s," *Psychology Today*, March:54–57.

Safrai, S. and M. Stern (eds.). 1974. *The Jewish People in the First Century*. Volume One. Philadelphia: Fortress Press.

Safrai, S. and M. Stern (eds.). 1976. *The Jewish People in the First Century*. Volume Two. Philadelphia: Fortress Press.

Sagi, Abraham, Marinus H. van Ijzendoorn, Ora Aviezer, Frank Donnell and Ofra Mayseless. 1994. "Sleeping Out of Home in a Kibbutz Communal Arrangement: It Makes a Difference for Infant-Mother Attachment," *Child Development*, 65(4):992–1004.

Sagi, Abraham, Marinus H. van Ijzendoorn, Ora Aviezer, Frank Donnell, Nina Koren-Karie, Tirtsa Joels, and Yael Harel. 1995. "Attachments in a Multiple-Caregiver and Multiple-Infant Environment: The Case of the Israeli Kibbutzim," *Monographs of the Society for Research in Child Development*, 60(2–3):71–91.

Saint-Jacques, Marie-Christine. 1995. "Role Strain Prediction in Stepfamilies," *Journal of Divorce and Remarriage*, 24(1/2):51–72.

Sanchez, L. and E. Thomson. 1997. "Becoming Mothers and Fathers: Parenthood, Gender and the Division of Labour," *Gender and Society*, 11(6):747–772.

Sander, William. 1993. "Catholicism and Intermarriage in the United States," *Journal of Marriage and the Family*, 55:1037–1041.

Sangree, W. 1980. "The Persistence of Polyandry in Irigwe, Nigeria," *Journal of Comparative Family Studies*, 11(3):325–334.

Sangree, W. and N. Levine. 1980. "Introduction," *Journal of Comparative Family Studies*, 11(3):i–iv.

Santelli, John S., Nancy D. Brener, Richard Lowry, Amita Bhatt and Laurie S. Zabin. 1998. "Multiple Sexual Partners among U.S. Adolescents and Young Adults," *Family Planning Perspectives*, 30(6):271–275.

Sathré, Freda S., Ray W. Olson and Clarissa I. Whitney. 1977. *Let's Talk: An Introduction to Interpersonal Communication*. Glenview: Scott, Foresman and Company.

Satzewich, V. 1993. "Migrant and Immigration Families in Canada: State Coercion and Legal Control in the Formation of Ethnic Families," *Journal of Comparative Family Studies*, 24, 3:315–338.

Saucier, Jean-Francois and Anne-Marie Ambert. 1986.* "Adolescents' Perception of Self and of Immediate Environment by Parental Marital Status: A Controlled Study," *Canadian Journal of Psychiatry*, 31:505–512.

Sawyer, R.G., P. J. Pinciaro and J.K. Jessell. 1998. "Effects of Coercion and Verbal Consent on University Students' Perception of Date Rape," *American Journal of Health Behavior*, 22:46–53.

Scanzoni, John. 1970. *Opportunity and the Family: A Study of the Conjugal Family in Relation to the Economic Opportunity Structure*. New York: The Free Press.

Scanzoni, John. 1972. *Sexual Bargaining: Power Politics in American Marriage*. Englewood Cliffs: Prentice Hall.

Scanzoni, John. 1978. *Sex Roles, Women's Work, and Marital Conflict*. Toronto: Lexington.

Scanzoni, John. 1979a. "Social Exchange and Behavioral Interdependence," in R.L. Burgess and T.L. Huston (eds.). *Social Exchange in Developing Relationships*. New York: Academic Press.

Scanzoni, John. 1979b. "Strategies for Changing Male Family Roles: Research and Practice Implications," *The Family Coordinator*, 28:435–442.

Scanzoni, John and William Marsiglio. 1993. "New Action Theory and Contemporary Families," *Journal of Family Issues*, 14:105–132.

Scanzoni, John H. 1972. *Sexual Bargaining: Power Politics in the American Family*. Englewood Cliffs: Prentice-Hall.

Scanzoni, John, Karen Polonko, Jay Teachman and Linda Thompson. 1989. *The Sexual Bond: Rethinking Families and Close Relationships*. Newbury Park: Sage.

Scarr, Sandra, Deborah Philips and Kathleen McCartney. 1989. "Working Mothers and their Families," *Social Behavior and Personality*, 44:1402–1409.

Schaaf, K. and T. McCanne. 1994. "Childhood Abuse, Body Image Disturbance, and Eating Disorders," *Child Abuse and Neglect*, 18(8):607–615.

Schaap, Cas, Bram Buunk and Ada Kerkstra. 1988. "Marital Conflict Resolution," in Patricia Noller and Mary A. Fitzpatrick (eds.). *Perspectives on Marital Interaction*. Philadelphia: Multilingual Matters Ltd.

Schachar, Russell J. and R. Wachsmuth. 1991.* "Family Dysfunction and Psychosocial Adversity: Comparison of Attention Deficit Disorder, Conduct Disorder, Normal and Clinical Controls," *Canadian Journal of Behavioural Science*, 23:332–348.

Schachar, Russell J. and R. Wachsmuth. 1991.* "Family Dysfunction and Psychosocial Adversity: Comparison of Attention Deficit Disorder, Conduct Disorder, Normal and Clinical Controls," *Canadian Journal of Behavioural Science*, 23:332–348.

Schellenberg, Grant and Christopher Clark. 1996.* "Boomers Today, Seniors Tomorrow," *Transition*, September:5–8.

Schlesinger, Benjamin. 1975.* "Women and Men in Second Marriages," in S.P. Wakil (ed.). *Marriage, Family and Society*. Scarborough: Butterworths.

Schnittger, Maureen H. and Gloria W. Bird. 1990. "Coping Among Dual-Career Men and Women Across the Life Cycle," *Family Relations*, 39:199–205.

Schoen, Robert. 1992. "First Unions and the Stability of First Marriages," *Journal of Marriage and the Family*, 54:281–284.

Schoen, Robert and Robin M. Weinick. 1993. "Partner Choice in Marriages and Cohabitations," *Journal of Marriage and the Family*, 55:408–414.

Schottland, C. I. 1967. "Government Economic Programs and Family Life," *Journal of Marriage and the Family*, 29:71–123.

Schreiber, E.M. 1975.* "The Social Bases of Opinions on Woman's Role in Canada," *Canadian Journal of Sociology*, 1:61–74.

Schreurs, Karlein M.G. and Bram P. Bunk. 1995. "Intimacy, Autonomy, and Relationship Satisfaction in Dutch Lesbian Couples and Heterosexual Couples," *Journal of Psychology and Human Sexuality*, 7:41–57.

Schroeder, P. 1989. *Champion of the Great American Family*. New York: Random House. Chapter 18.

Schuler, Corinna. 1990.* "Dangerous Dating," *The Edmonton Journal*. August 27:C1.

Schultz, David A. 1972. *The Changing Family*. Englewood Cliffs: Prentice-Hall.

Schumm, Walter R. 1985. "Beyond Relationship Characteristics of Strong Families: Constructing a Model of Family Strengths," *Family Perspective*, 19:1–9.

Schumm, Walter R., Anthony P. Jurich, Stephen R. Bollman and Margaret A. Bugaighis. 1985. "His and Her Marriage Revisited," *Journal of Family Issues*, 6:221–227.

Schumm, Walter R., Howard L. Barnes, Stephen R. Bollman, Anthony P. Jurich and Margaret A. Bugaighis. 1986. "Self-Disclosure and Marital Satisfaction Revisited," *Family Relations*, 35:241–247.

Schusky, Ernest L. 1965. *Manual for Kinship Analysis*. New York: Holt, Rinehart and Winston.

Schusky, Ernest L. 1974. *Variation in Kinship*. New York: Holt, Rinehart and Winston.

Schwartz, M. 1987. "Repeated Spousal Assaults in the National Crime Survey," paper presented at the American Society of Criminology, Montreal.

Schwartz, M. 1994. "Negative Impact of Sexual Abuse on Adult Male Gender: Issues and Strategies of Intervention," *Child and Adolescent Social Work Journal*, 11(3):179–194.

Scott, D. 1988.* "Theoretical Approaches to the Problem of Wife Assault: A Critique and Modest Reformulation." M.A. thesis in social studies, University of Regina.

Scott, Katherine. 1996.* *The Progress of Canada's Children, 1996*. Ottawa: Canadian Council on Social Development.

Scott, William A. and Ruth Scott. 1989.* "Family Correlates of High School Adjustment: A Cross-Cultural Study," *Australian Journal of Psychology*, 41:269–284.

Scott, William A., Ruth Scott and Morag McCabe. 1991.* "Family Relationships and Children's Personality: A Cross-Cultural, Cross-Source Comparison," *British Journal of Social Psychology*, 30:1–20.

Sebald, Hans. 1986. "Adolescent's Shifting Orientation Toward Parents and Peers: A Curvilinear Trend over Recent Decades," *Journal of Marriage and the Family*, 48:5–13.

Seccombe, Karen 2002. "'Beating The Odds' Versus 'Changing The Odds': Poverty And Family Policy," *Journal of Marriage and Family* 64:384–394.

Secret, Mary, Ginny Sprang and Judith Bradford. 1998. "Parenting in the Workplace: Examining a Unique Infant Care Option," *Journal of Family Issues*, 19(6):795–815.

Seifeddine, Samia. 1994.* *Changing Mosaic: A Needs Assessment of Immigrant Youth in Edmonton*. Edmonton: The Mennonite Centre for Newcomers.

Seligman, J. 1990. "Variations on a Theme: Gay and Lesbian Couples," *Newsweek*, 114 (Special issue):38–46.

Seligson, Marcia. 1974. *The Eternal Bliss Machine: America's Way of Wedding*. New York: Bantam Books.

Seltzer, Judith A. 1991. "Relationships between Fathers and Children Who Live Apart: The Father's Role after Separation," *Journal of Marriage and the Family*, 53:79–101.

Seltzer, Judith A. and Suzanne M. Bianchi. 1988. "Children's Contact with Absent Parents," *Journal of Marriage and the Family*, 50:663–677.

Seltzer, Judith A. and Suzanne M. Bianchi. 1988. "Children's Contact with Absent Parents," *Journal of Marriage and the Family*, 50:663–677.

Seltzer, Judith A. and Yvonne Brandreth. 1994. "What Fathers Say about Involvement with Children after Separation," *Journal of Family Issues*, 15(1):49–77.

Sevér, Aysan. 1992.* *Women and Divorce in Canada, A Sociological Analysis*. Toronto: Canadian Scholars' Press.

Shackleford, T.K. and Buss, D.M. 1998. "Anticipation Of Marital Dissolution As A Consequence Of Spousal Infidelity." *Journal of Social and Personal Relationships* 14:793–808.

Shah, Farida and Melvin Zelnick. 1981. "Parent and Peer Influence on Sexual Behaviour, Contraceptive Use and Pregnancy Experience of Young Women," *Journal of Marriage and the Family*, 43:339–348.

Shannon, C. E. and W. Weaver. 1949. *The Mathematical Theory of Communication*. Urbana: University of Illinois Press.

Shapiro, Adam D. 1996. "Explaining Psychological Distress in a Sample of Remarried and Divorced Persons: The Influence of Economic Distress," *Journal of Family Issues*, 17(2):186–203.

Shapiro, Brenda and J. Conrad Schwarz. 1997. "Date Rape: Its Relationship to Trauma Symptoms and Sexual Self-Esteem," *Journal of Interpersonal Violence*, 12:407–419.

Shaver, Philip and Clyde Hendrick. 1987. *Sex and Gender*. Newbury Park: Sage.

Shaw, Susan. 1988. "Gender Differences in the Definition and Perception of Household Labor," *Family Relations*, 37:333–337.

Sheehan, Michael M. 1971. "The Formation and Stability of Marriage in Fourteenth-Century England: Evidence of an Ely Register," *Medieval Studies*, 33:228–263.

Shehan, Constance L., E. Wilbur Bock and Gary R. Lee. 1990. "Religious Heterogamy, Religiosity and Marital Happiness: The Case of Catholics," *Journal of Marriage and the Family*, 52:73–79.

Sherman, Lawrence W. and Ellen G. Cohn. 1990. "The Effects of Research on Legal Policy in the Minneapolis Domestic Violence Experiment," in Douglas J. Bersharov (ed.). *Family Violence: Research and Public Policy Issues*. Washington: The AEI Press.

Shields, Nancy M. and Christine R. Hanneke. 1983. "Battered Wives' Reactions to Marital Rape," in David Finkelhor, Richard J. Gelles, Gerald T. Hotaling and Murray A. Strauss (eds.). *The Dark Side of Families: Current Family Violence Research*. Beverly Hills: Sage.

Shihadeh, Edward S. 1991. "The Prevalence of Husband-Centered Migration: Employment Consequences for Married Mothers," *Journal of Marriage and the Family*, 53:432–444.

Shorter, Edward. 1975. *The Making of the Modern Family*. New York: Basic Books.

Shotland, R. Lance and Lynne Goodstein. 1983. "Just Because She Doesn't Want to Doesn't Mean It's Rape," *Social Psychology Quarterly*, 46: 220–232.

Shuey, Kim and Melissa Hardy (2003). "Assistance To Aging Parents And Parent-In-Law: Does Lineage Affect Family Allocation Decisions?" *Journal of Marriage and Family* 65:418–431.

Shulz, David A. 1972. *The Changing Family, Its Function and Future*. Englewood Cliffs: Prentice-Hall, 41.

Siddique, M. 1983.* "Changing Family Patterns: A Comparative Analysis of Immigrant Indian and Pakistani Families of Saskatoon, Canada," in George Kurian and Ram P. Srivastava (eds.). *Overseas Indians: A Study in Adaptation*. New Delhi: Vikas Publishing.

Siggner, Andrew J. 1986.* "The Socio-Demographic Condition of Registered Indians," in J. Rick Ponting (ed.). *Arduous Journey: Canadian Indians and Decolonization*. Toronto: McClelland and Stewart.

Sigler, Robert T. 1989. *Domestic Violence in Context*. Lexington: Lexington Books.

Signorielli, Nancy. 1989. "Television and Conceptions About Sex Roles: Maintaining Conventionality and the Status Quo," *Sex Roles*, 21:341–360.

Silverman, A. B., H. Z. Reinherz, and R. M. Giaconia. 1996. "The Long-Term Sequelae of Child and Adolescent Abuse: A Longitudinal Community Study," *Child Abuse & Neglect*, 20:709–723.

Silverman, R. and L. Kennedy. 1993. *Deadly Deeds: Murder in Canada*. Scarborough: Nelson.

Skrypnek, B. J. and J. E. Fast. 1996. "Work and Family Policy in Canada: Family Needs, Collective Solutions," *Journal of Family Issues*, 17 (6):793–812.

Small, S.A., and D. Kerns. 1993. "Unwanted Sexual Activity among Peers during Early and Middle Adolescence: Incidence and Risk Factors," *Journal of Marriage and the Family*, 55:941–952.

Smith, D. E. 1993. "The Standard North American Family: SNAF as an Ideological Code," *Journal of Family Issues*, 14:50–65.

Sorenson, A. M., and D. Brownfield. 1991. "The Measurement of Parental Influence: Assessing the Relative Effects of Father and Mother," *Sociological Methods and Research*, 19:511–535.

South, Scott J., and Kim M. Lloyd. 1992. "Marriage Markets and Nonmarital Fertility in the United States," *Demography*, 29:247–264.

South, Scott J., Trent, Katherine and Yang Shen. 2001. "Changing Partners: Toward a Macrostructural-Opportunity Theory of Marital Dissolution," *Journal of Marriage and Family* 63:743–754.

Spanier, Graham B. 1983. "Married and Unmarried Cohabitation in the United States: 1980," *Journal of Marriage and the Family*, 45:277–288.

Spanier, Graham B. and Linda Thompson. 1987. *Parting: The Aftermath of Separation and Divorce*. Newbury Park: Sage.

Spanier, Graham B. and Paul C. Glick. 1981. "Marital Instability in the United States: Some Correlates and Recent Changes," *Family Relations*, 31:329–338.

Spanier, Graham B. and Randie L. Margolis. 1983. "Marital Separation and Extramarital Sexual Behaviour," *Journal of Sex Research*, 19:23–48.

Spanier, Graham B. and Robert E. Lewis. 1980. "Marital Quality: A Review of the Seventies," *Journal of Marriage and the Family*, 42:825–839.

Spanier, Graham B. 1976a. "Formal and Informal Sex Education as Determinants of Premarital Sexual Behaviour," *Archives of Sexual Behaviour*, 5:39–67.

Spanier, Graham B. 1976b. "Measuring Dyadic Adjustment: New Scales for Assessing the Quality of Marriage and Similar Dyads," *Journal of Marriage and the Family*, 38:15–28.

Speiser, S.M., 1970. "Recovery for Wrongful Death." Pp. 196–206 in *Economic Handbook*. Rochester, New York: Lawyers Co-operative Publication Committee.

Spiro, Melford E. 1956. *Kibbutz: Venture in Utopia*. Cambridge: Harvard University Press.

Spiro, Melford E. 1958. *Children of the Kibbutz*. Cambridge: Harvard University Press.

Sprecher, Susan. 1994. "Two Sides to the Breakup of Dating Relationships," *Personal Relationships*, 1:199–222.

Sprecher, Susan and Diane Felmlee. 1992. "The Influence of Parents and Friends on the Quality and Stability of Romantic Relationships: A Three-Wave Attitudinal Investigation," *Journal of Marriage and the Family*, 54:888–900.

Sprecher, Susan and P.C. Regan. 1998. "Passionate and Companionate Love in Courting and Young Married Couples," *Sociological Inquiry*, 68:163–185.

Sprecher, Susan and Pamela C. Regan. 1996.* "College Virgins: How Men and Women Perceive Their Sexual Status," *The Journal of Sex Research*, 25(3):261–288.

Sprecher, Susan. 2002. "Sexual Satisfaction In Premarital Relationships: Associations With Satisfaction, Love, Commitment, And Stability," *Journal of Sex Research* 39:190–196.

Sprey, Jetse. 1979. "Conflict Theory and the Study of Marriage and the Family," in Wesley R. Burr, Reuben Hill, F. Ivan Nye, Ira L. Reiss (eds.). 1979. *Contemporary Theories about the Family, Volume II*. New York: The Free Press, Chapter 4.

Spruijt, Ed and Martijn de Goede. 1997. "Transitions in Family Structure and Adolescent Well-Being," *Adolescence*, 32(128):897–911.

Srivastava, R. P. 1975.* "Family Organization and Change Among the Overseas Indians with Special Reference to Indian Immigrant Families of British Columbia, Canada." Pp. 369–91 in G. Kurian (Ed.) *Family in India: A Regional View*, Mouton: the Hague.

Stacey, Deborah and Meredith Kost. 1992.* "The Costs of the Trade-Off," *Transition*, June 11.

Stacey, Judith. 1993. "Good Riddance to 'The Family': A Response to David Popenoe," *Journal of Marriage and the Family*, 55:545–547.

Stack, S., 1981. "Divorce and Suicide, a Time Series Analysis, 1933–1970," *Journal of Family Issues*, 2(1):77–90.

Stack, Steven. 1994. "The Effect of Geographic Mobility on Premarital Sex," *Journal of Marriage and the Family*, 56:204–208.

Stahl, P.M. 1986. "Attitudes and Beliefs About Joint Custody: Findings of a Study," *Conciliation Courts Review*, 24:41–46.

Stainton, M. Colleen. 1985. "The Fetus: A Growing Member of the Family," *Family Relations*, 34:321–336.

Stanbury, W.T. 1975.* *Success and Failure: Indians in Urban Society*. Vancouver: University of British Columbia Press.

Stanley, S. 1986. "Commitment and the Maintenance and Enhancement of Relationships," unpublished doctoral dissertation, University of Denver.

Stanley, Scott M., Howard J. Markman, Michelle St. Peters and B. Douglas Leber. 1995. "Strengthening Marriages and Preventing Divorce: New Directions in Prevention Research," *Family Relations*, 44(4):392–401.

Stanton, Max E. 1995. "Patterns of Kinship and Residence," in Bron B. Ingoldsby and Suzanna Smith (eds). *Families in Multicultural Perspective*. New York: Guilford Press. Pp. 97–116.

Statistics Canada. 1994.* *Women in the Labour Force*. Ottawa, ON: Minister of Industry, Science and Technology.

Statistics Canada (1995), Catalogue No. 71F0004XCB.

Statistics Canada. 1995.* *Women In Canada*, Third Edition, Catalogue 89–503E, August 8.

Statistics Canada. *Health Reports.** *Therapeutic Abortions, 1990 and 1997*. Ottawa, ON: Ministry of Industry, Catalogue 82–219–XPB, Table 17.

Statistics Canada, 1993.* *Families: Social and Economic Characteristics*. Catalogue No. 93–320. Ottawa: Ministry of Industry, Science and Technology.

Statistics Canada. 1995. *Visible Minorities: A Diverse Group*. *The Daily*, August 15.

Statistics Canada. 1996. *Family Incomes, 1995*. *The Daily*, December 11.

Statistics Canada. *Vital Statistics, Births and Deaths*. Catalogue No. 84–210. Canada, 1991–1995.*

Statistics Canada. 1980.* *Canada's Female Labour Force*. Catalogue No. 98–804E. Ottawa: Supply and Services Canada.

Statistics Canada. 1981. *Census of Canada Public Use*. Sample Tape.

Statistics Canada. 1984.* *The Elderly in Canada*. Ottawa: Supply and Services Canada.

Statistics Canada. 1984.* *Women in the Work World*. Catalogue No. 99–940. Ottawa: Supply and Services Canada.

Statistics Canada. 1986 *Census of Canada Public Use*. Sample Tape.

Statistics Canada. 1986.* "Births to Unwed Mothers," *Canadian Social Trends*, Summer: 29–31.

Statistics Canada. 1987.* *Families*. Catalogue No. 93–101. Ottawa: Supply and Services Canada.

Statistics Canada. 1987.* *The Nation: Age, Sex and Marital Status*. Catalogue No. 93–101. Ottawa: Supply and Services Canada.

Statistics Canada. 1987.* *The Nation: Families, Part 1*. Catalogue No. 93–106. Ottawa: Supply and Services Canada.

Statistics Canada. 1988.* *Profiles, Urban and Rural Areas, Canada, Provinces and Territories, Part 1*. Catalogue No. 94–129. Ottawa: Supply and Services Canada.

Statistics Canada. 1988.* *Vital Statistics, Volume 1, Births and Deaths, 1986*. Ottawa: Supply and Services Canada.

Statistics Canada. 1989.* *Labour Force Annual Averages 1981–1988*. Catalogue No. 71–529. Ottawa: Supply and Services Canada.

Statistics Canada. 1990.* "Births to Unmarried Women," in Craig McKie and Keith Thompson (eds.). *Canadian Social Trends*. Toronto: Thompson Educational Publishing.

Statistics Canada. 1990.* *Health Reports*, Supplement No. 14, Volume 2 (1), Births 1987–1988. Ottawa: Supply and Services Canada.

Statistics Canada. 1990a.* *Postcensal Annual Estimates of Population by Marital Status, Age, Sex and Components of Growth for Canada, Provinces and Territories, June, 1, 1990.* Ottawa: Ministry of Industry, Science and Technology.

Statistics Canada. 1991.* *Characteristics of Dual-Earner Families, 1989.* Catalogue No. 13–215. Ottawa: Ministry of Industry, Science and Technology.

Statistics Canada. 1992.* *Families: Number, Type and Structure.* 1991 Census of Canada. Catalogue No. 93–312. Ottawa: Supply and Services Canada.

Statistics Canada. 1992.* "Therapeutic Abortions, 1990." *Health Reports,* Supplement No. 9, 3 (4). Catalogue No. 82–003S9. Ottawa: Supply and Services Canada.

Statistics Canada. 1992.* "Births, 1990." *Health Reports,* Supplement No. 14, 4 (1). Catalogue No. 82–003S14. Ottawa: Supply and Services Canada.

Statistics Canada. 1992.* "Divorce 1990." *Health Reports,* Supplement No. 17, Catalogue No. 820 S16. Ottawa: Ministry of Industry, Science and Technology.

Statistics Canada. 1992.* *Labour Force Annual Averages, 1991.* Catalogue No. 71–220. Ottawa: Ministry of Industry, Science and Technology.

Statistics Canada. 1992a.* "The Service Sector from 1976 to 1991," in *Labour Force Annual Averages, 1991.* Catalogue No. 71–229. Ottawa: Ministry of Industry, Science and Technology.

Statistics Canada. 1992a.* *The Nation: Age, Sex and Marital Status.* Catalogue No. 93–310. Ottawa: Ministry of Industry, Science and Technology.

Statistics Canada. 1992b.* *Selected Marriage Statistics, 1921–1990.* Catalogue No. 82–552. Ottawa: Supply and Services Canada.

Statistics Canada. 1992b.* *The Nation: Dwellings and Households.* Ottawa: Ministry of Industry, Science and Technology.

Statistics Canada. 1992c.* "Marriages 1990," *Health Reports,* Supplement No. 16, Catalogue No. 82–003S16. Ottawa: Ministry of Industry, Science and Technology.

Statistics Canada. 1992c.* *The Nation: Families: Number, Type and Structure.* Catalogue No. 93–312. Ottawa: Ministry of Industry, Science and Technology.

Statistics Canada. 1993.* *Families: Social and Economic Characteristics.* Catalogue No. 93–320. Ottawa: Ministry of Industry, Science and Technology.

Statistics Canada. 1993.* *Labour Force Annual Averages, 1992.* Catalogue No. 71–220 Annual. Ottawa: Ministry of Industry, Science and Technology.

Statistics Canada. 1993a.* *Labour Force Activity of Women by Presence of Children,* Catalogue No. 93–325. Ottawa: Ministry of Industry, Science and Technology.

Statistics Canada. 1993b.* *Language, Tradition, Health, Lifestyle and Social Issues.* Catalogue No. 89–533. Ottawa: Ministry of Industry, Science and Technology.

Statistics Canada. 1993c.* *The Nation: Labour Force Activity.* Catalogue No. 93–324. Ottawa: Ministry of Industry, Science and Technology.

Statistics Canada. 1993d.* *1991 Census Technical Reports: Age, Sex, Marital Status and Common-Law Status.* Catalogue No. 92–325E. Ottawa: Ministry of Industry, Science and Technology.

Statistics Canada. 1995.* *Births and Deaths, 1995.* Catalogue No. 84–210–XPB.

Statistics Canada. 1996.* *Canadian Families: Diversity and Change. The Daily,* June 19, 1995.

Statistics Canada. 1997.* "1996 Census: Marital Status, Common-Law Unions and Families," *The Daily,* October 14, 1997.

Statistics Canada. 1997.* *Canadian Families: Diversity and Change.* Catalogue No. 12F0061XPE. www.statcan.ca

Statistics Canada. 1997.* *Births and Deaths, 1995.* Catalogue No. 84–210–XMB, Ottawa: Ministry of Industry, Science and Technology.

Statistics Canada.* *Women In Canada,* Third Edition, Catalogue No. 89–503E, August 8, 1995.

Steel, Freda M. 1988.* "An Overview of Federal and Provincial Maintenance Enforcement Legislation," 1988 National Family Law Program, Vol. 2–E–1–1–E–1–62. The Federation of Law Societies of Canada and the Canadian Bar Association.

Steinberg, Laurence. 1987. "Bound to Bicker," *Psychology Today,* September:36–39.

Steinmetz, Suzane K. 1977. "The Battered Husband Syndrome," *Victimology,* 2:499–509.

Stephens, Linda S. 1996. "Will Johnny See Daddy This Week?: An Empirical Test of Three Theoretical Perspectives of Postdivorce Contact," *Journal of Family Issues,* 17(4):466–494.

Stephenson, Andy L., Carolyn S. Henry and Linda C. Robinson. 1996. "Family Characteristics and Adolescent Substance Use," *Adolescence,* 31(121): 59–77.

Sternberg, Robert J. 1986. "A Triangular Theory of Love," *Psychological Review,* 93:119–135.

Sternberg, Robert J. 1988. "Triangulating Love," in Robert J. Sternberg and Michael L. Barnes (eds.). *The Psychology of Love.* New Haven: Yale University Press.

Stets, Jan. 1992. "Interactive Processes in Dating Aggression: A National Study," *Journal of Marriage and the Family,* 54:165–177.

Stets, Jan E. 1990. "Verbal and Physical Aggression in Marriage," *Journal of Marriage and the Family,* 52:501–514.

Stets, Jan E. 1991. "Cohabiting and Marital Aggression: The Role of Social Isolation," *Journal of Marriage and the Family*, 53:669–680.

Stets, Jan E. 1992. "Interactive Processes In Dating Aggression: A National Study," *Journal of Marriage and the Family* 54:165–177.

Stets, Jan E. and Debra A. Henderson. 1991. "Contextual Factors Surrounding Conflict Resolution While Dating: Results from a National Study," *Family Relations*, 40:29–36.

Stevens, Gillian. 1986. "Sex-Differentiated Patterns of Intergenerational Occupational Mobility," *Journal of Marriage and the Family*, 48:153–163.

Stier, Haya and Yossi Shavit. 1994. "Age at Marriage, Sex-Ratios, and Ethnic Heterogamy," *European Sociological Review*, 10:79–87.

Stinnett, N. 1979. "Strengthening Families," *Family Perspective*, 13:3–9.

Stinnett, N. and K.H. Sauer. 1977. "Relationship Characteristics of Strong Families," *Family Perspective*, 11:3–11.

Stinnett, N., G. Sanders, J. DeFrain and A. Parkhurst. 1982. "A Nationwide Study of Families Who Perceive Themselves as Strong," *Family Perspective*, 16:15–22.

Stinnett, Nick and John DeFrain. 1985. *Secrets of Strong Families*. New York: Berkley Books.

Stirtzinger, Ruth and Lorraine Cholvat. 1991. "The Family Home as Attachment Object for Preschool Age Children After Divorce," *Journal of Divorce and Remarriage*, 15:105–124.

Stoller, Eleanor P. 1983. "Parental Caregiving by Adult Children," *Journal of Marriage and the Family*, 45:851–858.

Stolley, Kathy Shepherd and Elaine J. Hall. 1994. "The Presentation of Abortion and Adoption in Marriage and Family Textbooks," *Family Relations*, 43:267–273.

Stone, Lawrence, 1965. *The Crisis of the Aristocracy, 1558–1641*. Oxford: Oxford University Press.

Stone, Lawrence. 1977. *The Family, Sex and Marriage in England, 1500–1800*. New York: Harper and Row.

Storm, Christine, Thomas Storm and Janet Strike-Schurman. 1985.* "Obligations for Care: Beliefs in a Small Canadian Town," *Canadian Journal on Aging*, 42:75–85.

Stott, D.H. 1977.* "Children in the Womb: The Effects of Stress," *New Society*, May 19:328–331.

Stott, D.H. and Sandra A. Langford. 1976.* "Prenatal Antecedents of Child Health, Development and Behavior," *Journal of the American Academy of Child Psychiatry*, January:161–191.

Stout, Cam. 1991.* "Common Law: A Growing Alternative," *Canadian Social Trends*, Winter:18–20.

Straus, Murray. 1994. "State-to-State Differences in Social Inequality and Social Bonds in Relation to Assaults on Wives in the United States," *Journal of Comparative Family Studies*, 25(1):7–25.

Straus, Murray A. 1978. "Wife-Beating: How Common and Why?" in John M. Eekelaar and Sanford N. Katz (eds.). *Family Violence: An International and Interdisciplinary Study*. Toronto: Butterworths.

Straus, Murray A. 1979. "Measuring Intrafamily Conflict and Violence: The Conflict Tactics (CT) Scales," *Journal of Marriage and the Family*, 41:75–88.

Straus, Murray A. 1980. "Victims and Aggressors in Marital Violence," *American Behavioral Scientist*, 23:681–704.

Straus, Murray A. and Carrie L. Yodanis. 1996.* "Corporal Punishment in Adolescence and Physical Assaults on Spouses in Later Life: What Accounts for the Link?" *Journal of Marriage and the Family*, 58(4):825–841.

Straus, Murray A. and Richard J. Gelles. 1986. "Is Family Violence Declining? A Comparison of the 1975 and 1985 National Survey Rates," paper presented at the American Society of Criminology, San Diego.

Straus, Murray A. and Richard J. Gelles. 1988. "How Violent are American Families? Estimates from the National Family Violence Resurvey and Other Studies," in Gerald T. Hotaling, David Finkelhor, John T. Kirkpatrick and Murray A. Straus (eds.). *Family Abuse and Its Consequences: New Directions in Research*. Newbury Park: Sage.

Straus, Murray A., Richard J. Gelles and Susan K Steinmetz. 1980. *Behind Closed Doors: Violence in the American Family*. New York: Anchor/Doubleday.

Straus, Murray A., Sugarman, D. and Gils-Sims, J. (1997). Spanking By Parents And Subsequent Antisocial Behavior Of Children," *Archives of Pediatrics and Adolescent Medicine* 151:761–767.

Strike, Carol. 1987.* "The Incidence of Sexually Transmitted Disease in Canada," *Canadian Social Trends*, Summer:11–14.

Strike, Carol. 1989.* "Residential Care," *Canadian Social Trends*, 14:25–27.

Strike, Carol. 1991.* "AIDS: Into the 1990s," *Canadian Social Trends*, Winter:22–24.

Strong, Bryan and Christine DeVault. 1994. "Response to Stolley and Hall," *Family Relations*, 43:274–276.

Stuart, Richard B. 1980. *Helping Couples Change: A Social Learning Approach to Marital Therapy*. New York: The Guilford Press.

Stull, Donald E., Karen Bowman and Virginia Smerglia. 1994. "Women in the Middle: A Myth in the Making," *Family Relations*, 43:319–324.

Suitor, J. Jill. 1991. "Marital Quality and Satisfaction with the Division of Household Labor Across the Family Life Cycle," *Journal of Marriage and the Family*, 53:221–230.

Supreme Court of Canada. 1993.* *Canada (Attorney General) v. Mossop*. File No. 22145. February 25, 1993.

Surra, Catherine A. and Molly Longstreth. 1990. "Similarity of Outcomes, Interdependence, and Conflict in Dating Relationships," *Journal of Personality and Social Psychology*, 59:501–516.

Swanson, J. 1986. "Ethnicity, Marriage and Role Conflict," in Asswad, B. and B. Bilge (eds.). *Family and Gender Among American Muslims*. Philadelphia: Temple University Press. Pp. 241–249.

Sweeney, Megan M. 1997. "Remarriage of Women and Men after Divorce: The Role of Socioeconomic Prospects," *Journal of Family Issues*, 18(5):479–502.

Swenson, Donald 1999.* *Society, Spirituality, and the Sacred: A Social Scientific Introduction*. Peterborough, On.: Broadview.

Symons, Douglas K. and Peter J. McLeod. 1993.* "Maternal Employment Plans and Outcomes After the Birth of an Infant in a Canadian Sample," *Family Relations*, 42(4):442–446.

Symons, Gladys L. 1983.* "Innovative Gender Roles in the Dual-Career Family: A Cross-Cultural Perspective," presented at the annual meeting of the Canadian Sociology and Anthropology Association, Vancouver, June 1983.

Szinovacz, Maximiliane E. 1983. "Using Couple Data as a Methodological Tool: The Case of Marital Violence," *Journal of Marriage and the Family*, 45:633–644.

Szinovacz, Maximiliane E. 1987. "Family Power," in Marvin B. Sussman and Suzanne K. Steinmetz (eds.). *Handbook of Marriage and the Family*. New York: Plenum Press, Chapter 24.

Tanfer, Koray. 1987. "Patterns of Premarital Cohabitation Among Never-Married Women in the United States," *Journal of Marriage and the Family*, 49:483–497.

Taylor, G. Rattray. 1959. *Sex in History*. London: Thomes and Hudson.

Taylor, Robert J., Linda M. Chatters, M. Belinda Tucker and Edith Lewis. 1991. "Developments in Research on Black Families," in Alan Booth (ed.). *Contemporary Families: Looking Forward, Looking Back*. Minneapolis: National Council on Family Relations, 275–296.

Teachman, Jay 2003. "Premarital Sex, Premarital Cohabitation, and the Risk of Subsequent Marital Dissolution Among Women," *Journal of Marriage and Family* 65, 444–455.

Teachman, Jay 2002. "Stability Across Cohorts in Divorce Risk Factors," *Demography* 39:331–351.

Tein, Jenn-Yun, Mark W. Roosa and Marcia Michaels. 1994. "Agreement Between Parent and Child Reports on Parental Behaviors," *Journal of Marriage and the Family*, 56(2):341–355.

Teixera, Carlos. 1995. "The Suburbanization of Portuguese Communities in Toronto and Montreal: From Isolation to Residential Integration?" in Laprerriere, A. et al. (eds.). *Immigration and Ethnicity in Canada*. Montreal: Association for Canadian Studies. Pp. 181–202.

Termote, Marc. 1990.* "The Aged and the Family Environment," *Canadian Studies in Population*, 17:45–51.

Terman, Lewis 1938. *Psychological Factors in Marital Happiness*. New York: McGraw-Hill Publishing.

The Associated Press. 1992.* "Finding Backs Theory Sexual Orientation May be Set by Nature," *The Edmonton Journal*, August 1:A5.

The Canadian Press. 1992.* "Growing Number of Women Have AIDS Virus—Health Officials," *The Edmonton Journal*, August 18:A3.

The Canadian Press. 1993.* " 'Sandwich Generation' Sacrificing Careers—Study," *The Edmonton Journal*, March 23:A3.

The Daily, July 7, 1992.* Ottawa: Statistics Canada.

The Daily, March 12, 1992a.* "Therapeutic Abortions, Canada, 1990." Ottawa: Statistics Canada, 2.

Thistlethwaite, S. 1981. "Battered Women and the Bible: From Subjection to Liberation," Christianity and Crisis, November 16:311.

Thoen, M. (1993), *The Value of Household Production in Canada 1981, 1986, Discussion Paper*, National Accounts and Environment Division, Statistics Canada, Ottawa.

Thoits, Peggy A. 1986. "Multiple Identities: Explaining Gender and Marital Status Differences in Distress," *American Sociological Review*, 51:259–272.

Thomas, Derrick. 1990.* *Immigrant Integration and the Canadian Identity*. Ottawa: Employment and Immigration Canada.

Thomilison, B., M. Stephens, J. Cunes, R. Grinnell Jr. and J. Krysik. 1991. "Characteristics of Canadian Male and Female Child Sexual Abuse Victims," *Journal of Child and Youth Care*, Special Issue:65–76.

Thompson, Anthony P. 1983. "Extramarital Sex: A Review of the Research Literature," *The Journal of Sex Research*, 19:1–22.

Thompson, Anthony P. 1984. "Emotional and Sexual Components of Extramarital Relations," *Journal of Marriage and the Family*, 46:35–42.

Thompson, B. and E. Disch. 1992. "Feminist, Anti-racist, Anti-oppression Teaching: Two White Women's Experience," *Radical Teacher*, 41:4–10.

Thompson, Linda. 1991. "Family Work: Women's Sense of Fairness," *Journal of Family Issues*, 12:181–196.

Thompson, Linda and Alexis J. Walker. 1989. "Gender in Families: Women and Men in Marriage, Work and Parenthood," *Journal of Marriage and the Family*, 51(Nov): 845–871.

Thompson, Linda and Alexis J. Walker. 1995. "The Place of Feminism in Family Studies," *Journal of Marriage and the Family*, 57(4):847–865.

Thompson, Ronald W., Crystal R. Grow, Penney R. Ruma, Daniel L. Daly and Raymond V. Burke. 1993. "Evaluation of a Practical Parenting Program with Middle- and Low-Income Families," *Family Relations*, 42(1):21–25.

Thornberry, Terence P., Carolyn Smith and Gregory J. Howard. 1997. "Risk Factors for Teenage Fatherhood," *Journal of Marriage and the Family*, 59 (3):505–522.

Thorne, Barrie. 1982a. "Feminist Rethinking of the Family: An Overview," in Barrie Thorne and Marilyn Yalom (eds.). *Rethinking the Family: Some Feminist Questions*. New York: Longman, 1–24.

Thorne, Barrie and Marilyn Yalom (eds.). 1982b. *Rethinking the Family: Some Feminist Questions*. New York: Longman.

Thorne-Finch, Ron. 1992.* *Ending the Silence: The Origins and Treatment of Male Violence against Women*. Toronto: University of Toronto Press.

Thornton, Arland. 1989. "Changing Attitudes toward Family Issues in the United States," *Journal of Marriage and the Family*, 51:873–893.

Thornton, Arland. 1991. "Influence of the Marital History of Parents on the Marital and Cohabitational Experiences of Children," *American Journal of Sociology*, 96:868–894.

Thornton, Arland and Donald Camburn. 1987. "The Influence of the Family on Premarital Sexual Attitudes and Behaviour," *Demography*, 24:323–340.

Thornton, Arland and Donald Camburn. 1989. "Religious Participation and Adolescent Sexual Behaviour and Attitudes," *Journal of Marriage and the Family*, 51:641–653.

Thornton, Arland, Linda Young-DeMarco and Frances Goldscheider. 1993. "Leaving the Parental Nest: The Experience of a Young White Cohort in the 1980s," *Journal of Marriage and the Family*, 55(1):216–229.

Tiejde, L., Wortman, C., Downey, G., Emmons, C., Biernat, M., and Lang, E. 1990. "Women with Multiple Roles: Role-compatibility Perceptions, Satisfaction and Mental Health," *Journal of Marriage and the Family*, 52:63–72.

Tierney, Kathleen J. and David L. Corwin. 1983. "Exploring Intrafamilial Child Sexual Abuse: A Systems Approach," in David Finkelhor, Richard J. Gelles, Gerald T. Hotaling and Murray A. Strauss (eds.). *The Dark Side of Families: Current Family Violence Research*. Beverly Hills: Sage.

Tiesel, Judy Watson and David H. Olson. 1992. "Preventing Family Problems: Troubling Trends and Promising Opportunities," *Family Relations*, 41:398–403.

Todd, Richard D., Barbara Geller, Rosalind Neuman, Louis W. Fox and Janice Hickok. 1996. "Increased Prevalence of Alcoholism in Relatives of Depressed and Bipolar Children," *Journal of the American Academy of Child and Adolescent Psychiatry*, 35(6):716–724.

Todres, Rubin. 1978. "Runaway Wives: An Increasing North-American Phenomenon," *The Family Coordinator*, 27:17–21.

Toffler, Alvin. 1970. *Future Shock*. New York: Random House.

Tong, Rosemary. 1989. *Feminist Thought: A Comprehensive Introduction*. Boulder: Westview Press.

Tönnies, F. 1963. *Gemeinshaft and Gesellschaft* (Trans. C. Loomis). New York: Harper and Row.

Toronto Star. 1983. "Editorial," September 25:F2.

Toronto Star. 1991. "Ann Landers," March 6:D8.

Toufexis, Anastasia. 1992. "When Kids Kill Abusive Parents," *Time*, November 23:64–65.

Toullatos, John and Mary Jo Czaplewski. 1992. *Inventory of Marriage and Family Literature*, Volume 17–1990/91. Anoka: DataTraq International Inc.

Transition. 1994.* "Heritage Culture and Immigration, the Family Connection," Vanier Institute of the Family.

Tremblay, Richard E., Bernard Boulerice, Phillip W. Harden, Pierre McDuff, Daniel Pérusse, Robert O. Pihl and Mark Zoccolillo. 1996. "Do Children in Canada Become More Aggressive as They Approach Adolescence?" *National Longitudinal Survey of Children and Youth*. Statistics Canada: Catalogue No. 89–550–MPE:127–137.

Troll, Lillian E. 1971. "The Family of Later Life: A Decade Review," *Journal of Marriage and the Family*, 33:263–290.

Trocme, N., MacLaurin, B., fallon, B. Daciul, J. Billingsley, D. Tourigny, M., Mayer, M., Wright, J., Barter, K., Burford, G., Hornick, J., Sullivan, R. and McKenzie, B. 2001. *Canadian Incidence Study of Reported Child Abuse and Neglect: Final Report*. Health Canada.

Troost, Kay Michael and Erik Filsinger. 1993. "Emerging Biosocial Perspectives on the Family," in Pauline G. Boss, William G. Doherty, Ralph LaRossa, Walter R. Schumm and Suzanne K. Steinmetz (eds.). *Sourcebook of Family Theories and Methods: A Contextual Approach*. New York: Plenum Press, Chapter 26.

Trost, Jan. 1981. "Cohabitation in the Nordic Countries," *Alternative Lifestyles*, 4:401–427.

Trotter, Robert J. 1987a. "The Play's the Thing," *Psychology Today*, January:27–34.

Trovato, Frank 1986.* "The Relationship Between Migration and the Provincial Divorce Rate in Canada, 1971 and 1978: A Reassessment," *Journal of Marriage and the Family* 48:207–216.

Trovato, Frank. 1988.* "A Macrosociological Analysis of Change in the Marriage Rate: Canadian Women, 1921–25 to 1981–85," *Journal of Marriage and the Family*, 50:507–521.

Trovato, Frank. 1991.* "Sex, Marital Status and Suicide in Canada: 1951–1981," *Sociological Perspectives*, 34:427–445.

Trovato, Frank and Gloria Lauris. 1989.* "Marital Status and Mortality in Canada: 1951–1981," *Journal of Marriage and the Family*, 51:907–922.

Trovato, Frank. 2000.* "The Probability of Divorce in Canada: 1981–1995," *Canadian Studies in Population 27*, 1:231-238.

Trumbach, Randolph. 1978. *The Rise of the Egalitarian Family.* New York: Academic Press.

Trussell, James and K. Vaninadha Rao. 1989.* "Premarital Cohabitation and Marital Stability: A Reassessment of the Canadian Evidence," *Journal of Marriage and the Family*, 51:535–540.

Trussell, James, David C. Warner and Robert A. Hatcher. 1992.* "Condom Slippage and Breakage Rate," *Family Planning Perspectives*, 24:20–23.

Tschann, Jeanne M., Janet R. Johnston and Judith S. Wallerstein. 1989. "Resources, Stressors, and Attachment as Predictors of Adult Adjustment After Divorce: A Longitudinal Study," *Journal of Marriage and the Family*, 51:1033–1046.

Tuchman, Barbara. 1978. *A Distant Mirror, The Calamitous 14th Century.* New York: Ballantine Books.

Tully, Patricia and Chris Mohl. 1995.* "Older Residents of Health Care Institutions," *Health Reports*, 7(3):27–30.

Turcotte, Pierre and Alain Bélanger. 1997 "Moving in Together: The Formation of First Common-Law Unions," *Canadian Social Trends*, 47:7–10.

Turcotte, Pierre. 1988.* "Common-Law Unions: Nearly Half a Million in 1986," *Canadian Social Trends*, Autumn:35–39.

Turke, Paul W. 1988. "Concealed Ovulation, Menstrual Synchrony, and Paternal Investment," in Erik E. Filsinger (ed.). *Biosocial Perspectives on the Family.* Newbury Park: Sage, Chapter 5.

Turner, R. Jay and John W. Gartrell. 1978. "Social Factors in Psychiatric Outcome: Toward the Resolution of Interpretive Controversies," *American Sociological Review*, 43:368–382.

U.S. Public Health Service. 1980. *The Health Consequences of Smoking for Women (a report of the Surgeon General)*, Washington, D.C.: U.S. Department of Health and Human Services.

U.S. Public Health Service. 1982. *The Health Consequences of Smoking: Cancer. A report of the Surgeon General.* Washington, D.C.: U.S. Department of Health and Human Services.

Ubelacker, Sheryl. 1993.* "AIDS Incidence More Serious Than Thought," *The Edmonton Journal*, January 12:A3.

Udry, J. Richard. 1971. *The Social Context of Marriage* (second edition). Philadelphia: J.B. Lippincott.

Udry, J. Richard. 1997. "Family Ties Keep Teens Out of Trouble." www.yahoo.com/headlines/970910/news/stories/teens1.html

Ulrich, Y. 1991. "Women's Reasons for Leaving Abusive Spouses," *Health Care Women's International*, 12(4): 465–473.

United States National Center for Health Statistics. 1982. *Reproductive Impairments Among Married Couples: United States.* Data from the National Survey of Family Growth Series 23, No. 11. Hyattsville: U.S. Department of Health and Human Services.

Ursel, J. 1992.* *Private Lives, Public Policy: 100 Years of State Intervention in the Family.* Toronto, ON: Women's Press.

Ursel, Jane. 1993.* "Family and Social Policies," in G.N. Ramu. *Marriage and the Family in Canada Today* (second edition). Scarborough: Prentice-Hall Canada.

Usher, Debora J. 1991.* *The Impact of Children on the Household Division of Labour and Labour Force Participation.* Unpublished thesis, Department of Sociology, University of Alberta, Edmonton.

Vachon, Mary L.S. 1976.* "Grief and Bereavement Following the Death of a Spouse," *Canadian Psychiatric Association Journal*, 21:35–44.

Vadasz, Mish. 1988.* "Family Abuse of the Elderly," in Benjamin Schlesinger and Rachel Schlesinger (eds.). *Abuse of the Elderly, Issues and Annotated Bibliography*, Toronto: University of Toronto Press.

Vaillant, Caroline O. and George E. Vaillant. 1993. "Is the U-Curve of Marital Satisfaction an Illusion? A 40–Year Study of Marriage," *Journal of Marriage and the Family*, 55:230–239.

Valois, Robert F., Sandra K. Kammermann and J. Wanzer Drane. 1997. "Number of Sexual Intercourse Partners and Associated Risk Behaviors Among Public High School Students," *Journal of Sex Education Therapy*, 22(2):13–22.

Van de Sande, Adje. 1995. "Native and Mainstream Parenting Programs," *Native Studies Review*, 10, no.1:20.

Van Hekken, Suus M.J., Langha de Mey and Hans-Joachim Schulze. 1997. "Youth Inside or Outside the Parental Home: The Case of the Netherlands," *Journal of Family Issues*, 18(6):690–707.

Van den Berghe, Pierre L. 1988. "The Family and the Biological Base of Human Sociality," in Erik E. Filsinger (ed.). *Biosocial Perspectives on the Family.* Newbury Park: Sage, Chapter 2.

Van den Haag, Ernest. 1962. "Of Happiness and Despair We Have No Measure," in Eric Josephson and Mary Josephson (eds.). *Man Alone: Alienation in Modern Society.* New York: Dell.

Van Roosmalen, Erica H. and Susan A. McDaniel. 1989.* "Peer Group Influence as a Factor in Smoking Behavior of Adolescents," *Adolescence*, 24:801–816.

Van Roosmalen, Erica H. and Susan A. McDaniel. 1992.* "Adolescent Smoking Intentions: Gender Differences in Peer Context," *Adolescence*, 27:87–104.

Vancouver Sun. 1992.* "No Society Tolerates Sex Between Relatives," *The Edmonton Journal*, November 22:A3.

VandenHeuvel, A. 1997. "Women's Roles After First Birth: Variable or Stable?" *Gender and Society*, 11(3):357–368.

Vanier Institute of the Family. 1992.* "Adoption in Canada: A Profile," *Transition*, September:4–5.

Vannoy, Dana and William W. Philliber. 1992. "Wife's Employment and Quality of Marriage," *Journal of Marriage and the Family*, 54:387–398.

Varia, R., R. Abidin and P. Dass. 1996. "Perceptions of Abuse: Effects on Adult Psychological and Social Adjustment," *Child Abuse and Neglect*, 20(6):511–526.

Vasta, E. 1980. "The Second Generation Italian Adolescents: At Home and at School," *New Education*, (11):95–102.

Veevers, Jean E. (ed). 1991b.* *Continuity and Change in Marriage and Family*. Toronto: Holt, Rinehart and Winston of Canada.

Veevers, Jean E. 1971.* *The Family in Canada*. Volume 5, Part 3, Bulletin 5.3–3. Catalogue No. 99–725. Ottawa: Statistics Canada.

Veevers, Jean E. 1980.* *Childless by Choice*. Toronto: Butterworths.

Veevers, Jean E. 1988.* "The 'Real' Marriage Squeeze: Mate Selection, Mortality and the Mating Gradient," *Sociological Perspectives*, 31:142–167.

Veevers, Jean E. 1991a. "Traumas versus Stress: A Paradigm of Positive versus Negative Divorce Outcomes," *Journal of Divorce and Remarriage*, 15:99–127.

Veevers, Jean E. 1991c.* "Introduction: Major Trends in the Changing Canadian Family," in Jean E. Veevers (ed.). *Continuity and Change in Marriage and Family*. Toronto: Holt, Rinehart and Winston of Canada, 1–32.

Veevers, Jean E. 2003. "Marriage Squeeze," In James Ponzetti et al. (Eds.) *International Encyclopedia of Marriage and Family, Second Editon*. New York: McMillan Reference USA. 11071107-11131113.

Vemer, E., M. Coleman, L.H. Ganong and H. Cooper. 1989. "Marital Satisfaction in Remarriage: A Meta-Analysis," *Journal of Marriage and the Family*, 51:713–725.

Verbrugge, Lois M. 1979. "Marital Status and Health," *Journal of Marriage and the Family*, 41:267–285.

Verdon, M. 1987. "The Stem Family: Towards a General Theory," *Journal Of Interdisciplinary History*, 10:87–105.

Veroff, J., E. Douvan and R. A. Kukla. 1981. *The Inner American: A Self-Portrait from 1957 to 1976*. New York: Basic Books.

Vijaya, Krishnan. 1993.* "Religious Homogamy and Voluntary Childlessness in Canada," *Sociological Perspectives*, 36(1):83–93.

Visher, Emily B. and John S. Visher. 1988. *Old Loyalties, New Ties, Therapeutic Strategies with Stepfamilies*. New York: Brunner and Mazel.

Visher, Emily B. and John S. Visher. 1990. "Dynamics of Successful Stepfamilies," *Journal of Divorce and Remarriage*, 14(1):3–12.

Visher, John S. 1994. "Stepfamilies: A Work in Progress," The *American Journal of Family Therapy*, 22(4):337–344

Von Bertalanffy, Ludwig. 1950. *General Systems Theory*. New York: George Braziller.

Voydanoff, Patricia. 1987. *Work and Family Life*. Newbury Park, CA: Sage Publications.

Voydanoff, Patricia. 1991. "Economic Distress and *Family Relations*," in Alan Booth (ed.). *Contemporary Families: Looking Forward, Looking Back*. Minneapolis: National Council on Family Relations, 429–445.

Wagner, Barry M., Robert E. Cole and Paul Schwartsman. 1995. "Psychosocial Correlates of Suicide Attempts Among Junior and Senior High School Youth," *Suicide and Life-Threatening Behavior*, 25(3):358–372.

Waite, Linda J. 1995. "Does Marriage Matter?" *Demography*, 32:483–507.

Wakil, S. Parvez, C.M. Siddique and F.A. Wakil. 1981. "Between Two Cultures: A Study in Socialization of Children of Immigrants," *Journal of Marriage and the Family*, 43:929–940.

Walby, S. 1990. *Theorizing Patriarchy*. Oxford: Blackwell.

Wald, Esther. 1981. *The Remarried Family: Challenge and Promise*. New York: Family Association of America.

Waldron, I., C.C. Weiss and M.E. Hughes. 1998. "Interacting Effects of Multiple Roles on Women's Health," *Journal of Health and Social Behavior*, 39(September):216–236.

Walker, Alexis J. 1993. "Teaching about Race, Gender, and Class Diversity in United States Families," *Family Relations*, 42:342–350.

Walker, Jim. 1992.* "Teens for Chastity: Selling the Virtues of Virginity," *The Edmonton Journal*, June 13:A11.

Walker, Lenore E. 1979. *The Battered Woman*. New York: Harper and Row.

Walker, Lenore E. 1984. *The Battered Woman Syndrome*. New York: Springer Publishing.

Walker, Lenore E. 1988. "The Battered Woman Syndrome," in Gerald T. Hotaling, David Finkelhor, John T. Kirkpatrick and Murray A. Straus (eds.). *Family Abuse and Its Consequences: New Directions in Research*. Beverly Hills: Sage.

Walker, Lenore E. 1989. *Terrifying Love*. New York: Harper Row.

Wallace, J. 1997. "It's About Time: A Study of Hours Worked and Work Spillover Among Law Firm Lawyers," *Journal of Vocational Behavior*, 50:227–248.

Waller, G. 1994. "Childhood Sexual Abuse and Borderline Personality Disorder in the Eating Disorders," *Child Abuse and Neglect*, 18:97–101.

Waller, Willard. 1937. "The Rating-Dating Complex," *American Sociological Review*, 2:727–734.

Wallerstein, Judith S. 1985. "The Overburdened Child: Some Long-Term Consequences of Divorce," *Social Work*, March–April:116–123.

Wallerstein, Judith S. 1992. "Children After Divorce: Wounds that Don't Heal," in Ollie Pocs (ed.). *Marriage and Family 92/93*. Guilford: Dushkin Publishing.

Wallerstein, Judith S. and Sandra Blakeslee. 1989. *Second Chances: Men, Women and Children a Decade after Divorce*. New York: Ticknor and Fields.

Walster, Elaine and G. William Walster. 1978. *A New Look at Love*. Don Mills: Addison-Wesley.

Ward, Sally K., Kathy Chapman, Ellen Cohn, Susan White and Kirk Williams. 1991. "Acquaintance Rape and the College Social Scene," *Family Relations*, 40:65–71.

Ward, W. Peter. 1990.* *Courtship, Love, and Marriage in Nineteenth-Century English Canada*. Montreal: McGill-Queen's University Press.

Warren, Charles W., John S. Santelli, Sherry A. Everett, Laura Kann, Jane L. Collins, Carol Cassell, Leo Morris and Lloyd J. Kolbe. 1998. "Sexual Behavior Among U.S. High School Students, 1990–1995," *Family Planning Perspectives*, 30(4):170–172, 200.

Watson, Roy E. L. 1983.* "Premarital Cohabitation vs. Traditional Courtship: Their Effects on Subsequent Marital Adjustment," *Family Relations*, 32:139–147.

Watson, Roy E.L. and Peter W. DeMeo. 1987.* "Premarital Cohabitation vs. Traditional Courtship and Subsequent Marital Adjustment: A Replication and Follow-Up," *Family Relations*, 36:193–197.

Watters, Jessie, Georgina White, Ruth Parry and Robert Bates. 1986.* "A Comparison of Child Abuse and Child Neglect," *Canadian Journal of Behavioural Science*, 18:449–459.

Weed, J.A. 1980. "National Estimates of Marriage Dissolution and Survivorship: United States," *Vital and Health Statistics: Series 3, Analytic Statistics: No. 19.* DHHS Publication No. (PHS) 81–1403. Washington, D.C.: U.S. Department of Health and Human Services.

Weigert, Andrew J. and Darwin L. Thomas. 1971. "Family as a Conditional Universal," *Journal of Marriage and the Family*, 33:188–194.

Weinberg, Martin S., Ilsa L. Lottes and Frances M. Shaver. 1995. "Swedish or American Heterosexual Youth: Who Is More Permissive?" *Archives of Sexual Behavior*, 24(4):409–437.

Weinreb, Maxine and Varda Konstam. 1995. "Birthmothers: Silent Relationships," *Affilia*, 10(3):315–327.

Weiss, R.S. 1975. *Marital Separation*. New York: Basic Books.

Weiss, Robert L. 1978. "The Conceptualization of Marriage from a Behavioral Perspective," in T.J. Paolino and B.S. McCrady (eds.). *Marriage and Marital Therapy: Psychoanalytic, Behavioral and Systems Theory Perspectives*. New York: Brunner and Mazel, 165–239.

Weiss, Robert S. 1969. "The Fund of Sociability," *Transaction*, 7:36–43.

Weissman, M.M., D. Gammon, K. John, K.R. Merikangas, V. Warner, B.A. Prusoff and D. Sholomskas. 1987. "Children of Depressed Parents: Increased Psychopathology and Early Onset of Major Depression," *Archives of General Psychiatry*, 44:847–853.

Weitzman, L.J. 1985. *The Divorce Revolution: The Unexpected Social and Economic Consequences for Women and Children in America*. New York: The Free Press.

Wellman, M. 1993. "Child Sexual Abuse and Gender Differences: Attitudes and Prevalence," *Child Abuse and Neglect*, 17:539–547.

Westoff, L.A. 1977. *The Second Time Round: Remarriage in America*. New York: Viking.

Weston, K. 1991. *Families We Choose: Lesbians, Gays, Kinship*. New York: Columbia University Press.

Wheaton, Robert. 1980. "Introduction," in Robert Wheaton and Tamara K. Hareven (eds.). *Family and Sexuality in French History*. Philadelphia: University of Pennsylvania Press.

Whelan, E.M. 1978. *The Pregnancy Experience: The Psychology of Expectant Parenthood*. New York: W.W. Norton.

White, James. 1987.* "Premarital Cohabitation and Marital Stability in Canada," *Journal of Marriage and the Family*, 49:641–647.

White, James. 1989.* "Reply to Comment by Trussell and Rao: A Reanalysis of the Data," *Journal of Marriage and the Family*, 51:540–544.

White, James M. 1991.* *Dynamics of Family Development: A Theoretical Perspective*. New York: The Guilford Press.

White, James M. 1992.* "Marital Status and Well-Being in Canada: An Analysis of Age Group Variations," *Journal of Family Issues*, 13:390–409.

White, James M. 1999.* "Work-Family Stage and Satisfaction with Work-Family Balance," *Journal of Comparative Family Studies* 30:163–175.

White, James M. and Klein, David M. 2002.* *Family Theories* (2nd Ed.). Thousand Oaks, CA: Sage Publications.

White, James M. 2003.* "Computers and Family," James Ponzetti et al. (Eds.), *International Encyclopedia of*

Marriage and Family (Vol. I.), New York: Macmillan Reference, 347–349.

White, James M. 2005.* *Advancing Family Theories.* Thousand Oaks, CA: Sage Publications.

White, L.K., A. Booth and J.N. Edwards. 1986. "Children and Marital Happiness: Why the Negative Correlations?" *Journal of Family Issues*, 7: 131–147.

White, Lynn K. and Agnes Riedmann. 1992. "When the Brady Bunch Grows Up: Step/half- and Full Sibling Relationships in Adulthood," *Journal of Marriage and the Family*, 54(February):197–208.

White, Lynn K. and Alan Booth. 1991. "Divorce Over The Life Course: The Role Of Marital Happiness." *Journal of Family Issues* 12:5–21.

White, Lynn K. and Alan Booth. 1985a. "The Quality and Stability of Remarriages: The Role of Stepchildren," *American Sociological Review*, 50:689–698.

White, Lynn K. and Alan Booth. 1985b. "Transition to Parenthood and Marital Quality," *Journal of Family Issues*, 6:435–450.

White, Lynn K., Alan Booth and John N. Edwards. 1986. "Children and Marital Happiness: Why the Negative Correlation?" *Journal of Family Issues*, 7:131–147.

White, Lynn K., David Brinkerhoff and Alan Booth. 1985. "The Effect of Marital Disruption on Child's Attachment to Parents," *Journal of Family Issues*, 6:5–22.

White, S.W. and B.L. Bloom. 1981. "Factors Related to the Adjustment of Divorcing Men," *Family Relations*, 30:349–360.

Whitechurch, Gail G. and Larry L. Constantine. 1993. "Systems Theory," in Pauline G. Boss, William G. Doherty, Ralph LaRossa, Walter R. Schumm and Suzanne K. Steinmetz (eds.). *Sourcebook of Family Theories and Methods*: A Contextual Approach. New York: Plenum Press, Chapter 14.

Whitehead, Barbara Dafoe. 1993. "Dan Quayle was Right," *The Atlantic Monthly*, April:47–84.

Whitehead, Barbara Dafoe. 1996. "The Decline of Marriage as the Social Basis of Childrearing," in Popenoe, David, Jean Bethke Elshtain, and David Blankenhorn (eds.). *Promises to Keep: Decline and Renewal of Marriage in America.* London, England: Rowman and Littlefield Publishers, Chapter 1.

Whitehead, Barbara Dafoe. 1997. *The Divorce Culture.* New York: Alfred A. Knopf.

Whitehurst, R.N. and G.V. Booth. 1980.* *The Sexes: Changing Relationships in a Pluralistic Society.* Toronto: Gage.

Whitehurst, Robert N. 1974.* "Violence in Husband–Wife Interaction," in Suzanne K. Steinmetz and Murray A. Straus (eds.). *Violence in the Family.* New York: Dodd, Mead and Co.

Whiteley, D.E.H. 1974. *The Theology of St. Paul*, Oxford: Blackwell.

Wickrama, K.A.S., F.O. Lorenz, R.D. Conger and L. Matthews. 1997. "Linking Occupational Conditions to Physical Health Through Marital, Social, and Intrapersonal Processes," *Journal of Health and Social Behavior*, 38(December):363–375.

Widmer, Eric D. 1997. "Influence of Older Siblings on Initation of Sexual Intercourse," *Journal of Marriage and the Family*, 59(4):928–938.

Wilcox, Brian L. and Mary Uyeda. 1988. "Federal Mental Health Policy: Its Unhappy Past and Uncertain Future," in Elam W. Nunnally, Catherine S. Chilman and Fred M. Cox (eds.). *Mental Illness, Delinquency, Addictions and Neglect: Families in Trouble Series, Volume IV.* Beverly Hills: Sage, Chapter 11.

Wilke, Arthus S. 1976. "Family and Civilization: Thirty Years Later," *International Journal of Contemporary Sociology*, 13:224–238.

Williams, Dori G. 1988. "Gender, Marriage and Psychosocial Well-Being," *Journal of Family Issues*, 9:452–468.

Williams, Kirk R. 1992. "Social Sources of Marital Violence and Deterrence: Testing an Integrated Theory of Assaults Between Partners," *Journal of Marriage and the Family*, 54:620–629.

Williams, L.M. 1994. "Recall of Childhood Trauma: A Prospective Study of Women's Memories of Child Sexual Abuse," *Journal of Consulting and Clinical Psychology*, 62(6):1167–1176.

Williams, Linda S. 1992.* "Adoption Actions and Attitudes of Couples Seeking In Vitro Fertilization," *Journal of Family Issues*, 13:99–113.

Williams, M. 1989. "Ladies on the Line: Punjabi Cannery Workers in Central California," in Asian Women United of California (ed.). *Making Waves: An Anthology of Writings by and About Asian American Women.* Boston: Beacon. Pp. 148–159.

Wilson, Barbara Foley and Sally Cunningham Clarke. 1992. "Remarriages: A Demographic Profile," *Journal of Family Issues*, 13(2):123–141.

Wilson, Sue J. 1991. *Women, Families and Work.* Toronto: McGraw-Hill Ryerson.

Wilson, Sue. J. 1986.* *Women, the Family, and the Economy* (second edition). Toronto: McGraw-Hill Ryerson.

Wilson, S.J. 1996.* *Women, Families and Work* (4th ed.). Toronto, ON: McGraw-Hill Ryerson Limited.

Winch, Robert. 1971. *The Modern Family.* New York: Holt Rinehart and Winston.

Wind, T.W. and L. Silvern. 1994. "Parenting and Family Stress as Mediators of the Long-Term Effects of Child Abuse," *Child Abuse and Neglect*, 18(5): 439–453.

Wineberg, Howard. 1992. "Childbearing and Dissolution of the Second Marriage," *Journal of Marriage and the Family*, 54(November):879–887.

Wineberg, Howard and James McCarthy. 1998. "Living Arrangements after Divorce: Cohabitation versus Remarriage," *Journal of Divorce and Remarriage*, 29(1/2):131–146.

Wirth, Louis. 1938. "Urbanism as a Way of Life," *American Journal of Sociology*, 44:1–24.

Wisensale, Steven K. 1992. "Toward the 21st Century: Family Change and Public Policy," *Family Relations*, 41: 417–422.

Wisensale, Steven K. and Kathlyn E. Heckart. 1993. "Domestic Partnerships: A Concept Paper and Policy Discussion," *Family Relations*, 42(2):199–204.

Wister, Andrew V. and Thomas K. Burch. 1983.* "Fertility and Household Status of Older Women in Canada," *Canadian Studies in Population*, 10:1–13.

Wolf, Rosalie S. and Karl A. Pillemer. 1989. *Helping Elderly Victims: The Reality of Elder Abuse*. New York: Columbia University Press.

Wolff, C. 1971. *Love Between Women*. New York: Harper and Row.

Wonderlich, S., R. Wilsnack, S. Wilsnack and R. Harris. 1996. "Childhood Sexual Abuse and Bulimic Behavior in a Nationally Representative Sample," *American Journal of Public Health*, 86(8):1082–1086.

Wood, J.R. 2003.* "An Examination of Heterogeneity in Child Outcomes for the Intact Family Group." Unpublished Master's thesis, University of British Columbia, Vancouver, Canada.

Wright, C.J.H. 1992. "Family," in David N. Freedman. *The Anchor Bible Dictionary: Vol. 2*. New York: Doubleday.

Wu, Zheng. 1995.* "Remarriage after Widowhood: A Marital History Study of Older Canadians," *Canadian Journal on Aging*, 14(4):719–736.

Wu, Zheng and Margaret J. Penning. 1997.* "Marital Instability After Midlife," *Journal of Family Issues*, 18(5):459–478.

Wu, Zheng and T.R. Balakrishnan. 1994.* "Cohabitation after Marital Disruption in Canada," *Journal of Marriage and the Family*, 56(August):723–734.

WuDunn, Sheryl. 1996. "Abortion in Japan: No Fury, Just Grief," *New York Times* News Service, January 28.

Wynn, Ruth and Christine Fletcher. 1987. "Sex Role Development and Early Educational Experiences," in D. Bruce Carter. *Current Conceptions of Sex Roles and Sex Typing*. New York: Praeger.

Yama, M., B. Fogas, L. Teegarden and B. Hastings. 1993. "Childhood Sexual Abuse and Parental Alcoholism: Interactive Effects in Adult Women," *American Journal of Orthopsychiatry*, 63(2):300–304.

Yamaguchi, Kazuo and Denise B. Kandel. 1997. "The Influence of Spouses' Behavior and Marital Dissolution on Marijuana Use: Causation or Selection," *Journal of Marriage and the Family*, 59(1):22–36.

Yankelovich, Daniel. 1981. *New Rules: Searching for Self-Fulfillment in a World Turned Upside Down*. New York: Random House.

Yllo, Kirsti and Murray A. Straus. 1981. "Interpersonal Violence Among Married and Cohabiting Couples," *Family Relations*, 30:339–347.

Young, M. and P. Wilmott. (1957). *Kinship and Family in East London*. London: Routledge and Kegan Paul, Ltd.

Young, Robert L., Wayne Godfrey, Barbara Matthews and Gerald R. Adams. 1983. "Runaways: A Review of Negative Consequences," *Family Relations*, 32:275–281.

Zetterberg, Hans L. (1965). *On Theory and Verification* (third edition). Ottawa: The Bedminister Press.

Zillman, Dolf and Jennings Bryant. 1988. "Effects of Prolonged Consumption of Pornography on Family Values," *Journal of Family Issues*, 9:518–544.

Zimmerman, Shirley L. 1988. *Understanding Family Policy: Theoretical Approaches*. Newbury Park: Sage.

Zimmerman, Shirley L. 1992. "Family Trends: What Implications for Family Policy?" *Family Relations*, 41:423–429.

Zimmerman, Shirley L. and Catherine S. Chilman. 1988. "Poverty and Families," in Catherine S. Chilman (ed.). *Employment and Economic Problems: Families in Trouble Series, Volume 1*. Newbury Park: Sage, Chapter 5 .

Zinn, Maxine B. and D. Stanley Eitzen. 1993. *Diversity in Families* (third edition). New York: Harper Collins.

Zlotnik, Hania. 1995. "Migration and the Family: The Female Perspective," *Asian and Pacific Migration Journal*, 4(2,3):253–271.

Name Index

Hensley, W., 127
Henton, J., 142
Hepburn, C. G., 233
Herbert, B., 104
Herold, E. S., 124, 130n, 135, 136, 137
Héron, 137
Herrenkohl, E. C., 339
Hervig, L., 343
Herzig, L., 337
Hetherington, E. M., 316, 317
Hill, 35
Hill, C. T., 119
Hill, M. S., 195, 309
Hill, R., 26, 35, 325, 326, 327n
Hilton, H. G., 339, 343
Himelein, M., 343
Hinch, R., 330
Hirschi, T., 333
Hirschman, C., 62
Ho, F. C., 157
Hobart, C. W., 81, 123, 124, 125, 125n,
    126, 126n, 127n, 131n, 132, 134,
    135, 138, 158, 177, 307, 308n, 314
Hochschild, A., 228
Hocker, J. L., 205
Hof, L. M., 215
Hogan, D. P., 254
Holahan, C. J., 327
Hollis, C., 260
Holstein, J. A., 6
Homans, G., 80
Homebase Magazine, 254
Honeycutt, J. M., 201
Hook, N., 33
Horwitz, A. V., 185, 186
Hotaling, G. T., 259
House, J. S., 232
Houseknecht, S. K., 349
Houts, R. M., 157
Howes, P. W., 250
Hubay, C. A., 154, 155
Huddleston, R. J., 309
Hughes, 226
Hughes, M., 185, 226
Hughes, S., 249
Huguley, S., 27
Hum, D. P. J., 302
Hundleby, J. D., 259
Hunt, D., 76, 77
Hurh, W. M., 106
Hurlburt, D., 330
Huston, T. L., 195, 251

Hutchinson, S., 40
Hutter, M., 100
Huxsahl, J., 341

I

Ingoldsby, B. B., 53, 54
Inkeles, A., 60
Insabella, G. M., 317
Inside Edition, 243
Ipsos/Reid, 9
Ironmonger, D., 229
Isaac, S. V., 136
Isaac, W. L., 136
Ishwaran, K., 58, 178
Israelashvili, R., 252

J

Jabbra, N., 102
Jaccard, J., 134
Jack, L., 333, 343
Jackson, J., 340, 343
Jaffe, P., 330
Jamieson, K., 98
Jang, D., 100
Janoff-Bulman, R., 343
Jasso, G., 210
Jaworski, T., 341
Jekielek, 309
Jensen-Campbell, L. A., 158
Jimenez, M., 148, 262
Jimenez, M., 148, 262
Johnson, D., 161, 163, 198, 352
Johnson, E. M., 251
Johnson, H., 329, 330, 332, 333
Johnson, J. S., 202
Johnson, L. C., 359
Johnson, M., 331
Johnson, M. P., 137, 182
Johnson, P. J., 101, 102
Johnson, R. C., 157
Journal of Marriage and the Family, 42
Judd, C., 38
Julian, T., 328, 332, 333

K

Kahn, A. J., 353
Kalbach, W. E., 14, 86
Kalish, R. A., 180
Kalleberg, A. L., 232
Kalmijn, M., 155
Kalmuss, D. S., 328
Kammerman, S. B., 353
Kammermann, S. K., 133

Kandel, D. B., 42
Kanin, E. J., 124
Kantor, D., 36–37
Karney, B. R., 192
Keith, B., 316
Keith, J., 274
Kelley, M. A., 246
Kelly, K., 139, 141, 142
Kendall-Tackett, K. A., 341
Kennedy, C. E., 309
Kennedy, G., 309
Kennedy, J., 307
Kennedy, L., 334, 343, 344
Kennedy, L. W., 279
Kenrick, D. T., 158
Kerckhoff, A. C., 150
Kern, J., 343
Kerns, D., 142
Kerr, D., 245–246
Kersten, K. K., 84
Kersten, L. K., 83–84
Kesner, J., 328, 332
Kibria, N., 101
Kidder, L. H., 38
Kilpatrick, A., 335
Kim, K. C., 106
Kimball, S. T., 58
King, A. J. C., 124, 133, 134, 135
King, D. W., 226
King, E. M., 62
King, E. M., 62
King, L., 176, 226
King, V., 281
Kingsbury, N., 29, 118
Kinnaird, K. L., 133
Kinsey, A. C., 208, 210–211
Kinzl, J., 342
Kitson, G., 303
Klein, D. M., 26, 27, 29, 30, 31, 32, 33, 35,
    36, 37, 68, 199
Klein, I., 343
Klein, R. D., 243
Kline, M., 317
Klomegah, R., 52
Kluwer, E. S., 219, 251
Knox, D., 123, 137
Knudsen, D. D., 342
Kofodimos, J., 226
Kohn, M. L., 233
Korman, S. K., 71, 139
Kossek, E. E., 226
Kourvetaris, G., 108

Subject Index

sex ratio, 151
social exchange framework, 158
Stimulus-Value-Role theory, 167
values, similarity in, 157
maternal employment, 195
matriarchal authority, 57
matrifocal family, 58–59
matrilineal systems, 54
matrilocal residence, 55
matrimonial law, 174
matripatrilocal residence, 55
mature love, 121–122
measurement
qualitative measures, 40
quantitative measures, 40–41
reliability, 41
validity, 41
variables, 41
median age at first marriage, 155f
mediation, 306–307
medieval English family, 75–76
men
see also gender differences
attitudes toward rape, 144
male violence, predictors of, 332
and parent-infant relationships, 252
sexual aggressiveness, and peer pressure, 135
menopause, 213
mental capacity, 172
microlevel theoretical frameworks
conflict approach, 30
described, 33
family development framework, 35–36
symbolic interaction framework, 33–34
systems framework, 36–37
microsystem level of analysis
described, 25–26
microlevel theoretical frameworks, 33–37
mispaha, 70
missing children, 259
mobicentric characteristics, 3
modern family, emergence of, 84–85
modernization
see also changes
and consanguineous marriage, 61–62
and family ties, 60–61
gender factor, 62–63
higher education *vs.* local tradition, 63–64
and kinship, 60–61
marriage timing, 62
and sibling relationships, 61
modular characteristics, 3
monitoring, 259
monogamy, 49, 52, 172
moral commitment, 182
moral reasoning, and premarital sex, 135–136
mother-centred families, 58–59
multicultural society, 361–362
multidimensional models of love, 122–123
multiple spouses. *See* polygamy
Murdoch case, 304
mutual dependency, 119
mutual love, 122

N
naïve curiosity, 37
national family policy, lack of, 353

Native Canadian Act, 98
Native Canadians. *See* Aboriginal Canadian families
natural physical-biological environment, 33
need fulfillment, and family, 3–4
negative communication and physiological responses, 202
neglect, 335–336
neohomemakers, 254
neolocal residence, 55
net family formation, 85
network interference, 137–138
the never-married elderly, 276
new action theory, 350
new beginnings. *See* remarriage; stepfamilies
New France, 77
"new morality," emergence of, 125–127
nominal variable, 41
non-fraternal polyandry, 53
non-parental care of young children
child development and, 252–253
day-care centres, 253
mothers' work situation, 252
non-probability samples, 41
non-sororal polygyny, 53
nonconventional values, 203
nonverbal communication, 201–202
normative definitions, 8–11
norms
defined, 8
family, definitions of, 8–11
marriage, definitions of, 8–11
and physical aggression, 328
Noyes, John Humphrey, 53
nuclear family, 6, 9, 57
null hypothesis, 38
nurturant care, 2
nurturant socialization, 9

O
objectivity, 23–24
observation, 40
occupational gender segregation, 223–224
oestrus cycle, 208
Old Age Security (OAS), 284
older individuals. *See* the elderly
Omaha kinship system, 50
Oneidan Perfectionists, 53
open family systems, 37
operationalize, 39
optimum parenting, 255
ordinal variable, 41
organizational culture, 239
orphans, 83
out-migration, 85

P
parent-adolescent connection, 257–258
parent-child relationship
grandparent relationships, 281–282
and later-life remarriage, 274
parent and adult-child relationships, 278–281
parent-infant relationships, 251–252
remarriage, impact of, 313–314
shift from, after marriage, 181
stepparent-stepchild relationship, 312–315
parent-infant relationships
attachment, 251

powerlessness, 341
pragma, 122, 123
pre-parenting programs, 356
predictor variables, 42
pregnancy, 249–250
preindustrial Canadian families, 82–83
premarital cohabitation. *See* cohabitation
premarital communication, 204
premarital enrichment programs, 356–357
premarital intervention programs, 213
premarital sex
    abstinence standard, 124, 126
    and alcohol use, 133
    among Canadian students, 130*t*
    Anglophone premarital sex standards, 125*f*
    changing standards, 124–132
    competing perspectives, 136
    correlates of behaviour, 133–136
    and dating relationship development, 134–135
    double standard, 124
    and drug use, 133
    factors contributing to changes, 132
    and family structure, 133
    Francophone premarital sex standards, 126*f*
    French Canadian attitudes, 81
    high approval level, 131–132
    in high school, 129
    and moral reasoning, 135–136
    "new morality," emergence of, 125–127
    normative orientations toward sexuality, 128*t*
    and peer-group relationships, 135
    permissiveness with affection, 124
    permissiveness without affection, 125
    rank ordering of standards, 127*t*
    and religion, 135–136
    and romantic love, 120, 138
    sexual attitudes, changes in, 124–129
    sexual behaviours, changes in, 129–131
    sexual revolution, 207
    and sexual socialization, 133–134
    social changes, 136
premarital variables, 192
prenuptial contracts, 175–176
PREP (Prevention and Relationship Enhancement Program), 213, 356
preventive caregiving, 354
preventive services, types of, 354
primary prevention, 354
primogeniture, 54, 58
principle of least interest, 152
prior-marriage experiences, 295*t*
private pension plans, 284
probability samples, 41
property settlements, 304
propinquity, 150
propositions, 27
Protestantism, 75\76, 78
psychological aging, 266
psychological theories of domestic violence, 328
Punic Wars, 72

Q
qualitative measures, 40
quantitative measures, 40–41
Quebec
    families in. *See* French Canadian families
    family policy, 355

Quebec Aboriginal families, 99
Quebec Pension Plan, 284
questionnaires, 40
Quiet Revolution, 81

R
racialized immigration policies, 100–101
radical feminism, 31
random family systems, 37
rape. *See* sexual assault
rapport, 119
real income, 283–284
reciprocity, 214
reduced work hours, 358
refined divorce rate, 297
relations, 39
relationship endings
    annulment, 296
    children, effect on, 315–317
    desertion, 296
    divorce. *See* divorce
    separation, 296
    widowhood, 278, 294–296
Relationship Enhancement, 213
relationships
    after marriage, 179
    close relationships. *See* close relationships
    parent-child relationships. *See* parent-child relationship
    sibling relationships, 61, 61*t*, 282, 314
    stepsibling subsystem, 314
relative poverty, 108–109
relatives, 56, 181
reliability, 41
religion
    Black women and, 136
    and enduring marriages, 215
    and higher standards of sexual purity, 136
    interfaith marriages, 154–156
    and marital commitment, 183–184
    and marital quality, 198
    and physical punishment, 257
    and premarital sex, 135–136
    and social status, 3
    and virginity, 136
religious homogamy, 154–155, 156*t*
remarriage
    children's adjustment problems, 317–318
    divorce rate, 315
    divorced individuals and, 295, 296, 310, 298*f*
    the elderly, 278
    extended families, impact on, 309
    gender differences in probability, 310–312
    later-life remarriage, 274
    in 19th and 20th century Canada, 92
    parent-child relationships and, 313–314
    parenting after, 313–314
    relationships, perceptions of, 308*t*
    shared child, birth of, 315
    simplest form, 312
remarriage kindred, 307–309
replacement level, 81, 249
replicability, 24
reproductive function, 2
reproductive technologies, 243–244
research anomaly, 192
research designs

symbolic interactionist framework
    dating aggression, 142–143
    described, 33–35
    divorce, 34
    family, definition of, 8
    reaction, importance of, 34
    stimulus-interpretation-response (SIR), emphasis on, 34
    vs. stimulus-response approaches, 34
systems framework
    closed family systems, 37
    described, 36–37
    divorce, 34
    focus of, 36
    open family systems, 37
    random family systems, 37

T
tax law, 175
teenage mothers, 112, 249
telecommuting, 358–359
tertiary prevention, 354
theoretical definitions of marriage and family, 8
theoretical frameworks
    assumptions, 27
    concepts, 27
    conflict framework, 29–30
    definition, 27
    ecological framework, 32–33
    family development framework, 35–36
    feminist framework, 30–32
    hypothesis, 27
    importance of, 27\28
    macrolevel, 29–33
    Marxist feminist theory, 31
    microlevel theoretical frameworks, 33–37
    propositions, 27
    psychological themes, 30
    social-psychological themes, 30
    symbolic interaction framework, 33–34
    systems framework, 36–37
    theorizing processes, 28
    underlying assumptions, 44n
theory
    vs. beliefs, 26
    definition, 28
    research question, source of, 37
throwaways, 259
total dependency ratio, 270
total fertility rate, 86–89, 248
traditional marriage, 203
traditionalist, 106
transition to marriage
    engagement, 177
    honeymoon, 178
    wedding ceremony, 177–178
transition to parenthood
    marital interaction, 250–251
    and parent-infant relationships, 251
    pregnancy, 249–250
    teenage parents, 249
transitional double standard, 124
traumatic sexualization, 341
treatment effect, 41
trends. *See* family trends and patterns
trial marriage, 352
    see also cohabitation

tribe, 70
trustee family, 68
two-sided system, 55

U
ultimogeniture, 54, 58
Unemployment Insurance Act, 358
unilineal systems, 54
United States
    birth rate, 247
    death rate, 247
    ethnic families, 101
    family policy, 355
    marriage rates, 88f
    parental leave, 358
    single mothers, and earning opportunities, 59

V
validity, 41
value similarity, and mate selection, 157
variables
    control variables, 42
    in data analysis, 42
    dependent variables, 42
    interval variable, 41
    nominal variable, 41
    ordinal variable, 41
    predictor variables, 42
    statistics, use of, 43
variation in Canadian families
    Aboriginal Canadian families, 96–99
    Canadian immigration policies, 100–101
    first-generation families, 101–107
    poverty, 108–113
    second-generation families, 107–108
    sources of variability, 95
verbal abuse of children, 336–337
Vietnamese refugees, 101
violence
    alcohol use, 333
    child abuse. *See* child abuse
    college and university undergraduates, survey of, 140–141
    cycle theory of violence, 331
    in dating relationships, 139–143
    elder abuse, 280–281, 344
    in families. *See* domestic violence
    rape. *See* sexual assault
    victims remaining in relationships, 142, 331
virginity
    glorification of, 74–75
    reasons for remaining virgins, 132t
    trend towards, 132
    young religious women, 136
vital marriages, 213–215
vital statistics, 247–248
voluntary childlessness, 244–245

W
wealth, production of, 180
wedding ceremony, 177–178
well-being. *See* health and well-being
well-family clinics, 360
widowhood, 278, 294–296
wife abuse. *See* domestic violence
wives' employment. *See* women's employment

women
    see also gender differences
    in Aboriginal Canadian families, 98
    abusive relationships. *See* domestic violence
    aging, "double jeopardy" of, 266
    in ancient Hebrew families, 71
    college and university, and dating violence, 140–141, 144
    dating and female freedom, 116
    divorce, impact of, 111
    and domestic work, 218–219
        see also division of domestic work; domestic work
    eldercare, 279–280
    emotional affairs, 212
    employer exploitation of, 105
    employment of. *See* women's employment
    English families since 18th century, 78
    first-generation families, and role changes, 105–107
    French families in 17th century, 76–77
    generational squeeze, 280
    in-group marriage, encouragement of, 107
    kin-keeping, 276
    labour force participation. *See* women's employment
    learned helplessness, 331
    left in home country, 100
    maternal substance use, 259
    in medieval English families, 75
    menopause, 213
    neohomemakers, 254
    in New France, 77
    occupational mobility, 225
    personal *vs.* marital happiness, 186
    in preindustrial Canadian families, 83
    Punic Wars, status after, 72–73
    split household, 100
    stay-at-home mothers, 253–254
    survivorship, 221
    teenage mothers, 112, 249
    timing of transition to marriage, 180
    in traditional French Canadian family, 81–82
    violence against. *See* domestic violence; violence
    and work. *See* women's employment
women's employment
    see also work and marriage; work-family balance
    availability for work, 221
    changing attitudes, 222
    and childbearing, 226
    choice, 238
    co-breadwinners, 238
    decision, 253–254
    dissatisfaction with available roles, 222
    and double burden, 219
    employed homemakers, 238
    equality, fight for, 223–225
    expressive exchange, 235
    female participation rate, 221
    and financial need, 221
    First World War, 220

    gender segregation within occupations, 224
    Great Depression, 220
    higher educational achievement, 221
    historical background, 219–221
    income factor, 236–237
    instrumental exchange, 235
    job opportunities, increase in, 221
    labour force activity, 220t
    leading female occupations in Canada, 224t
    and marital quality, 229–231, 237
    and marital relationships, 234–237
    maternal employment, 195
    meanings of employment, 238
    new mothers, well-being of, 239
    and non-parental care of young children, 252–254
    occupational gender segregation, 223–224
    occupational mobility, 225
    part-time employment, 238
    pay inequality, 225
    power of working wives, 235
    reasons for increase in, 221–223
    Scanzoni's model, 235
    second shift, 228
    Second World War, 220–221
    sexual harassment, 225
    since the 1950s, 221–223
    unpaid work, 218
work and marriage
    career success, 237–238
    family-friendly work policies, 358–359
    future directions, 238–239
    parental employment, 233–234
    remedial programs and policies, 239
    research, 238–239
    women's employment. *See* women's employment
work-family balance
    childbearing, 226
    conventional pattern, 226
    as critical measurement construct, 226
    division of domestic work, 227–232
    research on, 226
    role-sharing pattern, 226
    second shift, 228
    strategies, 227
    work-family stress, 226
work-family stress, 226
Workers Compensation Act, 173
working from home, 358
working poor, 109

Y
young adult children
    delayed home leaving, 261
    leaving home, 260–261
    returning home, 262

Credits

Chapter 1: p. 7, Box 1.1, Bould, Sally. 1993. "Familial Caretaking: A Middle-Range Definition of Family in the Context of Social Policy," Journal of Family Issues, 14(1):133–151. Reprinted by Permission of Sage Publications; p. 15, Table 1.1 and 1.2, adapted from the Statistics Canada publication "Common-law Status (3), Age Groups (18A) and Sex (3) for Population, for Canada, Provinces, Territories, Census Metropolitan Areas and Census Agglomerations, 2001 Census - 100% Data," Catalogue 95F0405, January 22, 2003; p. 16, Table 1.3, adapted from Statistics Canada, Cansim database <http://cansim2.statcan.ca>. Table 051-0010; p. 18, Table 1.4, adapted from Statistics Canada website: <http://www12.statcan.ca/english/census01/products/highlight/PrivateHouseholds/page.cfm?Lang=E&geo=PR&View=1a&Table=1&StartRec=1&Sort=2&B1=Counts>; p. 19, Table 1.5, adapted from the Statistics Canada publication "Number of Children at Home (8) and Family Structures (7) for Census Families in Private Households, for Canada, provinces, Territories, Census Metropolitan Areas and Census Agglomerations, 2001 Census - 20% Sample data," Catalogues 95F0312, October 22, 2002.

Chapter 3: p. 61, Cicirelli, Victor G. 1994. "Sibling Relationships in Cross-Cultural Perspective," Journal of Marriage and the Family, 56(1):7–20. Copyrighted 1994 by the National Council on Family Relations, 3989 Central Avenue NE, Suite 550, Minneapolis, MN 55421.

Chapter 4: pp. 86 and 87, Table 4.1 and 4.2, adapted from the Statistics Canada publication "Historical Statistics of Canada, Second Edition," Catalogue 11-516, 1983, Series A67-69; p. 90, Table 4.3, adapted from the Statistics Canada publication "Historical Statistics of Canada, Second Edition," Catalogue 11-516, 1983; p. 91, Table 4.4, adapted from the Statistics Canada publication "Historical Statistics of Canada, Second Edition," Catalogue 11-516, 1983, Series A254-259;

Chapter 5: p. 96, Table 5.1, Adapted from the Statistics Canada website <http://www12.statcan.ca/english/census01/products/highlight/Aboriginal/Page.cfm?Lang=E&Geo=PR&View=1a&Table=1&Sort=2&B1=Counts01&B2=Total>; p. 97, Table 5.2, adapted from the Statistics Canada publication "Aboriginal Identity Population (3), Registered Indian Status (3), Age Groups (11B), Sex (3), and Area of Residence (7) for Population, for Canada, provinces and territories, 2001 Census - 20% Sample data," Catalogue 97F0011, January 21, 2003; p. 103, Table 5.3, Adapted from the Statistics Canada website <http://www12.statcan.ca/english/census01/products/highlight/ETO/Table1.cfm?Lang=E&T=501&GV=1&GID=0>; p. 104, Table 5.4, adapted from the Statistics Canada publication "Visible Minority Groups (15), Sex (3) and Age Groups (8) for Population, for Canada, Provinces, Territories, Census Metropolitan Areas and Census Agglomerations, 2001 Census - 20% Sample data," catalogue 95F0036, April 23, 2003; p. 109, Table 5.5, National Council of Welfare Estimates of Statistics canada's Before-Tax Low Income Cut-Offs (1992 base) for 2002. Reproduced with the permission of the Minister of Public Works and Government Services Canada, 2003; p. 110, Table 5.6, adapted from the Statistics Canada publication "Family Income Groups (22) in Constant (2000) Dollars and Census Family Structure (12) for Census Families in Private Households, for Canada, Provinces, Territories, Census Metropolitan Areas and Census Agglomerations, 1995 and 2000 - 20% Sample Data," catalogue 97F0020, May 13, 2003; p. 112, Figure 5.1, Aboriginal Children in Poverty in Urban Communities: Social Exclusion and the Growing Racialization of Poverty in Canada: Notes for Presentation to Subcommittee on Children and Youth at Risk of the Standing Committee on Human Resources Development and the Status of Persons with Disabilities on Wednesday, March 19th 2003, John Anderson, Canadian Council on Social Development, (http://www.ccsd.ca/pr/2003/aboriginal.htm). Adapted in part from the Statistics Canada 1996 Census,
custom tabulations; p. 112, Box 5.1, adapted from Fullton, E. Kaye. 1993.* "Babies Having Babies: Teenage Mothers Face a Bleak Future," Maclean's, February 22:32–33.

Chapter 6: p. 132, Table 6.5, Sprecher, Susan and Pamela C. Regan. 1996.* "College Virgins: How Men and Women Perceive Their Sexual Status," The Journal of Sex Research, 25(3):261–288. Copyright 2004 by the Society for the Scientific Study of Sexuality. Reproduced with permission of the Society for the Scientific Study of Sexuality in the format Textbook via Copyright Clearance Centre.

Chapter 7: p. 153, Table 7.1, Atkinson, Maxine P. and Becky L. Glass. 1985. "Marital Age Heterogamy and Homogamy, 1900 to 1980," Journal of Marriage and the Family, 47:685–691. Copyrighted 1985 by the National Council on Family

Relations, 3989 Central Ave. NE, Suite 550, Minneapolis, MN 55421. Reprinted by permission; p. 159, Figure 7.4, Adapted from the Statistics Canada publication "Changing Conjugal Life in Canada," 2001, Catalogue 89-576, July 11, 2002, p. 4; p. 164, Figure 7.5, adapted from the Statistics Canada publication "Changing Conjugal Life in Canada," 2001, Catalogue 89-576, July 11, 2002, p. 6.

Chapter 8: p. 174, Figure 8.1, adapted from the Statistics Canada publications "The Daily," Catalogue 11-001, October 14, 1997, and from "Age, Sex and Marital Status," Catalogue 93-101, 1987.

Chapter 9: p. 193, Figure 9.1, reprinted with the permission of The Free Press, a Division of Simon & Schuster Adult Publishing Group, from Contemporary Theories about the Family, Volume 1, edited by Wesley R. Burr, Reuben Hill, F. Ivan Nye, and Ira L. Reiss. Copyright 1979 by The Free Press. All Rights Reserved; p. 203, Table 9.2, Fitzpatrick, Mary Anne. 1988c. *Between Husbands and Wives: Communication in Marriage*. Newbury Park: Sage. Copyright 1988 by Sage Publications Inc. Reprinted by permission of Sage Publications Inc.

Chapter 10: p. 220, Table 10.1, Women's History Month 2000, Status of Women Canada. Reproduced with the permission of the Minister of Public Works and Government Services Canada, 2003; p. 222, Table 10.2, adapted from the Statistics Canada CANSIM database <http://cansim2.statcan.ca>, Table 282-0002; p. 224, Table 10.3, United Nations Platform for Action Committee Manitoba, Women and the Economy, http://www.unpac.ca/ca; p. 225, Figure 10.1, adapted from the Statistics Canada publication "Canada Year Book," 2001, Catalogue 11-402, March 2001; p. 227, Box 10.1, Schnittger, Maureen H. and Gloria W. Bird. 1990. "Coping Among Dual-Career Men and Women Across the Life Cycle," Family Relations, 39:199–205. Copyrighted 1990 by the National Council on Family Relations, 3989 Central Ave. NE, Suite 550, Minneapolis, MN 55421. Reprinted by permission; p. 228, Figure 10.2, adapted from the Statistics Canada publication "Labour Force Survey microdata file," Catalogue 71M0001, various years; p. 230, Table 10.4, adapted from Statistics Canada, General Social Survey, 1998. http://www.statcan.ca/english/Pgdb/ famil36a.htm.

Chapter 11: p. 246, Table 11.1, and p. 247, Table 11.2, adapted from the Statistics Canada website <http://www12.statcan.ca/ English/census01/products/analytic/ companion/abor/tables/total/livarrang.cfm#1>; p. 252, Box 11.2, Adler, Jerry. 1997. "It's a Wise Father Who Knows . . . His Child," *Newsweek*, Special Issue: Your Child, From Birth to Three, Spring/Summer:73. From *Newsweek*, 1997 copyright 1997 Newsweek, Inc. All rights reserved. Reprinted by permission.

Chapter 12: p. 267, adapted from the Statistics Canada publication "Legal Marital Status (6), Age Groups (18A) and Sex (3) for Population, for Canada, provinces, Territories, Census Metropolitan Areas and Census Agglomerations, 2001 Census - 100% Data," Catalogue 95F0407, October 22, 2002; p. 270, Table 12.2, adapted in part from the Statistics Canada publication "Age, Sex, and Marital Status (data products: nation series: 1991 Census of Population)" 1991, Catalogue 93-310, July 1992; p. 272, Table 12.3, Adapted from the Statistics Canada website <http://www12.statcan.ca/English/census01/ products/analytic/companion/fam/livarrang.cfm>; p. 283, Figure 12.1, adapted from the Statistics Canada publication "Low Income After Tax," 1997, Catalogue 13-592, August 1999; p. 285, adapted from the Statistics Canada publication "A Portrait of Seniors in Canada," 3rd edition, Catalogue 89-519, 1997.

Chapter 13: p. 295, adapted from the Statistics Canada publication "Marriage and Conjugal Life in Canada," 1991, Catalogue 91-534, April 1992; p. 298, Figure 13.1, adapted from the Statistica Canada Censuses of Canada, 1901-1986, Vital Statistics and Health Reports, 1973-1991; p. 299, Table 13.2, adapted from Ambert, A.M., *Divorce: Facts, Causes and Consequences*, The Vanier Institute of the Family, Table 1, www.vifamily.ca. © 2003; p. 300, Table 13.3, adapted from Statistics Canada publications "The Daily" Catalogue 11-001, December 2, 2002, and from "Divorces-Shelf tables'- 1999-2000, Catalogue 84F0213, December, 2002; p. 301, Table 13.4, Adapted from Statistics Canada publications "The Daily" Catalogue 11-001, December 2, 2002, and from "Divorces-Shelf tables'- 1999-2000, Catalogue 84F0213, December, 2002; p. 302, Table 13.5, www.divorcereform.org/gul.html. Reprinted with permission; p. 308, Table 13.6, Hobart, Charles. 1990. "Relationships Between the Formerly Married," Journal of Divorce and Remarriage, 14:1–25. Reprinted with permission of The Haworth Press; p. 311, Figure 13.2, adapted from Statistics Canada publication "Marriage and conjugal life in Canada", 1991, Catalogue 91-534, April, 1992; p. 312, Figure 13.3, adapted from the Statistics Canada publication "The Daily," Catalogue 11-001, June 19, 1996; p. 319, Box 13.3, *The Globe and Mail*, July 13, 1997. Reprinted with permission from *The Globe and Mail*.

Chapter 14: pp. 336-339, Figures 14.3, 14.4, 14.5, and 14.7, Canadian Incidence of Reported Child Abuse and Neglect: Final Report, and Child Maltreatment in Canada: Selected Results from the Canadian Incidence Study of Reported Child Abuse and Neglect, Child Maltreatment Division, Health Canada, 2001. http://www.hc-sc.gc.ca/pphb-dgspsp/cm-vee/cishl01/index.html. Reproduced with the permission of the Minister of Public Works and Government Services Canada, 2004;